SPURGEON'S
EXPOSITORY ENCYCLOPEDIA

SPURGEON'S EXPOSITORY ENCYCLOPEDIA

SERMONS BY CHARLES H. SPURGEON

Classified and Arranged for Ready Reference

VOLUME XII

BAKER BOOK HOUSE
GRAND RAPIDS, MICHIGAN
1952

CONTENTS OF VOLUME XII

PETER
Christ's Prayer for Peter—Luke 22:32 9
Exposition of Luke 22:7-34; 54-62 18
Peter's Restoration—Luke 22:60-62 21
Peter after His Restoration—Luke 22:32 33
Peter's Prayer—Luke 5:8 45
Peter's Shortest Prayer—Matt. 14:30 55
Exposition of Matthew 6:5-34 64
What Was Become of Peter?—Acts 12:18 67
Exposition of II Peter 1 75

PRAISE
Praise Thy God, O Zion—Luke 19:37-40 81
The Happy Duty of Daily Praise—Ps. 145:1, 2 93
Open Praise and Public Confession—Ps. 138:1-3 . . . 105
Exposition of Psalm 138 115
Mary's Magnificat—Luke 1:46-47 117
Exposition of Luke 1:39-56 127
Homage Offered to the Great King—Ps. 72:15 129
"The Garment of Praise"—Isa. 61:3 141

PRAYER
Ask and Have—James 4:2, 3 155
Prayer—Its Discouragements and Encouragements Matt. 15:23 . 167
Exposition of Ephesians 2 177
Ejaculatory Prayer—Neh. 2:4 179
Restraining Prayer—Job 15:4 191
"The Throne of Grace"—Heb. 4:16 203
Prayerful Importunity—Luke 18:7 215
True and Not True—John 9:31 227
A Plain Talk upon an Encouraging Topic—Jonah 2:7 . . . 237
Exposition of Jonah 2 246

PREACHING
Rightly Dividing the Word of Truth—II Tim. 2:15 . . . 251
The Burden of the Word of the Lord—Mal. 1:1 263

PRESERVATION
The Preservation of Christians in the World—John 17:15 . . 277
Exposition of Isaiah 49:1-23 284

Enduring to the End—Matt. 10:22 289
Christians Kept in Time and Glorified in Eternity—Jude 24, 25 . 301
The Final Perseverance of the Saints—Job 17:9 313
Saints Guarded from Stumbling—Jude 24, 25 325
Exposition of Psalm 91 334
Preventing Grace—I Sam. 25:32, 33 337
Exposition of Jonah 1 346
Jude's Doxology—Jude 24, 25 349
Exposition of the General Epistle of Jude 357

PROMISES

All the Promises—II Cor. 1:20 363
Exposition of II Corinthians 1; 2:1 372
The Wide-Open Mouth Filled—Ps. 81:10 375
A Promise for the Blind—Jer. 31:8 387
Exposition of Matthew 9:27-35; 20:29-34 395
Spiritual Convalescence—Zech. 10:12 399

PROVIDENCE

An Instructive Truth—Jer. 10:23 411
Exposition of Jeremiah 10 420
The Hungry Filled, The Rich Emptied—Luke 1:53 . . . 423
Exposition of Luke 1.26-56 432
The Commissariat of the Universe—Ps. 104:28 435
Exposition of Psalm 34 444
Beggars Becoming Princes—I Sam. 2:8 447

REDEMPTION

The Great Liberator—John 8:36 459
The Royal Saviour—Acts 5:31 471
Exposition of Romans 10 480
"The Lamb of God"—John 1:29 483
Exposition of John 1:1-34 492
The Wordless Book—Ps. 51:7 495
Exposition of Psalm 51 503

PETER

- Christ's Prayer for Peter—Luke 22:32
- Exposition of Luke 22:7-34;54-62
- Peter's Restoration—Luke 22:60-62
- Peter after His Restoration—Luke 22:32
- Peter's Prayer—Luke 5:8
- Peter's Shortest Prayer—Matt. 14:30
- Exposition of Matthew 6:5-34
- What Was Become of Peter?—Acts 12:18
- Exposition of II Peter 1

CHRIST'S PRAYER FOR PETER.

A Sermon

DELIVERED BY

C. H. SPURGEON,

AT THE METROPOLITAN TABERNACLE, NEWINGTON,

On Lord's-day Evening, January 22nd, 1882.

"But I have prayed for thee, that thy faith fail not."—Luke xxii. 32.

SATAN has a deadly hatred towards all good men; and they may rest assured that, somewhere or other, he will meet them on their way to the Celestial City. John Bunyan, in his immortal allegory, placed him in one particular spot, and described him as Apollyon straddling across the road, and swearing by his infernal den that the pilgrim should go no further, but that there and then he would spill poor Christian's soul. But the encounter with Apollyon does not happen in the same place to all pilgrims. I have known some of them assailed by him most fiercely at the outset of their march to Zion. Their first days as Christians have been truly terrible to them by reason of the Satanic attacks they have had to endure; but, afterwards, when the devil has left them, angels have ministered to them, and they have had years of peace and joy. You remember that, in the case of our Saviour, no sooner was he baptized than he was led of the Spirit into the wilderness to be tempted of the devil. In like manner, there are those whose fiercest trials from the adversary come at the beginning of their public ministry. Others meet with their greatest conflicts in middle life; when, perhaps, they are too apt to think themselves secure against the assaults of Satan, and to fancy that their experience and their knowledge will suffice to preserve them against his wiles. I know some, like Martin Luther, in whose voyage of life the middle passage has been full of storm and tempest, and they have scarcely known what it was to have a moment's rest during all that period. Then there have been others, the first part of whose career has been singularly calm: their life has been like a sea of glass, scarcely a ripple has been upon the waters; and yet, towards the end, the enemy has made up for it, and he has attacked them most ferociously right up to the last. I have known many instances of eminent saints who have had to die sword in hand, and enter heaven—I was about to say, with the marks of their stern conflict fresh upon them. At any rate, they have been crowned on the battlefield, and have fallen asleep at the close of a tremendous fight.

With the most of us who are really going to heaven,—I will not say that it is a rule without any exception, but with the most of us, at some time or another, we shall know the extreme value of this prayer, "Lead us not into temptation of any kind, but deliver us from *the evil one*, who, beyond all others, is especially to be dreaded." There is little to be got out of him, even if we conquer him. He usually leaves some mark of his prowess upon us, which we may carry to our graves. It were better to leap over hedge and ditch, and to go a thousand miles further on our pilgrim-road, than ever to have a conflict with him, except for those great purposes of which I shall presently speak a moment. The fight with Apollyon is a terrible ordeal,—an ordeal, however, which a brave Christian will never think of shirking. Nay, rather will he rejoice that he has an enemy worthy of his steel, that true Damascus blade with which he is armed; and, in the name of God, he will determine, though he wrestles not with flesh and blood, that he will contend against principalities and powers, and with the very leader of them all, that there may be all the more glory to the great King who makes the weakest of his followers to be so strong that they put the old dragon himself to flight.

So, dear friends, rest assured that Satan hates every good man, and that, some time or other, he is pretty sure to show that hatred in a very cruel and deadly attack upon him.

Further, because of his hatred, Satan earnestly desires to put believers into his sieve, that he may sift them as wheat;—not that he wants to get the chaff away from them,—but simply that he may agitate them. You see the corn in the sieve, how it goes up and down, to and fro. There is not a single grain of it that is allowed to have a moment's rest; it is all in commotion and confusion, and the man who is sifting it takes care to sift first one way, and next another way, and then all sorts of ways. Now, that is just what Satan does with those whom he hates, when he gets the opportunity. He sifts them in all manner of ways, and puts their whole being into agitation and turmoil. When he gets a hold of us, it is a shaking and sifting indeed; he takes care that anything like rest or breathing-space shall be denied to us.

Satan desires thus to sift the saints in his sieve; and, at times, God grants his desire. If you look at the Revised Version, in the margin you learn the true idea of Satan having asked, or rather obtained by asking, the power to sift Peter as wheat. God sometimes gives Satan the permission to sift as wheat those who are undoubtedly his people, and then he tosses them to and fro indeed. That record in the Book of Job, of Satan appearing before God, is just repeated in this story of Peter; for the devil had obtained from God liberty to try and test poor boasting Peter. If Christ had not obtained of God, in answer to his intercession, the promise of the preservation of Peter, then had it gone ill indeed with the self-confident apostle. God grants to Satan permission to try his people in this way, because he knows how he will overrule it to his own glory and their good.

There are certain graces which are never produced in Christians, to a high degree, except by severe temptation. "I noticed," said one, "in what a chastened spirit a certain minister preached when he had been the subject of most painful temptation." There is a peculiar tenderness, without which one is not qualified to shepherdize Christ's sheep, and to feed his lambs,—a tenderness, without which one cannot strengthen his brethren, as Peter was afterwards to do, a tenderness which does not usually come—at any rate, to such a man as Peter, except by his being put into the sieve, and tossed up and down by Satanic temptation.

Let that stand as the preface of my sermon, for I shall not have so much to say upon that as upon another point.

First, observe, in our text, *the grand point of Satan's attack*. We can see that from the place where Jesus puts the strongest line of defence: "I have prayed for thee, that thy faith fail not." The point of Satan's chief attack on a believer, then, is his faith. Observe, secondly, *the peculiar danger of faith:* "That thy faith fail not." That is the danger,—not merely lest it should be slackened and weakened, but lest it should fail. And then observe, thirdly, *the believer's grand defence:* "I have prayed for thee, that thy faith fail not."

I. Notice carefully, in the first place, THE GRAND POINT OF SATAN'S ATTACK.

When he assails a child of God, his main assault is upon his faith; and I suppose that the reason is, first, *because faith is the vital point in the Christian.* We are engrafted into Christ by faith, and faith is the point of contact between the believing soul and the living Christ. If, therefore, Satan could manage to cut through the graft just there, then he would defeat the Saviour's work most completely. Faith is the very heart of true godliness, for "the just shall live by faith." Take faith away, and you have torn the heart out of the gracious man. Hence, Satan, as far as he can, aims his fiery darts at a believer's faith. If he can only destroy faith, then he has destroyed the very life of the Christian. "Without faith it is impossible to please God." Therefore, if the devil could but get our faith away from us, we should cease to be pleasing to God, and should cease to be "accepted in the Beloved." Therefore, brethren, look well to your faith. It is the very head and heart of your being as before God. The Lord grant that it may never fail you!

I suppose that Satan also attacks faith *because it is the chief of all our graces.* Love, under some aspects, is the choicest; but to lead the van in conflict, faith must come first. And there are some things, which are ascribed solely and entirely to faith, and are never ascribed to love. If any man were to speak of our being justified by love, it would grate upon the ears of the godly. If any were to talk of our being justified by repentance, those of us who know our Bible would be up in arms against such a perversion of the truth; but they may speak as long as they like of our "being justified by faith," for that is a quotation from the Scriptures. In the matter of justification, faith stands alone. It lays hold on Christ's sacrifice, and his righteousness, and thereby the soul is justified. Faith, if I may so say, is the leader of the graces in the day of battle, and hence Satan says to his demoniacal archers, "Fight neither with small nor great, save only with the king of Israel; shoot at faith, kill it if possible." If faith is slain, where is love, where is hope, where is repentance, where is patience? If faith be conquered, then it is as when a standard-bearer fainteth. The victory is virtually won by the arch-enemy if he is able to conquer faith, for faith is the noble chieftain among the graces of a saint.

I suppose, again, that Satan makes a dead set upon the faith of the Christian *because it is the nourishing grace.* All the other graces within us derive strength from our faith. If faith be at a low ebb, love is sure to burn very feebly. If faith should begin to fail, then would hope grow dim. Where is courage? It is a poor puny thing when faith is weak. Take any grace you please, and you shall see that its flourishing depends upon the healthy condition of faith in our Lord Jesus Christ. To take faith away, therefore, would be to take the fountain away from the stream; it would be to withdraw the sun from his rays of light. If you destroy the source, of course that which comes out of it thereupon ceases. Therefore, beloved, take the utmost possible care of your faith, for I may truly say of it that out of it are the issues of life to all your graces. Faith is that virtuous woman who clothes the whole household in scarlet, and feeds them all with luscious and strengthening food; but if faith be gone, the household soon becomes naked, and poor, and blind, and miserable. Everything in a Christian fails when faith ceases to nourish it.

Next to this, Satan attacks faith *because it is the great preserving grace.* The apostle says, "Above all,"—that is, "over all," "covering all,"—"taking the shield of faith, wherewith ye shall be able to quench all the fiery darts of the wicked." Sometimes, the Eastern soldiers had shields so large that they were like doors, and they covered the man from head to foot. Others of them, who used smaller shields, nevertheless handled them so deftly, and moved them so rapidly, that it was tantamount to the shield covering the entire person. An arrow is aimed at the forehead, up goes the shield, and the sharp point rings on the metal. A javelin is hurled at the heart, but the shield turns it aside. The fierce foe aims a poisonous dart at the leg, but the shield intercepts it. Virtually, the shield is all-surrounding; so it is with your faith. As one has well said, "It is armour upon armour, for the helmet protects the head, but the shield protects both helmet and head. The breastplate guards the breast, but the buckler or shield defends the breastplate as well as the breast." Faith is a grace to protect the other graces; there is nothing like it, and therefore I do not wonder that Satan attacks faith when he sees its prominent position and its important influence in the entire town of Mansoul.

I cannot help saying, also, that I wonder not that Satan attacks faith, *because it is the effective or efficient grace.* You know what a wonderful chapter that 11th chapter of the Epistle to the Hebrews is; it is a triumphal arch, erected in honour of what? Of faith. According to that chapter, faith did everything; it quenched the fire, stopped the mouths of lions, turned to flight the armies of the aliens, received the dead who were raised, and so on. Faith is the soul's right hand. Faith works by love; but, still, it is faith that works; and you can do nothing acceptably before God unless you do it by that right hand of faith. Hence, Satan cannot endure faith; he hates that most of all. Pharaoh tried to have all the male children thrown into the river because they were the fighting force of Israel. He did not mind having the women to grow up to bear burdens, it was the men whom he feared. And, in like manner, the devil says, "I must stamp out faith, for that is the secret of strength." He will not trouble himself so much about your other graces, he will probably attack them when he can; but, first of all he says, "Down with faith! That is the man-child that must be destroyed;" and he aims his sharpest and deadliest darts at it.

I believe, also, that faith is attacked by Satan, most of all, *because it is most obnoxious to him.* He cannot endure faith. How do I know that? Why, because God loves it; and if God loves faith, and if Christ crowns faith, I am sure that Satan hates it. What are we told concerning the work of Jesus being hindered by unbelief? "He could not do many mighty works there because of their unbelief." Now, I will turn that text round, and say of Satan, that he cannot do many mighty works against some men because of their faith. Oh, how he sneaks off when he discovers a right royal faith in a man! He knows when he has met his master, and he says, "Why should I waste my arrows upon a shield carried by such a man as that? He believes in God, he believes in Christ, he believes in the Holy Spirit; he is more than a match for me." To those that are under his leadership, he cries, "To your tents!" He bids them flee away, and escape, for he knows that there can be no victory for them when they come into collision with true God-given faith. He cannot bear to look at it. It blinds him; the lustrous splendour of that great shield of faith, which shines as though a man did hang the sun upon his arm, and bear it before him into the fray, blinds even the mighty prince of darkness. Satan does but glance at it, and straightway he takes to flight, for he cannot endure it. He knows it is the thing which most of all helps to overthrow his kingdom, and destroy his power; therefore, believer, cling to your faith! Be like the young Spartan warrior, who would either bring his shield home with him, or be brought home dead upon his shield. "Cast not away your confidence, which hath great recompence of reward." Whatever else you have not, "have faith in God;" believe in the Christ of God; rest your soul's entire confidence upon the faithful promise and the faithful Promiser; and, if you do so, Satan's attacks upon you will all be in vain.

That is my first point,—observe the grand point of Satanic attack.

II. Now, secondly, observe THE PECULIAR DANGER OF FAITH: "That thy faith fail not."

Did Peter's faith fail? Yes, and no; it failed in a measure, but it did not altogether fail. It failed in a measure, for he was human; but it did not altogether fail, for, at the back of it, there was the superhuman power which comes through the pleading of Christ. Poor Peter! He denied his Master, yet his faith did not utterly fail; and I will show you why it did not. If you and I, beloved, are ever permitted to dishonour God, and to deny our Lord, as Peter did, yet may

God in mercy keep us from the utter and entire failure of our faith, as he kept Peter!

Notice, first, there was still some faith in Peter, even when he had denied his Master, for when the Lord turned, and looked upon him, *he went out, and wept bitterly.* If there had not been the true faith in Peter still, the Master might have looked upon him long before a tear would have coursed down his cheeks. The Lord not only looked on Judas, but he gave him a sop with him out of the dish; and he even let the traitor put his lips to him, and kiss him; but all that had no weight with Judas. The reason why Christ's look had such an effect on Peter was because there was some faith in Peter still. You may blow as long as ever you like at the cold coals, and you will get no fire; but I have sometimes seen a servant kneel down when there has been just a little flame left in the coal in a corner of the grate, and she has blown it tenderly and gently so as to revive it. " It is not quite out," she says; and, at last, there has been a good fire once again. May God grant that we may never come to that sad condition; but, if we do, may he, of his grace, grant that there may still be that blessed little faith left, that weak and feeble faith which, through the breathing upon it of the Spirit of God, shall yet be fanned into a flame!

We are sure that there was this faith still in Peter, *or else, what would he have done?* What did Judas do? Judas did two things; first, he went to a priest, or to priests, and confessed to them, and then he went out, and hanged himself; the two things were strangely connected. Peter did neither; yet, if he had not had faith, he might have done both. To publicly deny his Master three times, and to support his denial with oaths and curses, even when that Master was close by, and in his greatest exigency, must have put Peter into most imminent peril; and if there had not been, within his heart, faith that his Master could yet pardon and restore him, he might, in his despair, have done precisely what the traitor Judas did. Or, if he had not gone to that extremity of guilt, he would have hidden himself away from the rest of the apostles. But, instead of doing so, we soon find him again with John;—I do not wonder that he was with John. They were old companions; but, in addition to that, the beloved John had so often leaned his head on the Master's bosom that he had caught the sweet infection of his Saviour's tenderness; and, therefore, he was just the one with whom Peter would wish to associate. I think that, if I had ever denied my Lord as Peter did, in that public way, I should have run away, and hidden myself from all my former companions; but he did not, you see. He seemed to say to himself, "The Master, with his dear tender heart, can still forgive me, and receive me;" so he clings to the disciples, and especially to John. Ay, and notice that, on the day of our Lord's resurrection, Peter was the first disciple to enter the sepulchre; for, though "the other disciple did outrun Peter," and reach the grave first, "yet went he not in" until Peter led the way. "The Lord is risen indeed, and hath appeared to Simon," is a remarkable passage. Paul, writing concerning Christ's resurrection, says that "he was seen of Cephas," that is, Peter. There was some special manifestation of our blessed Master to Simon Peter, who was waiting for it, and privileged to witness it; and this showed that his faith was kept from failing through the Saviour's prayers.

Now, beloved, I say no more about Peter, but I speak to you about your own faith. Are you greatly troubled? Then, I pray that your faith may not fail. It is shaken; it is severely tried; but God grant that it may not fail! Something whispers within your heart, "Give up all religion, it is not true." To that lie, answer, "Get thee behind me, Satan; for the religion of Jesus Christ is eternally, assuredly, infallibly true." Cling to it, for it is your life. Or, perhaps, the fiend whispers, "It is true enough to others; but it is not meant for you, you are not one of the Lord's people." Well, if you cannot come to Christ as a saint, come to him as a sinner; if you dare not come as a child to sit at his table, come as a dog to eat the crumbs that fall under it. Only do come, and never give up your faith.

If the arch-fiend whispers again, "You have been a deceiver; your profession is all a mistake, or a lie," say to him, "Well, if it be so, there is still forgiveness in Christ for all who come unto God by him." Perhaps you are coming to the Saviour for the first time; you mean to cast yourself upon the blood and merit of Jesus, even if you have never done so before. I pray for you, dear coming one. O gracious Saviour, do not let Satan crush out the faith of even the weakest of thy people! Blessed Intercessor, plead for that poor trembler, in whom faith is almost dying out! Great High Priest, intercede for him, that his faith may not utterly fail him, and that he may still cling to thee!

What is to become of us if we have not faith in Jesus? I know that there are some who seem to get on well without it. So may the dogs; so may the wild beasts; they get on well enough without the children's garments or the children's bread; but you and I cannot. The moment I am unbelieving, I am unhappy. It is not a vain thing for me to believe in Christ; it is my life, it is my strength, it is my joy. I am a lost man, and it were better for me that I had never been born, unless I have the privilege of believing. Give up faith? Remember what Satan said concerning Job, "Skin for skin, yea, all that a man hath will he give for his life;" and our life is wrapped up in our faith in Christ. We cannot give it up, and we will not give it up. Come on, fiends of hell, or mockers of earth, we will not give it up, we will hold it fast, for it is part of the very warp and woof of our being. We believe in God, and in his Son, our Lord and Saviour, Jesus Christ; and it is our great concern that our faith should be well guarded and protected, for we know the peculiar danger to which it is exposed when it is assailed by Satan.

III. Now I will close my discourse by speaking, for only a very few minutes, upon THE BELIEVER'S GREAT PERSERVATIVE AND DEFENCE.

What is the great protection of our faith? Our Saviour's intercession. Prayer is always good, it is ever a blessed thing; but notice that great letter-word in the text, "*I* have prayed for thee." It is the intercession of Christ that preserves our faith, and there are three things about it which make it precious beyond all price; it is prevalent, prevenient, and pertinent. First, it is *prevalent;* for, if Jesus pleads, he must prevail. It is *prevenient;* for, before the temptation comes to Peter, he says, "I have prayed for thee. Satan hath but obtained, by his asking, the permission to tempt thee; but I have already prayed for thee."

And, then, it was *pertinent;* that is, to the point. Christ had prayed the best prayer possible: "that thy faith fail not." Peter would not have known that this was to be the chief point of attack by Satan; he might have thought that Satan would attack his love. The Lord seems to hint at his thought about that by saying to him, afterwards, "Simon, son of Jonas, lovest thou me?" But the Saviour knew that the hottest part of the battle would rage around Fort Faith, and therefore he prayed that the fortress might be well garrisoned, and never be captured by the enemy; and it was not.

Whenever I begin to talk to you about the intercession of Christ, I feel inclined to sit down, and let you think, and look up, and listen, till you hear that voice, matchless in its music, pleading, pleading, pleading, with the Father. It were much better for you to realize it than for me to describe it. It was a blessed thing to hear one's mother pray;—by accident, as we say, to pass the door that was ajar, and to hear mother pleading for her boy or her girl. It is a very touching thing to hear your child praying for her father, or your wife breathing out her warm desires for her beloved. I do not know anything more charming than to hear, now and then, a stray prayer that was never meant to be heard on earth, but only in heaven; I like such eavesdroppings. Oh, but listen! It is Jesus who is praying; he shows his wounds, and pleads the merit of his great sacrifice; and, wonder of wonders, he pleads for me, and for thee! Happy man, happy woman, to have our faith preserved by such a mighty preservative as this,—the intercession of Christ!

I want you specially to notice that *this intercession is the pleading of One who,* in the text, *seems directly to oppose himself to the great adversary:* "Satan hath obtained thee by asking, that he may sift thee as wheat; but I have obtained thee by asking," (so I will venture to paraphrase it,) "that thy faith fail not." There stands Satan; you cannot see him, and you need not want to; but that grim monster, who has made kings and princes tremble, and has plucked angels from their spheres of light, and hurled bright spirits down from heaven to hell, stands there to assail you; and you may well be afraid, for God himself permits him to sift you. Ah! but there also stands the ever-blessed One, before whom an angel, fallen or unfallen, is but a tiny spark compared with the sun; there he stands, girt about the paps with the golden girdle of his faithfulness, robed in the fair white linen of his matchless righteousness, upon his head a crown of glory that far outshines all constellations of stars and suns; and HE opposes his Divine pleading to the demoniacal asking of the fallen one. Are you afraid now? It does seem to me unspeakably blessed to see it written here, "Satan hath desired to have thee that he may sift thee as wheat," and then to see over the top of it this word, "but *I* have prayed for thee." Oh, blessed " but "! How it seems to cast the fallen angel back again into the bottomless pit, and to bind him with chains, and set a seal upon his prison: "But *I* have prayed for thee." Tempt on, then, O devil; tempt at thy worst, for there is no fear now when this glorious shield of gold, the intercession of the Saviour, covers the entire person of the poor attacked one! "I have prayed for thee, that thy faith fail not."

And then my last word is this; *it is an intercession which is absolutely certain of success.* In fact, he who offers it anticipates its success, and discounts it by giving this precept to his servant: "and when thou art converted,"—sure pledge, then, that he will be converted, that he will be turned back, however far he wanders,—when thou art restored, "strengthen thy brethren." Then, for certain, he will be restored, or else the Saviour would not have given him a precept which could only be available if a certain unlikely contingency should occur. O thou who art a true child of God, thou mayest be drenched, but thou shalt never be drowned! O warrior of the cross, thy shield may be covered with fiery darts, thickly as the saplings of a young forest grow; but no dart shall ever reach thy heart! Thou mayest be wounded in head and hand and foot; thou mayest be a mass of scars; but thy life is given thee. To Christ art thou given as a prey, and thou shalt come out even from between the jaws of death, and thou shalt overcome Satan by Christ's power. Only trust Christ; only trust him. Cling to your faith, beloved; cling to your faith! I would like to get a hold of that young man who has lately been listening to sceptical teachers, and to whisper in his ear, "Cling to your faith, young man; for, in losing that, you will lose all."

And to you who, alas! have fallen into sin after having made a profession of religion, let me say that, however far you have gone astray, still believe that Jesus is able to forgive you; and come back to him, and seek his pardon now. And you, my hoary-headed brother, whose hair is whitening for heaven, are you sorely beset by all sorts of temptations? Well, give me your hand, for I, too, know what this warfare means. Let us believe in God, my brother; let us both believe in God. Though he should break us down worse than ever, though he should set us up as a target, and let the devil shoot at us all the arrows from his quiver, let us still believe in God; and come you to this pass, to which my soul has come full often, and to which Job came of old, "'Though he slay me, yet will I trust in him;' whatever he doeth to me,—if he shall never smile upon me again,—I will still believe him, I can do no other." I dare not doubt him; I must confide in him. Where is there any ground for confidence if it be not in the God that cannot lie, and in the Christ of the everlasting covenant, whom he hath set forth to be the propitiation for human sin, and in the Holy Ghost, whose work it is to take of the things of Christ, and reveal them unto us?

May the blessed Trinity save and keep us all, for our Lord Jesus Christ's sake! Amen.

Exposition by C. H. Spurgeon.

LUKE XXII. 7—34; AND 54—62.

Verses 7—20. *Then came the day of unleavened bread, when the passover must be killed. And he sent Peter and John, saying, Go and prepare us the passover, that we may eat. And they said unto him, Where wilt thou that we prepare? And he said unto them, Behold, when ye are entered into the city, there shall a man meet you, bearing a pitcher of water; follow him into the house where he entereth in. And ye shall say unto the goodman of the house, The Master saith unto thee, Where is the guestchamber, where I shall eat the passover with my disciples? And he shall shew you a large upper room furnished: there make ready. And they went, and found as he had said unto them: and they made ready the passover. And when the hour was come, he sat down, and the twelve apostles with him. And he said unto them, With desire I have desired to eat this passover with you before I suffer: for I say unto you, I will not any more eat thereof, until it be fulfilled in the kingdom of God. And he took the cup, and gave thanks, and said, Take this, and divide it among yourselves: for I say unto you, I will not drink of the fruit of the vine, until the kingdom of God shall come. And he took bread, and gave thanks, and brake it, and gave unto them, saying, This is my body which is given for you: this do in remembrance of me. Likewise also the cup after supper, saying, This cup is the new testament—*

(Or, covenant—)

20, 21. *In my blood, which is shed for you. But, behold, the hand of him that betrayeth me is with me on the table.*

What a shadow this revelation must have cast over that solemn feast, over the Saviour's heart, and over the minds of all his attached disciples! We can scarcely imagine what pangs tore his loving spirit. He could have used the language of David, with even deeper emphasis, and said, "It was not an enemy that reproached me; then I could have borne it: neither was it he that hated me that did magnify himself against me; then I would have hid myself from him: but it was thou, a man mine equal, my guide, and mine acquaintance." "The hand of him that betrayeth me is with me on the table." O beloved, I pray that you and I may never betray our Master; if ever we should so fall as to deny him, may the Lord stop us where Peter fell, and never suffer us to betray him as Judas did!

22. *And truly the Son of man goeth, as it was determined: but woe unto that man by whom he is betrayed!*

The decree of God does not lessen the responsibility of man for his action. Even though it is predetermined of God, the man does it of his own free will, and on him falls the full guilt of it.

23, 24. *And they began to enquire among themselves, which of them it was that should do this thing. And there was also a strife among them, which of them should be accounted the greatest.*

Be astonished, dear friends, as you read, in such a connection as this, "There was also a strife among them, which of them should be accounted the greatest." What! while yet the anxious question as to which of them was the traitor was being passed round, "Lord, is it I?" Is it so closely followed by another question, "Which of us shall be highest in the kingdom?" Oh, the awful intrusiveness of pride and ambition! How it will come in, and defile the very holy of holies! May God prevent our falling victims to it! The last question for a Christian ever to ask is, "How may I win honour among men?" The one question for a believer should be, "How can I glorify my Master?" Very often, that can best be done by taking the very lowest place in his church.

25, 26. *And he said unto them, The kings of the Gentiles exercise lordship over them; and they that exercise authority upon them are called benefactors. But ye shall not be so: but he that is greatest among you, let him be as the younger; and he that is chief, as he that doth serve.*

Let every respect be given to the elder, and let such as God honours be honoured among us; but let no man honour himself, or seek honour for himself. After all, in Christ's kingdom, the way to ascend is to descend. Did not the Master act thus? He descended, that he might ascend, and fill all things; and so must his disciples do. Less, and less, and less, and less, must we become; and so we shall really be, in his sight, more, and more, and more, and more.

27. *For whether is greater, he that sitteth at meat, or he that serveth? is not he that sitteth at meat? but I am among you as he that serveth.*

For he had just then taken a towel, and girded himself, and washed their feet, so becoming *Servus servorum*, the Servant of servants, though he was in very truth the King of kings.

28. *Ye are they which have continued with me in my temptations.*

There is a reward to the righteous, though they serve not for reward, for the Lord says :—

29, 30. *And I appoint unto you a kingdom, as my Father hath appointed unto me; that ye may eat and drink at my table in my kingdom, and sit on thrones judging the twelve tribes of Israel.*

Ah, but see what follows! No sooner, in this chapter, does the thought seem to rise than it is dashed down again; the brightness ever has a shadow cast across it.

31, 32. *And the Lord said, Simon, Simon, behold, Satan hath desired to have you, that he may sift you as wheat: but I have prayed for thee, that thy faith fail not: and when thou art converted, strengthen thy brethren.*

We are thinking about thrones, and about which of us shall have the loftiest throne, but see how the Master is thinking about the necessary while we are doting upon the superfluous. He thinks of our needs while we are dreaming of something great. What a blessing it is that we have our Saviour praying for us when we ourselves may be fancying that we need not pray! Our hands are ready for the sceptre, and we are anxious to sit down on the throne, when the Lord knows that our proper place is at the footstool, pleading for mercy still.

33. *And he said unto him, Lord, I am ready to go with thee, both into prison, and to death.*

That is bravely spoken, Peter; and yet it is very foolishly said, too. He spoke out of his very heart, and he meant what he said; but Peter did not know what a poor weak body Peter really was. His Master understood him far better.

34. *And he said, I tell thee, Peter, the cock shall not crow this day, before that thou shalt thrice deny that thou knowest me.*

And so it came to pass. Let us read a part of the sad story, beginning at the fifty-fourth verse.

54. *Then took they him, and led him, and brought him into the high priest's house. And Peter followed afar off.*

I do not think that he was to be blamed for that; I do not see how he could very well have followed any nearer, for he was already a marked man. That sword-cut of his upon the ear of Malchus had made him specially prominent amongst the apostles, even if he had not been well known before. He got into the crowd, and came after his Master at such a distance as seemed safe for him.

55. *And when they had kindled a fire in the midst of the hall, and were set down together, Peter sat down among them.*

I do think that he was to be blamed for that action, for it brought him into dangerous company. Better be cold, than go and warm your hands in ungodly society.

56. *But a certain maid beheld him as he sat by the fire, and earnestly looked upon him,—*

As the flame came flashing up every now and then, she looked at him, and Peter was troubled by her gaze: she "earnestly looked upon him,"—

56—59. *And said, This man was also with him. And he denied him, saying, Woman, I know him not. And after a little while another saw him, and said, Thou art also of them. And Peter said, Man, I am not. And about the space of one hour after another confidently affirmed, saying, Of a truth this fellow also was with him: for he is a Galilæan.*

For he got talking to this ill company, and his speech had betrayed him.

60. *And Peter said, Man, I know not what thou sayest.*

Another Evangelist tells us that he began to curse and to swear, as if that was the surest proof that he could possibly give that he did not know Jesus; for, when you hear a man swear, you know at once that he is no Christian, you may conclude that safely enough. So Peter thought that, to prove that he was no follower of Christ, he would use such ill language as the ungodly speak.

60, 61. *And immediately, while he yet spake, the cock crew. And the Lord turned, and looked upon Peter.*

God has all things in his hands, he has servants everywhere, and the cock shall crow, by the secret movement of his providence, just when God wills; and there is, perhaps, as much of divine ordination about the crowing of a cock as about the ascending of an emperor to his throne. Things are only little and great according to their bearings; and God reckoned not the crowing bird to be a small thing, since it was to bring a wanderer back to his Saviour, for, just as the cock crew, "the Lord turned, and looked upon Peter." That was a different look from the one which the girl had given him, but that look broke his heart.

62. *And Peter remembered the word of the Lord, how he had said unto him, Before the cock crow, thou shalt deny me thrice. And Peter went out, and wept bitterly.*

How many there are, who sin with Peter, but who never weep with Peter! Oh, if we have ever transgressed in such a way as he did, let us never cease to weep! Above all, let us begin at once to lament it, and rest not till the Master looks again, and says by that look, "I have blotted out all thy transgressions; return unto me."

PETER'S RESTORATION.

A Sermon

DELIVERED ON LORD'S-DAY MORNING, JULY 22ND, 1888, BY

C. H. SPURGEON,

AT THE METROPOLITAN TABERNACLE, NEWINGTON.

"And immediately, while he yet spake, the cock crew. And the Lord turned, and looked upon Peter. And Peter remembered the word of the Lord, how he had said unto him, Before the cock crow, thou shalt deny me thrice. And Peter went out, and wept bitterly."—Luke xxii. 60—62.

PETER had terribly fallen. He had denied his Master, denied him repeatedly, denied him with oaths, denied him in his presence, while his Master was being smitten and falsely charged; denied him, though he was an apostle; denied him, though he had declared that should all men forsake him, yet would he never be offended. It was a sad, sad sin. Remember what led up to it. It was, first, Peter's presumption and self-confidence. He reckoned that he could never stumble, and for that very reason he speedily fell. A haughty spirit goes before a fall. Oh, that we might look to the roots of bitter flowers, and destroy them! If presumption is flourishing in the soil of our hearts to-day, we shall soon see the evil fruit which will come of it. Reliance upon our firmness of character, depth of experience, clearness of insight, or matureness in grace, will, in the end, land us in disgraceful failure. We must either deny ourselves, or we shall deny our Lord; if we cleave to self-confidence, we shall not cleave to him.

Immediately, Peter's denial was owing to cowardice. The brave Peter in the presence of a maid was ashamed; he could not bear to be pointed out as a follower of the Galilean. He did not know what might follow upon it; but he saw his Lord without a friend, and felt that it was a lost cause, and he did not care to avow it. Only to think that Peter, under temporary discouragement, should play the coward! Yet cowardice treads upon the heels of boasting: he that thinks he can fight the world will be the first man to run away.

His sin also arose from his want of watchfulness. His Master had said to him, "What, could ye not watch with me one hour?" and no doubt there was more meaning in the words than appeared on the surface. The Lord several times said to him, "Pray, that ye enter not into temptation." The words were repeated with deep impressiveness, for they were greatly needed. But Peter had not watched: he had been warming his hands. He did not pray: he felt too strong in himself to be driven to special prayer. Therefore, when the gusts of temptation came, they found Peter's boat unprepared for the storm, and they drove it upon a rock.

When Peter first denied his Master a cock crew. Peter must have heard that crowing, or he would not have communicated the fact to the evangelists who recorded it. But though he heard it, he was an example of those who have ears, but hear not. One would have thought that the warning would have touched his conscience; but it did not; and when the cock crowed a second time, after he had committed three denials, it might not have awakened him from his dreadful sleep if a higher instrumentality had not been used, namely, a look from the Lord Jesus.

God keep us free from this spirit of slumber, for it is to the last degree dangerous! Peter was under the direful influence of Satan, for it was a night wherein the powers of darkness were specially active. "This is your hour," said Jesus, "and the power of darkness." That same influence which assailed the Saviour unsuccessfully—for, said he, "the prince of this world cometh, and hath nothing in me"—assailed Peter with sad result; for the evil one had something in Peter, and he soon found it out. The sparks from Satan's flint and steel fell upon our Lord as upon water; but Peter's heart was like a tinder-box; and when the sparks fell, they found fuel there. Oh, that we may be kept from the assaults of Satan! "Lead us not into temptation" is a necessary prayer; but the next petition is specially noteworthy—"but deliver us from the evil one." A man never gets anything out of the devil, even if he conquers him. You will find in combat with him that, even if you win the victory, you come off with gashes and wounds of which you will carry the scars to your grave. "All the while," says Mr. Bunyan, while Christian was fighting with Apollyon, "I did note that he did not so much as give one smile." Oh no! there is nothing to smile about when the arch-enemy is upon us. He is such a master of the cruel art of soul-wounding, that every stroke tells. He knows our weak places in the present, he brings to remembrance our errors in the past, and he paints in blackest colours the miseries of the future, and so seeks to destroy our faith. All his darts are fiery ones. It takes all a man's strength, and a great deal more, to ward off his cunning and cruel cuts. The worst of it is that, as in Peter's case, he casts a spell over men, so that they do not fight at all, but yield themselves an easy prey. Our Saviour said to Peter, "Simon, Simon, behold, Satan hath desired to have you, that he may sift you as wheat: but I have prayed for thee, that thy faith fail not." Peter was as much under the power of Satan as corn is in the hand of the man who winnows it. He went up and down in that sieve like a helpless thing, and so passed from simple falsehood to plain denials of his Master with oaths and cursings.

I desire in this discourse to speak chiefly of Peter's restoration. Peter was down; but he was soon up again. One writer says the story should rather be called Peter's restoration than Peter's fall. His fall was soon over: he was like a little child learning to walk, scarcely down before his mother has him up again. It was not a continuance in a sin, like that of David, who remained for months without repentance; but it was the quick speech of a man carried away by sudden temptation, and it was followed by a speedy repentance. Upon his restoration we are going to meditate.

It was brought about by two outward means. I like to think of the singular combination: the crowing of the cock, and a look from the Lord. When I come to preach to you, it almost makes me smile to think that God should save a soul through me. I may find a fit image of myself in the poor cock. Mine is poor crowing. But as the Master's look went with the cock's crowing, so, I trust, it will go with my feeble preaching. The next time you also go out to try and win a soul for Jesus, say to yourself, "I cannot do it: I cannot melt a hard, rebellious heart; but yet the Lord may use me; and if there come a happy conjunction of my feeble words with my Lord's potent look, then the heart will dissolve in streams of repentance." Crow away, poor bird: if Jesus looks whilst thou art crowing, thou wilt not crow in vain, but Peter's heart will break. The two things are joined together, and let no man put them asunder—the commonplace instrumentality and the divine Worker. Christ has all the glory, and all the more glory because he works by humble means. I trust that there will be this morning a conjunction of the weakness of the preacher with the strength of the Holy Spirit; so that stony hearts may be broken and God glorified.

This morning, first, *let us look at the Lord who looked;* and secondly, *let us look into the look which the Lord looked;* and then, thirdly, *let us look at Peter, upon whom the Lord looked.* We will be all the while looking: may our Lord look upon us. May his Holy Spirit work with his holy word!

I. First, LET US LOOK AT THE LORD, WHO LOOKED UPON PETER.

Can you picture him up there in the hall, up yonder steps, before the high priest and the council? Peter is down below in the area of the house warming his hands at the fire. Can you see the Lord Jesus turning round and fixing his eyes intently upon his erring disciple? What see you in that look?

I see in that look, first, that which makes me exclaim: *What thoughtful love!* Jesus is bound, he is accused, he has just been smitten on the face, but his thought is of wandering Peter. You want all your wits about you when you are before cruel judges, and are called upon to answer false charges; you are the more tried when there is no man to stand by you, or bear witness on your behalf: it is natural, at such an hour, that all your thoughts should be engaged with your own cares and sorrows. It would have been no reproach had the thoughts of our Lord been concentrated on his personal sufferings; and all the less so because these were for the sake of others. But our blessed Master is thinking of Peter, and his heart is going out towards his unworthy disciple. That same influence which made his heart drive out its store of blood through every pore of his body in the bloody sweat now acted upon his soul, and drove his thoughts outward towards that member of his mystical body which was most in danger. Peter was thought of when the Redeemer was standing to be mocked and reviled. Blessed be his dear name, Jesus always has an eye for his people, whether he be in his shame or in his glory. Jesus always has an eye for those for whom he shed his blood. Though now he reigns in glory, he still looks steadily upon his own: his delight is in them, and his care is over them. There was not a particle of selfishness about our Saviour. "He saved others; himself he could not save." He looked to others, but he never looked to himself. I see, then, in our Lord's looking upon Peter, a wondrously thoughtful love.

I exclaim, next, *What a boundless condescension!* If our Lord's eye had wandered that day upon "that other disciple" that was known to the high priest, or if he had even looked upon some of the servants of the house, we should not have been so astonished; but when Jesus turns, it is to look upon Peter, the man from whom we should naturally have turned away our faces, after his wretched conduct. He had acted most shamefully and cruelly, and yet the Master's eye sought him out in boundless pity! If there is a man here who feels himself to be near akin to the devil, I pray the Lord to look first at him. If you feel as if you had sinned yourself out of the pale of humanity by having cast off all good things, and by having denied the Lord that bought you, yet still consider the amazing mercy of the Lord. If you are one of his, his pitying eye will find you out; for even now it follows you as it did Hagar, when she cried, "Thou God seest me." But oh, the compassion of that look! When first I understood that the Lord looked on me with love in the midst of my sin, it did seem so wonderful! He whom the heavens adore, before whose sight the whole universe is stretched out as on a map, yet passes by all the glories of heaven that he may fix his tender gaze upon a wandering sheep, and may in great mercy bring it back again to the fold. For the Lord of glory to look upon a disciple who denies him is boundless condescension!

But then, again, *what tender wisdom do I see here!* "The Lord turned, and looked upon Peter." He knew best what to do: he did not speak to him, but looked upon him. He had spoken to Peter before, and that voice had called him to be a fisher of men; he had given Peter his hand before, and saved him from a watery grave when he was beginning to sink. But this time he gives him neither his voice nor his hand, but that which was equally effectual, and intensely suitable, he lent him his eye: "The Lord looked upon Peter." How wisely doth Christ always choose the way of expressing his affection, and working our good! If he had spoken to Peter then, the mob would have assailed him, or at least the ribald crowd would have remarked upon the sorrow of the Master and the treachery of the disciple: our gracious Lord will never needlessly expose the faults of his chosen. Possibly no words could have expressed all that was thrown into that look of compassion. Why, brethren, a volume as big as a Bible is contained within that look of Jesus. I defy all the tongues and all the pens in the world to tell us all that our divine Lord meant by that look. Our Saviour employed the most prudent, the most comprehensive, the most useful method of speaking to the heart of his erring follower. He looked volumes into him. His glance was a divine hieroglyphic full of unutterable meanings, which it conveyed in a more clear and vivid way than words could have done.

As I think of that look again, I am compelled to cry out: *What divine power is here!* Why, dear friends, this look worked wonders.

I sometimes preach with all my soul to Peter, and, alas! he likes my sermon and forgets it. I have known Peter read a good book full of most powerful pleading, and when he has read it through, he has shut it up and gone to sleep. I remember my Peter when he lost his wife, and one would have thought it would have touched him, and it did, with some natural feeling; yet he did not return to the Lord, whom he had forsaken, but continued in his backsliding. See, then, how our Lord can do with a look what we cannot do with a sermon, what the most powerful writer cannot do with hundreds of pages, and what affliction cannot do with even its heaviest stroke. The Lord looked, and Peter wept bitterly. I cannot help thinking with Isaac Williams that there is a majestic simplicity in the expressions here used—"The Lord turned, and looked upon Peter. And Peter went out, and wept bitterly." The passage reminds us of that first of Genesis: "And God said, Let there be light: and there was light." As the Lord looked unto the host of the Egyptians, and troubled the Egyptians, so did he now look into Peter's heart, and his thoughts troubled him. Oh, the power of the Lord Christ! If there was this power about him when he was bound before his accusers, what is his power now that he is able to save unto the uttermost them that come unto God by him, seeing he ever liveth to make intercession for them? In that look there was divinity. The Son of God looked upon Peter: the text does not use the name Jesus, but it expressly says, "The Lord turned, and looked upon Peter." That divine look did the deed.

Let me beg you to note *what sacred teaching is here.* The teaching is of practical value, and should be at once carried out by the followers of Jesus. You, dear friend, are a Christian man or a Christian woman; you have been kept, by divine grace, from anything like disgraceful sin. Thank God it is so. I dare say, if you look within, you will find much to be ashamed of; but yet you have been kept from presumptuous and open sins. Alas! one who was once a friend of yours has disgraced himself: he was a little while ago a member of the church, but he has shamefully turned aside. You cannot excuse his sin; on the contrary, you are forced to feel great indignation against his folly, his untruthfulness, his wickedness. He has caused the enemies of the Lord to blaspheme, and has done awful mischief to the cause of righteousness. Now I know what will be suggested to you. You will be inclined to cut his acquaintance, to disown him altogether, and scarcely to look at him if you meet him in the street. This is the manner of men, but not the manner of Jesus. I charge you, act not in so un-Christlike a manner. The Lord turned, and looked on Peter; will not his servants look on him? You are not perfect like your Lord; you are only a poor sinful creature like your fallen brother. What! are you too proud to look at the fallen one? Will you not give him a helping hand? Will you not try to bring him back? The worst thing you can do with a backslider is to let him keep on sliding back. Your duty should be your pleasure, and your duty is to "restore such a one in the spirit of meekness, remembering thyself also, lest thou also be tempted." O brothers and sisters, it is a very little thing that has kept some of us from turning aside unto folly. One grain more and the scale would have turned in favour of a great fall. Our steps have well-nigh slipped. When we are proud of our sure standing, the Lord may well be angry with us for our vanity, and he may justly say, "How can I endure this pride? I have taken great care of this man, and watched over him to keep him out of sin, and now he takes the credit of it all, and plays the great man, and fancies that he will be defiled if he associates with my poor wandering children." Which, think you, is worse in God's sight, the sudden fall into sin, or the long-continued pride, which boasts itself in the presence of the Lord, and looks contemptuously upon erring ones? It is not my office to become a measurer of sins; but I would earnestly enforce this plain duty: since our own Lord and Master looked on backsliding Peter, let us seek out our wandering brethren.

One more lesson: observe *what heavenly comfort is here:* "The Lord turned, and looked upon Peter"; yes, Jesus looks upon sinners still. The doctrine of God's omniscience is far oftener set forth in a hard way than in a cheering way. Have you never heard a sermon from "Thou God seest me," of which the pith was—Therefore tremble, and be afraid? That is hardly fair to the text; for when Hagar cried, "Thou God seest me," it was because the Lord had interposed to help her, when she had fled from her mistress. It was comfort to her that there she also had looked after him that had looked upon her. There is a dark side to "Thou God seest me"; but it is not half so dark as it would be if God did not see us. It is true, O sinner, that God has seen your sin, and all the aggravations of it; but it is also true that as he sees your ruin, your misery, your sadness, he has compassion on you. He sees your sin that he may remove it, and make you clean in his sight. As the Lord looked upon Peter, so he looks upon you. He has not turned his back on you; he has not averted the gaze of his pity. He sees to the bottom of your heart, and reads all your thoughts. You have not to go about to find out God—he is looking upon you. "He is not far from every one of us"; he is within eyesight. You are to look to him; and if you do, your eyes will meet his eyes, for already he looks upon you.

I think we have gathered much from this brief look at the Lord who looked upon Peter. I doubt not that, had we more time and more insight, we should see greater things than these.

II. Now let us go on to the second point, and see whether we cannot gather still more instruction. LET US LOOK INTO THE LOOK WHICH THE LORD GAVE TO PETER. Help us again, most gracious Spirit!

That look was, first of all, *a marvellous refreshment to Peter's memory.* "The Lord turned, and looked upon Peter." What a sight it must have been for Peter! Our dear Master's face was that night all red from the bloody sweat. He must have appeared emaciated in body; his eyes weary with want of sleep, and his whole countenance the vision of grief. If ever a picture of the Man of Sorrows could have been drawn, it should have been taken at that moment when the Lord turned and looked upon Peter. By torchlight and the flickering flame of the fire in the court of the hall of Caiaphas Peter saw a vision which would never fade from his mind. He saw the man whom he loved as he had never seen him before. This was he who called him, when he was fishing, to become a fisher of men; this was he who bade him spread the net, and caused him to take an incredible quantity of fishes, insomuch that the boat began to sink, and he cried out, "Depart from me; for I am a sinful man, O Lord"; this was he who had made him walk on the water, and at other times had rebuked the winds, and raised the dead. This was he with whom Peter had been upon the mount of transfiguration! Truly there was a wonderful change from the glistening whiteness of the mount to the ghastliness of that sad hour! Though the lineaments of that reverend face were distained with blood, yet Peter could tell that it was the selfsame Lord with whom he had enjoyed three years of intimate intercourse and tender unveiling. All this must in a moment have flashed upon poor Peter's mind; and I do not wonder that in the recollection of it all he went out and wept bitterly. He did love his Lord; his denial was not of the heart, but of the tongue; and, therefore, as all the grounds of his faith came before his mind anew, his heart was broken into a thousand pieces with grief that he should have been false to such a friend. Yes, that look awoke a thousand slumbering memories, and all these called upon the sincere heart of Peter to repent of its ungenerous weakness.

Next, that turning of the Master was *a special reminder of his warning words*. Jesus did not say it in words, but he did more than say it by his look. "Ah, Peter! did not I tell you it would be so? You said, 'Though all men shall be offended because of thee, yet will I never be offended.' Did I not tell thee that before cock-crowing thou wouldst deny me thrice?" No rebuke was uttered; and yet the tender eye of the Lord had revealed to Peter his own extreme folly, and his Master's superior wisdom. Now he saw his own character, and perceived his Lord's discernment. It was a prophecy, and, like all other prophecies, it was understood after it was fulfilled. We read that "Peter remembered the word of the Lord, how he said unto him, Before the cock crow, thou shalt deny me thrice." It is clear, then, that our Lord's look was a special reminder of his former words: it stirred up Peter's mind by way of remembrance, and made him see how foolish he had been, and how inexcusable was his fault.

Surely it was, also, *a moving appeal to Peter's heart*. I bade you notice just now, in the reading of the chapter, that this story of Peter is singularly interwoven into the narrative of our Saviour's passion: it is so interwoven because it constitutes an essential part of that passion. We must not regard it as an accidental incident, it was part and parcel of that grief which he had to bear when he stood in our place and stead. It was written of old, "Smite the shepherd, and the sheep shall be scattered"; and this scattering of the sheep, of which Peter was a notable instance, was one of the bitter ingredients of our Redeemer's mental anguish. "Lover and friend hast thou put far from me" is his complaint in the Psalm. When the Saviour showed himself to Peter with all those lines of grief upon his face, he seemed to say to him, "Canst thou deny me now? I am bound for thee, and dost thou deny me? I stand here to be adjudged to death for thee, and dost thou deny me? Now is the hour of mine agony, and dost thou deny me?" The Lord could not have looked at Peter without creating strong emotion in the breast of the weak disciple who now found himself in so sad a plight. That look touched very tender cords. There was no need for a single word of appeal: that look sufficed to stir the deeps of Peter's nature.

What do you think that look chiefly said? My thought about it, as I turned it over, was this: when the Lord looked upon Peter, though he did refresh his memory, and make an appeal to his conscience, yet there was still more evidently *a glorious manifestation of love.* If I may be permitted humbly and reverently to read what was written on my Master's face, I think it was this: "And yet I love thee, Peter, I love thee still! Thou hast denied me, but I look upon thee still as mine. I cannot give thee up. I have loved thee with an everlasting love, and, notwithstanding all thine ill-conduct towards me, I am looking for thee, and expecting to receive thee. I have not turned my back on thee. Behold, I look towards thee with tender regard, foreseeing that thou wilt yet serve me, and prove the truth of thy devotion to me. Despair not, O Peter, for I will receive thee again, and thou shalt glorify me." Judging what would break my heart the soonest if I had thus denied my Master, it seems to me that I should be most affected by his saying to me, "And yet, despite thy sin, I love thee still." Love is the great heart-breaker. Immutable love is that divine hammer which breaks the rock in pieces. Though a man should have sinned himself into great hardness of heart, yet almighty love can soften him. Who can resist the charms of grace unchangeable? Sharper than a sword is a look of love: more fierce than coals of juniper are the flames of love. One said, the other day, speaking of a person who has gone awfully astray after having been a preacher of the Word, "If I did not believe in the doctrine of unchanging love I do not think I dare pray for him; but since I believe that God will bring him back again, I pray with humble confidence that he will be restored." That which is an encouragement to prayer for others will be a help towards our return if we have gone astray. I love to believe that my Lord will bring his wanderers back. O ye who are anxious to return to him, let this cheer you—"Yet doth he devise means that his banished be not expelled from him." This doctrine wins men back. There are wicked men who turn it into an argument for continuing in sin; but their damnation is just. True men will see, in the measureless and unchanging love of Christ, a reason which will put wings to their feet when they hasten back to him from whom they have gone astray.

Again: this look *penetrated Peter's inmost heart.* It is not every look that we receive that goes very deep. I look with eyes of deep affection at men from this pulpit, and I perceive that they know my meaning; but they soon shake it off. But our Saviour has an eye to which the joints and marrow are visible. He looks into the secret chambers of the soul; for his look is a sunbeam, and bears its own light with it, lighting up the dark places of our nature by its own radiance. Peter could not help feeling, for he was pricked in the heart by the arrow of Christ's glance. How many persons are affected by religion only in the head! It does not affect their heart and life. I am grieved when I hear of some of you, who are regular hearers, and take pleasure in my preaching, and yet, after many years, you are not a bit better. You have had spasms of improvement, but they have ended in nothing. You go back to the mire after you have been washed. You are a hearer of the gospel, and yet a drunkard. Your voice is heard in a psalm, but it may also be heard in an oath. It is a shocking thing; but I have done my best. I can preach to your ears, but I cannot look into your hearts. Oh, that my Lord would give such a glance at you this morning as should dart light into you, and cause you to see yourself, and to see him, and then the tears would fill your eyes!

One fact may not escape our notice: our Lord's look at Peter was *a revival of all Peter's looking unto Jesus.* The Lord's look upon Peter took effect because Peter was looking to the Lord. Do you catch it? If the Lord had turned and looked on Peter, and Peter's back had been turned on the Lord, that look would not have reached Peter, nor affected him. The eyes met to produce the desired result. Notwithstanding all Peter's wanderings, he was anxious about his Lord, and therefore looked to see what was done with him. Even while he warmed his hands at the fire, he kept looking into the inner hall. His eyes were constantly looking in the direction of the Lord Jesus. While he wandered about among the maids and serving-men, and got talking to them, fool that he was; yet still he would perpetually steal a glance that way to see how it fared with the man he loved. He had not given up the habit of looking to his Lord. If he had not still, in a measure, looked to his Master, how would the look of Jesus have been observed by him? His eye must look through your eye to get to your heart. The remainders of faith are the sparks among the ashes of piety, and the Lord blows on these to raise a fire. If there is a poor soul here that, despite his backsliding, can yet feel, "I am trusting in Jesus, and if I perish, I will perish there," there is hope for that soul. If you have given up the outward forms of religion it is a grievous fault: but if you still inwardly look to the Crucified, there is something in you to work upon; there is an eye which can receive the look of Jesus. It is through the eye that looks to Jesus that Jesus looks, and lets fresh light and hope into the soul. Oh that you who have this lingering faith in the Lord may now receive a look from him which shall work in you a bitter, salutary, saving repentance, without which you can never be restored!

This look was altogether between the Lord and Peter. Nobody knew that the Lord looked on Peter, except Peter and his Lord. That grace which saves a soul is not a noisy thing; neither is it visible to any but the receiver. This morning, if the grace of God comes to any one of you in power, it will be unperceived by those who sit on either side of you in the pew: they will hear the same words, but of the divine operation which accompanies them they will know nothing: the eye of the Lord will not speak to them as it is speaking to the awakened one. Do you know anything of the secret love-look of the Lord Jesus?

The whole process may not have occupied more than a second of time. "The Lord turned, and looked on Peter." It took less time to do than it takes to tell. Yet in that instant an endless work was done.

How soon can Jesus change the heart! " He spake, and it was done:" I venture to alter that verse, and say, "He looked, and it was done." Lord, look on sinful Peter now! Work a miracle with thine eye! Even here, let some sinner look to thee because thou hast looked on him.

III. Now I must go to my third point: LET US LOOK AT PETER AFTER THE LORD HAD LOOKED AT HIM. What is Peter doing? When the Lord looked on Peter *the first thing Peter did was to feel awakened.* Peter's mind had been sleeping. The charcoal fire had not done him much good, the fumes of it are evil. The dust of Satan's sieve had got into his eyes. He was confused with very sorrow for his dear Master, whom he truly loved. Peter was hardly Peter that night. I think I had better say, Peter was too much Peter, and his mind had more of Peter's stone in it, than of Christ's flesh. He had forgotten that he was an apostle; he had forgotten that which he had declared when the Lord said to him, "Blessed art thou, Simon Barjona: for flesh and blood hath not revealed this unto thee." Again, I remind you how significantly it is written, "*The Lord* turned, and looked upon Peter"; for it hints that Peter now saw his Lord's Deity through the veil of his humiliation and anguish. He had forgotten his Lord's Deity, and thus he had, in thought, denied his Lord. He was off the lines, and was in a sleepy state. He was what Paul calls "bewitched," and under the influence of a spiritual soporific, administered by Satan. The Lord's look brought him to his better self, and aroused all the spiritual life which had been dormant in him: "Peter remembered," and by this remembrance he was restored.

The next effect was, *it took away all Peter's foolhardiness from him.* Peter had made his way into the high priest's hall, but now he made his way out of it. He had not felt in any danger though in the worst of company. What did he care for the girl that kept the door? Surely he was too much of a man to mind her remarks. What did he care for the men that were round the fire? They were rough fellows, but he had been a fisherman, and quite able to cope with the priest's bailiffs. But now the brag is gone out of him. No sooner had Jesus looked upon him than Peter declined all further risks.

Now he shows the better part of valour, and with great discretion quits the dangerous society of the high priest's palace. Revival of grace in the heart is the death of presumption. The man who runs risks with his soul is not in a right state of mind. Perhaps the Saviour's glance conveyed a hint to Peter that he had no business where he was. It may have seemed to say to him, "You had better be gone from these surroundings." At any rate, that was the effect it produced. That palace in which the Lord fared so badly could not be a fit place for a disciple. To be warming himself at the fire was quite inconsistent for Peter while Jesus was being mocked of his enemies. A sight of the Lord Jesus makes many things seem incongruous which else might appear right enough. All Peter's daring vanished; he turned his back on maids and men, and went out into the darkness of the night. We do not hear of his coming near the cross: in fact, we hear no more of him till the resurrection morning, for Peter was sensible enough to feel that he could not trust himself any more. He placed himself in the background, till his Lord summoned him to the front. I wish that some religious professors whose lives have been questionable had grace enough to do the same. When I see a man who has sinned grievously pushing himself speedily to the front, I cannot believe that he has a due sense of the evil he has wrought, or of his own unfitness to be in the place of peril.

Above all, shun the place where you have fallen. Do not linger in it for a moment. Go out, even though you leave the comfortable fire behind you. Better be in the cold than stay where your soul is in danger. Till Peter had received from the Lord's own mouth abundant assurance of his restoration to his office by the threefold charge to feed the sheep and lambs, we do not find him again in the forefront.

That look of Christ *severed Peter from the crowd*. He was no longer among the fellows around the fire. He had not another word to say to them: he quitted their company in haste. It is well for believers to feel that they are not of the world! They should flee out of Sodom. The Lord has severed us from the multitude by his divine choice, and the separation should be our choice.

Oh, that the arrows of the great Lord would this morning pierce some soul even as a huntsman wounds a stag! Oh, that the wounded soul, like Peter, would *seek solitude!* The stag seeks the thicket to bleed and die alone; but the Lord will come in secret to the wounded heart, and draw out the arrow. Alone is the place for a penitent. Out in the darkness is far better for you than around the fire, where coarse jokes are bandied while Christ is mocked. There must be confession and weeping alone. If Christ has looked upon you, you must get away from the men of the world, and indeed from all others; the solitude of your chamber will suit you best.

That look of Christ also *opened the sluices of Peter's heart:* he went out, and wept bitterly. There was gall in the tears he wept, for they were the washings of his bitter sorrow. Dear friends, if we have sinned with Peter, God grant us grace to weep with Peter. Many will think of Peter's wandering who forget Peter's weeping. Sin, even though it be forgiven, is a bitter thing; even though Christ may look away your despair he will not look away your penitence. "He went out, and wept bitterly." Oh, how he chided himself! "How could I have acted so!" How he smote on his breast, and sighed, "How can I ever look up? Yet is he very precious. That look forgave me; but I can never forgive myself." He remembered it all his life, and could never hear a cock crow without feeling the water in his eyes.

Yet I want you to notice that that look of Christ *gave him relief*. It is a good thing to be able to weep. Those who cannot weep are the people that suffer most. A pent-up sorrow is a terrible sorrow. The Lord touched a secret spring, and made Peter's grief flow out in floods; and that must have greatly eased him. I have frequently heard people say, "I had a good cry, and after that, I was able to bear it." People die of bursting hearts when no tears relieve them. I thank God for Peter that he could weep bitterly, for thus the

Holy Spirit came to him with comfort. O Master, look on some poor dry heart here—some poor heart that cannot feel its sinfulness, but would if it could—and give it feeling! Look on the heart which cannot repent, that is crying, "I would, but cannot feel contrition." Lord, thou didst make the rock yield water at the smiting of the rod, use thy poor stick of a servant this morning to smite the rocky heart, and let the waters of repentance flow out.

And now, to conclude, it *made Peter* as long as he lived, *ashamed to be ashamed*. Peter was never ashamed after this. Who was it that stood up at Pentecost and preached? Was it not Peter? Was he not always foremost in testifying to his Lord and Master? I trust that if any of us have been falling back, and especially if we have wandered into sin, we may get such a restoration from the Lord himself, that we may become better Christians ever afterwards. I do not want you to break a bone, I pray God you never may; but if you ever do, may the heavenly Surgeon so set it that it may become thicker and stronger than before. Courage was the bone in Peter which snapped; but when it was set, it became the strongest bone in his nature, and never broke again. When the Lord sets the bones of his people, they never break any more—he does his work so effectually. The man who has erred by anger becomes meek and gentle. The man who has erred by drink quits the deadly cup, and loathes it. The man who has sinned by shame becomes the bravest of the company.

O Lord Jesus, I have tried to preach thee this morning, but I cannot look with thine eye. Thou must look on erring ones thyself. Look, Saviour! Look, sinner! "There is life in a look AT the crucified One," because there is life in a look *from* the crucified One. May Jesus look, and the sinner look! Amen.

PETER AFTER HIS RESTORATION.

A Sermon

DELIVERED BY

C. H. SPURGEON,

AT THE METROPOLITAN TABERNACLE, NEWINGTON,

ON A THURSDAY EVENING.

"When thou art converted, strengthen thy brethren."—Luke xxii. 32.

PETER was to be sifted, so our Lord warned him; and Satan was to operate with the sieve. Satan had an intense desire to destroy Peter—indeed, he would like to destroy all the chosen of God—and therefore he desired to sift him as wheat, in the hope that he would be blown away with the husks and the chaff. To see a child of God perish would bring to the evil one a malicious joy, for he would have wounded the heart of God. If ever the fallen spirit can be happy, he would derive happiness from defeating the grace of God, and robbing the Lord Jesus of those whom he bought with his blood. "Satan hath desired to have you": it would be a satisfaction to him to have a believer in his power. He was anxious to get Peter into his clutches, to give him as tremendous a shaking as he could manage.

If Satan knows, as he no doubt does, concerning any one believer that he cannot quite destroy him, then he is especially anxious to worry him. If he cannot devour the chosen, he would at least defile them: if he cannot ruin their souls, he would break their quiet. As the Revised Version puts it, Satan even asks of God to have them that he may sift them as wheat. This is a curious statement, for it seems from it that the devil can pray; and that his petition may be granted him. The margin has it, "Satan hath obtained you by asking." The Lord may grant the request of the devil himself, and yet he would not prove thereby that he had any love towards him. The Lord's wisdom may grant Satan's desire, and in the very act overthrow his evil power. Let us not then stake our faith in the Lord's love upon his giving us the precise answer we desire, for what he gives to Satan he may see fit to deny to those whom he loves, and he may do so because he loves them.

It is a fact that the evil one is permitted to test the precious metal of God's treasury. The story in the Book of Job is no fiction, or piece of imagination. It is even so, that Satan desires to have choice ones of God put into his power that he may test them—that he may torment them, that he may, if possible, destroy them. The Lord may permit this, as he did in the case of Job, and as he did in the case of the apostles, and specially in the case of Peter. He may grant the tempter's request and allow him to touch our bone and our flesh, and see whether we will hold to our God in mortal agony.

We are not bound to know God's reasons for what he does or permits. It is sometimes sinful to enquire into those reasons. What the Lord does is right; let that be enough for us who are his children. But we can see sometimes a reason why the saints should be sifted as wheat; for *it appertains unto wheat to be sifted, because it is wheat.* Sifting brings a desirable result with it: it is *for the saints' good* that they should be tried. Satan doubtless wishes that he may let the good seed fall to the ground and be destroyed; but God overrules it to separate the chaff from the wheat, and to make the wheat into clean grain, fit for storage in the King's granary. Satan has often done us a good turn when he has meant to do us a bad one. After all, he is only a scullion in God's kitchen to clean his vessels; and some of them have received special scouring by means of his harsh temptations. God also may find a reason for allowing his saints to be tempted of Satan, and that reason may have more relation to others than to themselves. They may have to be tested *for other people's good.* The testing of their faith is "more precious than that of gold that perisheth, though it be tried with fire," and part of its preciousness is its usefulness. The child of God under temptation, behaving himself grandly, will become a standing example to those who are around him. "Ye have heard of the patience of Job"; but ye never would have heard of the patience of Job if Satan had not sifted him. This great treasury of instruction, the Book of Job, and all the truth taught us by Job's example, comes to us through God's having permitted Satan to put forth his hand and to press the patriarch so sorely. We also may be afflicted not so much for ourselves as for others; and this may be remarkably the case in the instances of those of you whom God makes useful to a large circle of friends. You live for others, and therefore suffer for others. The whole of your lives will not be accounted for by yourselves, but by your surroundings. As a minister I may have to be tempted because temptation is one of the best books in a minister's library. As a parent you may need affliction, because a father without a trial can give no counsel to a tempted child. Public workers may have to be tried in ways which, to a private Christian, are unnecessary. Let us accept remarkable discipline if thereby we are qualified for remarkable service. If by the roughness of our own road we are trained to conduct the Lord's sheep along their difficult pathway to the pastures on the hill-tops of glory, let us rejoice in every difficulty of the way. If apostles, and men like Peter, had to be put into Satan's sieve while they were being trained for their life-work, we may not hope to escape.

Observe, dear friends, what came before the sifting and went with the sifting. Note well that blessed "but." "*But I have prayed for thee.*" Not, "Thy brethren have prayed for thee." Not, "Thou hast prayed for thyself." But, "*I* have prayed for thee." Jesus, that master in the art of prayer, that mighty pleader who is our advocate above, assures us that he has already prayed for us. "I have prayed for thee," means—Before the temptation I have prayed for thee. I foresaw all the danger in which thou wouldst be placed, and concerning that danger I have exercised my function as high priest and intercessor. "I have prayed for thee." What a divine comfort is this to any who are passing through deep waters! You only go where Jesus has gone before you with his intercession. Jesus has made provision for all your future in a prayer already presented: "I *have* prayed for thee." You may be much comforted by the prayers of a minister, or of some Christian man who has power with God; but what are all such intercessions compared with the praying of your Lord? It were well to have Noah, Samuel, and Moses praying for us, but better far to have Jesus say, "I have prayed for thee." Blessed be God, Satan may have his sieve, but as long as Jesus wears his breastplate we shall not be destroyed by Satan's tossings.

Notice that the principal object of the prayer of our Lord was, "*that thy faith fail not.*" He knows where the vital point lies, and there he holds the shield. As long as the Christian's faith is safe the Christian's self is safe. I may compare faith to the head of the warrior. O Lord, thou hast covered my head in the day of battle, for thou hast prayed for me that my faith fail not. I may compare faith to the heart, and the Lord holds his shield over the heart that we may not be injured where a wound would be fatal. "I have prayed for thee, that thy faith fail not." Faith is the standard-bearer in every spiritual conflict; and if the standard-bearer fall, then it is an evil day: therefore our Lord prays that the standard-bearer may never fail to hold up his banner in the midst of the fray: "I have prayed for thee, that thy faith fail not." If faith fails, everything fails: courage fails, patience fails, hope fails, love fails, joy fails. Faith is the root-grace; and if this be not in order, then the leafage of the soul, which shows itself in the form of other graces, will soon begin to wither. "I have prayed for thee, that thy faith fail not."

Learn a lesson from this, my brother—that you take care to commend your faith unto your God. Do not begin to doubt because you are tempted: that is to lay bare your breast. Do not doubt because you are attacked: that is to loosen your harness. Believe still. "I had fainted," said David, "unless I had believed." It must be one thing or the other with us; believing, or fainting; which shall it be? "Above all, taking the shield of faith." Not only taking it so that it may cover all, but making this the vital point of holy carefulness. Watch thou in all things, but specially guard thy faith. If thou be careful about one thing more than another, above all be careful of thy faith. "I have prayed for thee, that thy faith fail not." Our Saviour's pleading goes to the point, and thus it teaches us where to direct our own desires and our own prayers. He asks for us far more wisely than we shall ever learn to ask for ourselves: let us copy his petitions.

Therefore it follows because of Christ's prayer that, though Peter may be very badly put to it, yet he shall be recovered, for Christ speaks of it as of an assured fact—"*When thou art converted.*" As much as to say—When thou comest back to thy old life and thy old faith, then exercise thyself usefully for thy Lord. He speaks of Peter's restoration as if it were quite sure to be. And is it not quite sure to be? If Jesus, the Beloved of the Father, prays for his people, shall he not win his suit with God? He will win it! He will uplift Peter from among the siftings where Satan has thrown him. We are sure he will, for in prospect thereof, he sets him a loving and suitable task: "When thou art converted, strengthen thy brethren." The establishment and confirmation of all the rest are to hinge upon the setting up in his place of poor thrice-denying Peter.

Now, beloved friends, I may be addressing a number of persons who believe on the Lord Jesus Christ as Peter did, but they have fallen into a bad state, and need a new conversion. I am very sorry for you, but I am by no means staggered at the sight of you, for you belong to a numerous class. When sitting to see enquirers I am constantly stumbling on backsliders, who come back very sincerely and very truly, and feel right pleased to find a Christian home again. I meet with many who have been outside in the world, some of them, for years, attending the house of God very irregularly, and seldom or never enjoying the light of God's countenance. They have wandered so that none can tell whether they are the Lord's or not, except the Lord himself, and he always knoweth them that are his. I bear happy witness that the Lord brings his own back again. Though the Lord's sheep stray, yet the Good Shepherd finds them. Though the Lord's children go into the far country, yet they each one in due time say, "I will arise, and go to my Father." It is not every prodigal that returns, but only the prodigal *son*. In due time, the son returns to the Father's house. It is not every bit of stuff that falls on the ground that is found again; but the woman's piece of money is sure to be discovered. She will not lose it: it is hers, and she values it; she sweeps the house, and makes any quantity of dust until she finds it. The Lord will find his own, even though Satan tries to prevent the gracious discovery.

It may be, some of you have wandered into error. May you be brought back very speedily; and if you are, we are going to say to you to-night, "Strengthen your brethren." Possibly there has been a general decay in grace within your soul; you have lost your joy, your peace, your love, your zeal. This is sad; may the Lord restore you in answer to the prayer of him that redeemed you; and then, when you are converted, seek to recover your brethren from the decay of their graces which has also injured them. You will not be converted in quite the same sense as you were at first, but yet you will be turned again to your old life, and hope, and then you are to strengthen your brethren by aiming at their restoration to their first love and earliest zeal. Perhaps you have been neglectful. I find that many who were good Christian people in the country, always at the house of prayer, and walking near to God, will come up to this wicked London to live, and the change is a serious injury to them. They get lost to Christian society, and by degrees they become deteriorated by the ungodliness of this modern Sodom. Nobody in the street wherein they live ever goes to a place of worship, and they do not know anybody at the chapel, or at the church, and so they give up going to public worship, and fall into the ways and habits of the ungodly world.

They are not happy. God's children never are happy when they leave their Father. If you have ever eaten the white bread of heaven, you will never rest content with the black ashes of earth. If the flavour of Christ's love has once been in your mouth, you are spoiled for a worldling. You will not make an expert sinner now, for your hand is out of it. Once converted, you must be a child of God, or nothing. You are ruined for this world; and if the world to come is not yours, where are you? The devil himself will not like you long: you are not of his sort. There is a something about you that will not suit Satan any more than Jonah suited the whale. The whale was quite as glad to part with Jonah as Jonah was to be set free from the whale. I see arrangements for your coming home again. The Lord deviseth means that his banished shall not perish: those tokens of disquiet, those startings in your sleep, those horrible forebodings, those inward hungerings, are all pulling at you to come home. You have been trying to feed upon the dust which is ordained to be the serpent's meat, and if the Lord had not loved you, you would have done so. A deceived heart has turned you aside, but in love to your soul the Lord has made you aware of it, and your cry is, "I will go and return to my first husband; for then was it better with me than now." These are tokens by which I am assured that the Lord will bring his own back. I rest confident that he will turn them, and they shall be turned; and I am going to talk to backsliders about what they are to do when they do come back again.

We are going to take it for granted that they will come back, and to speak to them now about what it is their privilege to attempt under such gracious circumstances. "When thou art converted, strengthen thy brethren." First, *it is the restored man's duty;* secondly, *he has a special qualification for it;* and thirdly, *it will be a great blessing to him to set about it.*

I. First, it is HIS DUTY. He has gone astray, and he has been brought back; what better can he do than to strengthen his brethren? *He will thus help to undo the evil which he has wrought.* Peter must have staggered his brethren. Some of them must have been quite frightened at him. John soon looked after him, but then they were not all Johns. Full of love, John soon hunted up Peter; but the others must have felt that he was a mere reed shaken by the wind. It must have staggered the faith of the weaker sort to see that Peter, who had been such a leader among them, was among the first to deny his Lord. Therefore, Peter, you must build what you have thrown down, and bind up what you have torn! Go and talk to these people again, and tell them how foolish and weak you were. Warn them not to imitate your example. You must henceforth be more bold than anybody else, that you may in some measure undo the mischief which you have done.

Now, do think of this, any of you who have been cold towards the Lord. You have wasted months, and even years, in backsliding. Try to recover lost ground. It will be almost impossible for you to do it, but do at least make a serious attempt. If anybody has been staggered by your backsliding, look after him, and try to bring him back, and strengthen him. Ask his pardon, and beg him to recover the strength of which you helped to rob him. This is the least that you can do. If almighty love has drawn you back again after sad wanderings, lay yourself out with all your heart to do good to those who may have been harmed by your sad turnings aside. Am I asking more of you than simple justice demands?

Besides, *how can you better express your gratitude to God* than by seeking to strengthen your weak brethren when you have been strengthened yourself? After our first conversion, you and I were found seeking earnestly after sinners like ourselves. We had been newly brought out of the house of bondage, and we longed to lead other slaves into the liberty wherewith Christ makes men free. This, I say, we ought to do when first brought to Jesus' feet; but if, to our disgrace, we have turned aside, and have backslidden; and if, to God's infinite glory, he has restored our souls, and made us strong again, then we ought to renew our zeal for the salvation of others, and we ought to have a special eye to backsliders like ourselves. We should say, " Lord, I will show how much I thank thee for restoring me, by endeavouring to find any that have been overtaken in a fault, that I may restore such in the spirit of meekness, remembering myself also, since I have been tempted, and have not stood against the temptation." Those of you whom the Good Shepherd has restored should have a quick eye for all the sickly ones of the flock, and watch over these with a sympathetic care. You should say, " This is the field which I shall try to cultivate. Because in my spiritual sickness the Lord has been pleased to deal so graciously with me, I would therefore lay myself out to cherish others who are diseased in soul."

Do you not think, too, that this becomes our duty, because, *doubtless, it is a part of the divine design?* Never let us make a mistake by imagining that God's grace is given to a man simply with an eye to himself. Grace neither begins with man nor ends with him with an object confined to the man's own self. When God chose his ancient people Israel, it was not merely that Israel might enjoy the light, but that Israel might preserve the light for the rest of the nations. When God saved you, he did not save you for your own sake, but for his own Name's sake, that he might through you show forth his mercy to others. We are windows through which the light of heavenly knowledge is to shine upon multitudes of eyes. The light is not for the windows themselves, but for those to whom it comes through the windows. Have you ever thought enough about this? When the Lord brings any of you back from your backsliding, it is decidedly with this view—that you may be qualified to sympathize with others and wisely guide them back to the fold. All your history, if you read it aright, has a bearing upon your usefulness to your fellow-men. If you have been permitted, in an hour of weakness, to grow cold, or turn aside, and if the Lord, in unspeakable compassion, has restored you to his ways, surely this must be his motive—that you may afterwards strengthen your brethren.

By the way, the very wording of the text seems to suggest the duty: we are to strengthen our "brethren." We must do so *in order that we may manifest brotherly love, and thus prove our sonship towards God.* Oh, what a blessed thing it is when we come back to God, and feel that we are still in the family! That was the point which we debated with ourselves: we feared that we were not the Lord's. Whatever some may say about that hymn—

> " 'Tis a point I long to know,
> Oft it causes anxious thought."

I do not give much for the man who has not sometimes had to sing it in the minor key. It is a pity that he ever should have to sing it; he will not if he walks before the Lord with care and watchfulness; but when he has been a naughty child, when his life has not been what it should be, if he does not doubt himself we must take leave to doubt for him. How can he help asking—

> "Do I love the Lord or no?
> Am I his or am I not?"

I am inclined to say with a good experimental writer—

> "He that never doubted of his state,
> He may—perhaps he may too late."

It is not an ill thing to try yourselves, and see whether your faith is gold or dross. To have a question about your position in the heavenly family is a very painful thing, and should not be endured one moment if it be in our power to solve the doubt. But if the Lord has brought you back as his child, you now know that you belong to the family, and it will be suggested at once to you to do something for *the brethren.* Naturally, you will look around to see whether there be any child of God to whom you can show favour for his Father's sake. You have injured all by your backsliding; and hence it is your duty, when restored to the family, to benefit them all by special consecration and double earnestness. Let it be your delight, as well as your duty, to strengthen your brethren. Prove that you are a brother by acting a brother's part; and claim your privilege as a child, and exercise it as a child should, by helping another child that is in need. I think that the text within itself contains this argument.

Let us see to it, dear friends, if we have been restored, that we try to look after our weak brethren, *that we may show forth a zeal for the honour and glory of our Lord.* When we went astray we dishonoured Christ. If any of these others go astray they will do the same. Therefore let us be watchful, that if we can we may prevent their being as foolish as we have been. Let us learn tenderness from our own experience, and feel a deep concern for our brethren. If one member of this church sins we all suffer—in our reputation, at any rate; and, specially, the best known among us have to bear a great deal because of the inconsistency of this person and of that. Do you want us to be wounded through you? My beloved friends, I do not think that one of you would wish to cast reproach upon your minister. Alas! Christ himself suffers. His worst wounds are those which he receives in the house of his friends. Peter, if you ever denied your Master, mind you look well to others who are growing presumptuous as you were before your great sin. If you meet anyone who is beginning to say, "I will go with thee to prison, and to death," give him a gentle jog, and say, "Mind, brother; you are going near a nasty hole into which I once fell. I pray you take warning from me." If you speak experimentally, you will have no cause to boast, but you will find in your own sin a reason why you should tenderly guard your brethren lest they should cause like dishonour to that dear Name which is more precious, I hope, to you than life itself. "When thou art converted, strengthen thy brethren." It is your duty.

II. Now secondly, HE HAS A QUALIFICATION FOR IT. This Peter is the man who, when he is brought back again, can strengthen his brethren. He can strengthen them by telling them of *the bitterness of denying his Master*. He went out and wept bitterly. It is one thing to weep; it is another thing to weep bitterly. There are sweet tears, as well as salt tears; but oh, what weeping a sin costs a child of God! I recollect a minister speaking very unguardedly: he said that the child of God lost nothing by sin except his comfort; and I thought, "Oh dear me! And is that nothing? Is that nothing?" It is such a loss of comfort that, if that were all, it would be the most awful thing in the world. The more God loves you, and the more you love God, the more expensive will you find it to sin. An ordinary sinner sins cheaply: the child of God sins very dearly. If thou be the King's favourite, thou must mind thy manners, for he will not take from thee what he will take from an enemy. The Lord thy God is a jealous God, because he is a loving God. He has such love for his own chosen that, if they turn aside, his jealousy burns like coals of juniper. May God keep us from ever provoking his sacred jealousy by wandering at any time into any kind of sin. Now Peter, because he could tell of the bitterness of backsliding, was the man to go and speak to anyone who was about to backslide, and say, "Do not so, my brother; for it will cost you dear."

Again, Peter was the man to tell another of *the weakness of the flesh*, for he could say to him, "Do not trust yourself. Do not talk about never going aside. Remember how I talked about it. I used to be very lofty in my talk and in my feelings, but I had to come down, I felt so sure that I loved my Lord and Master, that I put great confidence in myself, and could not think that I should ever wander from him. But see, see how I fell. I denied him thrice ere the time called cock-crowing." Thus, you see, Peter was wonderfully qualified, by having known the bitterness of sin, and by feeling the weakness of his own flesh, to go and strengthen others in these important points.

But he was also qualified to bear his personal witness to *the power of his Lord's prayer*. He could never forget that Jesus had said to him, "I have prayed for thee." He would say to any brother who had grown cold or presumptuous, "the Lord Jesus prayed for me, and it was because of his prayer that I was preserved from going farther, so that I was led back, and delivered from the sieve of the Evil One." Do you not think that this would strengthen any trembling one when Peter mentioned it. It is wonderful how men and women are helped by those who have had a similar experience to themselves. Theory is all very well, but to speak experimentally has a singular power about it. How one can comfort the bereaved if one has been bereaved himself! but how little can the young and inexperienced yield of consolation to those who are greatly tried, even though they are anxious to do so! And so, brethren, if the Lord has blessed you, and remembered you in his great mercy, and you know the power of the prayer of the great Intercessor, you can strengthen your brethren by reminding them of the perseverance of the Saviour's love.

And could not Peter speak about *the love of Jesus to poor wanderers?* The Lord turned and looked upon Peter, and that look broke Peter's heart, and afterwards the Lord spoke to Peter by the sea, and said to him, "Feed my sheep, and feed my lambs." O beloved, Peter would always remember that, and he would speak of it to any whom he found in a sad and weary condition. He would say, "My Lord was very good to me, and was willing to receive me back. Nay, he did not wait until I came back, but he came after me. He sent after me, saying, Go tell my disciples *and Peter;* and when he saw that I was penitent, he never rebuked me, except in such a gentle side-way that I was rather comforted than rebuked by what he said." Oh, you that have wandered, and Christ has restored you, comfort the wanderers when you see their tears! When you hear any word of doubt, or anything like despair from them, tell them that there is no truth in the suggestion of Satan that Christ is unwilling to forgive. Beseech them not to slander that dear heart of love, which is infinitely more ready to melt towards the penitent than the penitent's heart is to melt towards it. You know it. You know that you can speak not only what you have read in the Bible, but what you have felt in your own heart. You are qualified, therefore, to strengthen your brethren.

And could not Peter fully describe *the joy of restoration?* "Oh," he would say, "do not wander. There is no good in it. Do not go away from Jesus. There is no profit to be found there. Come back to him: there is such peace, such rest with him. Never, never go away again." Peter ever afterwards in his epistles—and we are sure that it must have been the same in his spoken ministry—would testify to the love and goodness of Christ, and urge the saints to steadfastness in the faith. I would appeal to any child of God here whether he ever gained anything by going away from Christ. No, brothers and sisters, the old proverb says that honesty is the best policy, but I will turn it to a higher use, and say, "Holiness is the best policy." Communion with Christ is the happiest life. If you gained all the world and did not lose your soul, but only lost the light of Christ's countenance for a few days, you would make a poor bargain. There is heaven in every glance of his eye. There is infinite joy in every word of his mouth when he speaks comfortably to his servants. Go not away from him. Be like Milton's angel, who lived in the sun. Abide in Christ, and let his words abide in you. Closer, closer, closer, this is the way to spiritual wealth. To follow afar off, and live at a distance from Christ, even if it does not make your soul to perish, yet it will wither up your joys, and make you feel an unhappy man, an unhappy woman. Therefore, all those who have tried it should bear their witness, and put their experience into the scale as they thus strengthen their brethren.

III. And now, lastly, the restored believer should strengthen his brethren, because IT WILL BE SUCH A BENEFIT TO HIMSELF. He will derive great personal benefit from endeavouring to cherish and assist the weak ones in the family of God.

Brother, do this continually and heartily, for thus you will be *made to see your own weakness.* You will see it in those whom you succour. As you see how they doubt, or grow cold, or become lukewarm, you will say to yourself, "These are men of like passions with myself. I see which way I shall drift unless the grace of God sustains me." It will lead you to throw out another anchor, and get a fresh hold, as you see how they yield to the tide. One man is wonderfully like another man, only that other men are better than we are; and when we are trying to strengthen them, we are not to look upon ourselves as superior beings, but rather as inferior beings, and say, "He fell yesterday, I may fall to-day; and if I do not fall to-day, I may to-morrow." All the weaknesses and follies you see in others, believe that they are in yourself, and that will tend to humble you. I think that a true minister is often excited to better work by what he sees of weakness in his people, because he says to himself, "Am I feeding this flock well?" Perhaps he thinks to himself, "If I had properly tended them they would not have shown all these weaknesses"; and then he will begin to blame his own ministry, and look to his own heart, and that is a good thing for us all. We very seldom, I think, blame ourselves too much, and it is a benefit to us to see our own failings in others.

But what *a comfort* it must have been to Peter *to have such a charge committed to him!* How sure he must have felt that Jesus had forgiven him, and restored him to his confidence, when the Lord, having asked him, "Lovest thou me?" said to him, "Feed my sheep; feed my lambs." Peter is all right again, or else Christ would not trust lambs to him. Peter must be all right, or else Jesus would not put the sheep under his care. It is a grand proof of our being fully restored to the divine heart, when the Lord entrusts us with work to do for his own dear children. If you and I are made the means of strengthening our brethren, what a comfort it will be to our hearts! I know that it is not the highest form of comfort, for Jesus would say of it, "Rejoice not in this, but rather rejoice that your names are written in heaven"; but still to a loving child of God it is no mean consolation to find that God is using him. I know, for my own part, that when I go to see our friends who are ill, and near to die, it is a supreme consolation to see how calm they always are, without any exception; yes, and how joyful they generally are—how triumphant in the departing hour! Then I say to myself, "Yes, my Master has owned my ministry." The seals of fresh conversions are very precious, but the surest seals are these dying saints, who have been nurtured in the gospel that we have preached. They prove the truth of it, for if they do not flinch when they stand looking into eternity, but even rejoice in the prospect of meeting their Lord, then what we preach is true, and our Master has not left us without witness. So you see that it is a great benefit to a man to strengthen his brethren, because it becomes a comfort to his own soul.

And, brethren, whenever any of you lay yourselves out to strengthen weak Christians, as I pray you may, *you will get benefit from what you do in the holy effort.* Suppose you pray with them. Well, then, you will pray a little more than if you only prayed for yourself; and anything that adds to your prayerfulness is a clear gain. I wish that you had the habit of making everybody pray with you that comes to your house, saying to them, "Now we have done our little business, let us have a word or two of prayer." Some even of God's people would look at you. It will do them good to look at you, and learn from you the blessed habit. With regard to those who are strangers to divine things there will often occur opportunities in which you have put them under an obligation, or they have come to you in trouble to ask advice, and then you may boldly say, "Do not let us part till we have prayed." We used to have an old member of this church who used to pray in very extraordinary places. Two women were fighting, and he knelt down between them to pray, and they gave over fighting directly. Before a door when there has been a noise in the house he has begun to pray. He was better than a policeman, for his prayer awed the most obstinate. They could not understand it: they thought it a strange thing, and they did not care to put themselves into direct opposition to the man of God. There is a wonderful power in prayer to bless ourselves, besides the blessings that it will bring upon others. Pray with the weak ones, and you will not be a weak one yourself.

Well, then, your example. If you use your example to strengthen the weak—if you carefully say to yourself, "No, I shall not do that because, though I may do it, I may do injury to some weak one"—this will do you good. If you hesitate, if you draw back from your own rights, and say, "No, no, no; I am thinking of the weak ones"—you will get good from that self-denial. If the poor, trembling, wandering backslider is much upon your mind, you will often be very tender how you act. You will look to see where your foot is going down next time, for fear of treading upon somebody or other; and in that way you will be winning for yourself the great gain of a holy carefulness of walk and conversation—no small gain to you.

And again, suppose that in trying to strengthen these weak ones, you begin to quote Scripture to them—quote a promise to them—this will bless you. Some of you do not know which promise to quote. You do not even know where to find it in the Word. But if you are in the habit of studying Scripture with a view to strengthening the weak, you will understand it in the best way, for you will get it in a practical form and shape. You will have the Bible at your fingers' ends. Moreover, one of these days the text that you looked out for old Mary will suit yourself. How often have we paid Paul with that which we meant to give to Peter! We have ourselves fed on the milk we prepared for the babes. Sometimes what we have laid up for another comes in handy for ourselves. We strangely find that we ourselves have been fed while we were feeding others, according to that promise, "He that watereth shall be watered also himself."

Now, I have said all this to you that have wandered and come back, and I want to say it right home to you. May the Holy Spirit speak to your inmost souls. You know who you are, and how far all this applies to you. The Lord bless you.

But, dear friends, if you have not wandered, if the Lord has kept you these twenty years close to him, and given you the light of his countenance all that time, then I think that you and I, and any of us of that sort, ought to strengthen our brethren still more. Oh, what we owe to sovereign grace! To be kept from wandering— what a blessing is that! Let us feel that instead of having a small debt to pay, we have a greater debt to acknowledge. Let us wake up to strengthen our brethren. I ask this of you, members of the church; because, in so large a church as this, unless there is a kind of universal mutual pastorate, what can we do? You that are converted, I beseech you to strengthen your brethren.

And then, once more, if all this ought to be done to those who are in the family, what ought we not to do for those outside—for those that have no Christ and no Saviour? If you are converted yourself, seek the salvation of your children, of your own brothers and sisters, and of all your household. Try to bring in your neighbours to hear the word. Get them, if you can, under the sound of the gospel. Why should we not fill up on Thursday night till the uppermost gallery is full? There are some friends up there to-night, and I am glad to see them. May God bless them. I hope that the day will come when every seat will be occupied there, so that when we are preaching the gospel we may scatter it broadcast, and find a field upwards as well as downwards where the seed may fall. Oh for a blessing! May we meet in heaven to praise the Lord our God. Amen.

PETER'S PRAYER.

A Sermon

DELIVERED BY

C. H. SPURGEON,

AT THE METROPOLITAN TABERNACLE, NEWINGTON.

On Thursday Evening, June 10th, 1869.

"When Simon Peter saw it, he fell down at Jesus' knees, saying, Depart from me; for I am a sinful man, O Lord."—Luke v. 8.

THE disciples had been fishing all night. They had now given over fishing; they had left their boats, and were mending their nets. A stranger appears. They had seen him, probably, once before, and they remembered enough of him to command respect. Beside, the tone of voice in which he spoke to them, and his manner, at once ruled their hearts. He borrowed Simon Peter's boat and preached a sermon to the listening crowds. After he had finished the discourse, as though he would not borrow their vessel without giving them their hire, he bade them launch out into the deep and let down their nets again. They did so, and, instead of disappointment, they at once took so vast a haul of fish that the boats could not contain all, and the net was not strong enough, and began to break. Surprised at this strange miracle, overawed probably by the majestic appearance of that matchless One, who had wrought it, Simon Peter thought himself quite unworthy to be in such company, and fell on his knees, and cried this strange prayer, "Depart from me, for I am a sinful man, O Lord." So I desire that, first of all, we shall hear:—

I. THE PRAYER IN THE WORST SENSE WE CAN GIVE TO IT.

It is always wrong to put the worst construction on anyone's words, and therefore we do not intend so to do, except by way of licence, and for a few moments only, to see what might have been made out of these words. Christ did not understand Peter so. He put the best construction upon which he said, but if a caviller had been there, a wrong interpretation would have been to this sentence: "Depart from me, for I am a sinful man, O Lord."

The ungodly virtually pray this prayer. When the gospel comes to some men, and disturbs their conscience, they say, "Go thy way for this time; when I have a more convenient season, I will send for thee." When some troublesome preacher tells them of their sins, when he puts a burning truth into their conscience, and rouses them so that they cannot sleep or rest, they are very angry with the preacher, and the truth that he was constrained to speak. And if they cannot bid him get out of their way, they can at least get out of his way, which comes to the same thing, and the spirit of it is, "We do not want to give up our sin; we cannot afford to part with our prejudices, or with our darling lusts, and therefore depart, go out of our coasts; let us alone; what have we to do with thee, Jesus, thou Son of God? Art thou come to torment us before our time?" Peter meant nothing of this sort, but there may be some here who do, and whose avoidance of the gospel, whose inattention to it, whose despite to it, and hatred of it, all put together virtually make up this cry, "Depart from us, O Christ."

Alas! I fear *there are some Christians* who do in fact, I will not say in intention, really pray this prayer. For instance: if a believer in Christ shall expose himself to temptation, if he shall find pleasure where sin mingles with it, if he shall forsake the assemblies of the saints, and find comfort in the synagogue of Satan; if his life shall be inconsistent practically, and also he shall become inconsistent by reason of his neglect of holy duties, ordinances, private prayer, the reading of the Word, and the like—what does such a Christian say but, "Depart from me, O Lord"? The Holy Spirit abides in our hearts, and we enjoy his conscious presence if we are obedient to his monitions; but if we walk contrary to him, he will walk contrary to us, and before long we shall have to say:—

"Where is the blessedness I knew
When first I saw the Lord?"

Why does the Holy Spirit withdraw the sense of his presence? Why, but because we ask him to go? Our sins ask him to go; our unread Bibles do, as it were, with loud voices ask him to be gone. We treat that sacred guest as if we were weary of him, and he takes the hint, and hides his face, and then we sorrow, and begin to seek him again. Peter does not do so, but we do. Alas! how often ought we to say, "Oh! Holy Spirit, forgive us, that we so vex thee, that we resist thy admonitions, quench thy promptings, and so grieve thee! Return unto us, and abide with us evermore."

This prayer in its worst is *sometimes practically offered by Christian churches.* I believe that any Christian church that becomes divided in feeling, so that the members have no true love one to another, that want of unity is an act of horrible supplication. It does as much as say, "Depart from us, thou Spirit of unity! Thou only dwellest where there is love: we will not have love: we will break thy rest: go from us!" The Holy Spirit delights to abide with a people that is obedient to his teaching, but there are churches that will not learn: they refuse to carry out the Master's will, or to accept the Master's Word. They have some other standard, some human book, and in the excellencies of the human composition they forget the glories of the divine. Now, I believe that where any book, whatever it may be, is put above the Bible, or even set by the side of it, or where any creed or catechism, however excellent, is made to stand at all on an equality with that perfect Word of God, any church that does this, in fact, say, "Depart from us, O Lord," and when it comes to actual doctrinal error, particularly to such grievous errors as we hear of now-a-days, such as baptismal regeneration, and the doctrines that are congruous thereto, it is, as it were, an awful imprecation, and seems to say, "Begone from us, O gospel! Begone from us, O Holy Ghost! Give us outward signs and symbols, and these will suffice us; but depart from us, O Lord; we are content without thee." As for ourselves, we may practically pray this prayer as a church. If our prayer-meetings should be badly attended; if the prayers at them should be cold and dead; if the zeal of our members should die out; if there should be no concern for souls; if our children should grow up about us untrained in the fear of God; if the evangelisation of this great city should be given over to some other band of workers, and we should sit still; if we should become cold, ungenerous, listless, indifferent—what can we do worse for ourselves? How, with greater potency, can we put up the dreadful prayer, "Depart from us: we are unworthy of thy presence: begone, good Lord! Let 'Ichabod' be written on our walls; let us be left with all the curses of Gerizim ringing in our ears."

I say, then, the prayer may be understood in this worst sense. It was not so meant: our Lord did not so read it: we must not so read it concerning Peter, but let us, oh! let us take care that we do not offer it thus, practically concerning ourselves.

But now in the next place we shall strive to take the prayer as it came from Peter's lips and heart:—

II. A PRAYER WE CAN EXCUSE, AND ALMOST COMMEND.

Why did Peter say, "Depart from me, for I am a sinful man, O Lord!" There are three reasons. First, *because he was a man*; secondly, *because he was a sinful man*; and again, *because he knew this, and became a humble man.*

So, then, the first reason for this prayer was that *Peter knew that he was a man,* and therefore, being a man, he felt himself amazed in the presence of such an one as Christ. The first sight of God, how amazing to any spirit, even if it were pure! I suppose God never did reveal himself completely, could never have revealed himself completely to any creature, however lofty in its capacity. The Infinite must overwhelm the finite. Now, here was Peter, beholding probably for the first time in his life in a spiritual way the exceeding splendour and glory of the divine power of Christ. He looked at those fish, and at once he remembered that night of weary toil, when not a fish rewarded his patience, and now he saw them in masses in the boat, and all done through this strange man who sat there, having just preached a still stranger sermon, of which Peter felt that never man spake like that before, and he did not know how it was, but he felt abashed; he trembled, he was amazed in the presence of such an one. I do not wonder, if we read that Rebecca, when she saw Isaac, came down from her camel and covered her face with her veil; if we read that Abigail, when she came to meet David, alighted from her ass and threw herself upon her face, saying, "My Lord, David!"; if we find Mephibosheth depreciating himself in the presence of King David, and calling himself a dog—I do not wonder that Peter, in the presence of the perfect Christ, should shrink into nothing, and in his first amazement at his own nothingness and Christ's greatness, should say he scarcely knew what, like one dazed and dazzled by the light, half-distraught, and scarcely able to gather together his thoughts and put them connectedly together. The very first impulse was as when the light of the sun strikes on the eye, and it is a blaze that threatens to blind us. "Oh! Christ, I am a man; how can I bear the presence of the God that rules the very fishes of the sea, and works miracles like this?" His next reason was, I have said, *because he was a sinful man*, and there is something of alarm, mingled with his amazement. As a man he stood amazed at the outshining of Christ's Godhead: as a sinful man he stood alarmed at its dazzling holiness. I do not doubt that in the sermon which Christ delivered there was such a clear denunciation of sin, such laying of justice to the line, and righteousness to the plummet such a declaration of the holiness of God, that Peter felt himself unveiled, discovered, his heart laid bare: and now came the finishing stroke. The One who had done this could also rule the fishes of the sea: he must, therefore, be God, and it was to God that all the defects and evils of Peter's heart had been revealed and thoroughly known, and almost fearing with a kind of inarticulate cry of alarm, because the criminal was in the presence of the Judge, and the polluted in the presence of the Immaculate, he said, "Depart from me, for I am *a sinful man*, O Lord."

But I have added that there was a third reason, namely, that *Peter was a humble man*, as is clear from the saying, because he knew himself, and confessed bravely that he was a sinful man. You know that sometimes there have been persons in the world who have suddenly found some king or prince come to their little cottage, and the good housewife, when the king himself was coming to her hut has felt as if the place itself was so unfit for him that, though she would do her best for his majesty, and was glad in her soul that he would honour her hovel with his presence, yet she could not help saying, "Oh! that your majesty had gone to a worthier house, had gone on to the great man's house a little ahead, for I am not worthy for your majesty should come here." So Peter felt as if Christ lowered himself almost in coming to him, as if it were too good a thing for Christ, too great, too kind, too condescending a thing, and he seems to say, "Go up higher, Master; sit not down so low as this in my poor boat in the midst of these poor dumb fishes; sit not down here, for thou hast a right to sit on the throne of heaven, in the midst of angels that shall sing thy praises day and night; Lord, do not stop here; go up; take a better seat, a higher place; sit among more noble beings, who are more worthy to be blessed with the smiles of thy Majesty." Don't you think he meant that? If so, we may not only excuse his prayer, but even commend it, for we have felt the same. "Oh!" we have said, "does Jesus dwell with a few poor men and women that have come together in his name to pray? Oh! surely, it is not a good enough place for him; let him have the whole world, and all the sons of men to sing his praises; let him have heaven, even the heaven of heavens: let the cherubim and seraphim be his servants, and archangels loose the latchets of his shoes: let him rise to the highest throne in glory, and there let him sit down, no more to wear the thorn-crown, no more to be wounded and despised, and rejected; but to be worshipped and adored for ever and ever." I think we have felt so, and, if so we can understand what Peter felt, "Depart from me, for I am a sinful man, O Lord."

Now, brethren and sisters, there are times when these feelings, if they cannot be commended in ourselves, are yet excused by our Master, and have a little in them. at any rate, which he looks upon with satisfaction. Shall I mention one?

Sometimes a man is *called to an eminent position of usefulness*, and as the vista opens before him, and he sees what he will have to do, and with what honour his Master will be pleased to load him, it is very natural, and I think it is almost spiritual for him to shrink and say, "Who am I that I should be called to such a work as this? My Master, I am willing to serve thee, but oh! I am not worthy." Like Moses, who was glad enough to be the Lord's servant, and yet he said, and he meant it so heartily, "Lord, I am slow of speech; I am a man of unclean lips, how can I speak for thee?" Or, like Isaiah, who was rejoiced to say, "Here am I, send me," but who felt, "Woe is me, for I am a man of uncircumcised lips; how shall I go?" Not like Jonah, who would not go at all, but must needs go off to Tarshish to escape working at Nineveh; yet perhaps with a little seasoning of Jonah's bitters, too, but mainly a sense of our own unworthiness to be used in so great a service, and we seem to say, "Lord, do not put me upon that; after all, I may slip, and dishonour thee; I would serve thee, but lest by any means I should give way under the strain, excuse thy servant, and give him a humbler post of service." Now, I say we must not pray in that fashion, but still, while there is some evil there, there is a sediment of good which Christ will perceive, in the fact that we see our own weakness and our own unsuitableness. He won't be angry with us, but, riddling the chaff from the wheat, he will accept what was good in the prayer, and forgive the ill.

Sometimes, again, dear friends, this prayer has been almost on our lips *in times of intense enjoyment* Some of you know what I mean, when the Lord draws near unto his servants, and is like the consuming fire, and we are like the bush that seemed to be altogether on a blaze with the excessive splendour of God realised in our souls. Many of God's saints have at such times fainted. You remember Mr. Flavel tells us that riding on horseback on a long journey to a place where he was to preach, he had such a sense of the sweetness of Christ and the glory of God, that he did not know where he was, and sat on his horse for two hours together, the horse wisely standing still, and when he came to himself he found that he had been bleeding freely through the excess of joy, and as he washed his face in the brook by the roadside he said he felt then that he knew what it was to sit on the doorstep of heaven, and he could hardly tell that if he had entered the pearly gates he could have been more happy, for the joy was excessive. To quote what I have often quoted before, the words of Mr. Welsh, a famous Scotch divine, who was under one of those blessed deliriums of heavenly light and rapturous fellowship, and exclaimed, "Hold, Lord! hold. it is enough! Remember, I am but an earthern vessel, and if thou give me more, I die!" God does sometimes put his new wine into our poor old bottles; and then we are half inclined to say, "Depart, Lord: we are not ready yet for thy glorious presence." It does not come to saying that: it does not amount to all that in words, but still, the spirit is willing, and the flesh is weak, and the flesh seems to start back from the glory which it cannot bear as yet. There are many things which Christ would tell unto us, but which he will not, because we cannot bear them now.

Another time, when this has passed over the mind, not altogether rightly, not altogether sinfully, like the two last, is *when the sinner is coming to Christ*, and has indeed in a measure believed in him, but when at last that sinner perceives the greatness of the divine mercy, the richness of the heavenly pardon, the glory of the inheritance which is given to pardoned sinners. Then many a soul has started back and said, "It is too good to be true; or if true, it is not true to me." Well do I remember a staggering fit I had over that business. I had believed in my Master, and rested in him for some months, and rejoiced in him, and one day, while revelling in the delights of being saved, and rejoicing in the doctrines of election, final perseverance, and eternal glory, it came across my mind, "And all this for *you*, for such a dead dog as you —how can it be so?" and for awhile it was a temptation stronger than I could overcome. It was just saying spiritually, "Depart from me; I am too sinful a man to have thee in my boat, too unworthy to have such priceless blessings as thou dost bring to me." Now, that, I say, is not altogether wrong, and not altogether right. There is a mixture there, and we may excuse, and somewhat commend, but not altogether. There are other times in which the same feeling may come across the mind, but I cannot stay now to specify them. It may be so with some here, and I pray them not to concern themselves utterly, nor yet to excuse themselves completely, but to go on to the next teaching of this prayer:—

III. A PRAYER THAT NEEDS AMENDING AND REVISING.

As it stood it was not a good one: now, let us put it in a different way, "Depart from me, for I am a sinful man, O Lord." Would it not be better to say, "Come nearer to me, for I am a sinful man, O Lord?" It would be a braver prayer, and a tenderer prayer withal: more wise, and not less humble, for humility takes many shapes. "I am a sinful man," here is humility. "Come nearer to me," here is faith, which prevents humility from degenerating into unbelief and despair. Brethren, that would be a good argument, for see: "Since, Lord, I am a sinner, I need purifying; only thy presence can truly purify, for thou art the Refiner, and thou dost purify the sons of Levi: only thy presence can cleanse, for the fan is in thy hand, and thou alone canst purge thy floor. Thou art like a refiner's fire, or like fuller's soap: come nearer to me, then, Lord, for I am a sinful man, and would not be always sinful; come, wash me from mine iniquity that I may be clean, and let thy sanctifying fire go through and through my nature till thou burn out of me everything that is contrary to thy mind and will." Dare you pray that prayer? It is not natural to pray it; if you can, I would say to you, "Simon Bar-jona, blessed art thou, for flesh and blood hath not taught thee this." Flesh and blood may make you say, "Depart from me"; it is the Holy Ghost alone that, under a sense of sin, can yet put a divine attraction to you in the purifying fire, and make you long, therefore, that Christ should come near to you.

Again, "Come near to me, Lord, since I am a man, and being a man am weak, and nothing can make me strong but thy presence. I am a man, so weak that if thou depart from me, I faint, I fall, I pine, I die; come near to me, then, O Lord, that by thy strength I may be encouraged and be fitted for service. If thou depart from me, I can render thee no service whatever. Can the dead praise thee? Can those with no life in them give thee glory? Come near me, then, my God, though I am so feeble, and as a tender parent feeds his child, and the shepherd carries his lambs, so come near to me."

Do you not think he might have said, "Come near to me, Lord, and abide with me, for I am a sinful man," in the recollection of how he had failed when Christ was not near? All through that night he had put the net into the sea with many a splash, and had drawn it up with many an eager look as he gazed through the moonlight, and there was nothing that rewarded his toil. In went the net again, and now when Christ came, and the net was full to bursting, would it not have been a proper prayer, "Lord, come near to me, and let every time I work I may succeed: and if I be made a fisher of men, keep nearer to me still, that every time I preach thy Word, I may bring souls into thy net, and into thy Church that they may be saved"?

What I want to draw out from the text—and I shall do so better if I continue bringing out these different thoughts—is this: that it is well when a sense of our unworthiness leads us, not to get away from God, in an unbelieving, petulant despair, but to get nearer to God. Now, suppose I am a great sinner. Well, let me seek to get nearer to God for that very reason, for there is great salvation provided for great sinners. I am very weak, and unfit for the great service which he has imposed upon me; let me not, therefore, shun the service or shun my God, but reckon that the weaker I am the more room there is for God to get the glory. If I were strong, then God would not use me, because then my strength would get the praise for it, but my very unfitness and want of ability, and all that I lament in myself in my Master's work, is but so much elbow-room for omnipotence to come and work in. Would it not be a fine thing if we could all say, "I glory not in my talents, not in my learning, not in my strength, but I glory in infirmity, because the power of God doth rest upon me; men cannot say, "That is a learned man, and he wins souls because he is learned"; they cannot say, "That is a man whose faculties of reasoning are very strong, and whose powers of argument are clear, and he wins sinners by convincing their judgments"; no, they say, "What is the reason of his success? We cannot discover it; we see nothing in him different from other men, or perhaps only the difference that he hath less of gift than they." Then glory be to God; he has the praise more clearly and more distinctly, and his head who deserves it wears the crown.

See, then, what I am aiming at with you, dear brethren and sisters. It is this—do not run away from your Master's work, any of you, because you feel unfit, but for that reason do twice as much. Do not give up praying because you feel you cannot pray, but pray twice as much, for you want more prayer, and instead of being less with God, be more. Do not let a sense of unworthiness drive you away. A child should not run away from its mother at night because it wants washing. Your children do not keep away from you because they are hungry, nor because they have torn their clothes, but they come to you just because of their necessities. They come because they are children, but they come oftener because they are needy children, because they are sorrowful children. So let every need, let every pain, let every weakness, let every sorrow, let every sin, drive you to God. Do not say, "Depart from me." It is a natural thing that you should say so, and not a thing altogether to be condemned, but it is a glorious thing, it is a God-honouring thing, it is a wise thing, to say, on the contrary, "Come to me, Lord; come nearer to me still, for I am a sinful man, and without thy presence I am utterly undone."

I shall say no more, but I would that the Holy Spirit would say this to some who are in this house, that have long been invited to come and put their trust in Jesus, but always plead as a reason for not coming, that they are too guilty, or that they are too hardened, or too something or other. Strange, that what one man makes a reason for coming, another makes a reason for staying away! David prayed in the Psalms, "Lord have mercy, and pardon mine iniquity, for it is great." "Strange argument," you will say. It is a grand one. "Lord, here is great sin, and there is something now that is worthy of a great God to deal with. Here is a mountain sin; Lord, have omnipotent grace to remove it. Lord, here is a towering Alp of sin; let the floods of thy grace, like Noah's flood, come twenty cubits over the top of it. I, the chief of sinners am; here is room for the chief of Saviours." How strange it is that some men should make this a reason for stopping away! This cruel sin of unbelief is cruel to yourselves; you have put away the comfort you might enjoy. It is cruel to Christ, for there is no pang that ever wounded him more than that unkind, ungenerous thought, that he is unwilling. Believe, believe that he never is so glad as when he is clasping his Ephraim to his breast, as when he is saying, "Thy sins, which are many, are all forgiven thee." Trust him. If you could see him, you could not help it. If you could look into that dear face, and into those dear eyes once red with weeping over sinners that rejected him, you would say, "Behold, we come to thee; thou hast the words of eternal life; accept us, for we rest in thee alone; all our trust on thee is stayed"; and that done, you would find that his coming to you would be like rain on the mown grass, as the showers that water the earth, and, through him, your souls should flourish; your sackcloth should be taken away, and you should be girt about with gladness, and rejoice in him world without end. The Lord himself bring you to this. Amen.

PETER'S SHORTEST PRAYER.

A Sermon

DELIVERED BY

C. H. SPURGEON,

AT THE METROPOLITAN TABERNACLE, NEWINGTON,

On Thursday Evening, October 2nd, 1873.

"Lord, save me."—Matthew xiv. 30.

I AM going to talk about the characteristics of this prayer in the hope that there may be many, who have never yet prayed aright, who may make this their own prayer to-night, so that from many a person here present this cry may silently go up, "Lord, save me."

Where did Peter pray this prayer? It was not in a place set apart for public worship, nor in his usual place for private prayer; but he prayed this prayer just as he was sinking in the water. He was in great peril, so he cried out, "Lord, save me." It is well to assemble with God's people for prayer if you can; but if you cannot go up to his house, it matters little, for prayer can ascend to him from anywhere all over the world. It is well to have a special spot where you pray at home; probably most of us have a certain chair by which we kneel to pray, and we feel that we can talk to God most freely there. At the same time, we must never allow ourselves to become the slaves even of such a good habit as that, and must always remember that, if we really want to find the Lord by prayer,—

"Where'er we seek him, he is found,
And every place is hallowed ground."

We may pray to God when engaged in any occupation if it is a lawful one; and if it is not, we have no business to be in it. If there is anything we do over which we cannot pray, we ought never to dare to do it again; and if there is any occupation concerning which we have to say, "We could not pray while engaged in it," it is clear that the occupation is a wrong one.

The habit of daily prayer must be maintained. It is well to have regular hours for devotion, and to resort to the same place for prayer as far as possible; still, the spirit of prayer is better even than the habit of prayer. It is better to be able to pray at all times than to make it a rule to pray at certain times and seasons. A Christian is more fully grown in grace when he prays about everything than he would be if he only prayed under certain conditions and circumstances. I always feel that there is something wrong if I go without prayer for even half an hour in the day. I cannot understand how a Christian man can go from morning to evening without prayer. I cannot comprehend how he lives, and how he fights the battle of life without asking the guardian care of God while the arrows of temptation are flying so thickly around him. I cannot imagine how he can decide what to do in times of perplexity, how he can see his own imperfections or the faults of others, without feeling constrained to say, all day long, "O Lord, guide me; O Lord, forgive me; O Lord, bless my friend!" I cannot think how he can be continually receiving mercies from the Lord without saying, "God be thanked for this new token of his grace! Blessed be the name of the Lord for what he is doing for me in his abounding mercy! O Lord, still remember me with the favour that thou showest unto thy people!" Do not be content, dear brethren and sisters in Christ, unless you can pray everywhere and at all times, and so obey the apostolic injunction, "Pray without ceasing."

I have already reminded you, dear friends, that Peter prayed this prayer when he was in circumstances of imminent danger: "Beginning to sink, he cried, saying, Lord, save me." "But," asks someone, "ought he not to have prayed before?" Of course he ought; but if he had not done so, it was not too late. Do not say, concerning any trouble, "Now I am so deeply in it, I cannot go to God about it." Why not? "Is anything too hard for the Lord?" It would have been well if the disciples had prayed before the first rough breath of the tempest began to toss their little barque, yet it was not too late to pray when the vessel seemed as if it must go down. As long as you have a heart to pray, God has an ear to hear. Look at Peter; he is "beginning to sink." The water is up to his knees, it is up to his waist, it is up to his neck, but it is not yet too late for him to cry, "Lord, save me;" and he has no sooner said it than the hand of Jesus is stretched out to catch him, and to guide him to the ship. So, Christian, cry to God though the devil tells you it is no use to cry; cry to God even if you are beneath the tempter's foot. Say to Satan, "Rejoice not against me, O mine enemy: when I fall, I shall arise;" but do not forget to cry unto the Lord. Cry to God for your children even when they are most ungodly, when their ungodliness almost breaks your heart. Cry to God on behalf of those whom you are teaching in the Sunday-school; even when you seem to think that their characters are developing in the worst possible form, still pray for them. Never mind though the thing you ask for them should appear to be an impossibility, for God "is able to do exceeding abundantly above all that we ask or think."

I would also say to any unconverted person who is here under conviction of sin,—Dear friend, if you are beginning to sink, yet still pray. If your sins stare you in the face, and threaten to drive you to despair, yet still draw near to God in prayer. Though it seems as if hell had opened its mouth to swallow you up, yet still cry unto God. "While there's life, there's hope."

"While the lamp holds out to burn,
The vilest sinner may return;"—

and the vilest sinner who returns shall find that God is both able and willing to save him. Never believe that lie of Satan that prayer will not prevail with God. Only go as the publican did, smiting upon your breast, and crying, "God be merciful to me a sinner," and rest assured that God is waiting to be gracious unto you.

I cannot help feeling that Peter's short, simple prayer was uttered in a most natural tone of voice: "Lord, save me." Let us always pray in just such a way as the Spirit of God dictates to us, and as the deep sorrow and humiliation of our heart naturally suggest to us. Many men who pray in public get into the habit of using certain tones in prayer that are anything but natural, and I am afraid that some even in private fail to pray naturally. Any language that is not natural is bad; the best tone is that which a man uses when he is speaking earnestly, and means what he says, and that is the right way to pray. Speak as if you meant it; do not whine it, or cant it, or intone it, but pour it out of your soul in the most simple, natural fashion that you can. Peter was in too great peril to put any fine language into his prayer; he was too conscious of his danger to consider how he might put his words together, but he just expressed the strong desire of his soul in the simplest manner possible: "Lord, save me;" and that prayer was heard, and Peter was saved from drowning, just as a sinner will be saved from hell if he can pray after the selfsame fashion.

I. Now, coming to Peter's prayer itself, and suggesting that it is a suitable prayer for all who are able to pray at all, my first observation upon it is that IT WAS A VERY BRIEF PRAYER.

There were only three words in it: "Lord, save me." I believe that the excellence of prayer often consists in its brevity. You must have noticed the extreme brevity of most of the prayers that are preserved in Scripture. One of the longest is the prayer of our Saviour recorded by John, which would, I suppose, have occupied about five minutes; and there is the prayer of Solomon at the dedication of the temple, which may have taken six minutes. Almost all the other prayers in the Bible are very short ones; and, probably, in our public services, we pray far longer than all of them put together. This may, perhaps, be excused when there are many petitions to be presented by one person on behalf of a large congregation; but at our prayer-meetings, where there are many to speak, I am certain that, the longer the prayer is, the worse it is. Of course, there are exceptions to this rule. The Spirit of God sometimes inspires a man in such a way that, if he would keep on praying all night, we should be glad to join with him in that holy exercise; but, as a general rule, the Spirit of God does no such thing. There are some who pray longest when they have least to say, and only go on repeating certain pious phrases which become almost meaningless by monotonous reiteration. Remember, dear friends, when you are praying, whether in public or in private, that you have not to teach the Lord a system of theology; he knows far more about that than you do. You have no need to explain to the Lord all the experience that a Christian ought to have, for he knows that far better than you do. And there is no necessity for you always to go round all the various agencies, and institutions, and mission stations. Tell the Lord what is in your heart in as few words as possible, and so leave time and opportunity for others to do the same.

I wonder if anyone here ever says, "I have no time for prayer." Dear friend, dare you leave your house in the morning without bowing the knee before God? Can you venture to close your eyes at night, and wear the image of death, without first commending yourself to the keeping of God during the hours of unconsciousness in sleep? I do not understand how you can live such a careless life as that. But, surely, you did not really mean that you had not time to offer such a prayer as Peter's "Lord, save me." How much time does that take, or this? "God be merciful to me a sinner." If you realized your true condition in God's sight, you would find time for prayer somehow or other, for you would feel that you must pray. It never occurred to Peter, as he was beginning to sink, that he had no time for prayer. He felt that he must pray; his sense of danger forced him to cry to Christ, "Lord, save me." And if you feel as you should feel, your sense of need will drive you to prayer, and never again will you say,"I have no time for prayer." It is not a matter of time so much as a matter of heart; if you have the heart to pray, you will find the time.

I would urge you to cultivate the habit of praying briefly all the day. I have told you before of the Puritan who, in a debate, was observed to be making notes; and when they were afterwards examined, it was found that there was nothing on the paper except these words, "More light, Lord! More light, Lord! More light, Lord!" He wanted light upon the subject under discussion, and therefore he asked the Lord for it, and that is the way to pray. During the day, you can pray, "Give me more grace, God. Subdue my temper, Lord. Tell me, O my God, what to do in this case! Lord, direct me. Lord, save me." Pray thus, and you will be imitating the good example of brevity in prayer which our text sets before you.

PETER'S SHORTEST PRAYER. 59

II. Notice, next, that, brief as Peter's prayer was, IT WAS WONDERFULLY COMPREHENSIVE, AND ADAPTED FOR USE ON MANY DIFFERENT OCCASIONS: "Lord, save me."
It covered all the needs of Peter at that time, and he might have continued to use it as long as he lived. When his Master told him that Satan desired to have him that he might sift him as wheat, he might well have prayed, "Lord, save me." When he had denied his Master, and had gone out, and wept bitterly, it would have been well for him to pray, "Lord, save me." When he was afterwards journeying to and fro, preaching the gospel, he could still pray, "Lord, save me;" and when, at last, he was led out to be crucified for Christ's sake, he could hardly find a better prayer than this with which to close his life, "Lord, save me."
Now, as Peter found this prayer so suitable for him, I commend it to each one of you. Have you been growing rich lately? Then, you will be tempted to become proud and worldly; so pray, "Lord, save me from the evils that so often go with riches; thou art giving me this wealth, help me to be a good steward of it, and not to make an idol of it." Or are you getting poor? Is your business proving a failure? Are your little savings almost gone? Well, there are perils connected with poverty; so pray, "Lord, save me from becoming envious or discontented; let me be willing to be poor rather than do anything wrong in order to get money." Do you, dear friend, feel that you are not living as near to God as you once did? Is the chilling influence of the world telling upon you? Then pray, "Lord, save me." Have you fallen into some sin which you fear may bring disgrace upon your profession? Well then, ere that sin grows greater, cry, "Lord, save me." Have you come to a place where your feet have well-nigh slipped? The precipice is just before you, and you feel that, if some mightier power than your own does not interpose, you will fall, to your serious hurt, if not to your destruction. Then, at once breathe the prayer, "Lord, save me." I can commend this prayer to you when you are upon the stormy sea, but it will be equally suitable to you upon the dry land: "Lord, save me." I can commend it as suitable to you when you are near the gates of death, but it is just as much adapted to you when you are in vigorous health: "Lord, save me." And if you can add to the prayer, "and, Lord, save my children, and my kinsfolk, and my neighbours," it will be even better. Still, for yourself personally, it is an admirable prayer to carry about with you wherever you go: "Lord, save me."

III. Peter's prayer had a third excellence, IT WAS VERY DIRECT. It would not have done for Peter just then to have used the many titles which rightly belong to Christ, or to have begun asking for a thousand things; but he went straight to the point of his immediate need, and cried, "Lord, save me." When one of our dear friends, who has lately gone to heaven, was very ill, one of his sons prayed with him. He began in a very proper way, "Almighty Father, Maker of heaven and earth, our Creator,"—but the sick man stopped him, and said, "My dear boy, I am a poor sinner, and I want God's mercy; say, 'Lord, save him.'" He wanted his son to get to the point, and I can sympathize with him; for, often, when some of our dear brethren have been praying here, and have been beating about the bush, I have wished that they would come to the point, and ask for what they really needed. They have kept on walking round the house, instead of knocking at the door, and seeking to enter. Peter's prayer shows us how to go direct to the very heart of the matter: "Lord, save me."

Many persons fail to receive answers to their prayers because they will not go straight to God, and confess the sins that they have committed. There was a member of a Christian church who had, on one occasion, fallen very shamefully through drink. He was very penitent, and he asked his pastor to pray for him, but he would not say what his sin had been. The pastor prayed, and then told the brother himself to pray. The poor man said, "Lord, thou knowest that I have erred, and done wrong," and so on, making a sort of general confession, but that brought him no peace of mind. He felt that he could not go away like that, so he knelt down again, and said, "Lord, thou knowest that I was drunk; it was a shameful sin that I committed, but I am truly grieved for it; O Lord, forgive me, for Jesus' sake!" and ere his prayer was finished, he had found peace because he had plainly confessed his sin to God, and had not sought to hide it any longer. You remember that David could get no peace until he came to the point, and prayed, "Deliver me from bloodguiltiness, O God, thou God of my salvation." Before that, he had tried to smother his great sin; but there was no rest for his conscience until he had made a full confession of his guilt, and after that he could say, "The sacrifices of God are a broken spirit: a broken and a contrite heart, O God, thou wilt not despise." Let our prayers, whether for ourselves or others, and especially our confessions of sin, go straight to the point, and not go beating about the bush. If any of you have been using forms of prayer, which have not obtained for you any answers to your supplications, put them all on one side, and just go and tell the Lord plainly what you want. Your prayer will then probably be something like this, "O God, I am a lost sinner! I have been careless about divine things; I have listened to the gospel, but I have not obeyed it. Lord, forgive me, save me, make me thy child, and let me and my household too be thine for ever." That is the way to pray so that God will hear and answer you.

IV. Another characteristic of Peter's prayer was that IT WAS A VERY SOUND-DOCTRINE PRAYER: "Lord, save me."

Peter does not appear to have had any idea of saving himself from drowning, he does not seem to have thought that there was sufficient natural buoyancy about him to keep him afloat, or that he could swim to the ship; but, "beginning to sink, he cried, Lord, save me." One of the hardest tasks in the world is to get a man to give up all confidence in himself, and from his heart to pray, "Lord, save me." Instead of doing that, he says, "O Lord, I do not feel as I ought; I want to feel my need more, I want to feel more joy, I want to feel more holiness." You see, he is putting feelings in place of faith; he is, as it were, laying down a track along which he wants God to walk instead of walking in the way which God has marked out for all - who desire to be saved. Another man is seeking to reform himself, and so to make himself fit for heaven; and he prays in harmony with that idea, and of course gets no answer. I like to hear such a prayer as this, "O Lord, I cannot save myself, and I do not ask thee to save me in any way that I prescribe; Lord, save me anyhow, only do save me! I am satisfied to be saved by the precious blood of Jesus. I am satisfied to be saved by the regenerating work of the Holy Spirit. I know I must be born again if I am ever to enter heaven; quicken me, O thou ever-blessed Spirit! I know I must give up my sins. Lord, I do not want to keep them, save me from them by thy grace, I humbly entreat thee. I know that only thou canst do this work; I cannot lift even a finger to help thee in it; so save me, Lord, for thy great mercy's sake!" This is sound doctrinal truth,—salvation all of grace, not of man, nor by man; "not of blood, nor of the will of the flesh, nor of the will of man, but of God;" salvation according to the eternal purpose of God, by the effectual working of the Holy Spirit, through the substitutionary sacrifice of Jesus Christ. When a sinner is willing to accept salvation on God's terms, then the prayer shall ascend acceptably to the Most High, "Lord, save me."

V. Notice also that PETER'S PRAYER WAS A VERY PERSONAL ONE: "Lord, save *me*."

Peter did not think of anybody else just then; and when a soul is under concern about its eternal interests, it had better at first confine its thoughts to itself, and pray, "Lord, save *me*." Yes, and in the Christian's after-life, there will come times when he had better, for a while, forget all others, and simply pray, "Lord, save *me*." Here we are, a great congregation, gathered together from very various motives; and perhaps some here, who are not yet personally interested in Christ, are vaguely hoping that God will bless somebody in this assembly; but if the Holy Spirit shall begin to work upon some individual heart and conscience, the convicted one will begin to pray, "Lord, save *me*. I hear of many others being brought to Jesus; but, Lord, save *me*. My dear sister has been converted, and has made a profession of her faith; but, Lord, save *me*. I had a godly mother, who has gone home to glory; and my dear father is walking in thy fear; let not their son be a castaway, Lord, save *me*."

I entreat everyone here to pray this personal prayer, and I beg you who do love the Lord to join me in pleading with him that it may be so. I see some little girls over there; will not each one of you, my dear children, pray this prayer? I pray the Holy Spirit to move you to cry, "Lord, save little Annie," or "Lord, save little Mary;" and may you boys be equally moved to pray, "Lord, save Tom," or "Lord, save Harry." Pray for yourself in just that simple way, and who knows what blessing may come to you? Then you mothers will surely not let your children pray for themselves, while you remain prayerless; will not each one of you cry, "Lord, save me"? And you working-men, whom I am so glad to see at a week-night service, do not go away without presenting your own personal petitions. The apostle Peter had to pray for himself, the most eminent servants of God had to pray for themselves, and you must pray for yourselves. If all the saints of God were to pray for you, with one united voice, as long as you live, you would not be saved unless you also cried to God for yourself. Religion is a personal matter, there is no such thing as religion by proxy. You must repent for yourselves, and pray for yourselves, and believe for yourselves if you would be saved. May God grant that you may do so!

VI. I want you to notice, next, that PETER'S PRAYER WAS A VERY URGENT ONE: "Lord, save me."

He did not say, "Lord, save me to-morrow," or "Lord, save me in an hour's time." He was "beginning to sink;" the hungry waves had opened their mouths to swallow him, and he would soon be gone. He had only time to cry, "Lord, save me;" but he no doubt meant, "Lord, save me now, for I am now in danger of being drowned. Lord, save me now; for, if thou shouldst delay, I shall sink to the bottom of the sea." "And immediately Jesus stretched forth his hand, and caught him," and so saved him. There are many people who would like Jesus to save them, but when? Ah! that is the point which they have not settled yet. A young man says, "I should like Christ to save me when I grow older, when I have seen a little more of life." You mean when you have seen a great deal more of death, for that is all you will see in the world; there is no real life there except that which is in Christ Jesus. Many a man in middle life has said, "I mean to be a Christian before I die, but not just yet." He has been too busy to seek the Lord, but death has come to him without any warning; and, busy or not, he has had to die quite unprepared.

There is hope for a sinner when he prays, "Lord, my case is urgent, save me now. Sin, like a viper, has fastened itself upon me; Lord, save me now from its deadly venom. I am guilty now, and condemned already, because I have not believed in Jesus; Lord, save me now, save me from condemnation, save me from the damning sin of unbelief. Lord, for aught I know, I am now upon the brink of death, and I am in danger of hell as well as of death as long as I am unforgiven. Therefore, be pleased to let the wheels of thy chariot of mercy hasten, and save me even now, O Lord!" I have known some, who have been so deeply under the influence of the Holy Spirit, that they have knelt down by their bedsides, and said, "We will never give sleep to our eyes, or slumber to our eyelids, till we have found the Saviour," and ere long they have found him. They have said, "We will wrestle in prayer until our burden of sin is gone;" and when they have reached that determination, it has not been long before they have obtained the blessing they desire. When nothing else succeeds, importunity will surely prevail. When thou wilt not take a denial from God, he will not give thee a denial; but as long as thou art content to be unsaved, thou wilt be unsaved. When you cry, with all the urgency of which you are capable, "I must have Jesus, or die; I am hungering, thirsting, pining, panting after him, as the hart panteth after the water-brooks;" it shall not be long before you clasp that priceless treasure to your heart, and say, "Jesus is my Saviour; I have believed in him."

VII. Now, lastly, I must remind you that PETER'S PRAYER WAS AN EFFECTUAL ONE: "Lord, save me," and Jesus did save him.

There may be comfort to some here present, in the thought that, although this was the prayer of a man in trouble, and a man in whom there was a mixture of unbelief and faith, yet it succeeded. Imperfections and infirmities shall not prevent prayer from speeding if it be but sincere and earnest. Jesus said to Peter, "O thou of little faith, wherefore didst thou doubt?" which shows that he did doubt although there was also some faith in him, for he believed that Christ could save him from a watery grave. Many of us also are strange mixtures, even as Peter was. Repentance and hardness of heart can each occupy a part of our being, and faith may be in our heart together with a measure of unbelief, even as it was with the man who said to Jesus, "Lord, I believe; help thou mine unbelief."

Do any of you feel that you want to pray, and yet cannot pray? You would believe in Jesus, but there is another law in your members which keeps you back. You would pray an effectual prayer, like that of Elijah, never staggering at the promise through unbelief; but, somehow or other, you cannot tell why, you cannot attain to that prayer. Yet you will not give up praying; you feel that you cannot do that. You linger still at the mercy-seat even when you cannot prevail with God in prayer. Ah, dear soul! it is a mercy that God does not judge thy prayer by what it is in itself; he judges it from another point of view altogether. Jesus takes it, mends it, adds to it the merit of his own precious blood, and then, when he presents it to his Father, it is so changed that you would scarcely recognize it as your petition. You would say, "I can hardly believe that is my prayer, Christ has so greatly altered and improved it." It has happened to you as it sometimes happens to poor people who are in trouble, as it did happen to one whom I knew some time ago. A good woman wanted me to send in a petition, to a certain government office, concerning her husband, who was dead, and for whose sake she wanted to get some help. She drew up the petition, and brought it to me. About one word in ten was spelt correctly, and the whole composition was unfit to send. She wanted me to add my name to it, and post it for her. I did so; but I first re-wrote the whole petition, keeping the subject matter as she put it, but altering the form and wording of it. That is what our good Lord and Master does for us only in an infinitely higher sense; he re-writes our petition, sets his own sign-manual to it, and when his Father sees that, he grants the request at once. One drop of Christ's blood upon a prayer must make it prosper.

Go home, therefore, you who are troubled with doubts and fears, you who are vexed by Satan, you who are saddened by the recollection of your own past sins; notwithstanding all this, go to God, and say, "Father, I have sinned against heaven, and before thee," and ask for his forgiveness, and his forgiveness you shall receive. Keep on praying in such a fashion as this, "Lord, save me, for Jesus' sake. Jesus, thou art the Saviour of sinners, save me, I beseech thee. Thou art mighty to save; Lord, save me. Thou art in heaven pleading for transgressors; Lord, plead for me." Do not wait till you get home, but pray just where you are sitting, "Lord, save me." May God give grace to everyone here to pray that prayer from the heart, for Jesus Christ's sake! Amen.

Exposition by C. H. Spurgeon.
MATTHEW VI. 5—34.

Verse 5. *And when thou prayest, thou shalt not be as the hypocrites are: for they love to pray standing in the synagogues and in the corners of the streets, that they may be seen of men.*

We ought to pray in the synagogue, and we may pray at the corners of the streets; but the wrong is to do it to "be seen of men," that is, to be looking for some present reward in the praises that fall from human lips.

5—7. *Verily I say unto you, They have their reward. But thou, when thou prayest, enter into thy closet, and when thou hast shut thy door, pray to thy Father which is in secret; and thy Father which seeth in secret shall reward thee openly. But when ye pray, use not vain repetitions, as the heathen do: for they think that they shall be heard for their much speaking.*

They seem to attribute a sort of power to a certain form of words, as if it were a charm, and they repeat it over and over again. Not only do the poor Mohammedans and heathen "use vain repetitions," but the members of the Romish and other churches that I might name do the same thing; words to which they attach but very slight meaning, and into which they put little or no heart, are repeated by them again and again, as if there could be some virtue in the words themselves. Let it not be so with you beloved. Pray as long as you like in secret, but do not pray long with the idea that God will hear you simply because you are a long while at your devotions.

8. *Be not ye therefore like unto them: for your Father knoweth what things ye have need of, before ye ask him.*

He does not need to be informed, nor even to be persuaded. Mere words are of no value in his ears. If you must needs use many words, ask men to lend you their ears, for they may have little else to do with them; but God careth not for words alone, it is the thought, the desire of the heart to which he ever hath regard.

9. *After this manner therefore pray ye:*

Here is a model prayer for you to copy as far as it is suited to your case:—

9—13. *Our Father which art in heaven, Hallowed be thy name. Thy kingdom come. Thy will be done in earth, as it is in heaven. Give us this day our daily bread. And forgive us our debts, as we forgive our debtors. And lead us not into temptation, but deliver us from evil: for thine is the kingdom, and the power, and the glory, for ever. Amen.*

And then, as if there was one part of the prayer that would be sure to arrest the attention of his hearers, namely, that concerning forgiving our debtors, the Saviour makes the following remarks:—

14, 15. *For if ye forgive men their trespasses, your heavenly Father will also forgive you: but if ye forgive not men their trespasses, neither will your Father forgive your trespasses.*

Therefore, in order to succeed in prayer, we must have a heart purged from a spirit of revenge and from all unkindness; we must ourselves be loving and forgiving, or we cannot expect that God will hear our supplications when we come to crave his forgiveness.

16. *Moreover when ye fast, be not, as the hypocrites, of a sad countenance: for they disfigure their faces, that they may appear unto men to fast.*

They seemed to say to everyone who looked at them, "We have been so engrossed with our devotions that we have not found time even to wash our faces." But the Saviour says to his followers, "Do not imitate those hypocrites; do not make public your private religious exercises; perform them unto God, and not unto men. As for those hypocrites,"—

16. *Verily I say unto you, They have their reward.*

And a poor reward it is.

17, 18. *But thou, when thou fastest, anoint thine head, and wash thy face; that thou appear not unto men to fast, but unto thy Father which is in secret: and thy Father, which seeth in secret, shall reward thee openly.*

May God give us that modest, unselfish spirit which lives unto him, and does not want to walk in the sham light of men's esteem! What matters it, after all, what men think of us? The hypocrite proudly boasts if he wins a little praise from his fellows, but what is it except so much wind? If all men should speak well of us, all that we should gain would be this, "Woe unto you, when all men shall speak well of you! for so did their fathers to the false prophets."

19, 20. *Lay not up for yourselves treasures upon earth, where moth and rust doth corrupt, and where thieves break through and steal: but lay up for yourselves treasures in heaven, where neither moth nor rust doth corrupt, and where thieves do not break through nor steal:*

Christ here first teaches us how to pray, and then teaches us how really to live. He turns our thoughts from the object in life which allures and injures so many, but which is, after all, an object unworthy of our search; and he bids us seek something higher and better: "Lay up for yourselves treasures in heaven,"—

21. *For where your treasure is, there will your heart be also.*

It is sure to be so; your heart will follow your treasure. Send it away therefore up to the everlasting hills, lay up treasure in that blessed land before you go there yourself.

22, 23. *The light of the body is the eye: if therefore thine eye be single, thy whole body shall be full of light. But if thine eye be evil, thy whole body shall be full of darkness. If therefore the light that is in thee be darkness, how great is that darkness!*

If thine eye be blocked up with gold dust, or if thou art living for self and this world, thy whole life will be a dark life, and the whole of thy being will dwell in darkness.

"But," says someone, "may I not live for this world and the next too?" Listen:—

24. *No man can serve two masters:*
He may serve two individuals, who have conflicting interests, but they cannot both be his masters.

24. *For either he will hate the one, and love the other; or else he will hold to the one, and despise the other. Ye cannot serve God and mammon.*
Either the one or the other will be master; they are so opposed to each other that they will never agree to a divided service. "Ye cannot serve God and mammon." It is the Lord Jesus Christ who says this, so do not attempt to do what he declares is impossible.

25. *Therefore I say unto you, Take no thought for your life,—*
It should be, "Take no distracting thought for your life,"—

25. *What ye shall eat, or what ye shall drink; nor yet for your body, what ye shall put on. Is not the life more than meat, and the body than raiment?*
You are obliged to leave your life with God, why not leave with him all care about your food and your raiment?

26. *Behold the fowls of the air: for they sow not, neither do they reap, nor gather into barns; yet your heavenly Father feedeth them. Are ye not much better than they?*
Do you believe that, after all your earnest labour and your industry, God will permit you to starve, when these creatures, that labour not, yet are fed?

27—29. *Which of you by taking thought can add one cubit unto his stature? And why take ye thought for raiment? Consider the lilies of the field, how they grow; they toil not, neither do they spin: and yet I say unto you, That even Solomon in all his glory was not arrayed like one of these.*
Christ asks then whether, by taking thought, they can add a single cubit to their lives, for I take his question to mean, whether they could, by any means, make the standard of existence any longer than it was. They could not do so; they could shorten it, and very often, carking care has brought men to their graves. Then Christ bade them note how the lilies grow, so that even Solomon could not excel them for beauty.

30—33. *Wherefore, if God so clothe the grass of the field, which to day is, and to-morrow is cast into the oven, shall he not much more clothe you, O ye of little faith? Therefore take no thought, saying, What shall we eat? or, What shall we drink? or, Wherewithal shall we be clothed? (For after all these things do the Gentiles seek:) for your heavenly Father knoweth that ye have need of all these things. But seek ye first the kingdom of God, and his righteousness; and all these things shall be added unto you.*

If you want string and brown paper, you need not go into a shop to buy them; but if you buy certain articles, you get string and brown paper into the bargain. So, when you go to God, seeking first his kingdom and his righteousness, these other things, which are but the packing, as it were, the string and the brown paper, are given to you into the bargain. He who giveth you the golden treasures of heaven will not allow you to want for the copper treasures of earth.

34. *Take therefore no thought for the morrow: for the morrow shall take thought for the things of itself. Sufficient unto the day is the evil thereof.*
You cannot live in to-morrow, so do not fret about to-morrow. You live in to-day, so think of to-day, spend to-day to God's glory, and leave the care about to-morrow until to-morrow comes.

WHAT WAS BECOME OF PETER?

A Sermon

DELIVERED BY

C. H. SPURGEON,

AT THE METROPOLITAN TABERNACLE, NEWINGTON.

"Now as soon as it was day, there was no small stir among the soldiers, what was become of Peter."—Acts xii. 18.

WE can very well understand that there would be great excitement. It was the most improbable thing in the world that Peter should escape from custody. In the innermost dungeon, securely chained, watched by a four-fold guard, with no powerful friends outside to attempt a rescue, it was marvellous that, in the morning, the bird was flown; the prison doors were closed, and the guards in their places, but Peter, where was he? We marvel not that "there was no small stir among the soldiers, what was become of Peter?"

We will use this striking narrative as an illustration; what if we make it an allegory? The sinner fast bound in his sin is, by the mercy of God, set free, brought out from his spiritual prison into the streets of the new Jerusalem, and then there is no small stir among his old companions, what has become of him. Many questions are asked, and many strange answers are given. They cannot understand it. The vain world esteems it strange; much it admires, but hates the change. The carnal mind cannot understand conversion. There is "no small stir, what has become of Peter."

We shall, first of all, dwell a little upon *the escape of Peter, as illustrating the salvation of certain sinners;* then upon *the consequent stir about it,* and then upon *the quiet conduct of the man who is the object of all this stir:* "What was become of Peter?"

I. First, then, THE IMPROBABLE EVENT.

Peter was *in prison*. It was a most unlikely thing that he should come forth from Herod's gaol, but it is a far more unlikely thing that sinners should be set free from the dungeons of sin. For the iron gate which opened into the city to turn upon its hinges of its own accord was wonderful, but for a sinful heart to loathe its sin is stranger far. Who can escape from the grasp of sin? No person is more straitly shut up than is the sinner in the prison-house of original depravity; it is not around us merely, but in us, compassing our path, whether we lie down or rise up. Stronger than granite walls and bars of iron are the forces of evil. Evil has penetrated our souls, it has become part of ourselves. Whither shall we fly from its presence, or how shall we escape from its power? Vain are the wings of the morning; they cannot enable us to fly from our own selves.

O marvellous thing, that the Ethiopian should escape from his blackness, and the leopard from his spots! There are some men in whom evil is more than ordinarily conspicuous. They have done violence to conscience; they have quenched, as far as possible, the inner light; they have defied the customs of society; they have resolved to sin at random, and they do so. What a miracle it is that such as these should be emancipated from the slavery they choose so eagerly; that these, whose feet are set fast in the stocks of vice, in the innermost dungeon of transgression, should ever be set at liberty! And yet how often this has happened! The foundations of the prison have been shaken, and the prisoner's bands have been loosed. The saints of God can, all of them, bless him for setting them at liberty from sin; the snare is broken, and they are escaped! Ay, and many of them can praise him for deliverance from very great sins, black sins, iron sins, sins which had entered into their souls, and held their spirits captive. No man can set another man free from iniquity, nor can any man burst down his own prison-doors. No Samson is strong enough for that; but there is One, "mighty to save," who has come to proclaim liberty to the captives of sin, and the opening of the prison to them that are bound by iniquity, and he has so proclaimed it that many of us are now free through his grace. O that many others, now shut up in the spiritual Bastille, may be set free!

But, besides being in prison, Peter was *in the dark.* All the lamps had been quenched for the night in his miserable place of confinement. Such is the estate, spiritually, of every unconverted sinner, he is in the dark; he does not know Christ, nor apprehend his own condition, nor comprehend eternal realities. What a state of darkness is he in who has never heard the gospel! But, alas! there are some who have heard it, often heard it, and yet their eyes are holden so that they cannot see the light, and they are as badly in the dark as those upon whom the lamp has never shone. Does it not seem impossible to convert such darkened ones? You have held up, as it were, the very sun in the heavens before their eye-balls, while you have preached salvation by Christ, and yet so blind are they that they have seen nothing! Can these blind eyes see? Can these prisoners of midnight escape from the prison through its long corridors and winding passages? The thousands in this city who never attend the house of prayer, is it possible to get at them? Can the grace of God ever come to them? Yes, we bless God that, as the angel came into Peter's prison, and brought a light with him, so the Spirit can come into the prison of man's sin, and bring heavenly illumination with him, and then he will see, in a moment, the truth as it is in Jesus, which he never knew before. Glory be to God, he can lead the blinded mind into daylight, and give it eyes to see and a heart to love the truth divine. We can testify of this, for so hath God wrought upon *us*, and why should he not thus work upon others? But it is a great marvel; and when it is performed, there is "no small stir."

Peter's case, in the third place, had another mark of hopelessness about it. He was in prison; he was in the dark; and *he was asleep*. How can you lead a man out of prison who is sound asleep? If you cannot enter and arouse him, what can you do for him? Suppose the doors were opened, and the chains were snapped, yet if he remained asleep how could he escape? We find that the angel smote Peter on the side. I daresay it was a hard blow, but it was a kind one. Oh, how I wish the Spirit of God would smite some sleeping sinner on the side at this moment! I would not mind how sharp or cutting the blow might be for the time being, if it made him start up and say, "How can I escape from this dreadful cell of sin?" My brethren, how difficult it is to arouse some minds from their indifference! The most indifferent people in this world are those who have prospered in business for a long time without a break; they are accumulating money as fast as they can count it, and they have not time to think about eternal things. Another very hardened class consists of those who have enjoyed good health for a long time, and have scarcely known an ache or a pain. They do not think about eternity. It is a great blessing to enjoy health, but it is also a great blessing to suffer sickness, for it is often the means of awakening the slumbering heart. Many dream that, because things go smoothly with them, they are all right; and yet they are peculiarly in danger. O Spirit of the living God, smite them on the side! I have known this smiting come to some by a sermon, to others by the personal remark of a friend, to others by the death of a companion, or by the loss of a dear child, or by great trouble and want. Well, if your souls are saved, you will not in after days be sorry for the awakening trouble which helped to bring you to the Saviour. Yes, the most indifferent have been awakened; and why should it not be so again? The church prayed for Peter, and those prayers brought the angel to awaken him; let us pray for indifferent sons and careless daughters; let us pray for the godless, Christless population around us, and God's Spirit will yet arouse them, and make them cry with a bitter cry, "Lord, save us, or we perish!"

There was further difficulty about Peter's case. He was in the prison, in the dark, asleep, and *he was also chained*. Each hand was fastened to a soldier's hand. How could he possibly escape? And herein is the difficulty with some sinners, they cannot leave their old companions. Suppose the gay young man should propose to think about religion? Why, this very night he would be ridiculed for it. Suppose he endeavoured to walk in the ways of holiness, is there not chained to his left hand an unholy companion? It may be some unchaste connection has been made; how shall he break away from it? Let a man be joined to an ungodly woman, or let a woman have once given herself up to an unholy alliance, and how hard it is to set them free! Yet Peter did come out of prison though he was chained to his guards; and Christ can save a sinner though he is bound hand and foot by his intimate association with other sinners as bad as himself. It seems impossible that he should be set at liberty; but nothing is impossible with God. There may be some here who have had to snap many an old connection, and get rid of many an evil association; but, by divine grace, it has been done. We give God the glory of it, and do not wonder at the "stir" which it has made.

In addition to all this, Peter was not only chained, but *he was guarded by soldiers placed outside the prison.* And, oh, how some sinners, whom God means to bless, are similarly guarded! The devil seems to have an inkling that God will save them one day, and therefore he watches them; fearful lest by any means they should escape out of his hands, he guards them day and night. When men receive a tender conscience, or have their minds a little aroused, Satan will not trust them to enter the house of prayer; or if they do come, he comes with them, and distracts their attention by vain thoughts or fierce temptations; or if they are able to hear the sermon attentively, he will meet them outside, and try to steal away the good seed from their hearts. He will assail the man with temptation here and temptation there; he will assault him through some chosen instrument, and then again by another messenger of a like character so that if, by any means, he may keep him from being saved.

But when the Lord means to save, he makes short work of the guards, the prison, the darkness, the chains, the devil and all his allies. If the Lord means to save you, man, whoever you are, he will overcome your old master and his guards; the Lord's eternal will shall assuredly overcome your will, and the will of Satan, and the lusts of the flesh, and your own resolves; and although you may have made a league with death and a covenant with hell, yet, if the eternal Jehovah wills it, he can break your covenant, and set you free, and lead you a captive at the wheels of his chariot of mercy; for with God nothing is impossible.

Once more, Peter was, in addition to all this, *on the eve of death.* It was his last night, the night before his execution. It is a very sweet thing to think of Peter sleeping. It reminds one of the saint whom we read of in Foxe's Book of Martyrs. When the gaoler's wife came in the morning to call him, he was so sweetly asleep that she had to shake him to arouse him. It was a strange thing to disturb a man and say, "It is time to get up and be burnt!" But he slept as sweetly as though he should be married that morning instead of meeting a cruel death. God can give his people the greatest peace in the most disturbing times. So Peter slept. But that is not the point I wish to dwell upon. The next morning he was to die; but God would not have him die. Perhaps someone who hears or reads these words is despairing,—so despairing that he is ready to lay violent hands upon himself; or perhaps there is one so sick that, if the Lord does not appear to him very soon, it will be too late. Blessed be God, he never leaves his elect to perish in sin. He never is before his time, but he never is behind it. He cometh in at the last moment, and when it seems as though eternal destruction would swallow up his chosen one, he stretches out his hand, and achieves his purpose. May this remark be a message from God to someone! Though you have gone far in sin, and are near your end, yet the Lord, who can do anything and everything, may come to you and save you even now, at the eleventh hour, and then there will be a "stir" indeed.

We have thus remarked upon a whole series of improbabilities, but I have noticed that it is often the most unlikely people who are saved. There are many of whom I thought, "Surely the Lord's anointed is before me," and I have been disappointed in them; and there are many others, who came to hear out of curiosity, and were the least likely to be impressed, who nevertheless have been met with by sovereign grace. Does not this encourage you to say, "Why should not the Lord meet with me?" Ah, dear soul, why not? And what is more, he will regard thee if thou listenest to this word of his, "He that believeth on the Son hath everlasting life." To believe on Jesus Christ is simply to trust him. Then do thou trust him; for if thou dost trust thy guilty soul entirely on Jesus, he *has* met with thee, thou *art* saved, *now*. Go and sin no more; thy sins, which are many, are forgiven thee! That is salvation in a nut-shell. Whosoever reposes his trust in Jesus is saved. God grant such faith to you!

II. Secondly, in consequence of this great event, THERE WAS NO SMALL STIR, "what was become of Peter." When the Lord saves an unlikely individual, there is sure to be a stir about it.

The text says, "There was no small stir *among the soldiers*." So, generally, the stir about a sinner begins among his old companions. "What has become of Peter? I thought he would have met us to-night at our drinking bout. What has become of Peter? We were going to the theatre together. What has become of Peter? We intended to have a jolly time of it at the horse-races. What has become of Peter? We had agreed to go to the dancing saloon together." Those who were his old companions say, "We did not believe he would ever have been made religious. He'll never make a saint! We'll fetch him back. He has got among those canting Methodists, but we'll make it too hot for him. We will jest at him and jeer at him till he can't stand it; and if that does not do, we will threaten him, cast doubts on his creed, and set fresh temptations before him." Ah! but if God has set him free from sin, he is free indeed, and you will never lead him back to prison again. When you meet him, you will find him a new man; and you will be glad to get away from him, for he will prove too strong for you. Often, when a man's conversion is thorough, not only is he rejoiced to get away from his old companions, but his old companions are wonderfully glad to keep clear of him. They do not like the manner of him. He is so strange a man to what he was before. They say, "What has become of Peter? His ways are not ours.

What has happened to him?" If a dog were suddenly turned into an angel, the other dogs would be puzzled, the whole kennel would take to howling at him.

But after the soldiers came *Herod*. Herod wondered, "What has become of Peter? Did I not put sixteen men to guard him? Did I not provide heavy chains for his feet? Did I not chain him wrist to wrist to a soldier? Did I not put him in the innermost ward of the prison? What has become of Peter?" Herod grew very wroth. He was delighted to have killed James, and he meant to have killed Peter, and therefore he cried, in great chagrin, "What has become of Peter?" What a sight it would be to see the devil when he has lost some chosen sinner, when he hears the man who once could swear beginning to pray, when he beholds the heart that once was hard as adamant beginning to melt! I think I hear him say to himself, "What has become of Peter? Another of my servants has deserted me! Another of my choice followers has yielded to my foe! What, has Christ taken another lamb from between the jaws of the lion? Will he leave me none? Shall I have no soldiers? Shall none of my black guard be left to me? Am I to be entirely deserted? What has become of Peter?" Oh, it is a glorious thing to cause a howling through the infernal regions, and to set devils biting their tongues because poor sinners have snapped their chains! Pray that, as the prayers of the church then set Peter free, and made Herod angry, so the prayers of the church now may set sinners free, and put the devil to shame.

But we must not forget *the Jews*. They had expected to see Peter die, and when they found that they would have to eat the Passover with the bitter herb of Peter's escape from prison, they began to say to one another, "What has become of Peter?" They could not understand his escape. Many in these days are like the Jews. They are outsiders; they do not associate with sinners in their grosser vices, but they look on. Whenever they hear of a man converted, if he be indeed really changed, they say, "What has come to him? We don't understand him!" They put him down as a fanatical fool. Their maxim is that, if you like to go to a place of worship, all well and good, and if you like to have a religion, all well and good, but don't make a fuss about it; don't get carried off your legs by it; keep it to yourself, and be quiet over it. They think that to be lukewarm is the finest condition of mind; whereas the Saviour has said, "Because thou art lukewarm, and neither cold nor hot, I will spue thee out of my mouth." When a man becomes genuinely converted, especially if he has been a notorious sinner, these irreligious religious people cry out, "What has become of Peter?" The Lord grant that there may be much of this outcry in these days!

And surely, also, there was no small stir *amongst God's own people*. There was a great stir in that prayer-meeting when Rhoda went back and said, "There's Peter at the gate!" "Never, never." "But I know his voice. He has been here many times; I can't be mistaken." "Ah!" said one, "it may be his ghost; it can't be Peter himself. It is impossible!" So, sometimes, when a sinner, who has been very notoriously evil, has been converted, after he had been the subject of many prayers, God's people will say, "What, that man converted? It cannot be." When Paul, who had persecuted the church, was brought to be a Christian, it was very hard to make the disciples believe it. They had heard by many of this man, how he had put the saints to death; surely he could not have become a disciple of Christ. There was no small stir what was become of Paul in those days. Christians could hardly think that his conversion was genuine. I pray the Lord, in these times, to convert some very terrible opposer of his gospel, some notorious enemy of the truth. I pray that some of those great philosophers of this learned age, who are always startling us with new absurdities, may be made to feel the power of the sovereign grace of God. I do not know why they should not. Let us pray for it, and it will come to pass. Let us ask the Lord to save even those who brandish their silly learning in the face of the eternal wisdom, and they may yet be brought down to sit humbly at the Saviour's feet, and then there will be no small stir in the church, "What has become of Professor this and that?" O Master, for thine own glory's sake, grant that it may be done!

III. The last point is this, THE QUIET CONDUCT OF THE MAN ABOUT WHOM THERE WAS ALL THIS STIR.

What had become of Peter? He was out of prison. Where was he? I will tell you. In the first place, *he had gone to a prayer-meeting.* It is a very good sign that a man has been really awakened when he goes uninvited to a prayer-meeting. I love to see a stranger come stealing in, and sit in a corner, where God's people are met for supplication. Any hypocrite may come to worship on a Sunday, but it is not every hypocrite who will come to the meeting for prayer. Anybody will come to listen to a sermon, but it is not everybody who will draw near to God in prayer. Surely, when the prayer-meeting comes to be loved, it is good and hopeful evidence. What has become of Peter? He is not at the gin-palace. What has become of Peter? He is not at the races. What has become of Peter? He is not with his old associates at the skittle ground. No, but he is drawing near to God, where humble believers are crying to the Most High for a blessing.

The next thing was, *he joined the Christians.* I do not say that Peter had not done so before; but, on this occasion, he went to the place where the Christians were, and sat down with them. So that sinner whom God sets free from sin straightway flies to his own company. "Birds of a feather flock together," and those who bear the true feather of the white dove, and have been washed in Christ's blood, "fly as a cloud, and as doves to their windows." You do not love Christ if you do not love his people. If you love the Lord who has saved you, you will love the people whom the Lord has saved, and you will, like Peter, find out your brethren, and join with them. See then, you who have been making a stir about what has become of the new convert, we have told you where he is. He has joined the church of God, he is going to be baptized, and he is following Christ through evil report and good report. What say you to that?

I will tell you yet further what has become of Peter. *He has begun to tell his experience at a church-meeting.* Peter did that very soon. He beckoned with his hand, and told them how the Lord had brought him out of the prison. What a delight it is to see a man, who was just now black in the mouth with blasphemy, stand up and bless the Lord for what is grace has done for him. "I should think it strange," says one, "if that ever happened to me." My dear hearer, I should not think it strange, but should bless God for it. God grant that it may appen, and that I may hear of it! No experience in the world is so sweet as that of a sinner who has been in captivity to evil, and has been brought out with a high hand and an outstretched arm. An uncommon sinner, who has been remarkably converted, tells a more than ordinarily encouraging story in our church-meetings, and we delight in such glad tidings. That is what has become of Peter.

And then, lastly, it was not long before *Peter was preaching the gospel of Jesus Christ.* And oh! you who have been wondering what has become of some ungodly companions of yours, I should not be surprised if you hear them telling others what God has done for their souls. I should like to have heard John Newton's first sermon after he had been a slave-dealer, with his life full of all manner of villainy, and God had met with him in mercy. Oh, it must have been a sweet sermon, wet with tears! I will be bound to say that there were no sleepy hearers. He would talk in a way that would melt others' hearts, because his own was melted. I should like to have heard John Bunyan, though under a hedge, preaching the gospel of Jesus, while he told what God had done for a drunken tinker, and how he had washed him in the precious blood of Jesus, and saved him. Those who know what sin is, and what the Saviour has saved them from, can speak "in demonstration of the Spirit and of power." Peter could say, "I was in prison, but I gained my liberty, and it was the work of God." He could bear good testimony to what God has done for him.

I hold up the blood-red standard at this time; I am a recruiting sergeant, and I want, in God's name, to enlist fresh soldiers beneath the standard of the cross. "Whom will you enlist?" says one. "What must their characters be?" They must be guilty; I will have nothing to do with the righteous. The Saviour did not come to save those who are not sinful; he came to save sinners. I looked out of my window last winter, when it had been raining for several months almost incessantly, and I saw a man with a garden-hose watering plants, and I looked at him again and again, and to this moment I cannot understand what he was at; it did seem to me an extraordinary thing that a man should be watering a garden when the garden had been watered by the rain for a hundred days or so with scarcely a pause. Now, I am not going to water you who are already dripping with your own self-righteousness. Nay,

nay, what need have you of grace? Christ did not come to save you good people. You must get to heaven how you can, on your own account. He has come to wash the filthy, and heal the sick; and O ye filthy ones, before you I hold up the gospel banner, and say again, "Who will enlist beneath it?" If you will, the great Captain of salvation will take your guilt away, and cast your sins into the depths of the sea, and make you new creatures through the power of his Spirit.

"Well," says one, "If I am enlisted, and become a new creature, what shall I do?" I will not say what you *shall* do; but, if the Lord saves you, you will love him so much that nothing will be too hard, or too heavy, or too difficult for you. You will not need driving, if you once receive his great salvation; you will be for doing more than you can, and you will pray for more grace and strength to attempt yet greater things for his name's sake. A man who has had much forgiven, what will he not attempt for the service and glory of him who has forgiven him? May I be fortunate enough to enlist beneath the Saviour's banner some black offender! That is the man for Christ's service; that is the man who will sound out his name more sweetly than anybody else. That is the man who will be afraid of no one. That is the man who will know the power of the gospel of Christ to a demonstration. Oh, that the Lord would bring such men among us, for we want them in these days,—men who will come right out, without doubt, fear, or quibbling, facing all criticisms, defying all opinions, and each one saying, "Sinners, Christ can save you, for he saved me. I was a drunkard and a thief, but God has forgiven, and cleansed, and washed me, and I know the power of his salvation." Pray, members of the church, that both among men and women there may be many such conversions, and that throughout this city of London there may be no small stir, "What has become of Peter," and may that stir be to the praise and glory of God! Amen.

Exposition by C. H. Spurgeon.
2 PETER I.

Verse 1. *Simon Peter, a servant and an apostle of Jesus Christ, to them that have obtained like precious faith with us through the righteousness of God and our Saviour Jesus Christ:*

Peter here uses both his names,—Simon or Simeon, which was his first name, and signifies "hearing with acceptance," and happy are they who have the hearing ear and the receptive heart; and then there is what I may call his Christian name, the name which Christ gave him, Petros, or Cephas, a rock or stone. Those who learn to hear well, since faith cometh by hearing, may hope to obtain even greater stability of character than Peter had. Observe that Peter calls himself "a servant of Christ." There is no higher honour than to be a servant of God. "To serve God is to reign." An ancient philosopher was the author of that maxim, and Christianity fully endorses it. He is a true king who is a servant of God.

In this respect, all believers are on a level with Peter, but here is his distinguishing title, "an apostle of Jesus Christ," a sent one, one who had seen the Lord, and who could bear personal testimony to the fact of his existence, his death, and his resurrection. Hence the apostleship has ceased, since there are no longer any who lived in our Lord's days upon the earth.

Mark the reason why this Epistle, like the first, is called "the general Epistle of Peter," since it is addressed, not to any one church, as Paul's Epistle to the Ephesians, but to all saints; not to the Hebrews alone, but to the Gentiles as well. It is a general Epistle, addressed to all those who have "obtained like precious faith." These words were written by the apostle Peter many centuries ago, yet they come to us as fresh as if he had written them but yesterday, and may God grant us grace to profit from them as they are read by us to-day! After the apostle's titles comes the salutation of his Epistle,—

2—5. *Grace and peace be multiplied unto you through the knowledge of God, and of Jesus our Lord, according as his divine power hath given unto us all things that pertain unto life and godliness, through the knowledge of him that hath called us to glory and virtue: whereby are given unto us exceeding great and precious promises: that by these ye might be partakers of the divine nature, having escaped the corruption that is in the world through lust. And beside this,—*

"Since it is God who, by his divine energy, has made you partakers of the divine nature, see that you use your grace-given energy; rest not idly upon your oars because the tide of grace carries your ship onward."

5. *Giving all diligence,—*

It is not man's effort that saves him; but, on the other hand, grace saves no man to make him like a log of wood or a block of stone; grace makes man active. God has been diligently at work with you; now you must diligently work together with him.

5—7. *Add to your faith virtue; and to virtue knowledge; and to knowledge temperance; and to temperance patience; and to patience godliness; and to godliness brotherly kindness; and to brotherly kindness charity.*

As you have seen the mason take up first one stone, and then another, and thus gradually build the house, so are you Christians to take first one virtue, and then another, and then another, and to pile up these stones of grace one upon the other until you have built a palace for the indwelling of the Holy Ghost.

Faith, of course, comes first, because faith is the foundation of all the graces, and there can be no true grace where there is no true faith. Then, "add to your faith virtue," which should have been translated "courage." True courage is a very great blessing to the Christian; indeed, without it, how will he be able to face his foes? "And to courage knowledge;" for courage without knowledge would be foolish rashness, which would lead you to the cannon's mouth when there was nothing to be gained by flinging away your life.

"And to knowledge temperance;" for there are some who no sooner get knowledge than they are carried away with the new doctrine which they have learned, and become like men intoxicated, for it is possible to be intoxicated even with truth. Happy is that Christian who has temperance with his knowledge; who, while holding one doctrine, does not push that to the extreme, but learns to hold other doctrines in due conformity with it. "And to temperance patience;" or endurance, so that we are able to endure the "trial of cruel mockings" or sharp pains, or fierce persecutions, or the usual afflictions of this life. He is a poor Christian who has no powers of endurance; a true Christian must "endure hardness as a good soldier of Jesus Christ."

"And to endurance godliness;" having a constant respect to God in all our ways, living to God, and living like God so far as the finite can be like the Infinite. "And to godliness brotherly kindness." O dear friends, let us be very kind to those who are our brothers in Christ Jesus; let the ties of Christian kinship unite us in true brotherhood to each other. "And to brotherly kindness charity;" let us have love to all men, though specially to the household of faith.

8. *For if these things be in you, and abound, they make you that ye shall neither be barren nor unfruitful in the knowledge of our Lord Jesus Christ.*

I am sure you do not wish to be barren; I cannot imagine that any of you will be content to be unfruitful; so seek after all these virtues, and may God help you to give diligence to the attainment of them.

9, 10. *But he that lacketh these things is blind, and cannot see afar off, and hath forgotten that he was purged from his old sins. Wherefore the rather, brethren, give diligence to make your calling and election sure: for if ye do these things, ye shall never fall:*

He who is diligent in seeking these graces is kept from falling. Every Christian is safe from a final fall, but he is not safe from a foul fall unless he is kept by grace.

11. *For so an entrance shall be ministered unto you abundantly into the everlasting kingdom of our Lord and Saviour Jesus Christ.*

In this life you shall enjoy all the privileges of the inheritors of the kingdom of heaven; and in the life to come you shall go into the harbour of eternal peace like a ship with all her sails full, speeding before a favourable wind, and not as one that struggles into harbour,—
"Tempest-tossed, and half a wreck."

12. *Wherefore I will not be negligent to put you always in remembrance of these things, though ye know them, and be established in the present truth.*

We are not merely to preach new truths which people do not know, but we are also to preach the old truths with which they are familiar. The doctrines in which they are well established are still to be proclaimed to them. Every wise preacher brings forth from the treasury of truth things both new and old;—new, that the hearers may learn more than they knew before; old, that they may know and practise better that which they do already know in part.

13, 14. *Yea, I think it meet, as long as I am in this tabernacle, to stir you up by putting you in remembrance; knowing that shortly I must put off this my tabernacle, even as our Lord Jesus Christ hath shewed me.*

In the last chapter of the gospel according to John, it is recorded how Christ prophesied concerning the death of Peter, that when he was old, he should stretch forth his hands, and another should gird him, and carry him whither he would not. The evangelist adds, "This spake he, signifying by what death he should glorify God." The prospect of crucifixion was thus always before Peter's mind; and knowing what was to happen to him, he was not alarmed, but was rather quickened to greater diligence in stirring up the saints to make their calling and election sure. Hear thou behind thee, O Christian, the chariot wheels of thy Lord; hear thou behind thee the whizzing of the arrow of death, and let this quicken thy pace! Work while it is called to-day, for the sun even now touches the horizon, and the night cometh when no man can work. If we knew how short a time we have to live, how much more earnest, how much more diligent should we be! Let us be up and doing. "Let us not sleep, as do others; but let us watch and be sober," working diligently until the Lord comes, or calls us home to himself.

15—18. *Moreover I will endeavour that ye may be able after my decease to have these things always in remembrance. For we have not followed cunningly devised fables, when we made known unto you the power and coming of our Lord Jesus Christ, but were eyewitnesses of his majesty. For he received from God the Father honour and glory, when there came such a voice to him from the excellent glory, This is my beloved Son, in whom I am well pleased. And this voice which came from heaven we heard, when we were with him in the holy mount.*

Peter and James and John were with Christ on the Mount of Transfiguration, and Peter here bears his witness that they were not deceived when they bowed down before Christ, and worshipped him as Lord, nor were they deluded in expecting his coming and believing in his power.

19, 20. *We have also a more sure word of prophecy; whereunto ye do well that ye take heed, as unto a light that shineth in a dark place, until the day dawn, and the day star arise in your hearts: knowing this first, that no prophecy of the scripture is of any private interpretation.*

Even the prophets themselves did not always know the full meaning of their own prophecies. Many prophecies have never been completely understood until they have been fulfilled. This passage also appears to me to mean that no prophecy is to be restricted to any one event, so as to say, "This prophecy has been entirely fulfilled."

21. *For the prophecy came not in old time by the will of man: but holy men of God spake as they were moved by the Holy Ghost.*

So that they sometimes spoke what they did not themselves understand; the prophecy carried its own key within itself, and the key could not be found until the prophecy was fulfilled. I believe that the prophecies in the Revelation, and in the books of Daniel and Ezekiel are very much of this character; and that, while it is quite right to watch for and expect the coming of the Lord, we shall spend our time more profitably in preaching the doctrines of the gospel than in meditating upon the mysterious prophecies of the Word. They will be understood when they are fulfilled, but we do not think they will be fully understood before that time.

PRAISE
Praise Thy God, O Zion—Luke 19:37-40
The Happy Duty of Daily Praise—Ps. 145:1, 2
Open Praise and Public Confession—Ps. 138:1-3
Exposition of Psalm 138
Mary's Magnificat—Luke 1:46-47
Exposition of Luke 1:39-56
Homage Offered to the Great King—Ps. 72:15
"The Garment of Praise"—Isa. 61:3

PRAISE THY GOD, O ZION.

A Sermon

Delivered on Sunday Morning, February 25th, 1866, by

C. H. SPURGEON,

AT THE METROPOLITAN TABERNACLE, NEWINGTON.

"And when he was come nigh, even now at the descent of the mount of Olives, the whole multitude of the disciples began to rejoice and praise God with a loud voice for all the mighty works that they had seen; Saying, Blessed be the King that cometh in the name of the Lord: peace in heaven, and glory in the highest. And some of the Pharisees from among the multitude said unto him, Master, rebuke thy disciples. And he answered and said unto them, I tell you that, if these should hold their peace, the stones would immediately cry out."—Luke xix. 37—40.

The Saviour was "a man of sorrows," but every thoughtful mind has discovered the fact that down deep in his innermost soul he must have carried an inexhaustible treasury of refined and heavenly joy. I suppose that of all the human race there was never a man who had a deeper, purer, or more abiding peace than our Lord Jesus Christ. "He was anointed with the oil of gladness above his fellows." Benevolence is joy. The highest benevolence must from the very nature of things have afforded the deepest possible delight. To be engaged in the most blessed of all errands, to foresee the marvellous results of his labours in time and in eternity, and even to see around him the fruits of the good which he had done in the healing of the sick and the raising of the dead, must have given to such a sympathetic heart as that which beat within the bosom of the Lord Jesus Christ much of secret satisfaction and joy. There were a few remarkable seasons when this joy manifested itself. "At that hour Jesus rejoiced in spirit and said, I thank thee, O Father, Lord of heaven and earth." Christ had his songs though it was night with him; and though his face was marred, and his countenance had lost the lustre of earthly happiness, yet sometimes it was lit up with a matchless splendour of unparalleled satisfaction, as he thought upon the recompense of the reward, and in the midst of the congregation sang his praise unto God.

In this, the Lord Jesus is a blessed picture of his Church on earth. This is the day of Zion's trouble: at this hour the Church expects to walk in sympathy with her Lord along a thorny road. She is without the camp—through much tribulation she is forcing her way to the crown. She expects to meet with reproaches. To bear the cross is her office, and to be scorned and counted an alien by her mother's children is her lot. And yet the Church has a deep well of joy, of which none can drink but her own children. There are stores of wine, and oil, and corn, hidden in the midst of our Jerusalem, upon which the saints of God are evermore sustained and nurtured; and sometimes, as in our Saviour's case, we have our seasons of intense delight, for "there is a river, the streams whereof make glad the city of our God." Exiles though we be, we rejoice in our King, yea in him we exceedingly rejoice: while in his name we set up our banners.

This is a season with us as a Church when we are peculiarly called upon to rejoice in God. The Lord Jesus, in the narrative before us, was going to Jerusalem, as his disciples fondly hoped, to take the throne of David and set up the long-expected kingdom. Well might they shout for joy, for the Lord was in their midst, in their midst in state, riding amidst the acclamations of a multitude who had been glad partakers of his goodness. Jesus Christ is in our midst to-day: the kingdom is securely his. We see the crown glittering upon his brow; he has been riding through our streets, healing our blind, raising our dead, and speaking words of comfort to our mourners. We, too, attend him in state to-day, and the acclamations of little children are not wanting, for from the Sabbath school there have come songs of converted youngsters, who sing gladly, as did the children of Jerusalem in days of yore, "Hosanna! Blessed is he that cometh in the name of the Lord!"

I want, dear friends, this morning, to stir up in all of us the spirit of holy joy, because our King is in our midst; that we may welcome him and rejoice in him, and that while he is working his mighty deeds of salvation throughout this congregation so graciously, he may not lack such music as our feeble lips can afford him. I shall therefore invite your attention to these four verses, by way of example, that we may take a pattern for our praise from this inspired description. We shall observe four things: first, *delightful praise;* secondly, *appropriate song;* thirdly, *intrusive objections;* fourthly, *an unanswerable argument.*

I. First, we shall observe here DELIGHTFUL PRAISE.

In the thirty-seventh verse every word is significant, and deserves the careful notice of all who would learn aright the lesson of how to magnify the Saviour. To begin with, the praise rendered to Christ was *speedy praise.* The happy choristers did not wait till he had entered the city, but "when he was come nigh, even now, at the descent of the mount of Olives, they began to rejoice." It is well to have a quick eye to perceive occasions for gratitude. Blind unbelief and blear-eyed thanklessness allow the favours of God to lie forgotten in unthankfulness, and, without praises, die; they walk in the noonday of mercy and see no light to sing by; but a believing, cheerful, grateful spirit, detects at once the rising of the Sun of mercy, and begins to sing, even at the break of day. Christian, if thou wouldst sing of the mercy thou hast already, thou wouldst soon have more. If twilight made thee glad, thou shouldst soon have the bliss of noon. I am certain that the Church in these days has lost much, by not being thankful for little. We have had many prayer-meetings, but few, very few, praise-meetings; as if the Church could cry loud enough when her own ends were to be answered, but was dumb as to music for her Lord. Her King acts to her very much as he did with the man with the pound. That man put not out the pound to interest, and therefore it was taken away. We have not thanked him for little mercies, and therefore even these have been removed, and Churches have become barren and deserted by the Spirit of God. Let *us* lift up the voice of praise to our Master, because he has blessed us these twelve years. We have had a continual stream of revival. The cries of sinners have sounded in our ears—every day we have seen souls converted—I was about to say almost every hour of the week, and that by the space of these twelve years, and of late, we have had a double portion. Benjamin's mess has been set near our place at the table; we have been made to feast on royal dainties, and have been filled with bread even to the fill. Shall we not then praise God? Ah! let us not require twice telling of it, but let our souls begin to praise him, even now, that he comes nigh unto Jerusalem.

It strikes us at once, also, that this was *unanimous* praise. Observe, not only the multitude, but the *whole multitude* of the disciples rejoiced, and praised him; not one silent tongue among the disciples—not one who withheld his song. And yet, I suppose, those disciples had their trials as we have ours. There might have been a sick wife at home, or a child withering with disease. They were doubtless poor, we know they were, indeed; and poverty is never without its pinches. They were men of like passions with ourselves; they had to struggle with inbred sin, and with temptation from without, and yet there seems to have been no one who on those grounds excluded himself from the choir of singers on that happy day. Oh, my soul, whatever thou hast about thee which might bow thee down, be thou glad when thou rememberest that Jesus Christ is glorified in the midst of his Church. Wherefore, my brother, is that harp of thine hanging on the willows? Hast thou nothing to sing about? Has he done nothing for thee? Why, if thou hast no personal reason for blessing God, then lend us your heart and voice to help *us*, for we have more praise-work on hand than we can get through alone—we have more to praise him for than we are able to discharge without extra aid. Our work of praise is too great for us, come and help us; sing on our behalf, if thou canst not on thine own; and then, mayhap, thou wilt catch the flame, and find something after all for which thou, too, must bless him.

I know there are some of you who do not feel as if you could praise God this morning: let us ask the Master to put your harp in tune. Oh be not silent! Be not silent! Do bless him! If you cannot bless him for temporals, do bless him for spirituals; and if you have not of late experimentally enjoyed many of these, then bless him for what he is. For that dear face, covered with the bloody sweat; for those pierced hands, for that opened side, will you not praise him? Why, surely, if he had not died for me, yet I must love him, to think of his goodness in dying for others. His kindness, the generosity of his noble heart in dying for his enemies might well provoke the most unbelieving to a song. I am, therefore, not content unless all of you will contribute your note. I would have every bird throw in its note, though some cannot imitate the lark or nightingale; yea, I would have every tree of the forest clap its hands, and even the hyssop on the wall wave in adoration. Come, beloved, cheer up. Let dull care and dark fear be gone. Up with harps and down with doubts. It must be praise from "the whole multitude." The praise must be unanimous—not one chord out of order to spoil the tune.

Next, it was *multitudinous*. "The whole multitude." There is something most inspiring and exhilarating in the noise of a multitude singing God's praises. Sometimes, when we have been in good tune, and have sung "Praise God from whom all blessings flow," our music has rolled upward like thunder to yon dome and has reverberated peal on peal, and these have been the happiest moments some of us have ever known, when every tongue was praise, and every heart was joy. Oh, let us renew those happy times; let us anticipate the season when the dwellers in the East and in the West, in the North and in the South, of every age and of every clime, shall assemble on the celestial hill-tops and swell the everlasting song, extolling Jesus Lord of all. Jesus loves the praise of many; he loves to hear the voices of all the bloodwashed.

"Ten thousand thousand are their tongues,"
But all their joys are one."

We are not so many as that, but we are counted by thousands, and let us praise his name—the whole multitude.

Still it is worthy of observation that, while the praise was multitudinous, it was quite *select*. It was the whole multitude "*of the disciples*." The Pharisees did not praise him—they were murmuring. All true praise must come from true hearts. If thou dost not learn of Christ, thou canst not render to him acceptable song. These disciples, of course, were of different sorts. Some of them had but just enlisted in the army—just learned to sit at his feet. Some had worked miracles in his name, and, having been called to the apostolic office, had preached the word to others; but they were all disciples. I trust that in this congregation there is a vast majority of disciples: well, then, all of you, you who have lately come into his school, you who have long been in it, you who have become fathers in Israel, and are teaching others, the whole multitude of disciples, I hope, will praise God. I could wish—God grant the wish—I could wish that those who are not disciples might soon become so. "Take my yoke upon you," saith he, "and learn of me, for I am meek and lowly in heart." A disciple is a learner. You may not know much, but you need not know anything in coming to Christ. Christ begins with ignorance, and bestows wisdom. If thou dost but know that thou knowest nothing, thou knowest enough to become a disciple of Christ Jesus. There is no matriculation necessary in order to enter into Christ's college. He takes the fools, and makes them know the wonders of his dying love. Oh that thou mayest become a disciple! "Write my name down, sir," say thou to the writer with the inkhorn by his side, and be thou henceforth a humble follower of the Lamb. Now, though I would not have those who are not disciples close their mouths when ever others sing, yet I do think there are some hymns in which they would behave more honestly if they did not join, for there are some expressions which hardly ought to come from unconverted lips; better far would it be if they would pray, "Lord, open thou my lips, and my mouth shall shew forth thy praise." You may have a very sweet voice, my friend, and may sing with admirable taste and in exquisite harmony any of the parts, but God does not accept the praise where the heart is absent. The best tune in the book is one called *Hearts*. The whole multitude of the disciples whom Jesus loves are the proper persons to extol the Redeemer's name. May you, dear hearer, be among that company!

Then, in the next place, you will observe that the praise they rendered was *joyful praise*. "The whole multitude of the disciples began to rejoice." I hope the doctrine that Christians ought to be gloomy will soon be driven out of the universe. There are no people in the world who have such a right to be happy, nor have such cause to be joyful as the saints of the living God. All Christian duties should be done joyfully; but especially the work of praising the Lord. I have been in congregations where the tune was dolorous to the very last degree; where the time was so dreadfully slow that one wondered whether they would ever be able to sing through the 119th Psalm; whether, to use Watts's expression, eternity would not be too short for them to get through it; and altogether, the spirit of the people has seemed to be so damp, so heavy, so dead, that we might have supposed that they were met to prepare their minds for hanging rather than for blessing the ever-gracious God. Why, brethren, true praise sets the heart ringing its bells, and hanging out its streamers. Never hang your flag at half-mast when you praise God; no, run up every colour, let every banner wave in the breeze, and let all the powers and passions of your spirit exult and rejoice in God your Saviour. They *rejoiced*. We are really most horribly afraid of being too happy. Some Christians think cheerfulness a very dangerous folly, if not a ruinous vice. That joyous Hundredth Psalm has been altered in all the English versions.

"All people that on earth do dwell,
Sing to the Lord with cheerful voice,
Him serve with fear, his praise forth tell,
Come ye before him and rejoice."

"Him serve with fear," says the English version; but the Scotch version has less thistle and far more rose in it. Listen to it, and catch its holy happiness:—

"Him serve with *mirth*, his praise forth tell;
Come ye before him and rejoice."

How do God's creatures serve him out of doors? The birds do not sit on a Sunday with folden wings, dolefully silent on the boughs of the trees, but they sing as sweetly as may be, even though the rain-drops fall. As for the new-born lambs in the field—they skip to his praise, though the season is damp and cold. Heaven and earth are lit up with gladness, and why not the hearts and houses of the saints? "Him serve with mirth." Well saith the Psalmist; "before him exceedingly rejoice." It was *joyful* praise.

The next point we must mention is, that it was *demonstrative* praise. They praised him with their voices, and with a *loud* voice. Propriety very greatly objects to the praise which is rendered by Primitive Methodists at times; their shouts and hallelujahs are thought by some delicate minds to be very shocking. I would not, however, join in the censure, lest I should be numbered among the Pharisees who said, "Master, rebuke thy disciples." I wish more people were as earnest and even as vehement as the Methodists used to be. In our

Lord's day we see that the people expressed the joy which they felt; I am not sure that they expressed it in the most tunable manner, but at any rate they expressed it in a hearty, lusty shout. They altogether praised with a *loud* voice. It is said of Mr. Rowland Hill that, on one occasion, some one sat on the pulpit stairs, who sang in his ears with such a sharp shrill voice, that he could endure it no longer, but said to the good woman, " I wish you would be quiet;" when she answered, "It comes from my heart." "Oh," said he, "pray forgive me—sing away: sing as loudly as you will." And truly, dear friends, though one might wish there were more melody in it, yet if your music comes from the heart, we cannot object to the loudness, or we might be found objecting to that which the Saviour could not and would not blame. Must we not be loud? Do you wonder that we speak out? Have not his mercies a loud tongue? Do not his kindnesses deserve to be proclaimed aloud? Were not the cries upon the cross so loud that the very rocks were rent thereby, and shall our music be a whisper? No, as Watts declares, we would—

" Loud as his thunders shout his praise,
And sound it lofty as his throne."

If not with loud voices actually in sound, yet we would make the praise of God loud by our actions, which speak louder than any words; we would extol him by great deeds of kindness, and love, and self-denial, and zeal, that so our actions may assist our words. " The whole multitude praised him with a loud voice." Let me ask every Christian here to do something in the praise of God, to speak in some way for his Master. I would say, speak to-day; if you cannot with your voice, speak by act and deed; but do join in the hearty shout of all the saints of God while you praise and bless the name of our ever-gracious Lord.

The praise rendered, however, though very demonstrative, was very *reasonable;* the reason is given—" for all the mighty works that they had seen." My dear friends, we have seen many mighty works which Christ has done. I do not know what these disciples had happened to see. Certain it is, that after Christ entered into Jerusalem, he was lavish of his miracles. The blind were healed, the deaf had their ears opened, many of those possessed with devils were delivered, and incurable diseases gave way at his word. I think we have the like reason in a spiritual sense. What hath God wrought? It has been marvellous—as our elders would tell you, if they could recount what God has done—the many who have come forward during the last fortnight to tell what God has done for their souls. The Holy Spirit has met with some whom hitherto no ministry had reached. Some have been convinced of sin who were wrapped up in self-righteous rags; others have been comforted whose desponding hearts drew nigh unto despair. I am sure those brethren who sat to see enquirers must have been astonished when they found some hundreds coming to talk about the things that make for their peace. It was blessed work, I doubt not, for them. They, therefore, would lead the strain. But you have all in your measure seen something of it. During the meetings we have held we have enjoyed an overpowering sense of the Divine presence. Without excitement there has been a holy bowedness of spirit, and yet a blessed lifting up of hope, and joy, and holy fervour. The Master has cast sweet smiles upon his Church, he has come near to his beloved, he has given her the tokens of his affection, and made her to rejoice with joy unspeakable. Any joy which we have towards Christ, then, will be reasonable enough, for we have seen his mighty works.

With another remark, I shall close this first head—the reason for their joy was a *personal* one. There is no praise to God so sweet as that which flows from the man who has tasted that the Lord is gracious. Some of you have been converted during the last two or three months. Oh! you *must* bless him, you *shall;* you must take the front rank now, and bless his name for the mighty work which you have seen in yourself. The things which once were dear to you you now abhor, and those things which seemed dry and empty are now sweet and full of savour. God has turned your darkness into light. He has brought you up out of the horrible pit, and out of the miry clay, and has set your feet upon a rock; shall not your established goings yield him a grateful song? You shall bless him. Others here present have had their own children saved. God has looked on one family and another, and taken one, and two, and three. He has been pleased to lay his hand upon the elders among us, and bless their families. Oh sing unto his name! Sing praises for the mighty works which we have seen.

This will be common-place talk enough to those of you who have not seen it; but those who have, will feel the tears starting to their eyes as they think of son and daughter, of whom they can say, "Behold, he prayeth." Saints of God, I wish I could snatch a firebrand from the altar of praise that burns before the great throne of God: I wish I could fire your hearts therewith, but it is the Master's work to do it. Oh! may he do it now. May every one of you feel as if you could cast your crown at his feet; as if you could sing like the cherubim and the seraphim, nor yield even the first place of gratitude to the brightest spirit before the eternal throne. This morning may it be truly said, "The whole multitude of the disciples rejoiced with a loud voice for all the mighty things which they had seen."

> "O come, loud anthems let us sing,
> Loud thanks to our Almighty King;
> For we our voices high should raise,
> When our salvation's rock we praise.
>
> Into his presence let us haste,
> To thank him for his favours past;
> To him address, in joyful songs,
> The praise that to his name belongs."

II. I shall now lead you on to the second point—their praise found vent for itself in AN APPROPRIATE SONG. "Blessed be the King that cometh in the name of the Lord. Peace in heaven, and glory in the highest."

It was an appropriate song, if you will remember that *it had Christ for its subject.* "My heart is inditing of a good matter: I speak of the things which I have made touching the king." No song is so sweet from believing lips as that which tells of him who loved us and who gave himself for us. This particular song sings of Christ in his character of King—a right royal song then—a melody fit for a coronation day. Crown him! crown him Lord of all! That was the refrain —" Blessed be the King." It sang of that King as commissioned by the Most High " who cometh in the name of the Lord." To think of Christ as bearing divine authority, as coming down to men in God our Father's name, speaking what he has heard in heaven, fulfilling no self-espoused errand, but a mission upon which the divine Father sent him according to his purpose and decree; all this is matter for music. Oh bless the Lord, ye saints, as ye remember that your Saviour is the Lord's anointed: he hath set him on his throne; he Jehovah, who was pleased to bruise him, has said, " Yet have I set my King upon my holy hill of Sion." See the Godhead of your Saviour. He whom you adore, the Son of Mary, is the Son of God. He who did ride upon a colt the foal of an ass, did also ride upon a cherub and did fly; yea, he rode upon the wings of the wind. They spread their garments in the way, and brake down branches; it was a humble triumph, but long ere this the angels had strewn his path with adoring songs. Before him went the lightnings, coals of fire were in his track, and up from his throne went forth hailstones and coals of fire. Blessed be the King! Oh praise him this day: praise the King, divine, and commissioned of his Father. The burden of their song was, however, of Christ *present in their midst*. I do not think they would have rejoiced so loudly and sweetly if *he* had not been there. That was the source and centre of their mirth—the King riding upon a colt the foal of an ass—the King triumphant. They could not but be glad when he revealed himself. Beloved, our King is here. We sang at the beginning of this visitation, " Arise, O King of grace, arise, and enter to thy rest!" You remember our singing the verse—

" O thou that art the Mighty One,
Thy sword gird on thy thigh."

And King Jesus has done so in state: he has ridden prosperously, and out of the ivory palaces his heart has been made glad; and the King's daughter, all-glorious within, standing at his right hand, cannot but be glad too. Loud to his praise wake every string of your heart, and let your souls make the Lord Jesus the burden of their song.

This was an appropriate song, in the next place, because *it had God for its object;* they extolled God, God in Christ, when they thus lifted up their voices. They said, " Peace in heaven, and glory in the highest." When we extol Christ, we desire to bless the infinite majesty that gave Christ to us. Thanks be unto the Father for his unspeakable gift. O thou eternal God, we thy creatures in this little world do unfeignedly bless thee for that great purpose and decree, by which thou didst choose us to be illustrious exhibitions of thy majesty and love. We bless thee that thou didst give us grace in Christ thy Son before the starry sky was spread abroad. We praise thee, O God, and magnify thy name as we enquire, " What is man, that thou art mindful of him, or the son of man, that thou visitest him?" How couldst thou deign to stoop from all the glory of thine infinity, to be made man, to suffer, to bleed, to die for us? " Give unto the Lord, O ye mighty, give unto the Lord glory and strength. Give unto the Lord the glory that is due unto his name." Oh that I could give place to some inspired bard, some seer of old, who standing before you with mouth streaming with holy eloquence, should extol him that liveth but once was slain, and bless the God who sent him here below that he might redeem unto himself a people who should show forth his praise.

I think this song to have been very appropriate for another reason, namely, because *it had the universe for its scope.* It was not praise within walls as ours this morning: the multitude sung in the open air with no walls but the horizon, with no roof but the unpillared arch of heaven. Their song, though it was from heaven, did not stay there but enclosed the world within its range. It was, "Peace in heaven; glory in the highest." It is very singularly like that song of the angels, that Christmas carol of the spirits from on high when Christ was born; but it differs, for the angels' song was, "Peace on earth," and this at the gates of Jerusalem was, "Peace in heaven." It is the nature of song to spread itself. From heaven the sacred joy began when angels sang, and then the fire blazed down to earth in the words, "Peace on earth;" but now the song began on earth, and so it blazed up to heaven with the words, "Peace in heaven: glory in the highest." Is not it a wonderful thing that a company of poor beings, like us here below, can really affect the highest heavens? Every throb of gratitude which heaves our hearts glows through heaven. God can receive no actual increase of glory from his creature, for he has infinite glory and majesty, but yet the creature manifests that glory. A grateful man here below, when his heart is all on fire with sacred love, warms heaven itself. The multitude sung of peace in heaven, as though the angels were established in their peaceful seats by the Saviour, as though the war which God had waged with sin was over now, because the conquering King was come. Oh let us seek after music which shall be fitted for other spheres! I would begin the music here, and so my soul should rise. Oh for some heavenly notes to bear my passions to the skies! It was appropriate to the occasion, because the universe was its sphere.

And it seems also to have been most appropriate, because it had *gratitude for its spirit.* They cried aloud, "*Blessed*"—"Blessed be the King." We cannot bless God, and yet we do bless him, in the sense in which he blesses us. Our goodness cannot extend to him, but we reflect the blessedness which streams from him as light from the sun. Blessed be Jesus! My brethren, have you never wished to make him happier? Have you not wished that you could extol him? Let him be exalted! Let him sit on high! I have almost wished even selfishly that he were not so glorious as he is, that we might help to lift him higher. Oh! if the crushing of my body, soul, and spirit would make him one atom more glorious, I would not only consent to the sacrifice, but bless his name that he counted me worthy so to do. All that we can do bringeth nothing unto him. Yet, brethren, I would that he had his own. Oh that he rode over our great land in triumph! Would that King Jesus were as well known here now as he was once in puritanic times! Would that Scotland were as loyal to him as in covenanting periods! Would that Jesus had his majesty visible in the eyes of all men! We pray for this, we seek for this; and among the chief joys our chiefest joy is to know that God hath highly exalted him, and given him a name which is above every name, that at the name of Jesus every knee should bow. We have thus said something about the appropriateness of the song; may you, each of you, light upon such hymns as will serve to set forth your own case and show forth the mercy of God in saving you, and do not be slack in praising him in such notes as may be most suitable to your own condition.

III. Thirdly, and very briefly—for I am not going to give much time to these men—we have INTRUSIVE OBJECTIONS. " Master, rebuke thy disciples." We know that voice—the old grunt of the Pharisee. What could he do otherwise? Such is the man, and such must his communications be. While he can dare to boast, " God, I thank thee that I am not as other men are," he is not likely to join in praises such as other men lift up to heaven.

But why did these Pharisees object? I suppose it was first of all because *they thought there would be no praise for them.* If the multitude had been saying, " Oh these *blessed* Pharisees! these excellent Pharisees! What broad phylacteries! What admirable hems to their garments! How diligently and scrupulously they tithe their mint and their anise and their cummin! What a wonder that God should permit us poor vile creatures to look upon these super-excellent incarnations of virtue!" I will be bound to say there would not have been a man among them who would have said, "Master, rebuke thy disciples." A proud heart never praises God, for it hoards up praise for itself.

In the next place, *they were jealous of the people.* They did not feel so happy themselves, and they could not bear that other people should be glad. They were like the elder brother who said, " Yet thou never gavest me a kid, that I might make merry with my friends." Was that a reason why nobody else should be merry? A very ill reason truly! Oh, if we cannot rejoice ourselves, let us stand out of the way of other people. If we have no music in our own hearts, let us not wish to stop those who have.

But I think the main point was that they were *jealous of Jesus;* they did not like to have Christ crowned with majesty. Certainly this is the drift of the human heart. It does not wish to see Jesus Christ extolled. Preach up morality or dry doctrine, or ceremonies, and many will be glad to hear your notes; but preach Jesus Christ up, and some will say, " Master, rebuke thy disciples!" It was not ill advice of an old preacher to a young beginner, when he said, " Preach nothing down but sin, and preach nothing up but Christ." Brethren, let us praise nothing up but Christ." Have nothing to say about your Church, say nothing about your denomination, hold your tongue about the minister, but praise Christ, and I know the Pharisees will not like it, but that is an excellent reason to give them more of it, for that which Satan does not admire, he ought to have more of. The preaching of Christ is the whip that flogs the devil; the preaching of Christ is the thunderbolt, the sound of which makes all hell shake. Let us never be silent then; we shall put to confusion all our foes, if we do but extol Christ Jesus the Lord. " Master, rebuke thy disciples!" Well, there is not much of this for Jesus Christ to rebuke in the Christian Church in the present day. There used to be—there used to be a little of what the world calls fanaticism. A consecrated cobbler once set forth to preach the gospel in Hindoostan. There were men who would go preaching the gospel among the heathen, counting not their lives dear unto them. The day was when the Church was so foolish as to fling away precious lives for Christ's glory. Ah! she is more prudent now-a-days. Alas! alas! for your prudence. She is so calm and so quiet—no Methodist's zeal now—even that denomination which did seem alive has become most proper and most cold. And we are so charitable too. We let the most abominable doctrines be preached, and we put our finger on our lip, and say, "There's so many good people who think so." Nothing is to be rebuked now-a-days. Brethren, one's soul is sick of this! Oh, for the old fire again! The Church will never prosper till it comes once more. Oh, for the old fanaticism, for that indeed was the Spirit of God making men's spirits in earnest! Oh, for the old doing and daring that risked everything and cared for nothing, except to glorify him who shed his blood upon the cross! May we live to see such bright and holy days again! The world may murmur, but Christ will not rebuke.

IV. We come now to the last point, which is this—AN UNANSWERABLE ARGUMENT. He said, "If these should hold their peace, the very stones would cry out."

Brethren, I think that is very much our case; if we were not to praise God, the very stones might cry out against us. We *must* praise the Lord. Woe is unto us if we do not! It is impossible for us to hold our tongues. Saved from hell and be silent! Secure of heaven and be ungrateful! Bought with precious blood, and hold our tongues! Filled with the Spirit and not speak! Restrain, from fear of feeble man, the Spirit's course within our souls! God forbid. In the name of the Most High, let such a thought be given to the winds. What, our children saved; the offspring of our loins brought to Christ! What, see them springing up like willows by the water courses, and no awakening of song, no gladness, no delight! Oh, then we were worse than brutes, and our hearts would have been steeled and become as adamant. We must praise God! What, the King in our midst, King Jesus smiling into our souls, feasting us at his table, making his word precious to us, and not praise him. Why if Satan could know the delight of Christ's company he might begin to love; but we, we were worse than devils if we did not praise the name of Jesus! What! the King's arm made bare, his enemies subdued, his triumphant chariot rolling through our streets, and no song! Oh Zion, if we forget to sing let our right hand forget her cunning; if we count not the King's triumph above our chiefest joy. What, the King coming! His advent drawing nigh, the signs of blessing in the sky and air around, and yet no song! Oh, we must bless him! Hosanna! Blessed is he that cometh in the name of the Lord!

But could the stones ever cry out? Yes, that they could, and if they were to speak they would have much to talk of even as we have this day. If the stones were to speak they could tell of their *Maker;* and shall not we tell of him who made us anew, and out of stones raised up children unto Abraham? They could speak of ages long since gone; the old rocks could tell of chaos and order, and the handiwork of God in various stages of creation's drama; and cannot we talk of God's decrees, of God's great work in ancient times, and all that he did for his Church? If the stones were to speak they could tell of their *breaker*, how he took them from the quarry, and made them fit for the temple; and cannot we tell of our Creator and Maker, who broke our hearts with the hammer of his word that he might build us into his temple? If the stones were to speak, they would tell of their *builder*, who polished them and fashioned them after the similitude of a palace; and shall not we talk of our Architect and Builder, who has put us in our place in the temple of the living God? Oh, if the stones could speak, they might have a long, long story to tell by way of *memorial*, for many a time hath a great stone been rolled as a memorial unto God; and we can tell of Ebenezers, stones of help, stones of remembrance. The broken stones of the law cry out against us, but Christ himself, who has rolled away the stone from the door of the sepulchre, speaks for us. Stones might well cry out, but we will not let them: we will hush their noise with ours, we will break forth into sacred song, and bless the majesty of the Most High all our days. Let this day and to-morrow be especially consecrated to holy joys, and may the Lord in infinite mercy fill your souls right full of it, both in practical deeds of kindness and benevolence and works of praise! Blessed be his name who liveth for ever and ever!

THE HAPPY DUTY OF DAILY PRAISE.

A Sermon

Delivered on Lord's-day Morning, May 30th, 1886, by

C. H. SPURGEON,

AT THE METROPOLITAN TABERNACLE, NEWINGTON.

"I will extol thee, my God, O King; and I will bless thy name for ever and ever. Every day will I bless thee; and I will praise thy name for ever and ever."—Psalm cxlv. 1, 2.

If I were to put to you the question, "Do you pray?" the answer would be very quickly given by every Christian person, "Of course I do." Suppose I then added, "And do you pray every day?" the prompt reply would be, "Yes; many times in the day. I could not live without prayer." This is no more than I expect, and I will not put the question. But let me change the enquiry, and say, "Do you bless God every day? Is praise as certain and constant a practice with you as prayer?" I am not sure that the answer would be quite so certain, so general, or so prompt. You would have to stop a little while before you gave the reply; and I fear, in some cases, when the reply did come, it would be, "I am afraid I have been negligent in praise." Well, then, dear friend, have you not been wrong? Should we omit praise any more than we omit prayer? And should not praise come daily and as many times in the day as prayer does? It strikes me that to fail in praise is as unjustifiable as to fail in prayer. I shall leave it with your own heart and conscience, when you have asked and answered the question, to see to it in the future that far more of the sweet frankincense of praise is mingled with your daily oblation of devotion.

Praise is certainly not at all so common in family prayer as other forms of worship. We cannot all of us praise God in the family by joining in song, because we are not all able to raise a tune, but it would be well if we could. I agree with Matthew Henry when he says, "They that pray in the family do well; they that pray and read the Scriptures do better; but they that pray, and read, and sing do best of all." There is a completeness in that kind of family worship which is much to be desired.

Whether in the family or not, yet personally and privately, let us endeavour to be filled with God's praise and with his honour all the day. Be this our resolve—"I will extol thee, my God, O King; and I will bless thy name for ever and ever. Every day will I bless thee; and I will praise thy name for ever and ever."

Brethren, praise cannot be a second-class business; for it is evidently due to God, and that in a very high degree. A sense of justice ought to make us praise the Lord; it is the least we can do, and in some senses it is the most that we can do, in return for the multiplied benefits which he bestows upon us. What, no harvest of praise for him who has sent the sunshine of his love and the rain of his grace upon us! What, no revenue of praise for him who is our gracious Lord and King! He doth not exact from us any servile labour, but simply saith, "Whoso offereth praise glorifieth me." Praise is good, and pleasant, and delightful. Let us rank it among those debts which we would not wish to forget, but are eager to pay at once.

Praise is an act which is pre-eminently characteristic of the true child of God. The man who doth but pretend to piety will fast twice in the week, and stand in the temple and offer something like prayer; but to praise God with all the heart, this is the mark of true adoption, this is the sign and token of a heart renewed by divine grace. We lack one of the surest evidences of pure love to God if we live without presenting praise to his ever-blessed name.

Praising God is singularly beneficial to ourselves. If we had more of it we should be greatly blest. What would lift us so much above the trials of life, what would help us to bear the burden and heat of the day, so well as songs of praise unto the Most High? The soldier marches without weariness when the band is playing inspiring strains; the sailor, as he pulls the rope or lifts the anchor, utters a cheery cry to aid his toil; let us try the animating power of hymns of praise. Nothing would oil the wheels of the chariot of life so well as more of the praising of God. Praise would end murmuring, and nurse contentment. If our mouths were filled with the praises of God, there would be no room for grumbling. Praise would throw a halo of glory around the head of toil and thought. In its sunlight the commonest duties of life would be transfigured. Sanctified by prayer and praise, each duty would be raised into a hallowed worship, akin to that of heaven. It would make us more happy, more holy, and more heavenly, if we would say, "I will extol thee, my God, O King."

Besides, brethren, unless we praise God here, are we preparing for our eternal home? There all is praise; how can we hope to enter there if we are strangers to that exercise? This life is a preparatory school and in it we are preparing for the high engagements of the perfected. Are you not eager to rehearse the everlasting hallelujahs?

"I would begin the music here,
And so my soul should rise:
Oh, for some heavenly notes to bear
My passions to the skies!"

Learn the essential elements of heavenly praise by the practice of joyful thanksgiving, adoring reverence, and wondering love; so that, when you step into heaven, you may take your place among the singers, and say, "I have been practising these songs for years. I have praised God while I was in a world of sin and suffering, and when I was weighed down by a feeble body; and now that I am set free from earth and sin, and the bondage of the flesh, I take up the same strain to sing more sweetly to the same Lord and God."

I wish I knew how to speak so as to stir up every child of God to praise. As for you that are not his children—oh, that you were such! You must be born again; you cannot praise God aright till you are. "Unto the wicked God saith, What hast thou to do to declare my statutes, or that thou shouldest take my covenant in thy mouth?" You can offer him no real praise while your hearts are at enmity to him. Be ye reconciled to God by the death of his Son, and then you will praise him. Let no one that has tasted that the Lord is gracious, let no one that has ever been delivered from sin by the atonement of Christ, ever fail to pay unto the Lord his daily tribute of thanksgiving

To help us in this joyful duty of praise we will turn to our text, and keep to it. May the Holy Spirit instruct us by it!

I. In our text we have first of all THE RESOLVE OF PERSONAL LOYALTY:—"I will extol thee, my God, O King." David personally comes before his God and King, and utters this deliberate resolution that he will praise the divine majesty for ever.

Note here, first, that *he pays homage to God as his King*. There is no praising God aright if we do not see him upon the throne, reigning with unquestioned sway. Disobedient subjects cannot praise their sovereign. You must take up the Lord's yoke—it is easy, and his burden, which is light. You must come and touch his silver sceptre and receive his mercy, and own him to be your rightful Monarch, Lawgiver, and Ruler. Where Jesus comes, he comes to reign: where God is truly known, he is always known as supreme. Over the united kingdom of our body, soul, and spirit the Lord must reign with undisputed authority. What a joy it is to have such a King! "O King," says David: and it seems to have been a sweet morsel in his mouth. He was himself a king after the earthly fashion; but to him God alone was King. Our King is no tyrant, no maker of cruel laws. He demands no crushing tribute or forced service: his ways are ways of pleasantness, and all his paths are peace. His laws are just and good; and in the keeping of them there is great reward. Let others exult that they are their own masters; our joy is that God is our King. Let others yield to this or that passion, or desire; as for us, we find our freedom in complete subjection to our heavenly King. Let us, then, praise God by loyally accepting him as our King; let us repeat with exultation the hymn we just now sang—

"Crown him, crown him,
King of kings, and Lord of lords."

Let us not be satisfied that he should reign over us alone: but let us long that the whole earth should be filled with his glory. Be this our daily prayer—"Thy kingdom come. Thy will be done, in earth as it is in heaven." Let this be our constant ascription of praise—"For thine is the kingdom, and the power, and the glory, for ever. Amen."

Note that the Psalmist, also, in this first sentence, *praises the Lord by a present personal appropriation of God to himself by faith:* "I will extol thee, my God." That word "my" is a drop of honey; nay, it is like Jonathan's wood, full of honey; it seems to drip from every bough, and he that comes into it stands knee-deep in sweetness. "My God" is as high a note as an angel can reach. What is another man's God to me? He must be my God or I shall not extol him. Say, dear heart, have you ever taken God to be your God? Can you say with David in another place, "This God is our God for ever and ever. He shall be our guide, even unto death"? Blessed was Thomas when he bowed down, and put his finger into the print of his Master's wounds, and cried, "My Lord and my God." That double-handed grip of appropriation marked the death of his painful unbelief. Can you say, "Jehovah is my God"? To us there are Father, Son, and Holy Spirit; but these are one God, and this one God is our own God. Let others worship whom they will, this God our soul adores and loves, yea, claims to be her personal possession. O beloved, if you can say, "My God," you will be bound to exalt him! If he has given himself to you so that you can say, "My Beloved is mine" you will give yourself to him, and you will add, "And I am his." Those two sentences, like two silken covers of a book, shut in within them the full score of the music of heaven.

Observe that David *is firmly resolved to praise God*. My text has four "I wills" in it. Frequently it is foolish for us poor mortals to say "I will," because our will is so feeble and fickle; but when we resolve upon the praise of God, we may say, "I will," and "I will," and "I will," and "I will," till we make a solid square of determinations. Let me tell you you will have need to say "I will" a great many times, for many obstacles will hinder your resolve. There will come depression of spirit, and then you must say, "I will extol thee, my God, O King." Poverty, sickness, losses, and crosses may assail you, and then you must say, "I will praise thy name for ever and ever." The devil will come and tell you that you have no interest in Christ; but you must say, "Every day will I bless thee." Death will come, and perhaps you will be under the fear of it; then it will be incumbent upon you to cry, "And I will praise thy name for ever and ever."

> "Sing, though sense and carnal reason
> Fain would stop the joyful song :
> Sing, and count it highest treason
> For a saint to hold his tongue."

A bold man took this motto—" While I live I'll crow"; but our motto is, " While I live I'll praise." An old motto was, "*Dum spiro spero*"; but the saint improves upon it, and cries, "*Dum expiro spero*." Not only while I live I will hope, but when I die I will hope : and he even gets beyond all that, and determines—"Whether I live or die I will praise my God." "O God, my heart is fixed, my heart is fixed ; I will sing and give praise."

While David is thus resolute, I want you to notice that *the resolution is strictly personal*. He says, "*I* will extol thee." Whatever others do, my own mind is made up. David was very glad when others praised God : he delighted to join with the great congregation that kept holy day; but still he was attentive to his own heart and his own praise. There is no selfishness in looking well to your own personal state and condition before the Lord. He cannot be called a selfish citizen who is very careful to render his own personal suit and service to his king. A company of persons praising God would be nothing unless each individual was sincere and earnest in the worship. The praise of the great congregation is precious in proportion as each individual, with all his heart, is saying, "I will extol thee, my God, O King." Come, my soul, I will not sit silent, because so many others are singing: however many songsters there may be, they cannot sing for me: they cannot pay my private debt of praise, therefore awake, my heart, and extol thy God and King. What if others refuse to sing, what if a shameful silence is observed in reference to the praises of God; then, my heart, I must bestir thee all the more to a double diligence, that thou mayest with even greater zeal extol thy God and King! I will sing a solo if I cannot find a choir in which I may take my part. Anyhow, my God, I will extol thee. At this hour men go off to other lords, and they set up this and that new-made god; but as for me, my ear is bored to Jehovah's door-post; I will not go out from his service for ever. Bind the sacrifice with cords, even with cords to the horns of the altar. Whatever happens, I will extol thee, my God, O King.

Now brothers and sisters, have you been losing your own personality in the multitude. As members of a great church, have you thought "Things will go on very well without me"? Correct that mistake: each individuality must have its own note to bring to God. Let him not have to say to you, "*Thou* hast bought me no sweet cane with money; neither hast *thou* filled me with the fat of *thy* sacrifices." Let us not be slow in his praise, since he has been so swift in his grace.

Once more upon this head, while David is thus loyally resolving to praise God, you will observe that *he is doing it all the time*. For the resolution to praise can only come from the man who is already praising God. When he saith, "I will extol thee," he is already extolling. We go from praise to praise. The heart resolves, and so plants the seed, and then the life is affected, and the harvest springs up and ripens. O brethren, do not let us say, "I will extol thee to-morrow"; or, "I will hope to praise thee when I grow old, or when I have less business on hand." No, no; thou art this day in debt; this day own thine obligation. We cannot praise God too soon. Our very first breath is a gift from God, and it should be spent to the Creator's praise. The early morning hour should be dedicated to praise: do not the birds set us the example? In this matter he gives twice who gives quickly. Let thy praise follow quickly upon the benefit thou dost receive, lest even during the delay thou be found guilty of ingratitude. As soon as a mercy touches our coasts, we should welcome it with acclamation. Let us copy the little chick, which, as it drinks, lifts up its head, as if to give thanks. Our thanksgiving should echo the voice of divine lovingkindness. Before the Lord our King, let us continually rejoice as we bless him, and speak well of his name.

Thus, then, I have set before you the resolve of a loyal spirit. Are you loyal to your God and King? Then I charge you to glorify his name. Lift up your hearts in his praise, and in all manner of ways make his name great. Praise him with your lips; praise him with your lives; praise him with your substance; praise him with every faculty and capacity. Be inventive in methods of praise: "sing unto the Lord a new song." Bring forth the long-stored and costly alabaster box; break it, and pour the sweet nard upon your Redeemer's head and feet. With penitents and martyrs extol him! With prophets and apostles extol him! With saints and angels extol him! Great is the Lord, and greatly to be praised.

II. And now I must conduct you to the second clause of the text, which is equally full and instructive. We have in the second part of it THE CONCLUSION OF AN INTELLIGENT APPRECIATION: "And I will bless thy name for ever and ever." Blind praise is not fit for the all-seeing God. God forbade of old the bringing of blind sacrifices to his altar. Our praise ought to have brain as well as a tongue. We ought to know who the God is whom we praise; hence David says, "I will bless *thy name*"; by which he means—thy character, thy deeds, thy revealed attributes.

First, observe that *he presents the worship of inward admiration*: he knows, and therefore he blesses the divine name. What is this act of blessing? Sometimes "bless" would appear to be used interchangeably with "praise"; yet there is a difference, for it is written, "All thy works shall praise thee, O Lord; and thy saints shall bless thee." You can praise a man, and yet you may never bless him. A great artist, for instance; you may *praise* him, but he may be so ungenerous to you and others that it may never occur to you to *bless* him. Blessing has something in it of love and delight. It is a nearer, dearer, heartier thing than *praise*. "I will bless thy name," that is to say—"I will take an intense delight in thy name: I will lovingly rejoice in it."

The very thought of God is a source of happiness to our hearts; and the more we muse upon his character the more joyous we become. The Lord's name is love. He is merciful and gracious, tender and pitiful. Moreover, he is a just God, and righteous, faithful, and true, and holy. He is a mighty God, and wise and unchanging. He is a prayer-hearing God, and he keepeth his promise evermore. We would not have him other than he is. We have a sweet contentment in God as he is revealed in holy Scripture. It is not everybody that can say this, for a great many professors nowadays desire a god of their own making and shaping. If they find anything in Scripture concerning God which grates upon their tender susceptibilities, they cannot abide it. The God that casts the wicked from his presence for ever—they cannot believe in him; they therefore make unto themselves a false deity, who is indifferent to sin. All that is revealed concerning God is to me abundantly satisfactory; if I do not comprehend its full meaning, I bow before its mystery. If I hear anything of my God which does not yield me delight, I feel that therein I must be out of order with him, either through sin or ignorance, and I say, "What I know not, teach thou me." I doubt not that perfectly holy and completely instructed beings are fully content with everything that God does, and are ready to praise him for all. Do not our souls even now bless the Lord our God, who chose us, redeemed us, and called us by his grace? Whether we view him as Maker, Provider, Saviour, King, or Father, we find in him an unfathomable sea of joy. He is God, our exceeding joy. Therefore we sit down in holy quiet, and feel our soul saying, "Bless the Lord! Bless the Lord!" He is what we would have him to be. He is better than we could have supposed or imagined. He is the crown of delight, the climax of goodness, the sum of all perfection. As often as we see the light, or feel the sun, we would bless the name of the Lord.

I think when David said, "I will bless thy name," he meant that *he wished well to the Lord.* To bless a person means to do that person good. By blessing us what untold benefits the Lord bestows! We cannot bless God in such a sense as that in which he blesses us; but we would if we could. If we cannot give anything to God, we can desire that he may be known, loved, and obeyed by all our fellow-men. We can wish well to his kingdom and cause in the world. We can bless him by blessing his people, by working for the fulfilment of his purposes, by obeying his precepts, and by taking delight in his ordinances. We can bless him by submission to his chastening hand, and by gratitude for his daily benefits. Sometimes we say with the Psalmist, "O my soul, thou hast said unto the Lord, Thou art my Lord: my goodness extendeth not to thee; but to the saints that are in the earth, and to the excellent, in whom is all my delight." Oh, that I could wash Jesus Christ's feet! Is there a believer here, man or woman, but would aspire to that office? It is not denied you: you can wash his feet by caring for his poor people, and relieving their wants. You cannot feast your Redeemer; he is not hungry: but some of his people are; feed them! He is not thirsty; but some of his disciples are. Give them a cup of cold water in the Master's name, and he will accept it as given to himself. Do you not feel to-day, you that love him, as if you wanted to do something for him? Arise, and do it, and so bless him. It is one of the instincts of a true Christian to wish to do somewhat for his God and King, who has done everything for him. He loved me, and gave himself for me; should I not give myself for him? Oh, for perfect consecration! Oh, to bless God by laying our all upon his altar, and spending our lives in his service!

It seems, then, dear friends, that David *studied the character and doings of God,* and thus praised him. Knowledge should lead our song. The more we know of God the more acceptably shall we bless him through Jesus Christ. I exhort you, therefore, to acquaint yourselves with God. Study his holy Book. As in a mirror you may here see the glory of the Lord reflected, especially in the person of the Lord Jesus, who is in truth the Word, the very name of the Lord. It would be a pity that we should spoil our praises by ignorance: they that know the name of the Lord will trust him and will praise him.

It appears from this text that David *discovered nothing after a long study of God which would be an exception to this rule.* He does not say, "I will bless thy name in all but one thing. I have seen some point of terror in what thou hast revealed of thyself, and in that thing I cannot bless thee." No; without any exception he reverently adores and joyfully blesses God. All his heart is contented with all of God that is revealed. Is it so with us, beloved? I earnestly hope it is.

I beg you to notice *how intense he grows over this—*" I will bless thy name for ever and ever." You have heard the quaint saying of "for ever and a day." Here you have an advance upon it: it is "for ever," and then another "for ever." He says, " I will bless thy name for ever." Is not that long enough? No; he adds, "and ever." Are there two for-evers, two eternities? Brethren, if there were fifty eternities we would spend them all in blessing the name of the Lord our God. "I will bless thy name for ever and ever." It would be absurd to explain this hyperbolical expression. It runs parallel with the words of Addison, when he says—

> "Through all eternity to thee
> My song of joy I'll raise ;
> But oh, eternity's too short
> To utter all thy praise ! "

Somebody cavilled at that verse the other day. He said, " Eternity cannot be too short." Ah, my dear friend, you are not a poet, I can see ; but if you could get just a spark of poetry into your soul, literalism would vanish. Truly, in poetry and in praise the letter killeth. Language is a poor vehicle of expression when the soul is on fire ; words are good enough things for our cool judgment ; but when thoughts are full of praise they break the back of words. How often have I stood here and felt that if I could throw my tongue away, and let my heart speak without these syllables and arbitrary sounds, then I might express myself! David speaks as if he scorned to be limited by language. He must overleap even time and possibility to get room for his heart. "I will bless thy name for ever and ever." How I enjoy these enthusiastic expressions ! It shows that when David blessed the Lord he did it heartily. While he was musing the fire burned. He felt like dancing before the ark. He was in much the same frame of mind as Dr. Watts when he sang—

> " From thee, my God, my joys shall rise
> And run eternal rounds,
> Beyond the limits of the skies,
> And all created bounds."

III. But time will fail me unless I pass on at once to the third sentence of our text, which is, THE PLEDGE OF DAILY REMEMBRANCE. Upon this I would dwell with very great earnestness. If you forget my discourse, I would like you to remember this part of the text. " Every day will I bless thee " : I will not do it now and have done with it ; I will not take a week of the year in which to praise thee, and then leave the other fifty-one weeks silent ; but " every day will I bless thee." All the year round will I extol my God. Why should it be so ?

The greatness of the gifts we have already received demands it. We can never fully express our gratitude for saving grace, and therefore we must keep on at it. A few years ago we were lost and dead ; but we are found and made alive again. We must praise God every day for this. We were black as night with sin ; but now we are washed whiter than snow : when can we leave off praising our Lord for this ? He loved me and gave himself for me : when can the day come that I shall cease to praise him for this ? Gethsemane and the bloody sweat, Calvary and the precious blood, when shall we ever have done with praising our dear Lord for all he suffered when he bought us with his own heart's blood ? No, if it were only the first mercies, the mercy of election, the mercy of redemption, the mercy of effectual calling, the mercy of adoption, we have had enough to begin with to make us sing unto the Lord every day of our lives. The light which has risen upon us warms all our day with gladness ; it shall also light them up with praise.

To-day it becomes us to sing of the mercy of yesterday. The waves of love as well as of time have washed us up upon the shore of to-day, and the beach is strewn with love. Here I find myself on a Sunday morning exulting because another six days' work is done, and strength has been given for it. Some of us have experienced a world of loving-kindness between one Sabbath and another. If we had never had anything else from God but what we have received during the last week, we have overwhelming reason for extolling him to-day. If there is any day in which we would leave off praising God, it must not be the Lord's day, for

> "This is the day the Lord hath made,
> He calls the hours his own;
> Let heaven rejoice, let earth be glad,
> And praise surround the throne."

Oh, let us magnify the Lord on the day of which it can be said—

> "To-day he rose and left the dead,
> And Satan's empire fell;
> To-day the saints his triumphs spread,
> And all his wonders tell."

When we reach to-morrow shall we not praise God for the blessing of the Sabbath? Surely you cannot have forgotten the Lord so soon as Monday! Before you go out into the world, wash your face in the clear crystal of praise. Bury each yesterday in the fine linen and spices of thankfulness.

Each day has its mercy, and should render its praise. When Monday is over, you will have something to praise God for on Tuesday. He that watches for God's hand will never be long without seeing it. If you will only spy out God's mercies, with half an eye you will see them every day of the year. Fresh are the dews of each morning, and equally fresh are its blessings. "Fresh trouble," says one. Praise God for the trouble, for it is a richer form of blessing. "Fresh care," says one. Cast all your care on him who careth for you, and that act will in itself bless you. "Fresh labour," says another. Yes, but fresh strength, too.

There is never a night but what there comes a day after it: never an affliction without its consolation. Every day you must utter the memory of his great goodness.

If we cannot praise God on any one day for what we have had that day, *let us praise him for to-morrow.* "It is better on before." Let us learn that quaint verse:—

> "And a new song is in my mouth,
> To long-lived music set:—
> Glory to thee for all the grace
> I have not tasted yet."

Let us forestall our future, and draw upon the promises. What if to-day I am down; to-morrow I shall be up! What if to-day I cast ashes on my head: to-morrow the Lord shall crown me with loving-kindness! What if to-day my pains trouble me, they will soon be gone! It will be all the same a hundred years hence, at any rate; and so let me praise God for what is within measurable distance. In a few years I shall be with the angels, and be with my Lord himself. Blessed be his name!

Begin to enjoy your heaven now. What says the apostle? "For our citizenship is in heaven"—not is to be, but is. We belong to heaven now, our names are enrolled among its citizens, and the privileges of the new Jerusalem belong to us at this present moment. Christ is ours, and God is ours!

"This world is ours, and worlds to come;
Earth is our lodge, and heaven our home."

Wherefore let us rejoice and be exceeding glad, and praise the name of God this very day.

"Every day," saith he, "will I bless thee." *There is a seasonableness about the praising of God every day.* Praise is in season every month. You awoke, the sunlight streamed into the windows, and touched your eyelids, and you said, "Bless God. Here is a charming summer's day." Birds were singing, and flowers were pouring out their perfume; you could not help praising God. But another day it was dark at the time of your rising; you struck a match, and lit your candle. A thick fog hung like a blanket over all. If you were a wise man, you said, "Come, I shall not get through the day if I do not make up my mind to praise God. This is the kind of weather in which I must bless God, or else go down in despair." So you woke yourself up, and began to adore the Lord. One morning you awoke after a refreshing night's rest, and you praised God for it: but on another occasion you had tossed about through a sleepless night, and then you thanked God that the weary night was over. You smile, dear friends, but there is always some reason for praising God. Certain fruits and meats are in season at special times, but the praise of God is always in season. It is good to praise the Lord in the daytime: how charming is the lark's song as it carols up to heaven's gate! It is good to bless God at night—how delicious are the liquid notes of the nightingale as it thrills the night with its music? I do therefore say to you right heartily, "Come, let us together praise the Lord, in all sorts of weather, and in all sorts of places." Sometimes I have said to myself, "During this last week I have been so full of pain that I am afraid I have forgotten to praise God as much as I should have done, and therefore I will have a double draught of it now. I will get alone, and have a special time of thankful thought. I would make up some of my old arrears, and magnify the Lord above measure. I do not like feeling that there can ever be a day in which I have not praised him. That day would surely be a blank in my life. Surely the sweetest praise that ever ascends to God is that which is poured forth by saints from beds of languishing. Praise in sad times is praise indeed. When your dog loves you because it is dinner-time, you are not sure of him; but when somebody else tempts him with a bone, and he will not leave you, though just now you struck him, then you feel that he is truly attached to you. We may learn from dogs that true affection is not dependent upon what it is just now receiving. Let us not have a cupboard love for God because of his kind providence; but let us love him and praise him for what he is, and what he has done. Let us follow hard after him when he seems to forsake us, and praise him when he deals hardly with us; for this is true praise. For my part, though I am not long without affliction,

I have no faults to find with my Lord, but I desire to praise him, and praise him, and only to praise him. Oh, that I knew how to do it worthily! Here is my resolve:—"I will extol thee, my God, O King; and I will bless thy name for ever and ever. Every day will I bless thee."

IV. The last sentence of the text sets forth, THE HOPE OF ETERNAL ADORATION. David here exclaims, "And I will praise thy name for ever and ever."

I am quite sure when David said that, *he believed that God was unchangeable;* for if God can change, how can I be sure that he will always be worthy of my praise? David knew that what God had been, he was, and what he was then he always would be. He had not heard the sentence, "Jesus Christ the same yesterday, and to-day, and for ever"; nor yet that other, "I am the Lord, I change not; therefore ye sons of Jacob are not consumed"; but he knew the truth contained in both these texts, and therefore he said, "I will praise thy name for ever and ever." As long as God is, he will be worthy to be praised.

Another point is also clear: *David believed in the immortality of the soul.* He says, "I will praise thy name for ever and ever." That truth was very dimly revealed in the Old Testament; but David knew it right well. He did not expect to sleep in oblivion, but to go on praising; and therefore he said "I will praise thy name for ever and ever." No cold hand fell upon him, and no killing voice said to him, "You shall die, and never praise the Lord again." Oh, no; he looked to live for ever and ever, and praise for ever and ever! Brethren, such is our hope, and we will never give it up. We feel eternal life within our souls. We challenge the cold hand of death to quench the immortal flame of our love, or to silence the ceaseless song of our praise. The dead cannot praise God; and God is not the God of the dead, but of the living. Among the living we are numbered through the grace of God, and we know that we shall live because Jesus lives. When death shall come, it shall bring no destruction to us: though it shall change the conditions of our existence, it shall not change the object of our existence. Our tongue may be silenced for a little while, but our spirit, unaffected by the disease of the body, shall go on praising God in its own fashion; and then, by-and-by, in the resurrection, even this poor tongue shall be revived; and body, soul, and spirit shall together praise the God of resurrection and eternal glory. "I will praise thy name for ever and ever." We shall never grow weary of this hallowed exercise for ever and ever. It will always be new, fresh, delightful. In heaven they never require any change beyond those blessed variations of song, those new melodies which make up the everlasting harmony. On and on, for ever telling the tale which never will be fully told, the saints will praise the name of the Lord for ever and ever.

Of course, dear friends, David's resolve was that, *as long as he was here below* he would never cease to praise God; and this is ours also. Brethren, we may have to leave off some cherished engagements, but this we will never cease from. At a certain period of life a man may have to leave off preaching to a large congregation. Good old John Newton declared that he would never leave off preaching while he had breath in his body; and I admire his holy perseverance; but it was a pity that he did not leave off preaching at St. Mary Woolnoth; for he often wearied the people, and forgot the thread of his discourse. He might have done better in another place. Ah, well, we may leave off preaching, but we shall never leave off praising! The day will come when you, my dear friend, cannot go to Sunday-school: I hope you will go as long as ever you can toddle there; but it may be you will not be able to interest the children, your memory will begin to fail; but even then you can go on praising the Lord. And you will. I have known old people almost forget their own names, and forget their own children; but I have known them still remember their Lord and Master. I have heard of one who lay dying, and his friends tried to make him remember certain things; but he shook his head. At last one said, "Do you remember the Lord Jesus?" Then the mind came into full play, the eyes brightened, and the old man eloquently praised his Saviour. Our last gasp shall be given to the praise of the Lord.

When once we have passed through the iron gate, and forded the dividing river, then we will begin to praise God in a manner more satisfactory than we can reach at present. After a nobler sort we will sing and adore. What soarings we will attempt upon the eagle wings of love! What plunges we will take into the crystal stream of praise! Methinks, for a while, when we first behold the throne, we shall do no more than cast our crowns at the feet of him that loved us, and then bow down under a weight of speechless praise. We shall be overwhelmed with wonder and thankfulness. When we rise to our feet again, we will join in the strain of our brethren redeemed by blood, and only drop out of the song when again we feel overpowered with joyful adoration, and are constrained again in holy silence to shrink to nothing before the infinite, unchanging God of love. Oh, to be there! To be there soon! We may be much nearer than we think. I cannot tell what I shall do, but I know this, I want no other heaven than to praise God perfectly and eternally. Is it not so with you? A heart full of praise is heaven in the bud; perfect praise is heaven full-blown. Let us close this discourse by asking grace from God that, if we have been deficient in praise, we may now mend our ways, and put on the garments of holy adoration. This day and onward be our watchword "Hallelujah! Praise ye the Lord!"

OPEN PRAISE AND PUBLIC CONFESSION.

A Sermon

DELIVERED BY

C. H. SPURGEON,

AT THE METROPOLITAN TABERNACLE, NEWINGTON,

On Thursday Evening, October 11th, 1883.

"I will praise thee with my whole heart: before the gods will I sing praise unto thee. I will worship toward thy holy temple, and praise thy name for thy lovingkindness and for thy truth: for thou hast magnified thy word above all thy name. In the day when I cried thou answeredst me, and strengthenedst me with strength in my soul."—Psalm cxxxviii. 1—3.

IT is a very grievous thing, to one who worships the only living and true God, to see others engaged in idolatrous worship. It stirs one's indignation to see a man worship—not his own hands, but what is even worse than that—the thing which he has made with his own hands, and which must therefore be inferior to himself. As the righteous soul of Lot in Sodom was vexed with the filthy conversation of the inhabitants of that guilty city, so the righteous soul of David was vexed when he saw the lords many and gods many before whom his neighbours were bowing down; and, in like manner, as long as we are in this world, we shall often be troubled through seeing how others turn aside from the living God, how they forget his truth, set up thoughts of their own in the place of the thoughts of God, and dishonour the Holy Scripture by thinking that their own vain ideas can equal, if not even excel, the revelation of God. David in this matter becomes a guide to us; what he did in the presence of the idols of the heathen is to a great extent what we should do in the presence of the false systems of religion and the errors which are all round about us. You, dear friends, cannot love the right if you do not hate the wrong. I would not give a penny for your love to the truth if it is not accompanied with a hearty hatred of error. I have taken this text as an instruction to myself as well as to you. What David did with all his heart, as a man who loved Jehovah, the only true God, that we also should do if, indeed, we love the Lord Jesus Christ, and all the glorious truths which cluster around his glorious Deity and his atoning sacrifice.

I. How, then, will we act? We will try to act exactly as David did, and if we do so, we shall, first of all, SING WITH WHOLE-HEARTED PRAISE: "I will praise thee with my whole heart: before the gods will

I sing praise unto thee." This seems a very singular thing to do; here is a man indignant with these false gods, one would suppose that he would begin to argue on behalf of the true God, that he would raise a controversy on behalf of Jehovah; but he does nothing of the kind. At least, this is not the first thing that he does; but he begins to praise God, and to sing that praise aloud : " I will praise thee with my whole heart : before the gods will I sing praise unto thee."

This was a very singular method of procedure, yet a very wise one; for, first, *his song would openly show his contempt for the false gods.* What does it matter to him what these idols really are? Men call them gods; so, for the nonce, he calls them gods, too; and he begins to sing, not to them, but to his own God, the only living and true God. He pitches the tune, he lifts up the strain, he sings a psalm, and this is the theme of his music : " Glorious art thou, O Jehovah!" And he does this in the very presence of the idol gods and their worshippers; as much as to say, " I take so little notice of them all that I will not even be disturbed about them. I was singing the praises of Jehovah, and I shall go on singing them. I was full of holy joy, and I intend still to be so. These gods of the heathen are nothing, but our God made the heavens; therefore, I will not rob him of his glory, or deprive him of his full revenue of praise, by turning aside even for a single moment to pay any attention to these mere blocks of wood and stone." It was a wise way of acting on the part of David, and it was also a generous way, because he did not in words pour contempt upon the idols, but he showed his contempt for them by presenting his praise to Jehovah alone.

Let us do the same, beloved. Do not worry yourself about those who turn aside from the truth, and run in their own crooked ways. Warn them as best you can, but remember David's advice on another occasion : "Fret not thyself because of evildoers." You have better work to do than to fret about them; begin to praise your God, and go on praising him. Sing as many songs unto him as ever you did, and let your heart be just as glad as ever it can be. " Why do the heathen rage, and the people imagine a vain thing? The kings of the earth set themselves, and the rulers take counsel together, against the Lord, and against his anointed, saying, Let us break their bands asunder, and cast away their cords from us. He that sitteth in the heavens shall laugh : the Lord shall have them in derision." And if the Lord laughs, let us not cry. If he treats them with such calm contempt, let us do the same, and lift up our voices again and again unto him whose mercy endureth for ever, and whose throne is so established that all the leaguered hosts of earth and hell cannot shake it for a single moment. " Say among the heathen that the Lord reigneth." "The Lord sitteth upon the flood; yea, the Lord sitteth King for ever." Wherefore, let no man's heart fail him, but let all who love the Lord show their contempt for his adversaries by pouring out their joyful adoration unto the Most High.

I like David's plan of dealing with the idols, by continuing his whole-hearted praise to God, because, next, *it would evince his strong faith in the true God.* I cannot tell any better way by which he could have shown his confidence in Jehovah. He had already poured contempt upon the false gods, but now his calm, happy singing proves his reverence for the Most High, and makes men see that, if they doubt, he does not; if they rail, he knows how vain their railing is. It proves to them that there is at least one man who has true faith in God, for he stands like a solid rock amid the surging sea. He is not moved; nay, he is not affected enough to postpone his music, but he keeps on still singing, and singing the more loudly, the more the sea roars, and the fulness thereof. The more shrill the noise of the tumultuous idolaters, the more does he proclaim aloud his holy joy and his unshaken confidence in his God. True faith is one of the best of sermons; he who is—

"Calm 'mid the bewildering cry,
Confident of victory,"—

has, by that trustful calmness, done more to inspire the timid with confidence than if he were the most eloquent of men, who had with great vehemence urged them to trust in God. Thank God, faith, as well as unbelief, is contagious; and if—

"One sickly sheep infects the flock,
And poisons all the rest,"—

there is another side to that truth. One true believer tends to strengthen all the rest, and to make them "strong in the Lord, and in the power of his might." He who can sing as he goes to battle, if he be a leader, is likely to lead a tribe of heroes in his train. He who can sing in the time of shipwreck is likely to put courage into every one of the crew, so that they do their best for the labouring vessel, and, if it be possible, bring her safely into the haven. Sing, then, brother; sing, my sister; for this will prove your childlike confidence in God, your implicit reliance upon him.

That is a second commendation of David's mode of action.

The next is that, by continuing to praise Jehovah in the presence of the idols, *he declared his all-absorbing zeal for God's glory.* He did not need to stand up, and say, "I love the Lord with all my heart." Hear him sing, "I will praise thee with my whole heart;" see what force he puts into every note, listen to his jubilant song, you can tell by the very sound of his voice that his praise of Jehovah comes up from his heart, and from his whole heart. He is enthusiastic, he is full of confidence; if he had a doubt concerning Jehovah, he could not sing like that; and if he were lukewarm, he would not sing like that. But, as he is singing with his whole heart, those who are opposed to him say to themselves, "It is no use to trouble ourselves about that man; we shall never turn him from the faith." They will sheer off, one by one, knowing that it is no use to attack such a firm believer. He who praises God with his whole heart, is like a man on fire, he is terrible to the adversaries of the Most High. When the great Spanish Armada was ready to swoop down upon the English coast, our brave Admiral Drake took some of his small ships, and placed them where the wind would carry them right among the Spanish fleet. He filled the vessels with combustible material, and set them alight. Then he had no need to go himself, for the wind just took the fire-ships, and drifted them up against the Spanish galleons that floated high out of the water, and exposed a vast surface to the air, and one and another of the big unwieldy monsters were soon in a blaze, and a great victory was won without a blow being struck. So, I like to get a red-hot Christian, full of music and praise unto Jehovah, and just let him go, by the influence of the Holy Spirit, right into the middle of the adversaries of the truth. They cannot make him out; they do not know how to handle a man on fire. If he would try to argue with them, they might overwhelm him with their logic; if he would fire a shot at them, they could shoot back at him; but he does nothing of the kind. He simply blazes and burns to the glory of God; and that is a most effective mode of warfare with the Lord's enemies. Suppose, my brethren, that you were to have your hearts all on fire, burning and glowing with the intense conviction that the gospel is true, and that the God of heaven and earth is the one living and true God, and that the atoning blood of the Divine Saviour is the one hope of guilty sinners, you might do grand work for God then. Tolerate no doubt in your spirit, believe right up to the hilt, with unstaggering confidence; and then sing out your praises of Jehovah with a joyful confidence. Those who hate the truth will not know what to make of you, they will probably get out of your way as quickly as possible; but, if they do not, then perhaps you will set them also on fire; and it may be, by the grace of God, that you will burn up some of their errors, and put them into a terrible state of confusion and anxiety if they still resolve to fight against the Lord of hosts.

It was a wise plan, this of David, of getting in among the heathen gods, and singing to the praise of Jehovah. They could not understand him, but they were affected by his singing all the same. If he could have walked through any temple where all the idol gods could have been gathered together, and if he could have sung there the words of our grand Doxology,—

"Praise God from whom all blessings flow,
Praise him all creatures here below,
Praise him above, ye heavenly host,
Praise Father, Son, and Holy Ghost,"—

I should not have wondered if old Dagon had come tumbling down to the ground; and if Chemosh, and Milcom, and Baal, and Ashtaroth, and all those other abominations of the heathen, had fallen prone upon the earth at the sound of this glorious song of praise unto Jehovah. Therefore, if we would overthrow the idols of our own day, let us imitate this wise mode of action on the part of the psalmist.

I believe, also, that David was quite right in singing with all his heart before the idol gods, because *it would shield him from all danger wherever he went.* To walk among the wicked is a dangerous exercise. It is as though a man had to go into infected air, or traverse the wards of a lazar-house; he is himself apt to become affected by the poisonous atmosphere, and to become infected with the deadly malady; but, oh, if you keep on, with all your heart, praising God all the day, you may go with confidence wherever duty calls you! Ah! you might go between the jaws of death itself, and yet suffer no injury, for an atmosphere of praise would be the best deodorizer and disinfectant wherever you might be bidden by the Lord to go. As long as you kept on praising God, and magnifying his holy name, no adversary could do you any harm. Remember how the hosts of Jehoshaphat triumphed in the valley of Berachah when they began to sing praises unto God; then were their adversaries routed. Recollect also how Paul and Silas could not be held in bonds when, at midnight, they sang praises unto God. Then the prison rocked, the chains were broken, and the doors flew open, for there must be liberty where men can sing unto Jehovah. Where whole-hearted songsters adore the Most High continually, the prisoners' fetters snap, and the foundations of dungeons are moved. Therefore, dear friends, mind that you keep up the spirit of praise.

I used to know, years ago, a poor old labouring man; he was a Methodist of the good old-fashioned school. I never met him, or spoke with him, without finding that, wherever he was, he was always singing. He was up in the morning at half-past five to get out to his farm-work, and he sang while he was dressing. He sang as he pulled on his corduroys, he sang as he put on his smock, he sang as he walked downstairs, he sang as he tramped off down the street, and he sang all day as he was at his work. He did not keep on singing while I was preaching, but he seemed almost as if he wanted to do that; and every now and then he would burst out with "Hallelujah!" or "Praise the Lord." He was so full of thanksgiving to God that he was obliged to give expression to his feelings sometimes even when it would have been more proper if he had kept quiet. He was one of the holiest men I ever knew, and I used to account very much for his simple gentleness, integrity, and happiness by the habit he had acquired of constantly singing the praises of God. He worked with some men who were in the habit of swearing, but he kept on singing; and, after a time, they began to think that it was not the right thing for them to swear. He went among men who drank, but he never left off singing; and, somehow, even among such men there was a kind of respect for him. It was so with all who knew him; his employer tried to put him where he would have easier tasks than others as he grew old, and everybody loved him.

I always wished that he had been a Baptist; that would have been just the finishing touch to make him perfect, and then we should have lost him, for all perfect people go to heaven at once. But if I mentioned that subject to him,—and sometimes I did,—he was not long before he began to sing, and he asked me to join with him, which I gladly did. His was a happy way of living; I wish that I and all of you could rise to it. Perhaps somebody says, "That good man was a very happy, gracious soul, but still he was very childish." Perhaps so, but I would like to be just as he was; I do not speak of him as having been child-*ish*, but child-*like*, ever praising God like a happy child who is always singing. You know, dear friends, you can keep on praising the Lord whatever else you may be doing; you can sit down in your house with the needle in your hand, or go abroad into the garden with the hoe, and still be praising God. We do not have half enough of praise, brothers and sisters; I am sure the devil would be more angry with us if we would begin to praise

God more; and we certainly are under no obligations to him to keep from irritating his temper, so let us sing unto the Lord as long as we live, and defy the devil to do his worst. As he likes neither music nor song in praise of Jehovah, let him have plenty of them both; let us continually do as David declared that he would do: "I will praise thee with my whole heart: before the gods (or before the devils, before the kings or before the beggars, before the drunkards, before the swearers, before anybody and everybody) will I sing praise unto thee."

That, then, was the first part of David's action,—singing unto Jehovah with whole-hearted praise.

II. The second thing that David did was to WORSHIP BY THE DESPISED RULE. Even in the presence of those who set up their idol gods, and their false systems, he declared to Jehovah, "I will worship toward thy holy temple."

Some said, "Worship this way." Others said, "Worship that way." In the present day, some say that the Old Testament is not inspired, that there is much that is very doubtful in the five books of Moses; some are going to worship in one way, some in another way of their own inventing; but if we are of David's mind, we shall say to the Lord, "I will worship toward thy holy temple." Let every other man have his own way of worshipping if he will; but, brethren, as for me, I say to the Lord, with David, "I will worship toward thy holy temple."

I admire this declaration, first, because *it is a quiet way of ignoring all will-worship.* "Oh!" says one, "I am resolved to worship God with all kinds of show, and ceremony, and flowers, and millinery." Another says, "I intend to worship God out in the fields, and never to mingle with his people at all." Very well, you go your own ways, but I ignore both of your ways, for my way is to worship toward God's holy temple,—that is the way in which the apostles and the early Christians worshipped Christ, not forsaking the assembling of themselves together, as the manner of some is,—the way in which they cheered their own hearts, and the hearts of their fellow-believers, with psalms and hymns and spiritual songs,—the way in which they spoke as the Spirit gave them utterance,—the way in which they gathered around the table of their Lord to remember his great love to them. You may go and set up whatever novelty you like, but I shall keep to that—

"Good old way, by our fathers trod,"—

and I trust that every true child of God will make this personal declaration to the Lord, "I will worship toward thy holy temple."

What did David mean by that expression, "thy holy temple"? Well, the temple, like the tabernacle in the wilderness, was *typical of the adorable person of our Lord Jesus Christ.* It was not that the tent in the wilderness or the temple on Mount Zion was anything of itself; but these were the places where God was specially pleased to reveal himself. Now, to-day, the temple of Jehovah is the body of our Lord and Saviour Jesus Christ which he himself expressly called "the temple." Let others worship saints and angels, if they will; but we will worship the incarnate Christ, and him alone. Let others worship the man, and think him nothing more than man; but we shall worship Christ as God. I was delighted to sing with you, a little while ago,—

"Jesus, my God! I know his name,
His name is all my trust;
Nor will he put my soul to shame,
Nor let my hope be lost."

Jesus is not only my Saviour, but he is also my God; and my prayers are to be presented to the Father through him, and to come up unto the Most High through the person of the God-man, the Mediator between God and men, Jesus Christ our Lord and Saviour. I will worship toward that shrine, the person of the Son of God, and God the Son.

But the temple was also *the place of sacrifice;* and we shall only praise God aright as we trust to the one great sacrifice. Oh, how many, nowadays, deny the great truth of vicarious suffering, the substitutionary sacrifice of Christ on Calvary, saying that he is our Exemplar, but not the Maker of propitiation and reconciliation by his blood. Well, do not trouble your head about these people, and begin to discuss with them; but say, "As for me, 'I will worship toward thy holy temple.' I have not any hope of my prayers speeding except through the sacrifice of Christ upon the cross. I can have no assurance of being accepted by God unless I am 'accepted in the Beloved.' So, I will offer no prayer but that which goes to God by the crimson road of the substitutionary death of Christ. 'I will worship toward thy holy temple.'" Keep to that declaration with unshaken firmness of resolve, and it will be the best answer that you can give to the idols, or to the devils, or to everyone else who may oppose the Most High.

III. Now notice, thirdly, what David did. He went on from singing and worshipping, to PRAISE THE QUESTIONED ATTRIBUTES,—the very attributes which are being questioned in this present age: "I will praise thy name for thy lovingkindness and for thy truth."

The true believer should praise God, first, for *his lovingkindness,* and for that lovingkindness in its universality. Some say that the God whom we preach cannot be a God of love because he banishes unbelievers into endless misery. If they refuse his Son, he gives them no hope that there can be any hereafter for them except that of eternal banishment from his presence and from the glory of his power. "The wicked shall be turned into hell, and all the nations that forget God." And there are some preachers who cover up, and try to hide this solemn truth, or speak as if they had velvet in their mouths when they come to deal with it. I shall not do so; by God's grace, I never shall do so. There is enough love in God to satisfy me; and I shall not want to make another god in order that I may believe in his lovingkindness. My heart delights to praise the very Jehovah of whom the psalmist sings, "To him that smote Egypt in their firstborn: for his mercy endureth for ever: and brought out Israel from among them: for his mercy endureth for ever: with a strong hand, and with a stretched out arm: for his mercy endureth for ever.

To him which divided the Red Sea into parts: for his mercy endureth for ever: and made Israel to pass through the midst of it: for his mercy endureth for ever: but overthrew Pharaoh and his host in the Red Sea: for his mercy endureth for ever." I am quite certain that he never executes judgment with a severity which will be questioned by right minds; and in the last great day, when the whole of this dispensation is wound up, it will be seen that "God is love." We may not be able to see it now; he may seem to be, as David says in another Psalm, "terrible out of his holy places." Jehovah himself declares that he is a jealous God, who will by no means clear the guilty; and there are many who cavil at that, but the day shall declare it. When the veil is rolled up, to the astonishment of all God's creatures, it will be seen that he did the best, the wisest, and the kindest thing which, all things considered, could have been done; and, therefore, though I cannot yet understand all his dealings with the sons of men, yet I believe that they are right, and I will praise his name for his lovingkindness.

There is a special note here, which bids us think of *God's loving-kindness in its speciality*. Many cavil at this great truth, which seems to me to be self-evident, that Christ should choose his own spouse; they want to have entrusted to them the selection of a bride for him. They want God to be lackey to the free will of man, and that none of his purposes should be carried out unless man permits it; their notion is that the great Creator must sit and wait till he gets his creature's permission to be gracious. But as for us, beloved, we adore the glorious truth of his electing love, we admire the sovereignty of his grace, and we delight to know that he does as he wills among the inhabitants of this lower world, and deals out his mercy, as Paul puts it, "according to the good pleasure of his will." Instead of disputing with idols, or devils, we begin to sing with all our heart concerning the special love of God to his chosen, and the favour which he bears towards them that put their trust in him. We cannot employ our time to better purpose; to argue and debate might be a waste of effort, and might depress our own spirit; but to bless the name of the Lord will do us good, and will also be to his honour and glory.

I find that the original bears another meaning: "I will praise thy name *for thy grace*, and for thy truth." Is it not a blessed thing to have that word "grace" always in the mouth? "Grace." Is it not one of the sweetest words that God ever permitted human lips to utter? And we often say "*free* grace", even if some tell us that is tautology. If one tap of the hammer will not suffice, we will give two. If men do not understand what "grace" means, we will call it "free grace"; and we will bless and praise the name of the Lord that we have two such words in the language as "free grace."

The other attribute for which David said that he would praise the name of the Lord is, *God's truth*. Our heart may well be sad as we see how men are pecking at God's truth. One part of the Bible is given up by one, and another part is rejected by another; one of our wise men says, "I have given up all the Old Testament, and a large part of the New." Well, sir, you might just as well give it all up, because you evidently have no part nor lot in it, or else you would not talk like that. Those gentlemen who want to mend the Bible, really need mending themselves; that is where the mischief lies in most cases. If they were savingly converted by the grace of God, they would love every letter of the Book from Genesis to Revelation, and find it food to their souls. But they do not know the inner meaning of it, and therefore they despise the Scripture as being but husks to them; and I greatly fear that is all that it is to many of them. But as for us, we shall glory in God's truth,—in the historic accuracy of every word of this blessed old Bible; in the absolute truth of everything that is recorded here; in the certainty of the fulfilment of every promise and every threatening that is in this Book; and, what is more, in the absolute correctness of every unfulfilled prophecy as being just as certain as certainty itself. There is where we mean to stand. We believe in plenary verbal inspiration, with all its difficulties, for there are not half as many difficulties in that doctrine as there are in any other kind of inspiration that men may imagine. If this Book be not the real solid foundation of our religion, what have we to build upon? If God has spoken a lie, where are we, brethren? And if this Book, for which the martyrs bled, and which sustained our sires in prison and on the death-bed,—if this precious Book, which is to-day hugged to the heart of many a dying saint, is to be rent away from us, it shall not go without a struggle, in which we will, if necessary, sacrifice even our lives. We will never give up the Bible; we will love it in life and in death, and we will still believe that it is the glorious and perfect revelation, as far as our imperfect minds can discern it, of the lovingkindness and truth of God, and for it we will praise and bless his holy name. This is what David said he would do, and I recommend all tried saints to do the same.

IV. Now, fourthly, there was another thing which David meant to do, and that was, to REVERENCE GOD'S WORD TO THE HIGHEST DEGREE. He puts it thus: "Thou hast magnified thy Word above all thy name." My text is such a great one that I need half-a-dozen nights to descant upon it, so I can only give you hints of what I would say if I had the time.

God's name, dear friends, is revealed in a measure in nature. In providence, that name may be spelt out; but David tells us here that the Lord has magnified his Word above all his name. That is to say, that revelation is made by God to be infinitely superior to creation and to providence as a revealing of himself, for, first, *it is more clear.* If a man paints grand pictures, even if I never saw the man, I know a little about him when I see his paintings. Ay, but if he writes me a letter, and in that letter tells me what is in his very heart, I know more about him by his words than I do by his works; and there is more of God in some passages of the Bible than in the whole universe besides. If science could be all known, it would not contain as much real light as there is in a single verse of Scripture, for the best light is in the Word. There is other light, too; but it is only moonlight as compared with the sunlight. God has magnified his Word, for its clearness, above every other method of revealing his name or character.

It is not only *more clear,* but it is also *more sure.* If we look into

God's works, one man sees one thing and another man sees another; but if you look into God's Word, and you have a childlike spirit, you will see what another childlike-spirited man sees. If you are God's child, you will see what others of God's children see there; and in the great fundamental truths discoverable in his Word, the saints are almost entirely agreed. The whole universe is not big enough to mirror God in all his glory. If he looks into the great and wide sea that he has made, the glass is too small to reflect more than a part of his glory. Suppose that God should reveal himself to the full in nature; it would soon be seen that the axles of the wheel would be all too weak to sustain the weight of Deity. It is only revelation that can manifest him truly to us.

Think again; God's Word is *more lasting* than his other works. The revelation of God in nature is not unique. If he has made one world, he can make another; if he has made one universe, he can make fifty universes; but after having given us one complete revelation of his will, he will never give another, that one stands alone. What God has made known in the book of nature will all pass away; there will come a day when the elements themselves shall be dissolved with fervent heat, and like a worn-out vesture, all this material creation shall be put away. But, "the Word of the Lord endureth for ever. And this is the Word which by the gospel is preached unto you;" so that God magnifies his Word by making it everlasting. "Heaven and earth shall pass away, but my words shall not pass away."

Does not God magnify his Word in your hearts, dear friends? You have sometimes been in the fields on the Sabbath, and a sweet sense of rest has stolen over you. In the time of harvest, or on a bright morning when the sun has risen, you have been overwhelmed with a sense of the glory of God; but, still, that sweet feeling never comes to the heart so as to affect its secret springs like a passage out of Scripture. A promise from God will cast more light into your soul than all the beauties of sea and land. I do not for a moment depreciate the wondrous glory of God in all his works; but, still, I do say God is seen better in his Word than in all his works besides; and he has magnified his Word above all his name. They say that we ought to alter Scripture because scientists have found out something or other. Yes, I know all about that kind of talk; scientists found out many things years ago, and within ten years somebody else rose up, and found out that they were all wrong. The history of so-called philosophy is the history of fools; and the philosophers of this day are no more right than those of fifty years ago. The men are coming to the front who will confute the positive assertions of the present; and, when they have made their own assertions, and made their bow, another set of wise men will be coming after them to confound them. They are all as the grass that withereth, but "the Word of the Lord endureth for ever." It has been tried in the furnace of earth, purified seven times; and here it remains, the pure refined metal still, and in this will we glory, and not be ashamed.

V. Lastly, David was going to PROVE ALL BY HIS OWN EXPERIENCE. A bit of experience is the best thing with which to close up my discourse. "In the day when I cried thou answeredst me, and strengthenedst me with strength in my soul."

Ah! brethren, men say that facts are stubborn things, and so they are; and when a man once gets a fact with regard to the religion of Jesus Christ, he becomes a stubborn man. The man who is in the habit of praying to God, and who is in the habit of having answers to his prayers, the man who lives a life of prayer, and consequently who is enriched by innumerable mercies, says to those who deny the efficacy of prayer, "You may say what you like, but you cannot trouble me about this matter, because I am daily testing and daily proving in my own experience what prayer can accomplish." "Well," they say, "you did not get out of the trouble; you prayed, but you did not escape from it." That is quite true, I did not; but God strengthened me with strength in my soul; and it is a grand thing when the mind becomes calm, when the soul grows strong, when courage increases, when confidence comes, when deep peace and quiet restfulness flow into the soul. All that is a blessed answer to prayer; and as long as God gives us that, we cannot desert his standard, or deny his faithfulness and his truth. Let those who will, go and leave the snows of Lebanon, and the pure flowing river of God for the broken cisterns that can hold no water, or for the muddy waters of Egypt; but we cannot, we dare not, we will not. God helping us, we will stand fast in our belief in the power of prayer. We have tried it, we have proved it, and we are not to be shaken from our confidence in its efficacy. The Lord give to every one of you, who do not at present know it, really to prove it yourselves, to try it to your heart's joy and satisfaction, and you also shall stand fast in your confidence in him even to the end! The Lord bless you, for Christ's sake! Amen.

Exposition by C. H. Spurgeon.
PSALM CXXXVIII.

Verse 1. *I will praise thee with my whole heart: before the gods will I sing praise unto thee.*

"Gods or no gods, whatever they may be, 'I will praise thee with my whole heart,' I will not be ashamed to declare my confidence in Jehovah, whoever may listen to me."

2. *I will worship toward thy holy temple, and praise thy name for thy lovingkindness and for thy truth: for thou hast magnified thy word above all thy name.*

Now was his time to speak. The gods of the heathen had their worshippers; then, should Jehovah be deserted by his loyal subjects? "No," says David, "I will worship thee, and I will praise thee, whoever may oppose me."

3. *In the day when I cried thou answeredst me, and strengthenedst me with strength in my soul.*

What worshipper of idols could ever say that of his god? "Ears have they," but they hear not the cries of their worshippers. "Hands have they," but they cannot deliver those who cry to them. "Feet have they," but they cannot come to the help of their votaries. But David declares that God had heard him in the day of his trouble, and strengthened him with strength in his soul.

4. *All the kings of the earth shall praise thee, O LORD, when they hear the words of thy mouth.*

He felt that he had had such good things to say concerning God, such blessed words of God to make known, that even the kings of the earth, when they began to listen to him, would become attentive, and would even become converts, and begin to praise Jehovah with him.

5. *Yea, they shall sing in the ways of the LORD: for great is the glory of the LORD.*

Think of that,—kings singing in the ways of the Lord, crowned princes becoming choristers in God's service. Someone has said that there are few in heaven who wore crowns on earth; and I am afraid it is true that, of all who are crowned on earth, few ever get to that land where all are kings and priests unto God. To have a crown on earth, and a crown above, is a rare thing; but David says that these kings "shall sing in the ways of Jehovah: for great is the glory of Jehovah;" and they shall be overpowered by that glory,—melted, subdued, wooed, won, converted by its power.

6, 7. *Though the LORD be high, yet hath he respect unto the lowly: but the proud he knoweth afar off. Though I walk in the midst of trouble, thou wilt revive me:—*

He was a king, yet he expected trouble; and do you complain when it comes to your cottage, after it had been to David's palace? "Though I walk in the midst of trouble, thou wilt revive me:"—

7. *Thou shalt stretch forth thine hand against the wrath of mine enemies, and thy right hand shall save me.*

He expected first to be revived, and afterwards to be protected. He believed that God would stretch out his hand, as men do when they make a supreme effort, and put forth all their force: "Thou shalt stretch forth thine hand against the wrath of mine enemies." David also expected ultimate preservation: "'Thy right hand shall save me.' Thou wilt do it; dexterously, readily, gladly, wilt thou do it: 'Thy right hand shall save me.'"

8. *The LORD will perfect that which concerneth me:*

"All that has to do with me—my business, my family, my work, my temporal and my eternal interests,—'that which concerneth me,' and that which troubles me, moves my heart with the deepest concern, Jehovah will perfect."

8. *Thy mercy, O LORD, endureth for ever: forsake not the works of thine own hands.*

And he will not do it; he will carry on unto completion the work which he has begun, blessed be his holy name!

MARY'S MAGNIFICAT.

A Sermon

DELIVERED BY
C. H. SPURGEON,
AT THE METROPOLITAN TABERNACLE, NEWINGTON,

On Thursday Evening, April 22nd, 1875.

"And Mary said, My soul doth magnify the Lord, and my spirit hath rejoiced in God my Saviour."—Luke i. 46, 47.

MARY's Magnificat was a song of faith. You have thought, perhaps, that you could easily have sung this song if you had been as highly favoured as she was; but are you sure that you could have done so? Have you ever realized the difficulties under which this hymn was composed and sung? If not, permit me to remind you that the wondrous birth, which had been promised to her, had not then been accomplished, and in her mind there must have been a consciousness that many would doubt her statements. The visitation of the angel, and all its consequences, would seem to be ridiculous and even impossible to many to whom she might venture to mention the circumstances; nay, more than that, would subject her to many cruel insinuations, which would scandalize her character, and that which conferred upon her the highest honour that ever fell to woman would, in the judgment of many, bring upon her the greatest possible dishonour. We know what suspicions even Joseph had, and that it was only a revelation from God that could remove them. Mary must have been sorely troubled if she had been influenced by her natural feelings, and had been swayed by external circumstances.

It was only her wondrous faith,— in some respects, her matchless faith, for no other woman had ever had such a blessed trial of faith as she had,—it was only her matchless faith that she should be the mother of the holy child Jesus, that sustained her. Truly blessed was she in believing that, and blessed indeed was she in that, even before there was an accomplishment of the things that were told her by the angel, she could sing, "My soul doth magnify the Lord, and my spirit hath rejoiced in God my Saviour." Unbelief would have said, "Wait." Fear would have said, "Be silent." But faith could not wait, and could not be silent; she must sing, and sing she did most sweetly. I call your attention to this fact because, when we ourselves have a song to sing unto the Lord, we may perhaps be tempted not to sing it till our hopes are accomplished, and our faith has been exchanged for fact. O brother, sister, if this is your case, do not wait, for your song will spoil if you do. There is another song to be sung for the accomplished mercy, but there is a song to be sung now for the promised mercy; therefore, let not the present hour lose the song which is due to it.

I am not going to expound the text so much as to ask you to practise it with me; so, firstly, *let us sing;* secondly, *let us sing after Mary's manner;* and, thirdly, *let us sing with Mary's matter.*

I. Firstly, then, LET US SING.

Let us sing, first, *because singing is the natural language of joy.* Do not even the ungodly sing when their corn and wine increase? Have they not their harvest hymns and vintage songs? Do they not sing right merrily when they go forth to the dance? And if the wicked sing thus, shall the righteous be silent? Are the jubilant songs all made for the ungodly, and the dirges for us? Are they to lift high the festive strain, and we to be satisfied with the "Dead March" in *Saul,* or some such melancholy music as that? No, brethren; if they have joy, much more have we. Their joy is like the crackling of thorns under a pot; but ours is the shining of a star that never shall be quenched. Let us sing then, for our joy abounds and abides. Therefore, "Rejoice in the Lord alway: and again I say, Rejoice." If the joy of the Lord be your strength, why not express it in holy song? Why should not your joys have a tongue as well as the joys of ungodly men? When warriors win victories, they shout; have we won no victories through Jesus Christ our Lord? When men celebrate their festivals, they sing; are there any festivals equal to ours,—our paschal supper, our passage of the Red Sea, our jubilee, our expectation of the coronation of our King, our hymn of victory over all the hosts of hell? Oh, surely, if the children of earth sing, the children of heaven ought to sing far more often, far more loudly, far more harmoniously than they do. Come, then, let us sing because we are glad in the Lord.

Let us sing, too, *because singing is the language of heaven.* It is thus that they express themselves up yonder. Many of the songs and other sounds of earth never penetrate beyond the clouds. Sighs and groans and clamours have never reached those regions of serenity and purity; but they do sing there. Heaven is the home of sacred song, and we are the children of heaven. Heaven's light is in us; heaven's smile is upon us; heaven's all belongs to us; and, therefore,—

"We would begin the music here,
And so our souls should rise:
Oh, for some heavenly notes to bear
Our passions to the skies!"

The music of joy and the music of heaven should often be upon our lips in the form of psalms, and hymns, and spiritual songs.

Let us also sing, *because singing is sweet to the ear of God.* I think I may venture to say that even the song of birds is sweet to him, for, in the 104th Psalm, where it is written, "The Lord shall rejoice in his works," it is also mentioned that the birds "sing among the branches." Is there anything sweeter in the world than to wake up, about four or five o'clock in the morning, just at this time of the year, and hear the birds singing as if they would burst their little throats, and pouring out, in a kind of contest of sweetness, their little hearts in joyous song? I believe that, in the wild places of the earth, where no human foot has ever defiled the soil, God loves to walk. When I have been alone among the fir trees, inhaling their sweet fragrance, or have wandered up the hill where the loudest voice could not be answered by another voice for no man was there, I have felt that God was there, and that he loved to listen to the song of birds that he had created. Yea, even the harshly croaking ravens he heareth when they cry.

I do not think that mere music is sweet to God's ear when it comes from man in lewdness, attended with lascivious thoughts; and even sacred music, which is sweet in itself, when used for mere amusement, must be an abomination to the Most High when it is so degraded. But he loves to hear us sing when we sing his praises from our hearts. Do you not delight to hear your own children sing, and is there anything sweeter than a song from a child? At the Orphanage, the other day, they brought me a little boy who had just been taken in. I felt a special interest in him because his father had been a minister of the gospel. They told him to sing to me, and it was a very sweet song—one of Mr. Sankey's hymns,—which came from his lips. His singing quite touched my heart. Had it been my own child, I do not doubt that it would have touched my heart still more; and God loves to hear his children sing. Even your discords, so long as they do not affect your heart, but are only of sound and not of soul, shall please him. What a beautiful simile is used in the 22nd Psalm: "O thou that inhabitest the praises of Israel!" Just as God's ancient people, during the feast of tabernacles, dwelt under booths made from the boughs of trees, so Jehovah is represented as having made for himself a tabernacle out of the praises of his people. They are only like fading boughs, that soon turn brown, yet the great Lord of all condescends to sit beneath them; and, as we each one bring a new bough, plucked from the tree of mercy, we help to make a new tabernacle for the Most High to dwell in.

One reason why they sing in heaven is *because all there are seeking to please the heart of God.* They sing not merely that they may practise psalmody, and have their voices in good order, or that they may interest the strangers who are constantly arriving from these nether lands, or even that they may please each other, and delight the angels; but unto the Lord is their perpetual song, for he delighteth in it. Let us also sing unto him as long as we live. Sometimes, it would be well for us to make hymns, rather than to repress the making of them, as we often do. The Moravians were accustomed to gather up, in their churches, the very poorest rhymes and ditties that were made by the brethren, and they used to shape them as best they could into something like singable form, and their hymn-book has in it a great number of hymns that I should not like to hear you sing; but, for all that, I like the spirit that was in the early Moravians. "Let us each one try to make a hymn," said they. "Let us encourage one another to express some personal experience of our life, for we have each one of us had some special point of God's grace illustrated in us." I would that the men, who can so well write popular songs, and give to the people attractive words and tunes to sing in the street or in the home, would consecrate their talents to a better purpose by writing hymns and spiritual songs to the praise and glory of God. We should then be the richer in our psalmody, as, indeed, we always are when God sends us a true revival of religion, for revivals of religion always bring with them new hymns and spiritual songs.

But if we cannot ourselves compose hymns, let us sing those that somebody else has made, and let us sing the right ones, those that suit us best. There are some hymns that I cannot sing at present; they are too high for me, but I shall sing them by-and-by. There are others that are too low for me; I cannot get down to such depths of doubt and trembling as the poets seem to have been in when they composed them. Every Christian should have some particular hymn that he loves best, so that, when his heart is merriest, he should sing that hymn. How many good old people I have known, who used to sit and sing, or walk about the house, just humming or crooning—

> "When I can read my title clear
> To mansions in the skies,
> I bid farewell to every fear,
> And wipe my weeping eyes."

Some have other favourites; but, whatever our choice is, I think it is well to have a hymn which, although we have not ourselves written it, has, nevertheless, been made our own by our circumstances and experiences. When we have fixed on such a hymn as that, let us sing it unto the Lord again and again.

Let us not be amongst those who make excuses for not singing. One says that he has no voice. Then, sing with your heart, brother. Perhaps even your voice would improve if you used it more; but if there be such a grating noise about it that you dare not sing when another person is listening, get alone, and sing unto the Lord.

Do not say that you are unable to sing because you are always in company. I would have you make it your general rule to sing in almost any company where your lot may be cast; though, sometimes, it is not meet to cast your pearls before swine. Watch your opportunity; if all in the room are silent, perhaps you had better be silent, too; but if one of your workfellows feels that he must needs sing a song, and he has taken the liberty to do it, now is your turn, and you may sing, too. I remember being on mount St. Bernard, spending a night with the monks at the hospice. There was a piano, which had been given by the Prince of Wales, and the different persons who were spending the night there, sang and played by turns. One sang a Spanish hymn, and another a German hymn, and when it came to our turn, we sang,—

"There is a fountain filled with blood
Drawn from Immanuel's veins."

And why should we not sing it? Had we not as good a right to sing as the other people had? Do not you abate your rights and privileges, dear friends; but, if others sing, do you sing, too, and never mind who listens; it will do no man any hurt to hear the praises of the Lord.

And do not say that you cannot sing because of your occupation. Your hands may be just as busy as usual even while the songs of Zion are rising from your lips. You may even be writing, or otherwise mentally occupied, and yet, at the same time, your heart may be ascending to God in praise.

Make no excuse because you are ill. Sometimes, a little song between the sheets is very sweet in the ears of God, even though it has to be accompanied by sighs and groans. Pain makes every note come out with great effort, yet I believe God bends down his ear to hear such singing as that. I have known birds in cages sing better than those outside; and the Lord sometimes puts us in a cage on purpose that he may hear us sing the sweeter. He loves to hear his sick children sing his praises upon their beds, and his high praises in the midst of the furnace of affliction. Are you very poor? Then, sing from your heart unto the Lord, and your music shall be better than silver and gold unto God. Even death itself need not stay our songs; let us sing right up to this side of the glory gate, there is no fear about our keeping on with our song on the other side. So long as we can sing here, let us do so, praising the Lord right up to the last hour of our lives, then shall our voices be tuned immediately to nobler songs, for, in a moment, we shall—

"Sing with rapture and surprise
His lovingkindness in the skies."

II. Now, passing on to our second point, LET US SING AFTER MARY'S MANNER, as far as that manner may be transferable to us. No bird ought to try to sing exactly like another. The blackbird ought not to imitate the thrush, nor the thrush the canary; let them all keep to their own notes, and let each one of us sing his own song unto the Lord. Yet I think we shall see that there is something about Mary's music that will suit us all.

First, *let us sing reverently.* Mary was very joyful, but there was nothing in her song that would strike you as being irreverent, vulgar, or commonplace. I am not squeamish about music, but I must confess that I hardly like to hear the high praises of God sung to the tune of a comic song or of a dance. There is a certain congruity about things that must be observed, and some good music may have associated with it such queer ideas that we had better let it alone till those associations have died out, lest, haply, while we are uttering holy words, some people may be reminded by the tune of unholy things. Mary sings very reverently, and so should we; and though I like some of the new tunes very well, and am glad that they are so popular, yet, for my own part, I like a good old psalm tune much better. It seems to me like going away from the snows of Lebanon to seek after the stale cisterns of earth, when we leave the old music, and the old hymns, and the old psalms, for any of your modern melodies. Still, if you can praise God better with the new songs, do so; but let it always be done reverently.

But, secondly, *Mary praised God with personal devotion.* Notice how intensely personal her song is. Elizabeth is there, yet Mary sings as though she were all alone: "My soul doth magnify the Lord, and my spirit hath rejoiced in God my Saviour." It seemed as though her song meant something like this, "Elizabeth is glad, but I, Mary, also am glad, and I have a gladness which is all my own, which even Elizabeth cannot know. 'My soul doth magnify the Lord.'" It ought to be so in our congregations; we should join with our fellow-Christians in their songs of praise, but we must always mind that our personal note is not omitted, "*My* soul doth magnify the Lord." Do you not think that some of you too often forget this? You come to hear sermons, and sometimes you do not come to the assembly as much as you ought for the purpose of directly and distinctly praising God in your own personality and individuality. The music is delightful to us as it rises from thousands of voices, but to God it can be pleasant only as it comes from each heart. "My soul"—whether other people are praising the Lord or not;—"my soul"—for I have a personal indebtedness to thee, my God, and there is a personal union between thee and me; I love thee, and thou lovest me; and, therefore, even if all other souls are dumb, "my soul doth magnify the Lord." In this fashion, dear brother or sister, have a song to yourself, and mind that it is thoroughly your own.

Thirdly, *in Mary's song we see great spirituality.* You observe how she puts this matter twice over: "My *soul* doth magnify the Lord, and my *spirit* hath rejoiced in God my Saviour." She is far from being content with mere lip service. Her language is poetic, but she is not satisfied with her language. I have no doubt that her voice was exceedingly sweet, but she does not say anything about that, but she does speak of "my soul" and "my spirit." O dear friends, let us never be satisfied with any kind of worship which does not take up the whole of our inner and higher nature. It is what you are within that you really are before the living God; and it is quite a secondary matter how loud the chant may be, or how sweet the tune of your hymn, or how delightfully you join in it, unless your spirit, your soul, truly praises the Lord. You can sometimes do this in "songs without words"; and he that hath no voice for singing can, after this fashion, magnify the Lord with his soul and spirit.

Mary also praised the Lord intelligently. Notice how she sings: "My soul doth magnify *the Lord,* and my spirit hath rejoiced in *God my Saviour.*" You observe that she varies the names which she uses, and she varies them with great propriety. She magnifies

Jehovah; she makes him great; which is the proper thing to do concerning Jehovah; but she rejoices in God her Saviour. In that aspect, her Lord comes nearer to her, and becomes more immediately the object of joy to her, so she rejoices in God her Saviour. She dwells first upon Jehovah's power to save: "My soul doth magnify *the Lord*." Then she dwells upon his willingness to save: "My spirit hath rejoiced in *God my Saviour*." She seems to see the two points,—the greatness and the goodness of the Lord; Jehovah, yet her Saviour; the Ruler and Lawgiver, yet the gracious One who pardons and blots out sin.

Mary praised God enthusiastically, for the reduplication of the terms, "My soul doth magnify the Lord, and my spirit hath rejoiced in God my Saviour," indicates the fervour and ardour of her praise. It is natural to us to repeat ourselves when we begin to glow with holy gladness, so Mary says, "My soul, my natural life;—my spirit, my newborn, my intenser, diviner life;—my soul, my mind, my intellect;—my spirit, my affections, my heart, my emotions, my entire being, my soul and spirit praise the Lord." She did not need to add that her body praised the Lord, for the very sound of her voice bore witness that her body was joining with her soul and spirit, and that so her triple nature was magnifying the Lord. There was enthusiasm in her song; and if ever any of us ought to be stirred to the very depths of our spirit, it is when we are praising the Lord. Sing, brethren, sing sweetly, but sing loudly, too, unto God your strength.

Further, we may sing, as Mary did, *divinely;* I mean, of course, with regard to the object of her song. So let it be with us. "My soul doth magnify"—a doctrine? a church? a priest? God forbid! "My soul doth magnify the Lord; and my spirit hath rejoiced in"— the success of my pastor's ministry? Yes, it may do so, but that is one of the inferior themes for joy. "My spirit hath rejoiced in" my own success in casting out devils, and working miracles? Ay, it may do that; but, still, it would be better to rejoice that our names are written in heaven. The subject of Mary's joy is nothing low, nothing less than heavenly: "My spirit hath rejoiced in God my Saviour." If that is your declaration, you may well lift up your voice and sing,—

"Go up, go up, my heart,
Dwell with thy God above."

Note, again, that *Mary sang evangelically*, and we must mind that we always do the same, for I am afraid that there are some popular hymns which have something that is not gospel in them; and whenever there is a hymn that has the slightest taint of that sort in it, we ought to abandon it for ever, however sweet its poetry may be. Mary sings, "My spirit doth rejoice in God my Saviour." She was no Socinian, and she was no Romanist; she knew that she needed a Saviour, and that she needed a God for her Saviour, so her spirit rejoiced in God her Saviour. When we reach the highest point in our devotions, we still need a Saviour. I do not at all like the boastful talk about "the higher life" in which some people seem to revel. We cannot have too high a life; but "God be merciful to me a sinner," is about as big a prayer as I can manage at present; and often does my soul pray with such earnestness the dying thief's prayer that his petition is forced to my lips, "Lord, remember me when thou comest into thy kingdom." The place of the perfect does not suit me yet, at any rate, but the place of the publican and of the penitent more becomes me, as I think it does the most of us. Oh, yes! we still need a Saviour; so, like Mary, we will sing about our Saviour; and even if we walk in the light, as God is in the light, we cannot do without the blood of Jesus Christ constantly cleansing us from all sin, for sin we do still.

Once more, *Mary praised the Lord with assurance.* It is a grand thing to be able to sing, "My soul *doth* magnify the Lord, and my spirit *hath* rejoiced in God"—"who will, I hope, and pray, and sometimes believe, be my Saviour"? I have spoilt the music—have I not,—by putting in those words of my own? It goes better as Mary sang it, "My spirit hath rejoiced in God my Saviour." She was quite assured of that fact, and had not any doubts or fears concerning it. It is well to get such a firm grip of the Saviour that we rest in him completely, and so can sing to his praise. "Oh!" saith one, "I cannot praise Jesus as I would, because of my sins;" and I reply to that remark,—But, my dear friend, would you praise him if you had no sins? Would he be needed by you and wanted by you then? Could he be of any use to you then? Would you feel any gratitude to him? If you were not sinners, of what use would a Saviour be to you? But we praise him because, though we are conscious of sin, we are equally conscious of cleansing in his precious blood. We take him to be our All-in-all because we ourselves are nothing at all. If we had been of any account, he would have been just so much less; but, since we are nothing, there is the opportunity for him to be All-in-all to us. Let us sing, then, to his praise; may God the Holy Spirit teach us to do so, even as he taught the Virgin Mary!

III. Now, thirdly, and briefly, LET US SING WITH MARY'S MATTER. That was twofold: "My soul doth magnify the Lord, and my spirit hath rejoiced in God my Saviour."

The first part of our matter, then, should be, "*Magnify the Lord.*" How can we do that? We cannot really make God great, though that is the meaning of the word. How, then, can we magnify him?

Well, first, let us think of his greatness; it will be really praising him if we thus think of him. You need not speak, but just ponder, weigh, consider, contemplate, meditate, ruminate upon the attributes of the Most High. Begin with his mercy if you cannot begin with his holiness; but take the attributes one by one, and think about them. I do not know a single attribute of God which is not wonderfully quickening and powerful to a true Christian. As you think of any one of them, it will ravish you, and carry you quite away. You will be lost in wonder, love, and praise as you consider it; you will be astonished and amazed as you plunge into its wondrous depths, and everything else will vanish from your vision. That is one way of making God great,—by often thinking about him.

The next way to make God great is by often drinking him into yourself. The lilies stand and worship God simply by being beautiful,—by drinking in the sunlight which makes them so charming, and the dewdrops which glisten upon them. Stand before the Lord, and drink him in; do you understand what I mean by this expression? You go down to the seaside, when you are sickly, and you get out on a fine morning, and there is a delightful breeze coming up from the sea, and you feel as if it came in at every pore of your body, and you seem to be drinking in health at every breath you breathe. Do just like that in a spiritual sense with God, go down to the great sea of Godhead; magnify it by thinking how great it is, and then take it into your very soul. God cannot be greater than he is, but he can be greater in you than he is at present. He cannot increase; there cannot be more of God than there is, but there may be more of God in you. More of his great love, more of his perfect holiness, more of his divine power may be manifested in you, and more of his likeness and light may be revealed through you. Therefore, make him great in that respect.

And when you have done that, by his help, then try to make him great by what you give forth, even as the rose, when she has satisfied herself with the sweet shower, no sooner does the clear shining come after the rain, than she deluges the garden all around with her delicious perfume. Do you the same; first drink in all you can of the Deity, and then exhale him; breathe out again, in your praise, in your holy living, in your prayers, in your earnest zeal, in your devout spirit, the God whom you have breathed in. You cannot make more of God than he is, but you can make God more consciously present to the minds of others, and make them think more highly of God by what you say and what you do.

I should like to be able to say, as long as I live, " My soul doth magnify the Lord." I should like to have this as the one motto of my life from this moment until I close my eyes in death, " My soul doth magnify the Lord." I would fain preach that way; I would fain eat and drink that way; I would even sleep that way, so that I could truthfully say, "I have no wish but that God should be great, and that I should help to make him great in the eyes of others." Will not you also, dear friends, make this the motto of your life-psalm?

Then Mary added, "*and my spirit hath rejoiced in God my Saviour.*" Is there any true praise without joy? Is not praise twin brother to joy? And do not joy and praise ever dwell together? Rejoice, then, beloved, not in the scenes you see, for they are fleeting, but rejoice in your Saviour,—in him above everything else. Never let any earthly thing or any human being stand higher in your joy than Jesus Christ of Nazareth. Rejoice in him as most surely yours; for, dear brother, as a believer, Christ is thine. If thou art resting in him, he belongs to thee; so rejoice in thine own Saviour, for all of Christ is thine,—not half a Saviour; not one of his wounds for thee, and one for me; but all his wounds for thee, and all for me; not his thoughtful head for thee, and his loving heart for me; but his head and his heart all for thee and all for me;—he is my Saviour, from his feet that were pierced by the nails to his head that was crowned with thorns.

Oh, how we ought to rejoice in him, whatever our union with him may cost us! Mary did not know what that wondrous visitation would cost her; and it was to cost her much, as Simeon said to her, "Yea, a sword shall pierce through thy own soul also;" but even though the sword must go through her soul, it mattered not to her, for unto her a child was to be born, unto her a son was to be given, who was to be called "Wonderful, Counsellor, the Mighty God, the Everlasting Father, the Prince of Peace." So, if the fact that Christ is ours involves the bearing of the cross, we are glad to bear it. It may involve suffering and shame, and a thousand temptations and trials; if it be so, each true believer can say with Mary, "'My spirit hath rejoiced in God my Saviour,'—in what he is, in what he is to me, in what he is to all his sons, in what he is to poor sinners, in what he is to God, in what he will be when he comes again, and in what he will be throughout eternity." If a little bird has nothing else to do but sing, it has a great deal to do; and if you and I should have, to-night, when we get home, nothing to do but to praise the Lord, we have the best employment out of heaven. We must not think that Christians are wasting time when they pray and praise. Some fussy folk seem to imagine that we must always be talking, or attending meetings, or giving away tracts. Well, do as much as ever you can of all good things; but, still, there must be times for quiet meditation, times for reading, times for praying, and times for praising. There is no waste about such times; they are among the best spent hours that we ever have. To work is the stalk of the wheat; but to praise, is the full corn in the ear. You and I, beloved, are the living to praise God. This is the culmination, the very apex of the pyramid of existence, pointing straight up to heaven,—that we praise God with all our heart and soul.

So then, to conclude, here is something for every child of God to do. You can all magnify the Lord, and you may all rejoice in him. You cannot all preach. If you could, who would there be to hear you? If all were preachers, where would be the hearers? But you can all praise God. If there is any brother or sister here who has only one talent, let not such an one say, "I cannot do anything." You can magnify the Lord, and you can rejoice in him. To be happy in him is to praise God. The mere fact of our being happy in the Lord makes music in his ears. If you are one of his children, you can be happy in him, so get out of those doleful dumps; cast out that spirit of murmuring and complaint which so often possesses you. Pray the Lord to help you to shake off your natural tendency to look on the dark side of everything, and say, "No, no; I must not do that. After all, I am not on the road to hell; I am on the way to heaven; and this world is the ante-room to heaven, so my-soul shall magnify the Lord, and my spirit shall rejoice in God my Saviour." I believe that, if we could brighten the faces of all the saints, and anoint them with the oil of gladness, we should do more than anything else could do to spread Christianity. I mean, if we could make the children of the King rejoice, we should cause worldlings to ask, "Where does this joy come from?" And as they asked this question, we would give them the answer, and so the gospel would be sure to spread.

My closing word is concerning those who cannot magnify the Lord, and cannot rejoice in God their Saviour, those who cannot sing to God's praise, and who never have any joy in the Lord. Then, how can they be his children? God has many children, and they have many infirmities; but he never had a dumb child yet. They can every one say, "God be merciful to me a sinner;" and they can all sing, "Worthy is the Lamb that was slain." Prayer and praise are two of the sure signs of a true-born heir of heaven. If thou dost never praise God, my friend, thou canst never go to heaven. Till the Lord has taken out of thee the praise of other things, and the love of other things, and given thee the grace to love himself, and praise himself, thou canst not enter into his glory. May some poor soul here, that has not anything for which it could praise itself, begin now to praise that God who freely forgives the greatest sin, and who is willing to cleanse the very blackest sinner, for he has given Christ to die, the Just for the unjust, that he may bring them unto God. Oh, begin to magnify him and rejoice in him now, and you will never want to leave off doing so, world without end. Amen.

Exposition by C. H. Spurgeon.
LUKE I. 39—56.

Verses 39—41. *And Mary arose in those days, and went into the hill country with haste, into a city of Juda; and entered into the house of Zacharias, and saluted Elisabeth. And it came to pass, that, when Elisabeth heard the salutation of Mary, the babe leaped in her womb; and Elisabeth was filled with the Holy Ghost:*

We do not read that Mary was filled with the Holy Ghost, possibly because she was always in that condition, living very near to God in hallowed fellowship. Some of us have occasional fillings with the Holy Spirit, but blessed are they who dwell in him, having been baptized into him, and enjoying continual nearness to God as the blessed result.

42, 43. *And she spake out with a loud voice, and said, Blessed art thou among women, and blessed is the fruit of thy womb. And whence is this to me, that the mother of my Lord should come to me?*

Those who are most holy are most humble; you will always find those two things go together. Elisabeth was the older woman, but, inasmuch as Mary was more highly favoured than she was, she asked, "Whence is this to me, that the mother of my Lord should come to me?" Genuine Christians do not exalt themselves above their fellow-believers, but they have a self-depreciatory spirit, and each one esteems others better than himself.

44, 45. *For, lo, as soon as the voice of thy salutation sounded in mine ears, the babe leaped in my womb for joy. And blessed is she that believed: for there shall be a performance of those things which were told her from the Lord.*

What a benediction that is! If any of us truly believe God's Word, we are blessed from that very fact, for God's promise never misses its due performance. Men find it convenient to forget their promises, but God never forgets; he takes as much delight in keeping his promise as he does in making it.

46. *And Mary said,—*
We do not read that she spoke with a loud voice. Occasionally, the visitation of the Spirit causes excitement. Thus, Elisabeth spoke with a loud voice; but Mary, though full of a rapturous joy, spoke calmly and quietly, in a royal tone of holy calm. "Mary said,"—

46. *My soul doth magnify the Lord,—*
She was weary, for she had come a long journey, but she was like Abraham's servant, who said, "I will not eat, until I have told mine errand." So Mary will not eat until she has sung the praises of her God : "My soul doth magnify the Lord,"—

47, 48. *And my spirit hath rejoiced in God my Saviour. For he hath regarded the low estate of his handmaiden: for, behold, from henceforth all generations shall call me blessed.*
Some have done so to the grief of genuine Christians, for they have apostatized from the faith, and made Mary into a kind of goddess; and, therefore, Protestant Christians have gone to the other extreme, and have not always given to her the respect which is due to her.

49, 50. *For he that is mighty hath done to me great things; and holy is his name. And his mercy is on them that fear him from generation to generation.*
Notice how Mary quotes Scripture. Her mind seems to have been saturated with the Word of God, as though she had learned the books of Scripture through, and had them "by heart" in more senses than one ; and it is significant that, though the Holy Spirit was speaking by her, yet even he quoted the older Scriptures in preference to uttering new sentences. What honour he put upon the Old Testament by so continually quoting it in the New Testament, even as the Lord Jesus also did. Let us, too, prize every part of God's Word ; let us lie asoak in it till we are saturated with Scriptural expressions ; we cannot find any better ones, for there are none.

51—53. *He hath shewed strength with his arm; he hath scattered the proud in the imagination of their hearts. He hath put down the mighty from their seats, and exalted them of low degree. He hath filled the hungry with good things; and the rich he hath sent empty away.*
Mary's song reminds us of the song of Hannah, yet there is a different tone in it. Hannah's has more of exultation over enemies cast down, but Mary's is more becoming to the new dispensation as Hannah's was to the old. There is a gentle quietness of tone about the Magnificat all through, yet even Mary cannot help rejoicing that the Lord "hath filled the hungry with good things; and the rich he hath sent empty away."

54—56. *He hath holpen his servant Israel, in remembrance of his mercy; as he spake to our fathers, to Abraham, and to his seed for ever. And Mary abode with her about three months, and returned to her own house.*
Wondrous as her future was to be, she would not neglect the duties of her home. When any of you are privileged to share high spiritual enjoyments, mind that you always return to your own home not unfitted for your domestic duties. We read that David, after he had danced before the ark, "returned to bless his household." We must never set up God's altar in opposition to the lawful duties of our home. The two together will make us strong for service, and enable us to glorify the name of the Lord.

HOMAGE OFFERED TO THE GREAT KING.

A Sermon

DELIVERED BY

C. H. SPURGEON,

AT NEW PARK STREET CHAPEL, SOUTHWARK.

"And he shall live, and to him shall be given of the gold of Sheba; prayer also shall be made for him continually; and daily shall he be praised."—Psalm lxxii. 15.

I BELIEVE we must refer the ultimate fulfilment of this prophecy to the times of the latter-day glory, when Jesus Christ shall again appear upon the earth. Then "he shall have dominion from sea to sea, and from the river unto the ends of the earth;" then "they that dwell in the wilderness shall bow before him, and his enemies shall lick the dust." It has been a great question as to whether Jesus Christ is to come again in person or by his Spirit. Many passages of Scripture seem to point to his actual and personal coming, and, somehow or other, it does delight my soul to anticipate that Christ may yet come to the scene of his former battles, and make it the scene of his future triumphs. I am rejoiced to think that the head, once crowned with thorns on earth, may on earth itself wear a crown of glory; and that the feet that were once wearied in his pilgrimage here with the flinty stones of Jerusalem may yet "stand on the mount of Olives," while he ushers in "the day of the Lord in the valley of decision;" and that the shoulders which once wore the purple robe in mockery may yet be visibly clothed with the royal attire of universal empire, when "the Lord shall be King over all the earth." I am somewhat confirmed in this conviction by the words of the text, "And he shall live." It does strike me that such a prophecy as that would not be necessary concerning Jesus Christ, either as God or man, if it were not that he is again to visit the earth. It is quite certain that, as God, "he shall live;" for God over all, blessed for ever, only hath in himself immortality, and it is quite impossible that the Godhead ever should expire; while, as man, Jesus Christ must live; for when the just are raised, they die no more, but have life eternal; and when they ascend up into heaven, as Jesus hath done, they have a life that God confers upon them, which becomes as immortal as the very life of Deity itself. So that it does appear to me that neither in respect to his manhood or his Godhead, would it have been necessary to say, "He shall live," unless we are to understand it in the same sense that we should read it if it was written of his first coming,—he shall live as the God-man, he shall live on earth as other men do, he shall live here below. And I do think that no exegesis can. fully explain the passage unless we interpret it as to his actually living, residing here as very man upon the earth once more.

Be that as it may, the text, we trust, hath a fulfilment in your ears this night, and hath been in a certain manner fulfilled ever since the time when it was written, "to him," to Christ Jesus, there is "given of the gold of Sheba," to him prayer is also made, and to him praise continually ascends. Here are three things which are, throughout all time, even till the dawning of eternity, always to be bestowed on Christ. The first is *the gift of property*, the gold of Sheba; the second is *the gift of prayer;* and the third is *the gift of praise.*

I. To commence with the first, I shall be allowed here to make some remarks with reference to THE PECUNIARY MATTERS OF THE CHRISTIAN CHURCH, because no man on earth will ever suspect me of making any personal allusion either to my own church or congregation, or with regard to myself or any institution connected with this place of worship. In nothing have I fault to find with my church and people. Let it go forth to Christendom at large that, in their collections and contributions to the cause of God, they stand second to no church beneath the blue sky. I have simply to tell them that such-and-such a thing is needed for sacred purposes, and forth comes their money. It is always bestowed at the time it is required, and, therefore, it cannot be suspected that, in anything I say, there is the least allusion to them, except it be to their honour.

It is written that "to him shall be given of the gold of Sheba." I think that this ought continually to be impressed upon the minds of all Christians. Since Jesus Christ is the Son of God and their Saviour, and has given himself for them, they are not their own, but are bought with a price; their possessions as well as themselves are the absolute property of their Redeemer; they have, in fact, nothing whatever in their own private right; they have made over themselves to the Lord Jesus, to have and to hold them through life, and even till death, and for ever and ever. They are not to call their own their purse, their lands, their houses, nor anything that they have; but to give up everything to their Lord. From the moment when he himself comes to them, and unfolds their interest in his covenant, they are henceforth to consider themselves as his servants, as his children, "having nothing, yet possessing all things," because they have all things in Christ.

Were this well considered, my friends, how much greater

liberality should we find among Christians, especially in the support of gospel ministers! When God sends an ambassador into the world, wherever he sends him, the people are bound to receive him in some kind of honour and respect. Jehovah himself hath said that the mouth of the ox that treadeth out the corn is by no means to be muzzled; but it is the disgrace of our denomination, as well as of many others, that not a few of the best of God's servants are toiling week-day after week-day, and Sabbath after Sabbath, upon a miserable pittance scarcely sufficient to maintain the family even of a day-labourer. I thought, the other day, when reading Martin Luther's "Table Talk," that it was rather too bad for him to say what he did, but since then I have myself felt similar indignation when I have thought upon this subject. He said, "If I were God, and the world were to behave so wickedly to me as it does to him, I would kick it all to atoms." I thought it was a dreadful thing to say; but I have myself been almost inclined to say that, had I been the everlasting God, and sent ambassadors down from heaven, and had they been treated as they are now, I would have called every one of them back straightway, and would have said, "Is that the way ye despise my sent servants? Will ye show them no honour? Will ye do them despite as ye have always done?" Yes, I thought, I would call them back, revoke their charters, and say, "Henceforth I will send no more ambassadors." But, beloved, ambassadors are not thus received by you, and they ought not to be anywhere. God's servants should have what they require, and it should always be said, "Christ liveth, and to him—in the person of his ministers,—is always given of the gold of Sheba."

It is a terrible thought to me that, although God's Word says, "Owe no man any thing," yet that the church should be more awfully in debt than any corporation in England. I do not think that the debts of all the people put together would equal the debts of professing Christians,—debts which they have entered into often on account of religion. I would stand fast by the practice of owing no man anything, and if I did not see the means of doing anything for my God, I would stop till I did. "Owe no man anything," is a Christian principle, and one that we are bound most decidedly and continually to observe. Wherefore should the churches be in debt? Why should there not be money to send forth missionaries abroad? It is just this,—there is not enough of the love of Christ in the church, and there is not enough of Christ-preaching; otherwise, there would be more of Christian giving. Where Christ is exalted, there will be a willing, generous people. I do not believe it is so much the fault of Christians that they have not given more to the cause of God, as it has been the fault of ministers that they have not more fully preached Jesus Christ. They have not extolled his name, but have kept back his doctrines, and put them in the background. This is why God has allowed his Church to become poor, and suffered her funds to dwindle down. And it serves her right; for if she does not love her Husband, she ought to be poor; and if she does not extol Jesus, there ought to be no funds. But can you find a Christ-exalting people, among whom the gospel is preached in all its fulness, whose necessities God does not supply? There may indeed be some cases where it is so, when God tries them for their good. But I believe, as a rule, that once let our pulpits have the clear gospel sound in them; once let the good old doctrines of the Puritans come forth; once let the gospel be preached in all its fulness, none of your shams, for we have abundance of them, but the blessed gospel of Christ; once let this fidelity prevail, and God will provide the funds, God will open the hearts of the people to pour the money into your coffers. The silver and the gold are his, and the cattle on a thousand hills, and it is the fault of the Church herself that she has become poor. When God restores to her the language of Canaan, when Christ is exalted in his people's hearts, and they can hear the sweet and savoury notes of Jesus Christ preached, then they will say, "Can we refuse to do anything for such a gospel as this?" Half-hearted preachers beget half-hearted professors; a lukewarm gospel has made people's hearts lukewarm. We must have a reform,—a lasting reform by the help of God's Spirit; otherwise, who knoweth whereunto this bankruptcy of Christendom shall tend? And who can tell what shall eventually become of the Church? Once let Jesus be preached thoroughly, here, there, and everywhere, and then "to him shall be given of the gold of Sheba," and as much as ever his Church shall want shall be continually offered as a willing tribute.

Thus much then about money I have felt constrained to say, for I do believe that many of my brethren are half ashamed to speak out about the temporal claims of religion. For myself, I always deem it one of the noblest things we can do to give to the cause of God. Everyone knows what value we attach even to some little flower given by the hand of a friend, and God loves the little gifts of his people. As one of our old divines says, "It is not the value of the gift so much as the intention of the giver that is prized. For we should keep an old cracked sixpence if given to us by a friend; not because we think much of the sixpence,—that, perhaps, we would scarcely have stooped to pick up,—but because a friend has given it to us, and for his sake we never spend it or give it away." So the littles that we give to God are of great esteem in his sight. Every little gift we give to him is remembered; and at last he will take us and say, "My child, on such-and-such a day thou gavest me this." "Why, Lord, I scarcely thought of it! I found such a cause requiring help, and I assisted it." "Ah, my child! there is thy gift; I have stored it up here to show to thee when thou camest to me. Have I forgotten thy little acts of affection? Nay; I have stored them up in the cabinet of my memory; they are tokens of thy love to me, even as thou hast had numberless tokens of my love to thee." But what a few memorials of your love some of you will have to look upon when you get there! You only give now and then a trifle; that is all. God grant that you may have the heart to give unto Jesus "of the gold of Sheba" in far greater abundance!

II. Then comes the second offering. The gold first, and THE PRAYER afterwards; not because the gold is the more valuable; but because, in some respects, gold when it is given with a true heart is the better test.

"Prayer also shall be made for him continually." Notice those words again, "Prayer also shall be made *for him.*" Now we all know that prayer is continually made *unto* Jesus Christ. We are accustomed to address the Second Person of the Trinity as God in the form of prayer, and more frequently prayer is made *through* him when we address the First Person of the united Godhead through the mediation of the Son. But the psalmist says, "Prayer also shall be made *for* him." We can understand how Jesus Christ should pray for us; but, at first, it does seem to stagger us that we should be allowed to pray for him. That he should be our Intercessor, that he should bend his knee on our behalf, and point to our names engraven on his breastplate, is a truth so frequently mentioned in Scripture that we receive it unhesitatingly; but for us to become intercessors for Christ, to bind the breastplate on our breast, to wave the censer on his behalf, to plead for him, and pray for him, and beg for him,— this does somewhat astonish us. And yet our surprise is due rather to the expression than the fact, for it is a thing we are doing every day. Prayer is made for Christ continually.

Let me tell you that you virtually pray for Christ, beloved, *whenever you pray for one of his people.* Will you understand me if I say that Jesus Christ has gone through a great many editions? Every one of the Lord's people is but another copy of their blessed Master. They are, as it were, particles of Christ beaten out into humanity again, pieces of that mighty wedge of gold beaten out into plate afterwards. They are partakers of Christ's nature, they are part of his fulness; and whenever we do a kindness to one of them we do it unto him; whenever we pray for one of his servants, we pray for Christ. You prayed for that poor miserable-looking penitent who was afraid to call himself a Christian, though he was so in deed and in truth. Do you know that you then prayed for Christ? You interceded for that simple-minded woman who did not know the way to heaven, and who asked you to put up a prayer to God that she might be taught. Do you know that you then prayed for Christ, for she was part of his flesh and blood, and was afterwards brought into his family? Do you know that, whenever you put up a petition, even for the weakest and most despised of his little ones, you are praying for him? What a physician does to the remotest member of my body, is done to the entire frame; whatever is done to any part of my flesh is done to myself; and when we pray for Christ's people, the members of his body, we are really praying for Christ.

We pray for Christ, also, *when we pray for the spread of the gospel, and for the increase of his kingdom.* When we implore of God, at our missionary prayer-meetings, that all his mighty promises may be fulfilled,—that the people may fall under him as willing captives,—that the idols may be hurled from their thrones,

—that the Mother of harlots and abominations may receive her sudden doom, and the merchandise of her seven-hilled city cease for ever,—that Mohammedanism and all false superstitions may be overturned,—when we pray in the simple words which our Saviour taught us, "Thy kingdom come. Thy will be done, in earth, as it is in heaven,"—then we are praying for Christ in full sympathy with all saints, by whom prayer is made for him continually. And, best of all, when we bend our knees, and cry out for his second coming,—when we beg of him to cleave the skies, and come to judgment,—or when, with other and more literal expectations, we ask him to come and reign upon the earth, and make his people kings and princes unto him,—when we ask the Ancient of days to come and reign on earth with his ancients gloriously, then we are praying for Christ.

We ought to do so. Recollect, O Christian! in thy prayers, whatever thou forgettest, always to pray for thy Redeemer. It is thy privilege to have thy name written in the list of those for whom he pleads, and it is thy honour to be allowed to plead for him. Stop a moment,—a worm pleading for God! The finite asking a blessing on the head of the Infinite! Less than nothing begging that the Eternal All may be blessed! Oh! were it not told thee in Scripture, it would be blasphemy to attempt it. Thou mayest pray to him with the most dread and solemn awe; and thou mayest prostrate thyself at his feet; but to pray *for* him, to beg on his behalf, how wonderful this seems! For Jesus to take thy petition to his Father gives a glory and a dignity to thy very poorest prayer; but for thee to turn petitioner to the King of kings on behalf of his own Son,—dost thou not admire the condescension that permits that? Methinks I see thee coming, poor, weak, helpless one, and God says, "For whom dost thou plead?" Thou sayest, "I plead for Jesus." "What, thou! a poor beggar? What, thou! full of sin, littleness, nothingness,—dost thou plead for my eternal Son? Art thou making supplication for him?" Dost thou not, thyself, think it wonderful that thou shouldst be allowed to ask for a blessing on his head? Ay, then never slight this privilege; never forget it; but with thy prayers continually mingle his name.

III. Now comes the last point, and here we must be somewhat longer, for we shall have, we hope, more thoughts: "Daily shall he be PRAISED." Jesus is not only continually to have gold and prayer, but he is to have praise daily ascribed to him. Let me go over the list of things which prove that Jesus Christ shall daily be praised.

First, methinks, *Jesus daily shall be praised as long as there is a Christian ministry.* There have been professed ministers who have never exalted Christ at all; there have been some who took upon themselves the office for a morsel of bread, not being called thereunto; but has there ever been a time when there have not been faithful men of God? Has there ever been a season when God has not sent his prophets throughout the land to speak in living words, from burning hearts and fervid souls, the very Word of God? No;

and there never shall be. If God should now put out those lights that shine in London or elsewhere,—if he were now to say to the churches, "Your candlesticks shall be removed out of their places, I will take those ministers away," by to-morrow he would send others. And if the enemy should come and cut off the heads of all those who now speak God's Word, would that be able to stop the perpetual thunders of the gospel? No; for God would find to-morrow men who should rise up, and even in the palaces of kings should yet dare to speak the name of God. Men have thought they could put down the gospel. They have used the rack, and brought forth the stake; but what have they accomplished? They have but spread it more. All they have ever done to stop that mighty stream, and bank it up, has failed. It has retarded it a little while till, with overwhelming might, the stream has swept away the rock, dashed down the hill-side, and carried everything before it. They have attempted to amalgamate the gospel with free will, carnal reason, natural philosophy, and such-like doctrines of men, which would, if it were possible, frustrate the counsels of God; they have spoken ill of the gospel; they have given hard names to those who preach it; but have they been able to stop it, or shall they? Nay, never, while there is a God, he shall have his Calvins and his Luthers, he shall have his Gills and his Scotts, he shall have his devoted servants who are not ashamed or afraid of the gospel of Christ. There never shall come a day when the Church shall be bereft of mighty champions for the truth, who shun not to declare the whole counsel of God; but continually, to the latest period of time, men shall be raised up to preach free grace in all its sovereignty, in all its omnipotence, in all its perseverance, in all its immutability. Until the sun grows dim with age, and the comets cease their mighty revolutions,—till all nature doth quake and totter with old age, and, palsied with disease, doth die away, the voice of the ministry must and shall be heard, "and daily shall he be praised." Men cannot put out the light of Christianity. The pulpit is still the Thermopylæ of Christendom; and if there were but two godly ministers, they would stand in the pass, and repulse a thousand, yea, ten thousand. All the hosts of mankind shall never vanquish the feeble band of Christ's followers, while he sends forth his ministers. On this we rely as a sure word of prophecy, "Thy teachers shall not be removed into a corner any more;" and we believe that, by this ministry, daily shall Christ be praised.

But suppose the pulpit were to fail, still we have got other means whereby Jesus Christ's name should still be praised. *The ordinances that he has instituted will ever continue to perpetuate his praise.* There are two Scriptural ordinances, in both of which Jesus Christ is very much praised. There is, first, that holy ordinance of believers' baptism, in which Jesus Christ is much honoured, for it has especial relation to him. "Know ye not, that so many of us as were baptized into Jesus Christ were baptized into his death? Therefore we are buried with him by baptism into death: that like as Christ was raised up from the dead by the glory of the Father, even so we also should walk in newness of life." When you descend into the pool at baptism, you hear those sacred words pronounced, "I baptize thee in the name of the Father, and of the Son and of the Holy Ghost;" and you are specially reminded there that, unless you have believed in Jesus with all your heart, you have no right to this sacred avowal of fellowship with Christ, but are sinning against God in so doing. The Scriptures have taught us that whoever dares to administer that ordinance to any but those who believe with their heart, and profess with their mouth, dares to touch with sacrilegious hands God's own institution, and is guilty of breaking down the hedges of the Church, and throwing open to the world that which was never intended but for the Lord's own family. We solemnly admonish you to have an eye to Jesus Christ in that blessed ordinance; we bid you, before ye come, to examine yourselves whether ye be in the faith; and when ye are there, we remind you that afterwards ye are bound to live unto Christ; ye have now passed the Rubicon of life; ye have now come on the other side of the flood that divides the world from the Church; ye have now, as it were, taken the veil, and renounced the world; ye are dead with Christ, ye have been buried with him by baptism into death. By that very ordinance you honour the name of the Saviour; and while that ordinance lasts, Jesus Christ shall be praised. Nor less at the blessed supper of the Lord shall the name of Jesus be praised. I think the moments we are nearest to heaven are those we spend at the Lord's table. I have sometimes looked at your faces, my brethren and sisters, at the Lord's table; and if anyone wanted to see men's faces when they looked as if angels themselves were smiling in their eyes, such have your faces been when I have broken the bread, and the wine has been passed to you. When those morsels have been in our lips, simple as the sign was,—and when we have drunk the wine, simple and unceremonious as the whole affair was, what a sweet and holy influence it has had upon our hearts, and how did we feel that we could praise God! I have thought, sometimes, that I could almost have leaped from the table, and have said, "Oh! let us praise the glorious Redeemer." When we have seen him on the cross, and beheld him as our Substitute, we have felt our hearts were burning hot, that they could scarcely be held within our bodies, and we wanted all to rise up and sing,—

> "All hail the power of Jesus' name!
> Let angels prostrate fall:
> Bring forth the royal diadem,
> And crown him Lord of all."

Even if the pulpit be gone, there still remain these two ordinances in each of which Jesus Christ "shall be praised."

But suppose that these were to cease; suppose it possible that we could not meet together in our public assemblies to celebrate these sweet memorials, or to hear the Word of God; yet there is another opportunity for praising God,—there is the family of Christians; and *while there is a family on earth where Christ's name is named, it shall be daily praised.* I trust there is no Christian man or woman here who has a house without a family altar. If I came into your house, and heard that you had no fireplace in the winter time, I should certainly advise you to build one; and if I heard that any of you had not a family altar, I should say, "Go home and lay the first brick to-night: it will be a good thing if you do so, I am sure." We had some beautiful instances, last night, at our church-meeting, of young persons, who, even though their parents were not godly, boldly started family prayer in the house; and we heard, in many cases, that the parents felt that they had no objection, and never wished to have it stopped. After they have once had the incense smoking in their house, they do not want to have it put out. My brethren and sisters, I cannot make out how you Christians live who have not family prayer in your houses. When I step into a Christian's house in the morning, and we have a passage of Scripture, and a little prayer to God, it seems to put the heart and mouth into play for the whole day; there is nothing like it. And when we sit and talk of what Jesus said and did, and suffered for us here below, as old Dyer says, it is like locking the heart up by prayer in the morning, and bolting the devil out. We cannot get on half so well when we have not had that prayer in the morning. And, then, how do you get through at night? I do not understand at all how you professing Christians can get through the day without prayer, and have no family prayer at night. I should feel like the good man, who stopped at an inn, and when he heard there was no family prayer, said, "Get my horses out! I can't stop in a house where there is no family prayer." It does seem to me terrible that you should go on without prayer, that there should be no morning and evening sacrifice. I cannot make out how you live without it. I could not. I cannot understand how your piety gets on, nor what it feeds upon. I do think, wherever there is a Christian family, there should be daily praise in it. And mark this, and solemnly hear me to-night,—and I do not speak unadvisedly with my lips,—you will find that, where sons and daughters have turned out a curse to their parents, when they have been a shame and disgrace to their parents, and those parents have been Christians, it might have been set down to this; that whilst the parents have been Christians, they were not Christians at home; they had not family prayer, they never reared a family altar. I believe nine out of ten of such cases can be explained in that way without in the least touching the text, "Train up a child in the way he should go, and when he is old, he will not depart from it."

Well, supposing we had no family prayer, suppose we had no ordinances in the house, and the altar did not smoke there; yet daily should Jesus Christ be praised, for still *there would be our own hearts, and we could praise Christ there.* If they put us in prison, and we could not speak to one another, we could still praise him; or if our tongues were dumb, there is a language of the heart which can be heard in heaven. With stammering words, or with actions which speak louder than words, our hearts shall always praise him. Beloved brethren and sisters, do you think you will ever have done praising Christ as long as you are alive? I knew a woman who said to me, "Sir, if Jesus Christ does save me, he shall never hear the last of it." I thought it was a good saying. And shall he ever hear the last of it from you, beloved? The last of it! Never! When we lie dying, the last word we give him on earth shall be praise, and the first word we begin in heaven shall be instinct with praise; and while eternity lasts, and immortality endures, we will ascribe praise, honour, and blessing to him for ever. Can we who are pardoned rebels, liberated slaves, can we whose souls are quickened from the dead by his Spirit, whose sins are washed away by his precious blood, can we ever cease to praise him? Nay; surely the very stones would speak if our lips were silent, or our hearts refused to pay him grateful homage. Daily, daily, daily, "Daily shall he be praised."

> "I'll praise him while he lends me breath,
> And when my voice is lost in death,
>   Praise shall employ my nobler powers;
> My days of praise shall ne'er be past,
> While life, and thought, and being last,
>   Or immortality endures."

But, then, supposing the innumerable company of his redeemed could perish, and their immortality were swallowed up in death, yet even then, daily Christ would be praised! If all of us had departed from the boundless sphere of being, look up yonder, see *the mighty cohorts of cherubs and seraphs.* Let men be gone, and they shall praise him; let the troops of the glorified cease their notes, and let no sweet melodies ever come from the lips of sainted men and women; yet the chariots of God are twenty thousand, even thousands of angels, who always chant his praise. There is an orchestra on high, the music of which shall never cease, even were mortals extinct and all the human race swept from existence.

> "Immortal angels, bright and fair,
> In countless armies shine!
> At his right hand, with golden harps,
> They offer songs divine."

Again, if angels were departed, still daily would he be praised; for, *are there not worlds on worlds, and systems on systems, that could for ever sing his praise?* Yes! The ocean—that place of storms—would beat to his glory; the winds would swell the notes of his praise with their ceaseless gales; the thunders would roll like drums in the march of the God of armies; the illimitable void of ether would become vocal with song; and space itself would burst forth into one universal chorus, "Hallelujah! Hallelujah! Hallelujah! for the Lord God omnipotent reigneth!" And if these were gone; if creatures ceased to exist, he who ever liveth and reigneth, in whom all the fulness of the Godhead bodily dwells, would still be praised; praised in himself, and glorious in himself; for the Father would praise the Son, and the Spirit would praise him, and mutually blessing one another, and rendering each other beatified, still daily would he be praised.

Now, dear friends, I am conscious that I have not been able to enter into this mighty subject; but here are three things which we, as Christians, are bound to give to Christ,—the gold of Sheba, our prayers, and our praises. It is for us just to see what we have given to him. I wish we could keep a little book to see what our gifts to Jesus Christ come to in a year. I am afraid, dearly-beloved, that with some of you it would be a very miserable amount. I would lend you a small piece of paper out of my waistcoat pocket to put it down on, and there would be room enough. But it is not so with some of you, I know. You often pray for Christ, you often praise him, and you are often ready to give him "of the gold of Sheba." That is well; but let me tell you this one thing, there are none of you who need be afraid of praising Jesus Christ too much. We do sometimes praise men too much; we say so much in their favour, so much in their praise; and then, afterwards, we find out they never deserved it. But I will be bondsman for my blessed Master to-night that you will never praise him more than he deserves. If you like to speak of him in the most unmeasured phrases, if you borrow all the tongues of men and angels, and talk about him for ever; if you praise him, and call him God; if you call him the most perfect of men, if you style him the Wonderful, the Counsellor, the Mighty God, you will never say too much of him.

So, Christian, begin to praise Jesus Christ now. You need not be afraid that you will be too extravagant in the praise you bestow upon him; for when your hair begins to be white with the sunlight of heaven gleaming on it, you will find that you never said enough about him. Let the hoary-headed patriarch speak. Now he comes near his end; he totters and stoops, and lifts his eye to heaven, and says, "Praise Christ too much! I thought him lovely when I first knew him; I knew him to be lovely a little afterwards, when he helped me along, and I lived to prove that he was most lovely; but now I have got further still, and I can say, 'He is altogether lovely, and there is none to be compared with him.' I thought at first that each sweet mercy demanded a fresh song, and I did sometimes feel a glow of devotion to him; I then thought I must praise him more, and dedicate myself more to his service; and now," says he, "could I give my body to be burned for Jesus, I feel that he deserves it. His love in times past, his manifold helpings, his continual unchangeableness, render me devoted to him for ever." And, like the servant of whom we spoke on Monday night, the old Christian feels that he is ready to have his ear bored to the doorpost for ever: he never wants to go away now. I have said this because many persons nowadays say, "Ah! so-and-so is young; he'll be sobered down by-and-by." I am sure, beloved, it is a great pity if he should be. There are very few people in the present day who want much sobering with regard to religion. There is not so much fear of religious enthusiasm as there is of religious torpor and sleep. I should like to see a few enthusiastic Christians: "not drunk with wine, wherein is excess,—but filled with the Spirit." But what do men say? Why, "the man has got no moderation: he is mad." A person, passing by here the other day, said to another, "You know who preaches there, don't you?" "No, I do not." "Why, everybody knows that fellow; everybody goes to hear him; but, you know, he's rather touched in the brain." "Yes," said a friend of mine, "and I'll tell you another little thing, by way of a secret: he's rather touched in the heart, too; and that's better still." Well, beloved, we do not mind what they say about our being "touched in the brain;" we believe it is well to be "touched in the heart" too! We may be mad, but it is a sweet madness, it is a blessed delusion, it is a most excellent "touch." And we only pray that the Master may touch us all. "Touched in the brain!" Ah! we have precious need to be in these days, for the brains are wrong enough originally. "Touched in the brain!" Most decidedly we require it, for most men's brains are very far from what they should be. "Touched in the brain!" May God "touch" every man's brain, and every man's heart! And the more we are touched of God, whether it is touched in the brain, or touched in the hand, or touched in the purse, or touched anywhere, it is always good so long as we are touched of God.

You know it was objected against David that he must not go and fight Goliath, because his brother said he had come to see the battle in the pride of his heart. He did not stop to give an answer. The best answer he could give was to go and cut Goliath's head off, and bring it back in triumph. So, many of you, who are young in years, and full of zeal, are advised not to do this and that and the other. Do not mind what they say. Go forth, in the name of your God, and you shall do exploits. If the great and trained veterans are afraid of the battle, then raw and inexperienced recruits must stand in the forefront. While it is written, "Out of the mouth of babes and sucklings hast thou ordained strength," let it be known and proclaimed, let it be thundered forth from the skies, and let earth re-echo the sound, that Christ must and shall be praised. If one class of ministers will not do it, another shall; what the learned will not do, the ignorant must; what the polite and refined cannot do, the rough and untutored must; for, verily, it must and shall be done. If those who stand up with all their boasted prestige among men cannot exalt Christ, he will raise up humble but devoted followers, and by the weak things of the world confound the mighty. Of old he raised up a shepherd to be a king, a herdsman to be a prophet, and a fisherman to be an apostle. Those who dishonour him shall be lightly esteemed; but those who honour him he will honour. Go, Christian, and exalt Christ. Love him, and exalt him. Love your Master, talk about your Master, preach of your Master; and, by the help of the Spirit, you shall yet come off more glorious than your foes, if not here, yet in that day "when he shall come to be glorified in his saints, and to be admired in all them that believe."

"THE GARMENT OF PRAISE."

A Sermon

DELIVERED BY

C. H. SPURGEON,

AT THE METROPOLITAN TABERNACLE, NEWINGTON.

"The garment of praise for the spirit of heaviness."—Isaiah lxi. 3.

THE list of comforts which the Anointed has here prepared for his mourners is apparently inexhaustible. He seems as if he delighted to give "according to the multitude of his tender mercies" a very cloud of blessings. This is the third of his sacred exchanges—"the garment of praise for the spirit of heaviness": grace, like its God, delights to be a trinity. This is also the broadest of the blessings; for whereas the first adorned the face with beauty, and the second anointed the head with joy, this last and widest covers the whole person with a garment of praise. Man's first vesture was of his own making, and it could not cover his shame; but this garment is of God's making, and it makes us comfortable in ourselves, and comely in the sight of God and man. They are better adorned than Solomon in all his glory, to whom God giveth the garment of praise. May the blessed Spirit sweetly help us to bring out the rich meaning of this promise to mourners; for again I must remind you that these things are only given to them, and not to the thoughtless world.

We have noticed already the variety of the consolation which Jesus brings to mourners; the Plant of Renown produces many lovely flowers with rich perfume, and a multitude of choice fruits of dainty taste. Now, we would call your attention to their marvellous adaptation to our needs. Man has a spirit, and the gifts of grace are spiritual; his chief maladies lie in his soul, and the blessings of the covenant deal with his spiritual wants. Our text mentions "the spirit of heaviness," and gives a promise that it shall be removed. The boons which Jesus gives to us are not surface blessings, but they touch the centre of our being. At first we may not perceive their depth, but only know that beauty is given, instead of ashes: this might seem to be an external change. Further on, however, joy is given, instead of mourning, and this is inward; the thought has advanced, we are getting nearer the heart: but in the words before us the very spirit of heaviness, the fountain whence the mourning flows, the hearth whereon the ashes are burned, is dealt with and taken away, and instead thereof we receive the garment of praise. What a mercy it is that the blessings of the everlasting covenant belong to the realm of the spirit; for, after all, the outward is transient, the visible soon perishes. We are grateful for the food and raiment which our bodies require; but our sterner need is nourishment, consolation, and protection for our spirits. The covenant of grace blesses the man himself, the soul, which is the essence of his life. It puts away the sordid sackcloth of despondency, and robes the spirit in royal garments of praise. Judge ye your state by your estimation of such favours, for if ye have learned to prize them, they are yours. The worldling cares nothing for spiritual blessings; his beauty, and joy, and praise are found in things which perish in the using; but those who know their preciousness have been taught of God, and since they can appreciate them, they shall have them. Soul-mercy is the very soul of mercy, and he whom the Lord blesses in his spirit is blessed indeed.

I want you still further to notice how these blessings grow as we proceed. At first, out of the triplet of favours here bestowed there was beauty given, instead of ashes. There is much there: beauty of personal character before God is no mean thing; yet a man might have that, and by reason of his anxiety of heart he might scarcely be aware of it. Doubtless many who are lovely in the sight of God spend much of their time in bewailing their own uncomeliness. Many a saint sorrows over himself, while others are rejoicing in him; therefore, the next mercy given to the mourner in Zion is the oil of joy, which is a personal and conscious delight. The man rejoices. He perceives that he is made beautiful before God, and he begins to joy in what the Lord has done for him, and in the Anointed One from whom the oil of gladness descends. This is an advance upon the other, but now we come to the highest of all: seeing that God has made him glad, he perceives his obligations to God, and he expresses them in thankfulness, and so stands before the Most High like a white-robed priest, putting on praise as the garment in which he appears in the courts of the Lord's house, and is seen by his brethren. As you advance in the divine life, the blessings you receive will appear to be greater and greater. Some promising things become small by degrees and miserably less, but in the kingdom of heaven we go from strength to strength. The beginning of the Christian life is like the water in the pots at Cana, but in due time it blushes into wine. The pathway which we tread is at the first bright as the dawn; but if we pursue it with sacred perseverance, its refulgence will be as the perfect day. There shall be no going down of our sun, but it shall shine with increasing lustre till it shall be as the light of seven days, and the days of our mourning shall be ended.

I beg you also to mark that when we reach the greatest mercy, and stand on the summit of blessing, we have reached a condition of *praise*: praise to God invests our whole nature. To be wrapt in praise to God is the highest state of the soul. To receive the mercy for which we praise God is something; but to be wholly clothed with praise to God for the mercy received is far more. Why, praise is heaven, and heaven is praise! To pray is heaven below, but praise is the essence of heaven above. When you bow lowest in adoration, you are at your very highest. The soul full of joy takes a still higher step when it clothes itself with praise. Such a heart takes to itself no glory, for it is dressed in gratitude, and so hides itself. Nothing is seen of the flesh and its self-exaltation, since the garment of praise hides the pride of man. May you all who are heavy in spirit be so clothed upon with delight in the Lord, who hath covered you with the robe of righteousness, that you may be as wedding guests adorned for the palace of the King with glittering garments of adoring love.

Looking carefully into the words before us, we will dwell, first, upon *the spirit of heaviness*; secondly, upon *the promise implied in the text—that this shall be removed;* and then, thirdly, upon *the garment of praise which is to be bestowed.* First, let us muse upon :—

I. THE SPIRIT OF HEAVINESS.

We would not make this meditation doleful; and yet it may be as well to set forth the night side of the soul; for thus we may the better show a sympathetic spirit, and come more truly home to those who are in heaviness through manifold temptations. Some of us know by experience what the spirit of heaviness means. It comes upon us at times even now. There are many things in the body, there are many things in the family, there are many things in daily life which make us sad. Facts connected with the past, and with the future, cause us at times to hang our heads. We shall just now dwell upon those former times when we were under the spirit of heaviness on account of unpardoned sin. We cannot forget that we were in bondage in a spiritual Egypt. We would awaken our memories to remember the wormwood and the gall, the place of dragons and of owls.

Observe that *this heaviness is an inward matter*, and it is usually a grief which a man tries to keep to himself. It is not that he is sick in body, though his unbelieving friends fancy that he must surely be ailing, or he would not seem so melancholy. "He sitteth alone, and keepeth silence," and they say that he has a low fit upon him, and they invite him out into company, and try if they can jest him out of his distress. The fact is, that sin is pressing upon him, and well may the spirit be heavy when it has that awful load to carry. Day and night God's hand also is heavy upon him, and well may his spirit be loaded down. Conviction of sin makes us as a cart that is loaded with sheaves; but it is intensely inward, and therefore not to be understood of careless minds. "The heart knoweth its own bitterness, and a stranger intermeddleth not therewith." I have known persons who have been the subject of this heaviness most sedulously endeavour to conceal from others even the slightest appearance of it; and I cannot say that there has not been some wisdom in so doing, for ungodly men despise those who tremble at the Word of God. What do they care about sin? They can sin and rejoice in it as the swine can roll in the mire and feel itself at home. Those who weep in secret places because the arrows of the Lord have wounded them, are shunned by those who forget God, and they need not be sorry for it, since such company can furnish no balm for their wounds. Mourner, you are wise to keep your sorrow to yourself so far as the wicked are concerned; but remember, though perhaps you think not so, there are hundreds of God's children who know all about your condition, and if you could be bold enough to open your mind to them and tell them of your heaviness of spirit, you would be surprised to find how thoroughly they would sympathise with you, and how accurately some of them could describe the maze through which you are wandering. All are not tender of heart, but there are believers who would enter into your experience, and who might by God's blessing give you the clue to the labyrinth of your grief. The Lord comforted Paul by Ananias, and you may be sure that there is an Ananias for you. If you feel, as many do, that you could not unburden your soul to your parents or relatives, go to some other experienced believers, and tell them as far as you can your painful condition. I know, for I have felt the same, that all hope that you shall be saved is taken away, and that you are utterly prostrate; but yet there is hope.

While this heaviness is inward, notice in the next place that *it is real*. Heaviness of spirit is one of the most terribly true of all our griefs. He who is cheerful and light-hearted too often contemns and even ridicules him who is sad of soul. He says that he is "nervous," calls him "fanciful," "almost out of his mind," "very excitable," "quite a monomaniac," and so on. The current idea being, that there is really no need for alarm, and that sorrow for sin is mere fanaticism. If some persons had suffered half an hour of conviction of sin themselves, they would look with different eyes upon those who feel the spirit of heaviness; for I say it, and know what I am saying, that next to the torment of hell itself, there is but one sorrow which is more severe than that of a broken and a contrite spirit that trembles at God's word, but does not dare to suck comfort out of it. The bitterness of remorse and despair is worse; but yet it is unspeakably heart-breaking to bow at the mercy seat, and to fear that no answer will ever come; to lie at the feet of Jesus, but to be afraid to look up to him for salvation. To be conscious of nothing but abounding sin and raging unbelief, and to expect nothing but sudden destruction—this is an earthly Tophet. There are worse wounds than those which torture the flesh, and more cruel pangs arise from the broken bones of the soul than from those of the body. Sharp is that cut which goes to the very heart and yet does not kill, but makes men wish that they could die or cease to be. There is a prison such as no iron bars can make, and a fetter such as no smith can forge. Sickness is a trifle compared to it—it is to some men less endurable than the rack or the stake. To be impaled upon your own sins, pilloried by your own conscience, shot at by your own judgment as with barbed arrows—this is anguish and torment.

This heaviness of spirit *puts a weight upon the man's activity* and clogs him in all things. He is weighted heavily who bears the weight of sin. You put before him the precious promises, but he does not understand them, for the heaviness presses upon his mental faculties. You assure him that these promises are meant for him, but he cannot believe you, for heaviness of spirit palsies the grasping hand by which he might appropriate the blessing. "Their soul abhorreth all manner of meat, and they draw near to the gates of death." Troubled minds at times lose all their appetite. They need spiritual food, and yet turn from it. The most wholesome meat of the gospel they are afraid to feed upon, for their sadness makes them fearful of presumption. Heaviness brings on amazement, and this is but another word for saying that the mind is in a maze, and cannot find its way out.

They are weighted as to their understanding and their faith, for "the spirit of heaviness" presses there also. Their memory, too, is quick enough at recollecting sin, but to anything that might minister comfort, it is strangely weak; even as Jeremiah said, "Thou hast removed my soul far off from peace: I forget prosperity." Indeed, David was more oblivious still, for he says, "My heart is smitten and withered like grass, so that I forget to eat my bread." All the faculties become dull and inert, and the man is like one in a deadly swoon. I have heard persons, under conviction of sin, say, "I seem absolutely stupid about divine things." Like one that is stunned by a severe blow, they fall down, and scarcely know what they feel or do not feel. Were they in their clear senses, we could set the gospel before them, and point out the way of salvation, and they would soon lay hold of it; but, alas! they seem to have no capacity to understand the promise, or to grasp its consolation.

Now, this heaviness of spirit also *renders everything around the man heavy.* The external is generally painted from within. A merry heart maketh mirth in the dull November fog under a leaden sky, but a dull heart finds sorrow amidst May blossoms and June flowers. A man colours the world he lives in, to the tint of his own soul. "Things are not what they seem"; yet what they seem has often more influence upon us than what they are. Given a man, then, with heaviness of spirit, and you will find that his sorrows appear to be greater than he can bear. The common-place worries of life which cheerfulness sports with, are a load to a sad heart; yea, the grasshopper is a burden. The ordinary duties of life become a weariness, and slight domestic cares a torture. He trembles lest he should commit sin even in going in and out of his house. A man who bears the weight of sin has small strength for any other load. Even the joys of life become sombre. It matters not how much God has blest a man in his family, in his basket, or in his store; for as long as his heart is oppressed and his soul bowed down with sin, what are the bursting barns, and what are the overflowing wine vats to him? He pines for a peace and rest which these things cannot yield. If the eye be dark, the sun itself affords no light.

There is one thing, however, which we would say to mourners pressed down with guilt: whatever heaviness you feel, it is no greater heaviness than sin ought to bring upon a man, for it is an awful thing to have sinned against God. If the sense of sin should drive you to distraction—and cavillers often say that religion does this—it might reasonably do so if there were no other matters to think upon; no forgiving love and atoning blood. That which is the result of sin ought not to be charged upon religion; but true religion should be praised, because it brings relief to all this woe. Sin is the most horrible thing in the universe, and when a man sees how foully he has transgressed, it is no wonder that he is greatly troubled. To think that I, a creature that God has made, which he could crush as easily as a moth, have dared to live in enmity to him for many years, and have even become so hardened as to forget him, and perhaps defy him. This is terrible. When I have been told of his great love, I have turned on my heel and rejected it. Yes, and when I have even seen that love in the bleeding body of his dear Son, I have been unbelieving, and have done despite even to boundless grace, and gone from bad to worse, greedy after sin. Is it marvellous that, when they have seen the guilt of all this, men have felt their moisture turned into the drought of summer, and cried in desperation, "My soul chooseth strangling rather than life"? However low you are, beloved mourner, you are not exaggerating your guilt. Apart from the grace of God, your case is indeed as hopeless as you suppose. Though you lie in the very dust and dare not look up, the position is not lower than you ought to take. You richly deserve the anger of God; and when you have some sense of what that wrath must be, you are not more fearful of it than there is just need to be; for it is a fearful thing to fall into the hands of the living God. "He toucheth the hills and they smoke."

"The pillars of heaven's starry roof
Tremble and start at his reproof."

What will his wrath be when he puts on his robes of justice and comes forth to mete out justice to the rebellious? O God, how terrible is thy wrath! Well may we be crushed at the very thought of it.

Another reflection we would suggest here; and that is, that *if you have great heaviness of spirit on account of sin, you are by no means alone in it*; for some of the best servants of God have endured hard struggling before they have found peace with God. Read their biographies, and you will find that even those who have really believed in Christ have at some time or other felt the burden of sin pressing with intolerable weight upon their souls. Certain of them have recorded their experience in terrible sentences, and others have felt what they have not dared to commit to writing. "Weeping-cross," as the old writers call it, is a much-frequented spot; many roads meet at that point, and most pilgrims have there left a pool of tears.

There is this also to be added. Your Lord and Master, he to whom you must look for hope, knew what heaviness meant on account of sin. He had no sin of his own, but he bore the iniquity of his people, and hence he was prostrate in Gethsemane. We read that "he began to be sorrowful and to be very heavy." The spirit of heaviness was upon him, and he sweat as it were great drops of blood falling to the ground. This same heaviness made him cry upon the tree, "My God, my God, why hast thou forsaken me?" Jesus was sore amazed and very heavy; and it is to him as passing through that awful heaviness that I would bid you look in your hour of terror, for he alone is your door of hope. Through his heaviness, yours shall be removed, for "the chastisement of our peace was upon him, and with his stripes we are healed." So much, then, concerning heaviness of spirit. And now, secondly, let us:—

II. SEE THE HEAVINESS REMOVED, for of this the text contains a divine promise: the anointed Saviour will take it away. Only a word or two upon this.

Brethren, do you enquire how does Jesus remove the spirit of heaviness? We answer, he does it thus—by revealing to us with clearness and certainty that *our sin is pardoned*. The Holy Ghost brings us to trust in Christ, and the inspired word assures us that Christ suffered in the room, place, and stead of all believers, and therefore we perceive that he died for us, and also that nothing remains for us to suffer, because sin having been laid upon the Substitute, it is no more upon us. We rejoice in the fact of our Lord's substitution, and the transfer of our sins to him. We see that if he stood in our place we stand in his; and if he was rejected we are "accepted in the beloved." Then straight away this spirit of heaviness disappears, because the reason for it is gone.

"I will praise thee every day!
Now thine anger's turn'd away,
Comfortable thoughts arise
From the bleeding sacrifice."

Moreover, in the new birth *the Holy Spirit infuses into us a new nature*, and that new nature knoweth not the spirit of heaviness.

It is a thing of light, and life, and joy in the Holy Ghost. The new-born nature looks up and perceives its kinship with God. It rejoices in the favour of the Holy One, from whom it came. It rests in the Lord, yea, it joys and rejoices in him; and, whereas, the old sin-spirit still sinks us down according to its power, there being in us still the evil heart of unbelief, this new life wells up within us as a living fount of crystal, and buoys us up with the peace and joy which cometh of the Holy Ghost's indwelling. Thus the inner life becomes a constant remedy for heaviness of spirit.

And faith, too, that blessed gift of God, wherever it resides, works to the clearing away of heaviness; for faith sings, "All things are mine, why should I sorrow? All my sin is gone, why should I pine and moan? All things as to the present life are supplied me by the God of providence and grace, and the future is guaranteed to me by the covenant ordered in all things and sure." Faith takes the telescope and looks beyond the narrow range of time into the eternal heavens, and sees a crown laid up for the faithful. Ay, and her ears are opened so that she hears the songs of the redeemed by blood before the throne, thus she bears away the spirit of heaviness. If I see no joy with these poor optics, faith has other eyes with which she discovers rivers of delight. If flesh and blood afford me nothing but causes for dismay, faith knows more and sees more, and she perceives causes for overflowing gratitude and delight. Hope also enters with her silver light, borrowed from faithful promises. She expects the future glory, at which we hinted just now, and begins to anticipate it all; and so, again, she drives away the gloom of the heart. Love, also, the sweetest of the three, comes in and teaches us to be resigned to the will of God, and then sweetly charms us into acquiescence with all the divine purposes; and, when we reach that point, and so love God that, whatever he may do with us, we are resolved to trust him, and praise his name, then the spirit of heaviness must vanish.

Now, beloved mourners, I trust you know what this great uplifting means. It is a work in which the Lord is greatly glorified when he raises a poor, begrimed soul out of the sordid potsherds among which it has lain, and gives it to soar aloft as on the silver wings of a dove. Some of us can never forget the hour of our great deliverance; it was the day of our espousals, the time of love, and it must for ever remain as the beginning of days unto us. All glory be to him who has loosed our bonds and set our feet in a large room. But now we come to the third, and most prominent, point of the text; which is:—

III. THE GARMENT OF PRAISE BESTOWED, which takes the place of the spirit of heaviness. We suppose this may mean, and probably does mean, that the Lord gives us a garment that is honourable and worthy of praise: and what is this garment but *the righteousness of our Lord Jesus Christ?* The Lord arrays his poor people in a robe which causes them to be no more worthy of shame, but fit to be praised. They become unblameable in his sight. What a blessing this is! Did not the father, when he received the prodigal, say, "Bring forth the best robe and put it on him"? That was a praiseful garment, instead of the spirit of heaviness; and whenever a child of God begins to perceive his adoption, and to say, "Abba, Father," then he puts on a fit garment for a child to wear, an honourable dress, a garment of praise. When we realise that Christ has made us priests unto God, and we therefore put on the priestly garment of sanctification by beginning to offer the sacrifice of prayer and praise, then, again, we wear a praiseful garment. When we exercise the high prerogative of kings, for we are kings as well as priests, then, again, we wear not a sordid vesture of dishonour, nor the costume of a prison-house, nor the rags of beggary, nor the black robe of condemnation, but a garment of honour and of praise. Every child of God should be clothed with the garments of salvation: his Saviour has prepared them for this end, and let him wrap them about him and be glad, for these garments make him beautiful in the sight of God.

But I choose, rather, to follow the exact words of our version to-night, and speak of the garment of praise as meaning gratitude, thanksgiving, and adoration. The anointed Comforter takes away the spirit of heaviness, and he robes his people in the garment of praise.

Now, *this is something outward as well as inward.* A wise man endeavours to hide the heaviness of his spirit; but when the Lord takes that away, he does not wish to conceal his gratitude. I could not help telling those I lived with, when I found the Lord. Master John Bunyan informs us that he was so anxious to let someone know of his conversion that he wanted to tell the crows on the ploughed land all about it. I do not wonder. It is a piece of news which it would be hard to withhold. Whenever a man's inward heaviness is graciously removed, he puts on the outward manifestation of joy, and walks abroad in the silken robes of praise.

As we have already said, a garment is a thing which covers a man; so when a man learns to thank God aright, his praise covers him: he himself is hidden while he gives all the glory to God. The man is seen as clothed in praise from head to foot. Many persons very unfairly judge Christians when they begin to speak of the love and mercy of God to them, for they cry out that they are egotistical; but how can it be egotistical to talk of what the Lord has done for you? If you speak with any sort of confidence, captious individuals say that you are presumptuous. How can it be presumptuous to believe what God himself declares? It is presumptuous to doubt what God says, but it is no presumption to believe God; neither is it egotism to state the truth. If I were to say that God has not blest me abundantly, the pulpit on which I stand would cry out against me. Shall I conceal the mercy of God as if it were stolen goods? Never; but the rather will I speak the more boldly of the measureless love which has kept my soul from going down to the pit. "Him that glorieth, let him glory in the Lord."

Bless the Lord, O ye saints of his, and give thanks to his holy name. Show forth his salvation, compel men to see it, gird it about your loins, and wear it for your adorning in all companies.

While speaking of this garment of praise, let us enquire *of what it is made.*

Is not praise composed in a large measure of *an attentive observation of God's mercy*? Thousands of blessings come to us without our knowledge: we take them in at the back-door, and put them away in the cellar. Now, praise takes note of them, preserves the invoice of favours received, and records the goodness of the Lord. O friends, if you do this, you will never be short of reasons for praise. He who notices God's mercy will never be without a mercy to notice. This is the chief material of the garment of praise: attentive consideration of divine grace is the broadcloth out of which the garment of praise is made.

The next thing is *grateful memory.* Very much that God does for us we bury alive in the grave of oblivion. We receive his mercies as if they were common trash. They are no sooner come than they are gone, and the proverb saith true, "Bread eaten is soon forgotten." Why, my brethren, the Lord may give you a thousand favours, and you will not praise him, but if he smites you with one little stroke of the whip, you grumble at him. You write his mercies on the water, and your own trials you engrave on granite: these things ought not to be. Maintain the memory of his great goodness. "Forget not all his benefits." Call to remembrance your song in the night; and remember the loving-kindnesses of the Lord. In this also we find rich material for the garment of praise.

We are further aided *by rightly estimating mercy.* Is it not a great mercy to be alive, and not in hell; to be in your senses, and not in the lunatic asylum; to be in health, and not in the hospital; to be in one's own room, and not in the workhouse? These are great favours, and yet, perhaps, we seldom thank God for them. Then count up your spiritual mercies, if you can. Remember, on the other hand, what you deserved, and what it cost the Saviour to bring these blessings to you, how patient the Lord has been with your refusal of his love, and how continuously he has loaded you with benefits. Weigh his mercies, as well as count them, and they will help you to put on the garment of praise.

It is the telling out of the divine goodness which largely constitutes praise: to observe, to remember, to estimate, to prize, and then to speak of the Lord's gracious gifts—all these are essential. Praise is the open declaration of the gratitude which is felt within. How greatly do many fail in this: if you visit them, how readily they enlarge upon their troubles; in five minutes they have informed you about the damp weather, their aching bones, and their low wages. Others speak of the bad times and the decline of trade, till you know their ditty by heart. Is this the manner of the people of God? Should we not regale our visitors with something better than the bones of our meat, and the hard crusts of our bread? Let us set before them good tidings, and cheerfully tell of the divine goodness to us, lest they should go away under the impression that we serve a hard master. It would create an almost miraculous change in some people's lives if they made a point of speaking most of the precious things, and least of the worries and ills. Why always the poverty? Why always the pains? Why always the dying child? Why always the husband's small wages. Why always the unkindness of a friend? Why not sometimes—yea, why not always—the mercies of the Lord? That is praise, and it is to be our everyday garment, the livery of every servant of Christ.

Let us enquire, too, *who ought to wear this garment?* The answer may be suggested by another—whom does it fit? Truly there is garment of praise which exactly suits *me*, and I mean to wear it on my own person. It is so capacious that some of my brethren would wonder if they could see it spread out. I am so much in debt to my God that, do what I will, I can never give a fair acknowledgment of it. I freely confess that I owe him more than any man living, and am morally bound to praise him more earnestly than anyone else. Did I hear some of you claiming to be equal debtors? Do you demand to be allowed to praise him more than I? Well, I will not quarrel with you. Let the matter stand; and if you will excel me, I will praise my Lord for it. I once, in preaching, remarked that if I once entered heaven, I would take the lowest place, feeling that I owe more to God's grace than anybody else; but I found, when I left the pulpit, that I had several competitors, who would not yield the lowest place to me: They were each one ready to exclaim:—

> "Then loudest of the crowd *I'll* sing,
> While heaven's resounding mansions ring
> With shouts of sovereign grace."

Blessed be God, this is the only contention among the birds of Paradise—which owes the most, which shall love the best, which shall lie lowest, and which shall extol their Lord the most zealously. Charming rivalry of humility! Let us have more of it below. I again say there is a garment of praise that fits me. Brother, is there not one which fits you, exactly suiting your state and condition? If you are an heir of heaven, there is, there must be, a garment of praise which will rest most becomingly upon your shoulders, and you should put it on at once.

Then, *when shall we wear it?* We should certainly appear in it on high days and holidays. On Sabbath days and communion seasons the hours are fragrant with grateful memories. I heard of someone who did not attend public worship because his clothes were not fit to come in, and I replied, What can he mean? Does the Lord care for our outward dress? Let him put on the garment of praise, and he may come and welcome. The outer vestments matter little indeed, all garments of that sort are only proofs of our fall, and of the need to hide our nakedness for very shame.

Fine dress is unbecoming in the house of God, especially for those who call themselves "miserable sinners." The best adornment is humility of spirit, the robe of thanksgiving, the garment of praise. The Lord's day should always be the happiest day of the week, and the communion should be a little heaven to our souls. "Call the Sabbath a delight, the holy of the Lord, honourable."

We should wear the garment of praise on the most commonplace of days. It should be the peasant's frock, and the merchant's coat, the lady's dress, and the servant's gown: it is the best for wear, for comfort, and for beauty, and it never gets out of fashion. I once knew an old saint, a Methodist, a very quaint, original, rustic old man, who was celebrated for happiness. When he went out to day labour early in the morning, he was always singing as he went along the road. The country people used to call it "tooting to himself." Quietly he hummed a bit of a hymn wherever he was. When he used his spade or his hoe, he worked to the music of his heart, and never murmured when in poverty, or became angry when held up to ridicule. I wish we were all as spiritually minded and as full of praise as he. Bless the Lord! Bless the Lord! When should we not bless him? We will praise him when our beds refresh us: blessed be he who kept the night watches. When we put on our clothes in the morning, we will bless his name for giving us food and raiment. When we sit down to break our fast, we will bless the love which has provided a table for us. When we go forth to our work, we will bless the Lord who gives us strength to labour. If we must lie at home sore sick, with fierce pain or slow decay, let us praise him who heals and sanctifies all our diseases. Let us endeavour to display the sweet spirit of thankfulness from the rising of the sun to the going down of the same. Every moment may suggest a new verse of our life-psalm, and cause us to magnify him whose mercy endureth for ever.

Now, lastly, *why should we wear the garment of praise?* We should wear it as we wear other raiment, to keep us warm and comfortable, for there is no such vesture in the world as that of praise: it warms the inmost heart, and sends a glow through the whole man. You may go to Nova Zembla and not freeze in such a robe; in the worst cases, and in the most sorrowful plights, be you where you may, you are proof against outward circumstances when your whole being is enwrapped in praise. Wear it because it will comfort you. Wear it also because it will distinguish you from others. It will be livery to you, and men will know whose servants you are; it will be a regimental dress, and show to which army you belong; it will be a court dress, and manifest to what dignity you have attained. So arrayed, you will bear the tokens of your Lord, who often in the days of his sorrow lifted his eye and heart to heaven, and thanked the great Father for his goodness.

May some poor burdened soul lose its heaviness while thinking over our text, and henceforth wear this kingly robe—the garment of praise. Amen.

PRAYER
Ask and Have—James 4:2, 3
Prayer—Its Discouragements and Encouragements Matt. 15:23
Exposition of Ephesians 2
Ejaculatory Prayer—Neh. 2:4
Restraining Prayer—Job 15:4
"The Throne of Grace"—Heb. 4:16
Prayerful Importunity—Luke 18:7
True and Not True—John 9:31
A Plain Talk upon an Encouraging Topic—Jonah 2:7
Exposition of Jonah 2

ASK AND HAVE.

A Sermon

Delivered on Lord's-day Morning, October 1st, 1882, by

C. H. SPURGEON,

AT THE METROPOLITAN TABERNACLE, NEWINGTON.

"Ye lust, and have not: ye kill, and desire to have, and cannot obtain: ye fight and war, yet ye have not, because ye ask not. Ye ask, and receive not, because ye ask amiss, that ye may consume it upon your lusts."—James iv. 2, 3.

MAY these striking words be made profitable to us by the teaching of the Holy Spirit.

Man is a creature abounding in wants, and ever restless, and hence his heart is full of desires. I can hardly imagine a man existing who has not many desires of some kind or another. Man is comparable to the sea anemone with its multitude of tentacles which are always hunting in the water for food; or like certain plants which send out tendrils, seeking after the means of climbing. The poet says, "Man never is, but always to be, blest." He steers for which he thinks to be his port, but as yet he is tossed about on the waves. One of these days he hopes to find his heart's delight, and so he continues to desire with more or less expectancy. This fact appertains both to the worst of men and the best of men. In bad men desires corrupt into lusts: they long after that which is selfish, sensual, and consequently evil. The current of their desires sets strongly in a wrong direction. These lustings, in many cases, become extremely intense: they make the man their slave; they domineer over his judgment; they stir him up to violence: he fights and wars, perhaps he literally kills: in God's sight, who counts anger murder, he does kill full often. Such is the strength of his desires that they are commonly called passions; and when these passions are fully excited, then the man himself struggles vehemently, so that the kingdom of the devil suffereth violence, and the violent take it by force.

Meanwhile in gracious men there are desires also. To rob the saints of their desires would be to injure them greatly, for by these they rise out of their lower selves. The desires of the gracious are after the best things: things pure and peaceable, laudable and elevating. They desire God's glory, and hence their desires spring from higher motives than those which inflame the unrenewed mind. Such desires in Christian men are frequently very fervent and forcible; they ought always to be so; and those desires begotten of the Spirit of God stir the renewed nature, exciting and stimulating it, and making the man to groan and to be in anguish and in travail until he can attain that which God has taught him to long for. The lusting of the wicked and the holy desiring of the righteous have their own ways of seeking gratification. The lusting of the wicked developes itself in contention; it kills, and desires to have: it fights and it wars; while on the other hand the desire of the righteous when rightly guided betakes itself to a far better course for achieving its purpose, for it expresses itself in prayer fervent and importunate. The godly man when full of desire asks and receives at the hand of God.

At this time I shall by God's help try to set forth from our text, first, *the poverty of lusting,*—"Ye lust and have not." Secondly, I shall sadly show *the poverty of many professing Christians* in spiritual things, especially in their church capacity; they also long for and have not. Thirdly, we shall speak in closing, upon *the wealth wherewith holy desires will be rewarded if we will but use the right means.* If we ask we shall receive.

I. First, consider THE POVERTY OF LUSTING,—"*Ye lust, and have not.*" Carnal lustings, however strong they may be, do not in many cases obtain that which they seek after: as saith the text, "Ye desire to have, and cannot obtain." The man longs to be happy, but he is not; he pines to be great, but he grows meaner every day; he aspires after this and after that which he thinks will content him, but he is still unsatisfied: he is like the troubled sea which cannot rest. One way or another his life is disappointment; he labours as in the very fire, but the result is vanity and vexation of spirit. How can it be otherwise? If we sow the wind, must we not reap the whirlwind, and nothing else? Or, if peradventure the strong lustings of an active, talented, persevering man do give him what he seeks after, yet how soon he loses it. He has it so that he has it not. The pursuit is toilsome, but the possession is a dream. He sits down to eat, and lo! the feast is snatched away, the cup vanishes when it is at his lip. He wins to lose; he builds, and his sandy foundation slips from under his tower, and it lies in ruins. He that conquered kingdoms, died discontented on a lone rock in mid ocean; and he who revived his empire, fell never to rise again. As Jonah's gourd withered in a night, so have empires fallen on a sudden, and their lords have died in exile. So that what men obtain by warring and fighting is an estate with a short lease; the obtaining is so temporary that it still stands true, "they lust, and have not." Or if such men have gifts and power enough to retain that which they have won, yet in another sense they have it not while they have it, for the pleasure which they looked for in it is not there. They pluck the apple, and it turns out to be one of those Dead Sea apples which crumble to ashes in the hand. The man is rich, but God takes away from him the power to enjoy his wealth. By his lustings and his warrings the licentious man at last obtains the object of his cravings, and after a moment's gratification, he loathes that which he so passionately lusted for. He longs for the tempting pleasure, seizes it, and crushes it by the eager grasp. See the boy hunting the butterfly, which flits from flower to flower, while he pursues it ardently. At last it is within reach, and with his cap he knocks it down: but when he picks up the poor remains, he finds the painted fly spoiled by the act which won it. Thus may it be said of multitudes of the sons of men,—"Ye lust, and have not."

Their poverty is set forth in a threefold manner. "Ye kill, and desire to have, and cannot obtain," "Ye have not, because ye ask not," "Ye ask, and receive not, because ye ask amiss."

If the lusters fail, it is not because they did not set to work to gain their ends; for according to their nature they used the most practical means within their reach, and used them eagerly, too. According to the mind of the flesh the only way to obtain a thing is to fight for it, and James sets this down as the reason of all fighting. "Whence come wars and fightings among you? Come they not hence, even of your lusts that war in your members?" This is the form of effort of which we read, "*Ye fight and war, yet ye have not.*" To this mode of operation men cling from age to age. If a man is to get along in this world they tell me he must contend with his neighbours, and push them from their vantage ground; he must not be particular how *they* are to thrive, but he must mind the main chance on his own account, and take care to rise, no matter how many he may tread upon. He cannot expect to get on if he loves his neighbour as himself. It is a fair fight, and every man must look to himself. Do you think I am satirical? I may be, but I have heard this sort of talk from men who meant it. So they take to fighting, and that fighting is often victorious, for according to the text "*ye kill*"—that is to say, they so fight that they overthrow their adversary, and there is an end of him. They are men of great strength, young lions that can go forth and rend the prey, and yet it is said of them that they "lack and suffer hunger," while they that wait upon the Lord shall not want any good thing. These lusters are unrestrained in their efforts to gain their point; they stick at nothing, they kill, and desire to have. Moreover, they fight with great perseverance, for the text says, "Ye fight *and war.*" Now, war is a continuation of the act of fighting, prolonging it from campaign to campaign, and conducting it by the rules of military art till the victory is won. Multitudes of men are living for themselves, competing here and warring there, fighting for their own hand with the utmost perseverance. They have little choice as to how they will do it. Conscience is not allowed to interfere in their transactions, but the old advice rings in their ears, "Get money; get money honestly if you can, but by any means get money." No matter though body and soul be ruined, and others be deluged with misery, fight on, for there is no discharge in this war. If you are to win you must fight; and everything is fair in war. So they muster their forces, they struggle with their fellows, they make the battle of life hotter and hotter, they banish love, and brand tenderness as folly, and yet with all their schemes they obtain not the end of life in any true sense. Well saith James, "Ye kill, and desire to have, and cannot obtain; ye fight and war, yet ye have not."

When men who are greatly set upon their selfish purposes do not succeed they may possibly hear that the reason of their non-success is "*Because ye ask not.*" Is, then, success to be achieved by asking? So the text seems to hint, and so the righteous find it. Why doth not this man of intense desires take to asking? The reason is, first, because it is unnatural to the natural man to pray; as well expect him to fly. He despises the idea of supplication. "Pray?" says he. "No, I want to be at work. I cannot waste time on devotions; prayers are not practical, I want to fight my way. While you are praying I shall have beaten my opponent. I go to my counting-house, and leave you to your Bibles and your prayers." He hath no mind for asking of God. He declares that none but canting hypocrites care to pray, thus confessing that if he were to pray he would be a canting hypocrite. As for him, his praying is of quite another sort, and woe to those who come into his clutches; they will find that with him business is business, and pretty sharp business too. He will never stoop to pray, he is too proud. God-reliance he does not understand; self-reliance is his word. Self is his god, and to his god he looks for success. He is so proud that he reckons himself to be his own providence; his own right hand and his active arm shall get to him the victory. When he is very liberal in his views he admits that though he does not pray, yet there may be some good in it, for it quiets people's minds, and makes them more comfortable: but as to any answer ever coming to prayer, he scouts the idea, and talks both philosophically and theologically about the absurdity of supposing that God alters his course of conduct out of respect to the prayers of men and women. "Ridiculous," says he, "utterly ridiculous;" and, therefore, in his own great wisdom he returns to his fighting and his warring, for by such means he hopes to attain his end. Yet he obtains not. The whole history of mankind shows the failure of evil lustings to obtain their object.

For a while the carnal man goes on fighting and warring; but by-and-by he changes his mind, for he is ill, or frightened. His purpose is the same, but if it cannot be achieved one way he will try another. If he must ask, well, he will ask; he will become religious, and do good to himself in that way. He finds that some religious people prosper in the world, and that even sincere Christians are by no means fools in business, and, therefore, he will try their plan. And now he comes under the third censure of our text,—"*Ye ask and receive not.*" What is the reason why the man who is the slave of his lusts obtains not his desire, even when he takes to asking? The reason is because his asking is a mere matter of form, his heart is not in his worship. He buys a book containing what are called forms of prayer, and he repeats these, for repeating is easier than praying, and demands no thought. I have no objection to your using a form of prayer if you pray with it; but I know a great many who do not pray with it, but only repeat the form. Imagine what would come to our families if instead of our children speaking to us frankly when they have any need they were always to think it requisite to go into the library and hunt up a form of prayer, and read it to us. Surely there would be an end to all home-feeling and love; life would move in fetters. Our household would become a kind of boarding-school, or barracks, and all would be parade and formality, instead of happy eyes looking up with loving trust into fond eyes that delight to respond. Many spiritual men use a form, but carnal men are pretty sure to do so, for they end in the form. This man's prayer is asking amiss, because it is entirely for himself. He wants to prosper that he may enjoy himself; he wants to be great simply that he may be admired: his prayer begins and ends with self. Look at the indecency of such a prayer even if it be sincere. When a man so prays he asks God to be his servant, and gratify his desires; nay, worse than that, he wants God to join him in the service of his lusts. He will gratify his lusts, and God shall come and help him to do it. Such prayer is blasphemous, but a large quantity of it is offered, and it must be one of the most God-provoking things that heaven ever beholds. No, if a man will live to himself and his lusts, let him do so, and the further he gets off from God the more consistent he will be. Let him not mouth the Lord's prayer as though God were his father, or drag in Christ's sacred name to sanctify his greed, or invoke the Spirit's blessed power in connection with his personal aggrandizement, or his selfish ambition. If he does so, he will be no better off than he was at the beginning: he will ask, and have not. His asking will miss because he asks amiss, that he may consume it upon his lusts. If your desires are the longings of fallen nature, if your desires begin and end with your own self, and if the chief end for which you live is not to glorify God, but to glorify yourself, then you may fight, but you shall not have; you may rise up early and sit up late, but nothing worth gaining shall come of it. Remember how the Lord hath spoken in the thirty-seventh Psalm: "Cease from anger, and forsake wrath: fret not thyself in any wise to do evil. For yet a little while, and the wicked shall not be: yea, thou shalt diligently consider his place, and it shall not be. But the meek shall inherit the earth; and shall delight themselves in the abundance of peace."

So much upon the poverty of lusting.

II. Secondly, I have now before me a serious business, and that is, to show HOW CHRISTIAN CHURCHES MAY SUFFER SPIRITUAL POVERTY, so that they too "desire to have, and cannot obtain." Of course the Christian seeks higher things than the worldling, else were he not worthy of that name at all. At least professedly his object is to obtain the true riches, and to glorify God in spirit and in truth. Yes, but look, dear brethren, all churches do not get what they desire. We have to complain, not here and there, but in many places, of churches that are nearly asleep, and are gradually declining. Of course they find excuses. The population is dwindling, or another place of worship is attracting the people. There is always an excuse handy when a man wants one; but still there stands the fact,—public worship is almost deserted in some places, the ministry has no rallying power about it, and those who put in an appearance are discontented or indifferent. In such churches there are no conversions. If they had half-a-dozen added to them in a year, they would want to sing the "Hallelujah Chorus"; but as to bringing thousands to Christ, they secretly fear that this would be an undesirable thing, for it might involve excitement, and they are so proper that they dread anything of that sort. To do nothing, and let men be damned, is in their judgment proper and respectable, but to be alive and energetic is a perilous state of affairs, for it might lead to fanaticism and indecorum. They are specially afraid of anything like "sensationalism." That ugly-looking word they set before us very much as the Chinese try to frighten their enemies by painting horrible faces on their shields. Never mind that terrible word; it will hurt no one. These churches "have not," for no truth is made prevalent through their zeal, no sin is smitten, no holiness promoted, nothing is done by which God is glorified. And what is the reason of it?

First, *even among professed Christians, there may be the pursuit of desirable things in a wrong method.* "Ye fight and war, yet ye have not." Have not churches thought to prosper by competing with other churches? At such and such a place of worship they have a very clever man: we must get a clever man, too; in fact, he must be a little cleverer than our neighbour's hero. That is the thing,—a clever man! Ah me, that we should live in an age in which we talk about clever men in preaching the gospel of Jesus Christ! Alas, that this holy service should be thought to depend upon human cleverness!

Churches have competed with each other in architecture, in music, in apparel, and in social status. The leaders fancy that to succeed they must have something more handsome, artistic, or expensive than their neighbours: hence they build Gothic edifices in which the minister's voice gets up among the timbers, and is never properly heard, or else they purchase an organ with every stop except the full one. The opinion would seem to be widely spread that there is a deal of grace in an organ. To pray to God with a windmill like the Tartars would be very absurd; but to praise God with wind passing through a set of pipes is eminently proper. I never have seen the distinction, and do not see it now. Organ or no organ is not now the question, but I speak of instances in which these machines are set up as a matter of rivalry. Is it not the design of many to succeed by a finer building, better music, and a cleverer ministry than others? Is it not as much a matter of competition as a shop front and a dressed window are with drapers? Is this the way by which the Kingdom of God is to grow up among us?

In some cases there is a measure of bitterness in the rivalry. It is not pleasant to little minds to see other churches prospering more than their own. They may be more earnest than we are, and be doing God's work better, but we are too apt to turn a jealous eye towards them, and we would rather they did not get on quite so well. "Do ye think that the Scripture saith in vain, The spirit that dwelleth in us lusteth to envy?" If we could see a disturbance among them, so that they would break up and be ecclesiastically killed, we would not rejoice. Of course not; but neither should we suffer any deadly sorrow. In some churches an evil spirit lingers. I bring no railing accusation, and, therefore, say no more than this: God will never bless such means and such a spirit; those who give way to them will desire to have, but never obtain.

Meanwhile, what is the reason why they do not have a blessing? The text says, "*Because ye ask not*"; I am afraid there are churches which do not ask. Prayer in all forms is too much neglected. Private prayer is allowed to decay. I shall put it to the conscience of every man how far secret prayer is attended to; and how much of fellowship with God there is in secret among the members of our churches. Certainly its healthy existence is vital to church prosperity. Of family prayer it is more easy to judge, for we can see it. I fear that in these days many have quite given up family prayer. I pray you do not imitate them. I wish you were all of the same mind as the Scotch labourer who obtained a situation in the house of a wealthy farmer who was known to pay well, and all his friends envied him that he had gone to live in such a service. In a short time he returned to his native village, and when they asked him why he had left his situation, he replied that he "could not live in a house which had no roof to it." A house without prayer is a house without a roof. We cannot expect blessings on your churches if we have none on your families.

As to the congregational prayer, the gathering together in what we call our prayer-meetings, is there not a falling off? In many cases the prayer-meeting is despised, and looked down upon as a sort of second-rate gathering. There are members of churches who are never present, and it does not prick their consciences that they stay away. Some congregations mix up the prayer-meeting with a lecture, so as to hold only one service in the week. I read the other day an excuse for all this: it is said that people are better at home, attending to family concerns. This is idle talk, for who among us wishes people to neglect their domestic concerns? It will be found that those attend to their own concerns best who are diligent to get everything in order, so that they may go out to assemblies for worship. Negligence of the house of God is often an index of negligence of their own houses. They are not bringing their children to Christ, I am persuaded, or they would bring them up to the services. Anyhow, the prayers of the church measure its prosperity. If we restrain prayer we restrain the blessing. Our true success as churches can only be had by asking it of the Lord. Are we not prepared to reform and amend in this matter? Oh for Zion's travailing hour to come, when an agony of prayer shall move the whole body of the faithful.

But some reply, "There are prayer-meetings, and we do ask for the blessing, and yet it comes not." Is not the explanation to be found in the other part of the text, *"Ye have not, because ye ask amiss"?* When prayer-meetings become a mere form, when brethren stand up and waste the time with their long orations, instead of speaking to God in earnest and burning words, when there is no expectation of a blessing, when the prayer is cold and chill, then nothing will come of it. He who prays without fervency does not pray at all. We cannot commune with God, who is a consuming fire, if there is no fire in our prayers. Many prayers fail of their errand because there is no faith in them. Prayers which are filled with doubt, are requests for refusal. Imagine that you wrote to a friend and said, "Dear friend, I am in great trouble, and I therefore tell you, and ask for your help, because it seems right to do so. But though I thus write, I have no belief that you will send me any help; indeed, I should be mightily surprised if you did, and should speak of it as a great wonder." Will you get the help, think you? I should say your friend would be sensible enough to observe the little confidence which you have in him; and he would reply that, as you did not expect anything, he would not astonish you. Your opinion of his generosity is so low that he does not feel called upon to put himself out of the way on your account. When prayers are of that kind you cannot wonder if we "have not, because we ask amiss." Moreover, if our praying, however earnest and believing it may be, is a mere asking that our church may prosper because we want to glory in its prosperity, if we want to see our own denomination largely increased, and its respectability improved, that we may share the honours thereof, then our desires are nothing but lustings after all. Can it be that the children of God manifest the same emulations, jealousies, and ambitions as men of the world? Shall religious work be a matter of rivalry and contest? Ah, then, the prayers which seek success will have no acceptance at the mercy-seat. God will not hear us, but bid us begone, for he careth not for the petitions of which self is the object. "Ye have not, because ye ask not, or because ye ask amiss."

III. Thirdly, I have a much more pleasing work to do, and that is to hint at THE WEALTH WHICH AWAITS THE USE OF THE RIGHT MEANS, namely, of asking rightly of God.

I invite your most solemn attention to this matter, for it is vitally important. And my first observation is this, *how very small after all is this demand which God makes of us.* Ask! Why, it is the least thing he can possibly expect of us, and it is no more than we ordinarily require of those who need help from us. We expect a poor man to ask; and if he does not we lay the blame of his lack upon himself. If God will give for the asking, and we remain poor, who is to blame? Is not the blame most grievous? Does it not look as if we were out of order with God, so that we will not even condescend to ask a favour of him? Surely there must be in our hearts a lurking enmity to him, or else instead of its being an unwelcome necessity it would be regarded as a great delight.

However, brethren, whether we like it or not, remember, *asking is the rule of the kingdom.* "Ask, and ye shall receive." It is a rule that never will be altered in anybody's case. Our Lord Jesus Christ is the elder brother of the family, but God has not relaxed the rule for him. Remember this text: Jehovah says to his own Son, "Ask of me and I will give thee the heathen for thine inheritance, and the uttermost parts of the earth for thy possession." If the royal and divine Son of God cannot be exempted from the rule of asking that he may have, you and I cannot expect the rule to be relaxed in our favour. Why should it be? What reason can be pleaded why we should be exempted from prayer? What argument can there be why we should be deprived of the privilege and delivered from the necessity of supplication? I can see none: can you? God will bless Elijah and send rain on Israel, but Elijah must pray for it. If the chosen nation is to prosper Samuel must plead for it. If the Jews are to be delivered Daniel must intercede. God will bless Paul, and the nations shall be converted through him, but Paul must pray. Pray he did without ceasing; his epistles show that he expected nothing except by asking for it. If you may have everything by asking, and nothing without asking, I beg you to see how absolutely vital prayer is, and I beseech you to abound in it.

Moreover, it is clear to even the most shallow thinker that *there are some things necessary for the church of God which we cannot get otherwise than by prayer.* You can get that clever man I spoke about—the less, perhaps, you pray about him the better; and that new church, and the new organ, and the choir, you can also get without prayer; but you cannot get the heavenly anointing: the gift of God is not to be purchased with money. Some of the members of a church in a primitive village in America thought that they would raise a congregation by hanging up a very handsome chandelier in the meeting-house. People talked about this chandelier, and some went to see it, but the light of it soon grew dim. You can buy all sorts of ecclesiastical furniture, you can purchase any kind of paint, brass, muslin, blue, scarlet, and fine linen, together with flutes, harps, sackbuts, psalteries, and all kinds of music—you can get these without prayer; in fact, it would be an impertinence to pray about such rubbish; but you cannot get the Holy Ghost without prayer. "He bloweth where he listeth." He will not be brought near by any process or method at our command apart from asking. There are no mechanical means which will make up for his absence. If the Holy Spirit be not there, what is the use of that clever man of yours? Will anybody be converted? Will any soul be comforted? Will any children of God be renewed in spiritual life without the Holy Spirit? Neither can you get communion with God without prayer. He that will not pray cannot have communion with God. Yet more, there is no real, spiritual communion of the church with its own members when prayer is suspended. Prayer must be in action, or else those blessings which are vitally essential to the success of the church can never come to it. Prayer is the great door of spiritual blessing, and if you close it you shut out the favour.

Beloved brethren, do you not think that *this asking which God requires is a very great privilege?* Suppose there were an edict published that you must not pray: that would be a hardship indeed. If prayer rather interrupted than increased the stream of blessing, it would be a sad calamity. Did you ever see a dumb man under a strong excitement, or suffering great pain, and therefore anxious to speak? It is a terrible sight to see: the face is distorted, the body is fearfully agitated; the mute writhes and labours in dire distress. Every limb is contorted with a desire to help the tongue, but it cannot break its bonds. Hollow sounds come from the breast, and stutterings of ineffectual speech awaken attention, though they cannot reach so far as expression. The poor creature is in pain unspeakable. Suppose we were in our spiritual nature full of strong desires, and yet dumb as to the tongue of prayer, methinks it would be one of the direst afflictions that could possibly befall us; we should be terribly maimed and dismembered, and our agony would be overwhelming. Blessed be his name, the Lord ordains a way of utterance, and bids our heart speak out to him.

Beloved, we must pray: it seems to me that *it ought to be the first thing* we ever think of doing when in need. If men were right with God, and loved him truly, they would pray as naturally as they breathe. I hope some of us are right with God, and do not need to be driven to prayer, for it has become an instinct of our nature. I was told by a friend yesterday the story of a little German boy; a story which his pastor loved to tell. The dear little child believed his God, and delighted in prayer. His schoolmaster had urged the scholars to be at school in time, and this child always tried to be so; but his father and mother were dilatory people, and one morning, through their fault alone, he just left the door as the clock struck the hour for the school to open. A friend standing near heard the little one cry, "Dear God, do grant I may be in time for school." It struck the listener that for once prayer could not be heard, for the child had quite a little walk before him, and the hour was already come. He was curious to see the result. Now it so happened this morning that the master, in trying to open the schoolhouse door turned the key the wrong way, and could not stir the bolt, and they had to send for a smith to open the door. Hence a delay, and just as the door opened our little friend entered with the rest, all in good time. God has many ways of granting right desires. It was most natural that instead of crying and whining a child that really loved God should speak to him about his trouble. Should it not be natural to you and to me spontaneously and at once to tell the Lord our sorrows and ask for help? Should not this be the first resort?

Alas, according to Scripture and observation, and I grieve to add, according to experience, *prayer is often the last thing.* Look at the sick man in the one hundred and seventh Psalm. Friends bring him various foods, but his soul abhorreth all manner of meat: the physicians do what they can to heal him, but he grows worse and worse, and draws nigh to the gates of death: "Then they cry unto the Lord in their trouble." That was put last which should have been first. "Send for the doctor. Prepare him nourishment. Wrap him in flannels!" All very well, but when will you pray to God? God will be called upon when the case grows desperate. Look at the mariners described in the same psalm. The barque is well-nigh wrecked. "They mount up to the heaven, they go down again to the depths: their soul is melted because of trouble." Still they do all they can to ride out the storm; but when "they reel to and fro, and stagger like a drunken man, and are at their wit's end: then they cry unto the Lord in their trouble." Oh, yes; God is sought unto when we are driven into a corner and ready to perish. And what a mercy it is that he hears such laggard prayers, and delivers the suppliants out of their troubles. But ought it to be so with you and with me, and with churches of Christ? Ought not the first impulse of a declining church to be, "Let us pray day and night until the Lord appears for us: let us meet together with one accord in one place, and never separate until the blessing descends upon us"?

Do you know, brothers, *what great things are to be had for the asking?* Have you ever thought of it? Does it not stimulate you to pray fervently? All heaven lies before the grasp of the asking man; all the promises of God are rich and inexhaustible, and their fulfilment is to be had by prayer. Jesus saith, "All things are delivered unto me of my Father," and Paul says, "All things are yours, and ye are Christ's." Who would not pray when all things are thus handed over to us? Ay, and promises that were first made to special individuals, are all made to us if we know how to plead them in prayer. Israel went through the Red Sea ages ago, and yet we read in the sixty-sixth Psalm, "There did we rejoice in him." Only Jacob was present at Peniel, and yet Hosea says "There he spake with us." Paul wants to give us a great promise for times of need, and he quotes from the Old Testament, "For he hath said, I will never leave thee nor forsake thee." Where did Paul get that? That is the assurance which the Lord gave to Joshua: "I will never leave thee nor forsake thee." Surely the promise was for Joshua only. No; it is for us. "No Scripture is of private interpretation"; all Scripture is ours. See how God appears unto Solomon at night, and he says, "Ask what I shall give thee." Solomon asks for wisdom. "Oh, that is Solomon," say you. Listen. "If any man lack wisdom, let him ask of God." God gave Solomon wealth, and fame into the bargain. Is not that peculiar to Solomon? No, for it is said of the true wisdom, "Length of days is in her right hand, and in her left hand riches and honour"; and is not this much like our Saviour's word, "Seek ye first the kingdom of God and his righteousness, and all these things shall be added unto you." Thus you see the Lord's promises have many fulfilments, and they are waiting now to pour their treasures into the lap of prayer. Does not this lift prayer up to a high level, when God is willing to repeat the biographies of his saints in us; when he is waiting to be gracious, and to load us with his benefits?

I will mention another truth which ought to make us pray, and that is, that *if we ask, God will give to us much more than we ask.* Abraham asked of God that Ishmael might live before him. He thought "Surely this is the promised seed: I cannot expect that Sarah will bear a child in her old age. God has promised me a seed, and surely it must be this child of Hagar. Oh that Ishmael might live before thee." God granted him that, but he gave him Isaac as well, and all the blessings of the covenant. There is Jacob, he kneels down to pray, and asks the Lord to give him bread to eat and raiment to put on. But what did his God give him? When he came back to Bethel he had two bands, thousands of sheep and camels, and much wealth. God had heard him and done exceeding abundantly above what he asked. It is said of David, "The king asked life of thee, and thou gavest him length of days," yea, gave him not only length of days himself, but a throne for his sons throughout all generations, till David went in and sat before the Lord, overpowered with the Lord's goodness. "Well," say you, "but is that true of New Testament prayers?" Yes, it is so with the New Testament pleaders, whether saints or sinners. They brought a man to Christ sick of the palsy, and asked him to heal him, and he said, "Son, thy sins be forgiven thee." He had not asked that, had he? No, but God gives greater things than we ask for. Hear that poor, dying thief's humble prayer, "Lord, remember me when thou comest into thy kingdom." Jesus replies, "To-day shalt thou be with me in Paradise." He had not dreamed of such an honour. Even the story of the Prodigal teaches us this. He resolved to say, "I am not worthy to be called thy son; make me as one of thy hired servants." What is the answer? "This my son was dead, and is alive again: bring forth the best robe and put it on him; put a ring on his hands, and shoes on his feet." Once get into the position of an asker, and you shall have what you never asked for, and never thought to receive. The text is often misquoted: "God is able to do exceeding abundantly above all that we *can* ask, or even think." We *could* ask, if we were but more sensible and had more faith, for the very greatest things, but God is willing to give us infinitely more than we do ask.

At this moment I believe that God's church might have inconceivable blessings if she were but ready now to pray. Did you ever notice that wonderful picture in the eighth chapter of the Revelation? It is worthy of careful notice. I shall not attempt to explain it in its connection, but merely point to the picture as it hangs on the wall by itself. Read on —"When he had opened the seventh seal, there was silence in heaven about the space of half an hour." Silence in heaven: there were no anthems, no hallelujahs, not an angel stirred a wing. Silence in heaven! Can you imagine it? And look! You see seven angels standing before God, and to them are given seven trumpets. There they wait, trumpet in hand, but there is no sound. Not a single note of cheer or warning during an interval which was sufficiently long to provoke lively emotion, but short enough to prevent impatience. Silence unbroken, profound, awful reigned in heaven. Action is suspended in heaven, the centre of all activity. "And another angel came and stood at the altar, having a golden censer." There he stands, but no offering is presented: everything has come to a standstill. What can possibly set it in motion? "And there was given unto him much incense, that he should offer it with the prayers of all saints upon the golden altar which was before the throne." Prayer is presented together with the merit of the Lord Jesus. Now, see what will happen. "And the smoke of the incense, which came with the prayers of the saints, ascended up before God out of the angel's hands." That is the key of the whole matter. Now you will see: the angel begins to work: he takes the censer, fills it with the altar fire, and flings it down upon the earth, "and there were voices, and thunderings, and lightnings, and an earthquake." "And the seven angels which had the seven trumpets prepared themselves to sound." Everything is moving now. As soon as the prayers of the saints were mixed with the incense of Christ's eternal merit, and begun to smoke up from the altar, then prayer became effectual. Down fell the living coals among the sons of men, while the angels of the divine providence, who stood still before, sound their thunderblasts, and the will of the Lord is done. Such is the scene in heaven in a certain measure even to this day. Bring hither the incense. Bring hither the prayers of the saints! Set them on fire with Christ's merits, and on the golden altar let them smoke before the Most High: then shall we see the Lord at work, and his will shall be done on earth as it is in heaven God send his blessing with these words, for Christ's sake. Amen.

PRAYER—ITS DISCOURAGEMENTS AND ENCOURAGEMENTS.

A Sermon

DELIVERED BY

C. H. SPURGEON,

AT THE METROPOLITAN TABERNACLE, NEWINGTON,

On a Thursday Evening, in the summer of 1861.

"But he answered her not a word."—Matthew xv. 23.

WITH Christian men it is not a matter of question as to whether God hears prayer or not. There is no fact in mathematics which has been more fully demonstrated than this fact in experience—that God heareth prayer. About some other things in Christianity, young believers may have a question; but about the Lord's answering prayer, even they cannot entertain a doubt; while, to the old and advanced believer, who has tested the power of the mercy-seat, and proved it thousands of times, it is a matter about which he never allows a question, for he knows that, as surely as that he himself exists, and that God lives in heaven, the prayers of puny but believing man have power to move the almighty arm of God.

Probably, in the course of the past week, some of us have met with as many as a dozen special answers to prayer. Sceptics spend their sneers in vain upon us. Facts are blessed, as well as stubborn, things. Men may say that it is not possible that the cries and petitions of man can move the heart of God. They may question it, they may raise doubts about it; but doubts upon this matter never enter our minds, they never touch our inner consciousness, for we know that answers to prayer are a fact; and until we can doubt that we are men, until we can doubt that we breathe the air or live on food, until we can doubt that which we see with our eyes and touch with our hands, we cannot doubt that God is, " and that he is a Rewarder of them that diligently seek him."

Of course, our confidence that God answers prayer is not an argument to another man. He who has not tried it cannot have proved it for himself. But to those who have tried prayer, and proved it, we insist upon it that it amounts to a demonstration as clear as logic itself can make it, when, having called upon God, not merely once or twice, but thousands of times throughout their lives, they have invariably met with the same result, namely, a gracious answer from him who really does and will hear prayer. Yet there is, sometimes, a strange thing which puzzles the earnest believer. There are times when it does seem as if his prayer were not heard, for certainly it is not answered, or, at least, not answered as he expected. There are seasons, even with God's true children,—

"When at his feet they groan,
Yet bring their wants away."

They present their petition before the Lord, yet their request does not seem to be complied with there and then. To those who know that this is no strange thing which has happened unto them, it is not a matter which staggers their faith, for they can say, with Ralph Erskine, that—

"They're heard when answered soon or late;
Yea, heard when they no answer get;
Are kindly answered when refused,
And treated well when harshly used."

They understand that God's delays are not denials, and that his denials to particular requests are only intended to let us know that he will give us something richer and better than we have asked. If he doth not pay thy prayers in silver, he will pay them in gold; and if thy prayers be long in coming back, they shall be like a richly-laden ship which is all the longer on its way because of its costly freight, and which shall amply repay for the time spent on the voyage by the richness of the cargo it brings from the far country.

Yet I must again remind you that to some, and especially to young seekers, it is a staggering experience when, having long cried to Jesus, he answers them not a word; when, having prayed to him, they have seen no smile upon his benignant face, and have heard no word of comfort from those lips of his, which drop like honeycombs to others, but seem to be as dry wells to them. I am going to discuss this matter now as God the Holy Ghost may enable me, and I pray that he may make it comforting to many a distracted spirit. May some be graciously brought up out of the deep darkness of their prison-house, and be caused to rejoice in the liberty wherewith Christ makes his people free!

I shall speak of the text, first, in reference to *those who have been praying for themselves;* and, secondly, in regard to *those who have been praying for others.*

I. First, then, I am going to describe the case of SOME WHO HAVE BEEN PRAYING FOR THEMSELVES, but to whom, as yet, Christ has answered not a word.

I can describe the case of these people experimentally, for I have felt the same. As some of you know, I passed through five years of agony, during which my young spirit was crushed almost to despair. During those five years, if ever a child prayed to God, I did; and if ever a lad groaned, out of a longing spirit, to Jehovah in heaven, I did. You may remember that part of John Bunyan's "Grace Abounding" where he speaks of the exercises of his soul, and especially of his terror because his prayers seemed to reverberate from a brazen heaven, and not to pierce the skies. Such, too, was my experience. I am sure that I was sincere in my prayers, and in my groanings that could not be uttered; but yet, answers to my supplications there were none. I can speak, therefore, I trust, with all the more power because I can speak, sympathetically, of something which I have known and felt.

Poor soul, you have been praying for these last few months; and your complaint is, that you have not had one gracious answer to your petitions, or one precious promise applied with power to your soul. Let me remind you that the poor woman, of whom our text speaks, was in a similar condition. Indeed, not only did she not receive a promise, but she received a rebuff from Christ. Instead of a gracious invitation to come unto him, she had almost a command to go from him. When he did speak to her, he said, "I am not sent but unto the lost sheep of the house of Israel." Yours, then; is not a singular case. You must not sit down in despair because no promise has come home to your soul. Still continue to cry unto the Lord, still be constantly in prayer unto him. He will, he must, hear you by-and-by, and you shall have your heart's desire.

"Yes," you say, "but not only have I not had a promise, but I have not had any comforting sign whatever. The more I pray, the worse I feel; and the more I groan, the more it seems that I may groan. If my prayers are arrows, they are arrows that fall downwards, and return into my own heart instead of flying up to God's ear. I must pray, I cannot help it; my soul would burst if it did not express itself in words; yet my prayer does me little or no good. I rise from my knees more distressed than ever, and I come out of my closet, not as a man released from prison, but as he that passes from one dungeon to another. The Lord hath refused to listen to my supplication; he hath forgotten to be gracious, in anger he hath shut up the bowels of his compassion." Perhaps you even go further than this, and say, "I feel as if my prayer never would be answered. Something within me tells me that I may pray, but that, after all, I shall perish; that there may be mercy for all others in the world, but not for me. I may lift the knocker of mercy's gate, but the sound shall be only like that of a hammer upon my coffin; there shall be no music of hope as I rap at the golden gate. I know that God heareth prayer, but not the prayer of the wicked; that is an abomination unto the Lord. Such, I fear, is my prayer; and, therefore, he will not hear me.' Ah, poor soul! let me remind you that there is nothing that is so deluding as feelings. Christians cannot live by feelings, nor can you. Let me further tell you that these feelings are the work of Satan, they are not right feelings. What right have you to set up your feelings against the Word of Christ? He has expressly said, "For every one that asketh receiveth; and he that seeketh findeth; and to him that knocketh it shall be opened." It is not a question whether a man who truly prays shall be saved. He is saved, though he may not know it;

he has the germs of salvation in his prayer. "Behold, he prayeth," means, "Behold, he liveth; behold, he is accepted; behold, heaven openeth its gates for him." He prays; Jehovah hears; mercy answers; the man is blessed. I pray thee, then, let not thy feelings fly in the teeth of God's promises, but hope on; for, though thy case be very sad, it is not a strange one, and there is hope for thee.

Having thus described your case, let me now warn you of a danger. There is a danger to which all those are exposed who have prayed for any length of time without consciously receiving an answer from God, and that is, either to get despairing thoughts of themselves or else hard thoughts of Christ. That poor Canaanite was a brave woman. She came of an accursed race, but certainly there was a special blessing resting upon her. If you or I had been there when Christ spake to her so harshly, I wonder whether we should have taken his remarks so well as she did. Do you remember times when Christ has been silent to you? If so, you can imagine what her feelings must have been when "he answered her not a word." Some of you, who have quick tempers, would have said, if that had been your experience, "Is this the Messiah of whom we have heard so much, and who is said to be so ready to relieve the distressed? Here have we been crying to him in tones that seemed piercing enough to make a heart of adamant melt for us, yet he has not deigned to answer us. He seems to be stone deaf; or, if he hears us, he does not condescend to give us any reply. Is this the kind and tender spirit of which we have heard so much?" And when at last he spake, and said, "It is not meet to take the children's bread, and to cast it to dogs,"—some would have said, "If he would not grant us our request, he need not have used insulting epithets to us. Dogs, indeed! What means he by that term? He means that we do not belong to the favoured race of Israel; and a fine thing it would be for us if we did. Are they not oppressed under the Roman yoke, and cast off like withered branches?" The Canaanite woman might have said, "Why does he call me a dog? Am I not a woman, and an honest woman, too, and one who does not deserve such a title as that? I wish I had never asked for mercy at his hands. To get such an insult as to have the name of 'dog' thrown at me, is too bad; and I will not endure it." That may be a strong way of putting the matter, but you and I have probably put it in just that way. Have we not thought, because Christ has not answered our prayers, that there was a mistake about his graciousness,—that he was not the Christ that some said he was—that he did not mean his invitation when he said, "Come unto me, all ye that labour and are heavy laden, and I will give you rest;" that he desired to tantalize poor souls, making them pray and cry to him while he meant to be deaf to their requests? Have you not had hard thoughts of Christ like those? If you have, I pray you to put them all away from you, and not to fall into this snare of Satan. Jesus is the good Christ still. Though he may seem to be stony-hearted, he is not so in reality; he is always tender, he hath bowels of compassion. Slander him not, then; but be of good courage, and still cry unto him.

Possibly, Satan says to you, "Your prayer is not of the right sort; and, therefore, you never will be heard." Yes, but that Canaanitish woman's prayer to Christ was of the right sort, yet "he answered her not a word." Notice what her prayer was: "Have mercy on me, O Lord, thou Son of David." She gave him the right name. She might have said, "Thou Son of Abraham." That would have signified that he was the one in whom all the nations of the earth were to be blessed. That was the covenant which the Lord made with Abraham; but this woman said, "Thou Son of David." The covenant made with David related, not only to blessing and increase, but also to a kingdom, so this woman seemed to say to Christ, "Man of sorrows though thou art, thou art of royal blood; thy visage is more marred than that of any man, and thou wearest not a diadem, yet art thou King." She did, as it were, pay him the homage which Pilate unwittingly paid him when he placed over his head the inscription, "This is Jesus the King of the Jews." "Thou Son of David,"—she knew how to address him.

Then notice how she pleaded with him; she appealed, not to his justice, but to his mercy, to the love of his tender and compassionate heart: "Have mercy on me." This was the plea of the publican, the prayer by which he was justified, "God be merciful to me a sinner." There was nothing wrong in this woman's prayer to Christ, yet "he answered her not a word." So then, poor heart, thy prayers also may be right and proper, and yet not be answered. If they are not answered, faint not; but continue to pray. The Lord will yet reply to thy petition; he will open the windows of heaven, and shower down his mercy upon thee, and thou shalt receive it with a gladsome heart.

Now, having reminded you of your danger, let me call to your recollection the grounds of your comfort. What had this woman to comfort her? Well, first, she had Jesus Christ's face. He said to her, "It is not meet to take the children's bread, and to cast it to dogs." Now, my idea of the Saviour is that he could not utter that hard sentence without, somehow or other, letting the woman see, by the very expression of his countenance, that he was keeping something back, and that there was love yet in store for her. You know that your children can soon detect the meaning of what you say to them, for they can read your face as well as your words. So can poor beggars, and so could this poor woman who was begging of Christ so hard for her child. "Ay," she seemed to say, "thy lips may utter hard words, but thy loving eyes flash not the fire that should go with such severe sentences. I see a tear lifting up thine eyelids even now. I believe the language of thy face; that marred face—marred with sympathy for others' sorrows, marred with the cares and burdens of others, which have weighed thee down,—will not let me believe that thy heart is harsh." So, sinner, for thy comfort, let me beseech thee to look into the face of Jesus Christ. Dost thou believe that he—the Son of Mary, the Man of sorrows, grief's acquaintance, —can reject thee? O Christ, when I picture thee before my eyes, especially when I see thy face bedewed with bloody sweat in Gethsemane, and listen to thine agonized groanings in the garden,

I cannot, and I will not, believe that thou canst ever reject a supplicant who cries to thee, "Be merciful to me!"

Or, if that shall not be enough to cheer thee, remember that this poor woman had something more to comfort her, for she had heard the story of Christ's good deeds. She had been told, even in Tyre, what he had done in Capernaum, and she had heard, though far away, what he had done in Chorazin, so she believed that he, who had done such good deeds to others, could not be hard to her. So, sinner, let me tell thee of the good deeds that Christ hath done to others. I could bring thee hundreds, or even thousands, who could truly say, with the psalmist, "This poor man cried, and the Lord heard him." Speak with your eyes, my brethren, and bear witness to the fact which I now testify,—has not God heard your prayers, though you were sinners even as others, as vile by nature, and as hopeless by depravity? Did he not bring us up out of the horrible pit, out of the miry clay, and set our feet upon a rock, and establish our goings? Sinner, he who did this for us will and must do the like for you if you plead for mercy through the precious blood of his dear Son.

But you have one comfort which this poor woman never had; she could not be told that Christ had died for her. Sinner, thou who art seeking Christ, say not that he is harsh, and that he will not hear thee. Come thou with me, and by faith look upon him on the cross. Canst thou behold his thorn-crown, with its lancets piercing his blessed brow, and the tears streaming down his cheeks already crimsoned with his bloody sweat? Canst thou see his hands and feet as, pierced by the nails, they become founts of blood? There he hangs, naked, despised and rejected of men. Yet he endured all this agony that he might save sinners; then, how canst thou think so wickedly of him as to suppose that he, who once died, the Just for the unjust, now that he lives again, has an adamantine heart, and no bowels of compassion? No, by his wounds, I beseech thee to trust him; by his bloody sweat, I implore thee to continue thy supplication unto him; by his rent side, I urge thee to wrestle with him yet again, for he will hear thee, his mercy shall come unto thee, and thou shalt rejoice in it.

Lend me your ears while I give you a word of counsel as to what you ought to do. It is the Spirit of God who has taught you to pray. He has made you feel your need of a Saviour; it is he who has compelled you to fall upon your knees, and to cry for mercy. Now remember that it is your duty, as well as your privilege, to obey the voice of the Holy Spirit. What does that voice say to you? "Believe on the Lord Jesus Christ, and thou shalt be saved." That is to say, even though thy prayers be not answered, in the teeth of every hard thought and every harsh word, trust Christ with thy soul. If thou doest that, thou art saved there and then. The way of salvation is not, "Pray, and be saved;" but, "Believe, and be saved." Christ said, "He that believeth and is baptized shall be saved; but he that believeth not shall be damned." Remember that your main business is not with answers to prayer, but with your answer to God's call to you; and his call to you, poor conscience-stricken, awakened sinner, is, "Come unto me, and I will give you rest." Come, then, to Christ just as you are, and so shall you find that answer to your prayers which has been so long delayed. Still keep on wrestling with God, until your prayers are answered. Jericho's walls did not fall down the first day the hosts of Israel went round them; but they compassed the city seven days, and, on the seventh day, the walls fell flat to the ground. Elijah, on the top of Carmel, did not bring the rain the first time he prayed; but he said to his servant, "Go again seven times;" and there have been many other instances in which God has delayed the blessing, but has given it at the last.

I have thus preached, as God has enabled me, to poor seeking souls. O Spirit of God, apply the Word, and bring sinners to Christ, that they may find mercy in his wounds!

II. Now, for a few minutes, let us turn to the case of THOSE BELIEVERS, WHO HAVE LONG BEEN PRAYING FOR OTHERS WITHOUT ANY APPARENT RESULT.

There is a father here, who has been pleading with God for his daughter; and though years of supplication have passed away, she is still unconverted, and as hardened as ever. There is a mother here, who has laid her children upon her bosom, in prayer, as once she did for nourishment when they were but babes; and yet, though she cries day and night for them, they are not saved. My dear brothers and sisters, I beseech you never to give up praying for your children, or your other relatives, because, although God may not answer you for a while, you shall certainly yet have the desire of your heart. Let me just give you one or two instances in which the power of prayer has been distinctly proved.

There was a young man who, because of his love for sin, and his wish to be easy in it, became an infidel. As I have often said, infidelity is far more a matter of the heart than of the head. I am persuaded that men think there is no God because they wish there were none. They find it hard to believe in God, and to go on in sin, so they try to get an easy conscience by denying his existence. This young man was not only an infidel, but he was a very earnest one, and he used to distribute certain newspapers brought out by the infidel press. His employer was just as earnest a Christian as the young man was an infidel, and he used constantly to burn those papers whenever he could get hold of them; but the young man just as perseveringly procured others, and tried to lend them among the apprentices and journeymen, that he might advance his own views. He was always a bold blasphemer, and a desperate sinner. He cared little what others thought of him, and he was, at least, honest in his iniquities. One day, in a joke, he said to one of his companions, "I'll tell you what I will do. I'll show you that there is nothing in any of the Methodist cant and hypocrisy; the very first time there is a prayer-meeting at such-and-such a chapel, I'll go and offer myself to the minister to be prayed for by the members, and I shall get some fun out of them." He went; and, with all the impudence and coolness possible, told the minister that he was a poor troubled soul, who wished to find peace, and that he would be very glad if the brethren would pray for him. He did not know what he was doing; for, whether it was that the very deed awoke his slumbering conscience, or whether the Spirit of God was pleased to show the sovereignty of his grace at that moment, I cannot tell; but, as soon as one or two humble individuals had prayed for this young man, with tears in their eyes, he was down on his knees, with tears in his own eyes, praying for himself. Nay, not only did he pray then, but he never ceased to pray, and he is praying still, for he could not live without prayer. He found it no matter of fun, after all; he intended to tempt God, and to vex his people; but in that very act of sin he was arrested and converted. Do you think, then, if prayer only asked for in sport prevailed with God, that he will not hear your earnest cries for your own offspring? O Christians, be fervent in your supplications, for God will surely hear you, and your children shall be saved!

Another instance. There lived, in the village of Berwick St. John, in Wiltshire, a godly woman who had an ungodly husband. He not only hated good things, but he hated her for her goodness, for he turned her out of doors, on a Sabbath night, because she had gone to the meetinghouse. She, like a prudent woman, never told her neighbours, but walked the fields alone that she might not be noticed by others, and that her husband's shame might not be discovered. She was sometimes driven to the greatest straits, and to a sadness which seemed as if it would bring her to a premature grave. She resolved to pray for her husband, one hour a day, for a year. She did so; and, at the end of the year, he was as bad as before, if not worse. Then she thought she would try another six months; her faith was weak, and she was going to give her husband up then if her prayers were not heard. This was wrong, for we must not limit the Holy One of Israel. But it so happened that, ere the six months were over, her husband came home once, in the middle of the day, looking dejected and downcast. Like a true and tender wife, she asked what was the matter with him, but he could not tell her. He went upstairs, he did not want his dinner, and he did not return to his work that afternoon, for God was at work with him. When his wife got him to speak, he said, "O wife, I can't pray!" "Do you want to pray?" she asked, and he replied, "Oh, I must pray! I do not know how it was; but, about twelve o'clock to-day, such a strange feeling came over me. I feel that I am a lost man, for I cannot pray; will you pray for me?" You may guess what her feelings were when asked by that obdurate wretch to pray for him. She did pray, then they prayed together, and their united prayers were answered. The next Sabbath, they were both in God's house; and, in a few more Sabbaths, they were side by side at the Lord's table. The godly woman's prayers were heard at last, and God again proved that he has not said to the seed of Jacob, " Seek ye me in vain."

Yet another instance. There was a captain, whose name I will not give in full just now; I will call him Mitchell, for that will suffice. This captain was a godly man, and he once went to sea, leaving his wife at home expecting soon to give birth to their firstborn child. While he was at sea, one day, a time of deep solemnity came over him, in the course of which he penned a prayer. This prayer was for his wife and for his yet unborn child. He put the prayer into the oak chest in which he kept his papers. He never came home again, for he died at sea. His chest was brought home to his wife; she did not open it to look at his papers, but she thought they might be of use to her son when he should grow up. That son lived; and, at the age of sixteen, he joined a regiment at Boston. In that regiment, he became exceedingly debauched, profane, blasphemous, and sinful in every way. At the age of fifty-four, while he was living in sin with a wicked woman, it struck him that he would like to look through the contents of the old chest which his father had left. He opened it, and, at the bottom, found, tied up with red tape, a paper, on the outside of which was written, "The prayer of Mitchell K—— for his wife and child." He opened it, and read it; it was a most fervent plea with God that the man's wife and child might belong to Christ, written fifty-four years back, and before that child was born. He shut it up, and put it where it was before, and said that he would not look into "that cursed old chest" again. But that did not matter, for the prayer had got into his heart, and he could not lock his heart up in that chest. He became thoroughly miserable; and the wretched woman, with whom he lived, asked him what was the matter with him. He told her what he had read in that paper, and she said she hoped he would not become a hypocrite. All the jokes and frivolities of his companions could not take out the dart which God had sent into his heart; and, ere long, by true repentance and by living faith, that man was in Christ a saved soul, married honourably to the woman with whom he had lived in sin, and walking in uprightness, serving his father's God, as the result of a prayer which had lain in an old chest for fifty-four years, but which God's eye had seen all the while, and which, at last, he had answered when the set time had come.

Be of good courage, all ye who are pleading for your children, for God will yet answer your supplications. As one of the old divines says, "Prayer is the rope which hangs down on earth, and there is a bell in heaven which it rings, and which God hears." Pull that rope again to-night, praying father and mother. Make the great bell in heaven ring again and again, and let its notes be, "Save my children; save my husband; save my wife; save my brother; let my sister live before thee." Your prayers shall be heard, and God shall yet grant your requests. The instances I have given you are authenticated, and I could give you more which have come under my own notice; but time fails, and I have said enough upon that matter.

Let me just preach the gospel at the close plainly and simply, and then I have done. The gospel is this—Jesus Christ, of the seed of David, was born of the Virgin Mary, was crucified, dead and buried; the third day he rose again from the dead, and ascended into heaven. He came into the world to die for sinners; he hung upon the cross and bled for sinners. All that he died for will be saved: he died for sinners, and sinners will be saved.

Your only question is, are you in the true Scriptural sense of the term a confessed and acknowledged sinner? If so, Jesus died for you. On my door step the other night, when I reached home after preaching, stood a man. I asked him what he wanted, and he fell on his knees and cried, "I want to know what I must do to be saved." I thought the man was mad to be there at that time of night on such an errand; but he cried out concerning his sin, told me I did not know his guilt, that he had been near committing suicide, and that he dared not go home to rest till he was told the way of salvation. "Well," said I, "I will tell you;" but I could not make it plain to his poor darkened understanding until I told him a story which I have often told concerning an event which happened to me some time ago. One evening when sitting to see enquirers, there came an Irishman upstairs. "Well, Pat," I said. "How's your riverence?" said he. "Don't call me reverence," I said, "because I am no reverence at all: but how is it you have not gone to your priest?" Said he, "I have come here to ask you a question, and if you can answer it, that will do." "Well, what is the question?" "Why, you said, last Sunday, that God would forgive sin; what I want to know is how that can be, for I have been such a great sinner that if he doesn't punish me, he ought." Well, I thought I had got a sinner to deal with, and one who spoke from his heart what he felt. I said, "God pardons sinners for the sake of Jesus." But he replied, "I do not know what you mean." I told him that Jesus Christ died, and that for the sake of that, God pardoned sinners. Still he could not comprehend, and he said, "I want to know how God can be just: he ought to punish sin, and yet he does not; how can that be?" "Well," said I, "suppose you had been committing a murder, and the judge were to say you must be hanged." "I should deserve it," said he. "Well, how is Pat to be got off, and yet the sentence to be carried out?" "Faith!" says he, "that's what I don't exactly see." "Well," I continued, "suppose I go to the Queen, and say, 'Please, your Majesty, I am very fond of this poor Irishman; I admit he ought to be hanged, but I want him to live: will you be so good as to have me hanged instead?' Well, she couldn't say, "Yes," Pat; but suppose she did, and suppose I went to prison and were hanged instead of you, the murderer, would the Queen be unjust in letting you go afterwards?" "Faith!" says he, "I shouldn't ask that; how could she meddle with me afterwards? because I should say a gentleman was hung for me, and sure enough I was free. But," he added, "I don't see what that has to do with the matter." "Why just this," said I,—"Jesus Christ loved sinners so much that rather than they should perish he was content to die himself instead of them; and now, since Christ died for sinners, can you not see how God can be just in letting sinners go free?" "Oh, yes," says he, "I see it now; but then how am I to know that Christ died for me, so that I cannot be punished? You say there are some people that Christ died for, so that God could not punish them; then how am I to know whether I belong to them?" "Why, by this—are you a sinner? Because if you are—not in the matter of compliment, but if you are really so, and feel it, then Christ died in your stead, and you cannot die because God will never enforce the sentence twice; he will not ask payment first at the bleeding Surety's hands and then at ours." I think I see that man putting his hands together, and saying, "There! that's Bible, I know, that's true, that must be true; no man could have made that up; that's wonderful; I know it's God's Bible, for it just fits me; I am a poor sinner, and God has pardoned me." And he went on his way rejoicing. Now, doesn't that fit you, too? What would you give to-night if you could believe that Jesus Christ was punished instead of you, so that all your sins shall never be mentioned any more, but all be forgiven, because God punished Christ Jesus instead of you? I repeat, the only way you can tell is by answering this question—Are you a sinner? "Well, we are all sinners," says one. No, no; you are all sinners, but you are not all the sort of sinners that I mean. Some people say they are sinners, but they don't mean it. They are like the beggars in London apparently full of sores. Many a man we see in the streets with his leg tied up, and seeming desperately lame, will take off the bandage when he gets to his lodging house, and will dance before he goes to bed at night. Another man standing against the wall says he is stone blind; but he will see to count his money when he gets home, after begging all day. There are plenty of people of that sort. Now, if I invited the lame and the blind, do you think I should receive those who were only shamming? No, I would only have those who were really lame and blind. So Christ died only for those who are real sinners.

Exposition by C. H. Spurgeon.

EPHESIANS II.

Verse 1. *And you hath he quickened,—*

Is it so? Can anyone lay his hand on your shoulder, and say right into your ear, "You hath he quickened"? If so, why this deadness of spirit? Why this worldliness? Why these wanderings? "You hath he quickened,"—

1, 2. *Who were dead in trespasses and sins; wherein in time past ye walked according to the course of this world,—*

You were dead to all that was good, but you were alive enough to that which was evil. It seems, from this passage, that dead men walk, yet not in the way of God, but "according to the course of this world,"—

2, 3. *According to the prince of the power of the air, the spirit that now worketh in the children of disobedience: among whom also we all had our conversation in times past in the lusts of our flesh, fulfilling the desires of the flesh and of the mind; and were by nature the children of wrath, even as others.*

We were not in the least better, by nature, than the very worst of men; and if we were any better in practice, it was only because we were restrained by providence and by grace from going into gross sin, as others did. Look unto the hole of the pit whence ye were digged, and see how humble was your origin. If you are proud of your fine feathers, as the peacock is, remember his black legs; see whence you came, and recollect the sin from which you were delivered. Bless God for your deliverance, and be humble as you think of the grace that has caused you to differ from others.

4, 5. *But God, who is rich in mercy, for his great love wherewith he loved us, even when we were dead in sins, hath quickened us together with Christ, (by grace ye are saved;)*

This is a wondrous truth, that God loves the sinner even while he is dead in sin. This love is not caused by any goodness in him, for he is dead, he is wrapped up in the cerements of his sins. There is nothing lovable about him; yet God, "for his great love wherewith he loved us, even when we were dead in sins, hath quickened us together with Christ."

6—8. *And hath raised us up together, and made us sit together in heavenly places in Christ Jesus: that in the ages to come he might shew the exceeding riches of his grace in his kindness toward us through Christ Jesus. For by grace are ye saved through faith; and that not of yourselves: it is the gift of God.*

That great truth was put, in the 5th verse, into a parenthesis. Why did Paul write it twice? Because we cannot too often be reminded that we were saved by grace. It is a truth which we so soon forget that we had need to have it rung in our ears as by a peal of bells, "By grace are ye saved, through faith; and that not of yourselves, it is the gift of God."

9. *Not of works, lest any man should boast.*

God cannot endure boasting; and one great object of the plan of salvation by grace is to extinguish boasting, to shut it out. It is intolerable to God, he cannot endure it.

10. *For we are his workmanship,*

If we have anything good in us, it was all made by him.

10—12. *Created in Christ Jesus unto good works, which God hath before ordained that we should walk in them. Wherefore remember, that ye being in time past Gentiles in the flesh, who are called Uncircumcision by that which is called the Circumcision in the flesh made by hands; that at that time ye were without Christ, being aliens from the commonwealth of Israel, and strangers from the covenants of promise, having no hope, and without God in the world:*

That is a true description of our Anglo-Saxon forefathers, who were certainly heathen of the heathen, the wildest and most savage of men when Paul wrote this Epistle; and yet, by sovereign grace, we have been brought to the very forefront of the nations of the earth, and we are no longer without God, nor yet without hope, nor yet without Christ, neither are we now strangers to the covenants of promise, nor aliens from the commonwealth of Israel.

13—22. *But now in Christ Jesus ye who sometimes were far off are made nigh by the blood of Christ. For he is our peace, who hath made both one, and hath broken down the middle wall of partition between us; having abolished in his flesh the enmity, even the law of commandments contained in ordinances; for to make in himself of twain one new man, so making peace; and that he might reconcile both unto God in one body by the cross, having slain the enmity thereby: and came and preached peace to you which were afar off, and to them that were nigh. For through him we both have access by one Spirit unto the Father. Now therefore ye are no more strangers and foreigners, but fellow-citizens with the saints, and of the household of God; and are built upon the foundation of the apostles and prophets, Jesus Christ himself being the chief corner stone; in whom all the building fitly framed together groweth unto an holy temple in the Lord: in whom ye also are builded together for an habitation of God through the Spirit.*

Happy are the people who enjoy these high privileges.

EJACULATORY PRAYER.

A Sermon

Delivered on Lord's-Day Evening, September 9th, 1877, by

C. H. SPURGEON,

AT THE METROPOLITAN TABERNACLE, NEWINGTON.

"So I prayed to the God of heaven."—Nehemiah ii. 4.

As we have already seen in the reading of the Scripture, Nehemiah had made enquiry as to the state of the city of Jerusalem, and the tidings he heard caused him bitter grief. "Why should not my countenance be sad," he said, "when the city, the place of my fathers' sepulchres, lieth waste, and the gates thereof are consumed with fire?" He could not endure that it should be a mere ruinous heap—that city which was once beautiful for situation and the joy of the whole earth. Laying the matter to heart, he did not begin to speak to other people about what they would do, nor did he draw up a wonderful scheme about what might be done if so many thousand people joined in the enterprise; but it occurred to him that he would do something himself. This is just the way that practical men start a matter. The unpractical will plan, arrange, and speculate about what may be done, but the genuine, thorough-going lover of Zion puts this question to himself—"What can you do? Nehemiah, what can you do yourself? Come, it has to be done, and you are the man that is to do it—at least, to do your share. What can you do?" Coming so far, he resolved to set apart a time for prayer. He never had it off his mind for nearly four months. Day and night Jerusalem seemed written on his heart, as if the name were painted on his eyeballs. He could only see Jerusalem. When he slept he dreamed about Jerusalem. When he woke, the first thought was "Poor Jerusalem!" and before he fell asleep again his evening prayer was for the ruined walls of Jerusalem. The man of one thing, you know, is a terrible man; and when one single passion has absorbed the whole of his manhood something will be sure to come of it. Depend upon that. The desire of his heart will develop into some open demonstration, especially if he talks the matter over before God in prayer. Something did come of this. Before long Nehemiah had an opportunity. Men of God, if you want to serve God and cannot find the propitious occasion, wait awhile in prayer and your opportunity will break on your path like a sunbeam. There was never a true and valiant heart that failed to find a fitting sphere somewhere or other in his service. Every diligent labourer is needed in some part of his vineyard. You may have to linger, you may seem as if you stood in the market idle, because the Master would not engage you, but wait there in prayer, and with your heart boiling over with a warm purpose, and your chance will come. The hour will need its man, and if you are ready, you, as a man, shall not be without your hour. God sent Nehemiah an opportunity. That opportunity came, 'tis true, in a way which he could not have expected. It came through his own sadness of heart. This matter preyed upon his mind till he began to look exceedingly unhappy. I cannot tell whether others remarked it, but the king whom he served, when he went into court with the royal goblet, noticed the distress on the cupbearer's countenance, and he said to him, "Why is thy countenance sad, seeing thou art not sick? This is nothing else but sorrow of heart." Nehemiah little knew that his prayer was making the occasion for him. The prayer was registering itself upon his face. His fasting was making its marks upon his visage; and, though he did not know it, he was, in that way, preparing the opportunity for himself when he went in before the king. But you see when the opportunity did come there was trouble with it, for he says, "I was very sore afraid." You want to serve God, young man: you want to be at work. Perhaps you do not know what that work involves. It is not all pleasure. You are longing for the battle, young soldier: you have not smelt powder yet, but when you have been in a battle, and have had a few cuts, or a bullet or two have pierced you, you may not feel quite so eager for the fray. Yet the courageous man sets those things aside, and is ready to serve his country or his sovereign, and so the courageous Christian puts all difficulty aside, and he is ready to serve his comrades and his God, cost what it may. What if I should be sore afraid? yet so let it be, my God, if thus there shall be an opportunity to seek and to secure the welfare of Jerusalem for thy servant, who longs to promote it with all his heart.

Thus have we traced Nehemiah up to the particular point where our text concerns him. The king, Artaxerxes, having asked him why he was sad, he had an opportunity of telling him that the city of his fathers was a ruin. Thereupon the king asks him what he really wishes; by the manner of the question he would seem to imply an assurance that he means to help him. And here we are somewhat surprised to find that, instead of promptly answering the king—the answer is not given immediately—an incident occurs, a fact is related. Though he was a man who had lately given himself up to prayer and fasting, this little parenthesis occurs—"So I prayed to the God of heaven." My preamble leads up to this parenthesis. Upon this prayer I propose to preach. Three thoughts occur to me here, on each of which I intend to enlarge —*the fact that Nehemiah did pray just then; the manner of his prayer;* and, *the excellent kind of prayer he used.*

I. THE FACT THAT NEHEMIAH PRAYED CHALLENGES ATTENTION. He had been asked a question by his sovereign. The proper thing you would suppose was to answer it. Not so. Before he answered he prayed to the God of heaven. I do not suppose the king noticed the pause.

Probably the interval was not long enough to be noticed, but it was long enough for God to notice it—long enough for Nehemiah to have sought and have obtained guidance from God as to how to frame his answer to the king. Are you not surprised to find a man of God having time to pray to God between a question and an answer? Yet Nehemiah found that time. We are the more astonished at his praying, because he was so evidently perturbed in mind, for, according to the second verse, he was very sore afraid. When you are fluttered and put out you may forget to pray. Do you not, some of you, account it a valid excuse for omitting your ordinary devotion? At least, if anyone had said to you, "You did not pray when you were about that business," you would have replied, "How could I? There was a question that I was obliged to answer. I dared not hesitate. It was a king that asked it. I was in a state of confusion. I really was so distressed and terrified that I was not master of my own emotions. I hardly knew what I did. If I did not pray, surely the omission may be overlooked. I was in a state of wild alarm." Nehemiah, however, felt that if he was alarmed it was a reason for praying, not for forgetting to pray. So habitually was he in communion with God that as soon as he found himself in a dilemma he flew away to God, just as the dove would fly to hide herself in the clefts of the rock.

His prayer was the more remarkable on this occasion, because *he must have felt very eager about his object.* The king asks him what it is he wants, and his whole heart is set upon building up Jerusalem. Are not you surprised that he did not at once say, "O king, live for ever. I long to build up Jerusalem's walls. Give me all the help thou canst"? But no, eager as he was to pounce upon the desired object, he withdraws his hand until it is said, "So I prayed to the God of heaven." I confess I admire him. I desire also to imitate him. I would that every Christian's heart might have just that holy caution that did not permit him to make such haste as to find ill-speed. "Prayer and provender hinder no man's journey." Certainly, when the desire of our heart is close before us, we are anxious to seize it; but we shall be all the surer of getting the bird we spy in the bush to be a bird we grasp in the hand if we quietly pause, lift up our heart and pray unto the God of heaven.

It is all the more surprising that he should have deliberately prayed just then, because *he had been already praying for the past three or four months* concerning the selfsame matter. Some of us would have said, "That is the thing I have been praying for; now all I have got to do is to take it and use it. Why pray any more? After all my midnight tears and daily cries, after setting myself apart by fasting to cry unto the God of heaven, after such an anxious conference, surely at last the answer has come. What is to be done but to take the good that God provides me with and rejoice in it?" But no, you will always find that the man who has prayed much is the man to pray more. "For unto every one that hath shall be given, and he shall have abundance." If you do but know the sweet art of prayer, you are the man that will be often engaged in it. If you are familiar with the mercy-seat you will constantly visit it.

> "For who that knows the power of prayer
> But wishes to be often there?"

Although Nehemiah had been praying all this while, he nevertheless must offer another petition. " So I prayed to the God of heaven."

One thing more is worth recollecting, namely, that *he was in a king's palace*, and in the palace of a heathen king too ; and he was in the very act of handing up to the king the goblet of wine. He was fulfilling his part in the state festival, I doubt not, amongst the glare of lamps and the glitter of gold and silver, in the midst of princes and peers of the realm. Or even if it were a private festival with the king and queen only, yet still men generally feel so impressed on such occasions with the responsibility of their high position that they are apt to forget prayer. But this devout Israelite, at such a time and in such a place, when he stands at the king's foot to hold up to him the golden goblet, refrains from answering the king's question until first he has prayed to the God of heaven.

II. There is the fact, and I think it seems to prompt further enquiry. So we pass on to observe—THE MANNER OF THIS PRAYER.

Well, very briefly, it was what we call *ejaculatory prayer*—prayer which, as it were, hurls a dart and then it is done. It was not the prayer which stands knocking at mercy's door—knock, knock, knock ; but it was the concentration of many knocks into one. It was begun and completed, as it were, with one stroke. This ejaculatory prayer I desire to commend to you as among the very best forms of prayer.

Notice, how *very short* it must have been. It was introduced—slipped in—sandwiched in—between the king's question and Nehemiah's answer ; and, as I have already said, I do not suppose it took up any time at all that was appreciable—scarcely a second. Most likely the king never observed any kind of pause or hesitation, for Nehemiah was in such a state of alarm at the question that I am persuaded he did not allow any demur or vacillation to appear, but the prayer must have been offered like an electric flash, very rapidly indeed. In certain states of strong excitement it is wonderful how much the mind gets through in a short time. You may, perhaps, have dreamed, and your dream occupied, to your idea, an hour or two at the very least, yet it is probable —nay, I think certain—that all the dreaming is done at the moment you wake. You never dreamed at all when you were asleep : it was just in that instant when you woke that the whole of it went through your mind. As drowning men when rescued and recovered have been heard to say that while they were sinking they saw the whole panorama of their lives pass before them in a few seconds, so the mind must be capable of accomplishing much in a brief space of time. Thus the prayer was presented like the winking of an eye ; it was done intuitively ; yet done it was, and it proved to be a prayer that prevailed with God.

We know, also, that it must have been *a silent prayer* ; and not merely silent as to sounds but silent as to any outward signs—perfectly secret. Artaxerxes never knew that Nehemiah prayed, though he stood probably within a yard of him. He did not even move his lips as Hannah did, nor did he deem it right even to close his eyes, but the prayer was strictly within himself offered unto God. In the innermost shrine of the temple —in the holy of holies of his own secret soul—there did he pray. Short and silent was the prayer. It was a prayer on the spot. He did not go to his chamber as Daniel did, and open the window. Daniel was right, but this was a different occasion. Nehemiah could not have been permitted to retire from the palace just then. He did not even turn his face to the wall or seek a corner of the apartment. No, but there and then, with the cup in his hand, he prayed unto the God of heaven, and then answered the question of the king.

I have no doubt from the very wording of the text that it was *a very intense and direct prayer*. He says, "So I prayed to the God of heaven." That was Nehemiah's favourite name for God—the God of heaven. He knew whom he was praying to. He did not draw a bow at a venture and shoot his prayers anyhow, but he prayed to the God of heaven—a right straight prayer to God for the thing he wanted; and his prayer sped, though it occupied less, perhaps, than a second of time.

It was a prayer of *a remarkable kind*. I know it was so, because Nehemiah never forgot that he did pray it. I have prayed hundreds of times, and thousands of times, and not recollected any minute particular afterwards either as to the occasion that prompted or the emotions that excited me; but there are one or two prayers in my life that I never can forget. I have not jotted them down in a diary, but I remember when I prayed, because the time was so special and the prayer was so intense, and the answer to it was so remarkable. Now, Nehemiah's prayer was never, never erased from his memory; and when these words of history were written down he wrote that down, "So I prayed to the God of heaven"—a little bit of a prayer pushed in edgeways between a question and an answer—a mere fragment of devotion, as it seemed, and yet so important that it is put down in an historical document as a part of the history of the restitution and rebuilding of the city of Jerusalem, and a link in the circumstances which led up to that event of the most important character. Nehemiah felt it to be so, and therefore he makes the record—"So I prayed to the God of heaven."

III. Now, beloved friends, I come, in the third place, to recommend to you THIS EXCELLENT STYLE OF PRAYING.

I shall speak to the children of God mainly, to you that have faith in God. I beg you often, nay, I would ask you always to use this method of ejaculatory prayer. And I would to God, also, that some here who have never prayed before would offer an ejaculation to the God of heaven before they leave this house—that a short but fervent petition, something like that of the publican in the temple, might go up from you—"God be merciful to me a sinner."

To deal with this matter practically, then, *it is the duty and privilege of every Christian to have set times of prayer*. I cannot understand a man's keeping up the vitality of godliness unless he regularly retires for prayer, morning and evening at the very least. Daniel prayed three times a day, and David says, "Seven times a day will I praise thee." It is good for your hearts, good for your memory, good for your moral consistency that you should hedge about certain portions of time and say, "These belong to God. I shall do business with God at such-and-such a time, and try to be as punctual to my hours with him as I should be if I made an engagement to meet a friend." When Sir Thomas Abney was Lord Mayor of London the banquet somewhat troubled him, for Sir Thomas always had prayer with his family at a certain time. The difficulty was how to quit the banquet to keep up family devotion; but so important did he consider it that he vacated the chair, saying to a person near that he had a special engagement with a dear friend which he must keep. And he did keep it, and he returned again to his place, none of the company being the wiser, but he himself being all the better for observing his wonted habit of worship. Mrs. Rowe used to say that when her time came for prayer she would not give it up if the apostle Paul were preaching. Nay, she said, if all the twelve apostles were there, and could be heard at no other time, she would not absent herself from her closet when the set time came round. Well, I do not feel very sure that my scruples would go quite so far, for, I think, if I had the opportunity of hearing the apostle at the time when I am wont to pray, and could not at any other time hear him, I should postpone my prayer to hear the sermon, nor would there be any impropriety in the arrangement; probably it would show a little shrewd sense. Yet, as a general principle, it is desirable to be punctual and punctilious in respect to your private as well as your public devotions. Be not negligent, but vigilant; never remiss, but always regular in keeping up your appointed seasons of prayer.

But now, having urged the importance of such habitual piety, I want to impress on you the value of another sort of prayer; namely, *the short, brief, quick, frequent ejaculations* of which Nehemiah gives us a specimen. And I recommend this, because it hinders no engagement and occupies no time. You may be measuring off your calicoes, or weighing your groceries, or you may be casting up an account, and between the items you may say, "Lord, help me." You may breathe a prayer to heaven and say, "Lord, keep me." It will take no time. It is one great advantage to persons who are hard pressed in business that such prayers as those will not, in the slightest degree, incapacitate them from attending to the business they may have in hand. It requires you to go to no particular place. You can stand where you are, ride in a cab, walk along the streets, be the bottom sawyer in a saw pit, or the top one either, and yet pray just as well such prayers as these. No altar, no church, no so-called sacred place is needed, but wherever you are, just such a little prayer as that will reach the ear of God, and win a blessing. Such a prayer as that can be offered anywhere, under any circumstances. I do not know in what condition a man could be in which he might not offer some such prayer as that. On the land, or on the sea, in sickness or in health, amidst losses or gains, great reverses or good returns, still might he breathe his soul in short, quick sentences to God. The advantage of such a way of praying is that you can pray often and pray always. If you must prolong your prayer for a quarter of an hour you might possibly be unable to spare the time, but if it only wants the quarter of a minute, why, then, it may come again and again and again and again —a hundred times a day. The habit of prayer is blessed, but the spirit of prayer is better; and the spirit of prayer it is which is the mother of these ejaculations; and therefore do I like them, because she is a plentiful mother. Many times in a day may we speak with the Lord our God.

Such prayer may be suggested by all sorts of surroundings. I recollect a poor man once paying me a compliment which I highly valued at the time. He was lying in a hospital, and when I called to see him he said, "I heard you for some years, and now whatever I look at seems to remind me of something or other that you said, and it comes back to me as fresh as when I first heard it." Well, now, he that knows how to pray ejaculatory prayers will find everything about him helping him to the sacred habit. Is it a beautiful landscape? Say, "Blessed be God who has strewn these treasures of form and colour through the world, to cheer the sight and gladden the heart." Are you in doleful darkness, and is it a foggy day? Say, "Lighten my darkness, O Lord." Are you in the midst of company? You will be reminded to pray, "Lord, keep the door of my lips." Are you quite alone? Then can you say, "Let me not be alone, but be thou with me, Father." The putting on of your clothes, the sitting at the breakfast table, the getting into the conveyance, the walking the streets, the opening of your ledger, the putting up of your shutters—everything may suggest such prayer as that which I am trying to describe if you be but in the right frame of mind for offering it.

These prayers are commendable, *because they are truly spiritual.* Wordy prayers may also be windy prayers. There is much of praying by book that has nothing whatever to recommend it. When you have found the benefit of a manual of French conversation to anyone travelling in France without a knowledge of the language, then try how much good a manual of prayers will do a poor soul who does not know how to ask our heavenly Father for a boon or benefit that he needs. *A manual,* a handbook, forsooth! Tush! Pray with your heart, not with your hands. Or, if you would lift hands in prayer, let them be your own hands, not another man's. The prayers that come leaping out of the soul—the gust of strong emotion, fervent desire, lively faith—these are the truly spiritual; and no prayers but spiritual prayers will God accept.

This kind of prayer is free from any suspicion that it is prompted by the corrupt motive of being offered to please men. They cannot say that the secret ejaculations of our soul are presented with any view to our own praise, for no man knows that we are praying at all; therefore do I commend such prayers to you, and hope that you may abound therein. There have been hypocrites that have prayed by the hour. I doubt not there are hypocrites as regular at their devotions as the angels are before the throne of God, and yet is there no life, no spirit, no acceptance in their pretentious homage; but he that ejaculates—whose heart talks with God—he is no hypocrite. There is a reality, and force, and life about it. If I see sparks come out of a chimney I know there is a fire inside somewhere, and ejaculatory prayers are like the sparks that fly from a soul that is filled with burning coals of love to Jesus Christ.

Short, ejaculatory prayers are of great use to us, dear friends. Oftentimes they check us. Bad-tempered people, if you were always to pray just a little before you let angry expressions fly from your lips, why many times you would not say those naughty words at all. They advised a good woman to take a glass of water and hold some of it in her mouth five minutes before she scolded her husband. I dare say it was not a bad receipt, but if, instead of practising that little eccentricity, she would just breathe a short prayer to God, it would certainly be more effectual, and far more scriptural. I can recommend it as a valuable prescription for the hasty and the peevish; for all who are quick to take offence and slow to forgive insult or injury. When in business you are about to close in with an offer about the propriety of which you have a little doubt, or a positive scruple, such a prayer as "Guide me, good Lord" would often keep you back from doing what you will afterwards regret.

The habit of offering these brief prayers would also check your confidence in yourself. It would show your dependence upon God. It would keep you from getting worldly. It would be like sweet perfume burnt in the chamber of your soul to keep away the fever of the world from your heart. I can strongly recommend these short, sweet, blessed prayers. May the Holy Ghost give them to you!

Besides, they *actually bring us blessings from heaven.* Ejaculatory prayers, as in the case of Eliezer, the servant of Abraham, as in the case of Jacob when he said even in dying, "I have waited for thy salvation, O God,"—prayers such as Moses offered when we do not read that he prayed at all, and yet God said to him, Why cryest thou unto me; ejaculations such as David frequently presented, these were all successful with the Most High. Therefore abound in them, for God loves to encourage and to answer them.

I might thus keep on recommending ejaculatory prayer, but I will say one more thing in its favour. I believe it is very suitable to some persons of a peculiar temperament who could not pray for a long time to save their lives. Their minds are rapid and quick. Well, dear friends, time is not an element in the business, God does not hear us because of the length of our prayer, but because of the sincerity of it. Prayer is not to be measured by the yard, nor weighed by the pound. It is the might and force of it—the truth and reality of it—the energy and the intensity of it. You that are either of so little a mind or of so quick a mind that you cannot use many words, or continue long to think of one thing, it should be to your comfort that ejaculatory prayers are acceptable. And it may be, dear friend, that you are in a condition of body in which you cannot pray any other way. A headache such as some people are frequently affected with the major part of their lives—a state of body which the physician can explain to you—might prevent the mind from concentrating itself long upon one subject. Then it is refreshing to be able again and again and again—fifty or a hundred times a day—to address one's self to God in short, quick sentences, the soul being all on fire. This is a blessed style of praying.

Now, I shall conclude by just mentioning a few of the times *when* I think we ought to resort to this practice of ejaculatory prayer. Mr. Rowland Hill was a remarkable man for the depth of his piety, but when I asked at Wotton-under-Edge for his study, though I rather pressed the question, I did not obtain a satisfactory reply. At length the good minister said, "The fact is, we never found any. Mr. Hill used to study in the garden, in the parlour, in the bed-room, in the streets, in the woods, anywhere." "But where did he retire for prayer?" They said they supposed it was in his chamber, but that he was always praying—that it did not matter where he was, the good old man was always praying. It seemed as if his whole life, though he spent it in the midst of his fellow-men doing good, was passed in perpetual prayer. You know the story of his being over there in Walworth at Mr. George Clayton's chapel, where our brother Paul Turquand now is the pastor, and of his being seen in the aisles after everybody was gone, while he was waiting for his coachman. There was the old man toddling up and down the aisles, and as some one listened, he heard him singing to himself—

> "And when I shall die, receive me I'll cry,
> For Jesus has loved me, I cannot tell why;
> But this thing I find, we two are so joined,
> He won't be in heaven and leave me behind."

And with such rhymes and ditties, and choice words, he would occupy every moment of his life. He has been known to stand in the Blackfriars' road, with his hands under his coat tails, looking in a shop window, and if you listened you might soon perceive that he was breathing out his soul before God. He had got into a constant state of prayer. I believe it is the best condition in which a man can be—praying always, praying without ceasing, always drawing near to God with these ejaculations.

But if I must give you a selection of suitable times I should mention such as these. Whenever you have a great joy, cry, "Lord, make this a real blessing to me." Do not exclaim with others, "Am I not a lucky fellow?" but say, "Lord, give me more grace, and more gratitude, now that thou dost multiply thy favours." When you have got any arduous undertaking on hand or a heavy piece of business, do not touch it till you have breathed your soul out in a short prayer. When you have a difficulty before you, and you are seriously perplexed, when business has got into a tangle or a confusion which you cannot unravel or arrange, breathe a prayer. It need not occupy a minute, but it is wonderful how many snarls come loose after just a word of prayer. Are the children particularly troublesome to you, good woman? Do you seem as if your patience was almost worn out with the worry and harass? Now for an ejaculatory prayer. You will manage them all the better, and you will bear with their naughty tempers all the more quietly. At any rate your own mind will be the less ruffled. Do you think that there is a temptation before you? Do you begin to suspect that somebody is plotting against you? Now for a prayer, "Lead me in a plain path because of mine enemies." Are you at work at the bench, or in a shop, or a warehouse, where lewd conversation and shameful blasphemies assail your ears? Now for a short prayer. Have you noticed some sin that grieves you? Let it move you to prayer. These things ought to remind you to pray. I believe the devil would not let people swear so much if Christian people always prayed every time they heard an oath. He would then see it did not pay. Their blasphemies might somewhat be hushed if they provoked us to supplication. Do you feel your own heart going off the lines? Does sin begin to fascinate you? Now for a prayer—a warm, earnest, passionate cry, "Lord, hold thou me up." Did you see something with your eye, and did that eye infect your heart? Do you feel as if "your feet were almost gone, and your steps had well nigh slipped"? Now for a prayer—"Hold me, Lord, by my right hand." Has something quite unlooked for happened? Has a friend treated you badly? Then like David say, "Lord, put to nought the counsel of Ahithophel." Breathe a prayer now. Are you anxious to do some good? Be sure to have a prayer over it. Do you mean to speak to that young man as he goes out of the Tabernacle to-night about his soul? Pray first, brother. Do you mean to address yourself to the members of your class and write them a letter this week about their spiritual welfare? Pray over every line, brother. It is always good to have praying going on while you are talking about Christ. I always find I can preach the better if I can pray while I am preaching. And the mind is very remarkable in its activities. It can be praying while it is studying: it can be looking up to God while it is talking to man; and there can be one hand held up to receive supplies from God while the other hand is dealing out the same supplies which he is pleased to give. Pray as long as you live. Pray when you are in great pain; the sharper the pang then the more urgent and importunate should your cry to God be. And when the shadow of death gathers round you, and strange feelings flush or chill you, and plainly tell that you near the journey's end, then pray. Oh! that is a time for ejaculation. Short and pithy prayers like this: "Hide not thy face from me, O Lord"; or this, "Be not far from me, O God"; will doubtless suit you. "Lord Jesus, receive my spirit," were the thrilling words of Stephen in his extremity; and "Father, into thy hands I commend my spirit," were the words that your Master himself uttered just before he bowed his head and gave up the ghost. You may well take up the same strain and imitate him.

These thoughts and counsels are so exclusively addressed to the saints and faithful brethren in Christ that you will be prone to ask, "Is not there anything to be said to the unconverted?" Well, whatever has been spoken in their hearing may be used by them for their own benefit. But let me address myself to you, my dear friends, as pointedly as I can. Though you are not saved, yet you must not say, "I cannot pray." Why, if prayer is thus simple, what excuse can you have for neglecting it? It wants no measureable space of time. Such prayers as these God will hear, and ye have all of you the ability and opportunity to think and to express them, if you have only that elementary faith in God which believes "that he is, and that he is a rewarder of them that diligently seek him." Cornelius had, I suppose, got about as far as this, when he was admonished by the angel to send for Peter, who preached to him peace by Jesus Christ to the conversion of his soul. Is there such a strange being in the Tabernacle to-night as a man or woman that never prays? How shall I expostulate with you? May I steal a passage from a living poet who, though he has contributed nothing to our hymn books, hums a note so suited to my purpose, and so pleasant to my ear that I like to quote it—

> "More things are wrought by prayer
> Than this world dreams of. Wherefore let thy voice
> Rise like a fountain, flowing night and day:
> For what are men better than sheep or goats,
> That nourish a blind life within the brain,
> If, knowing God, they lift not hands of prayer,
> Both for themselves and those who call them friend?
> For so the whole round world is every way
> Bound by gold chains about the feet of God."

I do not suspect there is a creature here who never prays, because people generally pray to somebody or other. The man that never prays to God such prayers as he ought, prays to God such prayers as he ought not. It is an awful thing when a man asks God to damn him; and yet there are persons that do that. Suppose he were to hear you; he is a prayer-hearing God. If I address one profane swearer here I would like to put this matter clearly to him. Were the Almighty to hear you. If your eyes were blinded and your tongue were struck dumb while you were uttering a wild imprecation, how would you bear the sudden judgment on your impious speech? If some of those prayers of yours were answered for yourself, and some that you have offered in your passion for your wife and for your child, were fulfilled to their hurt and your distraction, what an awful thing it would be. Well, God does answer prayer, and one of these days he may answer your prayers to your shame and everlasting confusion. Would not it be well now, before you leave your seat, to pray, " Lord have mercy upon me; Lord, save me; Lord, change my heart; Lord, give me to believe in Christ; Lord, give me now an interest in the precious blood of Jesus; Lord, save me now"? Will not each one of you breathe such a prayer as that? May the Holy Spirit lead you so to do, and if you once begin to pray aright I am not afraid that you will ever leave off, for there is a something that holds the soul fast in real prayer. Sham prayers—what is the good of them? But real heart pleading—the soul talking with God—when it once begins will never cease. You will have to pray till you exchange prayer for praise, and go from the mercy-seat below to the throne of God above.

May God bless you all; all of you, I say; all who are my kindred in Christ, and all for whose salvation I yearn. God bless you all and every one, for our dear Redeemer's sake. Amen.

RESTRAINING PRAYER.

A Sermon

DELIVERED BY

C. H. SPURGEON,

AT THE METROPOLITAN TABERNACLE, NEWINGTON,

In the year 1863.

"Thou . . . . . . restrainest prayer before God."—Job xv. 4.

THIS is one of the charges brought by Eliphaz the Temanite against Job, "Yea, thou castest off fear, and restrainest prayer before God." I shall not use this sentence as an accusation against those who never pray, though there may be some in this house of prayer whose heads are unaccustomed to bow down, and whose knees are unaccustomed to kneel before the Lord their Maker. You have been fed by God's bounty, you owe all the breath in your nostrils to him, yet you have never done homage to his name. The ox knoweth his owner, and the ass his master's crib, but you know not, neither do you consider the Most High. The cattle on a thousand hills low forth their gratitude, and every sheep praiseth God in its bleatings; but these beings, worse than natural brute beasts, still continue to receive from the lavish hand of divine benevolence, but they return no thanks whatsoever to their Benefactor. Let such remember that that ground, which has long been rained upon, and ploughed, and sown, which yet bringeth forth no fruit, is nigh unto cursing, whose end is to be burned. Prayerless souls are Christless souls, Christless souls are graceless souls, and graceless souls shall soon be damned souls. See your peril, ye that neglect altogether the blessed privilege of prayer. You are in the bonds of iniquity, you are in the gall of bitterness. God deliver you, for his name's sake!

Nor do I intend to use this text in an address to those who are in the habit of formal prayer, though there are many such. Taught from their childhood to utter certain sacred words, they have carried through youth, and even up to manhood, the same practice. I will not discuss that question just now, whether the practice of teaching children a form of prayer is proper or not. I would not do it. Children should be instructed in the meaning of prayer, and their little minds should be taught to pray; but it should be rather the matter of prayer than the words of prayer that should be suggested; and I think they should be taught to use their own words, and to speak to God in such phrases and terms as their own childlike capacities, assisted by a mother's love, may be able to suggest. Full many there are who, from early education, grow up habituated to some form of words, which either stands in lieu of the heart's devotion, or cripples its free exercise. No doubt there may be true prayer linked with a form, and the soul of many a saint has gone up to heaven in some holy collect, or in the words of some beautiful liturgy; but, for all that, we are absolutely certain that tens of thousands use the mere language without heart or soul, under the impression that they are praying. I consider the form of prayer to be no more worthy of being called prayer than a coach may be called a horse; the horse will be better without the coach, travel much more rapidly, and find himself much more at ease; he may drag the coach, it is true, and still travel well. Without the heart of prayer, the form is no prayer; it will not stir or move, it is simply a vehicle that may have wheels that might move; but it has no inner force or power within itself to propel it. Flatter not yourselves that your devotion has been acceptable to God, you that have been merely saluting the ears of the Most High with forms. They have been only mockeries, when your heart has been absent. What though a parliament of bishops should have composed the words you use, what though they should be absolutely faultless, ay, what if they should even be inspired, or though you have used them a thousand times, yet have you never prayed if you consider that the repetition of the form is prayer. No! there is more than the chatter of the tongue in genuine supplication; more than the repetition of words in truly drawing near to God. Take care lest, with the form of godliness, you neglect the power, and go down to the pit, having a lie in your right hand, but not the truth in your heart.

What I do intend, however, is to address this text to the true people of God, who understand the sacred art of prayer, and are prevalent therein; but who, to their own sorrow and shame, must confess that they have restrained prayer. If there be no other person in this congregation to whom the preacher will speak personally, he feels shamefully conscious that he will have to speak very plainly to himself. We know that our prayers are heard; we are certain—it is not a question with us,—that there is an efficacy in the divine office of intercession; and yet (oh, how we should blush when we make the confession!) we must acknowledge that we do restrain prayer. Now, inasmuch as we speak to those who grieve and repent that they should so have done, we shall use but little sharpness; but we shall try to use much plainness of speech. Let us see how and in what respect we have restrained prayer.

I. Do you not think, dear friends, that we often restrain prayer IN THE FEWNESS OF THE OCCASIONS THAT WE SET APART FOR SUPPLICATION?

From hoary tradition and modern precedents, we have come to believe that the morning should be opened with the offering of prayer, and that the day should be shut in with the nightly sacrifice. We do ill if we neglect those two seasons of prayer. Do you not think that often, in the morning, we rise so near to the time of labour, when duty calls us to our daily avocation, that we hurry through the wonted exercises with unseemly haste, instead of diligently seeking the Lord, and earnestly calling upon his name? And even at night, when we are very weary and jaded, it is just possible that our prayer is uttered somewhere between sleeping and waking. Is not this restraining prayer? And throughout the three hundred and sixty-five days of the year, if we continue thus to pray, and this be all, how small an amount of true supplication will have gone up to heaven!

I trust there are none here present, who profess to be followers of Christ, who do not also practise prayer in their families. We may have no positive commandment for it, but we believe that it is so much in accord with the genius and spirit of the gospel, and that it is so commended by the example of the saints, that the neglect thereof is a strange inconsistency. Now, how often this family worship is conducted in a slovenly manner! An inconvenient hour is fixed; and a knock at the door, a ring at the bell, the call of a customer, may hurry the believer from his knees to go and attend to his worldly concerns. Of course, many excuses might be offered, but the fact would still remain that, in this way, we often restrain prayer.

And then, when you come up to the house of God,—I hope you do not come up to this Tabernacle without prayer,—yet I fear we do not all pray as we should, even when in the place dedicated to God's worship. There should always be a devout prayer lifted up to heaven as soon as you enter the place where you would meet with God. What a preparation is often made to appear in the assembly! Some of you get here half an hour before the service commences; if there were no talking, if each one of you looked into the Bible, or if the time was spent in silent supplication, what a cloud of holy incense would go smoking up to heaven!

I think it would be comely for you and profitable for us if, as soon as the minister enters the pulpit, you engaged yourselves to plead with God for him. For me, I may especially say it is desirable. I claim it at your hands above every other man. With this overwhelming congregation, and with the terrible responsibility of so numerous a church, and with the word spoken here published within a few hours, and disseminated over the country, scattered throughout all Europe, nay, to the very ends of the earth, I may well ask you to lift up your hearts in supplication that the words spoken may be those of truth and soberness, directed of the Holy Spirit, and made mighty through God, like arrows shot from his own bow, to find a target in the hearts that he means to bless.

And on going home, with what earnestness should we ask the Master to let what we have heard live in our hearts! We lose very much of the effects of our Sabbaths through not pleading with God on the Saturday night for a blessing upon the day of rest, and through not also pleading at the end of the Sunday, beseeching him to make that which we have heard abide in our memories, and appear in our actions. We have restrained prayer, I fear, in the fewness of the occasions. Indeed, brethren, every day of the week, and every part of the day, should be an occasion for prayer. Ejaculations such as these, "Oh, would that!" "Lord, save me!" "Help me!" "More light, Lord!" "Teach me!" "Guide me!" and a thousand such, should be constantly going up from our hearts to the throne of God. You may enjoy a refreshing solitude, if you please, in the midst of crowded Cheapside; or, contrariwise, you may have your head in the whirl of a busy crowd when you have retired to your closet. It is not so much where we are as in what state our heart is. Let the regular seasons for devotion be constantly attended to. These things ought ye to have done; but let your heart be habitually in a state of prayer; ye must not leave this undone. Oh, that we prayed more, that we set apart more time for it! Good Bishop Farrar had an idea in his head which he carried out. Being a man of some substance, and having some twenty-four persons in his household, he divided the day, and there was always some person engaged either in holy song or else in devout supplication through the whole of the twenty-four hours; never was there a moment when the censer ceased to smoke, or the altar was without its sacrifice. Happy shall it be for us when, day without night, we shall circle the throne of God rejoicing; but, till then, let us emulate the ceaseless praise of seraphs before the throne, continually drawing near unto God, and making supplication and thanksgiving.

II. But, to proceed to a second remark, dear friends, I think it will be very clear, upon a little reflection, that we constantly restrain prayer BY NOT HAVING OUR HEARTS IN A PROPER STATE WHEN WE COME TO ITS EXERCISE.

We rush into prayer too often. We should think it necessary, if we were to address the Queen, that our petition should be prepared; but, often, we dash before the throne of God as though it were but some common house of call, without even having a thought in our minds of what we are going for. Now, just let me suggest some few things which I think should always be subjects of meditation before our season of prayer, and I think, if you confess that you have not thought of these things, you will also be obliged to acknowledge that you have restrained prayer.

We should, *before prayer, meditate upon him to whom it is to be addressed*. Let our thoughts be directed to the living and true God. Let me remember that he is omnipotent, then I shall ask large things. Let me remember that he is very tender, and full of compassion, then I shall ask little things, and be minute in my supplication. Let me remember the greatness of his covenant, then I shall come very boldly. Let me remember, also, that his faithfulness is like the great mountains, that his promises are sure to all the seed, then I shall ask very confidently, for I shall be persuaded that he will do as he has said. Let me fill my soul with the reflection of the greatness of his majesty, then I shall be struck with awe; with the equal greatness of his love, then I shall be filled with delight. We should pray better than we do if we meditated more, before prayer, upon the God whom we address in our supplications.

Then, let me *meditate also upon the way through which my prayer is offered;* let my soul behold the blood sprinkled on the mercy-seat; before I venture to draw near to God, let me go to Gethsemane, and see the Saviour as he prays. Let me stand in holy vision at the foot of Calvary, and see his body rent, that the veil which parted my soul from all access to God might be rent too, that I might come close to my Father, even to his feet. O dear friends, I am sure, if we thought about the way of access in prayer, we should be more mighty in it, and our neglect of so doing has led us to restrain prayer.

And yet, again, *ought I not, before prayer, to be duly conscious of my many sins?* Oh! when I hear men pray cold, careless prayers, surely they forget that they are sinners, or else, abjuring gaudy words and flowing periods, they would smite upon their breast with the cry, "God be merciful to me a sinner;" they would come to the point at once, with force and fervency. "I, black, unclean, defiled, condemned by the law, make my appeal unto thee, O God!" What prostration of spirit, what zeal, what fervour, what earnestness, and then, consequently, what prevalence would there be if we were duly sensible of our sin!

If we can add to this *a little meditation upon what our needs are,* how much better we should pray! We often fail in prayer because we come without an errand, not having thought of what our necessities are; but if we have reckoned up that we need pardon, justification, sanctification, preservation; that, besides the blessings of this life, we need that our decaying graces should be revived, that such-and-such a temptation should be removed, and that through such-and-such a trial we should be carried, and prove more than conquerors, then, coming with an errand, we should speed before the Most High. But we bring to the altars bowls that have no bottom; and if the treasure should be put in them, it would fall through. We do not know what we want, and therefore we ask not for what we really need; we affect to lay our necessities before the Lord, without having duly considered how great our necessities are. See thyself as an abject bankrupt, weak, sick, dying, and this will make thee plead. See thy necessities to be deep as the ocean, broad as the expanse of heaven, and this will make thee cry. There will be no restraining of prayer, beloved, when we have got a due sense of our soul's poverty; but because we think we are rich, and increased in goods, and we have need of nothing, therefore it is that we restrain prayer before God.

How well it would be for us if, *before prayer, we would meditate upon the past with regard to all the mercies we have had during the day,* what courage that would give us to ask for more! The deliverances we have experienced through our life, how boldly should we plead to be delivered yet again! He that hath been with me in six troubles will not forsake me in the seventh. Do but remember how thou didst pass through the fires, and wast not burnt, and thou shouldst be confident that the flame will not kindle upon thee now. Christian, remember how, when thou passedst through the rivers aforetime, God was with thee; and surely thou mayst plead with him to deliver thee from the flood that now threatens to inundate thee. Think of the past ages too, of what he did of old, when he brought his people out of Egypt, and of all the mighty deeds which he has done,—are they not written in the book of the wars of the Lord? Plead all these, and say unto him in thy supplications:—" O thou that art a God that heareth prayer, hear me now, and send me an answer of peace!" I think, without needing to point that arrow, you can see which way I would shoot. Because we do not come to the throne of grace in a proper state of supplication, therefore it is that too often we restrain prayer before God.

III. Now, thirdly, it is not to be denied, by a man who is conscious of his own error, that, IN THE DUTY OF PRAYER ITSELF, WE ARE TOO OFTEN STRAITENED IN OUR OWN BOWELS, AND SO RESTRAIN PRAYER.

Prayer has been differently divided by different authors. We might roughly say that prayer consists, first, of *invocation;* " Our Father, which art in heaven." We begin by stating the title and our own apprehension of the glory and majesty of the Person whom we address. Do you not think, dear friends, that we fail here, and restrain prayer here? Oh! how we ought to sound forth his praises! I think, on the Sabbath, it is always the minister's special duty to bring out the titles of THE ALMIGHTY ONE, such as " King of kings, and Lord of lords!" He is not to be addressed in common terms. How should we endeavour, as we search the Scripture through, to find those mighty phrases which the ancient saints were wont to apply to Jehovah! And how should we make his temple ring with his glory, and make our closet full of that holy adoration with which prayer must always be linked! I think the rebuking angel might often say, " Thou thinkest that the Lord is such an one as thyself, and thou talkest not to him as to the God of the whole earth; but, as though he were a man, thou dost address him in slighting and unseemly terms." Let all our invocations come more deeply from our souls' reverence to the Most High, and let us address him, not in high-sounding words of fleshly homage, but still in words which set forth our awe and our reverence while they express his majesty and the glory of his holiness.

From invocation we usually go to *confession,* and how often do we fail here! In your closet, are you in the habit of confessing your real sins to God? Do you not find, brethren, a tendency to acknowledge that sin which is common to all men, but not that which is certainly peculiar to you? We are all Sauls in our way, we want the best of the cattle and the sheep; those favourite sins, those Agag sins, it is not so easy to hew them in pieces before the Lord. The right eye sin, happy is that Christian who has learned to pluck it out by confession. The right hand sin, he is blessed and well taught who aims the axe at that sin, and cuts it from him. But no, we say that we have sinned,—we are willing to use the terms of any general confession that any church may publish; but to say, " Lord, thou knowest that I love the world, and the things of the world; I am covetous;" or to say, " Lord, thou knowest I was envious of So-and-so, because he shone brighter than I did at such-

and-such a public meeting; Lord, I was jealous of such-and-such a member of the church, because I evidently saw that he was preferred before me;" and for the husband also to confess before God that he has been overbearing, that he has spoken rashly to a child; for a wife to acknowledge that she has been wilful, that she has had a fault,—this would be *letting out* prayer; but the hiding of these things is *restraining* prayer, and we shall surely come under that charge of having restrained prayer unless we make our private confessions of sin very explicit, coming to the point.

I have thought, in teaching children in the Sabbath-school, we should not so much talk about sin in general as the sins in which children most commonly indulge, such as little thefts, naughty tempers, disobedience to parents; these are the things that children should confess. Men in the dawn of their manhood should confess those ripening evil imaginations, those lustful things that rise in the heart; while the man in business should ever make this a point, to see most to the sins which attack business men. I have no doubt that I might be very easily led, in my confession, to look to all the offences I may have committed against the laws of business, because I should not need to deal very hardly with myself there, for I do not have the temptations of these men; and I should not wonder if some of you merchants will find it very easy to examine yourselves according to a code that is proper to me, but not to you. Let the workman pray to God as a workman, and confess the sins common to his craft. Let the trader examine himself according to his standing, and let each man make his confession like the confessions of old, when every one confessed apart,—the mother apart and the daughter apart, the father apart and the son apart. Let each one thus make a clean breast of the matter, and I am sure there will not be so much need to say that we have restrained prayer before God.

As to the next part of prayer, which is *petition*, lamentably indeed do we all fail. We have not, because we ask not, or because we ask amiss. We are ready enough to ask for deliverance from trial, but how often we forget to ask that it may be sanctified to us! We are quite ready to say, "Give us this day our daily bread;" how often, however, do we fail to ask that he would give us the Bread which cometh down from heaven, and enable us blessedly to feed upon his flesh and his blood! Brethren, we come before God with such little desires, and the desires we get have so little fervency in them, and when we get the fervency, we so often fail to get the faith which grasps the promise, and believes that God will give, that, in all these points, when we come to the matter of spreading our wants before God, we restrain prayer.

Oh, for the Luthers that can shake the gates of heaven by supplication! Oh, for men that can lay hold upon the golden knocker of heaven's gate, and make it ring and ring again as if they meant it to be heard! Cold prayers court a denial. God hears by fire, and the God that answers by fire let him be God. But there must be prayer in Elijah's heart first—fire in Elijah's heart first—before the fire will come down in answer to the prayer. Our fervency goeth up to heaven, and then God's grace, which gave us the fervency, cometh down, and giveth it the answer.

But you know, too, that all true prayer has in it *thanksgiving*. "Thine is the kingdom, and the power, and the glory, for ever and ever." What prayer is complete without the doxology? And here, too, we restrain prayer. We do not praise, and bless, and magnify the Lord as we should. If our hearts were more full of gratitude, our expressions would be far more noble and comprehensive when we speak forth his praise. I wish I could put this so plainly that every Christian might mourn on account of his sin, and mend his ways. But, indeed, it is only mine to speak; it is my Master's to open your eyes, to let you see, and to set you upon the solemnly important duty of self-examination. In this respect, I am sure even the prayers that you and I have offered to-day may well cry out against us, and say, "Thou hast restrained prayer."

IV. Yet, again, I fear also we must all join in acknowledging A SERIOUS FAULT WITH REGARD TO THE AFTER-PART OF OUR PRAYERS. When prayer is done, do you not think we very much restrain it?

For, *after prayer, we often go into the world immediately*. That may be absolutely necessary; but we go there, and leave behind us what we ought to carry with us. When we have got into a good frame in prayer, we should consider that this is like the meat which the angel gave to Elijah that he might go on his forty days' journey in its strength. Have we felt heavenly-minded? Yet, the moment we cross the threshold, and get into the family or business, where is the heavenly mind? Oh, to get real prayer, inwrought prayer,—not the surface prayer, as though it were a sort of sacred masquerading after all,—to have it inside, in the warp and woof of our being, till prayer becomes a part of ourselves; then, brethren, we have not restrained it. We get hot in our closets,—when I say "we", oh, how few can say so much as that!—but, still, we get hot in our closets, and go out into the world, into the draughts of its temptations, without wrapping ourselves about with promises, and we catch well-nigh our death of cold. Oh, to carry that heat and fervour with us! You know that, as you carry a bar of hot iron along, how soon it begins to return to its common ordinary appearance, and the heat is gone. How hot, then, we ought to make ourselves in prayer, that we may burn the longer; and how, all day long, we ought to keep thrusting the iron into the fire again, so that, when it ceases to glow, it may go into the hot embers once more, and the flame may glow upon it, and we may once again be brought into a vehement heat. But we are not careful enough to keep up the grace, and seek to nurture and to cherish the young child, which God seems to give in the morning into our hands that we may nurse it for him.

Old Master Dyer speaks of locking up his heart by prayer in the morning, and giving Christ the key. I am afraid we do the opposite, —we lock up our hearts in the morning, and give the devil the key, and think that he will be honest enough not to rob us. Ah! it is in bad hands when it is trusted with him; and he keeps filching all day long the precious things that were in the casket, until at night it is quite empty, and needs to be filled over again. Would God that we put the key in Christ's hands, by looking up to him all the day!

I think, too, that *after prayer, we often fail in unbelief.* We do not expect God to hear us. If God were to hear some of you, you would be more surprised than with the greatest novelty that could occur. We ask blessings, but do not think of having them. When you and I were children, and had a little piece of garden, we sowed some seed one day, and the next morning, before breakfast, we went to see if it was up; and the next day, seeing that no appearance of the green blade could be discovered, we began to move the mould to look after our seeds. Ah! we were children then. I wish we were children now, with regard to our prayers. We should go out, the next morning, to see if they had begun to sprout, and disturb the ground a bit to look after our prayers, for fear they should have miscarried. Do you believe God hears prayer?

I saw, the other day, in a newspaper, a little sketch concerning myself, in which the author, who is evidently very friendly, gives a much better description of me than I deserve; but he offers me one rather pointed rebuke. I was preaching at the time in a tent, and only part of the people were covered. It began to rain just before prayer, and one petition was, "O Lord, be pleased to grant us favourable weather for this service, and command the clouds that they rain not upon this assembly!" Now he thought this very preposterous. To say the least, it was rash, if not blasphemous. He admits that it did not rain a drop after it. Still, of course, he did not infer that God heard and answered the prayer. If I had asked for a rain of grace, it would have been quite credible that God would send that; but when I ask him not to send a temporal rain, that is fanaticism. To think that God meddles with the clouds at the wish of a man, or that he may answer us in temporal things, is pronounced absurd. I bless God, however, that I fully believe the absurdity, preposterous as it may appear. I know that God hears prayer in temporal things. I know it by as clear a demonstration as ever any proposition in Euclid was solved. I know it by abundant facts and incidents which my own life has revealed. God does hear prayer. The majority of people do not think that he does. At least, if he does, they suppose that it is in some high, clerical, mysterious, unknown sense. As to ordinary things ever happening as the result of prayer, they account it a delusion. "The Bank of Faith!" How many have said it is a bank of nonsense; and yet there are many who have been able to say, "We could write as good a book as Huntington's 'Bank of Faith,' that would be no more believed than Huntington's Bank was, though it might be even more true."

We restrain prayer, I am sure, by not believing our God. We ask a favour, which, if granted, we should attribute to accident rather than ascribe it to grace, and we do not receive it; then the next time we come, of course we cannot pray, because unbelief has cut the sinews of prayer, and left us powerless before the throne.

You are a professor of religion. After you have been to a party of ungodly people, can you pray? You are a merchant, and profess to be a follower of Christ; when you engage in a hazardous speculation, and you know you ought not, can you pray? Or, when you have had a heavy loss in business, and repine against God, and will not say, "The Lord gave, and the Lord hath taken away; blessed be the name of the Lord;" can you pray? Pity the man who can sin and pray, too. In a certain sense, Brooks was right when he said, "Praying will make you leave off sinning, or else sin will make you leave off praying." Of course, that is not meant in the absolute sense of the term; but as to certain sins, especially gross sins,—and some of the sins to which God's people are liable are gross sins,—I am certain they cannot come before their Father's face with the confidence they had before, after having been rolling in the mire, or wandering in By-path Meadow. Look at your own child; he meets you in the morning with a smiling face, so pleased; he asks what he likes of you, and you give it to him. Now he has been doing wrong, he knows he has; and you have frowned upon him, you have chastened him. How does he come now? He may come because he is a child, and with tears in his eyes because he is a penitent; but he cannot ask with the power he once had. Look at a king's favourite; as long as he feels that he is in the king's favour, he will take up your suit, and plead for you. Ask him to-morrow whether he will do you a good turn, and he says, "No, I am out of favour; I don't feel as if I could speak now." A Christian is not out of covenant favour, but he may be experimentally under a cloud; he loses the light of God's countenance; and then he feels he cannot plead, his prayers become weak and feeble.

Take heed unto yourselves, and consider your ways. The path of declension is very abrupt in some parts. We may go on gradually declining in prayer till faith grows weak, and love cold, and patience is exhausted. We may go on for years, and maintain a consistent profession; but, all of a sudden, the road which had long been descending at a gradual incline may come to a precipice, and we may fall, and that when we little think of it; we may have ruined our reputation, blasted our comfort, destroyed our usefulness, and we may have to go to our graves with a sword in our bones because of sin. Stop while you may, believer; stop, and guard against the temptation. I charge you, by the trials you must meet with, by the temptations that surround you, by the corruptions that are within, by the assaults that come from hell, and by the trials that come from heaven, "Watch and pray, lest ye enter into temptation." To the members of this church I speak especially. What hath God wrought for us! When we were a few people, what intense agony of prayer we had! We have had prayer-meetings in Park Street that have moved our souls. Every man seemed like a crusader besieging Jerusalem, each man determined to storm the Celestial City by the might of intercession; and the blessing came upon us, so that we had not room to receive it. The hallowed cloud rests o'er us still; the holy drops still fall. Will ye now cease from intercession? At the borders of the promised land, will ye turn back to the wilderness, when God is with us, and the standard of a King is in the midst of our armies? Will ye now fail in the day of trial? Who knoweth but ye have come to the kingdom for such a time as this? Who knoweth but that he will preserve in the land a small company of poor people who fear God intensely, hold the faith earnestly, and love God vehemently; that infidelity may be driven from the high places of the earth; that Naphtali again may be a people made triumphant in the high places of the field? God of heaven, grant this! Oh, let us restrain prayer no longer! You that have never prayed, may you be taught to pray! "God be merciful to me a sinner," uttered from your heart, with your eye upon the cross, will bring you a gracious answer, and you shall go on your way rejoicing, for—

> "When God inclines the heart to pray,
> He hath an ear to hear;
> To him there's music in a groan,
> And beauty in a tear."

"THE THRONE OF GRACE."

A Sermon

DELIVERED ON LORD'S-DAY MORNING, NOVEMBER 19TH, 1871, BY

C. H. SPURGEON,

AT THE METROPOLITAN TABERNACLE, NEWINGTON.

"The throne of grace."—Hebrews iv. 16.

THESE words are found embedded in that gracious verse, "Let us therefore come boldly unto the throne of grace, that we may obtain mercy, and find grace to help in time of need;" they are a gem in a golden setting. True prayer is an approach of the soul by the Spirit of God to the throne of God. It is not the utterance of words, it is not alone the feeling of desires, but it is the advance of the desires to God, the spiritual approach of our nature towards the Lord our God. True prayer, is not a mere mental exercise, nor a vocal performance, but it is deeper far than that—it is spiritual commerce with the Creator of heaven and earth. God is a Spirit unseen of mortal eye, and only to be perceived by the inner man; our spirit within us, begotten by the Holy Ghost at our regeneration, discerns the Great Spirit, communes with him, prefers to him its requests, and receives from him answers of peace. It is a spiritual business from beginning to end; and its aim and object end not with man, but reach to God himself.

In order to such prayer, the work of the Holy Ghost himself is needed. If prayer were of the lips alone, we should only need breath in our nostrils to pray: if prayer were of the desires alone, many excellent desires are easily felt, even by natural men : but when it is the spiritual desire, and the spiritual fellowship of the human spirit with the Great Spirit, then the Holy Ghost himself must be present all through it, to help infirmity, and give life and power, or else true prayer will never be presented, but the thing offered to God will wear the name and have the form, but the inner life of prayer will be far from it.

Moreover, it is clear from the connection of our text, that the interposition of the Lord Jesus Christ is essential to acceptable prayer. As prayer will not be truly prayer without the Spirit of God, so it will not be prevailing prayer without the Son of God. He, the Great High Priest, must go within the veil for us; nay, through his crucified person the veil must be entirely taken away; for, until then, we are shut out from the living God. The man who, despite the teaching of Scripture, tries to pray without a Saviour insults the Deity; and he who imagines that his own natural desires, coming up before God, unsprinkled with the precious blood, will be an acceptable sacrifice before God, makes a mistake; he has not brought an offering that God can accept, any more than if he had struck off a dog's neck, or offered an unclean sacrifice. Wrought in us by the Spirit, presented for us by the Christ of God, prayer becomes power before the Most High, but not else.

In order, dear friends, that I may stir you up to prayer this morning, and that your souls may be led to come near to the Throne of Grace, I purpose to take these few words and handle them as God shall give me ability. You have begun to pray; God has begun to answer. This week has been a very memorable one in the history of this church. Larger numbers than ever before at one time have come forward to confess Christ,—as plain an answer to the supplications of God's people, as though the hand of the Most High had been seen stretched out of heaven handing down to us the blessings for which we asked. Now, let us continue in prayer, yea, let us gather strength in intercession, and the more we succeed, the more earnest let us be to succeed yet more and more. Let us not be straitened in our own bowels, since we are not straitened in our God. This is a good day, and a time of glad tidings, and seeing that we have the King's ear, I am most anxious that we should speak to him for thousands of others; that they also, in answer to our pleadings, may be brought nigh to Christ.

In trying to speak of the text this morning, I shall take it thus: First, *here is a throne;* then, secondly, *here is grace;* then we will put the two together, and we shall see *grace on a throne;* and putting them together in another order, we shall see *sovereignty manifesting itself, and resplendent in grace.*

I. Our text speaks of A THRONE,—" The Throne of Grace." God is to be viewed in prayer as our Father; that is the aspect which is dearest to us; but still we are not to regard him as though he were such as we are; for our Saviour has qualified the expression "Our Father," with the words "who art in heaven;" and close at the heels of that condescending name, in order to remind us that our Father is still infinitely greater than ourselves, he has bidden us say, "Hallowed be thy name; thy kingdom come;" so that our Father is still to be regarded as a King, and in prayer we come, not only to our Father's feet, but we come also to the throne of the Great Monarch of the universe. The mercy-seat is a throne, and we must not forget this.

If prayer should always be regarded by us as an entrance into the courts of the royalty of heaven; if we are to behave ourselves as courtiers should in the presence of an illustrious majesty, then we are not at a loss to know the right spirit in which to pray. If in prayer we come to a throne, it is clear that our spirit should, in the first place, be one of *lowly reverence.* It is expected that the subject in approaching to the king should pay him homage and honour. The pride that will not own the king, the treason which rebels against the sovereign will should, if it be wise, avoid any near approach to the throne. Let pride bite the curb at a distance, let treason lurk in corners, for only lowly reverence may come before the king himself when he sits clothed in his robes of majesty. In our case, the king before whom we come is the highest of all monarchs, the King of kings, the Lord of lords. Emperors are but the shadows of his imperial power. They call themselves kings by right divine, but what divine right have they? Common sense laughs their pretensions to scorn. The Lord alone hath divine right, and to him only doth the kingdom belong. He is the blessed and only potentate. They are but nominal kings, to be set up and put down at the will of men, or the decree of providence, but he is Lord alone, the Prince of the kings of the earth.

> "He sits on no precarious throne,
> Nor borrows leave to be."

My heart, be sure that thou prostrate thyself in such a presence. If he be so great, place thy mouth in the dust before him, for he is the most powerful of all kings; his throne hath sway in all worlds; heaven obeys him cheerfully, hell trembles at his frown, and earth is constrained to yield him homage willingly or unwillingly. His power can make or can destroy. To create or to crush, either is easy enough to him. My soul be thou sure that when thou drawest nigh to the Omnipotent, who is as a consuming fire, thou put thy shoes from off thy feet, and worship him with lowliest humility.

Besides, he is the most Holy of all kings. His throne is a great white throne, unspotted, and clear as crystal. "The heavens are not pure in his sight, and he charged his angels with folly." And thou, a sinful creature, with what lowliness shouldst thou draw nigh to him. Familiarity there may be, but let it not be unhallowed. Boldness there should be, but let it not be impertinent. Still thou art on earth and he in heaven; still thou art a worm of the dust, a creature crushed before the moth, and he the Everlasting: before the mountains were brought forth he was God, and if all created things should pass away again, yet still were he the same. My brethren, I am afraid we do not bow as we should before the Eternal Majesty; but, henceforth, let us ask the Spirit of God to put us in a right frame, that every one of our prayers may be a reverential approach to the Infinite Majesty above.

A throne, and therefore, in the second place, to be approached with *devout joyfulness.* If I find myself favoured by divine grace to stand amongst those favoured ones who frequent his courts, shall I not feel glad? I might have been in his prison, but I am before his throne: I might have been driven from his presence for ever, but I am permitted to come near to him, even into his royal palace, into his secret chamber of gracious audience, shall I not then be thankful? Shall not my thankfulness ascend into joy, and shall I not feel that I am honoured, that I am made the recipient of great favours when I am permitted to pray? Wherefore is thy countenance sad, O suppliant, when thou standest before the throne of grace? If thou wert before the throne of justice to be condemned for thine iniquities, thy hands might well be on thy loins; but now thou art favoured to come before the King in his silken robes of love, let thy face shine with sacred delight. If thy sorrows be heavy, tell them unto him, for he can assuage them; if thy sins be multiplied, confess them, for he can forgive them. O ye courtiers in the halls of such a monarch, be ye exceeding glad, and mingle praises with your prayers.

It is a throne, and therefore, in the third place, whenever it is approached, it should be with *complete submission*. We do not pray to God to instruct him as to what he ought to do, neither for a moment must we presume to dictate the line of the divine procedure. We are permitted to say unto God, "Thus and thus would we have it," but we must evermore add, "But, seeing that we are ignorant and may be mistaken—seeing that we are still in the flesh, and, therefore, may be actuated by carnal motives—not as we will, but as thou wilt." Who shall dictate to the throne? No loyal child of God will for a moment imagine that he is to occupy the place of the King, but he bows before him who has a right to be Lord of all; and though he utters his desire earnestly, vehemently, importunately, and pleads and pleads again, yet it is evermore with this needful reservation: "Thy will be done, my Lord; and, if I ask anything that is not in accordance therewith, my inmost will is that thou wouldst be good enough to deny thy servant; I will take it as a true answer if thou refuse me, if I ask that which seemeth not good in thy sight." If we constantly remembered this, I think we should be less inclined to push certain suits before the throne, for we should feel, "I am here in seeking my own ease, my own comfort, my own advantage, and, peradventure, I may be asking for that which would dishonour God; therefore will I speak with the deepest submission to the divine decrees."

But, brethren, in the fourth place, if it be a throne, it ought to be approached with *enlarged expectations*. Well doth our hymn put it:

> "Thou art coming to a king:
> Large petitions with thee bring."

We do not come, as it were, in prayer, only to God's almonry where he dispenses his favours to the poor, nor do we come to the back-door of the house of mercy to receive the broken scraps, though that were more than we deserve; to eat the crumbs that fall from the Master's table is more than we could claim; but, when we pray, we are standing in the palace, on the glittering floor of the great King's own reception room, and thus we are placed upon a vantage ground. In prayer we stand where angels bow with veiled faces; there, even there, the cherubim and seraphim adore, before that selfsame throne to which our prayers ascend. And shall we come there with stunted requests, and narrow and contracted faith? Nay, it becomes not a King to be giving away pence and groats, he distributes pieces of broad gold; he scatters not as poor men must, scraps of bread and broken meat, but he makes a feast of fat things, of fat things full of marrow, of wines on the lees well refined. When Alexander's soldier was told to ask what he would, he did not ask stintedly after the nature of his own merits, but he made such a heavy demand, that the royal treasurer refused to pay it, and put the case to Alexander, and Alexander in right kingly sort replied, "He knows how great Alexander is, and he has asked as from a king; let him have what he requests." Take heed of imagining that God's thoughts are as thy thoughts, and his ways as thy ways. Do not bring before God stinted petitions and narrow desires, and say, "Lord, do according to these," but, remember, as high as the heavens are above the earth, so high are his ways above your ways, and his thoughts above your thoughts, and ask, therefore, after a God-like sort, ask for great things, for you are before a great throne. Oh that we always felt this when we came before the throne of grace, for then he would do for us exceeding abundantly above what we ask or even think.

And, beloved, I may add, in the fifth place, that the right spirit in which to approach the throne of grace, is that of *unstaggering confidence.* Who shall doubt the King? Who dares impugn the Imperial word? It was well said that if integrity were banished from the hearts of all mankind besides, it ought still to dwell in the hearts of kings. Shame on a king if he can lie. The veriest beggar in the streets is dishonoured by a broken promise, but what shall we say of a king if his word cannot be depended upon? Oh, shame upon us, if we are unbelieving before the throne of the King of heaven and earth. With our God before us in all his glory, sitting on the throne of grace, will our hearts dare to say we mistrust him? Shall we imagine either that he cannot, or will not, keep his promise? Banished be such blasphemous thoughts, and if they must come, let them come upon us when we are somewhere in the outskirts of his dominions, if such a place there be, but not in prayer, when we are in his immediate presence, and behold him in all the glory of his throne of grace. There, surely, is the place for the child to trust its Father, for the loyal subject to trust his monarch; and, therefore, far from it be all wavering or suspicion. Unstaggering faith should be predominant before the mercy-seat.

Only one other remark upon this point, and that is, that if prayer be a coming before the throne of God, it ought always to be conducted with the *deepest sincerity,* and in the spirit which makes everything *real.* If you are disloyal enough to despise the King, at least, for your own sake, do not mock him to his face, and when he is upon his throne. If anywhere you dare repeat holy words without heart, let it not be in Jehovah's palace. If a person should ask for audience with royalty, and then should say, "I scarce know why I have come, I do not know that I have anything very particular to ask; I have no very urgent suit to press;" would he not be guilty both of folly and baseness? As for our great King, when we venture into his presence, let us have an errand there. As I said the other Sabbath, let us beware of playing at praying. It is insolence towards God. If I am called upon to pray in public, I must not dare to use words that are intended to please the ears of my fellow-worshippers, but I must realise that I am speaking to God himself, and that I have business to transact with the great Lord. And, in my private prayer, if, when I rise from my bed in the morning, I bow my knee and repeat certain words, or when I retire to rest at night go through the same regular form, I rather sin than do anything that is good, unless my very soul doth speak unto the Most High. Dost thou think that the King of heaven is delighted to hear thee pronounce words with a frivolous tongue, and a thoughtless mind? Thou knowest him not. He is a Spirit, and they that worship him must worship him in spirit and in truth. If thou hast any empty forms to prate, go and pour them out into the ears of fools like thyself, but not before the Lord of Hosts. If thou hast certain words to utter, to which thou dost attach a superstitious reverence, go and say them in the bedizened courts of the harlot Rome, but not before the glorious Lord of Zion. The spiritual God seeks spiritual worshippers, and such he will accept, and only such; but the sacrifice of the wicked is an abomination unto the Lord, and only a sincere prayer is his delight.

Beloved, the gathering up of all our remarks is just this,—prayer is no trifle. It is an eminent and elevated act. It is a high and wondrous privilege. Under the old Persian Empire a few of the nobility were permitted at any time to come in unto the king, and this was thought to be the highest privilege possessed by mortals. You and I, the people of God, have a permit, a passport to come before the throne of heaven at any time we will, and we are encouraged to come there with great boldness; but still let us not forget that it is no mean thing to be a courtier in the courts of heaven and earth, to worship him who made us and sustains us in being. Truly, when we attempt to pray, we may hear the voice saying, out of the excellent glory, " Bow the knee." From all the spirits that behold the face of our Father who is in heaven, even now, I hear a voice which saith, " Oh, come let us worship and bow down, let us kneel before the Lord our Maker; for he is our God, and we are the people of his pasture and the sheep of his hand. O worship the Lord in the beauty of holiness; fear before him all the earth."

II. Lest the glow and brilliance of the word " throne " should be too much for mortal vision, our text now presents us with the soft, gentle radiance of that delightful word—" GRACE." We are called to the throne *of grace*, not to the throne of law. Rocky Sinai once was the throne of law, when God came to Paran with ten thousand of his holy ones. Who desired to draw near to that throne? Even Israel might not. Bounds were set about the mount, and if but a beast touched the mount, it was stoned or thrust through with a dart. O ye self-righteous ones who hope that you can obey the law, and think that you can be saved by it, look to the flames that Moses saw, and shrink, and tremble, and despair. To that throne we do not come now, for through Jesus the case is changed. To a conscience purged by the precious blood there is no anger upon the divine throne, though to our troubled minds—

> " Once 'twas a seat of burning wrath,
> And shot devouring flame;
> Our God appeared consuming fire,
> And *jealous* was his name."

And, blessed be God, we are not this morning to speak of the throne of ultimate justice. Before that we shall all come, and as many of us as have believed will find it to be a throne of grace as well as of justice; for, he who sits upon that throne shall pronounce no sentence of condemnation against the man who is justified by faith. But I have not to call you this morning to the place from whence the resurrection-trumpet shall ring out so shrill and clear. Not yet do we see the angels with their vengeful swords come forth to smite the foes of God; not yet are the great doors of the pit opened to swallow up the enemies who would not have the Son of God to reign over them. We are still on praying ground and pleading terms with God, and the throne to which we are bidden to come, and of which we speak at this time, is the throne of grace. It is a throne set up on purpose for the dispensation of grace; a throne from which every utterance is an utterance of grace;

the sceptre that is stretched out from it is the silver sceptre of grace; the decrees proclaimed from it are purposes of grace; the gifts that are scattered adown its golden steps are gifts of grace; and he that sits upon the throne is grace itself. It is the throne of grace to which we approach when we pray; and let us for a moment or two think this over, by way of consolatory encouragement to those who are beginning to pray; indeed, to all of us who are praying men and women.

If in prayer I come before a throne of grace, then *the faults of my prayer will be overlooked.* In beginning to pray, dear friends, you feel as if you did not pray. The groanings of your spirit, when you rise from your knees are such that you think there is nothing in them. What a blotted, blurred, smeared prayer it is. Never mind; you are not come to the throne of justice, else when God perceived the fault in the prayer he would spurn it,—your broken words, your gaspings, and stammerings are before a throne of grace. When any one of us has presented his best prayer before God, if he saw it as God sees it, there is no doubt he would make great lamentation over it; for there is enough sin in the best prayer that was ever prayed to secure its being cast away from God. But it is not a throne of justice I say again, and here is the hope for our lame, limping supplications. Our condescending King does not maintain a stately etiquette in his court like that which has been observed by princes among men, where a little mistake or a flaw would secure the petitioner's being dismissed with disgrace. Oh, no; the faulty cries of his children are not severely criticised by him. The Lord High Chamberlain of the palace above, our Lord Jesus Christ, takes care to alter and amend every prayer before he presents it, and he makes the prayer perfect with his perfection, and prevalent with his own merits. God looks upon the prayer, as presented through Christ, and forgives all its own inherent faultiness. How this ought to encourage any of us who feel ourselves to be feeble, wandering, and unskilful in prayer. If you cannot plead with God as sometimes you did in years gone by, if you feel as if somehow or other you had grown rusty in the work of supplication, never give over, but come still, yea and come oftener, for it is not a throne of severe criticism, it is a throne of grace to which you come.

Then, further, inasmuch as it is a throne of grace, *the faults of the petitioner himself shall not prevent the success of his prayer.* Oh, what faults there are in us! To come before a throne how unfit we are—we, that are all defiled with sin within and without! Dare any of you think of praying were it not that God's throne is a throne of grace? If you could, I confess I could not. An absolute God, infinitely holy and just, could not in consistency with his divine nature answer any prayer from such a sinner as I am, were it not that he has arranged a plan by which my prayer comes up no longer to a throne of absolute justice, but to a throne which is also the mercy-seat, the propitiation, the place where God meets sinners, through Jesus Christ. Ah, I could not say to you, "Pray," not even to you saints, unless it were a throne of grace, much less could I talk of prayer to you sinners; but now I will say this to every sinner here, though he should think himself to be the worst sinner that ever lived, cry unto the Lord and seek him while he may be found. A throne of grace is a place fitted for you: go to your knees; by simple faith go to your Saviour, for he, he it is who is the throne of grace. It is in him that God is able to dispense grace unto the most guilty of mankind. Blessed be God, neither the faults of the prayer nor yet of the suppliant shall shut out our petitions from the God who delights in broken and contrite hearts.

If it be a throne of grace, then *the desires of the pleader will be interpreted.* If I cannot find words in which to utter my desires, God in his grace will read my desires without the words. He takes the meaning of his saints, the meaning of their groans. A throne that was not gracious would not trouble itself to make out our petitions; but God, the infinitely gracious One, will dive into the soul of our desires, and he will read there what we cannot speak with the tongue. Have you never seen the parent, when his child is trying to say something to him, and he knows very well what it is the little one has got to say, help him over the words and utter the syllables for him, and if the little one has half-forgotten what he would say, you have seen the father suggest the word: and so the ever-blessed Spirit, from the throne of grace, will help us and teach us words, nay, write in our hearts the desires themselves. We have in Scripture instances where God puts words into sinners' mouths. "Take with you words," saith he, " and say unto him, Receive us graciously and love us freely." He will put the desires, and put the expression of those desires into your spirit by his grace; he will direct your desires to the things which you ought to seek for; he will teach you your wants, though as yet you know them not; he will suggest to you his promises that you may be able to plead them; he will, in fact, be Alpha and Omega to your prayer, just as he is to your salvation; for as salvation is from first to last of grace, so the sinner's approach to the throne of grace is of grace from first to last. What comfort is this. Will we not, my dear friends, with the greater boldness draw near to this throne, as we suck out the sweet meaning of this precious word, " the throne of grace"?

If it be a throne of grace, then *all the wants of those who come to it will be supplied.* The King from off such a throne will not say, "Thou must bring to me gifts, thou must offer to me sacrifices." It is not a throne for receiving tribute; it is a throne for dispensing gifts. Come, then, ye who are poor as poverty itself; come ye that have no merits and are destitute of virtues, come ye that are reduced to a beggarly bankruptcy by Adam's fall and by your own trangressions; this is not the throne of majesty which supports itself by the taxation of its subjects, but a throne which glorifies itself by streaming forth like a fountain with floods of good things. Come ye, now, and receive the wine and milk which are freely given, yea, come buy wine and milk without money and without price. All the petitioner's wants shall be supplied, because it is a throne of grace.

And so, *all the petitioner's miseries shall be compassionated.* Suppose I come to the throne of grace with the burden of my sins; there is one on the throne who felt the burden of sin in ages long gone by, and has not forgotten its weight. Suppose I come loaded with sorrow; there is One there who knows all the sorrows to which humanity can be subjected. Am I depressed and distressed? Do I fear that God himself has forsaken me? There is One upon the throne who said, "My God, my God, why hast thou forsaken me?" It is a throne from which grace delights to look upon the miseries of mankind with tender eye, to consider them and to relieve them. Come, then; come, then; come, then, ye that are not only poor, but wretched, whose miseries make you long for death, and yet dread it. Ye captive ones, come in your chains; ye slaves, come with the irons upon your souls; ye who sit in darkness, come forth all blindfold as you are. The throne of grace will look on you if you cannot look on it, and will give to you, though you have nothing to give in return, and will deliver you, though you cannot raise a finger to deliver yourself.

"The throne of grace." The word grows as I turn it over in my mind, and to me it is a most delightful reflection that if I come to the throne of God in prayer, I may feel a thousand defects, but yet there is hope. I usually feel more dissatisfied with my prayers than with anything else I do. I do not believe that it is an easy thing to pray in public so as to conduct the devotions of a large congregation aright. We sometimes hear persons commended for preaching well, but if any shall be enabled to pray well, there will be an equal gift and a higher grace in it. But, brethren, suppose in our prayers there should be defects of knowledge: it is a throne of grace, and our Father knoweth that we have need of these things. Suppose there should be defects of faith: he sees our little faith and still doth not reject it, small as it is. He doth not in every case measure out his gifts by the degree of our faith, but by the sincerity and trueness of faith. And if there should be grave defects in our spirit even, and failures in the fervency or in the humility of the prayer, still, though these should not be there and are much to be deplored; grace overlooks all this, forgives all this, and still its merciful hand is stretched out to enrich us according to our needs. Surely this ought to induce many to pray who have not prayed, and should make us who have been long accustomed to use the consecrated art of prayer, to draw near with greater boldness than ever to the throne of grace.

III. But, now regarding our text as a whole, it conveys to us the idea of GRACE ENTHRONED. It is a throne, and who sits on it? It is grace personified that is here installed in dignity. And, truly, to-day grace is on a throne. In the gospel of Jesus Christ grace is the most predominant attribute of God. How comes it to be so exalted? We reply, well, grace has a throne *by conquest.* Grace came down to earth in the form of the Well-beloved, and it met with sin. Long and sharp was the struggle, and grace appeared to be trampled under foot of sin; but grace at last seized sin, threw it on its own shoulders, and, though all but crushed beneath the burden, grace carried sin up to the cross and nailed it there, slew it there, put it to death for ever, and triumphed gloriously. For this cause at this hour grace sits on a throne, because it has conquered human sin, has borne the penalty of human guilt, and overthrown all its enemies.

Grace, moreover, sits on the throne because it has established itself there *by right.* There is no injustice in the grace of God. God is as just when he forgives a believer as when he casts a sinner into hell. I believe in my own soul that there is as much and as pure a justice in the acceptance of a soul that believes in Christ as there will be in the rejection of those souls who die impenitent, and are banished from Jehovah's presence. The sacrifice of Christ has enabled God to be just, and yet the justifier of him that believeth. He who knows the word "substitution," and can spell its meaning aright, will see that there is nothing due to punitive justice from any believer, seeing that Jesus Christ has paid all the believer's debts, and now God would be unjust if he did not save those for whom Christ vicariously suffered, for whom his righteousness was provided, and to whom it is imputed. Grace is on the throne by conquest, and sits there by right.

Grace is enthroned this day, brethren, because Christ has finished his work and gone into the heavens. It is enthroned *in power*. When we speak of its throne, we mean that it has unlimited might. Grace sits not on the footstool of God; grace stands not in the courts of God, but it sits on the throne; it is the regnant attribute; it is the king to-day. This is the dispensation of grace, the year of grace: grace reigns through righteousness unto eternal life. We live in the era of reigning grace, for seeing he ever liveth to make intercession for the sons of men, Jesus is able also to save them to the uttermost that come unto God by him. Sinner, if you were to meet grace in the by-way, like a traveller on his journey, I would bid you make its acquaintance and ask its influence; if you should meet grace as a merchant on the exchange, with treasure in his hand, I would bid you court its friendship, it will enrich you in the hour of poverty; if you should see grace as one of the peers of heaven, highly exalted, I would bid you seek to get its ear; but, oh, when grace sits on the throne, I beseech you close in with it at once. It can be no higher, it can be no greater, for it is written " God is love," which is an *alias* for grace. Oh, come and bow before it; come and adore the infinite mercy and grace of God. Doubt not, halt not, hesitate not. Grace is reigning; grace is God; God is love. Oh that you, seeing grace is thus enthroned, would come and receive it. I say, then, that grace is enthroned by conquest, by right, and by power, and, I will add, it is enthroned in glory, for God glorifies his grace. It is one of his objects now to make his grace illustrious. He delights to pardon penitents, and so to show his pardoning grace; he delights to look upon wanderers and restore them, to show his reclaiming grace; he delights to look upon the broken-hearted and comfort them, that he may show his consoling grace. There is grace to be had of various kinds, or rather the same grace acting in different ways, and God delights to make his grace glorious. There is a rainbow round about the throne like unto an emerald, the emerald of his compassion and his love. O happy souls that can believe this, and believing it can come at once and glorify grace by becoming instances of its power.

IV. Lastly, our text, if rightly read, has in it SOVEREIGNTY RESPLENDENT IN GLORY,—THE GLORY OF GRACE. The mercy seat is a throne; though grace is there, it is still a throne. Grace does not displace sovereignty. Now, the attribute of sovereignty is very high and terrible; its light is like unto a jasper stone, most precious, and like unto a sapphire stone, or, as Ezekiel calls it, " the terrible crystal." Thus saith the King, the Lord of hosts, " I will have mercy on whom I will have mercy, and I will have compassion on whom I will have compassion." "Who art thou, O man, that repliest against God? Shall the thing formed say to him that formed it, Why hast thou made me thus?" "Hath not the potter power over the clay to make of the same lump one vessel unto honour and another unto dishonour?" These are great and terrible words, and are not to be answered. He is a King, and he will do as he wills. None shall stay his hand, or say unto him, What doest thou? But, ah! lest any of you should be downcast by the thought of his sovereignty, I invite you to the text. It is a throne,—there is sovereignty; but to every soul that knows how to pray, to every soul that by faith comes to Jesus, the true mercy seat, divine sovereignty wears no dark and terrible aspect, but is full of love. It is a throne of grace; from which I gather that the sovereignty of God to a believer, to a pleader, to one who comes to God in Christ, is always exercised in pure grace. To you, to you who come to God in prayer, the sovereignty always runs thus: "I will have mercy on that sinner; though he deserves it not, though in him there is no merit, yet because I can do as I will with my own, I will bless him, I will make him my child, I will accept him; he shall be mine in the day when I make up my jewels." On the mercy seat God never executed sovereignty otherwise than in a way of grace. He reigns, but in this case grace reigns through righteousness unto eternal life by Jesus Christ our Lord.

There are these two or three things to be thought of, and I have done. On the throne of grace sovereignty has placed itself under bonds of love. I must speak with words choice and picked here, and I must hesitate and pause to get right sentences, lest I err while endeavouring to speak the truth in plainness. God will do as he wills; but, on the mercy-seat, he is under bonds—bonds of his own making, for he has entered into covenant with Christ, and so into covenant with his chosen. Though God is and ever must be a sovereign, he never will break his covenant, nor alter the word that is gone out of his mouth. He cannot be false to a covenant of his own making. When I come to God in Christ, to God on the mercy-seat, I need not imagine that by any act of sovereignty God will set aside his covenant. That cannot be: it is impossible.

Moreover, on the throne of grace, God is again bound to us by his promises. The covenant contains in it many gracious promises, exceeding great and precious. "Ask and it shall be given you; seek and ye shall find; knock and it shall be opened unto you." Until God had said that word or a word to that effect, it was at his own option to hear prayer or not, but it is not so now; for now, if it be true prayer offered through Jesus Christ, his truth binds him to hear it. A man may be perfectly free, but the moment he makes a promise, he is not free to break it; and the everlasting God wants not to break his promise. He delights to fulfil it. He hath declared that all his promises are yea and amen in Christ Jesus; but, for our consolation when we survey God under the high and terrible aspect of a sovereign, we have this to reflect on, that he is under covenant bonds of promise to be faithful to the souls that seek him. His throne must be a throne of grace to his people.

And, once more, and sweetest thought of all, every covenant promise has been endorsed and sealed with blood, and far be it from the everlasting God to pour scorn upon the blood of his dear Son. When a king has given a charter to a city, he may before have been absolute, and there may have been nothing to check his prerogatives, but when the city has its charter, then it pleads its rights before the king. Even thus God has given to his people a charter of untold blessings, bestowing upon them the sure mercies of David. Very much of the validity of a charter depends upon the signature and the seal, and, my brethren, how sure is the charter of covenant grace. The signature is the handwriting of God himself, and the seal is the blood of the Only-begotten. The covenant is ratified with blood, the blood of his own dear Son. It is not possible that we can plead in vain with God when we plead the blood-sealed covenant, ordered in all things and sure. Heaven and earth shall pass away, but the power of the blood of Jesus with God can never fail. It speaks when we are silent, and it prevails when we are defeated. Better things than that of Abel doth it ask for, and its cry is heard. Let us come boldly, for we bear the promise in our hearts. When we feel alarmed because of the sovereignty of God, let us cheerfully sing—

> "The gospel bears my spirit up,
> A faithful and unchanging God
> Lays the foundation for my hope
> In oaths, and promises, and blood."

May God the Holy Spirit help us to use aright from this time forward "the throne of grace." Amen.

PRAYERFUL IMPORTUNITY.

A Sermon

DELIVERED BY

C. H. SPURGEON,

AT THE 100TH ANNIVERSARY OF AMERSHAM BAPTIST CHAPEL,

In November, 1857.

"And shall not God avenge his own elect, which cry day and night unto him, though he bear long with them?"—Luke xviii. 7.

You remember this is the conclusion of the parable of the importunate widow. Her husband was dead; he had left her perhaps a little property, and some adversary, very probably a lawyer, seized hold of it, and took from her all that she had. What was she to do? She went straightway to the judge, the appointed minister of justice, in the city. The first time she went, she met with a cold repulse. She went a second time; her poverty drove her, her necessity compelled her, to face the man again. Now the judge "neither feared God, nor regarded man," but at last seeing the vehemence of the woman, feeling that he should be exceedingly troubled by her constant importunity, he granted her request, and he did avenge her of her adversary. Jesus used this to show the power of importunity,—"Hear what the unjust judge saith,"—"And if the *unjust* judge did this, shall not God avenge his own elect, who cry day and night unto him?"

Now, in trying to discuss this text this evening, I shall first show what I believe to be *the primary application of it;* and, secondly, I shall try to enlarge upon *the general principle involved in it,*—that importunity is very prevalent with God.

I. To begin then,—WHAT WAS THE ABSOLUTE AND CLEAREST MEANING THAT OUR SAVIOUR WOULD CONVEY TO HIS DISCIPLES BY THE PARABLE?

Well, now, I think the whole sense of the parable, as far as we can make any special application of it, hinges upon the meaning of that word "avenge." What is it that Christ's Church is always praying for? The answer is, they are praying spiritually, for that which the poor widow prayed for actually,—they are praying to be avenged of their adversary. Now what did this mean in the poor woman's case? For, in some degree, it means just the same in the Church's case. I do not believe that that poor widow-woman, when she went to the judge, went for mere vengeance sake. I cannot conceive that our Saviour would have exhibited the perseverance of malice as an example to his people. I do not think that when she applied day after day to the court of the judge to be avenged, she applied to have her adversary punished, for the mere sake of his being punished. It strikes me there was no revenge whatever in the poor woman's spirit, and that what she went for was simply this: her husband was dead, he had left her a little property, it was all she had to bring his babes up upon and support herself; someone had seized this property, and what she wanted was, that the property might be restored unto her, that that which had been unlawfully taken from the weak by the mighty, might at once be taken from the clutches of the strong, and restored unto the rightful owner. I think any intelligent person reading the passage would at once conceive that that was what she was seeking for. Now the Church of Christ is seeking just the very same thing. Those that can cry day and night in heaven before the throne of God, do not cry out of a spirit of revenge. The saints, when they pray to God on earth, and girdle the globe with supplication, do not pray against the wicked out of a spirit of hatred. God forbid that any of us should ever fall on our knees and ask God to avenge us of our adversary in the common acceptation of that phrase! I am sure there is no Christian who is actuated by the Spirit of Christ, who would ever ask for vengeance, even on the head of the bloodiest persecutor, for if he should do so, methinks the lips of Jesus might rebuke him, for we know what Jesus said when he was dying, he did not wish to be avenged, for he said, "Father, forgive them, for they know not what they do."

Christ's Church is seeking after just what the poor widow-woman was seeking after, and we are to understand our text, "Shall not God avenge his own elect?" in that modified sense which the parable would convey to us. The fact is, Christ's Church is a widow; it is true her husband is alive; but she is in a widowed state, because he has departed from her. Our Lord Jesus Christ, who is the Bridegroom, was once with his people, and the Church could not mourn or fast when the Bridegroom was with her. But he said, "The day shall come when the Bridegroom shall be taken away, and then she shall fast." These are the days; "Our Jesus has gone up on high," he is not with us in person now, he has left his Church in the wilderness, it is true he has left the Comforter with her, but his own absolute, personal presence is not vouchsafed to her, he is not yet come a second time without a sin-offering unto salvation. Well, then, taking advantage of the absence of Christ, the Church's Husband, the kings, the princes, the rulers, spiritual wickednesses in high places, have sought to rob the Church of her rights and her privileges, and what the Church is always crying for is, that God would restore her her rights, that he would give to her the portion which her Husband left her in his last legacy, and which, in due time, when God shall have answered her prayers, he shall restore unto her. And what is that legacy?

My brethren, there are many things that Christ has left to his

Church of which the world has robbed us. The Church was once a united Church. When Christ was in this world, his prayer was, that they all might be one, even as he and his Father were one. Alas! the world has robbed us of our unity; and now, behold, the Church crieth day and night, "Restore, O Lord, the scattered of Israel, and bring us into one fold, and let us have one Shepherd!" The spirit of the world has crept into our midst, and split us into many denominations. God's children are not now called Christians; but they are called Baptists and Independents, Churchmen, Dissenters, and such-like names of distinction. Their oneness, although it really exists in the heart, yet is lost, at least in the outward appearance of it; and, to some degree, it is entirely lost. But the Church is crying for it every day; the true hearts in the midst of God's Zion and the glorified spirits above are crying, day without night, "O Lord, make thy Church one!"

Again, the Church was sent into this world to bring the world to a knowledge of the truth; and, one day, the kingdoms of this world shall become the kingdoms of our Lord and of his Christ. We may say that all the world is Christ's, though heathenism has a part of it, Mohammed has another, and the Pope another. The world is divided into different sections, under different false systems of religion, but all the world belongs by right to Christ. We can cast our eye round the world, from the river even to the ends of the earth, and we can say, "The kings of the isles shall bring tribute; the princes of Sheba and Seba shall offer gifts; kings shall yet be the nursing fathers of the Church, and queens the nursing mothers." But the world has robbed us of this; the different false religions have spoiled the Church's inheritance; the wild boar of the wood doth waste her, and doth devour her borders. Zion's banner should wave everywhere in every kingdom, but instead thereof the priests, the kings, the idol gods have taken the kingdoms unto themselves. Now this is the great thing, I believe, that the Church is praying for. You know the Church is one day to wear a crown. Christ's Church is Christ's royal bride, and she is to have a crown; but she can never have it until her prayer has been heard, until her Lord comes to revenge her wrongs. For, lo! the Church of God is trampled on and despised; the precious sons of Zion, comparable unto fine gold, how are they esteemed as earthen pitchers, the workings of the potter! God's chosen people are counted as the off-scouring of all things, instead of being, as indeed they are, considered as the blood royal of the universe,—the princes among men. Now, because of these lost rights, Christ's Church crieth day and night unto God, crying out, "O Lord, avenge us of our adversary, and restore unto thy widowed Church her rights!"

Put the Jew wherever you may, and he will always declare that the promised land belongs to his nation. There is a pride about the Jew, wherever he may be; he believes himself still to belong to that chosen family, whose were the covenants and the oracles. That is true of the Christian: he may be never so poor, never so despised, but knowing himself to belong to the chosen body, he claims that all things are his own. You may clothe him in fustian, and you may feed him on bread and water, but he will still say, "All things are mine." You may thrust him into a dungeon, and let no light come to him except through two iron bars, but he will still declare, "Mine are the valleys and the hills; mine by sacred right; my Father made them all." There is a royalty in a Christian which persecution cannot burn out, which shame cannot crush, which poverty cannot root up; there it is, and there it must be for ever; and conscious of his high rights and distinctive privileges, the Christian, the believer, will never cease to cry unto Christ, that he may yet have his rights, and possess what his God did give unto him. Now, dear friends, very often we are low-spirited and down-hearted; sometimes the Christian minister goes back from his pulpit, and says, "Ah! the gospel seems making very little progress, I do not see how the kingdoms of this earth are to belong to Christ." The Sunday-school teacher goes home from his class, and says, "This is weary work; if things go on as they do now, we shall always have to say, 'Who hath believed our report?' and how can the Church prosper if things be so?" And there are times with each of us when a kind of sickness seizes our spirits, we look at everything with a sad eye, and we say, "Ah! the millennium is many years off." Indeed, unbelief says it is quite impossible. "How shall the heathen bow before him? How shall they that dwell in the wilderness lick the dust?" Now, you, who have thought thus, and you who are thinking so now, hear the Saviour's argument for your consolation, the argument couched in the text,—The Church of God is crying unto him day and night. There where the burning lamps of heaven perpetually light the skies; high in the seventh heavens, above the stars, where angels cast their crowns before the Most High, the saints for ever cry to God, "O Lord, avenge thine own elect!" for prayer is made in heaven. The saints under the altar cry aloud, "O Lord, how long?" There is never a moment when the saints cease to pray; they have—

"Vials full of odour sweet,
And harps of sweeter sound."

And we remember that the saints on earth are always in prayer. You meet together in the evening for prayer; you scatter to your houses, and then your family fires begin to burn, and when your family fires are put out, and your private devotions have ceased, the sun is just rising in the other land across the western sea, and there they are beginning to pray again; and when the sun hath set, then it rises somewhere round the world in the far east, there by the Ganges river, there by the Himalaya steeps, the saints of God begin again, and when the sun windeth on its course, and again shineth somewhere else, then the saints of the Lord offer incense and a pure offering; so that there is never an hour when this world ceases to offer its incense, not one moment, even in the darkest shades of midnight, when prayer does not ascend from this lower world. And it would be ill for the world if there were a moment when prayer should be suspended; for remember what a poet says,

"Perhaps the day when this world shall be consumed will be a day unbrightened by a prayer." Perhaps it may be so, but certainly such a day as that has not yet rolled over the world, for day without night the world is girdled with prayer, and one sacred belt of supplication winds the whole globe round. Now, said Christ, if God's elect in heaven and on earth are day without night, without ceasing, crying to God to give the Church her empire, her reign, her splendours, her victories, rest assured the Church shall have what it asks for. Shall not God avenge his own elect that cry day and night unto him? Yes, beloved brethren, we may not live to see it, though sometimes I think there be some alive in this world that will live to see that bright day; and yet, if we live not to see it, the day shall come when Christ, who is the truth, shall have all power given unto him under heaven; as he hath even now really, he shall then have it given to him in the form and symbol and fashion of it also. The day is coming when Christ shall come in the clouds of heaven to reign upon this earth in the midst of his people. Then, when he shall come, the kingdoms of this world shall be converted unto him; all people shall flock to his colours; every knee shall bow before him, and every tongue confess that the Lord is God. I have sometimes thought that I may yet live to see that day, and some of you mayhap. We cannot tell when Christ shall come. We are very apt to forget that he comes as a thief in the night, in such an hour as we think not. It is a pleasing thought sometimes to recollect that there may be some standing here that will not die, for we know the Scripture says, "Behold, I tell you a mystery. We shall not all sleep, but we shall all be changed in a moment, in the twinkling of an eye at the last trump." When Christ shall come, we shall be alive and remain, perhaps, some of us; for he may come to-morrow, he may come to-night; before the word I am speaking reaches your ear, the trump of the resurrection and jubilee may startle us all, and we may behold Christ come in the clouds of heaven. But whether he cometh or not in our lifetime, there will be some alive when he shall come, and they, if they be his people, shall not die, they shall be changed, "the dead shall be raised incorruptible, and we shall be changed." "Then we which are alive and remain shall be caught up together with them in the clouds, to meet the Lord in the air: and so shall we ever be with the Lord."

O work on, minister; toil on, teacher; weep on, mourner; pray on, intercessor; hope on, believer; the hallowed day is coming! Some of the streaks of the grey light already mark the horizon; some of the sweet tidings of the Master's coming have already been announced to God's favourite people; some that have dwelt high on the mountain top of communion have declared that the time is approaching near. The chariot wheels of Christ are drawing nigh. But be it near, or be it far off, it must come; it shall come; the Church shall triumph; the world shall be subdued beneath her feet. God shall avenge his own elect, who cry day and night unto him. Now, I take that as the absolute meaning of the passage, the nearest and most appropriate way of explaining it.

II. And now I am going to try to work out THE PRINCIPLE OF THE TEXT. It is this,—*Importunity will prevail.* Now you must not smile while I give you two pictures, the pictures that Christ gave his disciples, worked out a little, so as to be more plain to you. Jesus Christ says, if you want anything of God, if you do not get it the first time, try again; and if you do not get it then, continue in prayer; for long continuing in prayer, you will prevail with God; and he gives you two pictures that we have had this evening.

The first is, the good man who had no bread in his house when his friend came. You may picture the scene. He says, "I am very glad to see you, but I have not a morsel of food in the house. If I had the richest dainties in the world, you should have them all, but I have not any." "Well, but," says his friend, "I have come a good many miles this day; I cannot go to rest without something to eat. I shall faint." "Well, but," he says, "I have nothing for you." "My dear friend," says the other, "cannot you obtain a morsel? I am famished by the way: I expected to have got to my resting-place at noontide, and now it is midnight; I have been travelling these twelve hours, and have had nothing at all to eat." "Well," says his friend, "I have something for your horse to eat, but I cannot give you anything;" but at length he says, "There is a friend of mine who lives down the street; I will go and get something from him. You shall not starve. I will not come away till I get something." Away he goes, and finds his friend asleep; he gives a great knock, the man is upstairs in bed, and he says, "My wife and my children are with me in bed." He does not want to hear that knock, and so he just sleeps on. Then there comes another tremendous knock. Says the man, "I cannot think who that can be." The question is asked by those who are upstairs, but he does not feel at all inclined to get out and look. It is a cold night, and what should he get up for? Then there comes another rap. "Well," he says, "there is somebody at the door." He still turns in his bed, and will not get up. He doesn't see why he should rise at such an untimely hour as that. Besides, after all, it may be only some drunken fellow going home late. Then there comes another tremendous knock. He goes to the window, puts his head out, and asks what is the matter. "Oh!" says the man, "I want some loaves of bread; a friend of mine has come to see me, and I have nothing for him." "What do you come to me for at such an hour as this? I cannot come down; my wife and my children are with me in bed; I cannot give you bread at this hour of the night." "But," says the other, "I must have it, and I hope you will give it to me. What a friend you have been to me in times past!" "Friend or no friend," he says, "I shall not give you anything at this time of night." "He will not rise and give to him because he is his friend." Then what does the poor man do? He says, "I will not go back." He thinks he sees that poor hungry man; and he cannot bear the thought of going back and saying that he has nothing for him. That was the only house where he could get bread; and so he knocks again. "Oh, dear me!" says the man, "I thought I had got rid of that fellow. I told him I couldn't get up at this hour, and I won't!" But then there comes another rap,—a tremendous one, and the child says, "Father, we can't go to sleep; hadn't you better go and give that man his bread?" but the father says, "No, I shall not; why does he trouble me in this way?" Then there comes another rap, and he goes to the window in great anger, and asks him, "Whatever do you want coming knocking here in this way? I tell you once for all I shall not give you anything!" "Well," says the man, "you must give me bread; I cannot go till you do: if you do not give me any, I mean to stop here and knock all night." "Well," says Jesus, "I tell you, though he will not arise and give it to him, because he is his friend, yet because of his importunity he will arise and give him as many as he needeth." So he comes downstairs, gets the loaves, opens the door, and says to the man, "Here, take as many as you want, and be off with you, and never come to disturb me any more at nights." So off he goes, and importunity gets what even friendship could not obtain.

Well, then the Saviour gives another picture. Importunity can get what even justice ought to get, but cannot. There is the poor widow; she is robbed of all she has: she had a little plot of ground, and a little cottage with just enough to keep her children through the winter, and there was a little field, or two, that she could let out for rent sufficient to keep her all the year; and now it is all pounced upon. She does not know what she is to do. Somebody will come in to claim it who has no right to it. She is turned out of house and home, and she and her poor children are on the streets. She goes off to the judge's house to see him,—rather a wild errand that; for, when she gets there, there stand the porters at the door, and the men with halberds; and they say, "Woman, what do you want?" "I want to see the judge." "You cannot see the judge; he has got plenty to do without seeing you." "But I must see him; here is a man that has been taking"—"I do not want to know anything at all about it; you cannot see him." "But I must see him," says the woman; and somehow or other, though the porters repulse her all day long, she manages to get into court, and just when some witness steps down, up comes the woman, and begins, "My lord." "What case is that, sergeant?" says the judge. "Oh, it has nothing to do with the court business to-day, my lord!" "Get down with you," says the judge to the woman. "O my lord!" she replies, "there is a man that has come and taken away"—"Now, you have no right here, I tell you you must go," and she goes down, sad at heart. But the next morning she comes again. As soon as ever the court house is open, there is the woman at the door. Before anybody can be found to enter, there she is. She had established herself there as soon as the people came to get the place ready. Well, before they can begin the business of the day, the woman begins crying out, "O my lord, my husband is dead"—"Did you not come here yesterday?" says the judge. "Yes, my lord." "Well, I thought I told you this was not the proper time and place to apply. I cannot attend to you." "O my lord, if you would but just hear my case a little "—" Bring the next case up," says the judge; and there is a case brought up, and the judge proceeds. There happens, however, to be an interlude in the business, such as the poor widow has been looking for a long time, and his honour is just going out of court for a little refreshment, and as he is going, the woman steps up, and says, "My lord"—"Now take that woman away; she is always coming here, and disturbing me." The poor woman is taken away, but she returns, and all day long the poor soul is there. She comes the next day, and when the judge arrives, there is the apparition of this poor woman to startle him again. What is to be done all day long? He knows that at every possible opportunity she can get she will be down upon him to ask him to avenge her of her adversary. At length he says, "Well, what is your case?" and as soon as it is stated, he thinks to himself, "I know that man very well, that has taken away her property; he is a friend of mine. I shall not interfere in the case. I neither fear God, nor regard man, but as a friend of mine has got her property, I shall not interfere;" and then, addressing the woman, "I absolutely forbid you ever to come to this place again." But she comes again, and again, and again, until one day she steps into the witness box, and says, "My lord, I am a woman of a sorrowful spirit"—"Now I do not want any more of that; you are always giving me your long sermons in court." "My lord," continues the woman, "I will have a hearing to-day. I am a woman of a sorrowful spirit; I have been here many times before, and you have sent me away, when I ought to have had justice at your hands; and now this day, unless I am dragged out of court by main force, I will stop until I get justice." Well, the judge thinks to himself a moment or two, and says, "If I were just to decide this woman's case, I should get rid of her. Well, come, my good woman, let us hear about it." So she tells the whole history of the case; the judge sends the officer of the court to enquire into it; and at last he says, "Though I fear not God, nor regard man, yet because this widow troubleth me, I will avenge her of her adversary." He accordingly sets all her accounts square, and she goes home to her cottage with a joyous heart, and her children are fed, and all is happy; for the judge has set her free from all her dilemmas. Now, friends, there you have a case of importunity even going before the claims of justice, as in the other case it went before the claims of friendship.

Now what are these two pictures to teach the sinner? They are to teach the sinner that if the importunate woman could prevail with an unjust judge, you will prevail with a loving Saviour; to teach you, that if by constant knocking the friend who at first would not rise, at last did rise and give bread, by your repeated prayers you shall at last find the salvation that you need. I am certain that somewhere within the compass of my voice, there is one who has been for weeks and months seeking the Saviour; but he or she has never yet found the Saviour; Satan has whispered perhaps, "God will never have mercy upon you; you may as well give up prayer; prayer is a useless employment if it hath no answer; never attend the house of God again; there is no mercy for you; never again come to the throne of grace, for God's ears are deaf to you, he will not hear your supplication." Now, poor heart, listen not to the temptation of the devil, but listen to this that I have to say unto thee,—go again seven times, and if that suffice not, seventy times seven; God hath not promised to answer thee the first time; he will answer thee, however, at the end; so continue thy prayers. When, with deep anxiety of spirit I sought the Saviour, many months I prayed before I could get an answer; and I heard my mother say, one day, that there never was a man in the world, she believed, so wicked as to say that he had sought God truly and earnestly in prayer, and God had not answered him. "Many black oaths," said she, "have been sworn, but I never heard of any man who was allowed to utter a sentence so derogatory to the love and mercy of God as that,—'I have sought God, and he would not save me.'" At once the thought struck me, "I will say that, for I know I have sought God, and I feel he has not heard me." I resolved that I would say it, and that she should hear me, for I felt my spirit vexed within me. I had sought God, and, I thought, with all my heart, and he had never vouchsafed to hear me. But then it occurred to me, "Would it not be better to try again before saying it?" That time I sought as I had not sought before, and that time I found and rejoiced in hope of the glory of God, because my supplication had been answered in my own heart, to my own soul's comfort. Now, if you are in the same position, and are labouring under the same temptation, try again. If thy knees have been bent seventy times in vain, remember thou hast seventy times the fewer to pray in vain; so try again; thou art so much nearer the appointed number which thou must reach before God will hear thee; give not up thine efforts. In fact, I know thou neither wilt nor canst give up, if God the Holy Spirit hath taught thee praying, for that is one of the things that Satan cannot do,—he cannot effectually stop a praying tongue,—he cannot for ever quench the desire of the soul; though he may for a time do it by despondency and despair, yet he cannot do it in the end. I want, before I have done, to take the hand of that young man, or that young woman, who is to-night seeking the Saviour, but, as yet, without having found him to his heart's joy, and I want to say a kind word to him. Dear brother, God will hear you; be of good courage; but in the meantime to keep your spirits up I will tell you a few things.

Consider what a great being God is, and what a little creature you are, and then you need not wonder that you have to wait. Why, poor people, when they go to see a rich man, will stop in his hall for hours, and if they are going to see a great lord, they will not mind waiting in the antechamber where there is no fire, till their feet are cramped with cold, so long as they have a hope that they shall get an audience at last. The pertinacity of the beggar in the streets is sometimes astonishing; you cannot get rid of him; you walk a little faster, and he walks a little faster too; he keeps talking to you about his wife, who is sick, and tells you that he is a poor man, that you will never miss what you give him, that God will bless you, and all that. Well, if a beggar will wait upon his fellow worm, if we would be content to wait upon the great of the earth for so long a season, oh! we need not murmur against God if he bids us wait in his halls, for we are poor miserable sinners who are good for nothing, and he is the eternal God. There is such a distance between him and us, that we need not murmur if he keeps us waiting.

Besides, let us recollect what a great blessing it is we are asking for. The beggar will stop at your door half an hour with the hope of getting perhaps a crust of bread; and men will go and wait in the halls of princes just to get a word. But ah! my friends, that which we are seeking is more than that; we are seeking for the salvation of our souls; we are seeking for the blood of Christ, for the pardon of sin, for a seat in paradise, for deliverance from the flames of hell; and for such a gift as this it were worth while waiting a thousand years if we might be sure of getting it at last.

But again, poor soul, be willing to wait, because, let me tell thee this, thou art sure to get what thou seekest. "Oh!" cries one, "I would not mind what I did if I thought I could be saved at last." Well, you will. There was never a soul that perished praying, never one who sought the Saviour who was at last cast away. Oh, if the Lord should keep you waiting till your head is silvered o'er with grey, his mercy would not come too late; he would be sure at last to give an ear to your supplication, and bestow upon you the blessing. Therefore be patient; though the promise tarry, wait for it, for it will be sure to come. But whilst you are waiting, do not do as some people have done. I had a hearer once who used to tell me that he was waiting, and I never could get him out of that idea say what I would, until at last I had to use a good illustration in order to prove to him that he was not waiting. "Now," said I, " suppose I came to your house one day to tea, and you said to me, 'My dear sir, how late you are! we have been waiting for you.' And suppose there was no fire in the grate, no kettle singing on the hob, and no tea made, I should say, 'I do not believe you.'" Waiting implies being ready; if a man is waiting for another, he is ready for him. If you are waiting for the coach, why, you have your hat on and great coat and your gloves, and your bag is packed up, and you are ready to start; if you are waiting for the train, you are standing on the platform, and looking out for its arrival. And when a man is waiting for Christ, he is ready for Christ. But when they say they are waiting, and they fold their arms in unconcern, it is a gross falsehood; they are waiting for God to destroy them, and nothing else. When men do really wait for the Lord, this is the way they wait,—they go where they hope to meet him. If they hear that Jesus is in the house of God, they go there; if they hear that he is to be found in the reading of the Word, they read it day and night; if they hear that some minister has been specially blest in the salvation of souls, they will go many miles to hear him, in order that they may see Jesus; they will go where Jesus goes, and when they get near Jesus, they will cry after him. They will do as the blind man did when he heard that Jesus of Nazareth passed by. Let us describe that scene for a moment. A poor man sat by the wayside one day; he could see nothing, but he heard a great noise and a lot of people coming his way, so he said to some of the crowd, "What is that?" and they replied, "It is Jesus of Nazareth that passes by." That he thinks is a fine opportunity, and he cries out as loud as ever he can, "Jesus, thou Son of David, have mercy on me." Jesus Christ is preaching to the crowd as he walks along, working miracles, and he takes no notice of the cry. Then there is another shout, "Thou Son of David, have mercy on me!" The disciples come and tell him to be still; that he is disturbing Christ in his preaching, and that he must not make that noise,—but so much the more, a great deal, he cries, "Thou Son of David, have mercy on me!" And that shout prevailed over the voice of Christ, and the tramping of the feet of the multitude; then Christ stood still, and looked at the blind man, opened his eyes, and gave him sight. Now you must do the same; you must cry to Christ, you must agonize in prayer, and wrestle on your knees before him when you think that you are near to him. Above all, study his promises, and read his Word. And if this sufficeth not, hear then the last advice and the best, go to thy chamber to-night, thou that hast sought the Saviour long, as thou thinkest, sought him in vain,—go to thy upper chamber, shut to thy doors, fall on thy knees, open his holy Word, turn to that passage which describes the death of Jesus, and when thou hast meekly and reverently read through the story of the crucifixion, shut up the Book, sit down and picture to your mind's eye the hill of Calvary,—see the cross in the midst of those two other crosses of the thieves. Picture to yourselves the Lord Jesus with the thorn crown on his head, with his hands all dropping blood, with his side distilling a purple torrent. Don't think of anything else. The first thing that will happen, God the Holy Spirit helping you, will be that you will begin to weep; tears will run down your cheeks at the sight of the dear bleeding Man; and after a while, faith will begin to kindle, and the thought will arise, "Many souls have been saved by trusting in him that died upon the cross, and why not I?" And it may be that you shall come down from that chamber of yours with a light heart and gladsome countenance, singing as you come down the stairs,—

> "Oh, how sweet to view the flowing
> Of his sin-atoning blood!
> With divine assurance knowing
> He hath made my peace with God!"

There is no way of getting peace like that. O thou that hast sought often, adopt this last resource! Thou canst but perish coming to Jesus; thou wilt perish if thou dost not come; but at his feet ne'er sinner died, and never sinner shall. "Come unto me all ye that labour and are heavy laden, and I will give you rest." Ye sin-bitten, conscience-stricken sons of men, hear the gospel: "This is a faithful saying, and worthy of all acceptation, that Christ Jesus came into the world to save sinners." This is the glorious gospel of the blessed God, that Christ died for sinners. Believe the gospel, and your souls shall live, you shall be saved, and rejoice in glory everlasting. Christ died for real sinners. You ask a man, "Do you take God's name in vain?" "No." "Do you honour other gods before the Lord Jehovah?" "No." "Do you ever break the Sabbath?" "No." "Do you always honour your father and mother?" "Yes, all these things have I kept from my youth up." Well then, Jesus Christ did not die for you at all; you are too good by half to go to heaven; you are not the sort of person the gospel is preached to. Jesus Christ says, "I came not to call the righteous, but sinners to repentance." He came to save him whose aching heart and bleeding spirit and tearful eye betray the man who feels himself a sinner. Now, may I write the word SINNER in great capital letters, and say, "Who is the man that this word depicts?" Suppose I were to do it, are there not some of you who would get up, and say from your hearts, "O sir, that is just my name; you may put that on me, I the chief of sinners am"? Well then, Jesus died for you. "But," says one, "if I had a few good works, I should think he did die for me." Then you would have no reason to think so. Your reason for believing that Christ died for you, must be grounded on your sins. "Christ Jesus came into the world to save sinners,"—that must be your only groundwork. "It is hard," says one, "to draw white from black." Ay, but though it is hard, that is what faith must do. You must infer the good from the seeming evil. You know Martin Luther's logic. He says, in his book on Galatians, that Satan once came to him and said, "Martin, you are a great sinner; you will be damned." "No," said he, "Satan: the first is true,—I am a great sinner; the second is not true,—for, because I am a great sinner, (and I thank thee for telling me of it,) and because I feel it, I shall be saved; for Christ came to save sinners, and so I cut thine head off with thine own sword." The greatest saints on earth often have come to this. "Oh!" saith the heir of heaven, "I am afraid I am no child of God;" and the short cut to comfort is this, "Well, if I am not a child of God, I am a sinner, and—

"'A sinner is a sacred thing,
The Holy Ghost hath made him so.'"

And straightway he comes to Christ, and cries,—

"Nothing in my hands I bring,
Simply to thy cross I cling."

Poor sinners, that is believing on Christ, believing that he died for you when there is no evidence that he did except your own sense of sin. Then, casting your black soul into the fountain, then bringing your naked soul to the heavenly wardrobe, then do you prove the power of faith, and then are you thus manifested to be the children of God in verity and truth.

May the Lord add his blessing! If there are any careless souls here, may he awaken them, for Jesus Christ's sake! Amen.

TRUE AND NOT TRUE.

A Sermon

DELIVERED BY

C. H. SPURGEON,

AT THE METROPOLITAN TABERNACLE, NEWINGTON.

On Lord's-day Evening, May 23rd, 1875.

"Now we know that God heareth not sinners."—John ix. 31.

I HAVE taken my text out of its connection, for a certain purpose. Part of the purpose will be answered immediately if I say how wrong it is to take any passage of Scripture away from that which comes before it, and that which follows after it; for you may, if you are so inclined, prove anything you like from the Bible if you wrench a line from its context, and hold it up by itself. You can, indeed, act in the same way with any other book. You may take an expression from any human being's writings, as some people do from these divine writings, and make the author say what he never meant. That is how many treat the Word of God. For instance, a man may say that he can prove from Scripture that God hath forsaken and forgotten his people. By turning to Isaiah xlix. 14, we find that Zion, in an unbelieving fainting fit said, "The Lord hath forsaken me, and my Lord hath forgotten me." It was not true, but was one of the falsehoods of unbelief. If you take from their connection the words in Psalm xiv. 1, "There is no God," you will have the opposite of what David wrote, "The fool hath said in his heart, There is no God." If you pick out a sentence from the New Testament, without the context, you may say that Scripture declares that our Lord Jesus Christ was a gluttonous man and a wine-bibber, because his enemies falsely said so; and you may declare that it is your duty to worship the devil, because Matthew records that he said to Christ, "Fall down and worship me." You see at once the absurdity and wickedness of wresting the Scriptures in that fashion.

Now take the words that I have chosen for my text, "We know that God heareth not sinners." Who said that? A man who was born blind, to whom Christ had given sight. And who believed it? A set of still blinder Pharisees. He was arguing with them, and he wished to convince them, so he used an argument which was specially suitable to them. It was their Pharisaic belief that God would not hear sinners. "Very well," he said; "but God has heard Christ; therefore, according to your own belief, Jesus Christ, who has opened my eyes, cannot be a sinner." It was a capital *argumentum ad hominem*, as we say, an argument to the men themselves. But we are not going to accept everything that this man said. We are not bound to do so, for he did not speak under any sort of inspiration. The evangelist was inspired to record what the man said, but we should be very foolish if we believed all that he said, shrewd as he proved himself to be.

Is it true that "God heareth not sinners"? *It is true, and it is not true.* It is true, most true as this man meant it; but it is utterly false in the sense in which some persons have understood it. So I am going to speak, first, upon *how it is true that God heareth not sinners;* and, secondly, upon *how it is not true.*

I. First, then, IT IS TRUE THAT GOD HEARETH NOT SINNERS IN THE SENSE IN WHICH THIS MAN USED THE EXPRESSION, namely, that, *if Christ had been an impostor, it is not possible to conceive that God would have listened to his prayer*, and given him the power to open the blind man's eyes, for that would have been for God, the just and the true, to set his seal to a lie, and that cannot be. The man was quite accurate in arguing, "If this Jesus of Nazareth is a deceiver, how is it that" (as the man supposed) "he has asked God to open the eyes of one born blind, and God has done it, thereby as good as saying that this deceiver was true?" It is not supposable that the Most High could have done anything of the kind. It can never be believed that God will listen to the prayers of men who ask him to support their falsehoods, and assist them in the propagation of that which is contrary to his own kingdom. That was the primary sense in which, I have no doubt, the man meant his statement, and in that sense it is true. God will back up the right and the true, and stand by the Christ whom he himself hath sent; but he will not support imposture and falsehood.

In another sense it is true that "God heareth not sinners;" that is to say, *he will hear none of us,*—no sinner among us, (and who among us is not a sinner?) *in and of ourselves.* If heard, it must be through the interposition of the Mediator between God and men, the Man Christ Jesus, for up to the immediate presence of the thrice-holy God the guilty sinner cannot come by himself. The fire of the divine holiness would burst forth, and utterly destroy the presumptuous rebel who might attempt such an intrusion; but Jesus meets us just where we are, we give our prayers into his hand, and he perfumes them and cleanses us with his own most precious blood, and then he presents both ourselves and our prayers before his Father's face. God could not hear those prayers of ours, neither could he have respect unto us or to our offering, apart from the mediation of Christ. He must—to use the language of one of our hymn-writers,—"look through Jesu's wounds" on us, and then, but not till then, can he regard us favourably. As a matter of absolute justice, irrespective of the Mediator, God could not and would not hear any prayer from any sinful being in the universe.

Our text is also quite true if we read it as meaning that *God heareth not wicked prayers.* Perhaps someone asks, "What are wicked prayers?" There are many sorts, but I will only mention one or two kinds now. Those are wicked prayers which men offer formally; I mean such as we often hear when solemn sounds are evidently uttered by thoughtless tongues,—when men bow their heads in the posture of devotion, but their hearts are gadding abroad after vanity,—when they bend the knee, morning and night, and repeat a form, but there is no heart in it. All that is an insult and a mockery to the Most High. What should we think if somebody presented to us a petition, and asked us to listen to it, yet did not mean it, but merely mocked us with empty sounds? Unless your heart is in your prayer, it is a wicked one, and God will not answer it. He must hear it, but it will be only in indignation, and he will say to you, "What have I done that you should thus provoke me to my face, and bring to me mere empty shells when the kernel of the heart is altogether absent?"

That is also a wicked prayer which a man offers simply because it is the custom to offer it, and there is something to be gained by it. All attendance upon religious ordinances, for the sake of thereby getting pecuniary profit or social position, must be abominable in the sight of God, yet there are many who have a keen eye for the loaves and fishes that Christ or his apostles have to distribute, and they say a prayer for what they can get, and they would swear an oath for twice as much, or perhaps for half as much, equally satisfied whichever they might do so long as the wages were pretty sure and liberal. It is detestable that religion should ever be a stalking-horse for gain or for position. We know that God hears not such prayers as those. Sounding brass and a tinkling cymbal must be more musical in his ears than the mere chattering of formalists, or the pretended prayers of those who hope to gain thereby. He hears not prayers in which men sin as they pray, and insult him when they appear to be devout.

It is quite certain, as you will see from various passages of Scripture which I will presently quote to you, that God does not, and will not hear the prayers of those who continue in their sins even while they pray. There are thousands of persons who would very much like to go to heaven, and they are dreadfully afraid of going to hell; but, then, if they do go to heaven, they would like to take their sins with them,—at least, most of the way. They would cut their acquaintance just a few yards before the brink of the river of death; but they feel that they must keep those sweet sins of theirs, and yet they hope to go to heaven! If this is what any of you are doing, be you sure of this, that God will not hear your prayers. He will hear your supplications if you repent of and forsake your sins; but if you come before him arm in arm with your sinful lusts, he will drive you from his presence. A man prays for forgiveness, yet continues to drink to excess; can God answer a prayer of that kind? It cannot be; he will never pander to our base passions by allowing us to indulge in sin, and yet to hope for mercy. I believe that there are many persons who do pray, after a fashion, for grace, and Christ, and heaven; they have never obtained an answer yet, and they never will as long as they continue to dally with their beloved sins. These must be given up; even if they were like their right arms, they must be cut off, or like their right eyes, they must be plucked out, for it is utterly impossible to keep sin and yet go to heaven. In this sense, "God heareth not sinners."

Do you wish to be saved from sin? Do you pray to be saved from intemperance, from dishonesty, from falsehood, from unchastity? Do you ask to be saved from everything that makes you unlike your God? Then he will hear such prayers as those; but to pray for pardon, yet continue to rebel,—to pray for forgiveness, yet still go on to provoke him,—such a prayer as that must be a stench in the nostrils of the Most High. You will find, in Isaiah's first chapter, 15th verse, that the Lord says, "When ye make many prayers, I will not hear: your hands are full of blood." There is a similar passage in Jeremiah xiv. 12, where the Lord says concerning the people who would not turn from their evil ways, "When they fast, I will not hear their cry; and when they offer burnt offering and an oblation, I will not accept them: but I will consume them by the sword, and by the famine, and by the pestilence." "Thus have they loved to wander, they have not refrained their feet, therefore the Lord doth not accept them; he will now remember their iniquity, and visit their sins."

Another true meaning may be attached to this passage, "God heareth not sinners;" that is to say, *God does not hear hypocrites.* Job knew this, and so did his friends; it hardly needs a revelation to make us know that it is true. If a man tries to play fast and loose with God,—if he pretends to be the Lord's servant, and all the while he is the servant of sin,—God will not grant the request that is made by his double tongue. Listen to these words of Job: "What is the hope of the hypocrite, though he hath gained, when God taketh away his soul? Will God hear his cry when trouble cometh upon him? Will he delight himself in the Almighty? will he always call upon God?" No; hypocrites will not always call upon God, and God will not always hear them when they do call upon him; I may truly say that he will never hear them, for he abhors the sacrifice that is presented to him without the devout heart of the offerer.

We have further proof that our text has much truth in it if we think of *another class of sinners that God will not hear, namely, the unforgiving.* When we pray, "Forgive us our trespasses, as we forgive them that trespass against us," we expressly ask that God will not forgive us till we have forgiven our fellow-men. You may kneel till your knees grow to be part of the very floor; you may weep till you make your bed to swim; but no answer of peace shall ever come from God to you as long as you retain one black malicious thought against your fellow-man, however much he may have offended you. Perhaps this explains why some of you, who have been awakened of late, have not been able to find peace with God. If it is so with thee, my friend, thou must first take thy hand from the throat of thy brother, who owes thee that little debt, and then mayest thou hope that God will suffer thee to find mercy at his hands concerning thy far greater debt to him. Bring not thy sacrifice unto the Lord, pollute not his altar with it; nay, dishonour not the floor of God's house by treading upon it while thou dost cherish an unforgiving spirit; but go home to thy brother, and say unto him, "I freely forgive thee for the wrong thou hast done to me. Let this quarrel be ended, for I cannot meet my God till first I can meet thee;" for "he that loveth not his brother whom he hath seen, how can he love God whom he hath not seen?"

I may here remark, by the way, that *God will not hear even his own people when they are living in known sin.* You must have noticed that remarkable declaration in Psalm lxvi. 18, "If I regard iniquity in my heart, the Lord will not hear me." Have you not found it so, my brethren and sisters who have been favoured with the presence of God? When you have backslidden, when you have grieved the Spirit of God, have not your prayers returned empty to you? You used to ask and receive; when you kept up constant, familiar intercourse with the Most High, you had but to express your desire, and it was granted unto you. But you grew cold, worldly, careless; and now, when you pray, it is like speaking into a brazen cauldron; your words reverberate, they resound in your own ears, but they do not reach the ears of God. You go to the mercy-seat, and groan, but you bring your wants away with you; they are not supplied, and so, groaning, and groaning, and groaning yet again, prayer has become a toilsome task with you, for no answer follows your supplication. Ask the Lord to cleanse your heart, my brother; then your power in prayer will come back to you. If you walk contrary to God, he will walk contrary to you, and your power in prayer will fail you when you in any way give place to sin. I do not think that the blind man, who had been cured by Christ, meant that, but it is true, and it is necessary that I should mention it.

There is another class of sinners whom God will not hear. In Proverbs xxviii. 9, we read, "He that turneth away his ear from hearing the law, even his prayer shall be abomination." That is to say, *if a man will not hear God, God will not hear him.* You have a Bible, but you will not read it; then, when you pray, you must not expect God to give you audience. You will not attend the means of grace when you might do so; if anybody tries to explain the gospel to you, you tell him to hold his tongue, for you are determined not to know anything about the way to heaven. Well then, friend, you may say what you like about praying, but while God's gospel is treated by you with such disrespect as this, you cannot expect that God will grant your requests. Shut your ear to God, and he will shut his ear to you; but incline your ear, and come unto him, and, sinner as you are, your soul shall live, for God will hear you.

Further, *God will not hear those who continue to harden their hearts against him.* There are some people who have often been impressed, and they have had great difficulty in throwing off those impressions. The battering-ram of the gospel has been hammering at the doors of some of your hearts, and it has given such tremendous blows that you have thought that the door must be wrenched from its hinges, and the posts must be torn from their sockets; yet you have managed to strengthen your inside defences, and to keep up the barrier. Soul, let me solemnly warn you that you may do that once too often; you may put one bolt too many on that door; and, one of these days, the Lord will turn away from you, and say, "Because I have called, and ye refused; I have stretched out my hand, and no man regarded; but ye have set at nought all my counsel, and would none of my reproof; I also will laugh at your calamity; I will mock when your fear cometh." The Lord will not always strive with men. He waits long in matchless patience, but he will not always wait; and the day shall come when the refusers shall cry, "Lord, Lord, open unto us," but he will say, "Depart from me; I never knew you;" and they will hear the fatal sentence, "Too late; too late; ye cannot enter now." We know that God heareth not sinners when once they depart out of this life. Once driven by death beyond the verge of mercy, once shut up in hell, this man's words will be most emphatically true concerning them, "We know that God heareth not sinners."

II. Having thus shown you that there are some senses in which this declaration is true, I am going into the other side of the question, and shall show you that THERE ARE SENSES IN WHICH THIS TEXT IS NOT TRUE, but the very reverse of true.

First, it is not true that God hears not those who have been, and still are, in a measure, sinful; because, my brethren, *if he did not hear sinners, he would not hear any human being*, for " all have sinned, and come short of the glory of God." Solomon truly said, "There is no man that sinneth not;" and David wrote, under the inspiration of the Spirit, "There is none that doeth good, no, not one." We have all erred, and gone astray from the right road; and when we approach God in prayer, we must feel this, and confess it. It is not true, therefore, that the Lord does not hear those who have sinned,—those who still call themselves sinners, though they are saved by sovereign grace. Look at the long line of his people, and note how he has heard their prayers. Many beside David have said, "This poor man cried, and the Lord heard him, and saved him out of all his troubles." Even after his people have gone astray from him, he has heard them when they have repented, and returned unto him. The 51st Psalm is a sinner's prayer, is it not? Yet how graciously the Lord listened to it, and restored his penitent servant to his favour. If I thought that God did not hear sinners, that is to say, those who have any sin, then would it be of no use for me to open my lips in prayer, or to lift my eyes to heaven. But, blessed be his name, not only has he heard some of us, sinners though we are, but he has washed us from our sins, clothed us with the righteousness of Christ, and we are "accepted in the Beloved;" and now, when we plead with him, we prevail; we delight ourselves in him, and he gives us the desire of our heart. We dare not say that we are not sinners still; for, though we strive after perfection, and shall never be satisfied with anything short of it, and believe that we shall assuredly have it through Jesus Christ our Lord, yet we have not at present obtained it. We labour after it, not as though we had attained it, or were already perfect, for we still confess that there is iniquity about our holy things, unholiness in our holiness, unbelief in our faith, and something to be repented of in our repentance. Yet the Lord graciously heareth us, blessed be his name, so that it is not true absolutely that God heareth not sinners.

Neither is it true that God does not sometimes hear and answer the prayers of unregenerate men. I am going to speak upon a subject as to which there may be a difference of opinion, but I cannot help that; I am merely relating what I regard as facts. While I was but a child, and knew not the Lord in a saving sense, I was taught by my parents that God heard prayer; and I distinctly remember, as a boy, offering a prayer upon a very unimportant matter. If I were to tell you what it was, it would make you smile; but to me, as a child, it was a very great matter, and I prayed to God many times about it. I know that I was not then born again, neither had I true faith in the Lord Jesus Christ, but I did devoutly believe that God would hear me in that matter, and I asked him again and again, and he gave me my desire. The result upon my mind was wonderfully beneficial, for it confirmed my belief in the existence of God, and helped to arm me against any doubts of the infidel kind that might afterwards assail me, for the first, and what was to me a very remarkable, answer to my prayers, always anchored me fast. On one occasion, in my early ministry, I mentioned this circumstance when I was addressing some Sunday-school children in a chapel where the brethren were of the "very sound" sort; they believed in Calvinistic doctrine, not as I do, reckoning sixteen ounces to the pound, but allowing eighteen or nineteen ounces, and those extra ounces were not good for the people to feed upon. While I was speaking to the children, upstairs in the gallery were some of these divines, and this remark of mine quite shocked them. They considered me to be as bad as Andrew Fuller, and to them he was, doctrinally, about the most horrible person that could be; so, outside the chapel gate, I was assailed with questions about God hearing the prayers of unregenerate people. I was very young at the time, and was rather bothered by those old fellows, but I found a very valiant defender. A poor woman, wearing a red cloak, pushed her way into the throng, and addressed the old men thus, "Fools, and slow of heart to believe what the Holy Spirit has written in the Word." I looked in astonishment at her, wondering what she was going to say. "Did you never read," she said, "that God feedeth the young ravens which cry? Are they regenerate? Do they pray spiritual prayers? Is it not the most natural prayer in the world that comes from a hungry young raven; and if God hears them, and satisfies their desire, do you not think that he will hear a man who is made in his own image, even though he is unregenerate?" The woman won the day for me, and I went away rejoicing.

I know that God hears the sincere and earnest prayers even of unregenerate persons concerning common things. I read, yesterday, a story of Mr. Samuel Medley, of whose hymns we have many in our hymn-books, especially that one about God's lovingkindness. Mr. Medley, in his younger days, was an officer on board one of his majesty's men-of-war. There was a very sharp fight, in which a number of French vessels were destroyed, and young Medley was busy taking the minutes upon the quarter deck. One of the officers, passing by the place where he was sitting, said, "Mr. Medley, you are wounded." He had not perceived it, but the blood was streaming down his leg, and he had to be taken down to the cockpit. After the surgeon had examined him, he said to him, "You will have to lose your leg. I am afraid you cannot live unless amputation takes place." Now Mr. Medley had a godly mother and father, and other gracious people in his family, but he himself was a godless, Christless sinner, as wild as he could be; yet he turned his face to the wall of his little bedroom, and besought the Lord to spare him that leg. When the doctor came to him, the next morning, he said, "I never saw such a case as this before; there has been more healing done, in the last twelve hours, than I ever knew to take place in a leg in my life. I think you will not need to have it off, after all." That remarkable answer to prayer made a deep impression on young Medley's heart, and I believe that biographies will show that, in many cases, God has heard the prayers of unregenerate persons because he meant eventually to save them; and hearing their prayers led them to believe in him, and helped them to exercise that real spiritual faith which brought salvation to their souls.

Let me say, however, that *God sometimes hears the prayers of intensely wicked men out of no love to them.* You remember how he heard the cry of the children of Israel when they said, "Who shall give us flesh to eat?" The Lord sent them quails in great abundance; but "while the flesh was yet between their teeth, ere it was chewed, the wrath of the Lord was kindled against the people, and the Lord smote the people with a very great plague." Again and again, the Lord granted the requests of Pharaoh, cruel Pharaoh, hard-hearted, proud Pharaoh, who was afterwards destroyed in the Red Sea. Jehovah removed one plague after another from him, thus giving him (oh, dreadful thought!) an opportunity to exhibit the hardness of his heart, and to increase it by sinning against the answered prayer. I beseech any man or woman here, who, though not yet converted, has asked God for something, and has received an answer to that petition, not to abuse that answer. I pray you to follow it up. It may be that there are designs of matchless love in store for you, and that, loving you with an amazing love, even while you are dead in sin, God has given you a token that it is even so. But if, after having presented your request to the Lord, and had it granted, you continue to be his enemy, and even grow worse, it may be that the next communication from God to you will be the fatal sentence out of the lips of infinite justice, "You did pray to me, but you never sought anything but temporal things;

and now, since you have rejected me, and have not sought the treasures of my grace, and have sinned against light and knowledge, I will depart from you, and leave you to that final hardness of heart which will irrevocably seal your doom."

Finally,—and here I want to throw the whole force of my message,—*it is not true that God will not hear sinners when they pray to him for mercy, confessing their sins, and believing in Jesus Christ his Son.* I have known three or four persons, quite recently, who have been perplexed with this idea. They have said, "It is no use for us to pray, for God heareth not sinners." My dear friend, how can you, in the teeth of God's Word, believe that statement, understanding it in the sense you give to it? For, if it were so, we should be under the law, not under the gospel; and it would be necessary for us to be righteous before we could ask God for anything; and that is the teaching of Sinai, not of Calvary. It is the glory of the gospel that God does hear sinners, and that he does grant their requests. For you to say that he will not hear a sinner, when he confesses his sin, and forsakes it, and cries to him for mercy, is to contradict the gospel, which is not sent to the righteous, but to sinners,—is not meant for the good, but for the bad, for those who are unrighteous, ungodly, in fact, "sinners."

Look, for instance, at Manasseh, who "made Judah and the inhabitants of Jerusalem to err, and to do worse than the heathen." The Lord rebuked him, yet he would not hearken; but when he was carried away to Babylon, in his affliction, "he besought the Lord his God, and humbled himself greatly before the God of his fathers, and prayed unto him: and he was intreated of him, and heard his supplication, and brought him again to Jerusalem into his kingdom." Look also at the dying thief upon the cross, and let not the thought that God heareth not sinners ever enter into your heads. There was a sinner dying as a malefactor, yet he said to Jesus, "Lord, remember me when thou comest into thy kingdom;" and Jesus said unto him, "To-day shalt thou be with me in paradise." Never say that God heareth not sinners. Have you not read the parable of the publican who "would not lift up so much as his eyes unto heaven, but smote upon his breast, saying, God be merciful to me a sinner"? God did hear him, but he did not hear the Pharisee who thanked God that he was not as other men were. Do you say that God heareth not sinners? Read again the familiar story of the prodigal son. Here he comes, fresh from the swine-trough, filthy without and within, ragged, disgraced; but he has scarcely had time to say, "Father, I have sinned," before he is heard even more fully than he has prayed, and the kiss of acceptance is on his lip, and the best robe has covered him. It is a lie, concocted in the bottomless pit, to say that "God heareth not sinners." If they do but cry, "O God, forgive us, for Jesus' sake," he must hear them; it would be contrary to his nature to turn away from them. Why, sirs, to deny this is to fly in the face of all the invitations and promises of the Word of God. Take this one, for instance, "Seek ye the Lord while he may be found, call ye upon him while he is near; let the wicked forsake his way, and the unrighteous man his thoughts; and let him return unto the Lord, and he will have mercy upon him; and to our God, for he will abundantly pardon." What does that mean but that God invites sinners to pray to him, and bids them come to him, plainly implying that he will not reject them? Then there is that gracious invitation, "Come now, and let us reason together, saith the Lord: though your sins be as scarlet, they shall be as white as snow; though they be red like crimson, they shall be as wool." Does that mean that God will not hear sinners? Why, my Lord Jesus came into the world on purpose to hear sinners,—he came here to seek and to save sinners.

Last Friday night, I was speaking at Moody and Sankey's meeting at Bow Road Hall, and I used an illustration which I will use here now. I said that, if somebody were to ring at my bell at one or two o'clock in the morning, and I put my head out of the window, and asked, "What do you want?" and the answer came, "My wife is very ill, and I have come to ask you to take her case into your hands," I should say, "Bless you, good man! I am not a doctor; why have you come to me?" The man would not be welcome at all, for it is not my business to prescribe for the sick; but there is another house, not very far from mine, where there is a red lamp over the door, for there is a doctor living there. If the man will ring the bell at that house, and say what he wants, he will be welcome, and the doctor will say, "I will be there directly, for it is my business to try to heal the sick." Now, my Lord Jesus Christ has, as it were, a red lamp over his door. He is the Physician for sin-sick souls; it is his business to cure them. A doctor, who never had any patients, would be a poor doctor, would he not? And Jesus Christ (I say this with the utmost reverence,) could not be a great Saviour if there were no great sinners; and he could not be a great Saviour if there were not a great many sinners to be saved. Anybody, who is not a sinner, cannot help Christ in this business. A man, who is not ill, would have to say to a doctor, "I do not need your skill, for there is nothing the matter with me;" but the man who is ill is the one the doctor wants; and the more ill he is, the more does he add to the fame of the physician if a cure is wrought upon him. As for you who think yourselves very good people, Christ does not want you; you do not want him, and he does not want you. But you sinful people, you who know that you are sinners, you who, when I read my text, said, "Ah! that is a death-blow to all our hopes," you are the very people whom Jesus Christ wants. He came into the world to save sinners,—just the sort of people that you are; and let the news be published over the whole earth, that whosoever believeth on him is not condemned. He has shed his precious blood for those who are condemned through sin, that the condemnation might pass away from them through their believing on him. It is gloriously true that God heareth sinners, all sinners who come unto him through Jesus Christ his Son. Let the blind man say what he likes, we have tried it, and proved it for ourselves, and I hope that hundreds of you will prove, at this very moment, that he does hear sinners, for he has heard you.

A PLAIN TALK UPON AN ENCOURAGING TOPIC.

A Sermon

DELIVERED BY

C. H. SPURGEON,

AT THE METROPOLITAN TABERNACLE, NEWINGTON.

"When my soul fainted within me I remembered the LORD: and my prayer came in unto thee, into thine holy temple."—Jonah ii. 7.

THE experience of the saints is the treasure of the Church. Every child of God who has tried and proved the promises of God, when he bears his testimony to their truth, does as it were hang up his sword and spear on the temple walls; and thus the house of the Lord becomes "like the tower of David builded for an armoury, whereon there hang a thousand bucklers, all shields of mighty men." "The footsteps of the flock" encourage others who are following their track to the pastures above. Every preceding generation of saints has lived and suffered to enrich us with its experience. One great reason why the experience of saints in olden time is of such use to us, is this,—they were men of like passions with ourselves. Had they been otherwise, we could not have been instructed by what they suffered. They endured the same trials, and pleaded the same promises before the self-same God, who changes not in any measure or degree; so that we may safely infer that what they gained by pleading may also be obtained by us when surrounded by the same circumstances. If men were different, or if the promises were changed, or if the Lord had varied, all ancient experience would be but an idle tale to us; but now, whenever we read in Scripture of what happened to a man of faith in the day of trial, we conclude that the like will happen to us; and when we find God helping and delivering his people, we know that he will even now show himself strong on our behalf, since all the promises are yea and Amen in Christ Jesus unto the glory of God by us. The covenant has not changed, it abideth firm as the eternal hills. The preacher, therefore, feels quite safe in directing you to the experience of

Jonah, and in inviting you to make its lessons a practical guide to yourselves.

We shall use the lesson of the text, first, *for the child of God;* and, secondly, *for the sinner awakened and aroused.*

I. OUR TEXT HAS AN EVIDENT BEARING UPON THOSE WHO FEAR THE LORD, for such was Jonah. With all his mistakes, he was a man of God; and though he sought to flee from the service of his Master, yet his Master never cast him off; he brought back again his petulant messenger to his work, and honoured him in it, and he sleeps amongst the faithful, waiting for a glorious reward.

Think, then, of *the saints' condition.* In Jonah's case, as set forth before us, the child of God sees what a plight he may be brought into,—his soul may faint in him.

Jonah was certainly in a very terrible condition in the belly of the fish, but the position itself was probably not so dark as his own reflections, for conscience would say to him, "Alas, Jonah! you came here by your own fault, you must needs flee from the presence of God, because in your pride and self-love you refused to go to Nineveh, that great city, and deliver your Master's message." It gives a sting to misery when a man feels that he himself is alone responsible for it. If it were unavoidable that I should suffer, then I could not repine; but if I have brought all this upon myself, by my own folly, then there is a double bitterness in the gall. Jonah would reflect that now he could not help himself in any way. It would answer no purpose to be self-willed now; he was in a place where petulance and obstinacy had no liberty. If he had tried to stretch out his arm, he could not; he was immured in a dungeon which imprisoned every sense as well as every limb, and the bolts of his cell his hand could not draw; he was cast into the deep in the midst of the seas, the waters compassed him about even to the soul, the weeds were wrapped about his head. His state was helpless, and, apart from God, it was hopeless.

Children of God may be brought into a similar condition, and yet be dear to his unchanging heart. They may be poor and needy, and have no helper. No voice may speak a word of sympathy to them, and no arm may be stretched out to succour them. The best of men may be brought into the worst of positions. You must never judge of character by circumstances. Diamonds may be worried upon the wheel, and common pebbles may bathe at ease in the brook. The most wicked are permitted to clamber to the high places of the earth, while the most righteous pine at the rich man's gate, with dogs for their companions. Choice flowers full often grow amid tangled briars. Who has not heard of the lily among thorns? Where dwell the pearls? Do not the dark depths of the ocean conceal them, amid mire and wreck? Judge not by appearances, for heirs of light may walk in darkness, and princes of the celestial line may sit upon dung-hills. Men accepted of God may be brought very, very low, as Jonah was.

Let me remark that the hearts of God's servants may sometimes faint within them; yes, absolutely faint in them, and that, first, through a renewed sense of sin. In this matter, my tongue will not outrun my experience. Some of us have enjoyed for years a full assurance of our pardon and justification. We have walked in the light as God is in the light, and we have had fellowship with the Father and with the Son, and the blood of Jesus Christ his Son hath cleansed us from all sin. We have often felt our hearts dance at the assurance that "there is therefore now no condemnation to them which are in Jesus Christ." We have stood at the foot of the cross, and seen the records of our sins nailed to the tree, as the token of their full discharge. Yet, at this time, we may be suffering an interval of anxious questioning, and unbelief may be lowering over us. It is possible that our faith is staggered, and, therefore, our old sins have risen up against us, and are threatening our peace. At such times, conscience will remind us of our shortcomings, which we cannot deny, and Satan will howl over the top of these shortcomings, "How can you be a child of God? If you were born from above, how could you have acted as you have done?" Then, if for a moment we look away from the cross, if we look within for marks of evidences, the horrible bog of our inward corruptions will be stirred, and there will pour into the soul such dark memories and black forebodings that we shall cry, "I am utterly lost, my hope is hypocrisy; what can I do? What shall I do?" Let me assure you that, under such exercises, it is no wonder if the soul of the Christian faints within him. Be it remembered, also, that soul-fainting is the worst form of fainting. Though Jonah in the whale's belly could not use his eyes, he did not need them; and if he could not use his arms or his feet, he did not require to do so. It mattered not if they all failed him; but for his soul to faint,—this was horror indeed! So is it with us. Our other faculties may go to sleep if they will, but when our faith swoons, and our confidence staggers, things go very hard with us. Do not, however, my brother, when in such a state, write yourself down as a hypocrite, for many of the most valiant soldiers of the cross know by personal experience what this dark sensation means.

> "What though Satan's strong temptations
>   Vex and tease thee day by day?
> And thy sinful inclinations
>   Often fill thee with dismay?
>   Thou shalt conquer,
>   Through the Lamb's redeeming blood.
>
> "Though ten thousand ills beset thee,
>   From without and from within;
> Jesus saith he'll ne'er forget thee,
>   But will save from hell and sin;
>   He is faithful
>   To perform his gracious word.
>
> "Though distresses now attend thee,
>   And thou tread'st the thorny road,
> His right hand shall still defend thee,
>   Soon he'll bring thee home to God:
>   Therefore praise him,
>   Praise the great Redeemer's name."

The came faintness will come over us, at times, through the prospect of prolonged pain or severe trial. You have not yet felt the cruel smart, but you are well aware that it must come, and you shudder at the prospect. As it is true that "we feel a thousand deaths in fearing one," so do we feel a thousand trials in the dread of one single affliction. The soldier is often braver in the midst of the battle than before the conflict begins. Waiting for the assault is trying work; even the crash of the onslaught is not so great a test of endurance. I confess that I feel an inward faintness in the prospect of bodily pain; it creates a swooning sickness of heart within me to consider it for a moment; and, beloved friend, it is no strange thing that is happening to you if your soul also faints because of difficulties or adversities that lie before you. May you have wisdom to do what Jonah did—to remember the Lord,—for there and only there your great strength lieth.

Faintness will also come upon true Christians in connection with the pressure of actual sorrow. Hearts may bear up long, but they are very apt to yield if the pressure be continuous from month to month. A constant drip is felt even by a stone. A long day of drizzling rain is more wetting than a passing shower of heavy drops. A man cannot always be poor, or always be sick, or always be slandered, or always be friendless, without sometimes being tempted to say, "My heart is faint and weary; when will the day break and the shadows flee away?" I say again, the very choicest of God's elect may, through the long abiding of bitter sorrow and heavy distress, be ready to faint in the day of adversity.

The like has happened to earnest Christians engaged in diligent service, when they have seen no present success. To go on tilling a thankless soil, to continue to cast bread upon the waters, and to find no return, has caused many a true heart to faint with inward bleeding. Yet this is full often the test of our fidelity. It is a noble thing to continue preaching, like Noah, throughout a lifetime, amid ridicule, reproach, and unbelief; but it is not every man who can do so. The most of us need success to sustain our courage, and we serve our Master with most spirit when we see immediate results. Faint hearts of that kind there may be among my fellow-soldiers, ready to lay down the weapons of their warfare because they win no victory at this present; my brethren, I pray you do not desert the field of battle, but, like Jonah, remember the Lord, and abide by the royal standard still.

It may be that enquiries will be made as to why and wherefore we should thus enlarge upon the different ways in which Christians faint. Our reply is, we have been thus particular in order to meet the temptation, so common among young Christians, to fancy that they are singular in their trials. "Surely no one has felt as I feel," says many a young Christian; "I don't suppose another person ever hung down his head and his hands, and became so utterly overcome as I am." Do not listen to that suggestion, for it is devoid of truth. Faintness is very common in the Lord's hosts, and some of his mightiest men have been the victims of it. Even David himself, that hero of Judah, in the day of battle waxed faint, and had been slain if a warrior had not come to the rescue. Do not give way to faintness; strive against it vehemently; but, at the same time, should it overcome thee, cast not away thy confidence, nor write thyself down as rejected of God or one fatally fallen.

And now, brethren, we will notice *the saints' resort.* Jonah, when he was in sore trouble, tells us, "I remembered the Lord." What is there for a faint heart to remember in the Lord? Is there not everything? There is, first, his nature. Think of that. When I am faint with sorrow, let me remember that he is very pitiful, and full of compassion; he will not strike too heavily, nor will he forget to sustain. I will, therefore, look up to him, and say, "My Father, break me not in pieces. I am a poor weatherbeaten barque which can scarcely escape the hungry waves; send not thy rough wind against me, but give me a little calm that I may reach the desired haven." By remembering that the Lord's mercies are great, we shall be saved from a fainting heart.

Then I will remember his power. If I am in such a strait that I cannot help myself, *he* can help me. I have exigencies and sharp pinches, but there are no such things with him. There are no emergencies and times of severe pressure with God. With him all things are possible, therefore, will I remember the Lord. If the difficulty be one which arises out of my ignorance, though I know not which way to take, I will remember his wisdom. I know that he will guide me; I will remember that he cannot mistake, and committing my way unto him my soul shall take courage. Beloved, all the attributes of God sparkle with consolation to the eye of faith. There is nothing in the Most High to discourage the man who can say, "My Father, my God, in thee do I put my trust." None who have trusted in him have ever been confounded; therefore, if thy soul sink within thee, remember the nature, and character, and attributes of God.

When you have remembered his nature, then remember his promises. What has he said concerning souls that faint? Think of these texts if you think of no other:—"I will never leave thee, nor forsake thee." "Thy shoes shall be iron and brass; and as thy days, so shall thy strength be." "My grace is sufficient for thee: for my strength is made perfect in weakness." "Trust in the Lord, and do good: so shalt thou dwell in the land, and verily thou shalt be fed." "No good thing will he withhold from them that walk uprightly." When we get upon this strain, and begin to talk of the promises, we need hours in which to enlarge upon the exceeding great and precious words, but we mention only these, we let fall this handful for some poor Ruth to glean. When your soul is faint, catch at a promise, believe it, and say unto the Lord, "Do as thou hast said," and your spirit shall speedily revive.

Remember, next, his covenant. What a grand word that word "covenant" is to the man who understands it! God has entered into covenant with his Son, who represents us, his people. He has said, "As I have sworn that the waters of Noah should no more go over the earth; so have I sworn that I would not be wroth with thee, nor rebuke thee. For the mountains shall depart, and the hills be removed; but my kindness shall not depart from thee, neither shall the covenant of my peace be removed." Truly, we may say with good old David, "Although my house be not so with God; yet he hath made with me an everlasting covenant, ordered in all things, and sure." When everything else gives way, cling in the power of the Holy Spirit to covenant mercies and covenant engagements, and your spirit shall be at peace.

> " With David's Lord, and ours,
>   A covenant once was made,
> Whose bonds are firm and sure,
>   Whose glories ne'er shall fade;
> Signed by the Sacred Three in One,
> In mutual love ere time begun.
>
> "Firm as the lasting hills,
>   This covenant shall endure,
> Whose potent *shalls* and *wills*
>   Make every blessing sure:
> When ruin shakes all nature's frame,
> Its jots and tittles stand the same."

Again, when we remember the Lord, we should remember what he has been to us in past times. When any of us fall to doubting and fearing, we are indeed blameworthy, for the Lord has never given us any occasion for doubting him. He has helped us in sorer troubles than we are passing through at this time. We have tested his faithfulness, his power, and his goodness at a heavier rate than now, and though hardly tried, they have never failed us yet; they have borne the strain of many years, and show no signs of giving way; wherefore, then, are we distrustful? Many saints have proved the Lord's faithfulness for fifty, sixty, or even seventy years; how can they be of doubtful mind after this? What! has your God been true for seventy years, and cannot you trust him a few more days? Has he brought you to seventy-five, and cannot you trust him the few months more that you are to remain in the wilderness? Call to remembrance the days of old, the love of his heart, and the might of his arm, when he came to your rescue, and took you out of the deep waters, and set your feet upon a rock, and established your goings. He is the same God still; therefore, when your soul fainteth within you, remember the Lord, and you will be comforted.

Thus I have shown you the saint's plight and the saint's resort; now observe *the success of his prayer*. Jonah was so comforted with the thoughts of God that he began to pray, and his prayer was not drowned in the water, nor choked in the fish's belly, neither was it held captive by the weeds that were about his head, but up it went like an electric flash, through waves, through clouds, beyond the stars, up to the throne of God, and down came the answer like a return message. Nothing can destroy or detain a real prayer; its flight to the throne is swift and certain. God the Holy Ghost writes our prayers, God the Son presents our prayers, and God the Father accepts our prayers, and with the whole Trinity to help us in it, what cannot prayer perform? I may be speaking to some who are under very severe trials,—I feel persuaded that I am,—let me beg them to take this promise to themselves as their own; and I pray God the Holy Ghost to lay it home to their hearts, and make it theirs, "I will never leave thee, nor forsake thee." God will not fail you though you fail yourself. Though you faint, he fainteth not, neither is weary. Lift up your cry, and he will lift up his hand. Go to your knees, you are strongest there; resort to your chamber, and it shall be to you none other than the gate of heaven. Tell your God your grief; heavy to you, it will be light enough to him. Dilemmas will all be plain to his wisdom, and difficulties will vanish before his strength. Oh, tell it not in Gath that Israel cannot trust in God; publish it not in the streets of Askelon that trouble can dismay those who lean upon the eternal arm. With Jehovah in the van, O hosts of Israel, dare ye fear? "The Lord of hosts is with us; the God of Jacob is our refuge." What man's heart shall quail, or what soul shall faint? "Lift up the hands which hang down, and the feeble knees." Say unto the feeble in heart, "Be strong; fear not. God is with you; he will help you, and that right early."

II. Now we must change the subject altogether. Having addressed the people of God, we feel very anxious to speak to those concerning whom the Lord has designs of love, but who are not yet made manifest. THE SINNER, WHEN GOD COMES TO DEAL WITH HIM, IS BROUGHT INTO THE SAME PLIGHT AS JONAH. His soul faints in him. What does that show?

It shows very much which we are glad to see. When a man's soul faints within him, it is clear that *his carelessness is gone*. He used to take things very easily, and as long as he could make merry from day to day, what cared he about heaven or hell? The preacher's warnings were to him so much rant, and his earnestness fanaticism; but now the man feels an arrow sticking in his own loins, and he knows that there is a reality in sin, it is to him in very deed an evil and a bitter thing. Now the cup of gall is put to his own lips, and he feels the poison in his own veins. His heart faints within him, and he remains careless no longer; which is no small gain in the preacher's estimation.

His faintness also shows that *he will be self-righteous no longer.* Once he hoped he was as good as other people, and perhaps a little better; and for all that he could see, he was every whit as excellent as the saints themselves. They might speak about their trusting in Jesus Christ, but he was working for himself, and expected by his regular habits to win as good as place in the world to come as the best of believers. Ah! but now God has dealt with him, and let the daylight into his soul, and he sees that his gold and silver are cankered, and that his fair linen is filthy and worm-eaten; he discovers that his righteousnesses are as filthy rags, and that he must have something better than the works of the law to trust in, or he must perish. So far so good. Things are hopeful when there is no more self-reliance left in the sinner. The worst of human nature is that, though it cannot lift a finger for its own salvation, it thinks it can do it all; and though its only place is the place of death, and it is a mercy when it comes to burial, yet that same human nature is so proud that it would, if it could, be its own redeemer. When God make man's conscience a target for his fiery arrows, then straightway he feels that his life is no longer in him, and that he can do nothing, and he cries out, "God be merciful to me." Oh, that the two-edged sword of the gospel would slay all our spiritual self-reliance, and lay us in the dust at the feet of the crucified Saviour.

Perhaps I speak to some who faint because, though they have given up all self-righteousness now, and relinquished all self-dependence, they yet *have not laid hold upon Christ and his salvation*. "I have been trying to believe," says one, "but I cannot succeed." Well do I remember the time when I laboured to believe. It is a strange way of putting it, yet so it was. When I wished to believe, and longed to trust, I found I could not. It seemed to me that the way to heaven by Christ's righteousness was as difficult as the way to heaven by my own, and that I could as soon get to heaven by Sinai as by Calvary. I could do nothing, I could neither repent nor believe. I fainted with despair, feeling as if I must be lost despite the gospel, and for ever driven from Jehovah's presence, even though Christ had died. Ah! I am not sorry if you also have come to this condition. The way to the door of faith is through the gate of self-despair. Till thou hast seen thy last hope destroyed, thou wilt never look to Christ for all things, and yet thou wilt never be saved until thou dost; for God has laid no help on you, he has laid help upon One that is mighty, even Jesus only, who is the sole Saviour of sinners. Here, then, we have before us the sinner's plight; and I will venture to call it, though it is a very wretched one, a very blessed one; and I heartily wish that every unconverted man were brought into such a condition that his soul fainted within him.

Now, hear ye the gospel, incline your ear to it, and ye shall live. The way of salvation to you is the way which Jonah took. When his soul fainted, he remembered the Lord. I beseech you, by the living God, now to remember the Lord; and if you ask me what it is you should remember, I will tell you in a few words. Remember the Lord Jesus Christ, the Son of God, the Saviour of sinners; remember him who suffered in the room of the guilty. Know, assuredly, that God has visited upon him the transgressions of his people. Now, the sufferings of such an one as Jesus must have power to cleanse away sins. He is God, and if he deigns to die, there must be such merit in his death that he is able to save to the uttermost all them that come unto God by him. You are bidden, at this moment, in God's name, to trust your soul in those hands that were nailed to the cross, and rest your life with him who poured out his soul unto death that you might live. In yourself, you may well despair; but remembering his name, coupled with the names of Gethsemane and Golgotha, remembering all his pains, and griefs, and woes unutterable,—remembering these by faith, there shall be salvation for you at this moment. Do I hear you sigh, "Oh! but I have nothing good within me"? Know, then, that all good is in him for thee; and go to him for it. "But I am unworthy." He is worthy; go to him for worthiness. "But I do not feel as I should." He felt as he should; go to him for all that thou shouldst feel. If thou bringest a rusty farthing of thine own, God will not have it; it would only insult the precious gold of Ophir, which Jesus freely gives thee, if he should allow thy cankered counterfeits to be mixed therewith. Away with thy filthy rags! Wouldst thou add them to the spotless garment which Christ has woven? Dross and dung, the apostle says our best works are, if we venture to put them side by side with the merits of our Redeemer. None but Jesus can save; remember him, and live!

"But," says one, "I have tried to remember the Lord; but I find that, while I can trust him to pardon my sins, yet I have such a hard heart, and so many temptations, and I am so weak for all that is good, that I still despair." Hearken, then, yet again: remember the Lord. At this time remember the Holy Ghost. When Jesus ascended on high, the Holy Ghost was given, and he has never been recalled. The Holy Ghost is here in this assembly now, and in the Holy Ghost is your hope against indwelling sin. You complain that you cannot pray, but the Spirit helpeth our infirmities. You mourn that you cannot believe, but faith is the gift of God and the work of the Holy Spirit. A tender heart, a penitential frame of mind, a right spirit,—these are the work of the Holy Ghost in you. You can do nothing, but the Holy Ghost can work everything in you. Give yourself up to those dear hands that were pierced, and the power of the Holy Spirit shall come upon you. A new heart will he give you, and a right spirit will he put within you; you shall learn his statutes, and walk in his ways. Everything is provided for the believer that he can possibly want. O young man, anxious to be saved, the salvation of Jesus Christ precisely suits your case! O seeking soul, whatever it is thou cravest to make thee fit to dwell where God is for ever, it is all to be had, and to be had for the asking, for it is all provided in the covenant of grace; and if thou wilt remember Jesus the Lord, and the Holy Ghost,—the Indweller who renews the mind,—thou wilt be cheered and comforted!

Yet let me not forget another Person of the sacred Majesty of heaven,—remember the Father as well as the Son and the Spirit; and let me help thee to remember him. Thou, trembling sinner, must not think of God as severe or stern, for he is love. Wouldst thou be glad to be saved? He will be gladder still to save thee. Dost thou wish to return to thy God to-night? Thy God already meets thee, and bids thee come. Wouldst thou be pardoned? The absolution is on his lips. Wouldst thou be cleansed? The fountain of atoning blood was filled by his mercy, and filled for all who believe in his Son. Come and welcome, come and welcome! The child is glad to be forgiven, but the Father is gladder still to forgive. Jehovah's melting bowels yearn to clasp his Ephraim to his breast. Seek him at once, poor souls, and ye shall not find him hard and cold, but waiting to be gracious, ready to forgive, a God delighting in mercy. If you can thus remember God, the Son, the Spirit, and the Father, though your soul faint within you, you may be encouraged.

And so I close by bidding you, if such be the case, to imitate Jonah's example, and send up a prayer to heaven, for it will come up even to God's holy temple. Jonah had no prayer-book, and you need none. God the Holy Ghost can put more living prayer into half-a-dozen words of your own than you could get out of a ton weight of paper prayers. Jonah's prayer was not notable for its words. The fish's belly was not the place for picked phrases, nor for long-winded orations. We do not believe that he offered a long prayer either, but it came right up from his heart, and flew straight up to heaven. It was shot by the strong bow of intense desire and agony of soul, and, therefore, it speeded its way to the throne of the Most High. If you would now pray, never mind your words, it is the soul of prayer that God accepts. If you would be saved, go to your chamber, and rise not from your knees till the Lord has heard you. Ay, where you now are, let your souls pour out themselves before God, and faith in Jesus will give you immediate salvation.

Exposition by C. H. Spurgeon.
JONAH II

Verse 1. *Then Jonah prayed unto the* LORD *his God out of the fish's belly.*

What a strange place for prayer! Surely this is the only prayer that ever went up to God out of a fish's belly. Jonah found himself alive;— that was the surprising thing, that he was alive in the belly of a fish;— and because he was alive, he began to pray. It is such a wonder that some people here should continue to live that they ought to begin to pray. If you live with death so near, and in so great peril, and yet you do not pray, what is to become of you?

This prayer of Jonah is very remarkable because it is not a prayer at all, in the sense in which we usually apply the word to petition and supplication. If you read the prayer through, you will see that it is almost all thanksgiving; and the best prayer in all the world is a prayer that is full of thankfulness. We praise the Lord for what he has done for us, and thus we do, in effect, ask him to perfect the work which he has begun. He has delivered us; so we bless his holy name, and by implication we beseech him still to deliver us.

Notice that it says here, "Then Jonah prayed *untother* Lord his God." He was a runaway; he had tried to escape from the presence of God; yet the Lord was still his God. God will not lose any of his people; even if, like Jonah, they are in the belly of a fish, Jehovah is still their God: "Then Jonah prayed unto the Lord his God out of the fish's belly,"—

2. *And said, I cried by reason of mine affliction unto the* LORD, *and he heard me;—*

You see that this is not praying, it is telling the Lord what he had done for his disobedient servant. Jonah had prayed, and the Lord had heard him, yet he was still in the fish's belly. Unbelief would have said, "You have lived so long, Jonah; but you cannot expect to live to get out of this dreary, damp, fetid prison." Ah, but faith is out of prison even while she is in it. Faith begins to tell what God has done before the great work is actually accomplished; so Jonah said, "I cried by reason of mine affliction unto the Lord, and he heard me;"—

2. *Out of the belly of hell cried I, and thou heardest my voice.*
He was like a man in the unseen world among the dead. He felt that he was condemned and cast away; yet God had heard him, and now he sings about it in the belly of the fish. No other fish that ever lived had a live man inside him singing praises unto God.

3. *For thou hadst cast me into the deep, in the midst of the seas;*
The word Jonah used implies that God had violently cast him away into the deep. "Cast me not off," prayed David; but here is a man who says that God did cast him out like a thing flung overboard into the vasty deep: "Thou hadst cast me into the deep, in the midst of the seas;"—

3. *And the floods compassed me about:*
"They rolled all over me, beneath me, above me, around me: 'The floods compassed me about:'"—

3. *All thy billows and thy waves passed over me.*
Jonah had evidently read his Bible; at least, he had read the 42nd Psalm, for he quotes it here. It is a blessed thing to have the Bible in your mind and heart so that, wherever you may be, you do not need to turn to the Book because you have the Book inside you. Here is a man inside a fish with a Book inside of him; and it was the Book inside of him that brought him out from the fish again.

4. *Then I said, I am cast out of thy sight; yet I will look again toward thy holy temple.*
What grand faith Job displayed when he said, "Though he slay me, yet will I trust in him;" and here is another splendid manifestation of faith, "'I said, I am cast out of thy sight; yet I will look again toward thy holy temple.' If God does not look at me, I will still look towards the place where he dwells. As I am being flung away from him, I will give one more look towards his holy temple."

5. *The waters compassed me about, even to the soul:—*
They seemed to get right into his spirit; his heart became waterlogged: "The waters compassed me about, even to the soul:"—

5. *The depth closed me round about, the weeds were wrapped about my head.*
Like his winding-sheet,—as if the cerements of the grave were wrapped about his mouth, and ears, and eyes, and he was consigned to a living tomb. This narrative is a graphic description of the natural motion of the great fish which had swallowed Jonah. When the fish found this strange being inside him, the first thing that he did was to plunge as deep as ever he could into the waters. You will see that Jonah did go down very deep indeed. The next thing was for the fish to make for the weeds; as certain creatures eat weeds to cure them when they feel very ill, this fish went off to the weedy places to see if he could get a cure for this new complaint of a man inside him.

6. *I went down to the bottoms of the mountains;—*
To the very roots and foundations of the mountains, where the big jagged rocks made huge buttresses for the hills above: "I went down to the bottoms of the mountains;"—

6. *The earth with her bars was about me for ever:*
Down went the fish, as deep as he could go: and, of course, down went Jonah too, and he might well imagine that he was in a vast prison from which there was no way of escape.

6. *Yet hast thou brought up my life from corruption, O LORD my God.*

And, dear friend, God can bring you up, however low you may have gone. Though, in your own feelings, you feel as if you had gone so low that you could not go any lower, God can, in answer to prayer, bring you up again. O despairing one, take heart, and be comforted by this story of Jonah! God is dealing with you as he was with him. There may be a great fish, but there is a great God as well. There may be a deep sea, but there is an almighty God to bring you up out of it.

7. *When my soul fainted within me I remembered the LORD:*

It is a blessed memory that serves us faithfully in a fainting fit. Mostly, when the heart faints, the memory fails; but Jonah remembered the Lord when his soul fainted within him.

7. *And my prayer came in unto thee, into thine holy temple.*

Think of Jonah's prayer going right within the veil, and reaching the ear and heart of God in his holy temple. He said that he was cast out of God's sight, yet his prayer went into God's temple. Oh, the prevalence of a bold believing prayer! "My prayer came in unto thee, into thine holy temple."

8. *They that observe lying vanities forsake their own mercy.*

If you trust anywhere but in God, you will run away from your own mercy. God is the only really merciful One who can always help you; but if you trust in your own righteousness, if you trust in priestcraft, if you trust in any superstition, you are observing lying vanities, and forsaking your own mercy. God is the source of your mercy; do not run away from him to anyone or anything else.

9. *But I will sacrifice unto thee—*

"I long to do so. I cannot do it just now, but I would if I could; and I will do it when thou shalt grant me deliverance from my present peril."

9. *With the voice of thanksgiving; I will pay that that I have vowed. Salvation is of the LORD.*

That is one of the grandest utterances that any man ever made: "SALVATION!" Write it in capital letters. It is a very emphatic word in the Hebrew, and I might read it, "Mighty salvation is of Jehovah." This is real, old-fashioned Calvinistic doctrine spoken centuries before John Calvin was born. The whale could not endure it, and he turned Jonah out directly he said, "Salvation is of the Lord." The world does not like that doctrine, and there are many professing Christians who do not like it. They say, "Salvation is of man's free will; salvation is of the works of the law; salvation is of rites and ceremonies;" and so on. But we say, with Jonah, "Salvation is of the Lord." He works it from beginning to end, and therefore he must have all the praise for it for ever and ever.

10. *And the LORD spake unto the fish, and it vomited out Jonah upon the dry land.*

God has only to speak, and even sea-monsters obey him. I know not how he spoke to the fish; I do not know how to talk to a fish, but God does; and as the Lord could speak to that fish, he can speak to any sinner here. However far you may have gone from all that is good, he who spoke to that great fish, and made it disgorge the prophet Jonah, can speak to you, and then you will give up your sins as the whale gave up Jonah. God grant that it may be so this very hour!

That is the prayer of an ancient mariner; may it be ours, as far as it is suited to our circumstances, and may we be brought by God's grace to cry, with Jonah, "Salvation is of the Lord"!

PREACHING
Rightly Dividing the Word of Truth—II Tim. 2:15
The Burden of the Word of the Lord—Mal. 1:1

RIGHTLY DIVIDING THE WORD OF TRUTH

A Sermon

Delivered on Lord's-Day Evening, December 27th, 1874, by

C. H. SPURGEON,

AT THE METROPOLITAN TABERNACLE, NEWINGTON.

"Rightly dividing the word of truth."—2 Timothy ii. 15.

Timothy was to divide rightly the word of God. This every Christian minister must do if he would make full proof of his ministry, and if he would be clear of the blood of his hearers at the last great day. Of the whole twenty years of my printed sermons, I can honestly say that this has been my aim—rightly to divide the word of truth. Wherein I have succeeded I magnify the name of the Lord, wherein I have failed I lament my faultiness. And now once more we will try again, and may God the Holy Spirit, without whose power nothing can be done aright, help us rightly to divide the word of truth.

The expression is a very remarkable one, because it bears so many phases of meaning. I do not think that any one of the figures by which I shall illustrate it will be at all strained, for they have been drawn from the text by most eminent expositors, and may fairly be taken as honest comments, even when they might be challenged as correct interpretations of the text. "Rightly dividing the word of truth" is our authorised version, but we leave it for a little to consider other renderings. Timothy was neither to mutilate, nor twist, nor torture, nor break in pieces the word, nor keep on the outside of it, as those do who never touch the soul of a text, but rightly to divide it, as one taught of God to teach others.

I. The vulgate version translates it—and with a considerable degree of accuracy—"Rightly HANDLING the word of truth." What is the right way, then, to handle the word of truth? It is like a sword, and *it was not meant to be played with.* That is not rightly to handle the gospel. It must be used in earnest and pushed home. Are you converted, my friends? Do you believe in Jesus Christ? Are you saved, or not? Swords are meant to cut and hack, and wound, and kill with, and the word of truth is for pricking men in the heart and killing their sins. The word of God is not committed to God's ministers to amuse men with its glitter, nor to charm them with the jewels in its hilt, but to conquer their souls for Jesus. Remember, dear hearers, if the preacher does not push you to this—that you shall be converted, or he will know the reason why; if he does not drive you to this—that you shall either wilfully reject, or cheerfully accept Christ, he has not yet known how rightly to handle the great "sword of the Spirit, which is the word of God." Now, then, where are you personally at this moment? Are you unbelievers, upon whom the wrath of God abideth, or are you believers, who may lay claim to that gracious word, "Verily, verily, I say unto you, he that believeth in me hath everlasting life." Oh that the Lord would make his all-discerning word go round this place and strike at every conscience and lay bare every heart with its mighty power.

He that rightly handles the word of God will *never use it to defend men in their sins*, but to slay their sins. If there be a professing Christian here who is living in known sin, shame upon him; and if there be a non-Christian man who is living in sin, let his conscience upbraid him. What will he do in that day when Christ comes to judge the hearts of men, and the books shall be opened, and every thought shall be read out before an assembled universe? I desire to handle the word of God so that no man may ever find an excuse in my ministry for his living without Christ, and living in sin, but may know clearly that sin is a deadly evil, and unbelief the sure destroyer of the soul. He has indeed been made to handle the word aright who plunges it like a two-edged sword into the very bowels of sin.

The gospel ought *never to be used for frightening sinners from Christ.* I believe it is so handled sometimes. Sublime doctrines are rolled like rocks in the sinner's way, and dark experiences set up as a standard of horror which must be reached before a man may believe in Jesus: but rightly to handle the word of life is to frighten men *to* Christ rather than *from* him, yea, to woo them to him by the sweet assurance that he will cast out none that come, that he asks no preparations of them, but if they come at once as they are he will assuredly receive them. Have I not handled the word of truth in this way hundreds of times in this house? Has it not been a great magnet attracting sinners? As a magnet has two poles, and with one pole it repels, so, no doubt, the truth of God repels the prejudiced, rebellious heart, and thus it is a savour of death unto death; but our object is so to handle it that the attractive pole may come into operation through the power of the Spirit of God, and men may be drawn to Christ.

Moreover, if we rightly handle the word of God *we shall not preach it so as to send Christians into a sleepy state.* That is easily done. We may preach the consolations of the gospel till each professor feels "I am safe enough; there is no need to watch, no need to fight, no need for any exertion whatever. My battle is fought, my victory is won, I have only to fold my arms and go to sleep." No, no, men, this is not how we handle the word of God, but our cry is, "Work out your own salvation with fear and trembling; for it is God which worketh in you both to will and to do of his good pleasure. Watch and pray that ye enter not into temptation. Reckon not yourselves to have attained unto perfection, but forget the things that are behind, and reach forward to that which is before, ever looking unto Jesus." This is rightly to handle the word of God.

And, oh, beloved, there is one thing that I dread above all others—lest I should ever handle the word of God *so as to persuade some of you that you are saved when you are not.* To collect a large number of professors together is one thing; but to have a large number of true saints built together in Christ is quite another thing. To get up a whirl of excitement, and to have people influenced by that excitement, so that they think full surely that they are converted, has been done a great many times; but the bubble has, by-and-by, vanished. The balloon has been filled until it has burst. God save us from that. We want sure work, lasting work, a work of divine grace in the heart. If you are not converted, pray do not pretend that you are. If you have not known what it is to be brought down to see your own nothingness, and then to be built up by the power of the Spirit upon Christ as the only foundation, oh, remember that whatever is built upon the quicksand will fall with a crash in the hour of trial. Do not be satisfied with anything short of a deep foundation, cut in the solid rock of the work of Jesus Christ. Ask for real vital godliness, for nothing else will serve your turn at the last great day. Now, this is rightly to handle the word of God; to use it to push truth home upon men for their present conversion, to use it for the striking down of their sins, to use it to draw men to Christ, to use it to arouse sinners, and to use it to produce, not mere profession, but a real work of grace in the hearts of men. May the Holy Ghost teach all the ministers of Christ after this fashion to handle the two-edged sword of the Spirit, which is the word of God.

II. But now, secondly, my text has another meaning. It has an idea in it which I can only express by a figure. "Rightly dividing, or STRAIGHT CUTTING." A ploughman stands here with his plough, and he ploughs right along from this end of the field to the other, making a straight furrow. And so Paul would have Timothy make a straight furrow right through the word of truth. I believe there is no preaching that God will ever accept but that which goes decidedly through the whole line of truth from end to end, and is always thorough, honest, and downright. As truth is a straight line, so must our handling of the truth be straightforward and honest, without shifts or tricks. There are two or three furrows which I have laboured hard to plough. One is the furrow of *free grace.* "Salvation is of the Lord,"—he begins it, he carries it on, he completes it. Salvation is not of man, neither by man, but of grace alone. Grace in election, grace in redemption, grace in effectual calling, grace in final perseverance, grace in conferring the perfection of glory; it is all grace from beginning to end. If we say at any time anything which is really contrary to this distinct testimony that salvation is of grace, believe us not. This furrow must be ploughed fairly, plainly, and beyond all mistake. Sinner, you cannot be saved by any merit, penance, preparation, or feeling of your own. The Lord alone must save you as a work of gratis mercy, not because you deserve it, but because he wills to do it to magnify his abundant love. That is the straight furrow of the Word.

We endeavour always to make a straight furrow upon the matter of *human depravity*—to preach that man is fallen, that every part and passion of his nature is perverted, that he has gone astray altogether, is sick from the crown of his head to the sole of his foot, yea, is dead in trespasses and sins, and corrupt before God. "There is none that doeth good, no, not one." I have noticed some preachers ploughing this furrow very crookedly, for they say, "There are some very fine points about man still, and many good things in him which only need developing and educating." You may have read in the history of Mr. Whitfield's time what a howl was made at him because he once said that man was half beast and half devil. I do not think he ever got nearer the truth than when he said that; only I would beg the beast's pardon, for a beast would scarcely become so evil and vile as human nature becomes when it is left alone fully to develop itself. O pride of human nature, we plough right over thee! The hemlock stands in thy field, and must be cut up by the roots. Thy weeds smile like fair flowers, but the ploughshare must go right through them all till all human beauty is shown to be a painted Jezebel, and all human glorying a bursting bubble. God is everything, man is nothing. God in his grace saves man, but man by his sin utterly ruins himself until God's grace interposes. I like to plough a straight furrow here.

Another straight furrow is that of *faith*. We are sent to tell men that he that believeth and is baptised shall be saved, and our duty is to put it so. "Salvation is not of works;" that is not the furrow: not of prayers, that is not the furrow: not of feelings—that is not the gospel furrow: not of preparations and amendments and reforms; but by faith in Jesus Christ. He that believeth on him is not condemned. As we begin the new life by faith, we must abide in it by faith. We are not to be saved by faith up to a certain point, and then to rely upon ourselves. Having begun in the gospel we are not to be perfected by the law. "The just shall live by faith." We live by faith at the wicket-gate, and we live by faith until we enter into our eternal rest. *Believe!*—that is the grand gospel precept, and we trust we have never gone out of this furrow, but have tried to plough right across the gospel field from end to end, crying, "Look unto me and be ye saved, all ye ends of the earth, for Jehovah is God, and beside him there is none else."

Another furrow which some do not much like to plough, but which must be distinctly marked if a man is an honest ploughman for God, is that of *repentance*. Sinner, you and your sins must part. You have been married long, and you have had a merry time of it perhaps; but you must part. You and your sins must separate, or you and your God will never come together. Not one sin may you keep. They must all be given up; they must be brought out like the Canaanitish kings from the cave, and hanged up before the sun. Not one darling must be spared. You must forsake them, loathe them, abhor them, and ask the Lord to overcome them. Do you not know that the furrow of repentance runs right through the Christian's life? He sins, and as long as he sins he repents of his sin. The child of God cannot love sin: he must loathe it as long as he sees any of it in existence.

There is the furrow of *holiness*, that is the next turn the ploughman takes " Without holiness no man shall see the Lord." We have preached salvation by grace, but we do not preach salvation to those who still continue in sin. The children of God are a holy people, washed, purged, sanctified, and made zealous for good works; and he who talks about faith, and has no works to prove that his faith is a living faith, lies to himself and lies before God. It is faith that saves us, not works, but the faith that saves us always produces works: it renews the heart, changes the character, influences the motives, and is the means in the hand of God of making the man a new creature in Christ Jesus. No nonsense about it, sirs: you may be baptised and re-baptised, you may attend to sacraments, or you may believe in an orthodox creed; but you will be damned if you live in sin. You may become a deacon, or an elder, or a minister, if you dare; but there is no salvation for any man who still harbours his sins. "The wages of sin is death"—death to professors as well as to non-professors. If they hug their sins in secret God will reveal those sins in public, and condemn them according to the strict justice of his law. These are the furrows we have tried to plough—deep, sharp cut, and straight. Oh, that God might plough them himself in all your hearts that you may know experimentally how the truth is rightly divided.

III. There is a third meaning to the text. "Rightly dividing the word of truth" is, as some think, an expression taken from the priests dividing the sacrifices. When they had a lamb or a sheep, a ram or a bullock to offer, after they had killed it, it was cut in pieces, carefully and properly; and it requires no little skill to find out where the joints are, so as to cut up an animal discreetly. Now, the word of truth has to be taken to pieces wisely; it is not to be hacked or torn as by a wild beast, but rightly divided. There has to be DISCRIMINATION AND DISSECTION. It is a great part of a minister's duty to be able to dissect the gospel—to lay one piece there, and another there, and preach with clearness, distinction, and discrimination.

Every gospel minister must divide between the covenant of works and the covenant of grace. It is a very nice point that, and many fail to discern it well; but it must always be kept clear, or great mischief will be done. Confusion worse confounded follows upon confusing grace and law. There is the covenant of works—"This do, and thou shalt live," but its voice is not that of the covenant of grace which says, "Hear and your soul shall live." "You shall, for I will:" that is the covenant of grace. It is a covenant of pure promise unalloyed by terms and conditions. I have heard people put it thus—"Believers will be saved if from this time forth they are faithful to grace given." That savours of the covenant of works. "God will love you"—says another,—"*if you*—." Ah, the moment you get an "*if*" in it, it is the covenant of works, and the gospel has evaporated. Oil and water will sooner mix than merit and grace. When you find the covenant of works anywhere, what are you to do with it? Why, do what Abraham did, and what Sarah demanded, " cast out the bond-woman and her son, for the son of the bondwoman shall not be heir with my son, even with Isaac." If you are a child of the free-grace promise, do not suffer the Hagar and Ishmael of legal bondage and carnal hope to live in your house. Out with them; you have nought to do with them. Let law and gospel keep their proper places. The law is the schoolmaster to bring us to Christ, but when we have come to Christ we are no longer under a schoolmaster. Let the law principle go its way to work conviction in sinners, and destroy their ill-grounded hopes, but do you abide in Christ Jesus even as you have received him. If you are to be saved by works then it is not of grace, otherwise work is no more work; and if saved by grace then it is not of human merit, otherwise grace is no more grace. To keep clear here is of the first importance, for on the rocks of legality many a soul has been cast away.

We need also to keep up a clear distinction between the efforts of nature and the work of grace. It is commendable for men to do all they can to improve themselves, and everything by which people are made more sober, more honest, more frugal, better citizens, better husbands, better wives, is a good thing; but that is nature and not grace. Reformation is not regeneration. "Ye must be born again" still stands for the good as well as for the bad. To be made a new creature in Christ Jesus is as necessary for the moral as for the debauched; for, when flesh has done its best, "that which is born of the flesh is flesh;" and men must be born of the Spirit, or they cannot understand spiritual things, or enter into heaven. I have always tried to keep up this distinction, and I trust none of you will ever mistake the efforts of nature for the works of divine grace. Do what you can for human reformation, for whatsoever things are honest and of good repute you are to foster; but, still, never put the most philanthrophic plan, or the most elevating system in the place of the work of sovereign grace, for, if you do, you will do ten times as much mischief as you can possibly do good. We must rightly divide the word of truth.

It is always well, too, for Christian men to be able to distinguish one truth from another. Let the knife penetrate between the joints of the work of Christ for us, and the work of the Holy Spirit in us. Justification, by which the righteousness of Christ is imputed to us, is one blessing; sanctification, by which we ourselves are made personally righteous, is another blessing. I have known some describe sanctification as a sort of foundation, or at least a buttress for the work of justification. Now, no man is justified because he is sanctified: he is justified because he believeth in him that justifieth the ungodly. Sanctification follows justification. It is the work of the Spirit of God in the soul of a believer, who first of all was justified by believing in Jesus while as yet he was unsanctified. Give Jesus Christ all the glory for his great and perfect work, and remember that you are perfect in Christ Jesus and accepted in the Beloved, but, at the same time, give glory to the Holy Spirit, and remember that you are not yet perfect in holiness, but that the Spirit's work is to be carried on and will be carried on all the days of your life.

One other point of rightly dividing should never be forgotten, we must always distinguish between the root and the fruit. He is a very poor botanist who does not know a bulb from a bud, but I believe that there are some Londoners who do not know which are roots and which are fruits, so little have they seen of anything growing ; and I am sure there are some theologians who hardly know which is the cause and which is the effect in spiritual things. Putting the cart before the horse is a very absurd thing, but many do it. Hear how people will say—" If I could feel joy in the Lord I would believe." Yes, that is the cart before the horse, for joy is the result of faith, not the reason for it. " But I want to feel a great change of heart, and then I will believe." Just so ; you wish to make the fruit the root. " Believe in the Lord Jesus Christ," that is the root of the matter ; change of life and joy in the Lord will spring up as gracious fruits of faith, and not otherwise. When will you discriminate?

Thus I have given you three versions of my text—rightly handling, straightly furrowing, and wisely discriminating.

IV. The next interpretation of the apostle's expression is, practically CUTTING OUT the word for holy uses. This is the sense given by Chrysostom. I will show you what I mean here. Suppose I have a skin of leather before me, and I want to make a saddle. I take a knife, and begin cutting out the shape. I do not want those parts which are dropping off on the right, and round this corner ; they are very good leather, but I cannot just now make use of them. I have to cut out my saddle, and I make that my one concern. Or, suppose I have to make a pair of reins out of the leather. I must take my knife round, and work away with one object, keeping clearly before me what I am aiming at. The preacher, to be successful, must also have his wits about him, and when he has the Bible before him he must use those portions which will have a bearing upon his grand aim. He must make use of the material laid ready to his hand in the Bible. Every portion of the word of God is very blessed, and exceedingly profitable, but it may not happen to be connected with the preacher's immediate subject, and therefore he leaves it to be considered another time ; and, though some will upbraid him for it, he is much too sensible to feel bound to preach all the doctrines of the Bible in each sermon. He wants to have souls saved and Christians quickened, and therefore he does not for ever pour out the vials, and blow the trumpets of prophecy. Some hearers are crazy after the mysteries of the future. Well, there are two or three brethren in London who are always trumpeting and vialing. Go and hear them if you want it, I have something else to do. I confess I am not sent to decipher the Apocalyptic symbols, my errand is humbler but equally useful, I am sent to bring souls to Jesus Christ. There are preachers who are always dealing with the deep things, the very deep things. For them the coral caves of mystery, and the far descending shafts of metaphysics have a mighty charm. I have no quarrel with their tastes, but I do not think the word of God was given us to be a riddle-book. To me the plain gospel is the part which I cut out, and rightly cut out of the word of God. There is a soul that wants to know how to find peace with God. Some other brother can tell him where predestination falls in with free agency, I do not pretend to know ; but I do know that faith in Jesus brings peace to the heart. My business is to bring forth that which will save souls, build up saints, and set Christians to work for Christ. I leave the mysteries, not because I despise them; but because the times demand that we first, and above all other things, seek the souls of men. Some truths press to be heard; they must be heard now, or men will be lost. The other truths they can hear to-morrow, or by-and-by, but *now* escape from hell and fitness for heaven are their immediate business. Fancy the angels sitting down with Lot and his daughters inside Sodom, and discussing predestination with them, or explaining the limits of free agency. No, no, they cry, "Come along," and they take them by the arm and lead them out, saying, "Flee, flee, flee, for fire is coming down from heaven, and this city is to be destroyed." This is what the preacher has to do; leaving certain parts of truth for other times, he is now rightly dividing the word of truth when he brings out that which is of pressing importance. In the Bible there are some things that are essential, without which a man cannot be saved at all: there are other things which are important, but still men are saved, notwithstanding their ignorance of those things; is it not clear that the essentials must have prominence? Every truth ought to be preached in its turn and place, but we must never give the first place to a second truth, or push that to the front which was meant to be in the background of the picture. "We preach Christ," said the apostle, "Christ and him crucified," and I believe that if the preacher is rightly to divide the word, he will say to the sinner, "Sinner, Christ died, Christ rose again, Christ intercedes; look to him. As for the difficult questions and nice points, leave them for awhile. You shall discuss them by-and-by, so far as they are profitable to you, but just now believing in the Lord Jesus Christ is the main matter." The preacher must thus separate the vital from the secondary, the practical from the speculative, and the pressing and immediate from that which may be lawfully delayed; and in that sense he will rightly divide the word of truth.

V. I have given you four meanings. Now I will give you another, leaving out some I might have mentioned. One thing the preacher has to do is to ALLOT TO EACH ONE HIS PORTION; and here the figure changes. According to Calvin, the intention of the Spirit here is to represent one who is the steward of the house, and has to apportion food to the different members of the family. He has rightly to divide the loaves so as not to give the little children and the babes all the crust; rightly to supply each one's necessities, not giving the strong men milk, nor the babes hard diet; not casting the children's bread to the dogs, nor giving the swine's husks to the children, but placing before each his own portion. Let me try and do it.

Child of God, your portion is the whole word of God. Every promise in it is yours. Take it: feed on it. Christ is yours; God is yours; the Holy Spirit is yours; this world is yours, and worlds to come. Time is yours; eternity is yours; life is yours; death is yours; everlasting glory is yours. There is your portion. It is very sweet to give you your royal meat. The Lord give you a good appetite. Feed on it; feed on it. Sinner, you who believe not in Jesus, none of this is yours. While you remain as you are the threatenings are yours. If you refuse to believe in Jesus, neither this life nor the next is yours, nor time, nor eternity. You have nothing good. Oh, how dreadful is your portion now, for the wrath of God abideth on you. Oh, that you were wise, that your character might be changed, for until it is, we dare not flatter you, there is not a promise for you, nor a single approving sentence. You get your food to eat and your raiment to put on; but even that is given to you by the abounding longsuffering of God, and it may become a curse to you unless you repent. I am sorry to bring you such a portion but I must be honest with you. That is all that I can give you. God has said it—it is an awful sentence—"I will *curse* their *blessings*." Oh, sinner, the curse of the Lord is in the house of the wicked.

We have also to divide a portion to the *mourners*, and oh, how sweet a task that is, to say to those that mourn in Zion that the Lord will give them beauty for ashes. "Blessed are they that mourn, for they shall be comforted." The Lord will restore peace unto his mourners. Fear not, neither be dismayed, for the Lord will help you. But when we have given the mourners their sweet meats we have to turn round upon the *hypocrites* and say to them, "You may hang your heads like bulrushes, you may rend your garments and pretend to fast, but the Lord, who knows your heart, will suddenly come and unmask you, and if you are not sincere before him, if you are weighed in the balances and found wanting, he will deal out the gall of bitterness to you for ever. For his mourners there is mercy, but for the deceiver and the hypocrite there is judgment without mercy." It is a very pleasant thing, moreover, to deal out a portion to the *seeker*—when we say, "He that seeketh findeth, and to him that knocketh it shall be opened." "Come unto me all ye that labour and are heavy laden," saith Christ, "for I will give you rest." Take your portion and be glad.

We have to turn round, and say to others who think they are seekers, but *who are delaying*, "How long halt ye between two opinions?" How is it that you continually hesitate and refuse to believe in Jesus, and stay in the condition of unbelief, when the gospel mandate is, "Believe—believe now and live!" So we have to give to one comfort, to another counsel; to one reproof, to another encouragement; to one the invitation, to another the warning; and this is rightly to divide the word of truth.

Yes, and sometimes God enables his servants to give the word very remarkably to some men. I believe that if I were to tell a few of the things which have happened to me during the last one-and-twenty years they would not be believed, or if I were to tell you of passages of history which are known to me that have occurred in this Tabernacle to people who have come here, and to whom I have spoken the exact word, not knowing them for a moment, the facts would sound like fictions. I will give you one instance. Some of you will remember my preaching from the text, "What if thy father answer thee roughly?" There came into the vestry after that sermon a venerable Christian gentleman, bringing with him a young foreigner whom he was anxious to satisfy upon one point. He said, "Sir, I want you kindly to answer this question—have you seen me concerning this young gentleman?" "No, sir, certainly not," I said; and assuredly, though I knew the gentleman who addressed me, he had never spoken to me about the foreign stranger whose very existence was up to that moment unknown to me. Said he, "This young gentleman is almost persuaded to be a Christian. His father is of quite another faith, and worships other gods, and our young friend knows that if he becomes a Christian he will lose his father's love. I said to him, when he conversed with me, come down and hear Mr. Spurgeon this morning. Here we came, and your text was, 'What if thy father answer thee roughly?' Now, have you ever heard a word from me about this young gentleman?" "No, never," I said. "Well," said the young man, "it is the most extraordinary thing I ever heard in my life." I could only say, "I trust it is the voice of God to your soul. God knows how to guide his servants to utter the word most fitted to bless men."

Some time ago a town missionary had in his district a man who never would suffer any Christian person to come into his house. The missionary was warned by many that he would get a broken head if he ventured on a visit. He therefore kept from the house, though it troubled his conscience to pass it by. He made a matter of prayer of it, and one morning he boldly ventured into the lion's den, and the man said, "What have you come here for?" "Well, sir," he said, "I have been conversing with people in all the houses along here, and I have passed you by because I heard you objected to it; but somehow I thought it looked cowardly to avoid you, and therefore I have called." "Come in," the man said; "sit down, sit down. Now, you are going to talk to me about the Bible. Perhaps you do not know much about it yourself. I am going to ask you a question, and if you can answer me you shall come again. If you do not answer it, I will bundle you downstairs. Now," said he, "do you take me?" "Yes," said the other, "I do take you." "Well, then," said he, "this is the question—where do you find the word '*girl*' in the Bible, and how many times do you find it?" The city missionary said, "The word 'girl' occurs only once in the Bible, and that is in the Book of Joel, the third chapter and the third verse. 'They sold a girl for wine.'" "You are right," said he, "but I would not have believed you knew it, or else I would have asked you some other question. You may come again." "But," said the missionary, "I should like you to know how I came to know it. This very morning I was praying for direction from God, and when I was reading my morning chapter I came upon this passage, 'And they sold a girl for wine;' and I took down my concordance to see whether the word 'girl' was to be found anywhere else. I found that the word 'girls' occurs in the passage, 'There shall be girls and boys playing in the streets of Jerusalem,' but the word did not occur as 'girl' anywhere but in Joel." The result, however, of that story, however odd it seems, was that the missionary was permitted to call, and the man took an interest in his visits, and the whole family were the better; the man, and his wife, and one of his children becoming members of a Christian church some time afterwards. What an extraordinary thing it seems; yet, I can assure you that such extraordinary things are as commonplaces in my experience. God does help his servants rightly to divide the word, that is to say, to allot a special portion to each special case, so that it comes as pat upon the man as if everything about him was known. Before I came to London, a man met me one Sunday, in a dreadful state of rage. He vowed he would horsewhip me for bullying him from the pulpit. What had I said, I asked. "What have you said? You looked me in the face, and said, 'What more can God do for you? Shall he give you a good wife? You have had one: you have killed her by bad treatment: you have just got another, and you are likely to do the same by her.'" "Well," I said, "did you kill your first wife by your bad treatment?" "They say so; but I was married on Saturday," said he. "Did you not know it?" "No, I did not, I assure you," I replied; "I have no knowledge whatever of your family matters, and I am sure I wish you joy of your new wife." He cooled down a great deal; but I believe that I had struck the nail on the head that time—that he had killed his wife with his unkindness, and he scarcely liked to bring his new wife to the place of worship to be told of it. The cap fitted him; and if any cap fit you, I pray you wear it, for so far from shrinking from being personal, I do assure you I try to be as personal as ever I can, for I long to see the word go home to every man's conscience, and convict him and make him tremble before God and confess his sin and forsake it.

VI. You must give me a few more minutes while I take the last point, which is this. Rightly to divide the word of truth means to TELL EACH MAN WHAT HIS LOT AND HERITAGE WILL BE IN ETERNITY. Just as when Canaan was conquered, it was divided by lot among the tribes, so the preacher has to tell of Canaan, that happy land, and he has to tell of the land of darkness and of death-shade, and to let each man know where his last abode will be. You do know it; you who come here do know it. Need I repeat a story that we have gone over and over a thousand times? As many as believe in Jesus, and are renewed in heart, and are kept by the grace of God through faith unto salvation, shall inherit eternal life; but as for those who believe not on God, who reject his Son, who abide in their sins, there remaineth nothing for them but "a fearful looking for of judgment and of fiery indignation." "The wicked shall be turned into hell with all the nations that forget God." "These shall go away into everlasting punishment; but the righteous into life eternal." "Beware," saith God,—" Beware, ye that forget God, lest I tear you in pieces and there be none to deliver." Oh, the wrath to come! the wrath to come!

Believer, there is your portion—in the blessed land. Sinner, except you repent, there is your portion—in the land of darkness and of weeping, and of wailing, and of gnashing of teeth. I take a religious newspaper from America, and the last copy I had of it bore on it these words at the end, in good large type, printed in a practical, business-like, American way: "If you do not want to have this paper, discontinue it NOW. If you wish to have it for the year 1875, send your subscription NOW. If you have any complaint against it, send your complaint NOW. If you have removed, send a notice of your change of residence NOW." There was a big "NOW" at the end of every sentence. As I read it I thought, well, that is right: that is common sense. And it struck me that I would say to you on this last night of the year, if you wish to forsake your sins, forsake them NOW. If you would have mercy from God through Jesus Christ, believe on him now. What fitter time than ere the dying year is gone—now, now, now? In that very paper I read a story concerning Messrs. Moody and Sankey to the same point. The story is that, while they were preaching in Edinburgh, there was a man sitting opposite to them who was very deeply interested, and was drinking it all in. There was a pause in the service, and the man went out with his friend; but when he reached the door he stopped, and his friend said, " Come away, Jamie." " No," he said, " I will go back. I came here to get good to my soul, and I have not taken it all in yet, I must go back again." He went back, and sat in his old place, and listened again. The Lord blessed him. He found Christ, and so found salvation. Being a miner, he went down the pit the next day to his work, and a mass of rock fell on him. He was taken out; but he could not recover. He said to the man who was helping him out, " Oh, Andrew, I am so glad it was all settled last night. Oh, mon," said he, " it was all settled last night." Now, I hope those people who were killed in the railway accident on Christmas Eve could say—" It was all settled the night before." What a blessed thing it will be for you, if you should meet with an accident to-morrow, to say, " Blessed be God, it was all settled last night. I gave my heart to Jesus, I yielded myself to his divine love and mercy, and I am saved." O Holy Spirit, grant it may be so, and thou shalt have the praise. Amen and amen.

THE BURDEN OF THE WORD OF THE LORD.

A Sermon

DELIVERED BY

C. H. SPURGEON,

AT THE METROPOLITAN TABERNACLE, NEWINGTON.

"The burden of the word of the Lord." Malachi i. 1.

THE prophets of old were no triflers. They did not run about as idle tellers of tales, but they carried a burden. Those who at this time speak in the name of the Lord, if they are indeed sent of God, dare not sport with their ministry or play with their message. They have a burden to bear—"The burden of the word of the Lord"; and this burden puts it out of their power to indulge in levity of life. I am often astounded at the way in which some who profess to be the servants of God make light of their work: they jest about their sermons as if they were so many comedies or farces. I read of one who said, "I got on very well for a year or two in my pulpit, for my great-uncle had left me a large store of manuscripts, which I read to my congregation." The Lord have mercy on his guilty soul! Did the Lord send him a sacred call to bring to light his uncle's mouldy manuscripts? Something less than a divine call might have achieved that purpose. Another is able to get on well with his preaching because he pays so much a quarter to a bookseller, and is regularly supplied with manuscript sermons. They cost more or less according to the space within which they will not be sold to another clerical cripple. I have seen the things, and have felt sick at the sorry spectacle. What must God think of such prophets as these? In the old times, those whom God sent did not borrow their messages. They had their message directly from God himself, and that message was weighty—so weighty that they called it "the burden of the Lord." He that does not find his ministry a burden now will find it a burden hereafter, which will sink him lower than the lowest hell. A ministry that never burdens the heart and the conscience in this life, will be like a millstone about a man's neck in the world to come.

The servants of God mean business; they do not play at preaching, but they plead with men. They do not talk for talking's sake; but they persuade for Jesus' sake. They are not sent into the world to tickle men's ears, nor to make a display of elocution, nor to quote poetry:

theirs is an errand of life or death to souls immortal. They have a something to say which so presses upon them, that they must say it. "Woe is unto me if I preach not the gospel!" They burn with an inward fire, and the flame must have vent; for the Word of the Lord is as fire in their bones, consuming them. The truth presses them into its service, and they cannot escape from it. If, indeed, they be the servants of God they must speak the things which they have seen and heard. The servants of God have no feathers in their caps, but burdens on their hearts.

Furthermore, the true servants of God have something to carry, something worth carrying. There is solid truth, precious truth in their message. It is not froth and foam, phrases and verbiage, stories and pretty things, poetry and oratory, and all that; but there is weight in it of matters which concern heaven and hell, time and eternity. If ever there were men in this world who ought to speak in earnest, they are the men. Those who speak for God must not speak lightly. If there is nothing in what a man has to say, then God never commissioned him, for God is no trifler. If there is no importance in their message—yea, if their message be not of the first and last importance—why do they profess to speak in the name of God? It is constructive blasphemy to father God with our nonsense. The true servant of God has no light weight to bear; he has eternal realities heaped upon him. He does not run merrily as one that has a feather-weight to carry, but he treads firmly and often slowly as he moves beneath "the burden of the word of the Lord."

Yet, do not let me be misunderstood at the beginning. God's true servants, who are burdened with his word, right willingly and cheerfully carry that burden. We would not be without it for all the world. Sometimes, do you know, we get tempted, when things do not go right, to run away from it; but we view it as a temptation not to be tolerated for an hour. When some of you do not behave yourselves, and matters in our church get a little out of order, I say to myself, "I wish I could give this up, and turn to an employment less responsible, and less wearing to the heart"; but then I think of Jonah, and what happened to him when he ran away to Tarshish; and I remember that whales are scarcer now than they were then, and I do not feel inclined to run that risk. I stick to my business, and keep to the message of my God; for one might not be brought to land quite so safely as the runaway prophet was. Indeed, I could not cease to preach the glad tidings unless I ceased to breathe. God's servants would do nothing else but bear this burden, even if they were allowed to make a change. I had sooner be a preacher of the gospel than a possessor of the Indies. Remember how William Carey, speaking of one of his sons, says, "Poor Felix is shrivelled from a missionary to an ambassador." He was a missionary once, and he was employed by the government as an ambassador; his father thought it no promotion, but said, "Felix has shrivelled into an ambassador." It would be a descent indeed from bearing the burden of the Lord, if one were to be transformed into a member of Parliament, or a prime minister, or a king. We bear a burden, but we should be sorry indeed not to bear it.

The burden which the true preacher of God bears is for God, and on Christ's behalf, and for the good of men. He has a natural instinct which makes him care for the souls of others, and his anxiety is that none should perish, but that all should find salvation through Jesus Christ. Like the Christ who longed to save, so does the true Malachi, or messenger of God, go forth with this as his happy, joyful, cheerfully-borne burden—that men may turn unto God and live. Yet, it is a burden, for all that; and of that I am going to speak to you. Much practical truth will come before us while we speak of "the burden of the word of the Lord." Pray that the Holy Spirit may bless the meditation to our hearts.

I. And why is the word of the Lord a burden to him that speaketh it? Well, first, it is a burden BECAUSE IT IS THE WORD OF THE LORD. If what we preach is only of man, we may preach as we like, and there is no burden about it; but if this Book be inspired—if Jehovah be the only God, if Jesus Christ be God incarnate, if there be no salvation save through his precious blood—then there is a great solemnity about that which a minister of Christ is called upon to preach. It hence becomes a weighty matter with him. Modern thought is a trifle light as air; but ancient truth is more weighty than gold.

And, first, the word of the Lord becomes *a burden in the reception of it.* I do not think that any man can ever preach the gospel aright until he has had it borne into his own soul with overwhelming energy. You cannot preach conviction of sin unless you have suffered it. You cannot preach repentance unless you have practised it. You cannot preach faith unless you have exercised it. You may talk about these things, but there will be no power in the talk unless what is said has been experimentally proved in your own soul. It is easy to tell when a man speaks what he has made his own, or when he deals in second-hand experience. "Son of man, eat this roll": you must eat it before you can hand it out to others. True preaching is Artesian: it wells up from the great depths of the soul. If Christ has not made a well within us, there will be no outflow from us. We are not proper agents for conveying truth to others, if grace has not conveyed it to us. When we get God's word in our studies, we feel it to be a load which bows us to the ground. We are, at times, obliged to get up and walk to and fro beneath the terror of the threatenings of God's word; and often are we forced to bow our knee before the glory of some wonderful word of the Lord which beams with excessive grace. We say to ourselves, "These are wonderful truths: how they press upon our hearts!" They create great storms within us; they seem to tear us to pieces. The strong wind of the mighty Spirit blows through the messenger of God, and he himself is swayed to and fro in it as the trees of the forest in the tempest. Hence, even in the reception of the message of God, it is a burden.

The Word of God is *a burden in the delivery of it.* Do you think it an easy thing to stand before the people and deliver a message which you believe you have received from God? If you so imagine, I wish you would try it. He that finds it easy work to preach, will find it hard work to give an account of his preaching at the last great day. One has carefully to look around, and think while he is preaching, "I must mind that I do not put this truth in such a way as to exaggerate it into a falsehood. I must not so encourage the weak that I dwarf the strong; nor so commend the strong as to grieve the weak. I must not so preach the grace of God as to give latitude to sin: I must not so denounce sin as to drive men to despair." Our path is often narrow as a razor's edge, and we keep on crying in our spirit, while we are speaking, "Lord, direct me! Lord, help me to deal wisely for thee with all these souls!" The anxieties which we feel in connection with our pulpit work are enough to make us old before our time. I have heard of one who thought he would give up his ministry because he had so small a chapel, into which he could not get more than two hundred people; but a good old man said to him, "You will find it quite hard enough to give a good account of two hundred at the last great day." It is an idle ambition to desire a large congregation, unless that desire is altogether for God's glory; for we only increase our responsibilities when we increase the area of our influence. Still, some are responsible for *not* having a large congregation. If their dulness keeps people from hearing, they do not thereby escape from responsibility. To speak aright God's Word beneath the divine influence is, in the speaking as well as in the getting of the message, the burden of the Lord.

When we have preached, the gospel becomes *a burden in after consideration.* "Well, now, it is all done," says one. Is it? Is it all done? You, dear teacher, when you have taught your class to-day, have you done with your children? You have thought of them upon the Sabbath; will there be no care for them all the week? If your soul is towards your children or your congregation as it ought to be, you will bear them always on your heart. They will never be far away from you. The mother is gone from home. She is out to-day, seeing her sister: surely she is not caring about her babe; is she? Is SHE NOT? Why, wherever she is, the tender mother, if she does not bear her child outside her bosom, bears it inside her heart; her babe is always in her mind. "Can a woman forget her sucking child?" Can a soul-winner forget his charge? If God sends any of us to do good to our fellow-men, and to speak in his name, the souls of men will be a perpetual burden to us, and we shall constantly cry for their salvation, and perpetually, with entreaties and tears, go to God for them, and ask him to bless the message we have delivered.

Oh, that we may have, in all pulpits, ministers who bear the burden of the Lord in the study, in the pulpit, and when the discourse is finished! Once truly a minister you are always a minister; your burden clings to you. May you, my brethren and sisters, partakers in the holy service of our Lord Jesus Christ, each of you, in your measure, bear the burden of the Word of the Lord, and that continually.

II. I pass to a second point. It is not only a burden because it is so solemnly the Word of the Lord, and therefore weighty and overwhelming; but next, BECAUSE OF WHAT IT IS. What is it that the true servant of God has to bear and to preach?

Well, first, *it is the rebuke of sin.* I have heard of hirelings who preach, but never think of rebuking sin. It is with them like as in the story of the old negro preacher, a very popular preacher, indeed, among his coloured brothers. His master said, "I am afraid some of your people steal chickens, for I am always losing mine. I wish you would next Sunday give them a word about it." "Master," said the preacher, "it would throw such a damp over the congregation if I were to say anything about stealing chickens." So the black preacher avoided that subject. It seems to me that stealing chickens was the very thing that he ought to have preached about, if that was the sin his brethren were guilty of. If a man bears the burden of the Word of the Lord, he speaks most to his people upon the evil of which they are most guilty. Somebody once said to me, "Sir, you were very personal." I answered, "Sir, I tried to be. Do not think that I am going to apologize for it. If I knew anything that would come home to your heart and conscience concerning sin, I would be sure to say *that*—just that very thing." "And what if I should be offended?" "Well, I should be very sorry that you refused reproof, and should feel all the more sure that it was my duty to be very faithful with you. If after much love and prayer you refused the word, I could do no more; but I certainly should not speak with bated breath to please you; and you would despise me if I did." I remember one in Oliver Cromwell's day who complained to a preacher. He said, "The squire of the parish is very much offended by some remarks you made last Sabbath day about profane swearing." "Well," said the Puritan preacher, "is the squire in the habit of swearing?" It was admitted that he was, and that he therefore thought himself pointed out by the minister. The Puritan replied to the complaining tenant, "If your lord offends my Lord, I shall not fail to rebuke him for it; and if he is offended, let him be offended." So must every true preacher be careless of man's esteem, and speak faithfully; but this is a burden to one of a tender spirit. If there is any topic upon which we must of necessity dwell, it must be upon that sin which is most grieving to the Lord; for we must by no means leave an erring brother unwarned. This is not a work to be coveted. It is neither pleasant to the hearer, nor pleasant to the speaker; and yet to rebuke sin, and to rebuke it sharply, is part of the work of him whom God sends; and this makes the Word of the Lord his burden.

And, next, *the Word of the Lord gives a rebuff to human pride.* The doctrines of the gospel seem shaped on purpose, among other objects, to bring into contempt all human glory. Here is a man who is morally of a fine and noble nature, but we tell him that he is born in sin and shapen in iniquity: this is a stern duty. Here is a man of a grand righteous character in his own opinion, and we tell him that his righteousness is filthy rags: he will not smile on us for this. Here is a man that can go to heaven by his own efforts, so he thinks, and we tell him that he can do nothing of the sort—that he is dead in trespasses and sins: this will bring us no honour from him. He hopes that, by strong resolves, he may change his own nature and make himself all that God would have him; but we tell him that his resolutions are so much empty wind, and will end in nothing: this is likely to earn us his hate. Behold, the axe is laid at the root of the tree. Man stands a convicted criminal, and if saved must owe his salvation entirely to the gratuitous mercy of God. Condemned and ruined, if he ever escapes from his ruin it must be through the work of the Spirit of God in him, and not by his own works. Thus, you see, human nature does not like our message. How it writhes in wrath, how it grinds its teeth against the doctrine which humbles man, crucifies his pride, and nails his glory to the gibbet! Hence, such preaching becomes the burden of the Lord.

And then the true preacher has *to come into contact with the vanity of human intellect.* We ask of man, "Canst thou by searching find out God?" Thou sayest, "I know." What knowest thou, poor blind worm? Thou sayest, "I am a judge, and I can discern." What canst thou discern, thou that art in the dark, and alienated from God by thy wicked works? The things of God are hidden from the wise and prudent, but revealed unto babes; and the wise and prudent are indignant at this act revealed of divine sovereignty. "Well," says one, "I quarrel with the Bible." Do you? The only real argument against the Bible is an unholy life. When a man argues against the Word of God, follow him home, and see if you cannot discover the reason of his enmity to the Word of the Lord. It lies in some form of sin. He whom God sends cares nothing at all about human wisdom, so as to fawn upon it and flatter it; for he knows that "the world by wisdom knew not God"; and that human wisdom is only another name for human folly. All the savants and the philosophers are simply those who make themselves to be wise, but are not so. Yet to face false science with "the foolishness of preaching," and to set up the cross in the teeth of learned self-sufficiency, is a burden from the Lord.

The most heavy burden of the Word of the Lord, however, is *that which concerns the future.* If thou be sent of God, and if thou preachest what God has revealed in his Word, then thou sayest, "He that believeth not shall be damned," and thou dost not hesitate to say that the wrath of God abides on the rejectors of the Saviour. Thou dost not hesitate to say—

> "There is a dreadful hell
> And everlasting pains,
> Where sinners must with devils dwell
> In darkness, fire, and chains."

All the romance of the age runs against this. Everybody says, "Be quiet about the wrath to come, or you will have everybody down upon you." Be down upon me, then! I will not soften God's word to please anybody; and the Word of the Lord is very clear on this matter. If you receive not the Lord Jesus Christ, you will die in your sins. If you believe not in him, you must perish from his presence. There is a day coming when you will die; after this comes another day when you must appear before the judgment-seat of Christ, and all your actions shall be published, and you shall be judged for the things done in the body, whether they be good, or whether they be evil; and then you shall receive the sentence of, "Come, ye blessed," or, "Depart, ye cursed." Do you think we like to preach this? Do you think that it is any pleasure to the servant of God to deliver these heavy tidings? Oh, no! we speak in the bitterness of our spirit, very often; but we speak because we dare not refrain. It is infinitely better that men should be told the truth than that they should be flattered by a lie into eternal ruin. He ought to have the commendation of all men, not who makes things pleasant, but who speaks things truly. Somebody is preaching of how to get people out of hell. I preach about how to keep them out of hell. Don't go there. Keep you clear of the fire which never can be quenched. Escape for your lives: look not behind you; stay not in all the plain, but haste to Christ, the mountain of salvation, and put your trust in him. This is it which is the burden of the Word of the Lord. We have grief of heart because of the dreadful future which men prepare for themselves, namely, "everlasting punishment." We are heavy at heart for the many who will not turn to God, but persist in destroying their own souls for ever. Oh, why will they die? The prospect of their future is a present misery to us.

III. Now, dear friends, I have in the third place to say that it is a burden not only because it is the Word of the Lord, and because of what it is, but BECAUSE OF THE CONSEQUENCES OF OUR BEARING IT TO YOU.

Suppose that we do not preach the gospel, and warn the wicked man, so that he turn not from his iniquity, what then? Hear this voice: "He shall perish, but his blood will I require at thine hand." What will my Lord say to me if I am unfaithful to you? "Where is the blood of those people who gathered at Newington Butts? Where is the blood of that crowd which came together to hear you speak, and you did not preach the gospel to them?" Oh, it were better for me that I had never been born than that I should not preach the gospel! "Woe is unto me if I preach not the gospel" of Christ, for men perish where there is not the Word of God! I remember Mr. Knill's portrait which was once in *The Evangelical Magazine*, that it had written at the bottom of it, "Brethren, the heathen are perishing: will you let them perish?" So is it with men that hear not the glad tidings; they die in sin. Worse still, men are perishing in this country: in the blaze of the light they sit in darkness. Oh, that we might go and find them, and tell them of the gospel! for, if we carry it not to them, "How shall they believe in him of whom they have not heard? and how shall they hear without a preacher? And how shall they preach except they be sent?" What makes it more of a burden to me is, that men may die if they do hear the word of salvation; men may go from these pews quick into perdition. Those eyes that look on me to-night, oh, how intently and earnestly! O sirs, if you do not look to Christ, you will be lost, however well you may have attended to me. Now, you listen to each word I utter; but I pray you listen to the Word of God, the heavenly Father, who bids you repent and believe in his dear Son; for "except ye repent, ye shall all likewise perish." So said the Saviour. And this, I say, makes the burden of the message, lest some of you should not receive it. I cannot bear that one of you should die unforgiven. I look along these pews, and I remember some of you a good many years ago; you were then in a hopeful state, but you have not received Christ yet. Most faithful hearers you have been, but you have not been doers of the word. Do not think that I charge you too severely. Have you repented and believed? If not, woe is me that I should bear to you a message which will be a savour of death unto death unto you because you refuse it; for how shall we escape if we neglect so great salvation? When it has been freely proclaimed to us year after year, what will become of us if we reject it? Do not still refuse to come to Jesus. Do not make me a messenger of death to you. I implore you, receive the message of mercy, and be saved.

And, then, it becomes a great burden to me to preach the gospel when I think of *what those lose who will not have it*. That heaven above—what tongue can describe it? What painter can ever picture it—the heaven above, where all is love, and joy, and peace, and everlasting blessedness? What if you should be shut out? What if against you the door should be closed! There is no opening that door again, remember. Even though you stand and cry, "Lord, Lord!" yet will he not open it to you. May no one of us miss eternal felicity! May no one among us fall into eternal misery! But here lies the burden of the Lord—in the consequences of our ministry. I recollect walking out to preach nigh unto forty years ago, just when I began my witnessing for the Lord Jesus. As I trudged along with a somewhat older brother, who was going to preach at another village station, our talk was about our work, and he said to me, "Does it not strike you as a very solemn thing that we two local preachers are going to do the Lord's work, and much may depend even upon the very hymns we give out, and the way in which we read them?" I thought of that, and I prayed—and often do pray—that I may have the right hymn, and the right chapter, as well as the right sermon. Well do I remember a great sinner coming into Exeter Hall, and I read the hymn beginning, "Jesu, lover of my soul," and that first line pierced him in the heart. He said to himself, "Does Jesus love my soul?" He wept because he had not loved the Saviour in return; and he was brought to the Saviour's feet just by that one line of a hymn. It does make it the burden of the Lord when you see life, death, and hell, and worlds to come, hanging, as it were, upon the breath of a mortal man, by whom God speaks to the souls of his fellows. This is serious burden-bearing. At least, I find it more and more so the longer I am engaged in it.

IV. But I pass on to notice one thing more now. It is often the burden of the Lord, because of THE WAY IN WHICH MEN TREAT THE WORD OF GOD. Upon this I will be very brief. Some trifle with it. I was reading last night an account of how people are said to behave who go to church. It was written by a canon. I dare say he knows. Certainly, some people who go to Nonconformist places are as bad. A servant was asked by her mistress about the sermon. She said it was a very good sermon. "Where was the text, Martha?" "Somewhere in the Bible, ma'am." "What was it about?" She did not recollect a word of it. One question after another is put to her; she tells her mistress that it was a very nice sermon, but she really does not know what it was all about. And the writer goes on to say that a large proportion of our people go off at a tangent while we are talking, and their minds are thinking about something else. I hope that it is not quite true of you to-night. A man once went to hear Mr. Whitefield.

He was a shipbuilder, and he said, "Oh, that man! I never heard such a preacher as that before. When I have been to other places, I have built a ship from stem to stern—laid the keel, and put the mast in, and finished it all up, while the parson has been preaching; but this time I was not able to lay a timber. He took me right away." This pre-occupation of human minds makes it such a burden when we are in earnest to reach the heart and win the soul. Our people are sitting here in body, but they are far away in spirit. Yonder sits a good woman who is meditating as to how she shall leave her home to-morrow, long enough to get to the shop to buy those clothes for the children, ready for the spring weather. A gentleman here to-night wonders where he has left that diamond ring which he took off when he washed his hands. Do not let that bother you any more. Sell the stone, and give the money away; so that it will never trouble you again. All sorts of cares come buzzing around your brains, when I am wanting them to be quite clear to consider holy subjects. Little pettifogging cares intrude, and the preacher may speak his very soul out, but it all goes for nothing. This makes our work the burden of the Lord.

Then there is another. It is the number of those who do hear with considerable attention, but *they forget all that they hear*. The sermon is all done with when they have done hearing it. The last drop of dew is dried up when they get home. Nothing remains of that which cost the preacher so much thought and prayer. And is it not a hard thing to go on "pegging away and pegging away," and have done nothing? The pre-occupied mind is a slate, and we write on it; and then a sponge goes over it all, and we have to write each word all over again. Few would choose to roll the stone of Sisyphus, which always fell backward as fast as he laboriously heaved it up the hill-side. We are willing to do even this for our Lord; but we are compelled to admit that it is burdensome toil. Poor, poor work with some of you. Ah! it is the burden of the Lord to deal with your souls.

Alas! there are some others that *hear to ridicule*. They pick out some mannerism, or mistake, or something *outré* about the speaker's language, and they carry this home, and report it as raw material for fun. The preacher is in anguish to save a soul, and they are thinking about how he pronounces a word. Here is a man endeavouring to pluck sinners from the eternal burnings, and these very sinners are all the while thinking about how he moves his legs, or how he lifts his hand, or how he pronounces a certain syllable. Oh, it is sickening work—soul-sickening work! It is the "burden of the word of the Lord," when our life or death message is received in that way. But when it is received rightly, then are we in the seventh heaven! Oh, well do I remember one night preaching three sermons, one after the other; and I think that I could have preached thirty, if time had held out. It was in a Welsh village, where I had gone into the chapel and simply meant to expound the Scripture, while another brother preached. He preached in Welsh, and when it was done, the question was put whether Mr. Spurgeon would not preach. I had not come prepared, but I did preach, and there was a melting time; and then we sang a hymn. I think we sang one verse seven or eight times over: the people were all on fire. The sound seemed to make the shingles dance on the top of the chapel. When I had done, we asked those who were impressed to stop. They all stopped, and so I had to preach again; and a second time they all stopped, and I had to preach again. It got on to past eleven o'clock before they went away. Eighty-one came forward and joined the churches afterwards. It was but a few months before the terrible accident at Risca, and many of those converted that night perished in the pit. God had sent his Spirit on that glorious night to save them, that they might be ready when he should call them home. It was grand work to preach, for they sucked in the word as babes take in the milk. They took it into their hearts: it saved their souls. Would we had many such opportunities, and then the Word of the Lord would be no burden, but like the wings of a bird, to make us mount on high, and joy would fill every heart!

V. And now I must not detain you; but I want to say, in the fifth place, the Word of the Lord is the greatest burden to the true teacher's heart, because he remembers that HE WILL HAVE TO GIVE AN ACCOUNT. They are all down, those fifty-two Sabbaths; and those week-night opportunities, they are all down in the heavenly record, and the writing will be forthcoming when required. There will come a time when it will be said, "Preacher, give an account of your stewardship"; and at the same time a voice will be heard, "Hearers, give an account of your stewardship, too." What a mercy it will be if you and I together shall give in our accounts with joy, and not with grief! for a mournful account will be unprofitable for you. What sort of sermons shall I wish I had preached when I come to die? What sort of sermons will you wish that you had heard when you lie on your last beds? You will not wish that you had heard mere flimsy talk and clever speeches. Oh, no! you will say, as a dying man, "I bless God for weighty words, earnestly spoken, that were a blessing to my soul." I will say no more upon that, although it is the pressing point of the whole matter. Brethren, pray for the preacher. Brethren, pray for yourselves.

I have only these two or three practical words to say. We have to bear the burden of the Lord; but *there was one, the Head of our confraternity, the great Lord of all true gospel preachers, who bore a far heavier burden.* "He his own self bare our sins in his own body on the tree." Preacher, teacher, do you ever get weary? Look to him as he bows beneath his cross, take up your burden cheerfully, and follow after Jesus.

If this work be a burden, we also rejoice in *One who can help us.* There is One who can make the burden light, or strengthen the shoulder to bear the heavy yoke. Dear people, pray for us that this great Helper may enable us to bear the burden of his Word to your souls. Do not pray that it may not be a burden. Pray that it may be a burden that crushes your pastor to the very dust. God forbid that he should ever preach without its being a load to him! But pray that he may then be sustained under it; and for every true preacher of the gospel pray the same prayer. If the Lord be with us we shall not faint, but go from strength to strength.

Since it is a burden in itself. *I ask you not to make it any heavier.*

Do not make it intolerable. Some add to it greatly and wantonly. Who are these? Well, I will tell you. Inconsistent professors. When people point to such and such a member of the church, and say, "That is your Christian!"—this makes our burden doubly oppressive. What a spoil it is to our testimony for Christ when outsiders can point to one and another, and say, "That is how those Christians act!" Do not plunge us in this sorrow. I do not know why I should be blamed for all the offences of everybody that comes to hear me. Can I keep you all right? Are you like chessmen, that I can move at pleasure to any square on the board? I cannot be responsible for any one person; how can I be the guardian of all? Yet the preacher of God's truth is held responsible by many for matters over which he has no power; and this injustice makes his burden heavy.

And, next, *do not make our burden heavier by your silence.* There was a man of God who had been a very distinguished preacher, and when he lay dying he was much troubled in his mind. He had been greatly admired, and much followed. He was a fine preacher of the classical sort, and one said to him, "Well, my dear sir, you must look back upon your ministry with great comfort." "Oh, dear!" said he, "I cannot; I cannot. If I knew that even one soul had been led to Christ and eternal life by my preaching I should feel far happier; but I have never heard of one." What a sad, sad thing for a dying preacher! He died, and was buried, and there was a goodly company of people at the grave, for he was highly respected, and deservedly so. One who heard him make that statement was standing at the grave, and he noticed a gentleman in mourning, looking into the tomb, and sobbing with deep emotion. He said to him, "Did you know this gentleman who has been buried?" He replied, "I never spoke to him in my life." "Then what is it that so affects you?" He said, "Sir, I owe my eternal salvation to him." He had never told the minister this cheering news, and the good man's death-bed was rendered dark by the silence of a soul that he had blessed. This was not right. A great many more may have found the Lord by his means, but he did not know of them, and was therefore in sore trouble. Do tell us when God blesses our word to you. Give all the glory to God, but give us the comfort of it. The Holy Spirit does the work, but if we are the means in his hands, do let us know it, and we will promise not to be proud. It is due to every preacher of Christ that if he has been blessed to the conversion of a soul he should be allowed to see the fruit of his labours; and when he does not see it, it adds very sadly to "the burden of the Word of the Lord."

Do you not think that you add to my burden, too, *if you do not aid me in the Lord's work?* What a lot of idle Christians we have— Christian people who might sing, like mendicants in the street,

"And got no work to do,
And got no work to do!"

What a shameful chorus, when the world is dying for lack of true workers! There is a Sunday-school; do you know it? "Oh, yes, we know there is one of those excellent institutions" connected with our place of worship. Did you ever visit it? Have you ever helped in it? There is an Evangelists' Society, and young men go out to preach. "Oh, dear!" say you, "I never thought of that." Why do you not go out to preach yourself? Some of you could, if you would. What are you at? There are districts where there are tracts to be distributed. Do you know anything about house-to-house visitation? I speak to some who do nothing whatever, unless it be a little grumbling. I wonder whether we shall ever have a day such as the bees celebrate in its due season. You may, perhaps, have seen them dismissing the unproductives. It is a remarkable sight. They say to themselves, "Here is a lot of drones, eating our honey, but never making any; let us turn them out." There is a dreadful buzz, is there not? But out they go. I do not propose either to turn you out, or to make a buzz; but if ever those who do work for Christ should burn with a holy indignation against do-nothings, some of you will find the place too hot for you! I am sorrowfully afraid that it will thin my congregation, and lessen the number of church-members. I have but little to complain of among my people; but still, as there is a lazy corner in every village, there is the same in this community. You increase the burden of those who do work, if you are not working with them.

But the greatest increase of the burden comes from *those who do not receive the gospel at all*. May there not be one such here to-night, but may everyone now look to Jesus and live! I shall close by asking you to sing the gospel. Oh, that you may have it in your hearts! The final closing word is this—

> "There is life in a look at the Crucified One;
> There is life at this moment for thee;
> Then look, sinner—look unto him, and be saved—
> Unto him who was nail'd to the tree."

PRESERVATION
- The Preservation of Christians in the World—John 17:15
- Exposition of Isaiah 49:1-23
- Enduring to the End—Matt. 10:22
- Christians Kept in Time and Glorified in Eternity—Jude 24, 25
- The Final Perseverance of the Saints—Job 17:9
- Saints Guarded from Stumbling—Jude 24, 25
- Exposition of Psalm 91
- Preventing Grace—I Sam. 25:32, 33
- Exposition of Jonah 1
- Jude's Doxology—Jude 24, 25
- Exposition of the General Epistle of Jude

THE PRESERVATION OF CHRISTIANS IN THE WORLD.

A Sermon

DELIVERED BY
C. H. SPURGEON
AT NEW PARK STREET CHAPEL, SOUTHWARK,
On a Thursday Evening, in the year 1855.

"I pray not that thou shouldest take them out of the world, but that thou shouldest keep them from the evil."—John xvii. 15.

THE text, as we observed on a former occasion, contains two prayers,—a negative prayer, and a positive prayer. First, there is *the negative prayer:* "I pray not that thou shouldest take them out of the world." "There are wise ends to be observed by their remaining here. It will ultimately increase their happiness in heaven; it will give glory to God; it shall be the means of the conversion of others; therefore, 'I pray not that thou shouldest take them out of the world,' but I do pray"—and here comes *the positive prayer,*—"that, while they are in it, 'thou shouldest keep them from the evil.'"

I. Let us first, then, CONSIDER THE EVIL FROM WHICH CHRIST PRAYS THAT HIS PEOPLE MAY BE KEPT.

We have no hesitation in declaring that the only evil here intended is the evil of sin. It may be true that Jesus Christ pleads with his Father to preserve us from some of the direful afflictions which might be too much for our mortal frame to endure. It may be that, sometimes, the blows and attacks of the enemy are warded off by the arm of the intercession of Jesus. It may be that the great ægis of Almighty God is often held over our heads in matters of providence, to keep us from evil when we walk, and to guard us lest we dash our feet against a stone. We feel persuaded, however, that neither of these things is here intended; but that "the evil" so continually spoken of in Scripture, the evil pre-eminently here meant, is sin and nothing else: "I pray that thou shouldest keep them from the evil."

Afflictions are often beneficial, therefore Christ does not plead that we should be kept entirely from this kind of evil. Trial brings us to his feet, and gives new life to prayer, therefore Christ has not asked that this bitter-sweet might not be given to us. Death itself, which seems an evil, is a good thing for believers; so Christ does not ask that we may not die. The petition he here puts up for his people is, " I pray that thou shouldest keep them from the evil,"—the special evil, the particular, the deadly evil of sin.

Let us here remark that *sin is an unqualified evil.* It is *the* evil without the mitigation of any good in it. In sin there can be no good; it is evil, only evil, and that continually. The lowest form of sin is " the evil ", the highest is " the evil " more fully developed. Sin in an angel was " the evil ", for it turned him into a devil; sin in Eden was " the evil ", for it plucked up the fair trees by the roots, and blasted all their fruits, and sent Adam out to till the ground whence he was taken. Sin is always an evil; it brings no profit to anyone. It shall not profit a man if he shall gain the whole world, and lose his own soul; and in the Christian especially it is evil, nothing but evil; sin can never benefit him, it is an evil, only an evil, a powerful evil, and a dreadful evil; it is unmitigated evil, it is " the evil."

It is true, out of evil God bringeth good; sometimes, the very sins of God's people are overruled so as to preserve them from some greater sin, but that does not destroy " the evil." If God sends out bears from the wood to execute his commission, and they slay the mocking children, they are bears still; and if sin is sometimes made to be the means of honouring God, yet sin is sin notwithstanding any purpose that God may accomplish by it; and no false preaching can ever make us believe any doctrine which should take away the deadly character which by right belongs to sin. It is always hurtful and dangerous.

The Christian man, who trusts that, by any one sin, he may keep himself out of difficulty, or get himself out of difficulty, makes a terrible mistake. Sin cannot bring you good. " But," say you, " I am in great difficulties; my creditors are pressing me, what shall I do? If I could draw that accommodation bill, or forge that note, there might be some good in it." There cannot be any good in it. Sin is evil; it is " the evil "; it is " the evil " without a single particle of goodness; it is " the evil " without any mitigation whatsoever. " Oh! " says another, " if I were to do such-and-such a thing,—it is but a little evil,—I should then prosper in business; then I could dedicate myself to God, and serve him better; and so, out of the evil, I could bring a good. The end would justify the means." No; if the means be bad, they are bad; if the means be evil, they are evil. Sin is sin, and nothing but sin; and however there may, sometimes, appear to be temporary advantages in it, it is still evil, and only evil. What though the noxious draught may sometimes stimulate the man, and seem to make him mightier, it really weakens him, and it will ultimately destroy him. A man may fancy sin to be good; for a time, it may patch him up in respectability, and make him stand a little more favourably in the eyes of worldlings; but the house repaired with such rotten material as that shall fall, notwithstanding all that is done to prop it up.

All sin is unmitigated evil, and the only name we will give to it is "evil." Let the monster plead as it may, and ask us to call it good, we charge it with having slain our Lord; and we condemn it as an evil to be hated and avoided. A serpent may have beauteous azure hues upon his scales; but he is a deadly thing, and is to be crushed to the earth.

Next, we say that sin is "the evil" because it is *an unparalleled evil*. You can find nothing in the world so evil as sin. Nothing has so desolated this fair earth of ours as sin has. Tell me that war has slain its tens and hundreds of thousands, that earthquakes have shaken down vast cities, that pestilence has devoured millions; describe to me the concussion of the elements, speak to me of the wild uproar of nature abroad, and remind me of how it smites down man, and destroys his handiwork; but when you have written out the black catalogue of all the terrible things that have happened to man, I shall still tell you that sin stands up as the monster evil, the giant overtopping them all, head and shoulders above them, the most unqualified and unparalleled evil in the world. You ask me whether sin has done much evil, I answer you,—Yes. See Eden's garden blasted, a whole world drowned with water, even the tops of the mountains covered; see the earth open, and Korah, Dathan, and Abiram go down into the pit; see fire rained upon Sodom and Gomorrah, and see the cities of the plain, with all their inhabitants, destroyed. But sin has done more than that; it has digged a hell somewhere, we know not where,—not in the caverns of the earth. That were a direful thought, that this home of the righteous for a season should become the dwelling of the damned. If there be anything worse than that, sin is guilty of it, for it slaughtered Emmanuel, it slew the Lord of life and glory. Sin betrayed him, scourged him, put a crown of thorns upon his head, spit in his face, crucified him, nailed his hands and his feet to the accursed tree. Sin sat by, and watched him till he died; and that moment,—blessed be his name!—the sins of all his people were finished. Sin is unparalleled; no evil can compare with it. Find what evil you please, sin stands out first and foremost as "*the* evil."

Sin also, *in some sense, is an evil that has no remedy*. You may, perhaps, be somewhat startled by that thought, especially when you have so continually heard me say that the death of Christ takes away from a Christian the very guilt of his sin, so that he is not guilty before God, but stands accepted in Christ, with his Saviour's righteousness on, so that he can plead that before God, and even claim the merits imputed to him through Jesus. Still, what I have said is true,—that for sin there still remains no remedy, even to the Christian, when he has committed it. There is the remedy of forgiveness, so far as he is concerned; but there is no remedy for the sin itself. Where, for instance, is the remedy for a sinful word that I have spoken? Can my tears bring it back, and stop it from doing an injury to my fellow-creatures? Even though Christ has forgiven me, that will not end the wrong I may have done to others. When I drop a single stone of sin into the ocean of this universe, it will continue to make circle after circle, ever expanding. I may, through my whole life, labour with more than seraphic zeal, and with a Christ-like heart, to undo the evil I have done; but not if I might work throughout eternity could I untie those knots that I have tied, or dash down those mountains that I have piled, or dry up the rivers I have digged. True, the sin is all forgiven, it will never be laid to my charge; but, methinks, though Christ has forgiven me, I shall never forgive myself some things in which I may have disgraced his name, and dishonoured his blessed person. When some of you old blasphemers recollect that some in hell were damned by your means, you may thank God that you are saved, but you cannot undo that ruin to immortal souls. Sin is *the* evil. Well might Jesus pray for his people, "Father, keep them from the evil," for an evil it is, which, though it has a remedy as to itself, has no remedy as to its consequences upon others. God grant that any evils, which we may have wrought, may be as much remedied as it is possible they may be by the future holiness of our lives!

Once more, *sin is a most pestilent evil, because it brings every other evil with it.* Methinks, the worst evil sin has ever done to me is this, it has sometimes robbed me of the presence of my blessed Master. There have been seasons when the Spirit has been withdrawn from me. There have been times when I have sought my Beloved, and have not found him; when I have ardently desired his presence, but could not find it, and my only song was,—

"What peaceful hours I once enjoyed,
How sweet their memory still!
But now I find an aching void
The world can never fill."

Sin was that veil that came between me and my Lord. Dear old Joseph Irons used to say, "Christ often hides his face behind the clouds of dust his own children kick up." So we make dust by our sins, and Christ hides behind it; we build a wall by our transgressions, and our Beloved hideth behind that wall. Ah, sin, thou art indeed an evil, for thou hast robbed me of his sweet society, and taken away his blessed company! Thou hast been sitting on the throne of my heart, and he will not abide such an insult; he will not stop where sin is. Thou hast entered into my soul, and Jesus has said, "I will not tarry where there is sin; my presence shall drive out sin, or sin shall drive out my presence." "O sin, how much misery I experience through thee!" the Christian can say. Ah, sin! how many poor and fettered believers have had their fetters first forged by thee? Sin, thou art the anvil on which our doubts are welded; sin, thou art the fire in which our spirits are often molten down to grief. We could do all things were it not for thee. O sin, thou dost clip the wings of faith, thou dost damp the flame of love, thou dost destroy the energy of zeal; thou art "the evil"; my Master calls thee so, and such thou art. Thou needest not to be renamed; that name once given thou shalt bear for ever, and throughout eternity thou shalt be pointed at, in the pillory of scorn, by all the saints, as "the evil." Well might Christ ask his Father that, while he did not wish his children to be taken out of the world, he did wish that they might be kept from the evil.

I charge you, ye young converts, who are about to put on the Lord Jesus Christ, recollect that sin is "*the* evil." Through all your future lives, you must remember that this is "the evil" you are to shun. Fear not affliction, fear not persecution; rather, rejoice, and be exceeding glad if that should be your lot, for great is your reward in heaven; but, I charge you, fear sin. I commend you to the God of all grace, who is able to keep you from falling, and to present you faultless before the presence of his glory; but yet I beg you always to recollect that sin itself is "the evil" to you. It will always be so to you so long as you live, and, though forgiven, it is still sin pardoned. Shun it in the least degree, do not give way to little sins, and you will not give way to big ones. Remember the proverb, "Take care of the pence, and the pounds will take care of themselves;" beware of little sins, and you will not commit great ones. I charge you, keep your hearts in the love of God; and may God himself preserve you, according to our Saviour's prayer, "that thou shouldest keep them from the evil."

II. We can make only a very few remarks upon the second point; which is, THE DANGER TO WHICH CHRIST'S PEOPLE ARE EXPOSED.

Is there any danger of Christian men running into sin? After they have believed in Jesus, and after they have been pardoned, will they again commit sin? After they have been adopted into God's family, will they sin? Will they, can they, sin after all that? O beloved! I thought once, when my Lord first pardoned me, that I never could sin against him any more. When, black from head to foot, he spake the cleansing word, and made me white; when he took off my rags, and clothed me in royal garments, and kissed me with the kisses of his love, and showed me his deep, affectionate heart, I thought, "O thou blessed Jesus! can I ever again sin against thee? Can it be that I, a pardoned rebel, whom thou hast forgiven so much, could do such a thing?" "No, precious Jesus," the young convert thinks, "I can come and wash thy feet with my tears, and wipe them with the hairs of my head; but I cannot sin, I will not sin." Ah! how soon is that beautiful vision taken away! How soon the theory is spoiled by experience!

Beloved, do you not find that you are in danger of sinning now? Those of us who are young,—what danger of sinning we are in! While our passions are strong, and our lusts furious, we have need to be kept of God, or we shall sin against him. And you middle-aged gentlemen, to you also I have a word or two to say. You always pray so particularly for the young, and the young people are very much obliged to you; and they always intend to pray specially for you, because you are in the most dangerous position. I remind you of what I have told you before, that there is in Scripture no instance of a young man falling into sin, but there is more than one such instance of a middle-aged man.

Ye grandsires with snowy heads, whose hairs are whitened with age, know ye not that ye still have need of divine keeping, or ye will fall? O ye veterans in the army of the Lord, do you not acknowledge that, if his grace were withdrawn from you, you have enough tinder in your hearts to catch fire, for your souls are not yet perfectly purified? When I ask my old brethren whether sin is still present with them, each one of them always says, "Well, I thought I had a bad heart once, but I know I have now; I thought I was vile once, but I know I am now. I grow viler and viler as the years roll on, and I see myself to be more and more so every day." Is it not so with you? Ah! is it not just so with you perpetually? And will you not confess, till your last dying moment, that you will be kept if God keeps you; but that, if he were to leave you, you would be lost? I was pleased to hear some of the good answers the young people gave me when I asked them, "Do you think you will be kept faithful to Christ to the end?" "Yes; by God's grace," they said. "But suppose God should leave you?" I next asked, and how exceedingly proper the answer was! "God will not leave me, so I cannot tell anything about that." That was a sweet way of answering the question. He has promised that he will not leave us, nor forsake us; so, Christian, while we warn you of the danger if God should leave you, we comfort you by telling you that he will not leave you.

Mark the terrible threatening that those poor Arminians have been spoiling so much. Those who know nothing of the doctrines of grace make out that sinners fall, and come in again, and fall again, and come in again; but a more unscriptural doctrine cannot be propounded, for God solemnly declares that, if it were possible for a man, once regenerated and sanctified, to apostatize, he would be lost beyond all remedy, and there would remain no hope for him, "but a certain fearful looking for of judgment and fiery indignation." I charge you to recollect that, if it were possible for you thus to fall, there is the precipice over which you must drop. There is no ransom for you in such a case as that. If true conversion fails, God will never try twice; if once he puts his hand on you, and fails, he has done with you. But it is not possible, glory be to his name! He has not failed yet, and he never will. Still, we warn you, and Scripture tells us so to do, to remember that we shall be kept only through faith unto salvation, and that our Lord Jesus Christ said, "My sheep hear my voice, and I know them, and they follow me: and I give unto them eternal life; and they shall never perish, neither shall any man pluck them out of my hand. My Father, which gave them me, is greater than all; and no man is able to pluck them out of my Father's hand."

III. This brings us to speak, thirdly, concerning THE KEEPER OF CHRIST'S PEOPLE: "I pray that thou shouldest keep them from the evil."

We often get keeping ourselves, beloved, and a bad job we make of it, when we do that. If a Christian man tries to keep his own heart without asking the help of God, he will be just as good a keeper as those guards whom Herod set to watch the apostle Peter, and who, when they opened the prison doors in the morning, found that the prisoner had escaped. You may stand and watch your heart without God, but you will find that it has escaped, and gone after sin notwithstanding. The Christian must not trust to his guarding himself, because he will sometimes be asleep, and then the enemy will catch him unawares. People are often ready, as the saying is, to put a lock on the stable door when the horse is gone, and Christians are sometimes very careful after they have sinned. Ah! but the thing is to lock the door while the horse is in the stable, and to take care before you do sin. It is better to keep your house from being on fire, than to get the fire put out ever so quickly.

We all of us have need thus to be kept by God. We think we can keep ourselves, but we cannot, for poor flesh and blood will fail; though the spirit may be willing, the flesh is weak; and if it were possible for us to keep ourselves a little while, we should soon be overcome with spiritual slumber; and then, you know, the devil would come walking into the camp in the middle of the night, and if he caught us slumbering, and off our guard, he would, if allowed of God, hurry us away to perdition. If you trust yourselves to God, he will preserve you; but if you try to keep yourselves, you will fail. How many different schemes people have for keeping themselves from sin! Why do they not go and ask God to keep them, instead of binding themselves hand and foot to this thing and the other, and so thinking to avoid sin? Let us give our hearts to God thoroughly, for he will preserve his own people. Oh! what a gracious promise the Lord has given concerning his vineyard: " I the Lord do keep it; I will water it every moment; lest any hurt it, I will keep it night and day." Is not that a precious expression, " I the Lord do keep it"? The Lord seems to speak in his own defence, " They say I do not keep it, but I do. They say that I let my people fall away, but I do not. Look at my vineyard, ' I the Lord *do* keep it,' whatever they may say; ' I will water it every moment; lest any hurt it, I will keep it night and day.' " This is the only ground of our confidence, that God keepeth the feet of his saints, and none that trust in him shall be desolate.

We must now conclude, praying on behalf of the Lord's people that God would keep them. Recollect, believer, that *while it says God will keep you, he does it by means.* You must look after each other; I like to admonish you to look after your brethren and sisters. Why, there are some of you sitting with only a rail between you, and yet you do not know your next-door neighbours. Some of you, I know, talk too much sometimes; but I would rather you should talk a little too much than not talk at all. Oh, how little like Christians some of you are; sitting down side by side, and yet not knowing one another! The church is meant to be a place where we shall be like children at home. Be sure to look after these young friends who are coming into the church; try and take care of them. We want a few fathers who will lead them in the right way. Poor souls, you cannot expect them to know much; some of them, indeed, may have been long in the service of God, others have just commenced to run the Christian race;

you must look after the young ones, and then the prayer of Christ will be fulfilled in their case, "I pray that thou shouldest keep them from the evil."

Finally, *remember that the only Keeper of the saints is God,* and put your souls day by day into his hands. I beseech you, by the love of Christ, forget not his holy prayer of which I have been speaking to you. Often meditate upon the grace that put you into the Saviour's custody. Oh! forget not that you have been his from all eternity, and that it ill becomes you to sin; that you are elect in Christ, and it would be a disgrace to you to transgress. Recollect that you are one of the aristocracy of the universe, you must not mix with vile worldlings. Remember that the blood royal of heaven runs in your veins; therefore, do not disgrace yourselves by acts which might be tolerated in a beggar, but which would demean a prince of the heavenly household. Stand on your dignity, think of your future glory; recollect where you stand, and in whom you stand—in the person of Jesus. Fall at his feet daily; grasp his strength hourly, crying out,—

> "Oh, for this no power have I!
> My strength is at thy feet to lie."

O beloved, you who do not love the Lord, I cannot pray that God would keep you from the evil, because you are in it already; but I do pray God to take you out of it. There are some of you who do not feel sin to be an evil; and shall I tell you why? Did you ever try to pull a bucket up a well? You know that, when it is full of water, you can pull it easily so long as the bucket remains in the water; but when it gets above the water, you know how heavy it is. It is just so with you. While you are in sin, you do not feel it to be a burden, it does not seem to be evil; but if the Lord once draws you out of sin, you will find it to be an intolerable, a heinous evil. May the Lord, this night, wind some of you up! Though you are very deep down, may he draw you up out of sin, and give you acceptance in the Beloved! May you have new hearts and right spirits, which are alone the gift of God! Remember the words of the Lord Jesus: "Ask, and it shall be given you; seek, and ye shall find; knock, and it shall be opened unto you: for every one that asketh receiveth; and he that seeketh findeth; and to him that knocketh it shall be opened." God give you grace to ask, and seek, and knock, for Jesus' sake! Amen.

Exposition by C. H. Spurgeon.
ISAIAH XLIX. 1—23.

Verses 1, 2. *Listen, O isles, unto me; and hearken, ye people, from far; the* LORD *hath called me from the womb; from the bowels of my mother hath he made mention of my name. And he hath made my mouth like a sharp sword; in the shadow of his hand hath he hid me, and made me a polished shaft; in his quiver hath he hid me;*

Our Lord Jesus, that great Prophet of the Church, was in a special manner the Lord's in the matter of his birth. A wondrous holy mystery hangs about his birth at Bethlehem,—he was, in that respect, the Lord's in a very remarkable sense.

"He hath made my mouth like a sharp sword." You know how our Lord's mouth, or the word of his gospel that issues from his mouth, is like a sharp sword,—how it conquers,—how it cuts its way,—how, wherever it comes, it pierces "even to the dividing asunder of soul and spirit, and of the joints and marrow, and is a discerner of the thoughts and intents of the heart."

"In the shadow of his hand hath he hid me." You know how the protecting hand of God ever covered Christ, and how his gospel is ever sheltered by the providence of God.

3. *And said unto me, Thou art my servant, O Israel, in whom I will be glorified.*

It is wonderful condescension on Christ's part to take the name of his Church so that he himself is called "Israel" in this passage; and there is another passage, equally remarkable, where the Church is allowed to take one of the names of Christ: "This is the name wherewith she shall be called, The Lord our righteousness." Such an intermingling of interests, such a wonderful unity is there between Christ and his Church, that these twain are truly one.

4. *Then I said, I have laboured in vain, I have spent my strength for nought, and in vain: yet surely my judgment is with the LORD, and my work with my God.*

Our Saviour did, in his earthly ministry, to a large extent labour in vain. "He came unto his own, and his own received him not." He was sent to the lost sheep of the house of Israel, yet how few of them recognized him as the good Shepherd. He told his disciples that, after he returned to his Father, those who believed in him should do even greater things than he had done. That promise was fulfilled on the day of Pentecost; and since then it has been fulfilled over and over again in the history of the Christian Church.

5. *And now, saith the LORD that formed me from the womb to be his servant, to bring Jacob again to him, Though Israel be not gathered, yet shall I be glorious in the eyes of the LORD, and my God shall be my strength.*

What though the Jews still reject the Messiah, their sin does not affect his honour. His glory is still as great as ever it was in the esteem of the Most High.

6. *And he said, It is a light thing that thou shouldest be my servant to raise up the tribes of Jacob, and to restore the preserved of Israel: I will also give thee for a light to the Gentiles, that thou mayest be my salvation unto the end of the earth.*

What a blessed passage this is for you and for me, beloved! Strangers to the commonwealth of Israel were we; but, now, we who were afar off are made nigh by the blood of Jesus, and so are made fellow-heirs with the seed of Abraham, partakers of the self-same covenant blessing as the father of the faithful enjoys. In this let us exceedingly rejoice; and for this, let us praise and magnify the name of the Lord.

7. *Thus saith the LORD, the Redeemer of Israel, and his Holy One, to him whom man despiseth, to him whom the nation abhorreth,—*

What a true picture this is of the way in which the Jews still treat the promised Messiah! To this day, they gnash their teeth at the very mention of the name of Jesus of Nazareth; and the bitterest words of blasphemy that are ever uttered by human lips come from the mouth of Israel against the Lord Jesus: "him whom the nation abhorreth,"—

7. *To a servant of rulers, Kings shall see and arise, princes also shall worship, because of the* LORD *that is faithful, and the Holy One of Israel, and he shall choose thee.*

The Father has chosen Christ to be the precious corner-stone of the eternal temple, and he has also chosen all the living stones that are to be joined to him for ever.

8, 9. *Thus saith the* LORD, *In an acceptable time have I heard thee, and in a day of salvation have I helped thee: and I will preserve thee, and give thee for a covenant of the people, to establish the earth, to cause to inherit the desolate heritages; that thou mayest say to the prisoners, Go forth; to them that are in darkness, Shew yourselves. They shall feed in the ways, and their pastures shall be in all high places.*

Dear brethren, what honour the Lord has put upon Christ! In proportion as he has been the despised of men, and the abhorred of the Jewish nation, God has made him to be his own delight, his Well-beloved. He displays through him the marvels of his saving power for his own glory. I pray that it may be displayed in our midst just now, and in the way mentioned here: "I will preserve thee, and give thee for a covenant of the people, to establish the earth, to cause to inherit the desolate heritages; that thou mayest say to the prisoners, Go forth; to them that are in darkness, Shew yourselves." Come, beloved, after you receive such a message as this from God's mouth, what prison can hold you? What darkness can conceal you?. The word of Christ shall break your bonds asunder, and change your darkness into the glory of noonday. May this gracious work be done for any of you who are prisoners here!

10. *They shall not hunger nor thirst;—*

To the woman at the well, Christ said, "Whosoever drinketh of the water that I shall give him shall never thirst." That is a parallel to this passage: "They shall not hunger nor thirst;"—

10. *Neither shall the heat nor sun smite them: for he that hath mercy on them shall lead them, even by the springs of water shall he guide them.*

Oh, the wondrous sweetness of these exceeding great and precious promises! They are all concerning Christ, you see; undoubtedly, they are given with an eye to us, but yet much more with an eye to him, that he may be glorified in the deliverance and guidance of his people, in the protection of them from danger, and in the abundant provision for the supply of all their needs. It would not be for Christ's honour to let you die of thirst, poor thirsty one; it would not glorify him to lead you where there were no springs of water. Be sure, then, that God will always do that which will glorify his Son, and he will therefore deal well with you for his sake.

11, 12. *And I will make all my mountains a way, and my highways shall be exalted. Behold, these shall come from far: and, lo, these from the north and from the west; and these from the land of Sinim.*

From far-away China, they must come to Christ; the result of his death is not left to haphazard. Some say that his death did something or other, which, somehow or other, will benefit somebody or other; but we never speak in that indefinite way. We know that Christ, by his death, did eternally redeem his people, and we are quite sure that he will have all those for whom he laid down the ransom price. He died with a clear intent, a definite purpose; and "for the joy that was set before him," he "endured the cross, despising the shame." "He shall see of the travail of his soul, and shall be satisfied." The divine intent and purpose of the death of Christ cannot possibly be frustrated. He reigneth from the tree, and he shall win and conquer world without end.

13. *Sing, O heavens; and be joyful, O earth; and break forth into singing, O mountains: for the* LORD *hath comforted his people, and will have mercy upon his afflicted.*

How? Why, by the very coming of Christ, by his birth at Bethlehem, and all the blessings which come with the Incarnate God, his afflicted ones are consoled, and all his people are divinely comforted. Shall we not, then, rejoice in Christ, who is himself so full of joy that he teaches the very heavens to sing, and the mountains to break forth into praise?

14. *But Zion said,—*

Hear the lament of the poor Jewish Church, like a castaway left all alone,—

14. *The* LORD *hath forsaken me, and my Lord hath forgotten me.*

When we are glad in the Lord, and are singing out our heart's joy, there is pretty sure to be someone or other who sorrowfully sighs, "The Lord hath forsaken me."

People say that there never was a feast so well furnished but that somebody went away unsatisfied; but God will not have it so at his festivals; and hence, the rest of the chapter shows how the Lord comforted this poor Zion, whose lamentation and mourning he had heard. Notice how he begins:—

15. *Can a woman forget her sucking child, that she should not have compassion on the son of her womb?*

"Can a woman"—the tenderer parent of the two,—"forget her child,"—her own child, her feeble little child that still depends upon her for its nutriment and life,—"her sucking child,"—

15. *Yea, they may forget,—*

It is just possible; there have been such monstrosities: "they may forget,"—

15. *Yet will I not forget thee.*

> "Yet, saith the Lord, should nature change
> And mothers monsters prove,
> Sion still dwells upon the heart
> Of everlasting love."

How that gracious assurance should comfort the little handful, the "remnant weak and small" of God's people among the Jews! How it should also comfort any of God's servants who are under a cloud, and who have lost for a while the enjoyment of his presence!

16. *Behold, I have graven thee upon the palms of my hands;—*

Where they must be seen, and where he can do nothing without touching his people while doing it. When a name is engraven on the hand with which a man works, that name goes into his work, and leaves its impress on the work.

16, 17. *Thy walls are continually before me. Thy children shall make haste; thy destroyers and they that made thee waste shall go forth of thee.*

Jerusalem, the very Jerusalem that is in Palestine, shall be rebuilt. God will remember her walls, and the Church of God in Israel shall yet rise from that sad low estate in which it has been these many centuries; and all God's cast-down ones shall be comforted, and his churches, that seem to be left to die, shall be raised up again, for our God is no changeling. His heart does not come and go towards the sons of men.

> Whom once he loves, he never leaves,
> But loves them to the end."

18. *Lift up thine eyes round about, and behold: all these gather themselves together, and come to thee.*

What are all converted Gentiles doing, after all, but coming to the one Church? It is no longer a matter of Jew or Gentile, but all who believe are one in Christ Jesus. Let poor Zion rejoice that she herself is enriched by the conversion of these far-off sinners of the Gentiles.

18. *As I live, saith the LORD, thou shalt surely clothe thee with them all, as with an ornament, and bind them on thee, as a bride doeth.*

Converts are the garments of the church, her bridal array, her ornaments and her jewels. I wish that all churches thought so; but many of them think that gorgeous architecture, the garnishing of the material building in which they meet, and the sound of sweet music, and the smell of fragrant incense and choice flowers, make up the dignity and glory of a church; but they do no such thing. Converts are the true glory of a church: "Thou shalt surely clothe thee with them all, as with an ornament, and bind them on thee, as a bride doeth."

19, 20. *For thy waste and thy desolate places, and the land of thy destruction, shall even now be too narrow by reason of the inhabitants, and they that swallowed thee up shall be far away. The children which thou shalt have, after thou hast lost the other,—*

The children of thy childlessness,—so it runs,—the children of thy widowhood. It was strange that she should have children then; it is not so among men, but it is so with the Church of God: "The children which thou shalt have, after thou hast lost the other,"—

20—23. *Shall say again in thine ears, The place is too strait for me: give place to me that I may dwell. Then shalt thou say in thine heart, Who hath begotten me these, seeing I have lost my children, and am desolate, a captive, and removing to and fro? and who hath brought up these? Behold, I was left alone; these, where had they been? Thus saith the Lord GOD, Behold, I will lift up mine hand to the Gentiles, and set up my standard to the people: and they shall bring thy sons in their arms, and thy daughters shall be carried upon their shoulders. And kings shall be thy nursing fathers, and their queens thy nursing mothers: they shall bow down to thee with their face toward the earth, and lick up the dust of thy feet;—*

I have heard this passage quoted as a reason why there should be a State Church,—that kings should nourish the Church,—Henry VIII., for instance, and George IV. It was poor milk, I am sure, that they ever gave the Church of God. Yet I have no objection whatever to this text being carried out to the full,—ay, to the very letter,—only mind where the kings are to be put. What place does the verse say that they are to occupy? "They shall bow down to thee with their face toward the earth, and lick up the dust of thy feet." There is no headship of the Church here, nothing of that sort; the kings are to be at the feet of the Church, and that is what the State ought to do, submit itself to God, and obey his commands, and give full liberty to the preaching of the gospel. This is all that the true Church of Christ asks, and all she can ever fairly take if she is loyal to her Lord.

23. *And thou shalt know that I am the LORD.*

"Jehovah." "Thou shalt understand the greatness of thy God, his infiniteness, his majesty, his all-sufficiency· 'Thou shalt know that I am the I AM.'"

23. *For they shall not be ashamed that wait for me.*

Glory be to his holy name, none that wait for him shall ever have cause to be ashamed; may we all be of that blessed number, for Christ's sake! Amen.

ENDURING TO THE END.

A Sermon

DELIVERED ON SUNDAY MORNING, FEBRUARY 14TH, 1364, BY THE
REV. C. H. SPURGEON,
AT THE METROPOLITAN TABERNACLE, NEWINGTON.

"He that endureth to the end shall be saved."—Matthew x. 22.

THIS particular text was originally addressed *to the apostles* when they were sent to teach and preach in the name of the Lord Jesus. Perhaps bright visions floated before their minds, of honour and esteem among men. It was no mean dignity to be among the twelve first heralds of salvation to the sons of Adam. Was a check needed to their high hopes? Perhaps so. Lest they should enter upon their work without having counted its cost, Christ gives them a very full description of the treatment which they might expect to receive, and reminds them that it was not the commencement of their ministry which would win them their reward, but "He that endureth to the end, the same shall be saved." It would be well if every youthful aspirant to the gospel ministry would remember this. If merely to put our hand to the plough proved us to be called of God, how many would be found so; but alas, too many look back and prove unworthy of the kingdom. The charge of Paul to Timothy, is a very necessary exhortation to every young minister: "Be thou faithful unto death." It is not to be faithful for a time, but to be "faithful *unto death*," which will enable a man to say, "I have fought a good fight." How many dangers surround the Christian minister! As the officers in an army are the chosen targets of the sharpshooters, so are the ministers of Christ. The king of Syria said to his servants, "Fight neither with small nor great, save only with the king of Israel;" even so the arch-fiend makes his main attack upon the ministers of God. From the first moment of his call to the work, the preacher of the Word will be familiar with temptation. While he is yet in his youth, there are multitudes of the softer temptations to turn the head and trip the feet of the youthful herald of the cross; and when the blandishments of early popularity have passed away, as soon they must, the harsh croak of slander, and the adder's tongue of ingratitude assail him, he finds himself stale and flat where once he was flattered and admired; nay, the venom of malice succeeds to the honeyed morsels of adulation. Now, let him gird his loins and fight the good fight of faith. In his after days, to provide fresh matter Sabbath after Sabbath, to rule as in the sight of God, to watch over the souls of men, to weep with them who weep, to rejoice with those who do rejoice, to be a nursing father unto young converts, sternly to rebuke hypocrites, to deal faithfully with backsliders, to speak with solemn authority and paternal pathos to those who are in the first stages of spiritual decline, to carry about with him the care of the souls of hundreds, is enough to make him grow old while yet he is young, and to mar his visage with the lines of grief, till, like the Saviour, at the age of thirty years, men shall count him nearly fifty. "Thou art not yet fifty years old, and hast thou seen Abraham?" said the adversaries of Christ to him when he was but thirty-two. If the minister should fall, my brethren; if, set upon a pinnacle, he should be cast down; if, standing in slippery places, he should falter; if the standard-bearer fall, as fall full well he may, what mischief is done to the Church, what shouts are heard among the adversaries, what dancings are seen among the daughters of Philistia! How hath God's banner been stained in the dust, and the name of Jesus cast into the mire! When the minister of Christ turns traitor, it is as if the pillars of the house did tremble; every stone in the structure feels the shock. If Satan can succeed in overturning the preachers of the Word, it is as if yon broad-spreading tree should suddenly fall beneath the axe; prone in the dust it lies to wither and to rot; but where are the birds of the air which made their nests among its boughs, and whither fly those beasts of the field which found a happy shadow beneath its branches? Dismay hath seized them, and they flee in affright. All who were comforted by the preacher's word, strengthened by his example, and edified by his teaching, are filled with humiliation and grief, crying, "Alas! my brother." By these our manifold dangers and weighty responsibilities, we may very justly appeal to you who feed under our ministry, and beseech you, "Brethren, pray for us." Well, we know that though our ministry be received of the Lord Jesus, if hitherto we have been kept faithful by the power of the Holy Ghost, yet it is only he who endureth to the end who shall be saved.

But, my brethren, how glorious is the sight of the man who does endure to the end as a minister of Christ. I have photographed upon my heart just now, the portrait of one very, very dear to me, and I think I may venture to produce a rough sketch of him, as no mean example of how honourable it is to endure to the end. This man began while yet a youth to preach the Word. Sprung of ancestors who had loved the Lord and served his Church, he felt the glow of holy enthusiasm. Having proved his capabilities, he entered college, and after the close of its course, settled in a spot where for more than fifty years he continued his labours. In his early days, his sober earnestness and sound doctrine were owned of God in many conversions both at home and abroad. Assailed by slander and abuse, it was his privilege to live it all down. He outlived his enemies, and though he had buried a generation of his friends, yet he found many warm hearts clustering round him to the last. Visiting his flock, preaching in his own pulpit, and making very many journeys to other Churches, years followed one another so rapidly, that he found himself the head of a large tribe of children and grandchildren, most of them walking in the truth. At the age of fourscore years, he preached on still, until laden with infirmities, but yet as joyful and as cheerful as in the heyday of his youth, his time had come to die. He was able to say truthfully, when last he spake to me, "I do not know that my testimony for God has ever altered, as to the fundamental doctrines; I have grown in experience, but from the first day until now, I have had no new doctrines to teach my hearers. I have had to make no confessions of error on vital points, but have been held fast to the doctrines of grace, and can now say that I love them better than ever." Such an one was he, as Paul, the aged, longing to preach so long as his tottering knees could bear him to the pulpit. I am thankful that I had such a grandsire. He fell asleep in Christ but a few hours ago, and on his dying bed talked as cheerfully as men can do in the full vigour of their health. Most sweetly he talked of the preciousness of Christ, and chiefly of the security of the believer; the truthfulness of the promise; the immutability of the covenant; the faithfulness of God, and the infallibility of the divine decree. Among other things which he said at the last was this, which is, we think, worth your treasuring in your memories. "Dr Watts sings—

> 'Firm *as the earth* thy gospel stands,
> My Lord, my hope, my trust.'

What, Doctor, is it not firmer than that? Could you not find a better comparison? Why, the earth will give way beneath our feet one day or another, if we rest on it. The comparison will not do. The Doctor was much nearer the mark, when he said—

> 'Firm *as his throne* his promise stands,
> And he can well secure
> What I've committed to his hands.
> 'Till the decisive hour.'"

"Firm as his throne," said he, "he must cease to be king before he can break his promise, or lose his people. Divine sovereignty makes us all secure." He fell asleep right quietly, for his day was over, and the night was come, what could he do better than go to rest in Jesus? Would God it may be our lot to preach the Word, so long as we breathe, standing fast unto the end in the truth of God; and if we see not our sons and grandsons testifying to those doctrines which are so dear to us, yet may we see our children walking in the truth. I know of nothing, dear friends, which I would choose to have, as the subject of my ambition for life, than to be kept faithful to my God to death, still to be a soul-winner, still to be a true herald of the cross, and testify the name of Jesus to the last hour. It is only such who in the ministry shall be saved.

Our text, however, occurs again in the twenty-fourth chapter of Matthew, at the fourteenth verse, upon which occasion it was not addressed to the apostles, but to the disciples. The disciples, looking upon the huge stones which were used in the construction of the Temple, admired the edifice greatly, and expected their Lord to utter a few words of passing encomium; instead of which, he, who came not to be an admirer of architecture, but to hew living stones out of the quarry of nature, to build them up into a spiritual temple turned their remarks to practical account, by warning them of a time of affliction, in which there should be such trouble as had never been before, and he added, "No, nor ever shall be." He described false prophets as abounding, and the love of many as waxing cold, and warned them that "He that endureth to the end, the same shall be saved." So that this solemn truth applies to every one of you.

The Christian man, though not called to the post of danger in witnessing publicly of the grace of God, is destined in his measure to testify concerning Jesus, and in his proper sphere and place, to be a burning and a shining light. He may not have the cares of a Church, but he hath far more, the cares of business: he is mixed up with the world; he is compelled to associate with the ungodly. To a great degree, he must, at least six days in the week, walk in an atmosphere uncongenial with his nature: he is compelled to hear words which will never provoke him to love and good works, and to behold actions whose example is obnoxious. He is exposed to temptations of every sort and size, for this is the lot of the followers of the Lamb. Satan knows how useful is a consistent follower of the Saviour, and how much damage to Christ's cause an inconsistent professor may bring, and therefore he emptieth out all his arrows from his quiver that he may wound, even unto death, the soldier of the cross. My brethren, many of you have had a far longer experience than myself; you know how stern is the battle of the religious life, how you must contend, even unto blood, striving against sin. Your life is one continued scene of warfare, both without and within; perhaps even now you are crying with the apostle, "O wretched man that I am! who shall deliver me from the body of this death?" A Christian's career is always fighting, never ceasing; always ploughing the stormy sea, and never resting till he reaches the port of glory. If my God shall preserve you, as preserve you he must, or else you are not his; if he shall keep you, as keep you he will if you have committed your souls to his faithful guardianship, what an honour awaits you! I have in my mind's eye, just now, one who has been for about sixty years associated with this Church, and who this week, full of years, and ripe for heaven, was carried by angels into the Saviour's bosom. Called by divine grace, while yet young, he was united with the Christian Church early in life. By divine grace, he was enabled to maintain a consistent and honourable character for many years; as an officer of this Church, he was acceptable among his brethren, and useful both by his godly example and sound judgment; while in various parts of the Church of Christ, he earned unto himself a good degree. He went last Sabbath day, twice to the house of God where he was accustomed of late years to worship, enjoying the Word, and feasting at the Communion-table with much delight. He went to his bed without having any very serious illness upon him, having spent his last evening upon earth in cheerful conversation with his daughters. Ere the morning light, with his head leaning upon his hand, he had fallen asleep in Christ, having been admitted to the rest which remaineth for the people of God. As I think of my brother, though of late years I have seen but little of him, I can but rejoice in the grace which illuminated his pathway. When I saw him, the week before his departure, although full of years, there was little or no failure in mind. He was just the picture of an aged saint waiting for his Master, and willing to work in his cause while life remained. I refer, as most of you know, to Mr. Samuel Gale. Let us thank God and take courage—thank God that he has preserved in this case, a Christian so many, many years, and take courage to hope that there will be found in this Church, many, at all periods, whose grey heads shall be crowns of glory. " He that endureth to the end," and only he " shall be saved."

But, dear friends, perseverance is not the lot of the few; it is not left to laborious preachers of the Word, or to consistent Church-officers it is the common lot of every believer in the Church. It must be so for only thus can they prove that they are believers. It must be so, for only by their perseverance can the promise be fulfilled, " He that believeth and is baptized, shall be saved." Without perseverance, they cannot be saved; and, as saved they must be, persevere they shall through divine grace.

I shall now, with brevity and earnestness, as God enables me, speak upon our text thus: *perseverance is the badge of saints—the target of our foes—the glory of Christ—and the care of all believers.*

I. First, then, PERSEVERANCE IS THE BADGE OF TRUE SAINTS. *It is their Scriptural mark.* How am I to know a Christian? By his words? Well, to some degree, words betray the man; but a man's speech is not always the copy of his heart, for with smooth language many are able to deceive. What doth our Lord say? " Ye shall know them *by their fruits.*" But how am I to know a man's fruits? By watching him one day? I may, perhaps, form a guess of his character by being with him for a single hour, but I could not confidently pronounce upon a man's true state even by being with him for a week. George Whitfield was asked what he thought of a certain person's character. " I have never lived with him," was his very proper answer. If we take the run of a man's life, say for ten, twenty, or thirty years, and, if by carefully watching, we see that he brings forth the fruits of grace through the Holy Spirit, our conclusion may be drawn very safely. As the truly magnetized needle in the compass, with many deflections, yet does really and naturally point to the pole; so, if I can see that despite infirmities, my friend sincerely and constantly aims at holiness, then I may conclude with something like certainty, that he is a child of God. Although works do not justify a man before God, they do justify a man's profession before his fellows. I cannot tell whether you are justified in calling yourself a Christian except by your works; by your works, therefore, as James saith, shall ye be justified. You cannot by your words convince me that you are a Christian, much less by your experience, which I cannot see but must take on trust from you; but your actions will, unless you be an unmitigated hypocrite, speak the truth, and speak the truth loudly too. If your course is as the shining light which shineth more unto the perfect day, I know that yours is the path of the just. All other conclusions are only the judgment of charity such as we are bound to exercise; but this is as far as man can get it, the judgment of certainty when a man's life has been consistent throughout.

Moreover, *analogy shows us that it is perseverance which must mark the Christian.* How do I know the winner at the foot-race? There are the spectators, and there are the runners. What strong men! what magnificent muscles! what thews and sinews! Yonder is the goal, and there it is that I must judge who is the winner, not here, at the starting-point, for "They which run in a race run all, but one receiveth the prize." I may select this one, or that other person, as likely to win, but I cannot be absolutely sure until the race is over. There they fly! see how they press forward with straining muscles; but one has tripped, another faints, a third is out of breath, and others are far behind. One only wins—and who is he? Why, he who continueth to the end. So I may gather from the analogy, which Paul constantly allows us, from the ancient games, that only he who continueth till he reaches the goal may be accounted a Christian at all. A ship starts on a voyage to Australia—if it stops at Madeira, or returns after reaching the Cape, would you consider that it ought to be called an emigrant ship for New South Wales? It must go the whole voyage, or it does not deserve the name. A man has begun to build a house, and has erected one side of it—do you consider him a builder if he stops there, and fails to cover it in or to finish the other walls? Do we give men praise for being warriors because they know how to make one desperate charge, but lose the campaign? Have we not, of late, smiled at the boasting despatches of commanders, in fights where both combatants fought with valour, and yet neither of them had the common sense to push on to reap the victory? What was the very strength of Wellington, but that when a triumph had been achieved, he knew how to reap the harvest which had been sown in blood? And he only is a true conqueror, and shall be crowned at the last, who continueth till war's trumpet is blown no more. It is with a Christian as it was with the great Napoleon: he said, "Conquest has made me what I am, and conquest must maintain me." So, under God, conquest has made you what you are, and conquest must sustain you. Your motto must be, "Excelsior;" or, if it be not, you know not the noble spirit of God's princes. But why do I multiply illustrations, when all the world rings with the praise of perseverance?

Moreover, *the common-sense judgment of mankind* tells us, that those who merely begin and do not hold out, will not be saved. Why, *if every man would be saved who began to follow Christ, who would be damned?* In such a country as this, the most of men have at least one religious spasm in their lives. I suppose that there is not a person before me, who at some time or other did not determine to be a pilgrim. You, Mr. Pliable, were induced by a Christian friend, who had some influence with you, to go with him some short way, till you came to the Slough of Despond, and you thought yourself very wise when you scrambled out on that side which was nearest to your own home. And even you, Mr. Obstinate, are not always dogged; you have fits of thoughtfulness and intervals of tenderness. My hearer, how impressed you were at the prayer meeting! how excited you were at that revival service! When you heard a zealous brother preach at the theatre what an impression was produced! Ah! yes; the shop was shut up for a Sunday or two; you did not swear or get drunk for nearly a month, but you could not hold on any longer. Now, if those who were to begin were saved, why you would be secure, though you are at the present time as far from anything like religion, as the darkness at midnight is from the blazing light of midday. Besides, common sense shows us, I say, that a man must hold on, or else he cannot be saved, because *the very worst of men are those who begin and then give up.* If you would turn over all the black pages of villany, to find the name of the son of perdition, where would you find it? Why, among the apostles. The man who had wrought miracles and preached the gospel, sold his Master for thirty pieces of silver—Judas Iscariot, betrays the Son of Man with a kiss. Where is a worse name than that of Simon Magus? Simon " believed also," says the Scripture, and yet he offered the apostles money if they would sell to him the Holy Ghost. What an infamous notoriety Demas has obtained, who loved the present evil world! How much damage did Alexander the coppersmith do to Paul? " He did me much evil," said he, " the Lord reward him according to his works." And yet that Alexander was once foremost in danger, and even exposed his own person in the theatre at Ephesus, that he might rescue the apostle. There are none so bad as those who once seemed to be good. " If the salt has lost its savour, wherewith shall it be seasoned?" That which is best when ripe, is worst when rotten; liquor which is sweetest in one stage, becomes sourest in another. " Let not him that putteth on his armour boast as though he putteth it off;" for even common sense teaches you, that it is not to begin, but to continue to the end which marks the time of the child of God.

But we need not look to analogy and to mere common sense. *Scripture is plain enough.* What says John ? " They went out from us." Why? Were they ever saints? Oh! no—"They went out from us, because they were not of us, for if they had been of us, doubtless they would have continued with us, but they went out from us, that it might be manifest that they were not of us." They were no Christians, or else they had not thus apostatized. Peter saith, " It hath happened unto them according to the proverb, the dog hath returned to its vomit, and the sow that was washed to her wallowing in the mire," indicating at once most clearly that the dog, though it did vomit, always was a dog. When men disgorge their sins unwillingly, not giving them up because they dislike them, but because they cannot retain them; if a favourable time comes, they will return to swallow once more what they seemed to abandon. The sow that *was* washed—ay, bring it into the parlour, introduce it among society; it *was washed,* and well-washed too; whoever saw so respectable a member of the honourable confraternity of swine before? Bring it in! Yes, but will you keep it there? Wait and see. Because you have not transformed it into a man, on the first occasion it will be found wallowing in the mire. Why? Because it was not a man, but a sow. And so we think we may learn from multitudes of other passages, if we had time to quote them, that those who go back into perdition are not saints at all, for perseverance is the badge of the righteous. " The righteous shall hold on his way, and he that hath clean hands shall wax stronger and stronger." We not only get life by faith, but faith sustains it; " the just *shall live* by faith;" " but if any man draw back, my soul shall have no pleasure in him."

What we have learned from Scripture, dear friends, has been abundantly confirmed *by observation*. Every day would I bless God that in so numerous a Church we have comparatively so few who have proved false; but I have seen enough, and the Lord knoweth, more than enough, to make me very jealous over you with a godly jealousy. I could tell of many an instance of men and women who did run well. "What did hinder them that they should not obey the truth?" I remember a young man of whom I thought as favourably as of any of you, and I believe he did at that time deserve our favourable judgment. He walked among us, one of the most hopeful of our sons, and we hoped that God would make him serviceable to his cause. He fell into bad company. There was enough conscience left, after a long course of secret sin, to make him feel uncomfortable in his wickedness, though he did not give it up; and when at last his sin stared him in the face, and others knew it, so ashamed was he, that, though he bore the Christian name, he took poison that he might escape the shame which he had brought upon himself. He was rescued—rescued by skill and the good providence of God; but where he is, and what he is, God only knoweth, for he had taken another poison more deadly still which made him the slave of his own lusts.

Do not think it is the young alone, however. It is a very lamentable fact that there are, in proportion, more backslidings among the old than the young; and, if you want to find a great sinner in that respect, you will find him, surely, nine times out of ten, with grey hairs on his head. Have I not frequently mentioned that you do not find in Scripture, many cases of young people going astray. You do find believers sinning, but they were all getting old men. There is Noah—no youth. There is Lot, when drunken—no child. There is David with Bathsheba,—no young man in the heat of passion. There is Peter denying his Lord—no boy at the time. These were men of experience and knowledge and wisdom. "Let him that thinketh he standeth, take heed lest he fall."

With sorrow do we remember one whom, years ago, we heard pray among us, and sweetly too; esteemed and trusted by us all. I remember a dear brother saying very kindly, but not too wisely, "If he is not a child of God, I am not." But what did he, my brethren, to our shame and sorrow, but go aside to the very worst and foulest of sins, and where is he now? Perhaps the ale-house may tell, or worse places still. So have we seen, that earth's sun may be eclipsed, earth's stars may go out, and all human glory melt into shame. No true child of God perishes—hold that fast; but this is the badge of a true child of God: that a man endures to the end; and if a man does not hold on, but slinks back to his old master, and once again fits on the old collar, and wears again the Satanic yoke, there is sure proof that he has never come out of the spiritual Egypt through Jesus Christ, his leader, and hath never obtained that eternal life which cannot die, because it is born of God. I have thus then, dear friends, said enough to prove, I think, beyond dispute, that the true badge of the Christian is perseverance, and that without it, no man has proved himself to be a child of God.

II. Secondly, PERSEVERANCE IS THEREFORE, THE TARGET OF ALL OUR SPIRITUAL ENEMIES.

We have many adversaries. Look at *the world!* The world does not object to our being Christians for a time; it will cheerfully overlook all misdemeanors in that way, if we will now shake hands and be as we used to be. Your old companions who used to call you such *good fellows*, when you were bad fellows, would they not very readily forgive you for having been Christians, if you would just go back and be as in days gone by? Oh! certainly, they would look upon your religion as a freak of folly, but they would very easily overlook it, if you would give it up for the future. "O!" saith the world, "come back; come back to my arms once more; be enamoured of me, and though thou hast spoken some hard words against me, and done some cruel deeds against me, I will cheerfully forgive thee." The world is always stabbing at the believer's perseverance. Sometimes she will bully him back; she will persecute him with her tongue—cruel mockings shall be used; and at another time, she will cozen him, "Come thou back to me; O come thou back! Wherefore should we disagree? Thou art made for me, and I am made for thee!" And she beckons so gently and so sweetly, even as Solomon's harlot of old. This is the one thing with her, that thou shouldst cease to be a pilgrim, and settle down to buy and sell with her in Vanity Fair.

Your second enemy, *the flesh*. What is its aim? "Oh!" cries the flesh, "we have had enough of this; it is weary work being a pilgrim, come, give it up." Sloth says, "Sit still where thou art. Enough is as good as a feast, at least, of this tedious thing." Then, lust crieth, "Am I always to be mortified? Am I never to be indulged? Give me at least, a furlough from this constant warfare?" The flesh cares not how soft the chain, so that it does but hold us fast, and prevent our pressing on to glory.

Then comes in the devil, and sometimes he beats the big drum, and cries with a thundering voice "There is no heaven; there is no God; you are a fool to persevere." Or, changing his tactics, he cries, "Come back! I will give thee a better treatment than thou hadst before. Thou thoughtest me a hard master, but that was misrepresentation; come and try me; I am a different devil from what I was ten years ago; I am respectable to what I was then. I do not want you to go back to the low theatre or the casino; come with me, and be a respectable lover of pleasure. I tell thee, I can dress in broad cloth as well as in corderoy, and I can walk in the courts of kings, as well as in the courts and alleys of the beggar. O come back!" he saith, and make thyself one of mine." So that this hellish trinity, the world, the flesh, and the devil, all stab at the Christian's perseverance.

His perseverance in service they will frequently attack: "What profit is there is in serving God? The devil will say to me sometimes, as he did to Jonah, "Flee thou unto Tarshish, and do not stop in this Nineveh; they will not believe thy word, though thou speak in God's name?" To you he will say, "Why, you are so busy all the six days of the week, what is the good of spending your Sunday with a parcel of noisy brats in a Sunday School? Why go about with those tracts in the streets? Much good you will get from it. Would not you be better with having a little rest?" Ah! that word *rest*—some of us are very fond of it; but we ought to recollect that we spoil it if we try to get it *here*, for rest is only beyond the grave. We shall have rest enough when once we come into the presence of our Lord. Perseverance in service, then, the devil would murder outright.

If he cannot stay us in service, he will try to prevent our perseverance *in suffering*. "Why be patient any longer?" says he; "why sit on that dunghill, scraping your sores with a potsherd?—curse God, and die. You have been always poor since you have been a Christian; your business does not prosper; you see, you cannot make money unless you do as others do. You must go with the times, or else you will not get on. Give it all up. Why be always suffering like this?" Thus the foul spirit tempts us. Or you may have espoused some good cause, and the moment you open your mouth, many laugh and try to put you down. "Well," says the devil, "be put down—what is the use of it? Why make yourself singularly eccentric, and expose yourself to perpetual martyrdom? It is all very nice," saith he, "if you will be a martyr, to be burnt at once, and have done with it; but to hang, like Lord Cobham, to be roasted over a slow fire for days, is not comfortable. Why," saith the tempter, "why be always suffering—give it up." You see, then, it is also perseverance in suffering which the devil shooteth at.

Or, perhaps, it is perseverance *in steadfastness*. The love of many has waxed cold, but you remain zealous. "Well," saith he, "what is the good of your being so zealous? Other people are good enough people, you could not censure them: why do you want to be more righteous than they are? Why should you be pushing the Church before you, and dragging the world behind you? What need is there for you to go two marches in one day? Is not one enough? Do as the rest do; loiter as they do. Sleep as do others, and let your lamp go out as other virgins do." Thus is our perseverance in steadfastness frequently assailed.

Or else, it will be *our doctrinal sentiments*. "Why," says Satan, "do you hold to these denominational creeds? Sensible men are getting more liberal, they are giving away what does not belong to them—God's truth; they are removing the old landmarks. Acts of uniformity are to be repealed, articles and creeds are to be laid aside as useless lumber, not necessary for this very enlightened age; fall in with this, and be an Anythingarian. Believe that black is white; hold that truth and a lie are very much akin to one another, and that it not does matter which we do believe, for we are all of us right, though we flatly contradict each other; that the Bible is a nose of wax to fit any face; that it does not teach anything material, but you may make it say anything you like. Do that," saith he, "and be no longer firm in your opinion."

I think I have proved—and need not waste more words about it—that perseverance is the target for all enemies. Wear your shield, Christian, therefore, close upon your armour, and cry mightily unto God, that by his Spirit you may endure to the end.

III. Thirdly, brethren, PERSEVERANCE IS THE GLORY OF CHRIST.

That he makes all his people persevere to the end, is greatly to his honour. If they should fall away and perish, every office, and work, and attribute of Christ would be stained in the mire. If any one child of God should perish, where were Christ's covenant engagements? What is he worth as a mediator of the covenant and the surety of it, if he hath not made the promises sure to all the seed? My brethren, Christ is made a leader and commander of the people, to bring many souls into glory; but if he doth not bring them into glory, where is the captain's honour? Where is the efficacy of the precious blood, if it does not effectually redeem? If it only redeemeth for a time and then suffereth us to perish, where is its value? If it only blots out sin for a few weeks, and then permits that sin to return and to remain upon us, where, I say, is the glory of Calvary, and where is the lustre of the wounds of Jesus? He lives, he lives to intercede, but how can I honour his intercession, if it be fruitless? Does he not pray, "Father, I will that they also, whom thou hast given me, be with me where I am;" and if they be not finally brought to be with him where he is, where is the honour of his intercession? Hath not the Pleader failed, and the great Mediator been dismissed without success? Is he not at this day in union with his people? But what is the value of union to Christ, if that union does not insure salvation? Is he not to-day at the right hand of God, preparing a place for his saints; and will he prepare a place for them, and then lose them on the road? Oh! can it be that he procures the harp and the crown, and will not save souls to use them? My brethren, the perishing of one true child of God, would be such dishonour to Jesus, that I cannot think of it without considering it as blasphemy. One true believer in hell! Oh! what laughter in the pit—what defiance, what unholy mirth! "Ah! Prince of life and glory," saith the prince of the pit, "I have defeated thee; I have snatched the prey from the mighty, and the lawful captive I have delivered; I have torn a jewel from thy crown. See, here it is! Thou didst redeem this soul with blood, and yet it is in hell." Hear what Satan cries—"Christ suffered for this soul, and yet God makes it suffer for itself. Where is the justice of God?" Christ came from heaven to earth to save this soul, and failed in the attempt, and I have him here;" and as he plunges that soul into deeper waves of woe, the shout of triumph goes up more and more blasphemously—"We have conquered heaven! We have rent the eternal covenant; we have foiled the purposes of God; we have defeated his decree; we have triumphed over the power of the Mediator, and cast his blood to the ground!" Shall it ever be? Atrocious question! It *can never be*. They who are in Christ are saved. They whom Jesus Christ hath really taken into union with himself, shall be with him where he is. But how are you to know whether you are in union with Christ? My brethren, you can only know it by obeying the apostle's words, "Give all diligence to make your calling and election sure."

IV. I close, therefore, with but a hint on the last point, PERSEVERANCE SHOULD BE THE GREAT CARE OF EVERY CHRISTIAN—his daily and his nightly care. O beloved! I conjure you by the love of God, and by the love of your own souls, be faithful unto death. Have you difficulties? You must conquer them. Hannibal crossed the Alps, for his heart was full of fury against Rome; and you must cross the Alps of difficulty, for I trust your heart is full of hatred of sin. When Mr. Smeaton had built the lighthouse upon the Eddystone, he looked out anxiously after a storm to see if the edifice was still there, and it was his great joy when he could see it still standing, for a former builder had constructed an edifice which he thought to be indestructible, and expressed a wish that he might be in it in the worst storm which ever blew, and he was so, and neither himself nor his lighthouse were ever seen afterwards. Now you have to be exposed to multitudes of storms; you must be in your lighthouse in the worst storm which ever blew; build firmly then on the Rock of Ages, and make sure work for eternity, for if you do these things, ye shall never fall. For this Church's sake, I pray you do it; for nothing can dishonour and weaken a Church so much as the falls of professors. A thousand rivers flow to the sea, and make rich the meadows, but no man heareth the sound thereof; but if there be one cataract, its roaring will be heard for miles, and every traveller will mark the fall. A thousand Christians can scarcely do such honour to their Master as one hypocrite can do dishonour to him. If you have ever tasted that the Lord is gracious, pray that your foot slip not. It would be infinitely better to bury you in the earth than see you buried in sin. If I must be lost, God grant it may not be as an apostate. If I must, after all, perish, were it not better never to have known the way of righteousness than after having known the theory of it, and something of the enjoyment of it, turn again to the beggarly elements of the world? Let your prayer be not against death, but against sin. For your own sake, for the Church's sake, for the name of Christ's sake, I pray you do this. But ye cannot persevere except by much watchfulness in the closet, much carefulness over every action, much dependance upon the strong hand of the Holy Spirit who alone can make you stand. Walk and live as in the sight of God, knowing where your great strength lieth, and depend upon it you shall yet sing that sweet doxology in Jude, "Now unto him that is able to keep you from falling, and to present you faultless before the presence of his glory with exceeding joy, to the only wise God our Saviour, be glory and majesty, dominion and power, both now and ever. Amen." A simple faith brings the soul to Christ, Christ keeps the faith alive; that faith enables the believer to persevere, and so he enters heaven. May that be your lot and mine for Christ's sake. Amen.

CHRISTIANS KEPT IN TIME AND GLORIFIED IN ETERNITY.

A Sermon

DELIVERED BY

C. H. SPURGEON,

AT THE METROPOLITAN TABERNACLE, NEWINGTON.

"Now unto him that is able to keep you from falling, and to present you faultless before the presence of his glory with exceeding joy, to the only wise God our Saviour, be glory and majesty, dominion and power, both now and ever. Amen."—Jude 24, 25.

OMITTING all preface, it will be well to observe in what state of mind Jude was when he penned this Doxology, what had been his previous meditations, and when we have done so, we will endeavour to come directly to the text, and observe what mercies he sums up in it, and what praise is due from us to him of whom he thus speaks.

I. Then, UNDER WHAT INFLUENCE WAS JUDE'S MIND WHEN HE PENNED THIS DOXOLOGY.

Our first observation is that in writing this very short but very full epistle, he had been led to consider the *grievous faults* of many others, and in contemplating those failures he could not resist the impulse of penning these words, "Now unto him that is able to keep us from falling." You observe in reading that he mentions the Israelites who came out of Egypt. That was a glorious day in which the whole host met at Succoth, having just escaped from the thraldom of Egypt, and now found themselves delivered from the whips and the lashes of the task-masters, and were compelled no longer to make bricks without straw, and to build up palaces and tombs for the oppressors. That was, if possible, a yet more glorious day when God divided the Red Sea to make a way for his people. The depths stood upright as an heap, when the elect multitude walked through. Do you not see them, as with songs and praises they are led all that night through the deep as on dry ground; they are all landed on the other side, and then their leader lifts up his rod, when immediately there comes a wind, and the waters return to their place. The infatuated Egyptian king, who with his hosts had followed them into the depths of the sea, is utterly destroyed; the depths have covered them. They sank as lead in the mighty waters, there is not one of them left. Then sang Moses and the children of Israel, saying, "I will sing unto the Lord for he hath triumphed gloriously; the horse and his rider hath he thrown into the sea."

Is it credible, is it not too sadly incredible, that this very people who stood by the Red Sea and marked the overthrow of God's enemies, within a few days were clamouring to go back into Egypt, and before many months had passed, were for taking to themselves a leader, that they might force their way back into the place of their bondage? Aye, and they who saw Jehovah's work and all his plagues in Zoan, made to themselves a calf, and bowed down before it, and said, "These be thy gods, O Israel, which brought thee up out of the land of Egypt." With tears in your eyes, look at the many griefs which studded the pathway of their forty years' wandering, and with many fears reflect that out of all that multitude which came out of Egypt, there were but two who lived to cross Jordan. Aaron must put off the breast-plate, for he has sinned against God, and even Moses the meekest of men, must go to the top of Nebo, and is only permitted to gaze upon the prospect of that land which he must never actually enjoy, for save Caleb and Joshua, there were none found faithful among all the tribes, and these alone shall enter into the goodly land which floweth with milk and honey.

Now when Jude thought of this, I do not wonder that he began to consider the case of himself and of his fellow-believers united with him in Church fellowship at Jerusalem and elsewhere; and knowing that all of them who were truly brought up out of Egypt by Jesus, shall surely enter into the promised rest, he cannot, he does not desire to resist the impulse of singing, "Now unto him that is able to keep you from falling, and to present you faultless before the presence of his glory with exceeding joy, to the only wise God our Saviour, be glory and majesty, dominion and power, both now and ever." If you read on to the next verse, you perceive that Jude had another example in his mind's eye—the angels that kept not their first estate. We do not know much of angels, but from what we gather in Holy Scripture—perhaps tinged in our reading with some of the half-inspired ideas of Milton—we believe that angels are spirits vastly superior to ourselves. In intelligence they may well be so, even if they had been created upon a par, for they have had many years in which to learn, and gather experience, whereas man's existence is but a handbreadth. We regard an angel with intense respect, and while never paying any worship to those noble beings, we cannot but feel how little we are when compared with them. One of these angels appears to have been named Lucifer, son of the morning—perhaps he was a leader in the heavenly host, and first among the princes of heaven. He, together with multitudes of others, fell from their allegiance to God. We know not how; we have no idea that they were tempted, unless one of them tempted the other; but they kept not their first estate—they were driven out of heaven, they were expelled from their starry thrones, and henceforth they are reserved in chains of darkness until the great day of account.

Now, my brethren, can you think of the fall of angels without trembling? Can you think of the morning stars put out in blackness? of the cherub whose head did wear a crown, cast into the mire, and his crown rolled into the dust? Can you think of these bright spirits transformed into the hideous fiends that devils are; their hearts, once temples for God, now become the haunt of every unclean thing, themselves the most unclean? Can you think of that without feeling a tremor of fear lest you, too, should fall from your first estate? and without another and a higher thrill of joy, when you think of him who is "able to keep you from falling, and to present you faultless before the presence of his glory with exceeding joy?"

>"When any turn from Zion's way,
>   (Alas! what numbers do,)
> Methinks I hear my Saviour say,
>   'Wilt thou forsake me too?'
>
> Ah, Lord! with such a heart as mine,
>   Unless thou hold me fast,
> I feel I must, I shall decline,
>   And prove like them at last."

But we can also sing right joyously—

>"The soul that on Jesus has leaned for repose,
> He will not, he will not, desert to its foes;
> That soul, though all hell should endeavour to shake,
> He'll never, no never, no never, forsake."

We might continue to follow Jude, but we will not do so; we prefer to add something which Jude has not put in his epistle. Our first parent, Adam, lived in the midst of happiness and peace in the garden. Unlike ourselves, he had no depravity—no bias towards evil. God made him upright; he was perfectly pure, and it was in his own will whether he should sin or not. The balance hung evenly in his hand. But you have not forgotten how on that sad day he took of the forbidden fruit, and ate, and thereby cursed himself and all of us. My brethren, as you think of Adam, driven out of the garden of Eden, sent out to till the ground whence he was taken, compelled in the sweat of his face to eat bread; when you recollect the bowers he left, the happiness and peace that have for ever passed away through his sin, do you not hear the voice that says to you, as a depraved and fallen creature, "Let him that thinketh he standeth, take heed lest he fall?" Conscious of your own weakness as compared with your parent Adam, you are ready to cry out, "O God, how can I stand where Adam falls!" But here comes the joyous thought—Christ, who has begun with you, will never cease till he has perfected you. Can you help singing with Jude, "Now unto him who is able to keep us from falling?" It strikes me that every time we mark an apostate, and see the fall of a sinner or of a fellow-professor, we should go down on our knees and cry, "Hold thou me up, and I shall be safe," and then rise up and sing—

>"To our Redeemer God
>   Eternal power belongs,
> Immortal crowns of majesty,
>   And everlasting songs.
>
> He will present our souls
>   Unblemished and complete
> Before the glory of his face,
>   With joys divinely great."

This partly accounts for the text before us; but on a further reference to the epistle we get another part of the thoughts which had exercised the apostle's mind. Observe, dear friends, that the apostle had a very vivid and distinct sense of the *nature of the place* into which those fell, and of their utter ruin and destruction. Notice, concerning the children of Israel, he says that "God destroyed them that believed not." What is it to be destroyed? Destroyed! This does not end with the whited skeleton and the bleached bones which lay in the wilderness, a horror to the passer-by; he means something more than even that. Brought out of Egypt, and yet destroyed! Take heed, professor. You may be brought into something like gospel liberty, and yet may perish. Take heed, thou carnal professor, I say! Thou mayest fancy thou hast escaped the bondage of the law, but yet thou shalt never enter into the rest which remaineth for the people of God, but thou shalt be destroyed. Let that word "destroyed" ring in your ears, and it will make you bless God, who is able to keep you from falling, if it shall lead thee to flee to him for help.

Next, he says of the fallen angels, that they are "reserved in everlasting chains under darkness unto the judgment of the great day." What that may be we can but roughly guess. Satan is allowed to go about the world, but still he wears his chains, he has a tether, and the Lord knows how to pull him in, both by providence and direct acts of power. We believe that these spirits are under darkness; a gloom, a thick darkness that may be felt, hangs perpetually over their minds wherever they may be, and they are waiting till Christ shall come to summon them as rebellious creatures before his bar, that they may receive their sentence, and begin afresh their dreadful hell. And remember, dear brethren and sisters, unless eternal love shall prevent it, this case must be yours. We too must enter into places reserved in darkness, wearing everlasting chains, to endure eternal fire. We should do so, we must do so, if it were not for him " who is able to keep us from falling, and present us faultless before the presence of his glory with exceeding joy." Nor is this all, for if you will patiently read the next verse, you will see that Jude has, if possible, introduced a more graphic picture. The cities of Sodom and Gomorrha are bright as the sun goes down. The inhabitants are merry with boisterous laughter, there is plenty in the barn, there is luxury in the hall, for the plain of Sodom was well watered and lacked for nothing. Down went that sun upon a disastrous eve, never to rise upon the most of those who were in that doomed city. At day-break, just as the sun is beginning to shine upon the earth, angels had hastened Lot and his family out of the city, and no sooner had they reached the little city of Zoar than straightway the heaven is red with supernatural flame, and down descends a terrific rain, as if God had poured hell out of heaven. He rained fire and brimstone upon the cities, and the smoke of their torment went up, so that Abraham far away to the west, could see the rolling cloud, and the terrible brightness of the fire, even at mid-day; and as men go to the "Lacus Asphaltites," or the Dead Sea, they see to this day where death has reigned. There are masses of asphalt floating still upon the surface of that sea, where there is nought that lives; no fish swim in its turbid streams; there are indubitable evidences there of some dread judgment of God. And as Jude thought of this, he seemed to say, " Oh God, preserve us from such a doom, for this is the doom of all apostates, either in this world, or in that which is to come, thus to be consumed with fire." And as he remembered that God would keep his people, he blessed that protecting hand which covers every saint, and he wrote down, "Now unto him that is able to keep you from falling."

I have a thought in my mind, I cannot of course tell whether it is right or not, but it strikes me just now—the author's name is Jude—Judas. Did he recollect Judas, his namesake that was called Iscariot, as he penned these words? He had known him, probably had respected him as the others had done; he had marked him that night when he sat at the table, and like others said, "Is it I?" Probably Jude was very surprised when he saw Iscariot take the sop and dip in the dish with the Saviour, and when he went out he could scarcely believe his own ears, when the Saviour said, that he that betrayed him had gone forth. He must have known how Judas kissed the Son of Man and sold him for thirty pieces of silver. He could not but be aware how in remorse he hanged himself, and how his bowels gushed out; and methinks the shadow of the doom of Judas fell upon this better Judas while he penned these words, and he seems to say with greater emphasis, "Unto him that is able to keep you from falling, unto him be glory for ever and ever." Thus you see, dear friends, we are getting into the track, I think, of Jude's thoughts—he thought about the failures of others, and the terrible way in which they had fallen.

Yet again, by your leave, Jude had a very clear view of the *greatness of the sins into which apostates fall.* Probably there is not in the whole compass of Holy Writ a more fearful picture of the sin of backsliders and apostates than in the epistle of Jude. I remember preaching to you one evening from that text, "Raging waves of the sea, foaming out their own shame; wandering stars, to whom is reserved the blackness of darkness for ever." I remember how you trembled, myself trembling most, with such a terrible message to deliver. Where could such a text or simile be found but in the book of Jude? The sins of apostates are tremendous. They are usually not content with the average of human guilt; they must make themselves giants in iniquity. None make such devils as those that were once angels, and none make such reprobates as those who once seemed to bid fair for the kingdom of heaven. These go into filthy dreams, into sensuality; "they give themselves over to fornication, and go after strange flesh," as he has put it. In fact, where can we set the bounds to which a man will go, when he crucifies the Lord that bought him, and puts him to an open shame? Oh, beloved, as I think of the sin into which these apostates have gone, I cannot but feel that you must bless God with Jude, that there is one "who is able to keep you from falling, and to present you faultless before the presence of his glory with exceeding joy."

II. I might continue in this strain, but perhaps I had better not. I would rather turn to THE BLESSINGS OF WHICH JUDE SPEAKS.

He seems to ascribe here in this doxology three blessings, at least, to the power of the Lord Jesus. The first is *ability to keep you from falling,* and for this, I am sure, the highest praise is due, when you consider for a moment *the dangerous way.* In some respects the path to heaven is very safe It is so as God made it, but in other respects there is no road so dangerous as the road to eternal life. It is beset with difficulties. In some of our mountain climbings, we have gone along narrow pathways, where there was but a step between us and death, for deep down beneath us was a gaping precipice, perhaps a mile in perpendicular descent. One's brain reels at the thought of it now, and yet we passed along quite safely. The road to heaven is much like that. One false step, (and how easy it is to take that, if grace be absent,) and down we go. What a slippery path is that which some of us have to tread.

You know that there are a million opportunities in a single week for your foot to slip, and for your soul to be ruined. There are some spots, I believe, upon some of the more difficult Swiss mountains where no man ought to go at all, I think, and where, if any must go, they should be only such as have become most accomplished mountaineers, through years of practice; for one has to cling to the rock side, to hold on, perhaps, by bushes or stones that may be there, with nothing for the feet to rest upon except, perhaps, an inch of projecting crag, and so we go creeping on with our backs to the danger, for to look down upon it would be to make the brain reel and cause us to fall, and the result of falling, of course, would be the end of life—the body would be dashed into a thousand pieces. Such is truly the way to heaven. You must all have passed some such difficult places, and, in looking back, I can only myself say, "Unto him that has kept me from falling, when my feet had well nigh gone, and my steps had almost slipped, unto him be glory for ever and ever."

But next, you have to think of the *weakness of the person*. Some men may travel roads which would not be safe for others, and what are you, my brother pilgrim, but a little babe. It is unsafe to trust you along the pathway to glory; in the best roads you are soon tripped up. These feeble knees of yours can scarce support your tottering weight. A straw might throw you, and a pebble stone could wound you. Oh, if you shall be kept, how must you bless the patient power which watches over you day by day. Reflect upon your tendency to sin. The giddiness of that poor brain, the silliness of that deceitful heart. Think, how apt you are to choose danger, how the tendency is to cast yourselves down, how you rather are inclined to fall than to stand, and I am sure you will sing more sweetly than you have ever done, "Glory be to him, who is able to keep me from falling." Then, you have to notice, further, the *many foes* who try to push you down. The road is rough enough, the child is weak enough, but here and there is an enemy who is in ambush, who comes out when we least expect him, and labours to trip us up, or hurl us down a precipice. I suppose you never did see a man fall from a precipice. Some of you may have been fools enough to go and see a man walk on a rope, in which case, I believe, you have incurred the guilt of murder; because if the man does not kill himself, you encourage him to put himself where he probably might do so. But if you have ever really seen a man fall over a precipice, your hair must surely have stood on end, your flesh creeping on your bones, as you saw the poor human form falling off the edge, never to stand in mortal life again: surely as you left the place where you stood, and fled away from the edge of the precipice, you cried, "O bless the

God that made me stand, and kept my feet from falling." How alarmed you would be, if you were in such a position and had seen one fall, and that same monster who had pushed him over, should come to hurl you over also, and especially if you felt that you were as weak as water, and could not resist the gigantic demon. Now, just such is your case; you cannot stand against Satan; yea, your own flesh will be able to get the mastery over your spirit. A little maid made Peter deny his Master, and a little maid may make the strongest among us tremble sometimes. Oh, if we are preserved in spite of such mighty enemies, who are ever waiting to destroy us, we shall have great cause to sing praise "unto him that is able to keep us from falling."

Christ has the power to take us into heaven. You may keep a man from starving, but you cannot take him into the king's palace, and present him at court. Suppose that a man had been a rebel, you might hide him from the pursuers, and aid in his escape, but you could not take him into the presence of the king, and cause him to live in the royal castle of the land. But you see that Christ preserves his people though they have offended God, and daily provoke his justice; and he does more, for he presents them to the King of kings in the high court of heaven itself. This it is which makes the other blessing so great. We are not anxious to live in this world always. We find ourselves in a strange land here, and would be glad to fly away, and be at rest. This is to us a wilderness state, and we rejoice to know that Canaan lies beyond. Our heavenly Joshua can lead us into it. He can fight for us against Amalek, and slay all our foes, and preserve us from falling; but better still, he can and he will take us into the promised land, and give us to see the "better country, even the heavenly," and thither will he conduct all the host, so that not one shall perish or be left behind. Christ gives preservation, but he adds glorification, and that is still better. Here then, my brethren, is a thought of incomparable sweetness, we are safe while in this world:—

"More happpy, but not more secure
The glorified spirits in heaven."

And we too shall be, before long, as happy as they are, because he will present us with them before the presence of his glory with exceeding joy.

We cannot, however, enlarge on this point, though there is much, very much that ought to be said. We proceed to notice *the condition in which the saints are to be when presented*—they are to be "faultless;" for our Lord never stops short of perfection in his work of love. That Saviour who means to keep his people to the end, will not present them at last just alive, all black and foul as when he helped them out of the miry places. He will not bring them in, as sometimes gallant men have to do those whom they have rescued from drowning, with just the vital spark within them. No, our Saviour will carry on his people safe from falling, through this life, and he will present them, how?—faultless. Oh, that is a wondrous word, "faultless;" we are a long way off from it now. Faulty, aye we are now faulty through and through, but Jesus Christ will never be content till we are faultless. And this he will make us in three ways: he will *wash us* till there is not a spot left, for the chief of sinners shall be as white and fair as God's purest angel; the eye of justice will look, and God will say, "No spot of sin remains in thee." You may have been a drunkard, a thief, an adulterer, and what not; but if Christ in mercy undertakes your case, he will wash you in his blood so thoroughly that you shall be faultless at the last; without spot, or wrinkle, or any such thing. Now we are defiled and covered with sin as if we had "lien among the pots." We have revelled in uncleanness till we are as if we had been "plunged in the ditch." Our own flesh must abhor us if we could but see how defiled we are by nature and by practice. Now all this shall be completely removed, and we shall be whiter than snow. You remember that when the disciples looked at Jesus on the mount of transfiguration, they saw that his garments were white and glistening, whiter than any fuller could make them; now, so shall we be hereafter, whiter and fairer than any earthly art can attain to. The sea of glass, clear as crystal, will not be whiter nor purer than we shall be when washed in the blood of the Lamb.

But that is only one way. If a man had no fault, yet it would be necessary for him to have some virtues. A man cannot enter heaven simply because transgression is put away. The law must be kept, there must be a positive obedience to divine precepts. Religion is no negation, an absence of things evil merely; it is the presence of the good, the true, the pure. But since even when we do our best we shall be unprofitable servants, we need something higher than we can ever produce by these our feeble and sinful powers: therefore *the Lord our God imputes to us the perfect righteousness of his Son Christ Jesus*, for

"Lest the shadow of a spot
Should on my soul be found;
He took the robe the Saviour wrought,
And cast it all around."

The righteousness of Jesus Christ will make the saint who wears it so fair that he will be positively faultless. Yes, perfect in the sight of God. There is a fulness in this which it delights my soul to dwell upon. A man may be faultless in my sight, but not in the sight of those who know him intimately. A Christian may be so holy as to escape the censure of all just men; but ministering spirits, who read the heart and deal with the inner man, can speak of evil which has not come to light before human eyes. But we know that God sees even more clearly than angelic spirits, for he charges them with folly. Now, God is to see no iniquity in us, no shortcoming. We shall be tried in his scales, and set in the light of his countenance, and be pronounced "*faultless*." God's law will not only have no charge against us, but it will be magnified in us, and honoured by us. We shall have imputed to us that righteousness which belongs to him who has done all this for us that he might "present us faultless before the presence of his glory."

And fourthly, and best, perhaps, *the Spirit of God will make new creatures of us*. He has begun the work and he will finish it. He will make us so perfectly holy, that we shall have no tendency to sin any more. The day will come when we shall feel that Adam in the garden was not more pure than we are. You shall have no taint of evil in you. Judgment, memory, will—every power and passion shall be emancipated from the thraldom of evil. You shall be holy even as God is holy, and in his presence you shall dwell for ever.

How altered we shall be; for look within, and see if your experience is not like the Apostle Paul's, who found a potent law in his members, so that when he would do good evil was present with him, and when he desired to escape some evil, he did at times the very thing he allowed not, but would most heartily condemn. So is it with us; we would be holy, but we are like a ball that has a bias in it, we cannot go in a straight and direct line. We try to hit the mark, but we are prone to start on one side like a deceitful bow. There is a black drop in our hearts which taints all the streams, and none of them can be pure; but it will be all changed one day, we shall be re-made, and all the evil gone, gone for ever. How joyous must have been the entrance of Naaman, the Assyrian, into his house after he had washed in Jordan's stream, and found his flesh restored to him as the flesh of a little child. I think I see him, as the watchman on the tower has given notice of his approach in the distance, the whole household are at the gate to meet him, and to see if he comes back in health. His wife, if eastern customs would not permit of her going forth in public, would look from her casement to catch a glimpse of his face, to see if the dread spot was gone. How joyful the shout, "He is cured and clean!" But this is nothing compared with the rapture of that hour when the everlasting doors will be lifted up, and we, made meet for the inheritance of the saints in light, shall enter into the joy of our Lord. Or take another illustration from Scripture, and try and realize the happiness which reigned in the family of the maniac out of whom the legion of devils had departed. Perhaps he had been home before when under the evil influence of the foul fiends; how terrified they doubtless were with the mad frenzy of the poor unhappy wretch as he cut himself with stones, and brake all bonds put on him in tenderness and love in order to restrain his self-imposed misery and wounds; and now that he comes once more to his house, they see him approach, and the old terror seizes them because they know not that he is a changed man, but suppose him still to be the demented being of days gone by; but as he enters the door, as calm and composed as if he had returned from a long journey, and were only anxious to relate the incidents of the pilgrimage and greet loved friends once more; with no fierce frenzy rolling in his eye, no loud discordant shrieks rending the air, but all is the demeanour of a well-regulated, joyful, yet chastened mind; as all this is realized by his friends, and they hear what great things the Lord has done for him, what joy must have been in that family circle. I should like to have seen it. I am sure it was a choice exhibition of real human bliss, such as earth only witnesses now and then. A beam of purest radiance lighting up the scene, like as the splendour which Saul of Tarsus saw on the road to Damascus lit up the day, when he was made a new creature in Christ Jesus. Here also we can most truthfully say, that the joy, though great, was not comparable to the joy which shall be ours when we are changed into new creatures, when we shall be clothed and in our right mind; no longer prone to wander among the black mountains of iniquity, no more tempted to abide amongst those dead in trespasses and sins, but ever holy, and always living unto God, and made like unto him. Oh this is joy indeed! **Not only will he keep us from falling, but present us faultless.** My brethren and sisters, at the thought of this I think you must join with Jude, and say, "Now unto him that is able to do all this, be glory and majesty, dominion and power, both now and ever."

I cannot speak to you as I would wish upon such a theme as this—who could? but when we get to heaven, there our song shall be more sweet, more loud, because we shall understand better the dangers from which we have escaped, and how very much we owe to him who has kept us, and brought us safely through all the vicissitudes of life, unto the place he has prepared for us. Meanwhile, never let us be forgetful of that mighty goodness which holds us fast, and will not let us go.

III. Still I have not done with the text. I have already forestalled my next thought, but I think it requires a special notice Observe, the apostle adds, "To present us faultless before his presence, WITH EXCEEDING GREAT JOY."

Who will have the joy? My brethren, *you* will have it. Have you ever mused upon the parable of the Prodigal Son? I know you have; no one can have diligently read the Bible without staying to think over, again and again, of that most tender and instructive of our Lord's parables. Now, I ask who was happy at that feast? Was not the prodigal, think you? What was the character of those thoughts filling his heart, and making it heave as if it would burst? How overjoyed he must have been. How utterly crushed down with his father's love, and all the unexpected marks of kindness and affection. He had had his days of feasting and sinful merriment, but no songs could ever have been so sweet as those which rung round the old roof-tree to welcome him home. No viands had ever tasted so delicious as that fatted calf, and no voice of boon companion or witching charmer at his guilty feasts, had ever sounded such dulcet notes in his ears, as those words of his father, "Let us eat and be merry." So will it be with us when we have been restored to ourselves, when wearied of the world, and hungering and thirsting after righteousness, we shall have been led to the Father's house by the cords of love which the Spirit shall cast around us. When safely brought through all the weary pilgrimage from the far-off country, we shall tread the golden streets and be safe inside the pearly gates, and have the past all gone for ever amongst the things we never shall meet again. What rapture will be ours; this will be heaven indeed. When sin shall be gone, Satan shut out, temptation over for ever, you shall have a joy of which you cannot now conceive. Rivers of pleasure shall flow into your soul; you shall drink such draughts of bliss as your soul has never known this side the grave. Oh, be joyful now with an antipast of the joy which is to be revealed; and afterwards you shall have the fulness of divine bliss for ever and ever. Who shall be happy? Why, the *minister* will be happy. What pleasure was there in the heart of the shepherd youth David, the son of Jesse, when he had gone forth to do battle with the lion and bear, in order to rescue the lamb out of their jaws, and when God had delivered him and made him successful in his attempt. How gladly he must have watched the little lamb run to the side of its dam, and in the mutual pleasure of these poor dumb animals I am sure he found a joy; and so shall all the shepherds in heaven, all who have been faithful pastors, who have cared for and tended their flocks, shall find a bliss unspeakable in welcoming to glory those darling ones preserved from the power of the devil, "who goeth about as a roaring lion seeking whom he may devour." Yes, ministers will be sharers in this happiness. I think we shall have a special joy in bringing our sheaves with us. If it may please God to keep me from falling; if I just get inside the door of heaven, with some of the many thousands that God has given to me as my spiritual children, I will fall prostrate before his feet, the greatest debtor to his mercy that ever lived, and one that has more cause than any other of his creatures to thank him, and ascribe to him glory and honour, dominion and power, for ever and ever. Here am I, and the children whom thou hast given me; unto thee be praise. And what will be the joy of *angels* too? How exceeding great their bliss will be. If there be joy among the angels over one sinner that repenteth, what will there be over ten thousand times ten thousand, not of repenting, but of perfected sinners, cleansed from every stain, set free from every flaw. Oh, ye cherubim and seraphim, how loud will be your music! How will ye tune your harps anew, how shall every string wake up to the sweetest music in praise of God. "Let the sea roar and the fulness thereof" at the thought of the glorious joy at God's right hand. Who will have joy, I ask again? Why *Christ* will have the most joy of all. Angels, and ministers, and you yourselves will scarce know such joy as he will have—all his sheep safely folded; every stone of the building placed in its proper position; all the blood-bought and blood-washed ones, all whom the Father gave him, delivered out of the jaw of the lion; all whom he covenanted to redeem effectually saved—his counsel all fulfilled, his stipulations all carried out: the covenant not only ratified, but fulfilled in all its jots and tittles. Verily, none will be so happy as the great Surety in that day. As the bridegroom rejoiceth over the bride, so shall Christ rejoice over you. You know it is written, that "for the joy set before him he endured the cross, despising the shame;" and also, "He shall see of the travail of his soul and shall be abundantly satisfied." Now this satisfaction and joy will be our Lord's, when the whole Church is faultless and complete in the presence of his glory; but not till then. In that hour, when all his jewels are reckoned up and none found missing, he shall rejoice anew in spirit, and shall thank God with yet more of joy than he did when here on earth, and thought of this day in prospect, and by that thought nerved himself for cruel suffering and a death of shame. Yes, Christ will be glad. Our Head will have his share of joy with all the members, and happily he will be able to bear more, as he most certainly deserves and will have more. Who will have joy? Why, *God himself* will have joy. It is no blasphemy to say that the joy of God on that occasion will be infinite. It is always infinite; but it will be then infinitely displayed before his creatures' gaze. Listen to these words—you cannot fathom them, but you may look at them. It is written, "The Lord thy God will rejoice over thee with joy; he will joy over thee with singing." As I have said on this platform before, I think that is the most wonderful text in the Bible in some respects—God himself singing! I can imagine, when the world was made, the morning stars shouting for joy; but God did not sing. He said it was "very good," and that was all. There was no song. But oh, to think of it, that when all the chosen race shall meet around the throne, the joy of the Eternal Father shall swell so high, that God, who filleth all in all, shall burst out into an infinite, godlike song.

I will only put in this one more thought, that all this, beloved, is about you. All this you have a share in, the least in the Church, the poorest in the family, the humblest believer—this is all true of you, he will keep you from falling, and present you spotless before his presence with exceeding great joy. Oh, cannot you join the song and sing with me, "To the only wise God and Saviour be glory and honour, dominion and majesty for ever. Amen."

For my part I feel like that good old saint, who said that if she got to heaven, Jesus Christ should never hear the last of it. Truly he never shall.

> "I'll praise my Saviour with my breath;
> And when my voice is lost in death,
> Praise shall employ my nobler powers:
> My days of praise shall ne'er be past,
> While life and thought and being last,
> Or immortality endures."

I want you to go away with a sense of your own weakness, and yet a belief in your own safety. I want you to know that you cannot stand a minute, that you will be damned within another second unless grace keep you out of hell, and yet I want you to feel that since you are in the hand of Christ you cannot perish, neither can any pluck you out thence. And, poor sinners, my heart's desire is that you may be put into the hand of Christ to-night, that you may have done with trusting yourselves. You can ruin, but you cannot save yourselves. "Oh Israel, thou hast destroyed thyself, but in me is thy help found." Christ alone can save you, oh look out of self to Christ; trust yourselves in his hands; he is "able to keep you from falling." You cannot even stand upright yourselves, and if he should set you upright you cannot keep so for a minute without his protecting care. If saints need to be kept, how much more need have you to seek the shelter of the Saviour's wounded side: flee thither as the dove to the cleft of the rock. If holy men of God cry daily for pardon, and profess to have no right of themselves to heaven, how much more urgent is your case. You must perish if you die as you are. You can never make yourself *faultless*, but Christ can. He wants to do it: he has opened a fountain for sin and for uncleanness: wash and be clean. Again, I say, look to Jesus. Away with self and cling to Christ, down with self-confidence and up with simple faith in Christ Jesus. I shall not let you go, dear friends, without singing one verse, which I think will express the feeling of each one of us:

> "Let me among thy saints be found,
> Whene'er the Archangel's trump shall sound,
> To see thy smiling face;
> Then loudest of the crowd I'll sing,
> While heaven's resounding mansions ring
> With shouts of sovereign grace."

THE FINAL PERSEVERANCE OF THE SAINTS.

A Sermon

Delivered on Lord's-Day Morning, June 24th, 1877, by

C. H. SPURGEON,

At the Metropolitan Tabernacle, Newington,

"The righteous also shall hold on his way."—Job xvii. 9.

THE man who is righteous before God has a way of his own. It is not the way of the flesh, nor the way of the world; it is a way marked out for him by the divine command, in which he walks by faith. It is the King's highway of holiness, the unclean shall not pass over it: only the ransomed of the Lord shall walk there, and these shall find it a path of separation from the world. Once entered upon the way of life, the pilgrim must persevere in it or perish, for thus saith the Lord, "If any man draw back, my soul shall have no pleasure in him." Perseverance in the path of faith and holiness is a necessity of the Christian, for only " he that endureth to the end, the same shall be saved." It is in vain to spring up quickly like the seed that was sown upon the rock, and then by-and-by to wither when the sun is up; that would but prove that such a plant has no root in itself, but "the trees of the Lord are full of sap," and they abide and continue and bring forth fruit, even in old age, to show that the Lord is upright. There is a great difference between nominal Christianity and real Christianity, and this is generally seen in the failure of the one and the continuance of the other. Now, the declaration of the text is that the truly righteous man shall hold on his way; he shall not go back, he shall not leap the hedges and wander to the right hand or the left, he shall not lie down in idleness, neither shall he faint and cease to go upon his journey; but he "shall hold on his way." It will frequently be very difficult for him to do so, but he will have such resolution, such power of inward grace given him, that he will "hold on his way," with stern determination, as though he held on by his teeth, resolving never to let go. Perhaps he may not always travel with equal speed; it is not said that he shall hold on his *pace*, but he shall hold on his *way*. There are times when we run and are not weary, and anon when we walk are thankful that we do not faint; ay, and there are periods when we are glad to go on all fours and creep upward with pain; but still we prove that "the righteous shall hold on his way." Under all difficulties the face of the man whom God has justified is steadfastly set towards Jerusalem; nor will he turn aside till his eyes shall see the King in his beauty.

This is a great wonder. It is a marvel that any man should be a Christian at all, and a greater wonder that he should continue so. Consider the weakness of the flesh, the strength of inward corruption, the fury of Satanic temptation, the seductions of wealth and the pride of life, the world and the fashion thereof: all these things are against us, and yet behold, "greater is he that is for us than all they that be against us," and defying sin, and Satan, and death, and hell, the righteous holds on his way.

I take our text as accurately setting forth the doctrine of the final perseverance of the saints. "The righteous shall hold on his way." Years ago when there was an earnest, and even a bitter controversy between Calvinists and Arminians it was the habit of each side to caricature the other. Very much of the argument is not directed against the real sentiment of the opposite party, but against what had been imputed to them. They made a man of straw, and then they burned him, which is a pretty easy thing to do, but I trust we have left these things behind. The glorious truth of the final perseverance of the saints has survived controversy, and in some form or other is the cherished belief of the children of God. Take care, however, to be clear as to what it is. The Scripture does not teach that a man will reach his journey's end without continuing to travel along the road; it is not true that one act of faith is all, and that nothing is needed of daily faith, prayer, and watchfulness. Our doctrine is the very opposite, namely, that the righteous shall hold on his way; or, in other words, shall continue in faith, in repentance, in prayer, and under the influence of the grace of God. We do not believe in salvation by a physical force which treats a man as a dead log, and carries him whether he will it or not towards heaven. No, "he holds on," he is personally active about the matter, and plods on up hill and down dale till he reaches his journey's end. We never thought, nor even dreamed, that merely because a man supposes that he once entered on this way he may therefore conclude that he is certain of salvation, even if he leaves the way immediately. No, but we say that he who truly receives the Holy Ghost, so that he believes in the Lord Jesus Christ, shall not go back, but persevere in the way of faith. It is written, "He that believeth and is baptized shall be saved," and this he cannot be if he were left to go back and delight in sin as he did before; and, therefore, he shall be kept by the power of God through faith unto salvation. Though the believer to his grief will commit many a sin, yet still the tenor of his life will be holiness to the Lord, and he will hold on in the way of obedience. We detest the doctrine that a man who has once believed in Jesus will be saved even if he altogether forsook the path of obedience. We deny that such a turning aside is possible to the true believer, and therefore the idea imputed to us is clearly an invention of the adversary. No, beloved, a man, if he be indeed a believer in Christ, will not live after the will of the flesh. When he does fall into sin it will be his grief and misery, and he will never rest till he is cleansed from guilt; but I will say this of the believer, that if he could live as he would like to live he would live a perfect life. If you ask him if, after believing, he may live as he lists, he will reply, "Would God I could live as I list, for I desire to live altogether without sin. I would be perfect, even as my Father in heaven is perfect." The doctrine is not the licentious idea that a believer may live in sin, but that he cannot and will not do so. This is the doctrine, and we will first *prove it;* and, secondly, in the Puritanic sense of the word, we will briefly *improve it,* by drawing two spiritual lessons therefrom.

I. LET US PROVE THE DOCTRINE. Please to follow me with your Bibles open. You, dear friends, have most of you received as a matter of faith the doctrines of grace, and therefore to you the doctrine of final perseverance cannot require any proving, because it follows from all the other doctrines. We believe that God has an elect people whom he has chosen unto eternal life, and that truth necessarily involves the perseverance in grace. We believe in special redemption, and this secures the salvation and consequent perseverance of the redeemed. We believe in effectual calling, which is bound up with justification, a justification which ensures glorification. The doctrines of grace are like a chain—if you believe in one of them you must believe the next, for each one involves the rest; therefore I say that you who accept any of the doctrines of grace must receive this also, as involved in them. But I am about to try to prove this to those who do not receive the doctrines of grace; I would not argue in a circle, and prove one thing which you doubt by another thing which you doubt, but "to the law and to the testimony," to the actual words of Scripture we shall refer the matter.

Before we advance to the argument it will be well to remark that those who reject the doctrine frequently tell us that there are many cautions in the word of God against apostatizing, and that those cautions can have no meaning if it be true that the righteous shall hold on his way. But what if those cautions are the means in the hand of God of keeping his people from wandering? What if they are used to excite a holy fear in the minds of his children, and so become the means of preventing the evil which they denounce. I would also remind you that in the Epistle to the Hebrews, which contains the most solemn warnings against apostasy, the apostle always takes care to add words which show that he did not believe that those whom he warned would actually apostatize. Turn to Hebrews vi. 9. He has been telling these Hebrews that if those who had been once enlightened should fall away, it would be impossible to renew them again into repentance, and he adds, "But, beloved, we are persuaded better things of you, and things that accompany salvation, though we thus speak." In the 10th chapter he gives an equally earnest warning, declaring that those who should do despite to the spirit of grace are worthy of sorer punishment than those who depised Moses' law, but he closes the chapter with these words, "Now the just shall live by faith: but if any man draw back, my soul shall have no pleasure in him. But we are not of them who draw back unto perdition; but of them that believe to the saving of the soul." Thus he shows what the consequences of apostasy would be, but he is convinced that they will not choose to incur such a fearful doom.

Again, objectors sometimes mention instances of apostasy which are mentioned in the word of God, but on looking into them it will be discovered that these are cases of persons who did but profess to know Christ, but were not really possessors of the divine life. John, in his first Epistle, ii. 19, fully describes these apostates: "They went out from us, but they were not of us; for if they had been of us, they would no doubt have continued with us: but they went out, that they might be made manifest that they were not all of us." The like is true of that memorable passage in John, where our Saviour speaks of branches of the vine which are cut off and cast into the fire: these are described as branches in Christ that bear no fruit. Are those real Christians? How can they be so if they bear no fruit? "By their fruits ye shall know them." The branch which bears fruit is purged, but it is never cut off. Those which bear no fruit are not figures of true Christians, but they fitly represent mere professors. Our Lord, in Matt. vii. 22, tells us concerning many who will say in that day "Lord, Lord," that he will reply, "I never knew you." Not "I have forgotten you," but "I never knew you": they were never really his disciples.

But now to the argument itself. First we argue the perseverance of the saints, most distinctly *from the nature of the life which is imparted at regeneration.* What saith Peter concerning this life? (1 Peter i. 23.) He speaks of the people of God as "being born again, not of corruptible seed, but of incorruptible, by the word of God, which liveth and abideth for ever." The new life which is planted in us when we are born again is not like the fruit of our first birth, for that is subject to mortality, but it is a divine principle, which cannot die nor be corrupt; and, if it be so, then he who possesses it must live for ever, must, indeed, be evermore what the Spirit of God in regeneration has made him. So in 1 John iii. 9 we have the same thought in another form. "Whosoever is born of God doth not commit sin; for his seed remaineth in him: and he cannot sin, because he is born of God." That is to say, the bent of the Christian's life is not towards sin. It would not be a fair description of his life that he lives in sin; on the contrary, he fights and contends against sin, because he has an inner principle which cannot sin. The new life sinneth not; it is born of God, and cannot transgress; and though the old nature warreth against it, yet doth the new life so prevail in the Christian that he is kept from living in sin. Our Saviour, in his simple teaching of the gospel to the Samaritan woman, said to her (John iv. 13), "Whosoever drinketh of this water shall thirst again: but whosoever drinketh of the water that I shall give him shall never thirst; but the water that I shall give him shall be in him a well of water springing up into everlasting life." Now, if our Saviour taught this to a sinful and ignorant woman, at his first interview with her, I take it that this doctrine is not to be reserved for the inner circle of full-grown saints, but to be preached ordinarily among the common people, and to be held up as a most blessed privilege. If you receive the grace which Jesus imparts to your souls, it shall be like the good part which Mary chose, it shall not be taken away from you; it shall abide in you, not as the water in a cistern, but as a living fountain springing up unto everlasting life.

We all know that the life given in the new birth is intimately connected with faith. Now, faith is in itself a conquering principle. In the First Epistle of John, which is a great treasury of argument (1 John v. 4) we are told, "Whatsoever is born of God overcometh the world: and this is the victory that overcometh the world, even our faith. Who is he that overcometh the world, but he that believeth that Jesus is the Son of God?" See, then, that which is born of God in us, namely, the new life, is a conquering principle; there is no hint given that it can ever be defeated: and faith, which is its outward sign, is also in itself triumphant evermore. Therefore of necessity, because God has implanted such a wondrous life in us in bringing us out of darkness into his marvellous light, because he has begotten us again unto a lively hope by the resurrection of Jesus Christ from the dead, because the eternal and ever blessed Spirit hath come to dwell in us, we conclude that the divine life within us shall never die. "The righteous shall hold on his way."

The second argument to which I shall call your attention shall be drawn *from our Lord's own express declarations.* Here we shall look to the gospel of John again, and in that blessed third of John, where our Lord was explaining the gospel in the simplest possible style to Nicodemus, we find him laying great stress upon the fact that the life received by faith in himself is eternal. Look at that precious verse, the fourteenth:—"As Moses lifted up the serpent in the wilderness, even so must the Son of man be lifted up: that whosoever believeth in him should not perish, *but have eternal life.*" Do men therefore believe in him and yet perish? Do they believe in him and receive a spiritual life which comes to an end? It cannot be, for "God gave his only begotten Son, that whosoever believeth in him should not perish": but he would perish if he did not persevere to the end; and therefore he must persevere to the end. The believer has eternal life, how then can he die, so as to cease to be a believer? If he does not abide in Christ, he evidently has not eternal life, therefore he shall abide in Christ, even to the end. "For God so loved the world, that he gave his only begotten Son, that whosoever believeth in him should not perish, but have everlasting life." To this some reply that a man may have everlasting life and lose it. To which we answer, the words cannot so mean. Such a statement is a self-evident contradiction. If the life be lost the man is dead; how, then, did he have everlasting life? It is clear that he had a life which lasted only for a while: he certainly had not everlasting life, for if he had it he must live everlastingly. "He that believeth on the Son hath everlasting life" (John iii. 36). The saints in heaven have eternal life, and no one expects them to perish. Their life is eternal; but eternal life is eternal life, whether the person possessing it dwells on earth or in heaven.

I need not read all the passages in which the same truth is taught; but further on, in John vi. 47, our Lord told the Jews, "Verily, verily, I say unto you, he that believeth on me hath everlasting life:" not temporary life, but "everlasting life." And in the 51st verse he said, "I am the living bread which came down from heaven: if any man eat of this bread, he shall live for ever." Then comes that famous declaration of the Lord Jesus Christ, which, if there were no other at all, would be quite sufficient to prove our point. John x. 28: "And I give unto my sheep eternal life, and they shall never perish, neither shall any" (the word "man" is not in the original) "pluck them out of my hand. My Father, which gave them me, is greater than all; and no man is able to pluck them out of my Father's hand." What can he mean but this, that he has grasped his people, and that he means to hold them securely in his mighty hand?

"Where is the power can reach us there,
Or what can pluck us thence?"

Over and above the hand of Jesus which was pierced comes the hand of the omnipotent Father as a sort of second grasp. "My Father, which gave them me, is greater than all; and no man is able to pluck them out of my Father's hand." Surely this must show that the saints are secure from anything and everything which would destroy them, and consequently safe from total apostasy.

Another passage speaks to the same effect—it is to be found in Matthew xxiv. 24, where the Lord Jesus has been speaking of the false prophets that should deceive many. "There shall arise false Christs, and false prophets, and shall shew great signs and wonders; insomuch that, if it were possible, they shall deceive the very elect;" which shows that it is impossible for the elect to be deceived by them. Of Christ's sheep it is said, "A stranger will they not follow, for they know not the voice of strangers," but by divine instinct they know the voice of the Good Shepherd, and they follow him.

Thus has our Saviour declared, as plainly as words possibly can express it, that those who are his people possess eternal life within themselves, and shall not perish, but shall enter into everlasting felicity. "The righteous shall hold on his way."

A very blessed argument for the safety of the believer is found in *our Lord's intercession.* You need not turn to the passage, for you know it well, which shows the connection between the living intercession of Christ and the perseverance of his people—"Wherefore also he is able to save them to the uttermost that come unto God by him, seeing he ever liveth to make intercession for them" (Hebrews vii. 25). Our Lord Jesus is not dead; he has risen, he has gone up into the glory, and now before the eternal throne he pleads the merit of his perfect work, and as he pleads there for all his people whose names are written on his heart, as the names of Israel were written on the jewelled breastplate of the high priest, his intercession saves his people even to the uttermost. If you would like an illustration of it you must turn to the case of Peter which is recorded in Luke xxii. 31, where our Lord said, "Simon, Simon, behold, Satan hath desired to have you, that he may sift you as wheat: but I have prayed for thee that thy faith fail not: and when thou art converted, strengthen thy brethren." The intercession of Christ does not save his people from being tried, and tempted, and tossed up and down like wheat in a sieve, it does not save them even from a measure of sin and sorrow, but it does save them from total apostasy. Peter was kept, and though he denied his Master, yet it was an exception to the great rule of his life. By grace he did hold on his way, because not only then, but many a time beside, though he sinned, he had an advocate with the Father, Jesus Christ the righteous.

If you desire to know how Jesus pleads, read at your leisure at home that wonderful 17th of John—the Lord's prayer. What a prayer it is! "While I was with them in the world, I kept them in thy name: those that thou gavest me I have kept, and none of them is lost, but the son of perdition; that the scripture might be fulfilled." Judas was lost, but he was only given to Christ as an apostle and not as one of his sheep. He had a temporary faith, and maintained a temporary profession, but he never had eternal life or he would have lived on. Those groans and cries of the Saviour which accompanied his pleadings in Gethsemane were heard in heaven, and answered. "Holy Father, keep through thine own name those whom thou hast given me"; the Lord does keep them by his word and Spirit, and will keep them. If the prayer of Christ in Gethsemane was answered, how much more that which now goeth up from the eternal throne itself!

> "With cries and tears he offered up
> His humble suit below;
> But with authority he asks,
> Enthroned in glory now.
>
> "For all that come to God by him,
> Salvation he demands;
> Points to their names upon his breast,
> And spreads his wounded hands."

Ah, if my Lord Jesus pleads for me I cannot be afraid of earth or hell: that living, intercessory voice hath power to keep the saints, and so hath the living Lord himself, for he hath said—"Because I live ye shall live also." (John xiv. 19.)

Now for a fourth argument. We gather sure confidence of the perseverance of the saints *from the character and work of Christ.* I will say little about that, for I trust my Lord is so well known to you that he needeth no word of commendation from me to you; but if you know him you will say what the apostle does in 2 Tim. i. 12,—"I know whom I have believed, and am persuaded that he is able to keep that which I have committed unto him against that day." He did not say "I know *in* whom I have believed," as most people quote it, but, "I know whom I have believed." He knew Jesus, he knew his heart and his faithfulness, he knew his atonement and its power, he knew his intercession and its might; and he committed his soul to Jesus by an act of faith, and he felt secure. My Lord is so excellent in all things that I need give you but one glimpse of his character and you will see what he was when he dwelt here among men. At the commencement of John xiii. we read, "Having loved his own which were in the world, he loved them unto the end." If he had not loved his disciples to the end when here we might conclude that he was changeable now as then; but if he loved his chosen to the end while yet in his humiliation below, it bringeth us the sweet and blessed confidence that now he is in heaven he will love to the end all those who confide in him.

Fifthly, we infer the perseverance of the saints from *the tenor of the covenant of grace.* Would you like to read it for yourselves? If so, turn to the Old Testament, Jeremiah xxxii., and there you will find the covenant of grace set forth at some length. We shall only be able to read the fortieth verse: "And I will make an everlasting covenant with them, that I will not turn away from them, to do them good ; but I put my fear in their hearts, that they shall not depart from me." He will not depart from them, and they shall not depart from him,— what can be a grander assurance of their perseverance even to the end? Now, that this is the covenant of grace under which we live is clear from the Epistle to the Hebrews, for the apostle in the 8th chapter quotes that passage to this very end. The question runs thus—"Behold, the days come, saith the Lord, when I will make a new covenant with the house of Israel and with the house of Judah : not according to the covenant that I made with their fathers in the day when I took them by the hand to lead them out of the land of Egypt; because they continued not in my covenant, and I regarded them not, saith the Lord. For this is the covenant that I will make with the house of Israel after those days, saith the Lord ; I will put my laws into their mind, and write them in their hearts: and I will be to them a God, and they shall be to me a people." The old covenant had an "if" in it, and so it suffered shipwreck ; it was—"If you will be obedient then you shall be blessed"; and hence there came a failure on man's part, and the whole covenant ended in disaster. It was the covenant of works, and under it we were in bondage, until we were delivered from it and introduced to the covenant of grace, which has no "if" in it, but runs upon the strain of promise ; it is "I will" and "You shall" all the way through. "I will be your God, and ye shall be my people." Glory be to God, this covenant will never pass away, for see how the Lord declares its enduring character in the book of Isaiah (liv. 10) : "For the mountains shall depart, and the hills be removed ; but my kindness shall not depart from thee, neither shall the covenant of my peace be removed, saith the Lord that hath mercy on thee." And again in Isaiah lv. 3 : "I will make an everlasting covenant with you, even the sure mercies of David." The idea of falling utterly away from grace is a relic of the old legal spirit, it is a going away from grace to come under law again, and I charge you who have once been manumitted slaves, and have had the fetters of legal bondage struck from off your hands, never consent to wear those bonds again. Christ has saved you, if indeed you are believers in him, and he has not saved you for a week, or a month, or a quarter, or a year, or twenty years, but he has given to you eternal life, and you shall never perish, neither shall any pluck you out of his hands. Rejoice ye in this blessed covenant of grace.

The sixth most forcible argument is drawn *from the faithfulness of God.* Look at Romans xi. 29 : what saith the apostle there, speaking by the Holy Ghost? "For the gifts and calling of God are without repentance," which means that he does not give life and pardon to a man and call him by grace and afterwards repent of what he has done, and withdraw the good things which he has bestowed. "God is not a man, that he should lie; neither the son of man, that he should repent." When he putteth forth his hand to save he doth not withdraw it till the work is accomplished. His word is, "I am the Lord, I change not; therefore ye sons of Jacob are not consumed " (Mal. iii. 6). "The Strength of Israel will not lie nor repent " (1 Sam. xv. 29). The apostle would have us ground our confidence of perseverance upon the confirmation which divine faithfulness is sure to bestow upon us. He says in 1 Cor. i. 8, "Who shall also confirm you unto the end, that *ye* may be blameless in the day of our Lord Jesus Christ. God is faithful, by whom ye were called unto the fellowship of his Son Jesus Christ our Lord." And again he speaks to the same effect in 1 Thess. v. 24, "Faithful is he that calleth you, who also will do it." It was of old the will of God to save the people whom he gave to Jesus, and from this he has never turned, for our Lord said (John vi. 39), "And this is the Father's will which hath sent me, that of all which he hath given me I should lose nothing, but should raise it up again at the last day." Thus you see from these passages, and there are numbers of others, that God's faithfulness secures the preservation of his people, and "the righteous shall hold on his way."

The seventh and last argument shall be drawn *from what has already been done in us.* I shall do little more than quote the Scriptures, and leave them to sink into your minds. A blessed passage is that in Jeremiah xxxi. 3 : "The Lord hath appeared of old unto me, saying, yea, I have loved thee with an everlasting love : therefore with lovingkindness have I drawn thee." If he did not mean that his love should be everlasting he would never have drawn us at all, but because that love is everlasting therefore with lovingkindness has he drawn us. The apostle argues this in a very elaborate manner in Romans v. 9, 10: "Much more then, being now justified by his blood, we shall be saved from wrath through him. For if. when we were enemies, we were reconciled to God by the death of his Son, much more, being reconciled, we shall be saved by his life." I cannot stop to show how every word of this passage is emphatic, but so it is : if God reconciled us when we were enemies, he certainly will save us now we are his friends, and if our Lord Jesus has reconciled us by his death, much more will he save us by his life; so that we may be certain he will not leave nor forsake those whom he has called. Do you need me to bring to your minds that golden chapter, the 8th of Romans, the noblest of all language that was ever written by human pen ? "Whom ye did foreknow, he also did predestinate to be conformed to the image of his Son. Moreover, whom he did predestinate, them he also called ; and whom he called, them he also justified ; and whom he justified, them he also glorified." There is no break in the chain between justification and glory : and no supposable breakage can occur, for the apostle puts that out of all hazard, by saying, "Who shall lay anything to the charge of God's elect ? It is God that justifieth. Who is he that condemneth ? It is Christ that died, yea rather, that is risen again, who is even at the right hand of God, who also maketh intercession for us. Who shall separate us from the love of Christ ?" Then he heaps on all the things that might be supposed to separate, and says, "For I am persuaded, that neither death, nor life, nor angels, nor principalities, nor powers, nor things present, nor things to come, nor height, nor depth, nor any other creature, shall be able to separate us from the love of God, which is in Christ Jesus our Lord." In the same manner the apostle writes in Philippians i. 6. "Being confident of this very thing, that he who hath begun a good work in you will perform it until the day of Jesus Christ." I cannot stay to mention the many other Scriptures in which what has been done is made an argument that the work shall be completed, but it is after the manner of the Lord to go through with whatever he undertakes. "He will give grace and glory," and perfect that which concerneth us.

One marvellous privilege which has been bestowed upon us is of peculiar significance : we are one with Christ by close, vital, spiritual union. We are taught of the Spirit that we enjoy a marriage union with Christ Jesus our Lord—shall that union be dissolved ? We are married to him. Has he ever given a bill of divorce ? There never has been such a case as the heavenly bridegroom divorcing from his heart a chosen soul to whom he has been united in the bonds of grace. Listen to these words from the prophecy of Hosea ii. 19, 20. "And I will betroth thee unto me for ever ; yea, I will betroth thee unto me in righteousness, and in judgment, and in lovingkindness, and in mercies. I will even betroth thee unto me in faithfulness : and thou shalt know the Lord."

This marvellous union is set forth by the figure of the head and the body : we are members of the body of Christ. Do the members of his body rot away ? Is Christ amputated ? Is he fitted with new limbs as old ones are lost ? Nay, being members of this body, we shall not be divided from him. "He that is joined unto the Lord," says the apostle, "is one spirit," and if we are made one spirit with Christ, that mysterious union does not allow of the supposition of a separation.

The Lord has wrought another great work upon us, for he has sealed us by the Holy Spirit. The possession of the Holy Ghost is the divine seal which sooner or later is set upon all the chosen. There are many passages in which that seal is spoken of, and is described as being an earnest, an earnest of the inheritance. But how an earnest if after receiving it we do not attain the purchased possession ? Think over the exceedingly weighty words of the apostle in 2 Corinthians i. 21, 22 : "Now he which stablisheth us with you in Christ, and hath anointed us, is God ; who hath also sealed us, and given the earnest of the Spirit in our hearts." To the same effect the Holy Spirit speaks in Ephesians i. 13, 14 : "In whom ye also trusted, after that ye heard the word of truth, the gospel of your salvation : in whom also after that ye believed, ye were sealed with that Holy Spirit of promise, which is the earnest of our inheritance until the redemption of the purchased possession, unto the praise of his glory." Beloved, we feel certain that if the Spirit of God dwelleth in us, he that raised up Jesus Christ from the dead will keep our souls and will also quicken our mortal bodies and present us complete before the glory of his face at the last.

Therefore we sum up the argument with the confident expression of the apostle when he said (2 Tim. iv. 18), "The Lord shall deliver me from every evil work, and will preserve me unto his heavenly kingdom; to whom be glory for ever and ever. Amen."

II. Now, how shall we IMPROVE THE DOCTRINE PRACTICALLY ?

The first improvement is *for encouragement to the man who is on the road to heaven.* " The righteous shall hold on his way." If I had to take a very long journey, say from London to John o' Groats, with my poor tottering limbs to carry me, and such a weight to carry too, I might begin to despair, and, indeed, the very first day's walking would knock me up: but if I had a divine assurance unmistakeably saying, " You will hold on your way, and you will get to your journey's end," I feel that I would brace myself up to achieve the task. One might hardly undertake a difficult journey if he did not believe that he would finish it, but the sweet assurance that we shall reach our home makes us pluck up courage. The weather is wet, rainy, blusterous, but we must keep on, for the end is sure. The road is very rough, and runs up hill and down dale; we pant for breath, and our limbs are aching; but as we shall get to our journey's end we push on. We are ready to creep into some cottage and lie down to die of weariness, saying, " I shall never accomplish my task;" but the confidence which we have received sets us on our feet, and off we go again. To the right-hearted man the assurance of success is the best stimulus for labour. If it be so, that I shall overcome the world, that I shall conquer sin, that I shall not be an apostate, that I shall not give up my faith, that I shall not fling away my shield, that I shall come home a conqueror—then will I play the man, and fight like a hero. This is one of the reasons why British troops have so often won the fight, because the drummer-boys did not know how to beat a retreat, and the rank and file did not believe in the possibility of defeat. They were beaten oftentimes by the French, so the French tell us, but they would not believe it, and therefore would not run away. They felt like winning, and so they stood like solid rocks amidst the dread artillery of the foe till victory declared on their side. Brethren, we shall do the same if we realize that we are preserved in Christ Jesus, kept by the power of God through faith unto salvation. Every true believer shall be a conqueror, and hence the reason for warring a good warfare. There is laid up for us in heaven a crown of life that fadeth not away. The crown is laid up for *us*, and not for chance comers. The crown reserved for me is such that no one else can wear it; and if it be so, then will I battle and strive to the end, till the last enemy is overcome, and death itself is dead.

Another improvement is this: what *an encouragement this is to sinners* who desire salvation. It should lead them to come and receive it with grateful delight. Those who deny this doctrine offer sinners a poor twopenny-halfpenny salvation, not worth having, and it is no marvel that they turn away from it. As the Pope gave England to the Spanish king—if he could get it—so do they proffer Christ's salvation if a man will deserve it by his own faithfulness. According to some, eternal life is given to you, but then it may not be eternal; you may fall from it, it may last only for a time. When I was but a child I used to trouble myself because I saw some of my young companions, who were a little older than myself, when they became apprentices and came to London, become vicious; I have heard their mother's laments, and seen their tears about them; I have heard their fathers expressing bitterest sorrow over the boys whom I knew in my class to be quite as good as ever I had been, and it used to strike me with horror that I perhaps might sin as they had done. They became Sabbath-breakers; in one case there was a theft from the till to go into Sunday pleasuring. I dreaded the very thought; I desired to maintain an unsullied character, and when I heard that if I gave my heart to Christ he would keep me, that was the very thing which won me; it seemed to be a celestial life assurance for my character, that if I would really trust Christ with myself he would save me from the errors of youth, preserve me amid the temptations of manhood, and keep me to the end. I was charmed with the thought that if I was made righteous by believing in Christ Jesus I should hold on my way by the power of the Holy Spirit. That which charmed me in my boyhood is even more attractive to me in middle life: I am happy to preach to you a sure and everlasting salvation. I feel that I have something to bring before you this morning which is worthy of every sinner's eager acceptance. I have neither "if" nor "but" with which to dilute the pure gospel of my message. Here it is: "He that believeth and is baptized *shall be saved*." I dropped a piece of ice upon the floor yesterday, and I said to one who was in the room, "Is not that a diamond?" "Ah," he said, "you would not leave it on the floor, I warrant you, if it were a diamond of that size." Now I have a diamond here—eternal life, everlasting life! Methinks you will be in haste to take it up at once, to be saved now, to be saved in living, to be saved in dying, to be saved in rising again, for ever and ever, by the eternal power and infinite love of God. Is not this worth having? Grasp at it, poor soul; thou mayest have it if thou dost but believe in Jesus Christ, or, in other words, trust thy soul with him. Deposit thine eternal destiny in this divine bank, then thou canst say, "I know whom I have believed, and I am persuaded that he is able to keep that which I have committed to him against that day." The Lord bless you, for Christ's sake. Amen.

SAINTS GUARDED FROM STUMBLING.

A Sermon

DELIVERED BY

C. H. SPURGEON,

AT THE METROPOLITAN TABERNACLE, NEWINGTON.

"Now unto him that is able to keep you from falling, and to present you faultless before the presence of his glory with exceeding joy, to the only wise God our Saviour, be glory and majesty, dominion and power, both now and ever. Amen."—Jude 24, 25.

THE point and pith of what I may have to say will lie in the alteration of this text caused by the revision of the New Testament. The Revised Version runs thus, "Now unto him that is able to guard you from stumbling." I am not going to speak at any length upon the rest of the text; but shall dwell mainly upon this remarkable alteration, which certainly gives the meaning of the original better than the rendering in the Authorized Version.

To begin, then, here is a doxology. Jude is writing upon very practical subjects indeed; his short epistle is of the most practical kind; but he cannot finish it without a doxology of praise. Is there any work which we should complete without praise to God? Prayer should always have praise mingled with it. The preaching of the gospel, or the writing of it, the teaching of the young, and every other form of Christian service, should be combined with the spirit of praise. I think that I may say of praise what we read of salt in the Old Testament, "salt without prescribing how much." You cannot have too much of praise. "With all thine offerings thou shalt offer salt," and "with all thine offerings thou shalt offer praise." It seems delightful to me to notice how the apostle Paul stops almost in the midst of a sentence to bow his knees, and utter a doxology of praise to his God. And here Jude, with burning words denouncing sin, and urging believers to purity, cannot conclude his epistle without saying, "Now unto him that is able to keep you from falling, and to present you faultless before the presence of his glory with exceeding joy, to the only wise God our Saviour, be glory and majesty, dominion and power, both now and ever. Amen."

Beloved friends, we may well continue to praise God, for our God continues to give us causes for praise. If we will only think, we shall begin to thank. If we will only consider even the mercies of the present, we shall break out with ascriptions of praise to him. At this very moment, every believer here has a reason for a doxology.

My text begins with "Now", and closes with "now and ever." The praise of God should be given at the present time; and it is to be perpetually carried on, therefore now is the time for it to be rendered: "both now and ever. Amen."

Consider, then, dear brother or sister, thou hast at this moment a cause for ascribing praise to God, and thou hast this reason for it, at any rate, that he is able to guard thee from stumbling; his ability is to be employed for thy good; his power is intended for thy keeping. Oh, sing unto the Lord a new song to-night, with heart and soul bless him, who is able to guard thee from stumbling, and to present thee faultless before the presence of his glory with exceeding joy!

I. Coming to the text at once, I shall notice, first, THE DANGER TO BE DREADED. It is "stumbling." What is that?

Well, first of all, it is *a lesser form of falling*. A horse may stumble and not fall; yet it is a sort of falling. If there is much stumbling, it will be a fall. Now, there are faults, to which the child of God is very liable, which do not amount to actual falling; but they are stumblings. Like David, we have to say, "My feet were almost gone; my steps had well nigh slipped." We are not actually down; it is a wonder that we are not. We have not broken our knees; but we were within an inch of doing so; a little more, and we should have fallen to our serious hurt. The text speaks of "Him that is able to guard you from stumbling," to preserve you from the smallest form of grieving the Spirit, or the faintest trace of sin, which would not amount to a fall. The Lord can keep you from that which is not a fall, but which might lead to it. I want to set a high standard before you to-night. Jude does not say that you are able to guard yourselves from stumbling, for you are not; but the ascription of praise is to him who is able to guard you even from stumbling, and to present you, not only pardoned, but faultless before the presence of his glory with exceeding joy.

Stumbling is, next, not only a form of falling, and a matter therefore to be grieved over, but it is *a prelude to falling*. Oftentimes, we first stumble, and then, after a while, down we go. If we could recover ourselves from the stumble, we should not have to gather ourselves up from the fall. Long before the child of God falls into public sin, and injures his character, those who watch him will have perceived his stumbling. He kept up, just kept up; but you wondered that he did. He kept on, perhaps for months; but as you looked at him, you said to yourself, "I am afraid that he will come to something worse. I feel sure that he will have a stumble, and another stumble, and then another stumble, and he will be down by-and-by." Oh, that a child of God could notice his own stumblings, then he would soon be delivered from them! But it is too often with us, to change the metaphor, as Hosea says, "Gray hairs are here and there upon him, yet he knoweth it not." He is getting feeble, he is becoming prematurely old; but he has not seen the change in the colour of his hair. He has not looked in the glass of the Word lately, so he is unconscious that he is declining. If Satan cannot conquer Mansoul by storming it, he sometimes triumphs by sapping and mining, gradually undermining the walls, and getting a secret entrance in that way. May the Lord make us very watchful, that we may not be ignorant of Satan's devices, and may our Saviour guard us even from stumbling, for then we shall be kept from falling!

I think that I can put this matter pretty plainly. You must have known, you must have read of, or you must have seen, some people, whom you believe to be true and real Christians; and in their lives there is nothing glaringly wrong, nothing that is so offensive that they can be excluded from the church, or for which their Christian friends would condemn them as hypocrites; yet, somehow, their lives are, to say the least, questionable, doubtful. There is good in them; but that good is blotted. We trust that there is in them a true desire to be right; but there are so many sad failures in their lives that they seem to stumble to heaven rather than to run there. Now, our desire is that our life may not be of that kind; and therefore we would lay hold upon this text, and plead it before the throne, "Lord, thou art able to guard us from stumbling, be pleased to do so, to the praise of the glory of thy grace!"

You will see that stumbling is *itself a form of evil*, if you think of another phase of it. There were some who stumbled at the doctrine of Christ in his own day. He had a number of followers who kept with him up to a certain point; but when the Saviour said, "Except ye eat the flesh of the Son of man, and drink his blood, ye have no life in you," they went back, and walked no more with him. They could not understand what he meant, and they murmured, saying, "How can this man give us his flesh to eat?" So, being staggered and stumbled at the depth of this great mystery, they turned aside, and walked no more with him. Beloved, we want God so to uphold us and guard us that, whatever the teaching of his Holy Word may be, we shall receive it without a demur. I know that there are some Christian people who stumble at one doctrine, especially if they hear somebody denounce it; and there are others who are staggered at another doctrine, because they have met some very wise man, who knows better than the Word of God, and says that it cannot be true. In these days, there is very great liability to this kind of stumbling, especially among Christians who do not read their Bibles much; and I am sorry to say that there are plenty of such Christians. They read magazines, or perhaps works of fiction, rather than the sure Word of God; and they are thus easily caught in the snare of the fowler. Many professing Christians do not know what God's Word really teaches, so they are not established in the faith; they do not know even the elements of the doctrines of Christ, they have not examined the immutable foundations of the faith, and they are staggered. And truly, the mysteries of the kingdom are so deep, and the teachings of Christ are so contrary to the reasonings of flesh and blood, that we need not wonder if some are stumbled. Let us cry to him who is able to guard us from stumbling that, with steady step, we may press on in the way of life, and never be ashamed of truth, lest truth should be ashamed of us. Let us believe what the Bible says, however difficult the believing may be, because God has said it. This should ever stand for us as the grand master-argument, not the reasonableness of the doctrine, not because it commends itself to our judgment, but the fact that God hath said it; that ends all debate. Christ is able to guard from stumbling as to doctrine.

Many others are stumbled at the cross. Strange to say, the cross of Christ has always been the stumbling-stone to the ungodly, and to mere professors. What! the cross of Christ an occasion of stumbling? Why, it is the very centre of apostolic teaching: "We preach Christ crucified." Nowadays, there are two great points of attack; the one is the inspiration of Scripture, and the other is the substitutionary work of our Lord Jesus Christ. The enemies of the cross will not have a crucified Saviour; they stumble at that which is the very foundation of our faith. The Lord will keep us from stumbling at Christ's cross, I am quite sure. It is the rock of our refuge, the pillar of our hope.

The cross that Christ carried involves one for us to carry. No sooner does a Christian man become a believer, and confess Christ in baptism, than he is sure to meet with some who straightway revile him. He has to take up his cross. A working-man among sceptical companions, a young girl in a book-folding warehouse, a wife who has an ungodly husband, as soon as they come out boldly on the side of Christ, straightway they have a cross to carry; and this causes a great many to stumble. Persecution and ridicule are too much for them; by-and-by they are offended, that is, they stumble at the cross. They would have Christ, but not any shame for Christ's sake; they are like Mr. Pliable, who set out to go to the Celestial City, but when he tumbled into the Slough of Despond with Christian, he said that, if he could only get out on the side nearest to his own house, Christian might have the Celestial City all to himself, for he could not go through a slough to get there. How many there are of this kind, fearful ones; cowardly ones! But there is a God who is able to guard us from stumbling, and I trust that he will do so. May we never be stumbled by anything that happens to us for Christ's sake! May we take joyfully the spoiling of our goods, if need be; yea, and suffer death itself, if it should ever come to that, sooner than turn aside from bearing the cross after the crucified Christ!

And this stumbling sometimes happens, not only at the doctrine of Christ, and at his cross, but at the precepts he has given. If we are to be Christ's, we must obey him. "Ye call me Master and Lord: and ye say well; for so I am." But one will stagger at one command of Christ, and another at another. Though Christ bids us love one another, there are some who can do anything but love. They can give their bodies to be burned, but they have no charity. When Christ bids us walk in integrity before all mankind, there are some who can do many good things, but they like little sly practices in trade, and they stumble at Christ because of those evil ways. You know there are many ways in which people try to be as little Christians as they can be, so as just to get into heaven. Miserable wretches, they want to save their souls, and yet after all to follow the ways of the world. So they stumble at the precepts of the Holy Christ. They cannot put up with commands like his, which lay the axe at the root of the tree. If you are kept by him who is able to guard you from stumbling, you will love every way of Christ, and every word of Christ, and your prayer will be, "Teach me thy statutes," and your heart will willingly obey every precept of the Lord.

Once more, there are some who are staggered by the experience of believers. I speak now especially to young beginners. You have begun to be believers in Christ, and you have been very, very happy. I am very glad that you are. Long may your happiness continue! But there is another who has been, perhaps, in the way of the Lord for a few months; and suddenly a depression of spirit has come over him, and he says to himself, "Oh, dear me, is this the way of God's people?" I remember that, within a week after I had found joy and peace in believing, I began to feel the uprisings of inbred sin, and I cried out, "O wretched man that I am! who shall deliver me from the body of this death?" I did not know that such a sigh and cry never could come out of an unbelieving heart, that there must be a new heart and a right spirit within the man to whom sin is a burden, and who loathes it. I did not know that then; and I wondered whether I could be a child of God at all. Oh, there are strange experiences for those who are on the road to heaven! You remember how John Newton sings—

> "I asked the Lord that I might grow
> In faith, and love, and every grace
> Might more of his salvation know,
> And seek more earnestly his face.
>
> "I hoped that in some favoured hour
> At once he'd answer my request,
> And by his love's constraining power,
> Subdue my sins, and give me rest.
>
> "Instead of this he made me feel
> The hidden evils of my heart,
> And let the angry powers of hell
> Assault my soul in every part."

The good man began to discover more and more his own sinfulness, and he said, "Lord, is this the way to holiness?" and he was stumbled for a moment. O beloved, it is only the grace of God that can make us feel that, whatever experiences we have within us, our faith looks to a living Christ, who never changes, and we rest in his finished work. Whether we are up or whether we are down, whether we sing or whether we sigh, we look beyond our changing moods unto him who loved us, and gave himself for us. Yet many have been stumbled by their own inner experiences, not understanding them. There is only One who can guard us from such stumblings.

So, then, dear friends, to close this description of stumbling, if we are guarded from stumbling we shall certainly be kept from falling. *This is an inclusive blessing.* It includes preservation from all falling into outward sin; and especially all final falling, all fatal falling. Christ is able to guard us from stumbling; much more is he able to preserve us from falling away, from utterly departing from the faith. But we should do that if it were not for his guardian care. There is nothing that the worst of men have done which the best of men could not do if they were left by the grace of God. Do not think so much of yourself as to imagine yourself incapable of even the greatest crime.

That very thought proves that you are capable of committing any crime. I think that it is Mr. Cecil who says, "I thought myself humble, one day, when I said that I did wonder that I should have sinned as I had done in such a way; whereas," said he, "if I had been truly humble, I should not have wondered that I sinned like that; I should have wondered at the grace of God that kept me from even greater sin; and I should have understood that my natural tendencies all went towards evil, and that the marvel was that they did not master me, and lead me farther into evil than I had gone." Oh, beloved, we must be kept by God himself, or else stumbling, falling, foully and fatally falling, will be our lot! From that, however, the Lord will preserve us who are truly his.

So much, then, upon the danger to be dreaded.

II. Now, I must be somewhat more brief on the second point, THE PRIVILEGE TO BE ENJOYED: "Now unto him that is able to guard you from stumbling."

Well, beloved friends, it is a great privilege to be guarded from stumbling, for *it is a privilege that we greatly need.* I was thinking of the many things that make us in danger of stumbling. There is, first, our weakness. It is the weak horse, you know, that stumbles and falls. It is out of condition, out of health, and down it goes. And we are weak, very weak. Then, consider the many roads that we have to travel. Here is a man who is a preacher, a husband, a father, a master. Some of you are tradesmen, or workmen; and beside your daily occupation, you have all your domestic relationships on you. Now, what you need is to be guarded all round from stumbling. We have heard of one who was all right at home, but he was very queer outside his house. I have heard of another who was an excellent man in the church; but if you had asked his wife about him, she would not have liked to describe him. A man may be a very good man at a prayer-meeting; but he may be a very poor hand when you get him at his work. I have known some move very slowly indeed at that time; nobody would have liked to pay them by the day. Now, it is an evil thing when a Christian is bad anywhere; but it is a grand thing, and only God can enable us to attain to it, when we do not stumble in any one of the ways which we have to go, but are kept walking uprightly always.

And then, you know, it is the pace that makes some people stumble. See the pace we have to go at now. When I think of our dear old fathers in the country, I almost envy their quiet lives; not up too early, and seldom going to bed very late, not much to do, leading very steady sort of lives. They travelled by broad-wheeled waggons, and we fly over the ground by express trains, and want to go twice as quickly as we can, and all the while we have so much to do.

And, then, it is not only the pace, dear friends, but it is the loads that some of you have to carry. Oh, the weights that are piled upon some of God's people in their business! Only God can keep an overloaded heart from stumbling; and the ways are very rough just now. You hardly meet anybody in trade who does not say, "Ah, we have a rough bit of ground to travel over now; stone in plenty, and no steam roller!" But there is One who is able to keep you from falling.

Perhaps there are some of you who have not to travel over a rough bit of road; your path is very smooth; you have all that heart can wish for, and every comfort that you could desire. You want to be guarded from stumbling, for you are on a very slippery road. If there has been a thaw, and then a frost comes on at night, the road may be very pretty to look at, but it is very bad for a horse's feet; and so prosperity is a very slippery way for God's people. The Lord must keep them from falling, or they will go down with a crash.

Then there is the length of the road as well as the other things I have mentioned. If we had to serve God only for a short time, one might easily do it; but we may have to go on for fifty years, sixty years, seventy years, eighty years. I think, sometimes, that if martyr days were to come, and they would burn me quickly, I could endure it; but it would be a terrible trial to be roasted at a slow fire; yet our lives are often so prolonged, and filled with trial and temptation, that it is like being roasted alive by a slow fire. The road is long, and the pace has become very trying, so we may easily stumble; but the text gives us good cheer, for it tells us of him that is able to guard us from stumbling.

It is not only needful for us to be kept, but *it is very gracious on Christ's part to keep us.* Beloved, what if you should have this text fulfilled in you, so that, through a long and trying life, you should so live that, when your enemies wanted to find fault with you, they would not know where to begin? Live so that if they look you up and down, they will have to say of you as they said of Daniel, "We shall not find any occasion against this Daniel, except we find it against him concerning the law of his God." Oh, if you should go down to the grave faultless,—not that we can any of us be in ourselves faultless in the sight of God,—but if you live such blameless lives that no one shall be able to say evil of you, but shall be compelled to confess that in you the life of Christ has been reflected in your measure, what a privilege it will be! And this is the privilege set before you in the text, that you shall not be stumbled.

What distress you will be saved from if you are guarded from stumbling! A stumbling Christian has to be a sorrowing Christian. When a child of God stumbles, and knows it, he very soon takes to weeping, and humbling himself in the presence of his God. But if you are kept by the grace of God, you will be saved from many a bitter pang, and helped to go from joy to joy, and grace to grace.

What a blessing such a person is to other people in the Church of God! Without saying anything against our fellow-Christians, we know where our respect and confidence usually go. When we have seen brothers and sisters, who have been upheld and sustained in trial and temptation, and have not stumbled, we take delight in them. Those of us who are younger and weaker, go and hide, as it were, under the shadow of their wing.

And what a blessing such people are to the world! Those are the true saints who help to spread the gospel of Christ. A holy life is a missionary enterprise. An unstumbling life is an incentive to others to run along the heavenly road, trusting in the divine power to guard them also from stumbling.

Best of all that I have to say is this, that *this privilege is attainable*: "Unto him that is *able* to guard you from stumbling." "Oh!" says one, "if I just get to heaven, it will satisfy me." Will it? I pray you, do not talk so. Just to get in, like a tempest-tossed barque, waterlogged, or like a wreck just towed into the harbour at last,—well, it is a great mercy to get to heaven anyhow; but that is a poor way of getting in. Better would it be to steam into the harbour, with a full cargo, and plenty of passengers on board, and all the flags flying to the honour of the Great King and Pilot, who has guarded you through the storm, that "so an entrance shall be ministered unto you abundantly into the everlasting kingdom of our Lord and Saviour Jesus Christ." May it be so with you! Oh, that we may not have to send off the tugs, and tow you into the harbour; but that instead thereof, you may come in, with a fleet of little ships behind you, able to say, "Here am I, and the children that thou hast given me"! This is a privilege worth having, and it cannot be attained except through him who is able to guard you from stumbling.

III. Now I will lead you on, in the third place, with great brevity, to remember THE POWER WHICH BESTOWS THIS PRIVILEGE.

To be guarded from stumbling throughout a long life, is *not of ourselves*. It is not to be found in our own experience; not even in the means of grace alone. That same power that made the heavens and the earth, and keeps the earth and heavens in their places, is needed to make a Christian, and to keep him standing before the sons of men.

"Unto him that is able to guard you from stumbling." God has this power. *He has power over all circumstances.* He can so arrange the trials of your life that you shall never be tempted beyond what you are able to bear; he has power also over Satan, so that, when he desires to have you to sift you as wheat, the Lord can keep him back. God will not allow him to overcome you.

Best of all, *God has power over our hearts.* He can keep us alive with holy zeal; he can keep us so believing, so loving, so hoping, so watching, so fully obedient, that we shall not stumble at his Word, or stumble at anything else.

Jude speaks of "the only wise God", so that, *God's power is joined with wisdom.* He knows your weakness, and he can guard you against it. He knows your tempters, and he can thrust them aside, or help you to overcome them. It is the wise God, as well as the strong God, who is able to guard you from stumbling, He knows where the stumbling-stones are, and where your weakness is; and he can and he will bring you safely through.

Yet once more, the One who guards us from stumbling is *our Saviour* as well as the only wise God. It is his business to save you. It is his office to save you, and save you he will. Commit yourself to-night to his guardian care, and walk with him. That is a high favour, that you may not only be kept from falling, but even be guarded from stumbling, to the praise and glory of his grace.

I have been very brief where I should have liked to enlarge.

IV. I finish with this point, THE GLORY WHICH IS DUE TO CHRIST FOR THIS PRIVILEGE. If we are guarded from stumbling, we may take no credit to ourselves; but we must lay the crown at the feet of him to whom the power belongs.

If he has kept us from stumbling until now, *let us praise him for the past.* Oh, what a mercy to have had this keeping year after year! Notwithstanding many imperfections and follies, which we have had to confess, yet we have been kept from any grievous stumbling that would have dishonoured the holy name of Christ. Bless God to-night that you have been kept from stumbling to-day. I do not know where you have been; but I have no doubt you have been where you might have slipped if you had been left by the Spirit of God. You have been in the shop; you have been in the home; you have been in the street; you have been on the Exchange; you have been among ungodly men. Ay, and even among Christian men, you can soon commit yourself, and trip up. If you have been kept to-day, do not say, "How good I am!" No, no, no; say, "Now unto him who has guarded me from stumbling, be glory and majesty, dominion and power, both now and ever."

Now, will you *begin to praise him for the future as well?* You have not experienced it yet; but remember that verse which we often sing,—

> "And a new song is in my mouth,
> To long-loved music set;
> Glory to thee for all the grace
> I have not tasted yet."

Begin to thank the Lord that he will keep you from falling in the future. Bless him that he will present you faultless before the presence of his glory with exceeding joy.

And the next time that danger comes to you, *praise him that he can guard you from stumbling.* To-morrow morning, perhaps, you have a difficult task before you. You are looking forward, in the course of the week, to something that will be very trying. Well, praise God now, that he is able to guard you from stumbling. But oh, what a song we will give him when we are once over the river! When we climb the celestial hills, when we enter heaven, and find ourselves among the white-robed, blood-washed throng, I wonder which of us will praise him most. Well, let us not wait till then; but let us begin here; let us rehearse the music of the spheres now. Let us say, "Now unto him that is able to guard us from stumbling, be glory and majesty, dominion and power, both now and ever."

This sermon does not belong to all of you, I am sorry to say. I wish that it did; but remember, dear hearer, that he who can keep the saint from stumbling, can bring the sinner into the right way. The same grace that can preserve the child of God from falling into sin can bring you out of sin; and as we have to look wholly to Christ, certainly you must do so. May the Lord lead you to look to-night out of yourself, and your feelings, and your doings, and trust to the Lord Jesus, who died, but lives again, and lives to save guilty men! Whosoever believeth in him hath everlasting life; and he will bring them into his way, and keep them from stumbling, and present them among the rest of his blood-washed, to praise his name for ever. The Lord bless this meditation, for Christ's sake! Amen.

Exposition by C. H. Spurgeon.
PSALM XCI.

Verse 1.—*He that dwelleth in the secret place of the most High shall abide under the shadow of the Almighty.*

It is not every man who dwells there; no, not even every Christian man. There are some who come to God's house; but the man mentioned here dwells with the God of the house. There are some who worship in the outer court of the temple; but "he that dwelleth in the secret place of the most High" lives in the Holy of Holies; he draws near to the mercy-seat, and keeps there; he walks in the light, as God is in the light; he is not one who is sometimes on and sometimes off, a stranger or a guest, but like a child at home, he dwells in the secret place of the most High. Oh, labour to get to that blessed position! You who know the Lord, pray that you may attain to this high condition of dwelling in the inner shrine, always near to God, always overshadowed by those cherubic wings which indicate the presence of God. If this is your position, you "shall abide under the shadow of the Almighty." You are not safe in the outer courts; you are not protected from all danger anywhere but within the veil. Let us come boldly there; and, when we once enter, let us dwell there.

2. *I will say of the LORD, He is my refuge and my fortress: my God; in him will I trust.*

This is a daring utterance, as if the psalmist would claim for himself the choicest privileges of any child of God. When you hear a glorious doctrine preached, it may be very sweet to others; but the honey lies in the particular application of it to yourself. You must, like the bee, go down into the bell of the flower yourself, and fetch out its nectar. "I will say of the Lord, He is my"—then come three my's, as if the psalmist could grasp the Triune Jehovah,—"my refuge, my fortress, my God; in him will I trust." What a grand word that is, "My God"! Can any language be loftier? Can any thought be more profound? Can any comfort be surer?

3. *Surely he shall deliver thee from the snare of the fowler,*

If you dwell near to God, you will not be deceived by Satan. In the light of the Lord you will see light; and you will discover the limed twigs and the nets and the traps that are set to catch you: "He shall deliver thee from the snare of the fowler."

3. *And from the noisome pestilence.*

The pestilence is something that you cannot see. It comes creeping in, and fills the air with death before you perceive its approach; but "He shall deliver thee from the noisome pestilence." There is a pestilence of dangerous and accursed error abroad at this time; but if we dwell in the secret place of the most High, it cannot affect us; we shall be beyond its power. "Surely," oh, blessed word! there is no doubt about this great truth, "Surely, he shall deliver thee from the snare of the fowler, and from the noisome pestilence."

4. *He shall cover thee with his feathers,*

The psalmist uses a wonderful metaphor when he ascribes "feathers" to God, and compares him to a hen, or some mother-bird, under whose wings her young find shelter. Yet the condescension of God is such that he allows us to speak of him thus: "He shall cover thee with his feathers."

4. *And under his wings shalt thou trust:*

God is to his people a strong defence and a tender defence. "His wings" and "his feathers" suggest both power and softness. God hides not his people in a casing of iron; their shelter is stronger than iron, yet it is soft as the downy wings of a bird for ease and comfort. As the little chicks bury their tiny heads in the feathers of the hen, and seem happy, and warm, and comfortable under their mother's wings, so shall it be with thee if thou dwellest with thy God : "He shall cover thee with his feathers, and under his wings shalt thou trust."

4. *His truth shall be thy shield and buckler.*
Twice is he armed who hath God's truth to be his shield and buckler.

5. *Thou shalt not be afraid for the terror by night;*
Nervous as you are, and naturally timid, when you dwell near to God, your fears shall all go to sleep. That is a wonderful promise : "Thou shalt not be afraid." If it had said, "Thou shalt have no cause for fear," it would have been a very comforting word; but this is even more cheering, "Thou shalt not be afraid for the terror by night."

5. *Nor for the arrow that flieth by day;*
Both night and day thou shalt be safe. Thy God will not leave thee in the glare of the sun, nor will he forsake thee when the damps of night-dews would put thee in peril. We, dear friends, may have secret enemies, who shoot at us, but we shall not be afraid of the arrow. There may be unseen influences that would ruin us, or cause us dishonour, or distress; but when we dwell with God, we shall not be afraid of them.

6, 7. *Nor for the pestilence that walketh in darkness; nor for the destruction that wasteth at noonday. A thousand shall fall at thy side, and ten thousand at thy right hand; but it shall not come nigh thee.*
When God takes his people to dwell in nearness to himself, and they have faith in this promise, I make no doubt that, literally, in the time of actual pestilence, they will be preserved. It is not every professing Christian, nor every believer who attains this height of experience; but only such as believe the promise, and fulfil the heavenly condition of dwelling in the secret place of the most High. How could cholera or fever get into the secret place of the most High? How could any arrows, how could any pestilence, ever be able to reach that secure abode of God? If you dwell there, you are invincible, invulnerable, infinitely secure.

8—10. *Only with thine eyes shalt thou behold and see the reward of the wicked. Because thou hast made the* LORD, *which is my refuge, even the most High, thy habitation; there shall no evil befall thee,*
"There shall no evil befall thee." It may have the appearance of evil; but it shall turn out to thy good. There shall be but the appearance of evil, not the reality of it: "There shall no evil befall thee."

10, 11. *Neither shall any plague come nigh thy dwelling. For he shall give his angels charge over thee, to keep thee in all thy ways.*
You remember how the devil misapplied this text to Christ. He was quite right in the application; but he was quite wrong in the quotation, for he left out the words "in all thy ways." God will help us in our ways if we keep in his ways. When we meet with trouble and accident, we ought to enquire whether we are in God's way. That famous old Puritan, holy Mr. Dodd, having to cross a river, had to change from one boat into another, and being little used to the water, he fell in, and, when he was pulled out, in his simplicity and wisdom he said, "I hope that I am in my way." That was the only question that seemed to trouble him. If I am in my way, then God will keep me. We ought to ask ourselves, "Now, am I in God's way? Am I really moving to-day and acting to-day as divine providence leads me, and as duty calls me?" He who travels on the king's business, by daylight, along the king's highway, may be sure of the king's protection. "He shall give his angels charge over thee, to keep thee in all thy ways."

Come here, Gabriel, Michael, and all the rest of you," says the great King of kings to the angels around his throne; and when they come at his call, he says, "Take care of my child. Watch over him to-day. He will be in peril; suffer no evil to come near him."

12. *They shall bear thee up in their hands, lest thou dash thy foot against a stone.*

What royal protection we have, a guard of angels, who count it their delight and their honour to wait upon the seed-royal of the universe, for such are all the saints of God!

13. *Thou shalt tread upon the lion and adder: the young lion and the dragon shalt thou trample under feet.*

Strength and mastery may be united: "The young lion and the dragon": but the child of God shall overcome them. Talk of St. George and the dragon! We ought to think more of the saint and the dragon. It is he that dwelleth in the secret place of the most High, who, by God's help, treads upon the lion and adder, and of whom it is written, "The young lion and the dragon shalt thou trample under feet."

14. *Because he hath set his love upon me, therefore will I deliver him:*

Does God take notice of our poor love? Oh, yes, he values the love of his people, for he knows where it came from; it is a part of his own love; the creation of his grace!

14. *I will set him on high, because he hath known my name.*

Does God value such feeble and imperfect knowledge of his name as we possess? Yes; and he rewards that knowledge: "I will set him on high."

15. *He shall call upon me, and I will answer him:*

Notice, that it is, "He shall," and "I will." The mighty grace of God "shall" make us pray, and the Almighty God of grace "will" answer our prayer: "He shall call upon me, and I will answer him." How I love these glorious shalls and wills!

15. *I will be with him in trouble;*

"Whatever that trouble is, I will be with him in it. If he be dishonoured, if he be in poverty, if he be in sickness, if that sickness should drive his best friend away from his bed, still, 'I will be with him in trouble.'"

15. *I will deliver him, and honour him.*

God puts honour upon us, poor dishonourable worms that we are. One old divine calls a man "a worm six feet long"; and it is rather a flattering description of him. But God says, "I will deliver him, and honour him."

16. *With long life will I satisfy him, and shew him my salvation.*

He will live as long as he wants to live. Even if he should have but few years, yet he shall have a long life; for life is to be measured by the life that is in it, not by the length along which it drags. Still, God's children do live to a far longer age than any other people in the world; they are on the whole a long-lived race. They who fear God are delivered from the vices which would deprive them of the vigour of life; and the joy and contentment they have in God help them to live longer than others. I have often noticed how long God's people live. Some of them are speedily taken home; still this text is, as a rule, literally fulfilled, "With long life will I satisfy him, and shew him my salvation." He shall see God's salvation even here; and when he dies, and wakes up in the likeness of his Lord, he will see it to the full. May that be the portion of each of us! Amen.

PREVENTING GRACE.

A Sermon

DELIVERED BY

C. H. SPURGEON,

AT THE METROPOLITAN TABERNACLE, NEWINGTON,

In the year 1862.

"And David said to Abigail, Blessed be the Lord God of Israel, which sent thee this day to meet me; and blessed be thy advice, and blessed be thou, which hast kept me this day from coming to shed blood, and from avenging myself with mine own hand"—1 Samuel xxv. 32, 33.

I MUST tell you the story, for if you do not realize the circumstances, you will not understand these words. David was in the position of an outlaw in his country. He knew that he was one day to be king over Israel, but he had such reverence for Saul, the Lord's anointed, that he would do nothing that should look like usurpation, or seem in any way to injure the reigning monarch. Some four hundred restless spirits, who had been impoverished by the tyrannical government of Saul, persons who were in debt, and generally discontented, came to him in the caves of Adullam, and there formed an army of freebooters of which David was the head. A little while afterwards two hundred others, men like-minded, came and united themselves with this force, so that David found himself at the head of an army of six hundred men of war, all of them valiant men, ready for exploits. You will see he was in a very difficult position; he must find work for these men; they were soldiers of fortune, and they must be employed, yet it was impossible for him to act like a traitor; he could not lead his men against his king; he could not begin a revolution, in order to provide for his followers.

What, then, must he do if he desired still to be loyal to the king, and, at the same time, not to disband his men? He occupied his forces in peacefully guarding the herds of the great sheep-masters who fed their flocks on the high steeps of Carmel. This is not a thing uncommon in the East even to-day. Certain sheikhs, with their body of followers, sometimes undertake to keep off the Bedouin Arabs, and other marauders who attack the flocks of the sheep-master, and of course they expect to have some kind of remuneration for their trouble.

Now, all through the time that the sheep were in the pasture, David and his men watched over the flocks of a certain sheep-master called Nabal. When the time came round for shearing the flocks, David sent some of his followers to Nabal, to the feast of sheep-shearing, presenting his request that some contribution might be sent for the support of his men on account of their having taken care of Nabal's flocks, which otherwise would certainly have been diminished by systematic plunder. But Nabal had got all the good he wanted from David, and he refrained not from answering David's messenger in a most uncourteous, surly manner. "There be many servants," he said, "now-a-days, that break away every man from his master; shall I then take my bread, and my water, and my flesh, that I have killed for my shearers, and give it unto men whom I know not whence they be?"

Such a churlish message could not fail to nettle David; indeed, we know that it stung him to the quick. He had not run away from his master, but his master had driven him away, and as one who was apart from Saul, but was not Saul's antagonist, he was doing the best he could to maintain the peace. His blood boiled over. "Have I guarded the flocks of this miserable wretch," said he, "all this time, and kept my men there merely to attend his sheep, when they might have been profitable at some other work, and now, when I send to him, instead of giving me a donation, he answers me in this churlish manner?" Then, turning to his men, he said, "Gird ye on every man his sword, we will show this fellow how to treat us." So, leaving two hundred men to guard the caves, four hundred marched out, David at the head, his hot blood all ablaze within him, his anger showing in his face. "God do so to me," said he, "and more also, if I leave so much as a dog of that man's house alive by the morning light." He sallied forth doubtless with the full intent to destroy Nabal, to make his house a heap of ruins, and then to devastate the sheep-master's estate. What a false position for a child of God! But David was naturally impulsive, and somehow men that have any life in them do sometimes get their temper roused. We hear of some people that are as quiet and as peaceful and as easy as a pond of stagnant water; certainly their peace does not flow like a river, and their righteousness is never lashed to fury like the waves of the sea. David was not one of these.

As the son of Jesse rashly pursues the man of Mount Carmel, he meets a woman, Nabal's wife; perhaps a hard thought comes over him to smite her, but no—she is a woman, David cannot strike her, and, what is more, she is at his feet, asking him to lay all the blame at her door. Then she goes on to tell him that her lord is a very foolish and churlish man, and she hopes David will not take offence at his words. She has brought him a present, and she tells him that when he shall come to be king, it will be a great ease to his mind to think he never fought his own battles, but only the Lord's. She reminds him of the future, and so she makes him forget the present. After a while his heart yields to quiet reflections; he acts rather as saint than as soldier, putting up his sword into the sheath, and leaving the matter with his God.

Righteous vengeance was soon asserted, when barbarous revenge was stayed, for ten days afterwards Nabal died. The Lord himself dealt out retributive justice to the adversary, while the Lord's servant was held back from indiscriminate slaughter.

That is all we shall have occasion to say about the narrative. It suggests our subject, which is "Preventing Grace," the grace which God sends to prevent saints and sinners from running into sin. I hope before the service is over, many of us in looking back upon our past lives will gratefully bless the Lord: bless his providence, and bless the man or the woman whom he has sent to teach us, and to keep us back from evil: that we shall thank him because we have oftentimes been turned back from doing the wrong thing, and by an overruling counsel been led of him in the paths of righteousness.

Of this preventing grace we shall speak in two ways. We will deal first of all with the people of God, and with them but briefly, though they are the only persons who will ever be able to recognize the value and feel thankfulness for this precious benefit. Then we shall see how grace often prevents even men who are not followers of Jesus.

I. Preventing grace is enjoyed by all the people of God.

Dear friends, some of us can bless God at this hour that preventing grace came to us in the shape of *a godly education*. We heard no blasphemies when we lay in the cradle, no curses startled us from our dreams; many of us saw no drunkenness beneath the roof of our father's house; no libidinous books were put in our way. Many of you were trained from your youth up to know the Scriptures like Timothy, and some of you have even heard something of the voice of God speaking to you as he did to Samuel. Blessed be God for a holy mother; blessed be God for an affectionate, prayerful father; blessed be ye of the Lord, ye that brought us forth for God, and blessed be your advice, for ye have kept us from many a sin.

Since then, preventing grace has come in the shape of *godly associations;* we need none of us be very proud of what we are, if we think what we might have been, had we been put in other positions. If, instead of being bound apprentice to a good master, and afterwards brought into association with religious people in the Sabbath-school, and in the Bible-class, and in the congregation, your lot had been thrown where you could pick up your education in the street and take your college degree in the coal-hole or the theatre, who can tell but you had been as black a sinner as those whom you now pass by in the street, wondering that they are so vile? Much of a man's character comes from other men. What we are is not all of ourselves. We are deep in debt to others. Indeed, what man is there upon whom there have not been a hundred fingers to mould him and a thousand influences to make his plastic character what it is? I know that the grace of God is a thing that makes a man right before God, but I know, also, that holy associations (or ever grace comes into our heart to renew us) prevent us from indulging in sins into which, under other circumstances, we should certainly have plunged.

In extolling preventing grace, what shall I say, dear friends, besides this, of the *providential circumstances* which have kept us from sin? There have been times with some of us in our younger days before we knew Christ, when the temptation was very strong, but the opportunity was not near, and at other times the opportunity has been before our eyes, but there was no temptation. God help the man that has the temptation and the opportunity at the same time. Many and many a man has received the preventing and restraining grace of God when the devil has been hindered throwing the two dice at one time. It is of grace that at one time there has been the fire in the heart, but no fuel, while at another there has been the fuel but the fire did not burn just at that time so as to make it convenient or desirable for the man to sin. Oh, friends, the river of our life has been winding and tortuous in its course. Had it wound in another way, it had been very different from what it is, and, perhaps, a word—as we say, an accident, a chance hit—may have turned the whole of it. Now we can say that our moral reputation is unblemished, whereas otherwise we should have had to lament that we had been immoral, debauched, and depraved, if it had not been for this preventing grace of God working through providential circumstances.

There is a fountain which is the father of two rivers, and these two rivers both take their rise in a tarn at the top of a hill. Both rivers start from the same place, but when they end their course they are some five hundred miles apart. Behold this drop of water; there it lies. Which way shall it go? Shall it go down that stream and find its way to yonder sea, or down this stream to another destiny? It needs but a motion of a bird's wing to move that drop either way, and it shall go rolling onward into yonder sea, or it shall find another channel and pursue its course far apart. So has it been with us. The grace of God—preventing grace—had much to do with the providence which puts us in such and such a channel, instead of casting us into another; that allowed us to come into contact with holy people rather than to associate us with the vilest of the vile. This is a hard blow at our self-righteousness. If we had not had our hearts changed and if providential circumstances had been a little different, we might have been lost ere now.

But besides the power of conversion to change life, how much believers owe to the grace of God exercised through *trial and suffering!* They would have gone astray, but they were barred down by affliction; they would have leaped the hedges of God's law, but they were clogged by some adversity. Some men owe much to the fact that they were never in good health. A blind eye, or a crippled leg, or a maimed arm, may have been in the hands of God a great blessing in keeping some of you back from iniquities, in which otherwise you might have indulged. We never know what innumerable streams of good flow from that well which we call Marah, but which God often maketh to be an Elim to our souls.

"Determined to save he watched o'er my path,
When, Satan's blind slave, I sported with death."

I suppose, dear brethren and sisters in Christ, that in looking back you can say, " I can see the finger of God in a great many places where I might have ruined myself—there, and there, and there—though I knew him not, his arms were underneath me; he guided me with his eye, he led me by his right hand, that I might not be utterly destroyed."

Now, Christian man, if thou couldest think of this a little, *thou shouldest be very grateful indeed to God for this*. I know if thou hadst sinned even more, the blood of Christ could wash thy guilt away; and if thine iniquities had been greater still, thou wouldest not have overreached the power of divine love. But think now how good it is for thee that thou wast not suffered—I speak of course only to some of you—to go so far. How much sorrow you have been spared! From what evil habits have you been saved! What temptations are now kept away from you which, if God had not kept you back from sin in former days, might else overwhelm you.

Perhaps there is a man here who is a Christian, and though he knows he is redeemed, he would give his right arm if he could forget his unregenerate days. There are some men who might say, " I would give my eyes if I could forget what they have seen, and lose my ears if I could remember no more what they have heard." Why, there is a snatch of an old song that will come over you when you are in prayer, and when you are trying to get right up to heaven there is some old black remembrance of the merriment or dissipation of the former days that checks your flight, and is as a clog to the eagle, and will not let it mount. There is many a man who might have been a leader in God's camp, who is afraid to come out, and who, if he had come out, would have but little force because of the weakness some old habit has brought upon him; he feels he cannot do what he would for Christ because of the past. If this be not your experience, then thank God for preventing grace.

I preached this morning to the chief of sinners, I was glad to do it, but whenever I do, I find some who wish they had been greater sinners, not because they love sin, but because they think they should then see a greater change in themselves when the grace of God lays hold of them. Instead of this, thank God most devoutly : you are big enough sinners as you are; there is enough of vileness and corruption, there is enough of base depravity, there is enough of abominable sin in you now. Thank God if you have not been allowed to give vent to the evil within you and run to an excess of riot. I write every day among my mercies that I was taught to run in wisdom's way.

But, once again, dear friend, if you have not been permitted to run into outrageous folly, *do not think that you are any nearer Christ because of this*. Do not imagine that you are to be saved in any different way from the most outrageous drunkard or the most depraved of harlots. There is the same way to heaven for you who are highly esteemed among men as for the man who lies for his crime rotting in a gaol. I tell you, sirs, you who think you have done no wrong, you must go to heaven by the blood and righteousness of Christ, as much as the convict at the hulks; and when you get to glory you shall have no more right to boast of your own merits or your own goodness than the thief who went from the cross to glory, or that woman that was a sinner and loved much because she was much forgiven. "Other foundation can no man lay than that is laid," and while it is cause for congratulation that you have not wandered so far into sin as others, it is also cause for trembling, for verily I say unto you, often publicans and harlots enter the kingdom of heaven before Pharisees. Some who were the vilest of the vile have come to Christ, have penitently accepted his righteousness, while others robed in their own righteousness have gone down to hell and perished with a double destruction, with the rags of their righteousness about them.

I hope I have in no way whatever said anything which on the one hand detracts from the value of an early religious training and preventing grace, nor anything on the other hand which detracts from the grace which saves the very vilest of the vile. I feel that sometimes, when we are preaching, we seem to look after the scum and the raff, and we forget many others. I would not forget one of you, my dear hearers, who hear me Sabbath after Sabbath; God is my witness, if I thought I had missed any one of you I would be too glad to preach a sermon only for that one person, if I might but win his soul. What did I say? Preach a sermon! I would preach fifty sermons, I would preach my whole life but to win one of you, and think myself well paid with such a blessed reward for such easy toil. But whether you are great sinners or little sinners outwardly, remember you are all vile in the inner nature, and the same grace is presented to you all. "Whosoever will, let him take of the water of life freely."

II. The second part of our discourse is to be addressed to those who as yet have not experienced the grace of God in its constraining and quickening power. They, too, in a very real sense have received the preventing grace of God, for THE PREVENTING GRACE OF GOD IS UNIVERSAL.

Without the preventing grace of God to restrain man he would be unbearable, and if it were not for the preventing grace of God in society a nation would be an impossibility, and a well-ordered commonwealth would be a thing for which we might long, but should never be able to realize. Men would be little better we believe, than the beasts of the forest, tearing and devouring one another, if the grace of God did not keep them in check; and this, I think, is proved by the fact that the further you recede from the light of the Gospel—the further you get from the agencies which preventing grace is most likely to use—the more cruel and savage men are, the one toward the other. I thank God that this is a land where preventing grace is felt even by the very worst. I do not believe there is a burglar or a murderer but has been the subject of it, but has had to strive against it and against his own conscience, before he could consummate his crime and give himself up to iniquity. You have had preventing grace keeping you back from sin. Sinner, if *thou* canst not thank God for this *we* can, we bless the Lord that he restrains you and does not permit you to be worse than you are. We pray that this preventing grace may never be taken from you, or else you shall be like some wild horse that has desired to dash over the precipice, who, when the rein is laid upon his neck, leapeth to his doom and destroyeth himself and as many as be attached unto him.

Yet, while it is universal, *this preventing grace of God is by some men much detested and abhorred.* Some can hardly tolerate the restrictions which Christianity has imposed upon the nation! they are vexed that they have to shut up shop on Sunday, and, by a sort of custom, are compelled to go and hear the Word of God; they wish they lived in some place where they could do just as they liked. The wife who wants her husband and family to go up and hear the Gospel is thought hardly of because of it. Some men would even like, if they could, to have a family that was all the devil's; but somehow or other God will not let them have their way. The godless man gets a godly wife, and he is angry; by-and-by it turns out that one of the children receives God's saving grace, and he cannot bear the thought of it. I have seen men in spiritual things just like madmen of Bedlam. God knew that these men would ruin themselves if they were let alone, so, first of all, he straightwaistcoated them with poverty, that they could not do what they would. Then, afterwards, when they began to tear and foam, he put them into a godly family, as maniacs are put into a padded room, so that, dash themselves as they will, they cannot hurt themselves. These men cannot get loose, but they will strain at their bonds and foam and gnash because God has hold of them, and will not let the devil get the full mastery of them as they would like. O sinner, the day may come when God will say of thee, "Let him have his own way." If he should give thee up, then thy doom will be sealed for ever and thy fate be more desperate than words can describe. God help thee, man, and keep thee from thyself, or else thou wilt soon destroy thyself and go post haste to destruction.

But to turn to a more cheerful view of it, *in many persons this preventing grace leads to something higher.* After preventing grace has kept thee back from sin, in comes quickening grace and shows thee the hatefulness of sin, and after that comes pardoning grace, and gives thee power to believe in Jesus, and, lo! thy sins are put away. May God grant that this may be the case with some of you who have got no further yet than preventing grace. Be grateful for that, thank God with all your heart for it. May it lead you to repentance; may it lead you to put your trust in Jesus and in him only! Then you will pass from the mere prevention in which grace is a shackle, to the liberty in which grace becomes a shield and a sword, the joy and the sun of your life. May the long-suffering of God lead thee to repentance!

But once again, to turn to the solemn chord once more, where it does not lead to higher things, *preventing grace increases the responsibility of the man who receives it.* If a man will go over hedge and ditch to hell, he shall find it a hard fall when he gets to the edge. If, when we put poison out of the way and remove everything with which a man can destroy himself, he yet will tear open his own veins, he is a suicide indeed; who shall pity him? And when

God hedges you about, if you break the hedges—when he puts a bit into your mouth if you stand champing it until at last you get it from your jaws, and turn to your own way—this will not be done without bringing on your head at the last thunders of execration from the universe that shall judge you, and the full lightnings of wrath from the hand of God who shall condemn you. I fear there are some here who are sinning against light. You are not without warnings in this land, not without calls and wooing invitations; the time was when you might have gone into many of the churches in London and not have heard the Gospel so that you could understand it, but now in the corners of the streets and in the theatres you may hear it if you will; and God is my witness when I say there is one place where you can hear it preached with earnestness, and I rejoice to know there are thousands of others. Souls, if you perish, it is not for want of invitations to Christ. If you will not have Christ it is a wilful rejection; if you will be lost, blame not the minister, lay it not at our door, we are clear of your blood, we shake our skirts of the dust of your souls, we will not be responsible for you; we warn you, we cry aloud to you, and if you will not hear, but will go and turn to the downward road, on your own heads be your doom for ever and ever.

But instead of enlarging on these and other points, I will try, as God shall help me, to give you a little advice, in the hope that some who have come up, perhaps to a cattle show, or the Handel Festival, or the Great Exhibition, may get more than they came for; who could tell, some of you may have to say in time and eternity, "Blessed be the Lord God of Israel, which sent thee this day to meet me, and blessed be thy advice?"

Now, young man fresh from the country, you have a scheme in your head, and you are going to carry it out to-morrow. If my prayer for you is heard you will not do so. You have come up to London to have a merry time of it; you will have a merry time of another sort, I hope. Consider your ways. Bethink yourself. Why will you go wilfully, and with your eyes open, into that sin? It may be the last sin you will ever commit; it may be that you will die in the act. Great God! how prophetic these words may be! Am I pronouncing the doom of some soul here? Such things have happened, and it may be that they will happen again. Oh, I pray thee, friend, stay thy hand. Shall I fall down upon my knees and pray thee to stop, for an impulse is upon me to speak thus —do not, do not, it is for thy life. Back with thy hand, man, for fear of the viper's tooth; thou art playing on the hole of the asp, but his tongue is ready and his fang shall envenom all thy veins. By God, by Christ, by heaven, by hell, I adjure thee, thou who has intended some sin, cease from it! May this advice be blessed to thee! Hast thou not had enough already? What, man! hast thou killed thyself, and is not that enough? Art thou a lost man to-night, and is not that enough? Wouldest thou bury deep in sin even thy last hope? The leprosy is in thee now, wouldest thou make it stare in men's faces on thy very forehead? Oh, stay thee! stay thee! thou hast gone far enough, the wonder is that thou art spared seeing thou hast gone so far. What has all thine indulgence hitherto brought thee in? Is there real pleasure in sin? What has been thine experience up till now? Is it not a rough road, though it promised to be a joyous one? Have you not had already enough to bear as the result of your evil conduct? Why, therefore, continue to spend your money for that which is not bread, and your labour for that which satisfieth not? As the voice of one crying in the wilderness would I now seek to prepare the way of the Lord into thy heart. Cease thou from evil, man. Consider this thy sin and repent of it, for I hope that to thee the kingdom of heaven is at hand.

What if, instead of going into sin to-night, thou shouldest take my advice and seek the Saviour and find him. If God bless thee, thou shalt be saved; but if thou hast shut thine ear to God's pleading it shall not be my fault. Man! man! thou art lost and ruined by the fall, but there is One that is able to save, even to the uttermost, those that come to him. To come to Christ is to trust him. I have preached this Gospel for many years, and I do not think I ever finished a sermon except in one way—by trying to explain what is meant by this simple trust in the Lord Jesus Christ. Young man, you have the idea that you are to do twenty things; you have been trying to get ready for Christ; that is not the Gospel, that is the law. The Gospel is, trust Jesus Christ, trust Jesus Christ. He died upon the tree that he might bear the punishment of the sins of all who believe in him. So to believe in him is to trust him. Trust him, and then it is certain that your sins were laid on Christ, and that he suffered in your room and stead. Come to Jesus, come to Jesus, sinner, come just now. What if this should be the time when the Lord shall meet with thee; write it down, ye angels, in your golden tablets, record the birthday of a soul; take down your harps, ye bright ones, strike the chords with a new and heaven-born ardour. Cherubim and seraphim, lift up your voices to notes untried as yet while God himself breaketh forth into a song, rejoicing in singing over them that come unto him through Jesus Christ his Son. "Believe on the Lord Jesus Christ and thou shalt be saved." Believe now, you in this area and you in these galleries. Oh! that you would believe in Jesus now! Thank God if you have not gone to the great lengths some have gone, but remember you cannot be saved except through faith in Jesus. If you have gone to the greatest lengths thank God you are not gone too far yet, for he can still reach you. He has a long arm, and he can find you in the very depths of your iniquity. Trust him, sinner, trust him now, and there shall be joy in heaven over sinners that repent more than over ninety and nine just persons that need no repentance. May God add his own blessing for Jesus' sake. Amen.

Exposition by C. H. Spurgeon.
JONAH I.

Verses 1—3. *Now the word of the Lord came unto Jonah the son of Amittai, saying, Arise, go to Nineveh, that great city, and cry against it; for their wickedness is come up before me. But Jonah rose up to flee unto Tarshish from the presence of the Lord, and went down to Joppa; and he found a ship going to Tarshish: so he paid the fare thereof, and went down into it, to go with them unto Tarshish from the presence of the Lord.*

Observe the misconduct of the prophet Jonah. He had a plain command from the Lord, and he knew it to be a command; but he felt that the commission given to him would not be pleasant and honouring to himself, and therefore he declined to comply with it. We see, from his action, how some, who really know God, may act as if they knew him not. Jonah knew that God was everywhere, yet he "rose up to flee unto Tarshish from the presence of the Lord." What strange inconsistencies there often are even in good men! Here is one, who is favoured with a divine commission,—one who knows God, and fears him; yet, for all that, he ventures on the fool's errand of endeavouring to escape from the Omnipresent. He "went down to Joppa," which was the port of his country, "and he found a ship going to Tarshish." Learn from this that providence alone is not a sufficient guide for our actions. He may have said, "It was very singular that there was a ship there going to Tarshish, just when I reached the port. I gather from this that God was not so very disinclined for me to go to Tarshish." Precepts, not providences, are to guide believers; and when Christian men quote a providence against a precept,—which is to set God against God,—they act most strangely. There are devil's providences as well as divine providences, and there are tempting providences as well as assisting providences, so learn to judge between the one and the other.

4. *But the Lord sent out a great wind into the sea, and there was a mighty tempest in the sea, so that the ship was like to be broken.*

Learn, hence, that "Omnipotence has servants everywhere." The Lord is never short of sheriff's officers to arrest his fugitives, and on that occasion he "sent out a great wind into the sea." "The wind bloweth where it listeth." That is true; but it is also true that the wind bloweth where God listeth, and he knew how to send that great wind to that particular ship. No doubt many ships were on the Mediterranean at that time; but, possibly, unto none of them was the storm sent save unto the one which carried Jonah, the son of Amittai. We say, "Every bullet has its billet," and this great wind was sent to pursue the fugitive prophet.

5. *Then the mariners were afraid, and cried every man unto his god,—*

If there is ever a special time for prayer, it is a time of need. Nature seems then to compel men to utter prayer of such a sort as it is, for it is but nature's prayer at the best: "The mariners were afraid, and cried every man unto his god,"—

5. *And cast forth the wares that were in the ship into the sea, to lighten it of them.*

Life is precious, and a man will give up everything else in order to save it. Satan spoke the truth when he said, "Skin for skin, yea, all that a man hath, will he give for his life." From the action of these mariners, we may learn that sometimes we may lighten our ship for the safety of our souls. When we have less to carry, probably we shall sail more safely. Losses and crosses may turn out to be our greatest gains. Let the ill-gotten ingots go to the bottom of the sea; and lo, the ship rights herself at once!

5. *But Jonah was gone down into the sides of the ship; and he lay, and was fast asleep.*

The greatest sinner on that ship appeared to be the least concerned about the storm which had come because of him; he did not even seem to know that there was a storm, for he had "gone down into the sides of the ship; and he lay, and was fast asleep."

6. *So the shipmaster came to him, and said unto him, What meanest thou, O sleeper? arise, call upon thy God, if so be that God will think upon us, that we perish not.*

It is hard when sinners have to rebuke saints, and when an uncircumcised Gentile can address a prophet of God in language like this.

7. *And they said every one to his fellow, Come, and let us cast lots, that we may know for whose cause this evil is upon us. So they cast lots, and the lot fell upon Jonah.*

We commend not the action of these men in casting lots, but we admire the providence by which "the lot fell upon Jonah." Solomon says, "The lot is cast into the lap," but he did not say that it was right that lots should be cast into the lap; and he very properly added, "but the whole disposing thereof is of the Lord."

8. *Then they said unto him, Tell us, we pray thee, for whose cause this evil is upon us; What is thine occupation? and whence comest thou? what is thy country? and of what people art thou?*

I do not know whether these men had traded with those who then lived in these islands, but they had a very English custom of not judging a man before they had heard him speak. It would be well if we all practised it more,—so that, before we condemn men, we were willing to hear their side of the question. Considering that there was such a storm raging, the questions put to Jonah were remarkably calm. They were very comprehensive, and went to the very root of the matter.

9. *And he said unto them, I am an Hebrew:*

That let them know whence he came, and what his country was.

9. *And I fear the Lord, the God of heaven, which hath made the sea and the dry land.*

That, I suppose, must be regarded as his occupation; and what a blessed occupation it is,—to be occupied with the fear of the Lord! So, you see that, though Jonah was not properly following his occupation while he was on board that ship, yet he did not hesitate to avow, "I am a Hebrew; and I fear the Lord, the God of heaven, which hath made the sea and the dry land." The child of God, even when he gets where he ought not to be, if you test him and try him, will stand to his colours. He will confess that he is, after all, a servant of the living God.

10. *Then were the men exceedingly afraid, and said unto him, Why hast thou done this?*

Jonah had to go through this catechism, question after question, and this was the hardest of them all: "Why hast thou done this?" Could you, dear friend, submit every action of your life to this test? "Why hast thou done this?" I am afraid that there are some actions, which we have performed, for which we could not give a reason, or the reasons for which we should not like to give to our fellow-men, much less to our God.

10, 11. *For the men knew that he fled from the presence of the Lord, because he had told them. Then said they unto him, What shall we do unto thee, that the sea may be calm unto us?*

Here is another question; the catechism is not yet finished, and this is one of the most difficult of all.

11, 12. *For the sea wrought, and was tempestuous. And he said unto them, Take me up, and cast me forth into the sea; so shall the sea be calm unto you:*

Notwithstanding all his faults, Jonah was an eminent type of Christ. We know that from our Lord's own words, for he was as long in the belly of the whale as Christ was in the heart of the earth. Here he seems to be a type of our Saviour: "Take me up, and cast me forth into the sea: so shall the sea be calm unto you:"

12, 13. *For I know that for my sake this great tempest is upon you. Nevertheless the men rowed hard to bring it to the land;*

They showed a deal of good feeling in all their treatment of Jonah. They could not bear to take away a fellow-creature's life, so they pulled and tugged in order to get the ship to land.

13. *But they could not: for the sea wrought, and was tempestuous against them.*

Their safety lay in the sacrifice,—not in the labour. They rowed hard to bring the ship to land, but their efforts were of no avail. If they would cast Jonah overboard, then they would be safe.

14, 15. *Wherefore they cried unto the LORD, and said, We beseech thee, O LORD, we beseech thee, let us not perish for this man's life, and lay not upon us innocent blood: for thou, O LORD, hast done as it pleased thee. So they took up Jonah,—*

Put the emphasis on the first word, "*So* they took up Jonah"; that is, with great reluctance, with much pity and sorrow, not daring to do such a deed as that wantonly and with a light heart. When men do deeds like this, on a far greater scale, and go to war with a light heart, they will have a heavy heart before long. If ever you have to cast a brother out of the Church,—if ever you have to relinquish the friendship of any man,—do it as these men did with Jonah, patiently, and carefully. Investigate the matter, and do not act until you are driven to it after consulting the Lord.

15, 16. *And cast him forth into the sea: and the sea ceased from her raging. Then the men feared the LORD exceedingly, and offered a sacrifice unto the LORD, and made vows.*

Jonah had been the means of causing a greater change than he expected. His conduct and punishment had been a warning to those thoughtless sailors. They could not but believe in the God who had thus followed up his fugitive servant.

17. *Now the LORD had prepared a great fish to swallow up Jonah.*

He prepared a storm, he prepared a fish, and we afterwards read that he prepared a gourd, and he prepared a worm. In the great things of life, and in the little things, God is ever present. The swimming of a great fish in the sea is, surely, not a thing that is subject to law. If ever there is free agency in this world, it must certainly be in the wanderings of such a huge creature that follows its own instincts, and ploughs its way through the great wastes of the wide and open sea. Yes, that is true; yet there is a divine predestination concerning all its movements. Over every motion of the fin of every minnow predestination presides. There is no distinction of little or great in God's sight; he that wings an angel guides a sparrow. "The Lord had prepared a great fish to swallow up Jonah."

17. *And Jonah was in the belly of the fish three days and three nights.*

So round about the truant prophet was the preventing grace of Jehovah.

JUDE'S DOXOLOGY.

A Sermon

DELIVERED BY

C. H. SPURGEON,

AT THE METROPOLITAN TABERNACLE, NEWINGTON,

On Lord's-day Evening, November 7th, 1875.

"Now unto him that is able to keep you from falling, and to present you faultless before the presence of his glory with exceeding joy, to the only wise God our Saviour, be glory and majesty, dominion and power, both now and ever. Amen."—Jude 24, 25.

PAUL'S writings abound in doxologies. You will find them in different forms scattered throughout all his Epistles. But he is not the only apostle who thus pauses to magnify the name of God. Here is "Judas, not Iscariot," but the true-hearted Jude, who has been writing an Epistle which seems all ablaze with lightning, it burns so terribly against certain orders of sinners. Almost every word that Jude writes seems to have the roll of thunder in it; he appears to be more like the Haggai of the Old Testament than the Jude of the New. Yet he cannot close his short Epistle until he has included some ascription of praise to God.

Learn from this, dear friends, that the sin of man, if we are ever called to denounce it, should drive us to adore the goodness and glory of God. Sin defiles the world; so, after you have done your best to sweep it out, resolve that, inasmuch as man has dishonoured the name of God, you will seek to magnify that name. It is true that you cannot actually redress the wrong that has been done; but, at any rate, if the stream of sin has been increased, you may increase the stream of loyal and reverent praise. Take care that you do so. Jude is not satisfied with having rebuked the sons of men for their sin, so he turns round to glorify his God.

Observe that these doxologies, wherever we meet with them, are not all exactly the same. They are presented to the same God, and offered in the same spirit; but there are reasons given for the doxology in the one case which are not given in the other. Our morning text told us of what God is able to do, and so does this. They both begin with praising God's ability; but while Paul spoke about the greatness of that ability in what it could do for us, Jude speaks of the greatness of that ability in preserving us from falling, and perfecting us so that we may be presented faultless before the presence of the glory of God. Let us, in an adoring frame of mind, think over this sublime subject.

I. First, LET US ADORE HIM WHO CAN KEEP US FROM FALLING.

I address myself, of course, now, only to God's own people. When shall we ever see a congregation in which it will be needless to make such a remark as that? I cannot call upon some of you to adore God for keeping you from falling; for, alas! you have not yet learned to stand upright. God's grace has never yet been accepted by you. You are not on the Rock of ages; you have not yet set out upon the heavenly pilgrimage. It is a wretched state for you to be in, in which you cannot worship him whom angels worship. It is a sad state of heart for any man to be in, to be excluded—self-excluded—from the general acclamations of joy in the presence of God, because you feel no such joy, and cannot, therefore, unite in such acclamations.

But, to the people of God, I have to say this. Dear brothers and sisters, *we need keeping;* therefore, let us adore him who can keep us. As saved souls, we need keeping from final apostasy. "Oh!" saith one, "I thought you taught us that those who are once saved shall never finally apostatize." I do believe that doctrine, and delight to preach it; yet it is true that the saved ones would apostatize, every one of them, if the Lord did not keep them. There is no stability in any Christian, in himself considered; it is the grace of God within him that enables him to stand. I believe that the soul of man is immortal, yet not in and of itself, but only by the immortality which God bestows upon it from his own essential immortality. So is it with the new life that is within us. It shall never perish; but it is only eternal because God continues to keep it alive. Your final perseverance is not the result of anything in yourself, but the result of the grace which God continues to give you, and of his eternal purpose which first chose you and of his almighty power which still keeps you alive. Ah, my brethren, the brightest saints on earth would fall into the lowest hell if God did not keep them from falling. Therefore, praise him, O ye stars that shine in the Church's sky, for ye would go out with a noxious smell, as lamps do for want of oil, did not the Lord keep your heavenly flame burning. Glory be unto the Preserver of his Church who keeps his loved ones even to the end!

But there are other ways of falling beside falling finally and fatally. Alas, brethren! we are all liable to fall into errors of doctrine. The best-taught man, apart from divine guidance, is not incapable of becoming the greatest fool possible. There is a strange weakness which sometimes comes over noble spirits, and which makes them infatuated with an erroneous novelty, though they fancy they have discovered some great truth. Men of enquiring and receptive minds are often decoyed from the old paths,—the good old ways; and while they think they are pursuing truth, they are being led into damnable error. He only is kept, as to his thoughts and doctrinal views, whom God keeps, for there are errors that would, if it were possible, deceive even the very elect; and there are men and women going about in this world, with smooth tongues and plausible arguments, who carry honeyed words upon their lips, though drawn swords are concealed behind their backs. Blessed are they who are preserved from these wolves in sheep's clothing. Lord, thou alone canst preserve us from the pernicious errors of the times, for thou art "the only wise God our Saviour."

And, dear friends, we need keeping from an evil spirit. I do not know which I should prefer,—to see one of my dear Christian brethren fall into doctrinal error, or into an un-Christian spirit. I would prefer neither, for I think this is a safe rule,—of two evils, choose neither. It is sad to hear some people talk as if they alone are right, and all other Christians are wrong. If there is anything which is the very essence and soul of Christianity, it is brotherly love; but brotherly love seems to be altogether forgotten by these people; and other Christians, who, in the judgment of sobriety, are as earnest, and as true-hearted, and as useful as themselves, are set down as belonging to a kind of Babylonian system;—I hardly know what they do not call it, but they give it all sorts of bad names, and this is thought to be a high style of Christianity. God grant that the man may be forgiven who thought it to be a worthy purpose of his life to found a sect whose distinguishing characteristic should be that it would have no communion with any other Christians! The mischief that man has done is utterly incalculable, and I can only pray that, in the providence of God, some part of it may die with him.

O brethren and sisters, I charge you, whatever mistakes you make, not to make a mistake about this one thing,—that, even if you have all knowledge, and have not charity, it profiteth you nothing; even if you could get a perfect creed, and knew that your mode of worship was absolutely apostolic, yet, if you also imbibed the idea that you could not worship with any other Christians, and that they were altogether outside your camp, your error would be far worse than all other errors put together, for to be wrong in heart is even worse than to be wrong in head. I would have you true to God's truth; but, above all, I would have you true to God's love. My brother, I think you are mistaken about this matter or that; but do you love the Lord Jesus Christ? If so, I love you. I have no doubt that I also am mistaken about some things; but do not therefore withdraw your hand, and say that you cannot have fellowship with me. I have fellowship with my Father who is in heaven, and with his Son, Jesus Christ, and with his blessed Spirit; and methinks that it ill becomes you, if you call yourself a son of that same God, to refuse to have fellowship with me when I have fellowship with him. God save you from this evil spirit; but you may readily enough fall into it unless the Lord shall keep you. Your very zeal for truth may drive you into a forgetfulness of Christian love; and if it does, it will be a sad pity. O Lord, keep us from falling in this way!

But there are falls of another sort which may happen to the brightest Christian; I mean, falls into outward sin. As you read Jude's Epistle through, you will see what apostates some professors became, and you will be led to cry, "Lord, keep me from falling!" And if you were the pastor of a large church like mine, you would see enough to convince you that traitors like Judas are not all dead,—that, amidst the faithful, the unfaithful are still found,—that there are bad fish to be thrown away, as well as good fish to be kept; and every time we execute an act of discipline,—every time we have to bemoan the fall of one who looked like a brother,—we may thank God that we have been kept, and may sing this doxology, "Unto him that is able to keep us from falling, be glory and power for ever."

And, dear friends, there is a way of falling, out of which people are not so often recovered as when they fall into overt sin; I mean, falling into negligence as to natural or Christian duties. I have known professors who have been very lax at home,—children who were not obedient to their parents,—husbands who did not love their wives as they ought,—wives who were quite at home at this meeting and that, but very negligent of their domestic duties. And, mark you, where that is the case, it is a thing to mourn over, for the Christian ought to be absolutely reliable in everything he has to do. I would not give twopence for your religion if you are a tradesman, but not fair in your dealings. I do not care if you can sing like David, or preach like Paul, if you cannot measure a yard of material with the proper number of inches, or if your scales do not weigh rightly, or your general mode of business is not straight and true, you had better make no profession of religion. The separation of what is called "religious" from the "secular" is one of the greatest possible mistakes. There is no such thing as a religion of Sundays, and of chapels and churches; at least, though there *is* such a thing, it is not worth having. The religion of Christ is a religion for seven days in the week,—a religion for every place and for every act; and it teaches men, whether they eat, or drink, or whatever they do, to do all in the name of the Lord Jesus Christ, and to the glory of God. I pray that you may be kept from falling away from that religion, and that you may be kept up to the mark in serving the Lord in all things, and attending diligently to the little commonplace matters of daily life.

And you know, dear friends, there is another sort of falling; that is, when the heart gets gradually cold,—when the Christian wanders away little by little,—when the life becomes more or less inconsistent with the profession. Oh, how many professors get into this state! They are like people who are not as well as they used to be. They do not know when they began to feel worse; it was months ago, and every day they have got weaker, till now you can see their bones, though once they were full of flesh. Now they discover that, whereas once they could have walked ten miles without fatigue, half a mile or less wearies them. Their appetite, too, has gradually gone; they scarcely know how. Ah, these are the sick folk with whom the physician has more trouble than he has with those who are suddenly seized by some well-known disease; and that gradual decline of spiritual health, which does not come all at once, but little by little, is one of the most perilous of evils;

and we have need continually to cry, "Lord, keep us from this;" and to praise his name that he is able so to keep us.

Thus I have shown you that we need keeping; and, brethren, *none but the Lord can keep us.* No man can keep himself; without God's grace, he will surely fail. And no place can keep us. Some people think that, if they could get into such-and-such a family, they could keep from sin, but they are mistaken. In every position which a man occupies, he will find temptation. We have heard of the hermit, who hoped to get rid of all sin by living in a cave. He took with him his little brown loaf and his jug of water, but he had hardly entered the cave before he upset his jug, and spilt the water. It was a long way to the well, and he got so angry with himself for what he had done, that he soon discovered that the devil could get into a cave as quickly as he could, so he thought he might as well go back, and face the trials of ordinary society. There is a story which they tell in Scotland of a family who were thriftless, and therefore did not succeed; but they thought it was one of the "brownies" that kept them from getting on; so they decided to "flit." They put all their things into the cart; but just as they were about to start, they heard a noise that made them cry out, "The brownie is in the churn;" so, wherever the churn went, the brownie would go too. And you may remove wherever you like, and think, "If I get into such a position, I shall escape from temptation;" but you will find that "the brownie is in the churn" still, and he will follow you wherever you may go. You cannot be kept from falling by choosing another situation. You had better stop where you are, brother, and fight the devil there, for perhaps the next place that you select as the scene of combat may not be as suitable as the one you have now.

"Ah!" says one, "I wish I could get to—

> "'A lodge in some vast wilderness,
> Some boundless contiguity of shade;
> Where rumour of oppression and deceit,
> Of unsuccessful or successful war,
> Might never reach me more.'"

Yes, yes; but that is not the way to conquer sin, is it? Suppose the battle of Waterloo is just beginning, and here is a soldier who wants to win a victory; so he runs away,—gets off to Brussels, and hides himself in a cellar! Is he likely to be numbered among the heroes of the day? No, brethren; and if there is any sin to be overcome in this world, there is no credit to the man who says, "I am going to hide somewhere out of the world." No, no, my brother; accept the lot that God has provided for you; take your place in the ranks of his soldiers; and whatever temptation comes, look up to him who is able to keep you from falling, but do not dream of running away, for that is the way to fall, that is being defeated before the battle begins. Nobody but God can keep you. You may join whatever church you like; you may wear a hat with a broad brim, and say "thou" and "thee"; you may meet with those who break bread, and preach nothing but the gospel of the grace of

God; you may dwell amongst the best people who ever lived; but you will still be tempted. Neither place nor people, neither manners nor customs can keep you from falling; God alone can do it.

But here is the mercy, *God can do it*. Notice how Jude's doxology puts it: "To the only wise God our Saviour." It is because he alone is wise that he alone is able to keep us from falling. He does it by teaching us the truth, by warning us against secret sin, and by his providential leading. Sometimes, he keeps temptation from us; at other times, he allows a temptation to come to us that, by overcoming it, we may be the stronger to meet another one. Oftentimes, he delivers us from temptation by letting affliction come upon us. Many a man has been kept from falling into sin by being stretched upon a bed of sickness. Had it not been for the loss of that eye, he would have looked upon vanity. Had it not been for that broken bone, he would have run in the ways of ungodliness. We little know how much preservation from falling we owe to our losses and crosses. The story of Sir James Thornhill painting the inside of the cupola of St. Paul's is probably well known to you. When he had finished one of the compartments, he was stepping backward that he might get a full view of it, and so went almost to the edge of the scaffolding, and would have fallen over if he had taken another step; but a friend, who saw his danger, wisely seized one of his brushes, and rubbed some paint over his picture. The artist, in his rage, rushed forward to save his painting, and so saved his own life. We have all pictured life; what a fairy picture we made of it; and as we admired it, we walked further and yet further away from God and safety, and got nearer and yet nearer to perilous temptation, when trial came, and ruined the picture we had painted; and then, though scarcely knowing why, we came forward and were saved. God had kept us from falling, by the trouble he had sent to us.

God has often kept us from falling by a bitter sense of our past sin. We have not dared to go near the fire again, for our former burns have scarcely healed. I have also noticed, in my own case, that when the desire for sin has come with force, the opportunity for sin has not been present; and when the opportunity of evil has been present, then the desire has been absent. It is wonderful how God prevents these two things from meeting, and so keeps his people from falling.

Above all, it is by the Divine Spirit that God bears us up as upon eagle's wings. The Spirit teaches us to hate sin, and to love righteousness, and so we are daily kept from falling.

Brethren, join with me in adoring the Lord that *he will keep us to the end.* Have we committed our souls into the hands of Jesus? Then, our souls are safe for ever. Are we trusting to him to keep us till the day of his appearing? If so, he will keep us; not one sheep or lamb out of his flock shall by any possibility be destroyed by the wolf, or the bear, or the roaring lion of hell. They shall all be his in the day when they pass again under the hands of him that telleth them.

II. Now, secondly, LET US ADORE HIM BECAUSE HE WILL, AT THE LAST, PRESENT US "FAULTLESS BEFORE THE PRESENCE OF HIS GLORY WITH EXCEEDING JOY."

There will come a day, brethren, when we must either be presented in the courts of God as his courtiers, or else be driven from his judgment-seat as rebels against his authority. We look forward with the confident expectation that we shall be presented as the friends of Christ unto God even the Father; and that is, indeed, a cause for adoring gratitude

Do you notice how Jude puts it? "To present you faultless." *There shall be none in heaven but those who are faultless.* There shall by no means enter into those holy courts anything that defileth. Heaven is perfectly pure; and if you and I are ever to get there, we must be pure as the driven snow. No taint of sin must be upon us, or else we cannot stand among the courtiers of God. His flaming throne would shoot forth columns of devouring fire upon any guilty soul that dared to stand in the courts of the Most High, if such a standing were possible. But we are impure,—impure as to our acts; and, worst of all, impure as to our very nature; how then can we hope ever to stand there? Yet, dear brethren and sisters, our confidence is that we shall. Why?

Is it not because *Christ is able to present us faultless there?* Come, Christian, think for a minute how faultless Christ has made you so far as your past sin is concerned. The moment you believed in him, you were so completely washed in his precious blood that not a spot of sin remained upon you. Try to realize that, whatever your past life has been, if you now believe in Jesus Christ, you are cleansed from all iniquity by virtue of his atoning sacrifice, and you are covered by a spotless robe of righteousness by virtue of his blessed life of perfect purity and obedience to his Father's will. You are now without fault so far as your past sin is concerned, for he has cast it all into the depths of the sea; but you feel that you are not without fault as to your nature.

"Oh!" say you, "I feel everything that is evil rising at times within me." But all that evil is under sentence of death. Christ nailed it to his cross. Crucifixion is a lingering and very painful death, and the culprit struggles ere he breathes his last; but your sins have had their death-blow. When Christ was nailed to the cross, your sins were nailed there too, and they shall never come down again. Die they must, even as he died. It will be a blessed hour when sin shall at last give up the ghost,—when there shall be not even the tendency to sin within our nature. Then shall we be presented faultless before the throne of God.

"Can that ever be?" asks one. Well may you ask that question, brother. Can it ever be that we shall not be tempted by one foul lust, nor be disturbed by one unbridled passion, nor feel the emotions of envy or of pride again? Yes, it shall surely be. Christ has secured this blessing to you. His name is Jesus, Saviour, "for he shall save his people from their sins." He must and will do this for all who trust him. Rejoice that he will do this, for no one but God can do it. It must be "the only wise God our Saviour" who can accomplish this; but accomplish it he will. Does your faith enable you to picture yourself as standing before the throne of God faultless? Well then, give to the Lord the glory which is due unto him for such a wondrous act of grace as that.

This is how you are to be presented by Christ in glory. There is a great stir in a family when a daughter is to be presented at court, and a great deal is thought of it; but, one day, you and I, who have believed in Jesus, shall be presented to the Father. What radiant beauty shall we then wear when God himself shall look upon us, and declare us to be without fault;—when there shall be no cause for sorrow remaining, and therefore we shall be presented with exceeding joy! It shall be so, my brother; it shall be so, my sister; therefore do not doubt it. How soon it shall be, we cannot tell; possibly, to-morrow. Perhaps, ere the sun rises again, you and I may be presented by Christ "before the presence of his glory with exceeding joy." We cannot tell when it will be, but we shall be there in his good time. We shall be perfect; we shall be "accepted in the Beloved;" and, therefore, "unto him be glory and majesty, dominion and power, both now and ever. Amen."

III. That is the note with which I have to close my discourse. LET US, BECAUSE OF THESE TWO GREAT BLESSINGS OF FINAL PRESERVATION AND PRESENTATION BEFORE HIS GLORY, OFFER UNTO THE LORD OUR HIGHEST ASCRIPTIONS OF PRAISE.

Jude says, "Both now and ever." Well, we will attend to the "ever" as eternity rolls on; but let us attend to the praise of God "now"—at this moment: "To the only wise God our Saviour be glory and majesty, dominion and power *now*." Come, brethren and sisters, think of what you owe to him who has kept you to this day, and will not let you go. Think of where you might have been; and think, I may say, of where you used to be, in your unregenerate state. Yet you are not there now; but here you are, without self-righteousness, made to differ from your fellow-men, entirely through the grace of God. You have been kept, perhaps twenty years; thirty years, forty years,—possibly, fifty years. Well, unto him be the glory; give him the glory even now.

How can you do it? Well, feel it in your hearts; speak of it to your neighbours; talk of it to your children. Tell everybody you meet what a good and blessed and faithful God he is, and so give him glory now. And be happy and cheerful; you cannot glorify God better than by a calm, quiet, happy life. Let the world know that you serve a good Master. If you are in trouble, do not let anyone see that the trouble touches your spirit;—nay, more, do not let it trouble your spirit. Rest in God; take evil as well as good from his hand, and keep on praising him. You do not know how much good you may do, and how greatly you may glorify God, if you praise him in your dark times. Worldlings do not care much about our psalm-singing unless they see us in pain and sorrow, and observe that we praise God then. I like, and the world likes, a religion that will wash,—a religion that will stand many showers, and much rough usage. Some Christians' joy disappears in the wear and tear of life; it cannot endure the world's rough handling.

Let it not be so with us, beloved; but let us praise, and bless, and magnify the name of the Lord as long as we have any being.

I know that, in speaking thus, I am only addressing a part of my congregation. I wish that every man and woman here were now praising the Lord, and I am sure that you could not have a better occupation to all eternity. Remember that, if you do not praise God, it is impossible for you ever to enter heaven, for that is the chief occupation of heaven; and remember also that praise from your lips, until those lips are divinely cleansed, would be like a jewel in a swine's snout, a thing altogether out of place. For you, dear unsaved hearer, the first thing is not praise, but prayer,—nay, not even prayer first, but faith. "Believe on the Lord Jesus Christ, and thou shalt be saved;" and then, in faith, pray the prayer which God accepts. But thou must first believe in Jesus. "And what does believing in Jesus mean?" thou askest. It means this: thy sin deserves punishment, for God, who is just, must punish sin. But his Son came into the world to suffer in the stead of those who trust him; and now, God can be just, and yet the Justifier of every soul that believes in Jesus. In the person of his Son, God hangs upon a tree, and dies a felon's death; wilt thou believe in the merit of that death, and in the love of God, who spared not his own Son in order that he might spare us? Canst thou trust Jesus as thy God and Saviour? Wilt thou do it now? Then thou art saved. The first moment of thus trusting God is the beginning of a new life,—a life which will drive out the old death of sin. The moment that thou dost thus trust thy God, thou wilt be placed upon a new footing with regard to him, thy whole aspect towards God will be changed. Repentance will take such possession of thy spirit that thou wilt be actuated by new motives, and swayed by new desires; in fact, thou wilt be a new man in Christ Jesus. This is being saved,—saved from the love of sin, saved from returning to sin, saved from falling, and so completely saved that Christ shall one day present thee "faultless before the presence of his glory with exceeding joy." May God do this for every one of you, my hearers, according to the riches of his grace! It is my heart's last, best, and strongest desire that every one of you may be saved. May we all meet in heaven, before the throne of God, never more to be parted! While I am away, listen with all earnestness to other heralds of the cross, and pray the Lord to bless their messages to your salvation, if mine have not been so blest. I pray that, by some instrumentality, you may all be saved in the Lord with an everlasting salvation. Amen.

Exposition by C. H. Spurgeon.

THE GENERAL EPISTLE OF JUDE.

Verse 1. *Jude.*

That is to say Judas, not Iscariot,—

1. *The servant of Jesus Christ, and brother of James,—*

He does not say, "and brother of our Lord," for we know that James and Judas were both of them among the Lord's kinsmen according to the flesh; but now, after the flesh, knoweth he even Christ no more, but is content and happy to be known as "the servant of Jesus Christ, and brother of James,"—

1. *To them that are sanctified by God the Father,*

For the decree of election, the setting apart of the chosen is usually ascribed unto God the Father.

1. *And preserved in Jesus Christ, and called:*

We have here a very blessed description of the whole work of our salvation,—set apart by the Father, joined unto Christ, and preserved in him, and then, in due time, called out by the Spirit of God.

2. *Mercy unto you, and peace, and love, be multiplied.*

Christian letters should be full of love and good will. The Christian dispensation breathes beneficence; it is full of benediction: "Mercy unto you, and peace, and love, be multiplied." May the Divine Trinity give you a trinity of blessings!

3. *Beloved, when I gave all diligence to write unto you of the common salvation, it was needful for me to write unto you, and exhort you that ye should earnestly contend for the faith which was once delivered unto the saints.*

In the sense of being once for all given to the saints, the faith of Christians is not a variable quantity. It is not a thing which changes from day to day, as some seem to suppose, vainly imagining that fresh light is bestowed upon each new generation. No, the truth was delivered once for all, it was stereotyped, fixed; and it is for us to hold it fast as God has given it to us.

4. *For there are certain men crept in unawares,—*

They did not boldly avow their heresy when they came in;—they would not have been allowed to enter if they had done so;—but they sneaked in, they climbed into the pulpit, professing to be preachers of the gospel, when they knew, all the while, that they intended to undermine it. Basest of all men are those who act thus: "There are certain men crept in unawares,"—

4. *Who were before of old ordained to this condemnation,*

Proscribed by God as traitors long ago. Those who have not the courage of their convictions probably have no convictions at all, but seek to undermine the faith which they profess to hold.

4. *Ungodly men, turning the grace of our God into lasciviousness, and denying the only Lord God, and our Lord Jesus Christ.*

Antinomians, "turning the grace of our God into lasciviousness," falsely declaring that the law has no binding force upon the Christian's life, and saying that we may do evil that good may come;—and Socinians, "denying the only Lord God, and our Lord Jesus Christ."

5. *I will therefore put you in remembrance, though ye once knew this, how that the Lord, having saved the people out of the land of Egypt, afterward destroyed them that believed not.*

If we have no real faith, we may appear to go a long way towards heaven, but we shall not enter the heavenly Canaan.

6. *And the angels which kept not their first estate, but left their own habitation, he hath reserved in everlasting chains under darkness unto the judgment of the great day.*

See, then, the need of stability, the need of abiding in the faith, and abiding in the practice of it, lest we should turn out to be like the Israelites, who, though they came out of Egypt, left their carcases in the wilderness, or like the angels, who, though they once stood in God's presence in glory, have fallen to the deeps of the abyss because of their apostasy.

7, 8. *Even as Sodom and Gomorrha, and the cities about them in like manner, giving themselves over to fornication, and going after strange flesh, are set forth for an example, suffering the vengeance of eternal fire. Likewise also these filthy dreamers defile the flesh, despise dominion, and speak evil of dignities.*

They cast off all restraint; they claim to have liberty to do whatever they like; and when reproved, they utter railing words against those who honestly rebuke them.

9. *Yet Michael the archangel, when contending with the devil he disputed about the body of Moses, durst not bring against him a railing accusation, but said, The Lord rebuke thee.*

To what does this refer? I am sure I do not know. I cannot think it refers to anything recorded in the Old Testament, but to some fact, known to Jude, who here speaks by revelation, and records it. We believe it, and learn from it that, when an archangel disputes with the devil, he does not use hard words even against him, for hard words are an evidence of the weakness of the cause which they are used to support. Hard arguments softly put, are the really effective weapons, but it takes some of us a long time to learn this; and generally, in our younger days, we wear away our own strength by the violence with which we use it.

10. *But these speak evil of those things which they know not: but what they know naturally, as brute beasts, in those things they corrupt themselves.*

It is a horrible thing when a man's sin goes the full length of his knowledge, and he sins up to the degree of his possibilities.

11, 12. *Woe unto them! for they have gone in the way of Cain, and ran greedily after the error of Balaam for reward, and perished in the gainsaying of Core. These are spots—*

"These are spoilers," so it may be rendered.

12. *In your feasts of charity,*

They spoil your love feasts at the communion table, they mar your fellowship when you gather together for worship.

12. *When they feast with you, feeding themselves without fear.*

Some of the best Christians, who come to the Lord's table, come there in great fear and trembling; and I have known some, who have had an undoubted right to be there, half afraid to come. Yet those very persons, who have a holy fear lest they should come amiss, are those who really ought to come. "Feeding themselves without fear" is the mark of those who are further off from God.

12. *Clouds they are without water, carried about of winds.*

They believe according to what is said to them by the last man who speaks to them; they are easily persuaded to this doctrine, and to that, and the other.

12. *Trees whose fruit withereth, without fruit,*

They seem to be bearing fruit, but it drops off before it ripens.

12, 13. *Twice dead, plucked up by the roots; raging waves of the sea,—*

They have nothing to say for Christ, yet they must say something, so they are "raging waves of the sea,"—

13. *Foaming out their own shame; wandering stars, to whom is reserved the blackness of darkness for ever.*

These are the false professors of religion, the members of the church for whom there are seats reserved in hell. This is a dreadful thought: "to whom is reserved the blackness of darkness for ever;"—not for the heathen, not for the open refusers of the gospel, but for such as creep into the churches unawares, teach false doctrine, live unholy lives.

14, 15. *And Enoch also, the seventh from Adam, prophesied of these, saying, Behold, the Lord cometh with ten thousands of his saints, to execute judgment upon all, and to convince all that are ungodly among them of all their ungodly deeds which they have ungodly committed, and of all their hard speeches which ungodly sinners have spoken against him.*

How Jude knew that Enoch said that, I cannot tell; it is another instance of inspiration.

16. *These are murmurers, complainers,*

You know the sort of people alluded to here; nothing ever satisfies them. They are discontented even with the gospel. The bread of heaven must be cut into dice pieces, and served on dainty napkins, or else they cannot eat it; and very soon their soul loatheth even this light bread. There is no way by which a Christian man can serve God so as to please them. They will pick holes in every preacher's coat; and if the great High Priest himself were here, they would find fault with the colour of the stones of his breastplate.

16—19. *Walking after their own lusts; and their mouth speaketh great swelling words, having men's persons in admiration because of advantage. But, beloved, remember ye the words which were spoken before of the apostles of our Lord Jesus Christ; how that they told you there should be mockers in the last time, who should walk after their own ungodly lusts. These be they who separate themselves, sensual, having not the Spirit.*

People who must, if they make a profession of religion at all, be continually breaking up churches, and holding themselves aloof from others, having no fellowship with anybody but those who can say "shibboleth" as plainly as they can, and sound the h pretty loudly.

20—22. *But ye beloved, building up yourselves on your most holy faith, praying in the Holy Ghost, keep yourselves in the love of God, looking for the mercy of our Lord Jesus Christ unto eternal life. And of some have compassion, making a difference:*

Some of those professors, who are not living consistently with their profession, in whom you can see signs and tokens of sin, yet there may be some trace of repentance, some reason to hope that they will forsake the evil when they see it to be evil: "have compassion" upon them.

23. *And others save with fear, pulling them out of the fire; hating even the garment spotted by the flesh.*

When you have to deal with unclean professors, there must be an abhorrence and detestation of their sin even when there is great gentleness towards the sinner. We must never be such believers in the repentance of the guilty as to be willing to wink at sin; for sin is a great evil in any case, and repentance cannot wipe it away; and though it behoves us to be tender to the sinner, we must never be tender to the sin.

How beautifully this short and sad Epistle ends! Having described the many who, after making a profession, yet turn aside, Jude bursts out with this jubilant doxology:—

24, 25. *Now unto him that is able to keep you from falling, and to present you faultless before the presence of his glory with exceeding joy, to the only wise God our Saviour, be glory and majesty, dominion and power, both now and ever. Amen.*

PROMISES

All the Promises—II Cor. 1:20
Exposition of II Corinthians 1; 2:1
The Wide-Open Mouth Filled—Ps. 81:10
A Promise for the Blind—Jer. 31:8
Exposition of Matthew 9:27-35; 20:29-34
Spiritual Convalescence—Zech. 10:12

ALL THE PROMISES.

A Sermon

DELIVERED BY

C. H. SPURGEON,

AT THE METROPOLITAN TABERNACLE, NEWINGTON,

On Thursday Evening, August 31st, 1882.

"For all the promises of God in him are yea, and in him Amen, unto the glory of God by us."—2 Cor. i. 20.

As the result of a very simple incident, a sublime truth may be proclaimed. It was so in the instance referred to in this chapter. These Corinthians had misrepresented the apostle Paul, and spoken ill of him. He might have ignored their unkindness, and said nothing about it; but, under the guidance of the Holy Spirit, he was led to act otherwise; and, while defending his own character for consistency, to vindicate also the consistency and truthfulness of God. We might never have had this precious verse if Paul had not been so ill-treated by these men of Corinth. They did him great wrong, and caused him much sorrow of heart, for a man who was so sincere and upright could not but be sorely vexed by their unjust suspicions and misrepresentations; yet you see how the evil was overruled by God for good, and through their unsavoury gossip and slander this sweet sentence was pressed out of Paul: "For all the promises of God in Christ are yea, and in Christ Amen, unto the glory of God by us." There are many things which, at first, we may regret, but for which we are afterwards exceedingly grateful. I have felt half inclined to thank the Pharisees and scribes for some of their cruel attacks upon our blessed Lord himself, for, in answering them, he has given us lessons which we now highly prize. Perhaps we might never have had those three wonderful parables of the lost sheep, the lost silver, and the lost son, if those cavillers had not spoken evil of him because all the publicans and sinners drew near unto him to hear him.

The fact was, that Paul had intended to visit the Christians at Corinth again, but he felt compelled to alter his decision, and he did not go to them, because he could only have gone in order to chastise or rebuke them, they had behaved so ill. In their folly, and in their coolness towards the apostle, they misconstrued his action, and they said, "We cannot rely upon his word, and we do not know what he will do; he promised that he would come to us, but he has changed his mind." The apostle declares here that he did not use lightness, or fickleness, either in giving his conditional promise, or in retracting it. He was not accustomed to speak without thinking what he was going to say. He was prompted by a worthy motive when he made the proposition to go to them, and an equally good motive swayed him when he resolved not to go. He tells them that his mind was not of the "yea and nay" order; but when he said "yea," he meant it, his yea was yea, and if he said "nay," he meant it, and his nay was nay.

This remark led the apostle further to say that the gospel which he preached was not of the "yea and nay" kind. It was something certain, settled, positive, fixed; it was not a variable gospel, nor a deceptive gospel. It was not a chameleon gospel, which changed its colour according to the light which fell upon it, but it was a clear and distinct gospel, given in all sincerity by the truthful and truth-loving Saviour who never used words in a double sense, but who said what he meant, and meant what he said. It was by this process of reasoning that the apostle was led up to the statement contained in our text concerning Christ: "All the promises of God in him are yea, and in him Amen, unto the glory of God by us." That is now to be the theme of our meditation.

I. The first thing I notice in the text is, THE DIGNITY OF THE PROMISES. Notice the apostle's words: "For all the promises *of God* in him are yea."

These promises were all made *according to the purpose of his own will.* We sometimes read, or hear, or speak of the promises written in God's Word, but do not give them as much credit as if they were the promises of a friend, or of our father, or our brother. If we valued them more, we should believe them better. We have many proverbs to remind us what poor and frail things the promises of men are; but those of which Paul writes are "the promises of God." Men often change their minds; even the apostle did that, and therefore he was wise to try to take the thoughts of those, to whom he was writing, off from the promises even of an apostle, which were liable to change, and which might very properly not be carried out because of altered circumstances, and lead them away to the promises of God, which are unfailing and unchangeable, and are always fulfilled to his glory and to our profit. We little know what solemn things we are trifling with when we say that we cannot believe a certain promise. What! Has it come to this,—that God's own children cannot believe him? Is it so, that we, who say that "we love him because he first loved us," yet add to that declaration, "but there are some of his promises which we cannot believe"? I am afraid that we talk far too flippantly about our unbelief, and that we seek to shelter one another in it, instead of whipping ourselves out of it. To be unbelieving may be painful; but there is a more serious consideration than that, for it is sinful; it is heinous to the last degree when we feel—much more when we express—any incredulity with regard to "the promises of

God." Just turn that thought over in your minds for a minute or two, and see whether it does not crimson your face with shame to think that you should have had any suspicion about the fulfilment of promises made by "God, that cannot lie."

Even in the case of a man, a promise is something which comes from him, and yet, in a sense, which still remains with him. He cannot speak of promise, and let it blow away with the wind. It is his promise after he has uttered it; and those to whom it was given can bring it back to him, and say, "That is your promise, will you not fulfil it?" If a man repudiates his own pledged word, he does, in fact, repudiate the fruit of himself, the outgoing of his own life; and every promise of God partakes of his nature, there is in it something divine, something which comes distinctly from God, and which he will continue to own as his. Though it may have been spoken two or three thousand years ago, or longer than that, yet it is still his promise, and part and parcel of himself. Well, then, if God will own it as his promise, shall I, to whom it is given in infinite mercy, doubt whether it is his promise or not? And shall I even venture to go further than that, and, knowing it to be his promise, shall I begin to question how he can fulfil it, or whether he will fulfil it or not? God forbid! The dignity of the promise must not be insulted by our doubting it.

Kindly observe the position of the promise, which is a very singular one. *It is a kind of link between the divine thought and the divine act.* It is not at all a necessary link so far as God is concerned, but it is often a most necessary and consoling link to us. There is the eternal purpose that has ever been in God's secret mind, and his promise is the shadow which that purpose casts upon the revealed page. It is the divine decree made manifest; and it stands there, bright and sparkling, between the decree, which our eyes cannot and dare not look upon, and the blessed fulfilment which is to be our joy and delight for ever. I confess that I cannot think of God's eternal purposes without the utmost awe and reverence; for, to me, there is something very solemn and impressive about them. I know that some people speak as though they would trample them in the mire if they could; but whenever I hear a word against the promises, the providences, the decrees, and the purposes of God, I feel inclined to do as a negro slave did, under certain circumstances, in the presence of his master. While waiting upon his master, who frequently took the name of God in vain, and blasphemed it most terribly in his cursing, the black man bowed his head. His master asked him why he did so, and he replied that it was because his soul was full of trembling at the very name of God, and he wished to do him reverence, even while he was being blasphemed and insulted. So, whenever I hear or read of anyone speaking or writing against the divine decrees, I feel anxious at once to bow my head, and to prostrate myself in homage before that eternal mind which knows no new thought,—for God knew all things from the beginning,—and to adore that infinite wisdom which has planned everything from the flitting of a sparrow to the flight of the archangel. It is very wonderful to me to think of a promise in the Scriptures being virtually the manifestation of God's everlasting purposes. I might compare the purpose to God himself,—invisible, and the promise to the Incarnate God, who was born at Bethlehem, and who came to earth to be seen of men.

Think yet again of the promise of God, and you will see how a sense of its dignity grows upon you while you are meditating upon it. Consider, next, that *the truth of God is irrevocably bound up with his promise.* If a man says, "Such a thing shall be done," he ought to do it if it is in his power. We have no right to break promises that we have made; we feel that, if we do, men will learn to distrust us, and soon will care nothing at all for our promises. But, beloved,— and we speak with the utmost reverence concerning the Most High,— his character for truthfulness would be lost if his promises were not kept; and, while it would be an awful loss to us to miss what he has promised, it would be a far greater loss to him to lose his truthfulness. We rejoice that, as a matter of fact, this is a thing which can never happen. All things except this are possible with God, but it is not possible for him to be God and yet to fail in the fulfilment of his promises. The two ideas will not run together at all. If he is God, he must be true to his truth, and he will be; so, when I read a promise in his Word, I read something which is as certain as a fact already accomplished, since, if it were not to come to pass, God's glory would suffer an eclipse, and his veracity would be impugned, and that can never be.

Nor is the truth of God the only attribute which would suffer if he failed to fulfil his promise, for *his immutability would also be put in jeopardy.* If he makes a promise, and yet does not fulfil it in due time, then he must have changed; the motives which led to the making of the promise have now no influence over him, and he has become something different from what he was when he made the promise. But God must be immutable. It cannot be possible for him to change for the better, for he is infinitely good; and, certainly, he cannot change for the worse, for, if he did, then he would be something less than he might be, and so he would not be God at all. Change is impossible to him; he can never change his will, and his promise, as one of the most solemn declarations of his will, must be fulfilled when he has once made it. Surely, no one of us would wish or dare to deny either the truthfulness or the unchangeableness of God.

Further, *his power is bound up with his promise.* Shall it ever be said that God failed to keep his promise because he could not keep it, or because he miscalculated his resources, or his arm waxed short, or the great deeps of his eternal Godhead became dried up? No; that cannot be, for what he has promised he will always be able to perform.

So, then, if we slight the promises of God, we slight also his truth, his immutability, and his power.

And we also seriously *compromise his mercy and his love.* It was love that moved him to give the promise. He might have bestowed the blessing without promising to do so, and that would have been a gracious proof of his love; but, because the promise has a sweet, consoling power in it, he has been pleased to give it to us as a further proof of his love; and if he does not grant the boon at once when he promises it, the delay is all for loving reasons; but, having given the promise, he must keep it because of his love. His love must be changed if it does not constrain him to fulfil what it caused him to promise; but that can never be, and we must not—we dare not—cast such a slight upon the promise of God as to imagine, for a moment, that it can remain unfulfilled.

So much, then, concerning the dignity of the promises.

II. Still keeping closely to the text, I want you to notice, next, THE RANGE OF THE PROMISES, for Paul here speaks of "*all* the promises of God."

There is a prospect for you: "All the promises." There are very many of them, and they are found in both the Old and the New Testaments. There was one given at the gates of the garden of Eden, very near the commencement of human history. There is another right at the end of the Revelation: "Surely I come quickly." The Bible is a Book of precious promises; all the way we have to travel, they seem to be like a series of stepping-stones across the stream of time, and we may march from one promise to another, and never wet our feet all the way from earth to heaven, if we do but know how to keep our eyes open, and to find the right promise to step upon. "All the promises," the Old Testament ones as well as those in the New Testament, are sure and steadfast. The conditional promises—if we believe, and if we repent,—God will certainly fulfil; and the unconditional ones—the promises of the everlasting covenant, in which he pledges himself to give men repentance, and to give them new hearts and right spirits,—he will keep them, too.

God will fulfil all temporal promises. Bread shall be given you, and water shall be assured unto you, if you are the Lord's children. He will keep his promises about temporal affairs as well as those which concern everlasting joys and blessings. "No good thing will he withhold from them that walk uprightly." You may speak of the promises in any way that you please, and then you may say that the Lord will keep them all; you may pick out the promise to the prisoner, the promise to the sinner, the promise to the backslider, the promise to the doubting one, the promise to the aged, the promise to the young, the promise to her that halteth, the promise to the barren woman, the promise to the strong, the promise to those who have full assurance of faith, the promise to those who love the Lord, the promise to those who delight themselves in the Lord, and then you may confidently declare, concerning all these promises to all sorts and conditions of people, that the Lord will surely keep every one of them.

"All the promises." Why, here is a grand granaryful! Who can sort them all out? Promises of pardon to the seeking sinner; promises of justification to the believing child; promises of sanctification to him who is struggling against sin; promises of the supply of all kinds of spiritual food to the flock of Christ; promises of guidance; promises of preservation; promises of holy education; promises of peace and joy; promises of hope; promises of the sustenance of our love; promises for death; promises for judgment; promises for glory; promises that reach to all eternity. "All the promises." What a range of vision this expression opens up! Go forth presently, and lift up thine eyes, and gaze upon the stars; see whether thou canst number them all, do they not far exceed all thy powers of numeration? Yet, if thou couldst count the stars, and weigh them in scales, and tabulate the measure of their light, thou couldst not count the promises of God, or estimate their true value, or know how infinitely precious is the light divine which streams from them into a believing soul. If God does not fulfil a single promise to me for the next fifty years, I shall be perfectly satisfied to live on the promises themselves, if my faith shall but be sustained by his grace. I may fairly talk thus, for you would say, "I do not need a single penny to spend, as long as ever I live, if I can but always have plenty of £5 notes; I shall never care if I do not see a sovereign again, so long as I can always have the promise of the Bank of England to pay me on demand all that I need." So let it be with the promises of God. Men's promises are but breath, they would never feed us; but God's promises can satisfy us, for they are the substance of the things hoped for; and faith, the evidence of things not seen, rejoices to see that which is invisible, to lay hold of that which it cannot touch, and to feed upon that which, as yet, it cannot taste. Faith works wonders. It enables a man to project himself right into eternity. He sits down, and sighs, and sorrows, and then he says to himself, "This will never do, I will trust in the Lord;" and, in an instant, by faith he walks the golden streets, and sings the everlasting songs. He is not obliged to live in this narrow sphere of time and sense, for, by faith, he spreads his wings, and, like the lark, he ascends and sings. He soars far more rapidly than even the eagle, and finds himself already enjoying the things which God has prepared for them that love him, and so he is happy in the Lord.

III. Now I must turn to my third point, which is in the very heart of the text: "For all the promises of God *in him are yea, and in him Amen.*" These words teach us THE STABILITY OF THE PROMISES.

The promises of God are very firm, for, first, *they are settled on an everlasting basis*, for they are promises in Christ. As I look at the text, I can see two words leaping up out of it; and as I look at it again, I see the same two words leaping up again: "*in him.*" "All the promises of God in him are yea, and in him Amen." There is a great thought which I cannot fully open up to you now, you must lie awake to-night, and think over it, and pray over it: "All the promises of God in him." What a great Christ you have, to have "all the promises of God" within himself! The range of the promises seems to be infinite, and yet Christ is great enough to be the circumference that shuts them all in. Do rejoice in this great truth, that "all the promises of God" are in Christ Jesus our Lord.

And in Christ they are said to be "Yea." That is a Greek word, so this is a message to Gentiles. "And in him Amen." That is a Hebrew word, and is therefore for the Jews. You may have noticed how, whenever the Holy Spirit wishes to impress any truth upon us with more than usual solemnity, he uses two languages, as in the case of "Abba, Father." In this way, all the saints of God, whether they be Jews or Gentiles, may have their portion of meat in due season.

"All the promises of God in him are "yea." That is, they are certain. "And in him Amen." That is, they are accomplished. We may say, after every promise of God, "Yea, so it is. Amen, so let it be." There is but a slight variation in the meaning of the words, but it is enough to let us see that there is no tautology here, not even if the words are translated, "All the promises of God are yea," that is, true; "and they are Amen;" that is, they shall be accomplished in Christ Jesus.

The stability of the promises in Christ is established beyond all hazard, first, because Christ is God's Witness. If anyone asks, "Did God make this promise?" Christ comes forward, and says, "Yes, I heard him say it." Christ is "the faithful and true Witness." He bears witness of God and for God to the sons of men; and he sets his seal to every divine promise, and certifies it with his "Yea and Amen."

Next, the promises are sure in Christ, because he is God's Representative. He is always doing the Father's will, even as he has done it in the past. When he came to earth, and died upon the cross, he accomplished the work of redemption upon which God's heart was set; and he is still doing the Father's will. Whatever Jesus has said, God has said, for he speaks the words of God. The Father sent him into the world as his Representative, and he spoke not merely his own words, but the words of the Father who sent him.

Then, next, Jesus is the Surety of the covenant. The promise was at first made to Adam. If Adam keeps the command of God, and does not touch the forbidden fruit, he and those whom he represents shall have all manner of good things. But Adam transgressed the law of the Lord, so that covenant was made void. The second covenant is on this wise. If Jesus Christ, the second Adam, will do this and that, then all whom he represents shall have the blessings guaranteed in the covenant. The Lord Jesus has done all that he agreed to do; he has kept the law, and so has honoured it, and he has also died, and borne the sentence of the law. He has thus offered both an active and a passive obedience to the law of God, and now all the promises of God must be kept to Christ, for they are "Yea and Amen" in him. Take those great promises in the fifty-third of Isaiah: "He shall see of the travail of his soul, and shall be satisfied: by his knowledge shall my righteous servant justify many; for he shall bear their iniquities. Therefore will I divide him a portion with the great, and he shall divide the spoil with the strong; because he hath poured out his soul unto death: and he was numbered with the transgressors; and he bare the sin of many, and made intercession for the transgressors." These are promises, first to the Head, and then to us the members of his mystical body; first to the second Adam, and then to all who, by a living faith, are included in his federal headship. So the promises are "Yea and Amen" in him.

And as long as Jesus Christ lives, they are also "Yea and Amen" in this sense,—that he is seeing to their being carried out. He is interceding before the throne for us that the promises of God may meet our distresses. O brethren, all the promises must be true in Christ, because God spared not his own Son, but freely delivered him up for us all; and, having given him, will he not, with him, also freely give us all things? If God had meant to run back from any promise, he would surely have run back from the promise to give his only-begotten Son; but, having fulfilled that, what promise is there that he will ever break? Moreover, in the gift of Christ, he has virtually and really given us all things; for if Christ is yours, all things are yours. All things are in Christ; so, having him, you possess all. There is no desire of your spirit, or need of your nature, that shall remain unsatisfied when once you have Christ as yours. You have heaven, and earth, and all things that are or ever shall be, encompassed in that blessed One whose very name is "the Amen, the faithful and true Witness." O beloved, rejoice with all your heart that every promise of God is sure in Christ Jesus to all his true seed!

IV. Now, let us consider the last words of the text: "For all the promises of God in him are yea, and in him Amen, *unto the glory of God by us.*" This impression teaches us THE RESULT OF THE PROMISES.

So then, dear friends, the promises of God are his glory. There is no pretended god that has ever been supposed to make promises like those of our God. Turn to the Koran, and see what Mohammed has promised. Ah, me! What a beggarly array of promises does he set before his followers! Turn to Brahma and Buddha, and read all the so-called sacred books written by their priests, and see what their gods are said to have promised. You can put the essence of it all into an egg-shell, and not see it even then. But our God has promised more than heaven and earth can hold. He has promised to give himself to his people. He is the great Promiser,—the mighty Promiser. I set the promises of God in comparison and contrast with all the promises that were ever made in connection with all false systems of religion under heaven, and unhesitatingly declare that there are none that can compare for an instant with the promises of the Most High.

It was greatly to God's glory to make those promises all sure, for they all depended at first upon the condition that Christ should obey the Father's will. But he has done it; and oh, what a glory it is to God that "he gave his only begotten Son, that whosoever believeth in him should not perish, but have everlasting life"! The gift of the Redeemer, the life of the Redeemer, the death of the Redeemer, the intercession of the Redeemer, the making the promises sure,—all this is greatly to the glory of God.

And now it is to the glory of God to keep every promise that he has made. There is not one which, if it were broken, would redound to his praise or increase his honour. Nay, and there is not one but, when it is kept, reflects fresh honour upon him, and brings still further renown to his ever-blessed name.

If I had time, I would enlarge upon all these points; but as it is already past our usual hour for closing the service, I must end my discourse with a brief reference to the last words in our text: "unto the glory of God by us." While I was thinking earnestly over my text, I fancied that those two little words, "by us," seemed to spoil that grand word "glory" and that greater word "God." "To the glory of God"—"by us;" what a contrast! It is even more marked than in that old story of the organ-blower who would persist in saying, "*We* did it," when all that he did was just to pump the air into the organ. Must we be mentioned at all? Is it not a pity to bring us in? But, as I turned the subject over in my mind, I thought, "Oh, no, no; it is quite right to bring us in here!" Now look. God wants to have the glory of being merciful; yes, but he cannot have that glory unless there is a sinner somewhere to whom he can show mercy; a sinner is an essential part of the whole business. Suppose that the king, who made the great supper, had said to his servants, "Go out into the highways and hedges, and compel them to come in;" and that they had come back to him, and said, "There is not a single creature under the hedges or in the highways; there is not even a solitary beggar anywhere about the streets or lanes of the city." Then he could not have had the feast, whatever dainties he might have prepared, if he had not anybody to eat them. It would have been a mournful business to have the oxen and fatlings killed, and heaped upon the tables, yet nobody to sit down to partake of them. Even the king, if he is to have honour, must be dependent for once on the beggars in the highways and hedges. Is not this wonderful? God wants to show his power in pardoning my sin, but he cannot do it if I have no sin to be pardoned; and if I do not come to him to be pardoned, and do not ask for his mercy, then it lies like dead capital never spent. The Lord delights to help the weak; it is his joy to do it; but suppose that there is no weak person anywhere, what is to happen then? Ah! but I think I hear the weak souls crying out, "By us! By us! 'To the glory of God by us.'" He delights to help the poor and needy, and he cannot do so if there are not some poor and needy ones for him to help; so, when we seek his aid, it is 'to the glory of God by us.'" And the Lord delights to make his strength perfect in our weakness. I think I hear Paul crying out, and he is the man who wrote these words, "by us,"—"God is glorified by my weakness." And I hear many of you, who are trying to serve your Lord and Master, saying, "Ah, then! that is why such weak ones as we feel ourselves to be are used, 'to the glory of God by us.'"

Come along, then, all you who need God's mercy; you have laid hold of one of his promises, and feel that you need and must have all that it includes. With utmost reverence would I say that God himself cannot be glorified by the promise without you. If he intends to feed the hungry, then the hungry are essential to the accomplishment of his purpose. If he would clothe the naked, then there must be naked ones for him to clothe. Is there not a mine of comfort here for you who have been almost without hope? I trust that some of you poor lost ones will say in your hearts, if you do not utter it with your voices, "Are we really essential to God's glory? Does God need our poverty, and our sinfulness, and our nothingness, in order that he may, through them, display the greatness of his grace? Then we will certainly come to him just as we are." Do so, I pray you. Come! Come!! Come!!! May the Holy Spirit, by his omnipotent grace, draw you now, for our Lord Jesus Christ's sake! Amen.

Exposition by C. H. Spurgeon.

2 CORINTHIANS I., AND II. 1.

Chapter i. Verse 1. *Paul, an apostle of Jesus Christ by the will of God, and Timothy our brother, unto the church of God which is at Corinth, with all the saints which are in all Achaia:*

Paul is very jealous of his apostleship. There were some in Corinth who denied it, and therefore he takes care, at the very commencement of this Epistle,—as he does in beginning most of his letters,—to write concerning himself, "Paul, an apostle of Jesus Christ by the will of God." But with what humility of mind does he associate Timothy with himself! Frequently he puts Timothy, his own convert, one so young, and so much beneath him in position and attainments, on a level with himself; and if we also can help our younger brethren, how willingly should we put ourselves side by side with them!

2. *Grace be to you and peace from God our Father, and from the Lord Jesus Christ.*

What a wonderful source of grace and peace! "God our Father." How can he give other than grace and peace to his own children? "And from the Lord Jesus Christ," our redeeming Saviour, who has given himself for us, and who has graven our names on the palms of his hands;—is there not an abundant supply of grace and peace to be found in the very music of his name?

3. *Blessed be God, even the Father of our Lord Jesus Christ, the Father of mercies, and the God of all comfort;*

Let me read those titles again: "The Father of our Lord Jesus Christ, the Father of mercies, and the God of all comfort." Do not the second and third titles derive much of their significance from the first one? It is because God is "the Father of our Lord Jesus Christ" that he becomes "the Father of mercies, and the God of all comfort."

4. *Who comforteth us in all our tribulation, that we may be able to comfort them which are in any trouble, by the comfort wherewith we ourselves are comforted of God.*

Experience teaches the first rank of God's servants, and their experience of sorrow and consolation is often the means of enabling them to be the means of blessing to others. Almost everything that the minister of the gospel enjoys or endures will be found to be sent to him for the elect's sake, that he may know how to teach them the lessons he has himself learned.

5. *For as the sufferings of Christ abound in us, so our consolation also aboundeth by Christ.*

Are we not willing to endure the greater suffering that we may enjoy the greater consolation?

6. *And whether we be afflicted, it is for your consolation and salvation, which is effectual in the enduring of the same sufferings which we also suffer: or whether we be comforted, it is for your consolation and salvation.*

We receive both suffering and consolation for the sake of others, and we are bound to give out again all that we receive. It is the essence of the true Christian life first to be dependent upon God for everything, and then to give forth to all around us that which God has poured into our spirit. The heart would soon die if it pumped in the blood, and never pumped it out again; but it is by that perpetual process of giving out what it has received that it continues in life; and the highest form of Christian life is the reception of all that comes to us out of the fulness of Christ, and then the free giving out of what he has bestowed.

7—10. *And our hope of you is stedfast, knowing, that as ye are partakers of the sufferings, so shall ye be also of the consolation. For we would not, brethren, have you ignorant of our trouble which came to us in Asia, that we were pressed out of measure, above strength, insomuch that we despaired even of life: but we had the sentence of death in ourselves, that we should not trust in ourselves, but in God which raiseth the dead: who delivered us from so great a death, and doth deliver: in whom we trust that he will yet deliver us;*

No doubt Paul did preach all the better and with the greater confidence in God because he preached, like Richard Baxter, "as a dying man to dying men." His life was frequently in danger, and on this occasion it was so in a very remarkable degree; so, when he was again able to testify for his Master, he realized that he had no time to waste, and therefore he wrote and spoke with the utmost earnestness. He felt himself in jeopardy every hour, and therefore he fell back upon his God, and trusted alone in him. Anything that works to this end for us also is an undisguised blessing.

11. *Ye also helping together by prayer for us, that for the gift bestowed upon us by the means of many persons thanks may be given by many on our behalf.*

Much prayer leads to much thanksgiving. It should be a great cause for joy when numbers of Christians unite in praying for any Christian minister, for they will unite also in praising God on his behalf, when that which they asked for him is granted.

12. *For our rejoicing is this, the testimony of our conscience, that in simplicity and godly sincerity, not with fleshly wisdom, but by the grace of God, we have had our conversation in the world, and more abundantly to you-ward.*

There had been whispers, among these Corinthians, that Paul had concealed a double meaning in some of his writings, and also that he had made a promise which he never intended to keep; so now he calls upon them to bear witness that he never was a man to act according to policy, but he was a straightforward, honest, plain-dealing man, full of godly sincerity and unselfishness. He had abundantly proved all this to the Corinthians, for, lest they should have any occasion for speaking against him, he would not take at their hands the support to which he was entitled, but he laboured at his trade of tent-making that they might not have anything to say concerning him except that he was disinterested in all his endeavours to serve them. Paul evidently felt their unkindness very much, but his conscience assured him that their accusations were unjust.

13, 14. *For we write none other things unto you, than what ye read or acknowledge; and I trust ye shall acknowledge even to the end; as also ye have acknowledged us in part, that we are your rejoicing, even as ye also are our's in the day of the Lord Jesus.*

See how Paul restrains himself in writing to these people. He had good cause to be offended, for they had touched him in a point about which he was very jealous, namely, his integrity; but here he speaks with great moderation of spirit, and herein lay his strength. Every Christian man, when he has to defend himself against false accusations, should use soft words and hard arguments.

15, 16. *And in this confidence I was minded to come unto you before, that ye might have a second benefit; and to pass by you into Macedonia, and to come again out of Macedonia unto you, and of you to be brought on my way toward Judæa.*

He had planned to see them in his going, and also in his returning; but he could not carry out the idea which was in his mind. The wisest of men often find their plans impracticable, and even an inspired man is not always inspired. God guides him when guidance is absolutely necessary; but, at other times, he leaves him to arrange according to his own judgment, and to find out that his judgment is not infallible. "I had a mind," says he, "to come and see you twice."

17. *When I therefore was thus minded, did I use lightness?*

"Did I make up my mind hastily, and then did I change it all of a sudden without good reason? Had I never thought before I decided, and therefore did I find it necessary to revoke my promise?"

17, 18. *Or the things that I purpose, do I purpose according to the flesh, that with me there should be yea yea, and nay nay? But as God is true, our word toward you was not yea and nay.*

He binds up his own ministry with himself, and he says, "You charge me with being fickle, but you know better; you are well aware that I am not one who says one thing to-day and another thing to-morrow. You know that I have been open and aboveboard in all my dealings with you, and that I have never stooped to policy and craftiness, but have spoken that which I believed, whatever might come of it."

19. *For the Son of God, Jesus Christ, who was preached among you by us, even by me and Silvanus and Timotheus, was not yea and nay, but in him was yea.*

He declares that he preached the truth straightforwardly and consistently, and that he did not say one thing one day and another thing a few days later.

20. *For all the promises of God in him are yea, and in him Amen, unto the glory of God by us.*

Christ is no quicksand, slipping and sliding away, and so ruining those who cling to him. He is the Rock of ages, and he stands fast for ever. His gospel is one and the same at all times. You see that, as Paul grows warm, he advances in his argument. If the Corinthians suspected his honesty in making a promise, the next thing they would do would be to suspect the gospel, and after that they would suspect Christ himself, who is the truth.

21—23. *Now he which stablisheth us with you in Christ, and hath anointed us, is God; who hath also sealed us, and given the earnest of the Spirit in our hearts. Moreover I call God for a record upon my soul, that to spare you I came not as yet unto Corinth.*

"If I had come, I should have been obliged to rebuke you and reprove you. I should have had to be like an armed man going to battle, or an officer of the law carrying out the sentence pronounced upon a criminal, and I could not bear to do that; so I felt it would be better and wiser to stay away, and therefore I did not visit you as I had proposed."

24. *Not for that we have dominion over your faith, but are helpers of your joy: for by faith ye stand.* Chapter ii. Verse 1. *But I determined this with myself, that I would not come again to you in heaviness.*

And they ought to have had enough confidence in him to know that he had a very good and sufficient reason for not fulfilling his conditional promise. Let us, dear friends, who are one in Christ, trust each other; for, if suspicion be once bred among the people of God, it will mean farewell to all fellowship.

THE WIDE-OPEN MOUTH FILLED.

A Sermon

DELIVERED BY

C. H. SPURGEON,

AT THE PASTORS' COLLEGE CONFERENCE,

On *Friday morning*, April 7*th*, 1876.

"I am the LORD thy God, which brought thee out of the land of Egypt: open thy mouth wide, and I will fill it."—Psalm lxxxi. 10.

You have, no doubt, met with various interpretations of this metaphor: "Open thy mouth wide, and I will fill it." You will find that several expositors say that there is an allusion here to a custom which is said to have been observed by the late Shah of Persia, who, being greatly pleased with one of his courtiers, made him open his mouth, and then began to fill it with diamonds, pearls, rubies, and emeralds. I should expect that, under such circumstances, the courtier would open his mouth very widely indeed.

Well, you may use that incident as an illustration, if you like to do so; and, certainly, the spiritual blessings, which God gives to his children, are far more precious than pearls, and diamonds, and rubies, and there is every inducement for you to open your mouth to receive such treasure as he is waiting and willing to give you. But I do not feel sure that the Holy Spirit intended the psalmist to allude to any such custom as this. It is too expensive an operation to be very frequently performed, and it strikes me that even such semi-maniacs as Shahs and Sultans usually are would not be likely often to attempt such a feat as that. In default of a more suitable illustration, it might be used, but it does not appear to me to be in accordance with the chaste and natural tone of the Word of God.

Another illustration of the text may be found in a custom which is much more common in the East. At Oriental feasts, when the head of the household wishes to select the best part of the joint for an honoured guest, he usually chooses the fattest portion he can find, as the Oriental mind conceives just what we should not conceive, namely, that a mass of fat, all dripping with grease, is the most delicious morsel that can possibly be given to a guest;

so the host searches for the fattest piece of meat in the dish, takes it in his hand, and puts it deliberately into the mouth of the principal guest, bidding him open his mouth wide that he may receive it. This seems a revolting practice to us, but it was evidently the custom then, as it still is in the East. Thus we have David saying, "My soul shall be satisfied as with marrow and fatness; and my mouth shall praise thee with joyful lips,"—as if the lips sucked it with delight even while the fat was still upon them.

But I am inclined to look for quite another explanation of the text, though admitting that the second one is probably that upon which the psalmist was thinking when he wrote these words. One springtime, I discovered a bird's nest, in which there were a number of little birds. They were not fledged enough to fly, and their judgments were not well developed, and therefore they mistook me for their mother or father. I would not touch them, but I held my fingers over them, and they opened their mouths wide,—nay, the little creatures seemed to me as if they were all mouth. I could not see any other part of their bodies; all seemed lost in one great vacuum. If you have ever seen the mother-bird come to the nest with a worm in its mouth, you have noticed that, in an instant, all her little ones are up, and eager to swallow that worm. She can only fill the mouth of one, and she can scarcely do that; for, no sooner has it swallowed what she gives it than it begins to gape again; so the parent-birds have to keep flying very fast, all day long, collecting food for their family; but, however many times they come, they never have to use the exhortation of our text. The little birds in their nests are far more sensible than we are. When God hovers over us with his wide-spread wings, and covers us with his warm feathers, he has need to say to each one of us, "Open thy mouth wide, and I will fill it;" but the little birds take good care, without any teaching, to open their mouths wide, that their mothers may fill them. This illustration may occur again during the sermon; for, whether it is the one to which the psalmist alludes, or not, it is a very useful one, and is full of instruction. It also has the further advantage that it does not appertain to either the East or the West alone; and, as this blessed Book is neither for East nor West alone, but for both, I like to find an illustration which, in all time, and in every clime, may open up the meaning of the Word. "Open thy mouth," then, as a bird opens its mouth when the mother-bird returns with its food, and he who, in the infinitude of his condescension, likens himself to birds, says, "I will fill it."

Let us imitate the inspired teachers in using things in nature to illustrate the meaning of the messages they have to deliver. Look from our Lord Jesus Christ, the Prince of preachers, through the long line of prophets, to evangelists, and apostles, and you will see that they did not utter the truth with their eyes closed; but, with large sympathy, they looked abroad upon the whole range of creation, both animate and inanimate, and yoked every creature to the chariot of truth, if, by any means, through the use of simile, and metaphor, and illustration, they might enable the divine message to ride triumphantly into the hearts of the people.

If any of us are to succeed in teaching, either few or many, we must imitate these masters of the art. God has given the preacher eyes as well as a tongue;—ay, two eyes to one tongue;—and he must take care to observe all that can be seen, and to make abundant use of his observation; otherwise, he will find his speech prove to be, as Shakespeare says, "stale, flat, and unprofitable." The true teacher should not seek to soar on the gaudy wings of brilliant oratory, pouring forth sonorous polished sentences in rhythmic harmony; but should endeavour to speak pointed truths,—things that will strike and stick,—thoughts that will be remembered and recalled, again and again, when the hearer is far away from the place of worship where he listened to the preacher's words.

The text naturally divides itself into three parts. First, there is *the exhortation:* "Open thy mouth wide." Secondly, there is *the promise:* "I will fill it;" and, thirdly, there is *the encouragement* contained in the name by which God speaks of himself: "I am Jehovah thy God, which brought thee out of the land of Egypt."

I. First, then, brethren, here is THE EXHORTATION: "Open thy mouth wide."

What does that expression mean? Well, I should have to open my mouth very wide indeed if I were to explain all it means. You probably will know, by putting it in practice, better than by any explanation that I can give you; but, certainly, first of all, I should say that it means that *there should be a great sense of your need.* The wide-open mouth means that you hunger. The little birds need no instruction in opening their mouths except the inward monitor. They feel a lack of food; they are growing, and growing fast, and feathers have to be made, and they need much food, and those strong needs of theirs make them open their mouths by instinct, as we say. Brethren, if we had more sense of our need, prayer would be more of an instinct with us; we should pray because we could not help praying; we should pray, perhaps, less methodically, but we should pray, probably, more truly, if we prayed because there were groanings within us, caused by intense pain, and moanings that came out of inward agony, and longings that came out of the consciousness of our dire necessities. Surely, this kind of opening of the mouth, by the sense of our need, ought to be easy to us, for our needs are very great. I must not say that they are infinite, for we are only finite beings; but they are so vast that only infinity can ever supply them. What is there that you do not need, my brother? Someone said in prayer, the other day, that we were "a bag of wants." That was a very accurate description. Are we all conscious of our many needs?

Dear brother, are you growing conscious of your own power? If so, pray against it with all your might. A much better thing is to become conscious of your own weakness. You will not open your mouth wide if you do not realize how weak you are. If you feel that you are strong, you will cease to cry to God for strength. Are you getting proud of your experience of divine things? Strive to hurl that pride down, for you will be no wiser than a wild ass's colt if you rely on your own experience. Do you feel that you have now attained to a very high degree of grace? You have certainly not attained it if you think you have. If you are still conscious of your own shortcomings, you are probably far ahead of your own belief; but if you are conscious of your attainments, you are far behind those attainments; rest assured of that. I do solemnly believe, brethren, that it is as good a test of a man's spiritual riches as can be found, namely, his own sense of his spiritual poverty. Oh, get less and less in your own esteem; grow poorer and poorer, weaker and yet weaker still; become, in yourselves, nothing, and less than nothing. This is a grand way of opening the mouth; because our needs, when they are truly felt, are really prayers, for prayers are merely the expression of the wants of our heart; and if, to the consciousness of our need, there is added the knowledge that God can supply that need, we have, at any rate, the basis of all true prayer. Oh, for a great sense of our spiritual poverty! Oh, for an awful vacuum within the soul, a consciousness most truly felt, that there is room for God! Oh, for a deep chasm to yawn within one's nature, which only Christ himself can fill!

The next way of opening the mouth will be *to increase the vehemence of desire.* How did the psalmist do this? He says, "I opened my mouth, and panted." This is what we need to do, to get such vehement desires after good things that we cannot take a negative answer to our petitions. We know that what we ask is for God's glory and our own good; and, therefore, we are not going to ask as men who may be put off, but our resolve is like that of Jacob at Jabbok,—

"With thee all night I mean to stay,
And wrestle till the break of day."

We cry, with good John Newton,—

"No,—I must maintain my hold,
'Tis thy goodness makes me bold;
I can no denial take,
When I plead for Jesus' sake."

Those prayers speed best that are fullest of holy vehemence. There is a naughty kind of vehemence which we must get rid of. I am not sure that all the expressions we sometimes hear in prayer are right; there is no need for us to seem to fight with God at the mercy-seat. I feel, sometimes, a sort of shivering when I hear brethren make a great noise in prayer without any evidence of corresponding earnestness deep down in their soul. Yet I know that our Lord Jesus said, "The kingdom of heaven suffereth violence, and the violent take it by force." If you want to have great things of God, you must want them terribly; you must get to want them more and more, your sense of want must keep on growing. You know also that our Lord Jesus said, "Blessed are they which do hunger and thirst"—hunger is bad enough, and thirst is awful, but hunger and thirst combined bring a man to the verge of death;—yet Jesus says, "Blessed are they which do hunger and thirst after righteousness: for"—Christ's promise is parallel to the text before us,—"they shall be filled." Get that blessed hunger and thirst, brethren. When you cannot live without conversions, you shall have conversions; when you *must* have them, you shall have them. May the Lord drive that "must" into us all! May he urge us on, with a passionate desire, to resolve that we will know the reason why if souls are not converted to God.

Another way of opening the mouth is *to ask for greater capacity*. If you have ever fed a lot of little birds—no doubt my friend, Archibald Brown, has often done it,—with pieces of egg, if you have some very small pieces, you drop them into the smaller mouths; but if you have a large piece of egg, where does it go? Into the biggest mouth you can find. You seem to feel, "That little bird must not have a large piece, because he has only a tiny mouth; but here is one, whose mouth yawns like the crater of a small volcano." So you drop into his mouth a larger piece; and I have no doubt the mother-birds exercise a good deal of discretion in feeding their young. They do not give the large worms to the little birds, but they drop the large ones into the large mouths; and, in like manner, if we get large capacities, we shall receive large blessings. What a wonderful difference there is in the capacity of different individuals! I have heard it said that a sinner sucks in happiness, such as it is, with the mouth of an insect, but that a believer drinks in bliss with the mouth of an angel; and it is so. The stream of mercy seems to run right over some men because there is no place for it to run in; it runs into others in driblets because there is only a little hole into which it can drip; but when the mouth is opened wide to receive the blessing of the Lord, how capacious it is! I should like, spiritually, to have my mouth like that of Behemoth, of which the Lord said to Job, "he trusteth that he can draw up Jordan into his mouth." Oh, for a mouth of such mighty capacity as to be capable of receiving a far greater blessing than we have ever yet received!

Dear brethren, we are not straitened in God; if we are straitened at all, it is in ourselves. No wise man will try to put a gallon of any liquid into a quart pot. You cannot expect to put a bushel of anything into a peck measure. "Be ye therefore enlarged," is still the message we need to hear; and one part of that enlargement must consist in the enlargement of the mouth in prayer and in holy vehemence. God grant to all of us far greater capacity! What little men we all are! We sometimes call one another great, and perhaps fancy that we are. I wonder what our Heavenly Father thinks of us. We see our little children, one of them three years old, and another only two, and another only a month or two; they think the baby is a very little thing, and that they themselves are ever so big, and they talk of their big brother, who is only four or five years old! It is very much like that with us; there is not much more difference between the greatest and the least of us than between those children. So, if we can, we must grow,—grow at the mouth, and grow all over. We need to have greater grace given to us; but the Lord will not give us great blessings until we are able to bear them. You remember how he said to his disciples, "I have yet many things to say unto you, but ye cannot bear them now;" and he might say to us, "I have yet many things to give unto you, but ye cannot bear them at present." If God were now to give to any man all the blessings that he means to bestow upon him in a few years' time, it would ruin him. When God has given us any success, it is a great addition to the mercy if he has first fitted us to bear it. Some of us can recollect brethren, taken almost straight from the miners' pit, and elevated suddenly into a position of great popularity, with no training for the ministry, and no persecution, no criticism from the public press, and no unkind remarks from Christian men; and we remember with sorrow how they failed. So, if you, while you are young men, have to run the gauntlet of a good deal of trial, and difficulty, and opposition, and non-success, you ought to thank God for it. You are now being made ready to receive the blessing for which you were not fit before. The Lord is increasing your capacity; and when the capacity is sufficient, he will fill it.

Next, dear brethren, I feel that the text must mean, *seek for greater blessings than any that you have yet received*. You have opened your mouth, and you have received something; possibly, you think that you have received a great deal; but the Lord "is able to do exceeding abundantly above all that we ask or think." I have heard people say in prayer, "Thou art able to do exceeding abundantly above all that we *can* ask or think." Well, I suppose that is true, but that is not what Paul was inspired to write. We can ask and can think a great deal; but Paul says that God is able to do exceeding abundantly above all that we actually do ask or think. Well, then, as this is the case, will we not ask for greater things than we have ever asked for before? It is a singular fact that the certainty of obtaining is in proportion to the largeness of what you ask. Some men go to God, and ask only for temporal favours; and, possibly, they do not obtain them. He who would be content with this world will probably never get it; but he who craves spiritual good may ask with the absolute certainty of receiving it. Christ's promise is, "Ask, and it shall be given you; seek, and ye shall find; knock, and it shall be opened unto you." If you ask only for temporal mercies, and can be satisfied with them, you may get what you ask. There are gushing springs from which you might drink if you would, but the muddy waters of Sihor are evidently good enough for you. But if you ask the Lord for spiritual blessings, he is sure to give them to you. It is more natural for God to give great things than little things; they are more in his line,—more in his way. You know that certain men have certain ways. There are men whom you can get to do anything if it is in their way, but they will not act in another way. Well, now, the Lord's ways are as high above our ways as the heavens are above the earth; yet David knew what God's ways were, for he said, "Then will I teach transgressors thy ways." One of the ways of God is to do great things for his people. Some of them sang, "The Lord hath done great things for us; whereof we are glad." So you are more sure of getting blessings from God if you ask him for great things; therefore, be sure to ask for very great things. When you do get to the mercy-seat, do not begin asking for littles, and go home with trifles; but ask for as big things as ever your soul can desire, and as big things as the promises of God cover. There you have a task before you that will tax your greatest powers, but give your heart and soul to it, and you will find it to be a very pleasant and profitable one.

Ask great things for yourselves, brethren. Ask to know all the truth of God; ask to know the fulness of God; ask to know the riches of his grace; ask to know "the love of Christ, which passeth knowledge;" and when you have asked for all that, ask for holiness, and do not ask for anything less than perfect holiness. Continue to open your mouth wide, that every grace may be given to you; adding "to your faith virtue; and to virtue knowledge; and to knowledge temperance; and to temperance patience; and to patience godliness; and to godliness brotherly kindness; and to brotherly kindness love;" and do not rest satisfied until you have all these Christian virtues. You may ask also for joy; and, oh, what an ocean of bliss is before you in the joy of the Lord! In "the peace of God, which passeth all understanding," what a wondrous depth of joy there is laid up in store for you! Our Lord Jesus said to his disciples, "These things have I spoken unto you, that my joy might remain in you, and that your joy might be full." It may be the same with you; therefore, ask for great things. Do not be satisfied with being little Christians, seek to come to the full stature of men in Christ Jesus. I will be thankful to get just inside the gate of heaven; but if I can sing more sweetly, and if I can have more fellowship with Christ, nearer his throne, why should I not get there? God grant that we may all have that high privilege!

Once more, I think that this exhortation, "Open thy mouth wide," means *attempt great things for God* as well as ask great things from God. Brethren, go in for something great. Go in for saving one soul; that is something great. Go in for preaching the whole truth of God; that is something great. Go in to be faithful to the teaching of the whole Word of God; that is something great. It is not sufficient if you have filled your own place;—a good many of you have not done that yet;—go in to preach the gospel somewhere else as well. Open some other building for worship; penetrate into some region where the gospel is not yet known. I wish that our College would open its mouth so wide as to include the whole world in the sphere of its operations. Brother Wigstone tells us that, if we open our mouth wide, we shall swallow up the whole of Spain and Portugal. Other brethren want us to open our mouth wide enough to absorb France, and Germany, and Russia, and all Europe. Some of our brethren have gone to India; there is a mouthful for us. If we open our mouth wide, India may be evangelized, and China, and the new world of America, and the far-distant world of Australia, will feel the power of the gospel that we take there in the name of the Lord. Let us pray, as David did, long ago, that the whole earth may be filled with God's glory. What is the whole earth, after all, compared with the greatness of God, and with the infinite sacrifice that Christ has offered? Well may the Lord say to each one of us, "Open thy mouth wide, and I will fill it."

I do like big prayers, brethren. I have some regard for the memory of William Huntington, though I should be sorry to endorse all that he said and did. He was a man whose prayers God heard and answered, but what were his prayers often? I smile, sometimes, as I think of what he asked of God: "Lord, give me a new pair of leather breeches;" or, "Give me a horse and carriage;" and he got them. William Carey cried, "India for Christ," and his prayer has kept on ringing right down the ages, and the Church of God is still praying, "India for Christ," and that prayer will be heard and answered in God's good time. Little boats, that carry small cargoes, come quickly home; but the big ships, that do business in great waters, are much longer in reaching the home port; but, then, they bring back much more precious loads. Huntington's prayer was the little boat that proved God's faithfulness; but Carey's prayer was the big ship, which will come home as surely as the other one did. So, "open thy mouth wide," brother, and ask something that will be honouring to God to give.

Did you ever think, dear friends, how wonderful is the condescension of God in hearkening to the voice of a man? That he should hear our prayers at all, shows that, in his condescension, he is as infinite as he is in his glory. Do you know, in your own soul, that God has ever heard your prayers? Then bless him, and love him, all your days. You know how the writer of the 116th Psalm put the matter: "I love the Lord, because he hath heard my voice and my supplications. Because he hath inclined his ear unto me, therefore will I call upon him as long as I live." It is truly marvellous that, though our prayer is so full of faultiness, and has to do with such insignificant worms as we are, yet that the Lord hears us, and grants our requests.

There are some who talk as if prayer was a meaningless form to us. "It is a beneficial thing, no doubt, for you to pray," say they. Surely, sirs, you must be measuring our corn with your bushel if you imagine that we could do such an idiotic thing as pray to a god who cannot hear us. That is an employment only fit for imbeciles; and if you tell us that no doubt it is a good thing for us to do, we reply that it would probably be a good thing for you to do it, for it could only be suitable to the imbecility which originated the charge brought against us. We assert, and rejoice to assert that, without working miracles, God still accomplishes his eternal purposes in answer to the supplications of his people. In earlier days, he wrought miracles for the deliverance of his servants; but, to-day, he does the same thing without the miraculous process, and as manifestly grants the requests of his suppliants as if miracles were as plentiful as the leaves upon the trees in summer.

II. Now, secondly, we turn to THE PROMISE: "I will fill it."

Great asking seems to me to be on a scale proportionate to the great things that are according to the very nature of God. I have never been able to believe in a little hell because I cannot find, in the Bible, any trace of a little heaven, or of a little Saviour, or of a little sin, or of a little God. I believe in a theology that is drawn to scale. If it is on the scale of an inch all round, I can receive it; but if it is on the scale of a foot in one place, I think it should be on the same scale throughout. Look, brethren, at the brightness of the Shekinah glory shining above the mercy-seat, and that mercy-seat red with such blood as was never spilt but once, and the Eternal Spirit leading us up to that mercy-seat;—can we go there to ask for a mere trifle? That does not seem to me to be at all congruous; far more congruous does it seem that, before the great God, with the great Mediator, and the great Spirit helping our infirmities, we should open our mouth wide, and expect God to fill it. O brethren, we may be quite sure that, in dealing with the infinite Jehovah, if we can rise to his scale of things, he will fill our mouths when we open them. It is hard work to fill a hungry mouth, for the food disappears down the throat in a moment; when once fed, it opens again, and is as empty as it was before. But God has the way of filling mouths that makes them keep full. He gives us water to drink, of so wondrous a kind, that we do not thirst again. Jesus said to the woman of Samaria, "Whosoever drinketh of the water that I shall give him shall never thirst; but the water that I shall give him shall be in him a well of water springing up into everlasting life." And God says to each child of his, "'Open thy mouth wide,' and though it seems to be like a horse-leech crying, 'Give, give,' 'I will fill it;' though it seems as insatiable as the grave, 'I will fill it.'" The great God himself says it; and, therefore, it must be true. If he had not said it, I would not have believed it; but having said it, he can do what seems to us impossible; he can satisfy our most insatiable cravings and longings; and he bids us keep on longing and craving, that he may keep on satisfying us again and again.

This promise is given by One who knows what we are going to ask. The Lord says, "Open thy mouth wide," and he knows what we desire to receive from him, and he has it all ready to give to us. Did you never bring home a present for your children, and ask them to wish for something, although they did not know that, all the while, it was in your pocket? You have brought them up to the point of asking for something that they want; then they go to bed, and when they wake in the morning, they are surprised to see the very thing they longed for lying on their pillow. In a similar manner, our Heavenly Father gives additional sweetness to his mercies by tempting us to long for various things that he has all ready to give to us. He may well say, "Open thy mouth wide," when he has so many good things ready to fill it.

What will he fill our mouths with? *Sometimes, he will fill them with prayer.* Do you not find, at times, that you cannot pray? Never mind, brother, if it is so with you; open your mouth wide, for he will fill it. He will fill your mouth with arguments. Kneel down, and groan because you cannot pray, agonize because you cannot pray, and the next day you will say, "I wish I felt as I did yesterday, for I never prayed with greater power than when I thought I was not praying at all." Open your mouth with a sense of want, a sense of desire. Open your mouth with the sensibility of insensibility; you can comprehend, by experience, the paradox that I cannot explain. God knows how to fill your mouth with prayer when you go to your pulpit. Perhaps, before the time for the service came, you thought you could not pray or preach at all. You remember how the Lord said to Ezekiel, "Eat this roll, and go speak unto the house of Israel;" and the prophet says, "So I opened my mouth, and he caused me to eat that roll." You also may be able to do the same thing. Sitting in your study, you may be anxious because you cannot get a subject to really lay hold of you. At any rate, brother, open your mouth with desire, and eagerness, and longing, as you sit there; and if the Lord sends a roll to you, and shows you how to eat it, when you go to talk to your people, you shall get that promise to Ezekiel fulfilled in your own experience, "I will open thy mouth, and thou shalt say unto them, Thus saith the Lord God." When you open your mouth in private, and eat the roll that the Lord gives you, he will open your mouth in public, and you shall tell the people the truth upon which you have privately feasted.

Next, *the Lord will fill our mouths with all manner of spiritual blessings.* David says that the Lord "satisfieth thy mouth with good things; so that thy youth is renewed like the eagle's." Time fails me to attempt any list of proof texts upon this point; I can only say that, when the Lord opens your mouth, you may be quite certain that anything he puts into it is wholesome and good; even though, sometimes, it is not according to your own taste, though it will be if your spiritual palate is in a healthy condition. If your taste is out of order, even sweet things will seem bitter to you. If your heart is not right with God, you will ask for that which would injure you if he granted your request. When the Israelites craved for flesh in the wilderness, they made a terrible mistake. It will be far wiser for you, when you open your mouth in prayer, not so much to go into details as to say, "Lord, I am a mass of wants; I hardly know what they really are, and what I think I want may be a mistake, but my mouth is open to receive whatever thou seest to be best for me." Then you may expect that he will fill it with all sorts of good things.

Further, *the Lord will fill your mouth with sacred joy.* When the Lord turned again the captivity of Zion, his people said, "Then was our mouth filled with laughter, and our tongue with singing." It is a blessed mouthful when you get such an amazing mercy that you cannot understand it. Have you not, sometimes, received a mercy that has been like Isaac, the child of laughter? It has come to us as Isaac came to Abraham, and we have heard the sound of the mercy, and have laughed for very joy. God will also fill your mouth with his praise. That was a wise prayer of the psalmist, "Let my mouth be filled with thy praise and with thy honour all the day." What a blessed mouthful it would be to have your mouth so full of the praise of God that you could not help letting it run out!

III. Now I must close by noticing THE ENCOURAGEMENT. "Open thy mouth wide, and I will fill it." Why? "Because I am Jehovah, thy God, which brought thee out of the land of Egypt."

Brother, *it is Jehovah who says to thee*, "*Open thy mouth wide.*" It does not do always to open your mouth wide to man, but the Lord says to you, "I am Jehovah, your God; open your mouth wide, and I will fill it." When you stand before men, ask little, and expect less; but when you stand before God, ask much, and expect more, and believe that he is able to do for you exceeding abundantly above all that you ask or think. "I am Jehovah." That is a boundless name; we know that our askings can never exceed his benevolence or his might. We are asking of a King; yea, of him who is King of kings, so let us open our mouths wide as we approach him; his very name prompts us so to do. Then he adds, "I am Jehovah, thy God;" so, will you not ask great things of the One who has given himself to you? Is God himself yours? Then, what is there that you may not ask of him? There is great force in Paul's argument, "He that spared not his own Son, but delivered him up for us all, how shall he not with him also freely give us all things?" There is equal force in this other argument,— As he spared not his own Deity, but freely gave himself up to be the God of his chosen ones, saying, "I will be their God, and they shall be my people," then he will not deny them anything that they ask of him if it is really for their good. Indeed, all things are yours already; since he is your God, you have only to ask him to give you that which is your own by his own gracious covenant. I should not feel afraid or ashamed to ask anyone to give me what really belonged to me, however big it was; and, in prayer, you have to ask from God what he has already given you in Christ Jesus, for "all things are yours," because "ye are Christ's; and Christ is God's."

Then he adds, "*which brought thee out of the land of Egypt.*" Notice this argument, brethren. Our own experience of deliverance from sin is a wonderful reason for asking great things of God. I speak with the utmost reverence, but it seems to me that God himself cannot give me anything more than he has already given me in the unspeakable gift of his only-begotten and well-beloved Son. His blessed Spirit has given unto us eternal life. All the embellishments and enrichments and sustenances of that life are not equal to the life itself; the life of God in the soul is the chief blessing, and that we have already received. Well, then, as God has given us life, surely he will give us all other great blessings that we need, and will deny us nothing that is for his own glory and our present and future good. Paul often uses this kind of argument; for instance, "While we were yet sinners, Christ died for us. Much more then, being now justified by his blood, we shall be saved from wrath through him. For if, when we were enemies, we were reconciled to God by the death of his Son, much more, being reconciled, we shall be saved by his life." The greater mercy having come, the lesser one will also surely come. So, ask God for large things; for you have already received larger things than you are ever likely to ask for, so you may rest assured that you will receive, in the future, whatever God sees that you really need.

God said to his ancient people, "I am the Lord thy God, which brought thee out of the land of Egypt." Might they not well ask large things of that God who smote Pharaoh with all those terrible plagues? Might they not well ask great things of him who darkened the sun at midday, who brought up the locusts till they covered the land, who made the very dust of Egypt to crawl with noxious life, and who sent terrific hailstorms, with fire mingled with the hail? Who would not ask great things of such a great God as that? Then think of his slaying the firstborn of Egypt, and dividing the sea, even the Red sea, and leading all the hosts of Israel through the deep and through the wilderness. He that could do all that could, in his infinite might, do all else that his people needed, so they might well ask great things at his hand. Moses sang, on the borders of the Red sea, "He is my God, and I will prepare him a habitation; my father's God, and I will exalt him." The Israelites might well ask great things of him who had overthrown all their adversaries; and you, who have experienced such a marvellous deliverance by the blood of Jesus Christ, ought surely to be bold when you go to the mercy-seat. The deliverance of Israel out of Egypt was by blood. The paschal lamb was slain, and its blood was sprinkled upon the houses of the Israelites; but you have not been redeemed with the blood of earthly lambs, "but with the precious blood of Christ, as of a lamb without blemish and without spot." Can it be possible, after such a redemption, that anything that is needed to bring you into the promised land, and to enrich you with all temporal and spiritual blessings, should ever be withheld from you? Let us each one go to the mercy-seat with our mouths wide open, and then let us go to our pulpits, and preach with our mouths wide open, even as Paul wrote, "O ye Corinthians, our mouth is open unto you, our heart is enlarged." Your mouths may well be open to your hearers because they have first been opened unto God. I am thankful that, throughout this Conference, I have seen no traces of doubt, and no signs of despondency. Every brother has seemed to have confidence in God, and to have hope, like a bright light, guiding him on his way. I have no doubt that some of you will see "greater things than these" even here on earth, while others will see them from the heights of heaven. As surely as we have the gospel with us, and the Holy Ghost with us, as surely as God has led us thus far through the wilderness, as surely as he keeps us knit together in love and unity, so surely will he lead us from strength to strength, and the Lord will be magnified in our mortal bodies whether by life or by death, and we shall, by his grace, all appear before him in Zion. God bless you, brethren! Amen.

A PROMISE FOR THE BLIND.

A Sermon

DELIVERED BY

C. H. SPURGEON,

AT THE BAPTIST CHAPEL, CHURCH STREET, BLACKFRIARS ROAD,

On Tuesday Evening, April 3rd, 1855,

On behalf of The Christian Blind Relief Society.

"Behold, I will bring them from the north country, and gather them from the coasts of the earth, and with them the blind and the lame, the woman with child, and her that travaileth with child together: a great company shall return thither."—Jer. xxxi. 8.

Poor Israel, as a nation, had its ups and downs. It was sometimes in captivity; and anon it experienced a deliverance. At one time, it was minished and brought low through affliction, persecution, or sorrow; at another, it was multiplied and increased exceedingly. It was the deliverance from one of these evil seasons that Jeremiah was commissioned to announce, by the promise that the Lord's people should come again to their own land.

Let us consider, for a few minutes, the circumstances of these Israelites. It must have been a sorrowful thing for them to dwell in a land that was not their own, to hear a language they understood not, to see the fierce inhabitants, their enemies, and the idolatrous worship of the heathen gods. We can well conceive of their mournful spirit, and the feeling with which they gave utterance to their plaintive song, "By the rivers of Babylon, there we sat down, yea, we wept, when we remembered Zion. We hanged our harps upon the willows in the midst thereof. For there they that carried us away captive required of us a song; and they that wasted us required of us mirth, saying, Sing us one of the songs of Zion. How shall we sing the Lord's song in a strange land?" But God sent among them prophets, who told them that they should be restored, and herein lay the glory of the promise, that it included *all* the captive people of God, whatever might be their rank or position. The blind, the halt, and the lame, should all come back. The hoary-headed man with his staff equally with the young and vigorous; the lame man as well as he who could run like the hart; all should come to the mount of the Lord; nor should even women be left behind: "The blind and the lame, the woman with child, and her that travaileth with child together: a great company shall return thither." Had the prophet not said that the blind and the lame should come, that their faces should be turned towards the holy city, had he not said that they should enter into the temple of the Lord; they might have thought that, being poor and blind, they would never be allowed to come unto the holy mountain, even Zion.

But, my friends, this text has a further prophetical signification in its reference to the gathering in of the Jews in the latter times; and with this we have more particularly to do. I believe in the restoration of the Jews to their own land in the last days. I am a firm believer in the gathering in of the Jews at a future time. Before Jesus Christ shall come upon this earth again, the Jews shall be permitted to go to their beloved Palestine. At present, they are only at the entrance gates. I am told that the Jews have a practice of bringing some of the soil of their own country to England, under the seal of the chief rabbi; and that, at their death, it affords them the highest joy to know that they will have a portion of this soil buried with them, even were it no more than sufficient to cover a sixpence. They have another idea,—of course, it is a very foolish one,—that every Jew dying in a foreign land travels underground direct to Palestine. It is because they love their country that they believe such a falsehood.

But whatever may be our opinion respecting the Jews, and their position, this I know,—though they ought not to be fettered and oppressed, though they ought to have a vote in Parliament, though they ought to be freed from civil disabilities, yet they never can amalgamate with other nations. The time will come when they shall leave their sordid ideas in the pursuit of gain to secure the treasures of paradise. They are a scattered people now, and must be till the last times; then suddenly they shall rise, touched by the influence of the Spirit of God, again to be his people. Their temple shall again resound with the worship of God, and old Zion will be again built. Then may we truly expect the latter-day glory shall come. Certainly, if I read my Bible aright, I must believe that the downtrodden, despised Jew shall again be glad; and poor old Judæa, that has been the scoff and scorn of mankind, shall again be lifted up and restored, and shall shine forth "fair as the moon, clear as the sun, and terrible as an army with banners."

If it be so, mark you, the blind Jew and the lame Jew will as surely go to Jerusalem as any of the rest of the Jews. They will all go; the blind, the lame, the woman travailing with child, will all meet in God's holy temple.

However, I leave this case of the Jews, their coming up from Babylon, and the last gathering in of Israel. I know very little of them; but would rather speak of my text under another aspect. You know that God has a peculiar people, as much a chosen nation as the Jews ever were; a called and elected people, whom the Father has chosen from before the foundation of the world; a redeemed people, whom Jesus has purchased with his precious blood; a sanctified people, because God has separated them from the rest of mankind. Well, all these people are to be brought in, to be gathered to Christ; every one whom God has chosen, redeemed, and sanctified shall come to mount Zion. Blessed be God, they shall all come to this city above. God's wheat shall all be gathered into God's garner. The ransomed of the Lord shall all join the throng around the throne, for ever—

"To bless the conduct of his grace,
And make his glories known."

My text says, the blind and the lame shall meet there.

Now I am about to speak, first of all, of *the characters named in the text;* and then I am going to try to show you *the duties of Christians to the persons so designated, or spoken of, as the lame and the blind.*

I. First, I am to speak of THE CHARACTERS NAMED IN THE TEXT: "the blind and the lame."

We will speak of the blind first. There are three classes of blind people: the physically blind, the mentally blind, and the spiritually blind. In illustration, I would take you to the London Road, and there you will find these three orders of blind people. There is the school for the blind, where you will find the physically blind. Just before you is the Roman Catholic Cathedral; there you will find the spiritually blind. And further on is the Bethlehem Hospital, commonly called Bedlam, where you will find the mentally blind. These are, then, the three divisions: the naturally, or physically blind; the mentally blind; and the spiritually blind.

Well, first, we refer to *the physically blind.* If chosen of God, they will love him, and they shall all come to heaven. Ah, poor Adam, how many are the infirmities which thy one sin has entailed upon thine offspring! Oh, mother Eve, how did thine act of transgression bring on us a train of woes! Lameness, blindness, deafness, with all the sad ailments of the paralytic, the dumb, the deformed! But all honour to the second Adam, he overcomes these infirmities; he saves "the blind and the lame." Through his sovereign grace, he loves many of the poor, darkened sons of men. Blind men are not chosen for soldiers, except in the army of God; but in that army, he enlists many blind warriors, and makes them the best of his soldiers. Yes, blind saints, God loves you, and will not exclude you from heaven. The man who has to go leaning on his crutch all through the journey of life, is not refused at heaven's door because of his crutches. Ye blind men, groping along in the world, when you arrive at heaven's gate, are you to be excluded because of the want of your eyes? Rather, the moment they come to its threshold, God speaks the word, and the withered limb regains its strength, the dim eye its lustre, and thus "the blind and the lame" become fitted to join the shining multitude around the throne.

We know that, if we die aged, we shall not be aged in heaven; there are no furrows on the brow of the glorified ones. Their eyes know no dimness; they know not what it is to have infirmities of body, for mortality is exchanged for immortality. It may be that we are weakly here; it may be that we have a feeble, diseased, emaciated body here; but there we shall have a spiritual body, like unto Christ's glorious body, clothed in light and majesty; we shall then be partakers of the bliss of heaven, shining as the stars in the firmament for ever and for ever. Now, ye physically blind, ye who do not see the glorious rays of the sun, do not be downcast, but remember that there have been many illustrious saints who have endured the same calamity. Chief and foremost, remember the blind bard of paradise, who, when his eyes were darkened, saw things that others never had imagined; I mean, Milton. Though you are deprived of your temporal sight, you may see far into the deep things of God. Others have been blind as well as you. Many blind men have been great men. Ye physically blind, rejoice that, blind though you are, if you look to Christ by faith, you will join "the general assembly and church of the firstborn, which are written in heaven."

But, then, secondly, *the mentally blind* shall be restored. I have referred to Bedlam for an illustration. I do not mean, by that, to refer to those who have suffered the entire loss of their reason. It would be a very doubtful question to discuss, whether a person born without the use of his natural reason can be an object of divine grace. It would lead to a great deal of discussion, without any practical result, so I leave it alone. But there is such a thing as practical mental blindness. There may be the master-mind, gigantic conceptions, a fruitful imagination, with the power of leading and governing other minds, and yet there may be a degree of mental blindness. We are all somewhat blind; we have all, we must confess, an imperfect vision; except the Pope, who claims to be infallible, and therefore proves that he is more blind than the rest of us. There are some of us who feel our fallibility in point of judgment, and who are obliged to acknowledge our ignorance and want of clear mental perception.

But, my friends, some of the mentally blind shall enter heaven. I now refer to those whose mental powers are very weak. I sometimes meet with these mentally blind people. They do not know much of their own language, and perhaps have never put as many as a half a dozen words together in their lives, in public. I once heard of one of these, an old woman, who had heard a most uninteresting discourse upon metaphysics, but she called it "a blessed sermon, for," she said, "the minister told us all about the Saviour being both meat and physic too." I think that was a good mistake. She, like many of the mentally blind, could not understand one-half of the words that are used by some of our preachers. She belonged to the somewhat mentally blind folk who have not had the benefit of teaching or training. Well, blessed be God, they do not need it to find the way to heaven. "The wayfaring men, though fools, shall not err therein."

Well, all these mentally blind shall come. There will be people in heaven who never read a word in their lives. I know not how low the grace of God can go. Some poor creatures, who know nothing of the things of earth, even these may understand the gospel, it is so plain. We do not need a giant intellect in order to grasp its doctrines. Its element and substance is, "He that believeth and is baptized shall be saved." Believer, ignorant though you may be, you can comprehend this grand scheme of man's redemption, so do not say that, because you are poor and ignorant, you will not enter heaven.

But, then, thirdly, there are *the spiritually blind*. Whenever you find a person spiritually blind, you ought to be very careful how you speak to him, or of him. I do think this is a matter in which we often fail. The discussion between Catholics and Protestants has been far from what it ought to have been. We seem bent upon forcing them to submit at once to our views, but this is wrong of us. We may condemn wrong principles, but let us always speak gently of the men who hold them. They are spiritually blind, so we should deal kindly with them, avoiding that bitterness of spirit which is so often manifested. Sick men will not take your medicine if you give them vinegar with it; give them something sweet with it, and they will take it. So be kind and loving to the spiritually blind, and they will be likely to give heed to you.

To say nothing of the Church of Rome, the Puseyites, or Arminians; to go no further than the present congregation, there are many spiritually blind here. Oh, man or woman, do you see your lost and ruined state by nature? No. Did you ever, by faith, see Christ crucified on the cross for man's redemption? No, you did not! Did you ever understand the sufficiency of the mediatorial sacrifice of Christ? No, you did not! Did you ever realize what vital union with the person of Christ means? No! Has the Holy Spirit ever spoken in your heart? You are obliged to confess that you know nothing about his purifying influence. Ah, then, you are blind, spiritually blind! Chapel-goer, church-goer, having the form of religion without the power, you are blind as a bat, which can only fly in the night; or like the owl, when daylight comes, you will not be able to find your way. Unless the scales are removed from your eyes, you will be exposed to the judgment of God; but if the Holy Ghost illuminates you, though *now blind*, you shall come to Zion with the rest of the chosen race.

But my text also mentions the lame. These are not so much the subject of our consideration to-night, and may therefore be passed over briefly. But many of the lame are to get to heaven. Who are they? Well, brethren, *there are some of God's people who are lame, because they are weak in faith.* We hear sometimes a great deal said about possessing a full assurance of being a child of God; and then, every now and then, we hear of others who have a doubt, or only a hope, concerning their salvation. As good Joseph Irons used to say, "They keep hope, hope, hoping,—hop, hop, hopping,—all their lives, because they can't walk." Little-faith is always lame. Yet, although some of you never could say, with certainty, that you are the people of God, yet one or another of you can say with sincerity,—

"A guilty, weak, and helpless worm,
　On thy kind arms I fall;
Be thou my strength and righteousness,
　My Jesus, and my all."

Ye lame ones, fear not; you will not be cast out. Two snails entered the ark; how they got there, I cannot tell. It must have taken them a long time. They must have started rather early, unless Noah took them part of the way. So, some of you are snails; you are on the right road, but it will take you a long while to get into the ark unless some blessed Noah helps you.

Again, *backsliders are lame.* There are Christians to be found who believe that it is possible to fall from a state of grace. Here I would speak cautiously. God's people cannot fall finally; but they can fall a long way. When a Christian falls, it is no light matter. I hear some talking of falling and getting up again, as if it were nothing; but let them turn to Hebrews vi. 4—6.* But we will rejoice that—

'Grace will complete what grace begins,
　To save from sorrows or from sins."

I do not say that a Christian man may not fall, and break a limb; but I do say that a child of God cannot fall, spiritually, and break his neck. He cannot fall without grievous injury. The result, in his experience, must be unhappiness and misery. Look at poor David; after falling into that great sin, his history was nothing but troubles from rebellious sons and enemies. Ye loving, living children of the blessed God, I know that you will not talk lightly of falling into sin. Backsliders, fallen ones, God will have mercy upon you if you are truly penitent. It is a glorious fact that the sorrowing backsliders shall not be left behind. Backsliders shall sing above, as God's restored children, whom he ever has loved. Blind and lame ones, believe in the Lord, and you shall be found amongst the followers of the Lamb at the last.

II. Now, secondly, and very briefly, WHAT ARE OUR DUTIES TO THESE BLIND PEOPLE?

I answer, first, *to the spiritually blind, our duty is to pray for them.* Yes, I believe we shall never do anything without this. However much you may profess to love them, yet if you do not pray for them, I cannot believe what you say. An infidel once met a Christian man, and said to him, "You don't believe in the Bible; you don't believe in the gospel." "I do," the Christian replied. "Well, then, how is it that, as I pass you in going to my business every day, you have never spoken to me concerning my soul? You don't believe the Bible." "I do." "I cannot believe you," he said, "for if you do, you are very unfeeling."

Now, Christians, if you believe that you have spiritually blind people around you, what is your duty towards them? Sirs, unless you feel a deep concern about their state, I fear that the heavenly Physician has not removed the spiritual cataract from your eyes. If we believe their position to be one of extreme peril, that they, for want of the light to guide them, are perishing, how we ought to exert ourselves on their behalf. The ministers do not feel enough for souls in this degenerate age, but keep on preach, preach, preaching; or read, read, reading their good-for-nothing manuscripts, and yet there is no increase to their churches. The minister is here in the pulpit, and the people are down below in the pews; there is no golden link of sympathy between them. We want more of this sympathy. We want more intense love to souls, the souls of the ungodly. We want to go more to God's throne to plead *for* you, and then to plead *with* you. As God's ambassadors, we say with Paul, "We pray you, in Christ's stead, be ye reconciled to God." It is no trifling matter to be spiritually blind. It is no light matter to have no eyes. No, the blind are sure not to enter heaven if they die spiritually blind. They must have their eyes enlightened by God if they are to be found above. May the ever-blessed and glorious God awaken all the spiritually blind! May we who are ministers, and all others who have the opportunity use it, under God's blessing, to throw light upon their dark minds! Try to get your neighbours to the house of God, but take care that it is a gospel ministry to which you invite them. Take care that you prove the value of the gospel you possess by your own consistent practice. Pray for them, and it may be that God will give unto them repentance unto life.

And then, next, *our duty to the mentally blind is to be very charitable, and try to instruct them.* We must manifest, in all our dealings with them, a kindness of disposition, never attempting to thrash them into what we believe to be right. I do not believe in the utility of bigoted denunciations. I sometimes differ from my Christian brethren, but I do not quarrel with them on that account; all I can say is, "Well, brother, if you can't see it, I cannot help it; it is in the Bible, and I can see it plainly enough." We, as Calvinists, believe that men cannot see the truth unless it is revealed to them by God; we should therefore be the last to condemn the ignorant, but should do our utmost to instruct them, and to open their eyes. It is of no use to attempt to force a man to believe. It has been said,—

> "Convince a man against his will,
> He's of the same opinion still."

So, whenever you get into an argument with a mentally blind man, suppose it to be a Roman Catholic, don't get cross with him. If you do, you will never make a friend of your opponent. Suppose others do not see as you do on some matters, on infant baptism or anything else,—and I think we Baptists very often err in our temper in some of our discussions,—well, don't try to compel them to see as you see. Brethren, that is not the way to convince them of the truth of our beliefs. Instead of acting like that, we should try to show our brethren the truth as it is in the Bible; and then, they must shut their eyes or else see it. "It is there," say you; "if you can't see it, I shall not be cross or out of temper with you." Never let us be cross with the mentally blind. You know that the policeman, when he meets a man at night, turns his lantern straight upon the man's eyes; so must we turn the light of truth upon these blind eyes, and not take out the truncheon to thrash them at once. We should also reflect that there was a time when we, too, knew nothing. It therefore behoves us to act kindly to the younger scholars in the school, seeing that we have not always ourselves been in the highest class.

But, now to conclude, we have to speak of *our duty to the physically blind*. There are some good people who would be glad to work for their living, but they are disabled through affliction; among these are the blind. When I go amongst the sick and poor, I find so many to relieve that, when I have given all I can afford, there is still more to do. Well, there they are, and to do them any permanent good you must give them something week by week. I was thinking, suppose another globe were created, and rolled up alongside this world, so that when any in this world became sick, or blind, or helpless, we could put them over into the other world to get rid of them. Well, suppose that were done, brethren; you would soon want them back again. "There is dear Sister So-and-so, she is entirely dependent upon the charity of her friends, but she has such rich deep experience; we have derived so much comfort from her society that we must have her back." Then, if these poor sufferers were in another world, you would have no way of doing good by relieving them, and then you would wish you could be doing something for them for the sake of the Lord Jesus Christ. You would then have to complain, "Here is this shilling; I don't know what to do with it. Here I have money that I cannot use because there are no objects of charity to whom I can give it. I wish Jesus Christ would come down to earth again; would I not minister to his necessities if he were here? Ay, that I would; I would give him the best of things that were to be found anywhere. Then I would sit at his feet, washing them with my tears, and wiping them with the hair of my head."

You say that, but if all these poor blind people were in another world, there would be no one to whom you could minister for his sake, so Jesus Christ has sent some of them to us that we may have the opportunity of doing good to them, and that, by-and-by, he may be able to say to us, "Inasmuch as ye have done it unto one of the least of these my brethren, ye have done it unto me." He has cast some blind people upon the Church on purpose to give us the treat of doing something for them. He has said, "The poor ye have always with you." He allows you the opportunity of evidencing your love to him by relieving those who need your help. When I hear of a church where they are all gentlemen, I always say farewell to that; for where there are no poor, the ship will soon sink. If there are no poor there, Christ will soon give them some if they are a real gospel church.

Now, the reason we have a Blind Society is simply this, there are some good people who cannot help themselves because they are blind and helpless; there is one from my church, and some from other churches. It is not a very large Society, it is all the better for that; for I find that, in the great Societies, there is so much influence needed, and so many votes required, that those who need help most cannot obtain it; and those who do not need it so much, but have the influence, get it all. Well, in this Christian Blind Relief Society, some of these poor blind people receive a trifle every week, and I assure you they are all needy and deserving objects of your charity.

This is what we ask you to-night to support. Jesus Christ stands at the door, and says to you as you retire, "Give me somewhat, this night, if you love me."

I have to appeal so often, and am followed so much by my own people, that I have not the face to ask you for anything to-night, so Christ shall ask instead, and I will ask next time.

Remember the poor! Take care of the blind!

Expositions by C. H. Spurgeon.
MATTHEW IX. 27—35; AND XX. 29—34.

Chapter ix. Verse 27. *And when Jesus departed thence, two blind men followed him, crying, and saying, Thou son of David, have mercy on us.*

No sooner does Jesus move than fresh candidates for his bounty appear: the blind seek sight from him. Two sightless men had become companions in affliction; they may have been father and son. They were in down-right earnest, for *they "followed him, crying, and saying, Have mercy on us."* Persevering, vehement, yet intelligent was their appeal. They were of one mind in reference to Jesus, and therefore they went one way, and used one prayer, to one and the same person. Our Lord is here called by his royal name: *"Thou Son of David."* Even the blind could see that he was a king's son. As Son of David, he is entreated to show mercy, and act according to his royal nature. It is *mercy* which gives us our faculties, and mercy alone can restore them.

This prayer suits us when we perceive our own darkness of mind. When we cannot see our way into truth, let us appeal to the Lord for gracious instruction; ever remembering that we have no claim except that which originates in his mercy.

28. *And when he was come into the house, the blind men came to him: and Jesus saith unto them, Believe ye that I am able to do this? They said unto him, Yea, Lord.*

They were most eager for the boon. They gave him no leisure: they pressed *into the house* where he had sought privacy and rest: they *came to him*, even to Jesus himself. The Lord would have them express their faith, and so he makes inquiry of them as to what they believe about himself. Jesus makes no inquiry about their eyes, but only about their faith: this is ever the vital point. They could not see, but they could believe; and they did so. They had a specific faith as to the matter about which they prayed; for our Lord put it plainly, "*Believe ye that I am able to do* THIS?" They had also a clear view of the character of him to whom they applied; for they had already styled him "*Son of David*", and now they called him "*Lord*."

29. *Then touched he their eyes, saying, According to your faith be it unto you.*

Again he arouses their faith; and this time he throws the whole responsibility upon their confidence in him. "*According to your faith be it unto you.*" He touched *them* with his hand; but they must also touch him with their faith. The word of power in the last sentence is one upon which he acts so continually, that we may call it, as to many blessings, a rule of the kingdom. We have the measuring of our own mercies; our faith obtains less or more according to its own capacity to receive. Had these men been mere pretenders to faith they would have remained blind. If we will not in very truth trust our Lord, we shall die in our sins.

30. *And their eyes were opened; and Jesus straitly charged them, saying, See that no man know it.*

They both saw: the double miracle was wrought at the same moment. Comrades in the dark, they are now companions in the light. Singular that for two souls there should thus be one destiny! It was a singular double fact, and deserved to be made widely known; but our Lord had wise reasons for requiring silence. He "*straitly charged them.*" He left them no option: he demanded complete silence. He that opened their eyes closed their mouths. Jesus did not desire fame; he wanted less crowding; he wished to avoid excitement; and therefore he was express and peremptory in his order: "*See that no man know it.*"

31. *But they, when they were departed, spread abroad his fame in all that country.*

They most industriously published what they were bidden to conceal, till "*all that country*" rang with the news. In this they erred greatly, and probably caused the Saviour so much inconvenience by the pressure of the crowd, that he had to remove from the town. We may not hope that we are doing right if we disobey our Lord. However natural disobedience may appear to be, it is disobedience, and must not be excused. Even if the results turned out to be advantageous, it would not make it right to break the command of our Lord. Silence is more than golden when our King commands it. He doth not seek applause, nor cause his voice to be heard in the streets that he may be known to be doing a great work. His followers do well to copy his example.

We do not wonder that our Lord's name became famous when there were such persons to advertise it. How earnestly and eloquently would the two formerly blind men tell the story of how he opened their eyes! *We* are not forbidden, but exhorted to make known the wonders of his grace. Let us not fail in this natural, this necessary, this useful duty. More and more let us "*spread abroad his fame.*"

32. *As they went out, behold, they brought to him a dumb man possessed with a devil.*

As a pair of patients leave the surgery, another poor creature comes in.

Note the "*behold.*" The case is striking. He comes not freely, or of his own accord: "*they brought*" him: thus should we bring men to Jesus. He does not cry for help, for he is "*a dumb man.*" Let us open our mouths for the dumb. He is not himself, but he is "*possessed with a devil.*" Poor creature! will anything be done for him?

33. *And when the devil was cast out, the dumb spake: and the multitudes marvelled, saying, It was never so seen in Israel.*

Our Lord does not deal with the symptoms, but with the source of the disorder, even with the evil spirit. "*The devil was cast out*"; and it is mentioned as if that were a matter of course when Jesus came on the scene. The devil had silenced the man, and so, when the evil one was gone, "*the dumb spake.*" How we should like to know what he said! Whatever he said it matters not; the wonder was that he could say anything. The people confessed that this was a wonder quite unprecedented; and in this they only said the truth: "*It was never so seen in Israel.*" Jesus is great at surprises: he has novelties of gracious power. The people were quick to express their admiration; yet we see very little trace of their believing in our Lord's mission. It is a small thing to *marvel*, but a great thing to believe.

O Lord, give the people around us to see such revivals and conversions, as they have never known before!

34. *But the Pharisees said, He casteth out devils through the prince of the devils.*

Of course, they had some bitter sentence ready. Nothing was too bad for them to say of Jesus. They were hard pressed when they took to this statement which our Lord in another place so easily answered. They hinted that such power over demons must have come to him through an unholy compact with "*the prince of the devils.*" Surely this was going very near to the unpardonable sin.

35. *And Jesus went about all the cities and villages, teaching in their synagogues, and preaching the gospel of the kingdom, and healing every sickness and every disease among the people.*

Chapter xx. Verses 29, 30. *And as they departed from Jericho, a great multitude followed him. And, behold, two blind men sitting by the way side, when they heard that Jesus passed by, cried out, saying, Have mercy on us, O Lord, thou son of David.*

On *Jericho* a curse had rested, but the presence of Jesus brought it a blessing. We suppose he must needs go through Jericho as once before he must needs go through Samaria. Our Lord *departed from Jericho*, and a vast crowd attended him; for his fame had spread far and wide. Nothing striking is noted concerning his doings till two beggars come upon the scene. Mercy needs misery to give it an occasion to work. *Behold, two blind men sitting by the way side.* They could not behold Jesus, but we are asked to behold *them*. They had taken up a hopeful position, *by the way side*, for there they would be likely to hear any good news, and there they would be seen by the compassionate. They had ears if they had not eyes, and they used their hearing well. On enquiry, they learned *that Jesus passed by*, and believing that he could restore their sight, they grew earnest in prayer to him: *they cried out*. Their plea was pity: "*Have mercy on us.*" Their appeal was to the royal heart of Jesus: "*O Lord, thou son of David.*" Our Lord's sermon was interrupted by the repeated outcries of these two blind beggars of Jericho; but this never displeased him; neither would true preachers of the gospel be disconcerted if some of their hearers were to cry out with similar eagerness for salvation.

31. *And the multitude rebuked them, because they should hold their peace: but they cried the more, saying, Have mercy on us, O Lord, thou son of David.*

The crowd desired to hear Jesus, but could not do so because of the shouts of the blind men : therefore *the multitude rebuked them.* Did they upbraid them for ill manners, or for noise, or for harshness of tone, or for selfishly wishing to monopolize Jesus? It is always easy to find a stick when you wish to beat a dog. The people wanted them to be quiet, and *hold their peace,* and found plenty of arguments why they should do so. This was all very well for those who were in possession of their faculties; but men who have lost their sight cannot be quieted if there is an opportunity of obtaining sight; and as that opportunity was rapidly passing away from these poor men, they became vehement in their earnestness. Unhindered by the threats of the crowd, *they cried the more.* Some men are urged onward by all attempts to pull them back. When we are seeking the Lord, we shall be wise to make every hindrance into a stimulus. We may well bear rebukes and rebuffs when our great aim is to obtain mercy from Jesus.

Unvarying was the blind beggars' cry: "*Have mercy on us, O Lord, thou son of David!*" Variety of words they had no time to study. Having asked for what they needed, in words which leaped from their hearts, they repeated their prayer and their plea, and it was no vain repetition.

32. *And Jesus stood still, and called them, and said, What will ye that I shall do unto you?*

Jesus stood still. At the voice of prayer, the Sun of righteousness paused in his progress. Believing cries can hold the Son of God by the feet. *He called them :* and this because they had called him. What comfort that call yielded them ! We are not told that they came to him: there is no need to tell us that. They were at his feet as soon as the words were uttered. How sadly blind are those who, being called a thousand times by the voice of mercy, yet refuse to come !

Our Lord enlightened minds as well as eyes, and so he would have the blind men intelligently feel and express their needs. He puts to them the personal enquiry : "*What will ye that I shall do unto you?*" It was not a hard question, yet it is one which many an attendant at our places of worship would find it difficult to answer. You say you " wish to be saved ": what do you mean by those words?

33. *They say unto him, Lord, that our eyes may be opened.*

Just so. They needed no time for second thoughts. Oh, that our people were as quick to pray, "*Lord, that our eyes may be opened*" ! They went straight to the point. There is not a word to spare in their explanatory prayer. No book was wanted, no form of words; the desire clothed itself in simple, natural, earnest speech.

34. *So Jesus had compassion on them, and touched their eyes : and immediately their eyes received sight, and they followed him.*

So, that is, since they thus stated their desire, and had so great a need, *Jesus had compassion on them,* pitying their loneliness in the dark, their deprivation of enjoyment, their loss of power to follow a handicraft, and their consequent poverty. *He touched their eyes.* What hands were those which undertook such lowly fellowship with human flesh, and wrought such deeds of power ! *Immediately their eyes received sight.* Only a touch, and light entered. Time is not necessary to the cures of Jesus. Proof of their sight was at once forthcoming, for *they followed him.* We best use our spiritual sight when we look to Jesus, and keep close to his heel.

Oh, that the reader, if he be spiritually blind, may ask for the touch of Jesus, and receive it at once, for immediately he will receive sight ! An inward light will in an instant shine forth upon the soul, and the spiritual world will become apparent to the enlightened mind. The Son of David still lives, and still opens the eyes of the blind. He still hears the humble prayer of those who know their blindness and their poverty. If the reader fears that he, too, is spiritually blind, let him cry unto the Lord at this very instant, and he will see what he shall see, and he will for ever bless the hand which gave sight to the eyes of his soul.

SPIRITUAL CONVALESCENCE.

A Sermon

DELIVERED BY

C. H. SPURGEON,

AT THE METROPOLITAN TABERNACLE, NEWINGTON,

On Thursday Evening, March 17th, 1864.

"And I will strengthen them in the LORD; and they shall walk up and down in his name, saith the LORD."—Zechariah x. 12.

ACCORDING to our own natural conceit, we are very strong; it is as hard for us to part with our belief in our own strength as with our trust in our own righteousness. It is a very painful cut which severs us from confidence in ourselves; but when the Spirit of God performs that most needful operation, then we discover that our supposed strength is utter weakness, and that our righteousnesses are but filthy rags. If our eyes have been opened to see ourselves as we are in God's sight, we know that we are weak as water, and that from us, unassisted by divine grace, there can never come any good thing. Our past experience might have been sufficient to teach us this lesson. The feeble way in which we have performed any duty that devolved upon us, the sad manner in which we have met any temptation that assailed us, the impatient and murmuring spirit in which we have endured any affliction that has come upon us,—all these must have shown us that, even after we are renewed by divine grace, though "the spirit indeed is willing," yet "the flesh is weak;" and though to will is present with us, yet how to perform that which is good we find not. We are not now like a stone which lies on the ground, and cares not to stir; but we are like a bird with a broken wing, which longs to soar into the clearer air above the clouds, but which is quite unable to reach that higher atmosphere. We know something of our weakness, but we probably do not yet know how weak we are, and I suppose it will be one of our life lessons to learn by experience how great our weakness is.

Perhaps some of you have been discouraged by the consciousness of your weakness; and, in looking forward to the future, you have been greatly distressed. You are anticipating some important duty for which you feel quite unfit, or it may be that the shadow of some impending trial is just beginning to fall upon you. Possibly you have come to the verge of the valley of the shadow of death, and you know that the way to the celestial city lies through it, and you intend to press through it; but you are half afraid of what will happen to you there, for you know how weak you are. And, perhaps, just at this juncture, Satan may have whispered in your ear, "It is no use for you to try to get through; you have started on a wild-goose chase, and see how you limp already; your arm is so weak that you will be no match for the giants you will have to fight. Give it up, man; how can a poor timid creature such as you are ever pass by the lions' dens and the mountains of leopards? Such weaklings as you are should not go on pilgrimage, leave that task to those who are stronger and braver than you are." Well, if such a temptation as that has come to you, the message of the text is peculiarly timely to you. It does not deny that you are weak, it implies that you are; it would not have you for a moment forget your weakness, it even reminds you of it. There would be no necessity for this promise if you were strong: "I will strengthen them in the Lord; and they shall walk up and down in his name, saith the Lord."

There are three things for us to notice in the text: first, *divine strengthening promised;* secondly, *Christian activity predicted;* and, thirdly, *both blessings divinely guaranteed.*

I. First then, here is DIVINE STRENGTHENING PROMISED: "I will strengthen them in the Lord."

Observe *the discrimination of the promise,* or what is not promised in it. It is not said, "They shall have no work to do; I will take them out of the vineyard in the middle of the day, and bid them sit down in the cool arbour, and rest and refresh themselves." No, there is no such promise as that; the Lord does not say, "I will take you away from your labours," but "I will strengthen you, so that you will be able to perform them." I do not remember any promise that the waters of trouble shall be dried up; but you all remember this one, "When thou passest through the waters, I will be with thee; and through the rivers, they shall not overflow thee." I have no recollection of any promise that the fires of trial shall be quenched; but the Lord has said, "When thou walkest through the fire, thou shalt not be burned; neither shall the flame kindle upon thee." If you had not to trudge along the pilgrim way, if you had not to carry the cross and fight for the crown, you would not need this promise. The Lord would not strengthen you in order that you might sit still, or put "the everlasting arms" beneath you so that you might lie down in blissful laziness. Oh, no! but as you are bidden to "put on the whole armour of God," you may be certain that there is stern fighting before you; and as the Lord promises to strengthen you, there must be no relaxation of watchfulness and no cessation of activity on your part. So, Christians, seek the promised strength, for you are sure to need it; seek it now, for you may need it to-night; seek to get as much of it as you can, for when you have the most of it that you can get, you will find that you will need it all.

Then notice, next, *the comprehensiveness of the promise*: "I will strengthen them in the Lord." You may view this promise in many different lights. Perhaps you have fallen into such a state of despondency that you question your interest in Christ, possibly you have almost begun to doubt the veracity of your God or his faithfulness to his promise. Well then, in your case, the promise of the text will apply to your faith. Come to God at this moment, and say, "Lord, thou hast said, 'I will strengthen them;' wilt thou not graciously strengthen my faith, which is now like a reed shaken by the wind, so that it shall become like an oak of the forest which fears not the stormiest wind that blows?"

Or it may be that your hope has grown dim; you cannot see afar off, you cannot—

"Read your title clear
To mansions in the skies."

Well then, take this promise to the Lord, and ask him to fulfil it to you; he will give you some heavenly eye-salve, and as soon as your eyes are anointed with it, your vision will become clear and strong, and you will be able to see the land of far distances where in due time you shall arrive, and "see the King in his beauty."

Possibly it is your courage that has declined. The fear of man has ensnared you; you cannot now face a hostile multitude as you once could; indeed, you are half ashamed to go back to the home where you are laughed at because of your religion. You are not now inclined to nail your colours to the mast; you would rather sail away to some peaceful shore than remain to fight the foe. O my brethren and sisters in Christ, plead this promise, "I will strengthen them," for so shall you get your courage renewed until you, who are now timid as the deer, shall become bold as a lion.

Is it your zeal that is flagging? Do you, who once gloried in being in the thickest of the fight, now try to hide away among the baggage? Then pray to God to restore to you your former fervour and devotion to his cause, and pleading this promise you shall surely get your heart's desire. The promise is such a comprehensive one that it not only includes the strengthening of any special part of our spiritual being that is weak, but also the thorough restoration and strengthening of the entire spiritual constitution. Lord, I would be made strong, not only in the hands of my faith, but also in the feet of my obedience; I would be so strengthened in the vitality of my spiritual life that my eyes should be able to see much that is now invisible to me, that my ears might hear the music of thy matchless voice, that my heart might dance at the sound of thy name, and that I might be like Elijah when he girded up his loins, and ran before King Ahab, because he heard the sound of an abundance of rain, the promise of those welcome showers which the Lord was about to pour down upon the thirsty land.

But we must not forget *the provision that is made for the fulfilment of this promise:* "I will strengthen them in the Lord." We know that it is the Holy Spirit's work to strengthen believers, and I trust that many of us have experienced his mysterious operations. We have sometimes felt so despondent that we did not know what to do; and then, though perhaps we had not been specially engaged in prayer, and had not been up to the house of God to worship, all of a sudden our spirits have become elastic as we have felt some precious promise applied with power to our soul, and the burden which threatened to bow us down to the earth has become light as a feather, and we have stood upright, and rejoiced "with joy unspeakable." There is no grief which the Holy Spirit cannot allay; that Divine Comforter knoweth so well how to get at the secret springs of our sorrow, and to put the comfort right into the spring itself, that there can never be a grief which can elude him, or which can baffle his skill.

Usually, however, the Holy Spirit is pleased to work by the use of means; and you know, dear friends, how often you have been strengthened in this way. What a strengthening cordial is prayer! When you have gone to cast your burden upon the Lord, many a time you have gone upstairs groaning, but you have come down singing. Oftentimes, you have received strengthening through this blessed Book. When you have opened it, your eyes have been full of tears; but as you have lighted upon some precious promise that has exactly met your case, your tears have all vanished, and your soul has been filled with joy. God has spoken to you through his Word, and so you have been strengthened. Or you have come up to the house of the Lord, and you have found something there that has strengthened you. I know that many of you find spiritual food in the services here on the Sabbath; but, by the time that Thursday night comes round, your soul is very hungry, and you are well-nigh famished; but the Holy Spirit graciously applies the Word to your heart, and you go out to meet the trials and engagements of the week feeling strong through the strength you have received from heaven. Yes, the Master is pleased, in the assembly of his saints, when we break the Bread of life, to feed the multitude to the full, and they go away refreshed. This is specially the case when we gather around the table of our Lord. I wish that all the saints would meet for communion on every "first day of the week." I cannot conceive it to be possible for them to meet thus too often. As for myself, unless sickness keeps me away, I find it most helpful to come to the Lord's table every Lord's day; for, although we believe neither in transubstantiation nor in consubstantiation, yet there is a very real sense in which we do spiritually eat the flesh and drink the blood of the Son of man, and so become "strong in the Lord and in the power of his might."

Nor are the means of grace the only channels by which we are spiritually strengthened. Christian society will often produce the same blessed results. Some Christians live too much alone. It is true that there is an evil of an opposite character, for some professors spend far too much time in one another's houses, wasting precious hours in idle gossip and chatter; but brethren and sisters in Christ ought to find opportunities for profitable conversation concerning their Lord and his work at home and abroad. Some of us might derive great benefit from the Christian experience of those who are older than we are, or who have been more deeply taught in the things of God; while others of us might be able to impart some spiritual gift to those who are less favoured than we are. In the olden days, "they that feared the Lord spake often one to another." Let this good practice be revived, for thereby, depend upon it, many will be strengthened in the Lord.

Still, dear friends, the best way of obtaining a renewal of spiritual strength is by getting near to Christ, and keeping near to him. He who layeth hold of Christ has grasped "very God of very God." He who can come so close to Christ as to lay his head upon Christ's bosom, and to say, "Let him kiss me with the kisses of his mouth," must grow stronger and stronger every moment that he is in the immediate presence of his Lord. We grow in grace as we grow in the knowledge of our Lord and Saviour Jesus Christ. The clearer view we have of Christ, the firmer confidence we have in his faithfulness and his power to save, the stronger will our spiritual nature grow, and the more like our Lord shall we become. They who live near to Christ must derive strength from him. Having waited upon the Lord, they shall renew their strength, they shall mount up with wings as eagles, they shall run, and not be weary, they shall walk, and not faint.

Before I pass from this point, I should like to emphasize the words of this part of the text; there are not many of them, but they are all significant: "*I* will strengthen them." You cannot strengthen yourselves, and your minister cannot strengthen you; it is God who first gives you spiritual life, and then sustains it by his grace; in fact, he is himself, as David says, the strength of our life. It is still true that power belongeth unto God, and that power he imparts to all as he pleases. Note, too, that he says, "I will strengthen them *in the Lord.*" They are not strengthened in themselves; there is no Christian who grows stronger through the force of his own personality, but he derives more and more strength from the Lord; he learns how to draw continually from the inexhaustible supplies of omnipotence, and so is himself strengthened in the Lord. Perhaps someone says, "I have been a Christian for thirty years, but I am not spiritually any stronger than I was when first I knew the Lord." No; nor will you be any stronger if you live for another thirty years unless you depend upon God to strengthen you. Is anyone here more able than in the past to live by faith upon the Son of God, and to drink deeper draughts from the fountain of infinite fulness? Then it is clear that, in your case, my brother or sister, the promise of the text has been fulfilled, and you have been strengthened in the Lord.

Now lay the emphasis on the divine "I will," "I *will* strengthen them in the Lord." This promise was true more than two thousand years ago, and it is just as true to-day. It has been fulfilled many thousands of times since then, but it is just as full of force as when it was first given. Suppose I take a note to the Bank of England, and get five pounds for it, that note will be cancelled, and I cannot get the cash for it a second time. But it is not so with God's promises; you may take a promise to the Bank of Heaven in the morning, and cash it, as it were; and you may take the same promise in the afternoon, and cash it again; and you may take it again at night, and once more get the full value for it. You may have pleaded that promise when you were a young man of twenty, but it is just as true now that you are an old man of eighty; and to the very last moment of your life you shall find that the promise shall be fulfilled in your experience: "I will strengthen them in the Lord."

Note, too, the comprehensiveness of the promise. The Lord does not say, "I will strengthen them up to such-and-such a point;" but it is implied that the strength will be sufficient for all their needs. So it will, my brother or my sister; "as thy days so shall thy strength be." You shall always have strength enough, but you shall never have any to spare. If you had any superfluous strength, you would only do mischief with it; but you will have all that you really need. When you come to the last river, you may feel, "If there is another river after this to be crossed, I shall be unable to cross it;" but there is not another, and your strength shall fail when you have no more need of it, but not before. Your strength shall be like the widow's oil; so long as there were any empty vessels, the oil kept on running; but as soon as her son said to her, "There is not a vessel more," the oil stayed; and until your life's task is complete the Lord will strengthen you. The manna kept falling until the children of Israel entered Canaan, and the manna of grace shall keep on falling into your heart until you shall enter the heavenly Canaan. Wherefore be of good courage, brethren and sisters in Christ, for you shall have just as much strength as you will require, for your Lord's promise concerning you is, "I will strengthen them in the Lord."

II. I must speak but briefly upon our second point, which is, CHRISTIAN ACTIVITY FORETOLD: "they shall walk up and down in his name, saith the Lord."

How strangely some people read their Bibles, and how wickedly they pervert its plainest teaching! They learn that salvation is all of grace, and then they say, "Therefore, as it is all of grace, we need not do anything at all. It is God which worketh in us both to will and to do of his good pleasure, so we can leave the working out to him also. God begins the work of grace, God carries it on, and God completes it, so we can be as careless and indifferent as we please." If they do not actually put their thoughts into words, this is practically what they think. They seem to imagine that divine grace is an excuse for human laziness, but I have never yet found any passage of Scripture to warrant such an assumption as that. Certainly our present text does not support that idea: "I will strengthen them in the Lord; and they shall walk up and down in his name." According to the lazy system, it ought to read, "I will strengthen them in the Lord; and they shall be carried to heaven in a sedan chair;" for that seems to be some people's notion of how they are to get there. May our tongue cleave to the roof of our mouth ere our preaching shall ever lead our hearers into such a state of spiritual slumber as that! Our doctrine may be as high as the Scriptures warrant us in teaching, but we shall never find there any ground for the infamous deduction that, because God worketh in us, we are to lie inert as if we were logs or stones. Oh, no! that is not his will concerning us, for the apostolic injunction is, "Work out your own salvation with fear and trembling, for it is God which worketh in you both to will and to do of his good pleasure."

So *true Christians are to be active*: "they shall walk up and down in his name, saith the Lord." Christianity has its meditative side, it has its passive stage, but these are the necessary preparation for an active life. A devout contemplation of the doctrine of divine sovereignty will be like the underlying rock which supports the good rich mould of holy gratitude and love which yields an abundant harvest both to God and man. True Christians delight in sacred activity; in that respect, they are like the angels of God, "that do his commandments, hearkening unto the voice of his word;" and like the glorified saints above, who "serve him day and night in his temple." A life of Christian activity down here is a fitting prelude to a life of heavenly activity up there. The best Christians are those who serve God the most. Ask the gardener which is the best apple tree in the garden, and he will tell you that it is not the one which has the best shape, but the one which yields the most fruit; and he is not the best Christian who occupies the highest position, or who talks the most about divine things, but it is he whose life is most fruitful in good works to the glory of God.

Further, *Christian activity is, as far as it is possible, incessant.* This is implied in the phrase, "they shall walk up and down," as though they were never to be inactive, and certainly never to be idle. The true Christian, when he is in a healthy spiritual state, has always some good work on hand,—something on the anvil, or something heating in the fire, or something cooling in the water,—something that he is planning for the future, something that has yet to be completed, or something that is just finished, and ready to be presented to God,—a prayer to offer, a hymn to sing, the sick to visit, the poor to relieve, the ignorant to instruct. He advances from one duty to another while he is about in the world, and serves his God there; and when he gets home, he still serves his God by gathering his family and servants together for prayer. As Satan is represented as a restless spirit continually going to and fro, walking up and down in the earth, so is it with the true Christian; he is constantly traversing the world, not seeking to do evil, but, like his Master, going about doing good.

The expression, "they shall walk up and down," also implies *variety of service.* They shall not only walk *up,* they shall also walk *down.* There are some departments of Christian service that we like, and others that we do not like. Many would far rather glorify God by preaching to hundreds or thousands from the pulpit than by lying alone in the chamber of affliction. Some like to serve God in what they regard as a respectable sort of way, but they do not care to work for Christ in the back slums, the cellars, or the garrets; but true Christians will be just as willing to go down as to go up. We must be ready to go anywhere and to do anything for Christ. It is just as great an honour to be employed in Christ's scullery as to serve him in his temple. If he allows us to wash his feet, even with our tears, let us count that as high a privilege as to anoint his head with oil. Happy is that servant who shall be permitted to kiss his Master's feet, but equally happy should he be who is bidden to unloose the latchet of his shoes. It should be a matter of no moment to us whether we go up or down so long as we are doing our Lord's will.

But do not forget to notice that *all is to be done in God's name:* "they shall walk up and down in his name." It is Jehovah who is speaking here; and it is in his name, under his authority, at his command, and to his praise and glory that all our service is to be rendered. It is all to be done as unto the Lord, and not unto men. I rejoice that so many, whom I am now addressing, are occupied in various forms of Christian activity; and I hope that each one of us who loves the Lord will continue thus to walk up and down in his name until he calls us to serve him in the upper sanctuary.

III. Now I close by briefly reminding you that BOTH THESE BLESSINGS ARE DIVINELY GUARANTEED: "I will strengthen them in the Lord; and they shall walk up and down in his name, saith the Lord."

Perhaps some Christian brother or sister here is thinking sorrowfully, "I never can be made strong enough to serve God as I would like to serve him." But, my dear friend, here you have a triple guarantee from the Lord himself; here is the divine "I will" of omnipotent grace, the divine "they shall" of consecrated free agency, and the divine "saith the Lord" of infallible faithfulness; what more can you want? Is not God's declaration of more value than the oaths of all the men who ever lived? Would you not sooner rely upon his divine assurance than trust to anything that you can see? Possibly you say that you would, but I am half afraid of you. When things go very pleasantly with you, it is easy for you to believe; but it is another matter when the sun has set, and it is very dark, and there are no stars to be seen. O beloved, seek to have a faith which can trust God as well in the dark as in the light! What a grand life that man leads who lives upon whatever is guaranteed to him by "Thus saith the Lord"! He never gets any poorer, because "Thus saith the Lord" never fails him; and he never needs to get any richer, for "Thus saith the Lord" is all that his spirit can possibly crave. Here is one of the promises which is guaranteed to us by "Thus saith the Lord:" "All things, whatsoever ye shall ask in prayer, believing, ye shall receive." That is enough for me; I will take that promise, and plead it at the throne of grace, and I know I shall not be sent empty away. Will you not, dear friends, do the same with the promises in our text? You need supernatural strength for the service to which your Lord has called you, and here he has promised it to you. "Thus saith the Lord" is surely sufficient for you; so, seeing this divine seal attached to the promise, do not be slow to secure the fulfilment of it; but to-night, ere you retire to rest, seek the strength you need from the Strong One, and then, on the morrow, go forth to walk up and down in his name.

But there are some here, I fear, who never think of God's promises, and that is a strange and sad state for anyone to be in. To one who has been brought out of nature's darkness into God's marvellous light, it does seem amazing that anyone can live without a thought of God and his many exceeding great and precious promises. It is most extraordinary that an immortal being, created by God, can be content to go on from day to day and from year to year without any care about pleasing his Creator. But if anyone here is feeling, "Oh, I wish that I could get to God! I would not for all the world have him as my enemy, and I long to know how I can come to him;"—I am thankful that you feel like that, and I am glad that I am commissioned to tell you the way to come to him. "No man cometh unto the Father but by me," said Christ. "There is one God, and one Mediator between God and men, the man Christ Jesus." Look first at the crucified Christ lifted up upon yonder tree, for—

"There is life for a look at the Crucified One,
There is life at this moment for thee."

Trust him as your Mediator, your Advocate with the Father, and you shall find that then God will receive you for Christ's sake, he will strengthen you in the Lord, and you shall walk up and down in his name; and, by-and-by, you shall dwell with him for ever. God grant it, for Jesus' sake! Amen.

PROVIDENCE

An Instructive Truth—Jer. 10:23
Exposition of Jeremiah 10
The Hungry Filled, The Rich Emptied—Luke 1:53
Exposition of Luke 1.26-56
The Commissariat of the Universe—Ps. 104:28
Exposition of Psalm 34
Beggars Becoming Princes—I Sam. 2:8

AN INSTRUCTIVE TRUTH.

A Sermon

PUBLISHED ON THURSDAY, JULY 21ST, 1904,

DELIVERED BY

C. H. SPURGEON,

AT THE METROPOLITAN TABERNACLE, NEWINGTON,

On Thursday Evening, June 22nd, 1876.

"O LORD, I know that the way of man is not in himself: it is not in man that walketh to direct his steps."—Jeremiah x. 23.

THIS declaration follows after Jeremiah's lamentation over the Lord's ancient people, who were about to be carried away captive into Babylon. The prophet speaks of a fact that was well known to him. It is always well, brethren, to know the truth, and to know it so certainly that you are able to remember it just when you most need it. There are some people, who are very much like that foolish captain of whom we have heard, who had a good anchor, but he left it at home when he went to sea, so it was no use to him. So, these people know what would comfort them, but they do not recollect it in the time of their distress. Jeremiah says, "O Lord, I know," and he utilizes his knowledge as a source of comfort in his hour of need.

What Jeremiah knew was this,—that the affairs of this world are not under the control of men, however much they may imagine that they are. There is a supreme authority to theirs, and a power which rules, and overrules, and works according to its own beneficent will, whatever men may desire or determine to do. Nebuchadnezzar was about to carry the Jews away from the land which flowed with milk and honey to his own far distant country; but the prophet consoled himself with the reflection that, whatever Nebuchadnezzar meant to do, he was only the instrument in the hands of God for the accomplishment of the divine purpose. He proposed, but God disposed. The tyrant of Babylon thought that he was working out his own will, yet he was really carrying out the will of God in chastising the idolatrous and rebellious nation. This was Jeremiah's consolation, "I do not know what Nebuchadnezzar may do; but I do know that 'the way of man is not in himself: it is not in man that walketh to direct his steps.' I know that, in God's eternal purposes, every step of Judah's way is mapped out, and he will make it all work for his own glory and the good of his chosen people in the end."

Child of God, will you, for a moment, reflect upon the overruling power of God even in the case of the most mighty and wicked of men? They sin grossly, and what they do is done of their own free will, and the responsibility for it lies at their own door. That we never can forget, for the free agency of man is a self-evident truth; but, at the same time, God is omnipotent, and he is still working out his wise designs, as he did of old, in the whirlwind of human wrath, in the tempest of human sin, and even in the dark mines of human ambition and tyranny, all the while displaying his sovereign will among men even as the potter forms the vessels on the wheel according to his own will.

This truth ought to be remembered by us, because it tends to take from us all fear of man. Why shouldst thou, O believer, be afraid of a man that shall die, or the son of man, who is but a worm? Thou art, as a child of God, under divine protection; so, who is he that shall harm thee while thou art a follower of that which is good? Remember that ancient promise, "No weapon that is formed against thee shall prosper; and every tongue that shall rise against thee in judgment thou shalt condemn. This is the heritage of the servants of the Lord." The most powerful enemy of the Church can do nothing without God's permission. He can put a bit into the mouth of leviathan, and do with him as he pleaseth. The almighty God is Master and Lord even over the men who imagine that all power is in their hands.

And while this truth should banish our fear of man, it should also ensure our submission to the will of God. Suppose that the Lord allows Nebuchadnezzar to devastate the land that he gave to his people by covenant; it is God who permits it, therefore think not thou so much of the instrument employed by him as of the hand in which that instrument is held. Art thou afflicted, poor soul, by some hard unkind spirit? Remember that God permits thee to be so tried, and be not angry with that which is only the second cause of thy trouble, but believe that the Lord permits this to happen to thee for thy good, and therefore submit thyself to him. A dog, when he is struck with a stick, usually bites the stick; if he had more sense, he would try to bite the man who holds the stick. So, your contention must not be against the instrument of your affliction. If there be any contention, it is really against God; and you would not, I trust, think of contending with your Maker. Rather, say, "It is the Lord; let him do what seemeth him good." Let your back be bared to the rod, and look up into your Heavenly Father's face, and say, "Show me wherefore thou contendest with me."

This truth ought also to strengthen our faith. When fear goes, faith comes in. It is an easy matter to trust God when everything goes smoothly; but genuine faith trusts God in a storm. When the land of Judah was hedged about by God's providence, and no enemy ventured to set foot upon the sacred soil, it was easy for a prophet to praise the Lord; but it was quite another matter to trust God when Nebuchadnezzar destroyed the villages, besieged the cities, and, by-and-by, took them, and gave them up to utter destruction, and carried away their inhabitants into captivity. To trust in God then, was not so easy; yet that was the time for the display of real faith. Faith in the storm is true faith; faith in a calm may be, or may not be, genuine faith. Summer-weather faith may be true, or may not be true; but wintry faith, that can bring forth fruit when the snows are deep, and the North wind blows, is the faith of God's elect. It proves that it has divine vitality in it, because it can master the circumstances which would have utterly crushed the faith which appertains only to flesh and blood. It is a severe trial, to a child of God, when he is mocked at home,—when someone, who ought to be kind to him, is quite the opposite,—when the ties of nature seem only to intensify the hatred that is felt against the heir of grace,—when Ishmael mocks Isaac, and grieves him continually. That is a severe trial, but it affords the opportunity for the tried one to recall this truth, that God has all things in his hand, and that this trial is only permitted, in his wisdom and love, for some good purpose towards his own child. It is still true that "all things work together for good to them that love God, to them who are the called according to his purpose;" and that "no good thing will he withhold from them that walk uprightly." If your enemy triumphs over you for a time, you should say to him, "Rejoice not against me, O mine enemy: when I fall, I shall arise." May the Holy Spirit help you so to do! The way of the persecutor is, after all, not left absolutely to his own will, but there is another and a higher will that overrules all.

We will not, however, tarry longer over the consideration of the context so far as it applies to Nebuchadnezzar, and other adversaries of the people of God, but we will endeavour to learn the lesson that is taught us in the latter clause of the text: "It is not in man that walketh to direct his steps." And, firstly, I will try to prove to you that *these words are true;* and, secondly, that *these words are instructive.*

I. First, then, THESE WORDS ARE TRUE: "It is not in man that walketh to direct his steps."

For, first, although man is an active individual, so that he can walk, he cannot direct his steps, *because there may be some obstacle in his way which he cannot surmount, and which will change the whole course of his life.* He may have determined, in his own mind, that he will do this or that, and that he will go here or there; but he cannot foresee every circumstance that may happen to him, and there may be circumstances that will entirely alter the direction of his life; there may be unexpected difficulties, or what many call accidents, which are really providences, which will prevent us from doing what we have resolved to do. Take the case of a young man, who is just beginning business life; though he is active and strong, is it in him to direct his steps? I know it was not in me to direct my own steps. I had certain plans concerning my life course, but they have not been fulfilled. No doubt, the highest desire I ever cherished has been granted to me; but my first plans and purposes were not realized. I am not, to-day, where I hoped to have been; there were difficulties in the way, which made it impossible for me to get there. I expect others have had a similar experience. A young man may try to choose his path in life, but we all know how seldom, if ever, he can get exactly what he wants. Perhaps he goes into a certain house of business, and he says, "I shall work my way up till I get to the top." Yet, how frequently it happens that something occurs, which jerks him off the line of rails which he had laid down for himself, and he has to go in quite a different direction. The path he had chosen was, apparently, a very proper one for him to choose; perhaps, he spent a good deal of earnest thought upon the matter, and, possibly, also a good deal of prayer; yet he finds, as many others have found, that "it is not in man that walketh to direct his steps." It is possible that the young man prospers so that he is able to go into business on his own account; but the same lesson has to be learned under different circumstances. He could not foresee what was going to happen, so he had purchased certain goods, relying upon an expected rise in the market; but there was a sudden fall, instead of a rise, and he became a loser, not a gainer. Going into business is often like going to sea; one may be much tossed about, and possibly may be wrecked, before reaching the desired haven. Many a man has found that he cannot get what he most confidently reckons upon.

Another man fails in health. He might have prospered; but, just when the full vigour of his physical strength was needed, and the greatest clearness of his mental vision was required, he was laid aside. As he sickened, he also became depressed in spirit, as he realized that his path must be that of an invalid, and perhaps of a poor man; yet he thought his career would have been that of a strong man, who would soon have reached a competence. I am sure that I must be addressing many, who know very well, from their own experience, that it is not of the slightest use for a man to say, "I will do this," or "I will do that," because something or other may occur, which will altogether prevent you from doing that which seems simple enough now. The mariner reckons on reaching port at a certain day or hour, but the wind may shift, or many things may happen to delay him. The mariner, however, can reckon even better than you can, for he has his chart, and he can find his way; he knows where the shoals are, and the quicksands, and the rocks, and where the deep channels run; but you do not know anything about your future life; you are sailing over a sea that no ship's keel has ever ploughed before. God knows all about it; everything is present to his all-seeing eye, but it is not present to your eye. It is not possible for a man to direct his own way absolutely, for he has not the power to do it; let him strive and struggle as he may, he must often be made to feel this.

Perhaps some of you are just now in this condition. Your affairs have got into a tangle, and you do not at all know how to unravel it. You are like a man in a maze or a labyrinth. You wish to take the course which is according to the will of God; but, whether you should turn to the right hand or to the left, you do not know.

Now, you have begun to realize what was always true, but what you did not perceive before, that is, that "it is not in man that walketh to direct his steps." You cannot direct your own way; you are quite perplexed as to which of two courses you should take. If this one be taken, it involves one form of trouble; and if the other course be chosen, that involves another kind of difficulty. What are you to do? Well, you know that the wisest thing for you to do is to take the matter to the Lord, and ask him to direct you. That is what you ought to do in every case; that ought to be the constant habit of your soul,—to look for the fiery-cloudy pillar which alone can guide you safely over the trackless wastes of life.

In the second place, man ought not to direct his way according to his own will, because *his will is naturally evil*. Ungodly men think that they can direct their own way. Ah, sirs! if you do that, you will direct your way down to the deeps of destruction. He who is his own guide is guided by a fool. He that trusteth to his own understanding proves that he has no understanding. If you will be your own director, you will be directed to the place where you will have bitter cause to rue it for ever and ever. If a man, starting out in life, says, "I shall follow my own will. I will say to my passions, 'You shall be indulged;' and to my desires, 'Eat, drink, and be merry;' and to my soul, 'Trouble not thyself with solemn and serious things; leave eternity till it comes, and make thou the best thou canst of time:' I will direct my own way as pleasure shall guide me, or as self-interest shall guide me,"—if you, sir, talk like that, I pray you to remember that "it is not in man that walketh to direct his steps;" and it ought not to be, for man is quite incompetent to perform such a task as that, because he has a natural bias towards that which is evil,—an inclination towards that which will be injurious to him, and to others also, and which will make him miss the chief end of his being, which is, to glorify God, and to enjoy him for ever.

I should like, before proceeding further with my subject, to urge everyone, who has hitherto depended upon himself, to pause, and lift up his heart to heaven, and say, "Gracious Spirit, thou shalt be my Guide, from this time, and for ever." For, young man, young woman, you will surely run upon the rocks, ere long, if you take the tiller of your life's vessel into your own hands. With such a heart as yours, you cannot expect to go right without the grace of God. The doctrine of the depravity of the human race, is not merely an article in the creed; it is a matter of everyday experience. There is in you, by nature, a tendency to put bitter for sweet, and sweet for bitter,—to put darkness for light, and light for darkness; and though you may think that you have a preference for good,—and it is possible that you have a preference for some forms of good,— yet there are critical points where self seeks to rule, where the weakness of your natural disposition will be discovered, sooner or later, and where the evil that lurks within your flesh will prove to be your ruin. I charge you, sons and daughters of Adam, to remember that, since your father, Adam, even in his state of innocence, could not direct his own way aright, but lost paradise for us all, there is no hope that, in your fallen state, you can find your way back to paradise. Nay, but you will keep on wandering further, and further, and further from the way of peace and holiness, for "it is not in man that walketh to direct his steps."

Let me give another meaning to the text, and still seek to prove it at the same time. It is not, and it ought not to be in man that walketh to direct his steps, because, not only is he naturally inclined to evil, but *even when grace has renewed his nature, his judgment is so fallible that it is a great mistake for him to attempt to direct his own way.* Dear brother or sister in Christ, the stony heart of unbelief has been removed from you, and you have had a new heart and a right spirit put within you; and, now, the living and incorruptible seed that is in you makes you seek after that which is good and right; but if you, even now, shall trust to your own judgment, you will find yourself brought into a thousand sorrows. Ah, my brother, you are an experienced Christian man, and others look up to you, and ask direction from you; but if you are really experienced, you will often say to them, "God helping me, I can direct you; but, as for myself, I feel that I have need of a director quite as much as the youngest babe in the family of God." Does not every man, who is truly wise, feel himself to be increasingly a fool apart from divine guidance, and is it not a token of growth in wisdom and grace when a man's self-confidence continues to grow less and less? Distrust yourself, dear friend, for you accurately gauge your own judgment when you do that. It is about little matters that wise men generally make their grosser mistakes. In what he considers a difficult matter, the wise Christian man always has resort to God in prayer; but when he gets what he regards as a very simple thing, which is perfectly clear, and which he thinks he can himself decide; then his folly is speedily discovered. He is like the Israelites were with the Gibeonites; they said, in effect, if not in words, "We do not need to pray about this matter. We must not make treaties with the Canaanites, but these men are not Canaanites, that is quite clear. We heard them say that they had come from a far country, and when we looked at their shoes we knew that they spoke the truth. They told us that they were quite new when they put them on, yet now they are old and clouted; they must have come a great many miles, you may depend upon it. And their bread—did you notice that? It has the blue mould all over it; we should not like to eat a mouthful of it, yet they told us that it was quite new when they started. There is no doubt that they are distinguished foreigners, who have come from a far country, so let us strike hands with them, and make a covenant with them." And so they did, for the case seemed so clear to them that they asked no counsel of God; and therein Israel made a great mistake. So, brothers and sisters, whenever any case appears to be very clear to you, be sure then to say, "Let us pray about it." You know the old proverb, "When it is fine weather, carry an umbrella. When it is wet, you can do as you like." So, when any case seems to be quite clear, pray over it. When it is more difficult, I dare not say that you may do as you like about praying then, unless I say it in the spirit of the proverb, which would imply that you would be sure to pray then. When you feel certain that you cannot go wrong, you certainly will go wrong unless you ask counsel of God about the matter. That was a good plan of the old Scotchman, who, when anything was in dispute, used to say, "Reach down yon Bible;" and when that was brought down, and the Scripture read, and prayer offered, the good man felt that he could see his way, and could go with firm step along the path to which the Lord had directed him. "It is not in man that walketh to direct his steps," for his judgment is fallible.

I think there is another meaning to be given to the text, for the gracious man feels that he must not direct his own steps, *because he cannot take even a step in the right way apart from divine help.* How can he talk about directing his own steps when he is absolutely dependent upon the grace of God for every step he takes? O brothers and sisters, if the Lord were to help us, by his grace, until we got up to the doorstep of heaven, we should never be able to get in unless he gave us the grace to take the last step! You cannot direct your own steps, for you are a cripple, and cannot take even one step except as strength is given you from on high. You are like a ship upon the sea; you can make no progress except as the breath of the Divine Spirit fills the sails of your barque. How can you direct your own way when you have no power to go in it, and are dependent upon God for everything? I pray you to confess your dependence, and not to talk of directing your own steps.

I must give you just one thought more under this head. *He that walketh need not think of directing his own steps, for there is One who will direct them for him.* What if sin inclines us to take the wrong path, and if a feeble judgment makes us err through inadvertence? There is no need for us to choose our own lot; but we may bow before the Lord, and say, "Thou shalt choose our inheritance for us." The choice is difficult for you, my brother; then do not choose your own way, but leave it to him who seeth the end from the beginning, and who is sure to make a wise choice. The burden of life is heavy, my sister, then do not try to carry it, but "cast thy burden upon the Lord, and he shall sustain thee." "Commit thy way unto the Lord; trust also in him; and he shall bring it to pass." Let it not be your choice, but let it be God's choice. That was a wise answer of a good old Christian woman, when she was asked whether she would choose to live or die. She said that she had no choice in the matter, but that she left it with the Lord. "But," said one, "suppose the Lord put it to your choice, which would you select?" "Neither," she replied; "I would ask him not to let me choose, but to choose for me so that it should be as he willed, not as I willed." Oh, if we could but once abandon our own choosings, and say to the Lord, "Not as I will, but as thou wilt," how much more happy we might be! We should not be troubled by the thought that we could not direct our own steps, but we should be glad of it, because our very weakness would entitle us to cry unto the Lord, "Now that I cannot direct my own way, what I know not teach thou me."

II. Time fails me, and therefore I will close my discourse by briefly mentioning the practical lessons of the text in order to prove to you that THESE WORDS ARE INSTRUCTIVE. It seems to me that they are instructive if we use them thus.

First, *avoid all positive resolutions about what you mean to do*, remembering that "it is not in man that walketh to direct his steps." Do not forget what the apostle James says about this matter, "Go to now, ye that say, To-day or to-morrow we will go into such a city, and continue there a year, and buy and sell, and get gain, whereas ye know not what shall be on the morrow." If you do make any plans, always make them in pencil, and have your indiarubber handy, so that you can rub them out quickly. Much mischief comes of making them in ink, and regarding them as permanent, and saying, "This is what I am sure I shall do." Cast iron breaks easily, so do not have any cast-iron regulations for your life. Do not say, "That is my plan, and I shall keep to it whatever happens." Be ready to alter your plan as God's providence indicates that alteration would be right. I have known people who have been very much given to change; I cannot commend them, for I remember that Solomon said, "As a bird that wandereth from her nest, so is a man that wandereth from his place." So, do not be in a hurry to wander. On the other hand, I have known some persons, who have resolved that they will never move at all. Do not make such a resolution as that, but recollect that, although "a rolling stone gathers no moss," it is equally true that "a sitting hen gets no barley;" and believe that there may come a time when it will be right for you to move. Do not make up your mind either that you will move, or that you will not move, but wait for guidance from God as to what he would have you do.

The next thing is, *never be too sanguine in your expectations*. I suppose we must have expectations; that old-fashioned benediction, "Blessed are they that expect nothing, for they shall not be disappointed," is very difficult to gain. Expect that, if God has promised you anything, he will be true to his word; but, beyond that, do not expect anything beneath the moon; for, if you do, you will be sure to be disappointed sooner or later. It is of the man whose heart is fixed, trusting in the Lord, that it is said, "He shall not be afraid of evil tidings;" but if his heart had been fixed merely on the attainment of certain worldly ends, he would have been overwhelmed when the evil tidings came. As to anything in this world, let this be the rule by which you are governed, "Having food and raiment, be therewith content," and never cherish too sanguine expectations.

Next, *avoid all security as to the present*. If you have anything that you prize very highly, hold it very loosely, for you may easily lose it. Read the word "mortal" plainly imprinted on the brows of all your children. Look into the dear eyes that are to you like wells in the desert, and remember that they may be closed in less than an hour, and the light of life be gone from them. Your beloved one and you yourself are alike mortal, and either of you may soon be taken from the other. Have you property? Remember that wealth has wings, and that it flies away, like a bird upon swift pinions. Have you health? Then think what a marvellous mercy it is that—

"A harp of thousand strings
Should keep in tune so long;"—

and remember that, very soon, those strings may be all jarring, and some of them may be broken. Hold everything earthly with a loose hand; but grasp eternal things with a death-like grip. Grasp Christ in the power of the Spirit; grasp God, who is your everlasting portion, and your unfailing joy. As for other things, hold them as though you held them not, even as Paul says, "It remaineth, that both they that have wives be as though they had none; . . . and they that use this world, as not abusing it: for the fashion of this world passeth away." Of everything below, it is wise for us to say, "This is not my abiding portion." It is very necessary to say this, and to realize that it is true, for everything here is covered with bird-lime, and the birds of paradise get stuck to it unless they are very watchful. Mind what you are doing, you prosperous people, you who have nice homes, you who are investing your money in the funds; mind that you do not get bird-limed. There is nothing permanently for you here, after all. Your home is in heaven; your home is not here; and if you find your treasure here, your heart will be here also; but it must not be so. You must keep all earthly treasures out of your heart, and let Christ be your treasure, and let him have your heart.

The next observation I would make is this,—*Bow before the divine will in everything.* "It is not in man that walketh to direct his steps." Why should it be? O Lord, thou art Master, thou art King; then why should we wish to have our own way? Is it right that the servant should take the master's place? There are some of you who are in trouble, and probably your chief trouble arises from the fact that you will not absolutely submit to the Lord's will. I pray that the Holy Spirit may enable you to do so, for trouble loses all its sting when the troubled one yields to God. If you had directed your own way, and this trouble had come upon you because of the choice that you had made, you might have cause to be distressed; but as the Lord has so directed and arranged your affairs, why should you be cast down? My dear friend, you know—or, at any rate, you ought to know—that you cannot be supreme; you must be content to be second. You must say to the Lord, "Thy will, not mine, be done." You will have to say it sooner or later; and if you are a child of God, you ought to have said it long ago, so say it at once. I heard one who, I thought, was a Christian, say, "I cannot think that God was right in taking away my dear mother from me." I replied, "My sister, you must not talk like that." Perhaps someone else says, "I did feel that it was hard when my dear child was taken from me." Yes, my dear friend, you may have felt that it was hard, but you ought to have felt that it was right. God must be free to do as he pleases, and he always does what is right; therefore, you must submit to his will, whatever he pleases to do.

My last observation is,—*Pray about everything.* Remember what Paul wrote to the Philippians, "Be careful for nothing; but in every thing by prayer and supplication with thanksgiving, let your requests be made known unto God." Pray about everything; I make no exception to this. Pray about waking in the morning, and pray about falling asleep at night. Pray about any great event in your life, but pray equally about what you call the minor events. Pray as Jacob did when he crossed the brook Jabbok; but do not forget to pray when there is no angry Esau near, and no special danger to fear. The simplest thing, that is not prayed over, may have more evil in it than what appears to be the direst evil when once it has been brought to God in prayer. I pray that all of you, who love the Lord, may commit yourselves afresh to Christ this very hour. I wish to do so myself, saying, "My Master, here am I; take me, and do as thou wilt with me. Use me for thy glory in any way that thou pleasest. Deprive me of every comfort, if so I shall the more be able to honour thee. Let my choicest treasures be surrendered if thy sovereign will shall so ordain." Let every child of God make a complete surrender here and now, and ask for grace to stand to it. Your greatest sorrow will come when you begin to be untrue to your full surrender to the Lord; so may you never prove untrue to it!

Exposition by C. H. Spurgeon.
JEREMIAH X.

Verses 1, 2. *Hear ye the word which the* LORD *speaketh unto you, O house of Israel: Thus saith the* LORD, *Learn not the way of the heathen, and be not dismayed at the signs of heaven; for the heathen are dismayed at them.*

Among the heathen, if certain stars were in conjunction, it was considered unlucky; and certain days of the week were also regarded as unlucky, just as to this day, there are people who think that it is very unfortunate to commence anything on a Friday. There are a great many foolish superstitions floating about this silly world, but you Christian people should never allow such follies to have any influence upon you. Neither the fiends of hell, nor the stars of heaven, can ever injure those who put their trust in God.

3, 4. *For the customs of the people are vain: for one cutteth a tree out of the forest, the work of the hands of the workman, with the axe. They deck it with silver and with gold; they fasten it with nails and with hammers, that it move not.*

Those ancient prophets seemed to take delight in heaping scorn upon the god-making of the heathen. Even the heathen poets made sport of the god-making; one of them very wisely said that it would be more reasonable to worship the workmen who made the god, than to worship the god which the workmen had made.

5. *They are upright as the palm tree, but speak not: they must needs be borne, because they cannot go.*

Pretty gods they must be, cannot move, and cannot even stand till they are nailed up, and cannot stir unless they are carried from place to place.

5—8. *Be not afraid of them; for they cannot do evil, neither also is it in them to do good. Forasmuch as there is none like unto thee, O* LORD; *thou art great, and thy name is great in might. Who would not fear thee, O King of* *nations? for to thee doth it appertain: forasmuch as among all the wise men of the nations, and in all their kingdoms, there is none like unto thee. But they are altogether brutish and foolish: the stock is a doctrine of vanities.*

To teach people to worship mere stocks and stones, may well be called "a doctrine of vanities."

9. *Silver spread into plates is brought from Tarshish, and gold from Uphaz, the work of the workman, and of the hands of the founder: blue and purple is their clothing: they are all the work of cunning men.*

Step into any Roman Catholic Joss-house in England, or on the Continent; or, for the matter of that, into any Anglican Joss-house, for they are all very much alike; and you will see that the modern "gods" are no better than those upon which the prophets of old poured scorn; and I think it is our duty to pour scorn upon these saints, and saintesses, and Madonnas, and Bambinos, and I know not what besides.

10—13. *But the* LORD *is the true God, he is the living God, and an everlasting king: at his wrath the earth shall tremble, and the nations shall not be able to abide his indignation. Thus shall ye say unto them, The gods that have not made the heavens and the earth, even they shall perish from the earth, and from under these heavens. He hath made the earth by his power, he hath established the world by his wisdom, and hath stretched out the heavens by his discretion. When he uttereth his voice, there is a multitude of waters in the heavens, and he causeth the vapours to ascend from the ends of the earth; he maketh lightnings with rain, and bringeth forth the wind out of his treasures.*

To what a height of sacred imagery does Jeremiah mount! He seems to shake off his usual melancholy spirit when he comes to sing the praises of the Lord. He uses very similiar language to that of Job, his fellow-sufferer.

14. *Every man is brutish in his knowledge:*

Every idolater proves that he knows no more than a brute beast when he worships a stock or a stone.

14, 15. *Every founder is confounded by the graven image: for his molten image is falsehood, and there is no breath in them. They are vanity, and the work of errors: in the time of their visitation they shall perish.*

The next verse brings out very vividly the contrast between these false gods and the one living and true God:—

16. *The portion of Jacob is not like them: for he is the former of all things; and Israel is the rod of his inheritance: The* LORD *of hosts is his name.*

What a blessed name that is for God: "The portion of Jacob"! And the other side of the truth is equally blessed: "Israel is the rod of his inheritance." God belongs to his people, and they belong to him; if we can but realize that these blessings are ours, we are building on the solid foundation of the richest possible happiness.

The form of the prophecy now changes; for God was about to send his people, because of their sin, into a long and sad captivity; so the prophet says, in the name of the Lord:—

17, 18. *Gather up thy wares out of the land, O inhabitant of the fortress. For thus saith the* LORD, *Behold, I will sling out the inhabitants of the land at this once, and will distress them, that they may find it so.*

They had fled to their fortresses for shelter, for the Babylonians were coming up against them; but no hope of deliverance was held out to them, and they were told to pack up their little bundles, to put their small stores as closely together as they could, for they had to go away into a far distant country as captives of the mighty king Nebuchadnezzar. God compares their captivity to the forcible ejection of stones from a sling: "I will sling out the inhabitants of the land at this once." How severely God chastened his people in Jeremiah's day! Yet, when we think of their innumerable provocations, and of how they revolted again and again against the Lord, we are not surprised that at last, the Lord sent them into captivity.

Now listen to Jeremiah's lamentation over the people whom he looks upon as already in captivity; he speaks in the name of the nation, and says:—

19. *Woe is me for my hurt! my wound is grievous: but I said, Truly this is a grief, and I must bear it.*

Ah, child of God, you also must learn to say that! There are some trials and troubles, which come upon you, against which you may not contend, but you must say, "Truly this is a grief, and I must bear it."

20. *My tabernacle is spoiled, and all my cords are broken: my children are gone forth of me, and they are not: there is none to stretch forth my tent any more, and to set up my curtains.*

Alas, poor Israel! she was like a tent removed, with none to set her up again. There are some churches, in the present day, that are in this sad condition; the faithful fail from among them, there are no new converts, and no earnest spirits, so that the church has to say, "My tent is spoiled, and all my cords are broken: my children are gone forth of me, and they are not: there is none to stretch forth my tent any more, and to set up my curtains." Yes, poor afflicted church, that may be all true, yet thy God can visit thee, and make the barren woman to keep house, and to be a joyful mother of children; and thou, who hast lost thy dearest ones, and seemest now to have no stay left,—thy children are all taken from thee, but thy God can build thee up; is he not better to thee than ten sons; and has he not said to thee, "Thy Maker is thy Husband; the Lord of hosts is his name"?

21, 22. *For the pastors are become brutish, and have not sought the LORD: therefore they shall not prosper, and all their flocks shall be scattered. Behold, the noise of the bruit is come,—*

"Bruit" is an old Norman word; one wonders how it got in here. It might be rendered, "The noise of the *tumult* is come,"—

22—24. *And a great commotion out of the north country, to make the cities of Judah desolate, and a den of dragons. O LORD, I know that the way of man is not in himself: it is not in man that walketh to direct his steps. O LORD, correct me, but with judgment; not in thine anger, lest thou bring me to nothing.*

What a suitable prayer this is for a sick man, for a tried believer, for the child of God in deep despondency of soul; I scarcely know any better words that any of us could use. The suppliant does not ask to go unchastised, but he says, "O Lord, correct me, but with judgment: not in thine anger; lest thou bring me to nothing."

25. *Pour out thy fury upon the heathen that know thee not, and upon the families that call not on thy name: for they have eaten up Jacob, and devoured him, and consumed him, and have made his habitation desolate.*

So he asks God, instead of smiting his own children, to smite his enemies; and knowing what we do about the Babylonians, we do not wonder that Jeremiah put up such a prayer as that.

THE HUNGRY FILLED, THE RICH EMPTIED.

A Sermon

DELIVERED BY
C. H. SPURGEON,
AT THE METROPOLITAN TABERNACLE, NEWINGTON,

On Thursday Evening, February 25th, 1869.

"He hath filled the hungry with good things; and the rich he hath sent empty away."—Luke i. 53.

DIVINE providence is like a wheel; and as the wheel revolves, that spoke which was highest becomes the lowest, and that which was lowest is elevated to the highest place. It seems to be one of the works in which God delights to cast down the lofty, and to lift up the lowly. He hurleth down princes from their thrones, and lifteth up beggars from the dunghill. "Every valley shall be exalted, and every mountain and hill shall be made low." Like the woodman with his axe, the providence of God is cutting down the high and goodly cedars, while making fruitful trees that were dry and withered. That which is full, God empties; and that which is empty, God fills. That which is something, he makes to be nothing; and that which is nothing, he makes to be something. That which is reckoned the wisdom of this world, God maketh to be utter folly; but base things of the world, and things which are despised, hath God chosen, that he may elevate them, and crown them with his glory.

I am going to take our text as one instance of the general providence of God, and to use it, first, *in reference to sinners;* then, *in reference to saints;* and, lastly, *in reference to saints in their capacity as workers for Christ.*

I. First, then, WITH REFERENCE TO SINNERS, it is true that "He hath filled the hungry with good things; and the rich he hath sent empty away."

"*The hungry*" are the poorest of the poor. When a man is homeless, he is poor; but he may still have something in his purse with which to supply his present necessities. When a man is penniless, he is certainly poor; yet he may have just satisfied the cravings of his hunger, and before the time shall come for another meal, he may be able to procure it. But when the hour has passed in which the man should have refreshed himself, and he is literally hungry, yet has no means of getting food, then he is one of the poorest of the poor. There are thousands, in London, who are very poor; but, still, they are not actually hungry. They are brought down to poverty; but yet, by some means or other, they are able to get their daily wants supplied; but the hungry man is worse off, and he represents the lowest degree of spiritual poverty. When a man has lost all his former treasures of self-righteousness, when he has no merits, no strength, no might whatever, when he is entirely empty, and his soul craves for what it cannot find in itself, nor earn of itself, nor by any possibility procure by its own merit or power, then is the man in the lowest state of spiritual destitution; and when he is brought to that state, then may he expect, in his experience, the fulfilment of the first part of our text, "He hath filled the hungry with good things."

More than that, the man who is hungry is not only abjectly poor, but *he feels his poverty in a way that does not permit him to forget it.* The man who has but few clothes upon his back may, by reason of the genial weather, scarcely realize that he is wearing the garb of poverty. A man who sleeps in a miserable hut may seldom have been better housed, and therefore may scarcely recognize that he is dwelling amongst the very poor. But he that is hungry has internal evidence that will not suffer him to deny, nor even for a moment to forget, his destitution. So is it with certain sinners. They have within them an insatiable hunger, which causes a desperate disquietness. There is no peace to them; neither by day nor by night can they be at ease. Their sins haunt them, and the fear of punishment dogs their heels. They long to find mercy, but know not how to seek it aright. They would be indeed thankful to be saved from the wrath to come, but they wonder whether salvation is possible to them. They know they are guilty in the sight of God; yet, possibly, they feel grieved to think that they do not feel as much grieved as they should; and are vexed to think that they are not more vexed on account of their sins. All this shows very clearly how utterly destitute they must be, and how truly they may write themselves down among the spiritually "hungry."

I hope I am now addressing some who are in this condition. Dear friends, you are well aware that there is no good thing in you, yet you wish there were; though, sometimes, you fear that you have not even the desire to be right. To be able to confess your sins with a proper tenderness of conscience, seems to be a task beyond your powers. You say that you wish you could repent, and could believe; and I think you are repenting and believing all the while. But even if you are not, this only proves how abjectly poor you are spiritually, and how far you have gone astray from God, and how lost, how undone you are; and then comes in this blessed message of our text, "He hath filled the hungry "—that is, such sinners as you are, so full of needs,—" he hath filled the hungry with good things."

How is it that the hungry get filled while the rich are sent empty away? I think it is, partly, because *the hungry are not to be satisfied with anything but bread.* There are many, in the world, who spend their money for that which is not bread, and they are contented when they get unsubstantial diet; but a really hungry soul knows that it needs bread, and will not be put off with anything else. When a soul really feels the pressure of sin, it wants to have it pardoned, and it will not be content with anything less than pardon. It wants peace with God, and it will never rest till it gets it. The soul that once hungers after God, the living God, will not be put off with ceremonies and so-called "sacraments." It wants Christ himself; it wants to hear him say, "Thy sins, which are many, are all forgiven; go in peace." You can pacify those whose desires are only whims; but when men's desires are based on such voracious appetites as the hungry have, you cannot satisfy them by the clatter of plates and dishes, and the rattling of knives and forks, or even with the sight of food. They must have it to eat; they will not be put off without it. They cry until they get it, and hence they do get it, for God hears their cry, and grants their request. If a man's prayer be of such a character that only sovereign grace, real pardon, and true salvation will content his soul, then he shall not be put off with anything else, but he shall have that for which his soul craves. Such a man prays, with one of our hymn-writers,—

"Gracious Lord, incline thine ear,
My requests vouchsafe to hear;
Hear my never-ceasing cry;
Give me Christ, or else I die.

"Lord, deny me what thou wilt,
Only ease me of my guilt;
Suppliant at thy feet I lie,
Give me Christ, or else I die.

"Thou hast promised to forg.v.
All who in thy Son believe;
Lord, I know thou canst not lie;
Give me Christ, or else I die."

How vain a thing it is for a man to boast of the privileges he enjoys rather than of the use which he has made of them! How many say, like the Jews of old, "The temple of the Lord, The temple of the Lord, The temple of the Lord are these;" because they think they belong to an orthodox denomination, or they are members of a church which is correct in its creed, or they attend a ministry which God has greatly blessed to the salvation of souls. Ah, sirs! but if the creed be not believed in your heart, and if the ministry be not blessed to you, your boasting is as vain as that of one who was clothed in rags, and died in poverty, but who boasted of the wealth of London, or of the man who shut his eyes, but who nevertheless boasted of the light that shone upon his countenance. Except you use your privileges, unless you get through the external husks into the very spirit and kernel of them, instead of boasting, you have reason to be ashamed, and to hide your heads. But the truly hungry soul is not satisfied with privileges and opportunities; he wants Christ. To sit in a place of worship to hear a gospel sermon, he counts to be a favour, for he is very humble, but it is a favour that cannot content him. His soul cries, "Lord, give me Christ; give me salvation; give me now to know that my many iniquities are cast behind thy back, to be remembered against me no more for ever." He cannot be content with anything short of a full Christ for his poor empty spirit.

Further, a hungry soul is likely to get the blessing it craves *because it is an importunate soul*. You know that our Lord Jesus Christ, in his parable of the widow and the unjust judge, set forth the prevalence of importunate pleading with God; and, on another occasion, our Lord used the figure of one, who though not himself hungry, was able to satisfy the hunger of a friend, who had unexpectedly called upon him when he had nothing to set before him; but, by his importunity, he obtained for his friend the food that he needed. Ay, and let a man really have the fear of hell before his eyes, and a sincere desire after reconciliation with God, let his soul be really hungering after peace with God through Jesus Christ, and he will be at mercy's door both night and day, he will hammer away at the knocker, and give God no rest until he puts forth his hand, and gives the Bread of life to that poor starving suppliant. Yes, it is holy importunity that wins the day, and the spiritually hungry man gets the blessing because his importunity gives success to his pleading with God.

I feel sure that there are some in this place who, knowing their need, being painfully conscious that they have no good thing of their own, are hungering after eternal life. I do trust that this hunger will grow into a craving that will never be satisfied until you get what your spirit wants. I pray God that you may never be comforted till Christ comforts you, never get peace till he becomes your peace, never feel that you are safe till you get into the very heart of Christ, and never suppose that you are clean till you are washed in the fountain filled with blood. Beware of getting peace apart from Christ; always be afraid of a hope that is not grounded upon him; for it is better far to continue to hunger and to thirst than to be satisfied with the dust and ashes of this world's religion, or this world's pleasures. O ye hungry ones, hear the words of the text, and be encouraged: "He hath filled the hungry." Look at that blessed word "filled." He has not merely given them a little refreshment, or administered some temporary consolation to them; but "he hath *filled* the hungry,"—given them all that they can wish for, all that their souls really need. Turn to this blessed Book of God, and see what promises are there for needy souls. Do they need pardon? There is plenteous forgiveness. Do they need adoption? "They shall be my sons and my daughters, saith the Lord Almighty." Do they need comfort? There is the Holy Spirit himself to be their Comforter. Do they need anything on earth or in heaven? Then it shall not be denied to them, seeing that, in giving Christ to them, God has given them all things. "He hath filled the hungry."

It is a blessed thing to see the man, who once was spiritually hungry, after he has had his soul filled by God. How he rejoices!

He dances like David did before the ark; nay, more than that, his soul seems as though it would dance into heaven itself with glorious leaps of overwhelming joy. As Christ is mine, and Christ is all, I have in Christ all that I can ever desire. It is a blessed fulness, a divine satiety, a heavenly satisfaction which the Lord gives to us when he makes our youth to be renewed like the eagle's by filling our mouth with good things.

We must notice one other word in the text: "He hath filled the hungry with *good* things." I shall not be altering the text, but only giving its true sense, if I say that he fills the hungry soul with the best of things. They are positively good; and they are good comparatively, better than all the good things of the world; and they are superlatively good, for even heaven itself hath no better things than God giveth to poor hungry souls when they come unto him by faith in Jesus. We are apt to think that, if men are starving, the commonest kind of food will do for them so long as they are able to keep away from death's door; but it is not thus that God deals with the spiritually hungry. He spreads the table bounteously, royally, with the best of food; and filleth the hungry with good things;—not simply with a good thing, but the word is in the plural, "with good things." Their needs are many, so the mercies given to them shall also be many. Their needs seem to be as many as their moments, but the mercies of God exceed their utmost needs. All their capacious souls can wish, they shall find in Jesus Christ, who shall be their All-in-all.

The text, you observe, refers to the past, but it may be taken for granted that what God did yesterday he will do to-day, and what he does to-day he will do for ever, so far as it is needful and right; and as he is "the same yesterday, and to-day, and for ever," all the blessings that he gives to his people shall be continued to them as long as they need them. Some of us can say that we were filled with these good things twenty years ago, and we have never again hungered as we hungered then. The Lord hath satisfied our souls by giving us Christ, and we are fully content with him. His own word is true to us, "Whosoever drinketh of the water that I shall give him shall never thirst; but the water that I shall give him shall be in him a well of water springing up into everlasting life." God is still filling the hungry with good things. There are many, in this house, who can testify that, in answer to prayer, they have had their griefs assuaged, and heavenly comforts granted to them; and, poor sinner, God is willing to do the same for you. If you are hungering and thirsting, come unto him, for there is as much grace in him to-day as ever there was; so come, just as you are, and trust him, rely upon him, and you too shall be filled with good things.

The other half of the text, in its reference to sinners, I shall touch upon very briefly: "The rich he hath sent empty away." Oh, how many sinners there are who think themselves rich! According to their own valuation, they are rich in merit; but the gospel has nothing to do with merit, it only deals with misery, and therefore it sends them away empty, because it does not conduct its business on the lines that they approve. There are many sinners, who are so rich in their own estimation, that they will not take Christ and his cross for nothing. David knew enough to say to the Lord, "With the froward thou wilt shew thyself froward. For thou wilt save the afflicted people; but wilt bring down high looks." If a man thinks that he is so good that he does not need the gospel, God regards him as so vile that the gospel brings no message of mercy to him until he humbles himself and repents. Jesus said, "They that are whole have no need of the physician, but they that are sick: I came not to call the righteous, but sinners to repentance."

Of all the sins that can happen to us, perhaps the deadliest of all is that of not being conscious of having any sin. A good old Scotchman used to say that there was no devil in the world so bad as having no devil at all, and that not to be tempted was the worst sort of temptation. So I think; and not to be conscious of any sin is, perhaps, to be at the furthest point from God to which any human being can go; for, the nearer we are to God, the more conscious we are of our own shortcomings, and the more earnestly do we struggle to overcome every atom of sin which we discover to be within our souls.

"The rich" are those who are far from being hungry; they have enough, and to spare. Instead of going down upon their knees, like beggars, to ask mercy from God as a charity, they talk proudly about what they deserve, and what good deeds they have done, and what they mean to do in the future; and, therefore, they thank God that they are not as other men are.

Now, what becomes of these sinners, who think themselves so rich that they have no need of the good things with which God fills the hungry? The text does not simply say that they are not fed; it does not say that the door of mercy is shut in their faces; but it says that they are sent right away from mercy's door because they have no right to stand there. Why should a man be allowed to pray when he has nothing to pray for? These rich people are sent away from mercy's table because they do not want to feed on mercy's fare. Why should they sit there, and uselessly occupy places where hungry ones might sit and feast? So they are sent away.

And, mark you, it is an awful thing to be sent away from the gospel; and it is a remarkable thing that the only people who are sent away from the gospel are those who consider themselves spiritually rich. You who think yourselves so excellent, moral, and amiable, you who cannot see any fault in yourselves, you who think you are going to heaven because of your good deeds,—the gospel not only does not open its door to you, but it even sends you away from its door; and how does it send you away? The text says, "The rich he hath sent *empty* away." Empty even of what you once thought you had. I only hope that the gracious meaning of the text may be fulfilled to some of you, and that, while listening to the gospel, you may be made to feel that, after all, you are not spiritually rich, but that you are "wretched, and miserable, and poor, and blind, and naked." It will be the best day's work that was ever done for you if you are brought to realize your true position, and come to Christ confessing your abject poverty; for, as Joseph Hart well says,—

> "'Tis perfect poverty alone
> That sets the soul at large;
> While we can call one mite our own,
> We have no full discharge."

We know what happened to the two debtors,* "When they had nothing to pay, he frankly forgave them both;" but if they had had anything with which they could pay, there would have been no forgiveness vouchsafed to them. Oh, for such an emptying that you may afterwards be filled with good things!

But there are some, who are sent away from hearing the gospel with the same conceit of fulness as they had before, and they are suffered to remain empty without discovering their true condition. This is a dreadful state for anyone to be in,—to go on deceiving one's self, and thinking all is well for time and eternity, and only to find out one's fatal mistake where the discovery will come too late. "Woe is me!" cries the self-righteous professor, when he wakes up in the world to come, and finds that he is shut out of heaven;—"Woe is me, that I should ever have fancied that I had a sufficient store of good things for eternity, yet now I have not so much as a drop of water to cool my tongue, and I am tormented in this flame! Woe is me, that I am banished for ever from the presence of God, and from the glory of his power,—'sent empty away'!"

O my dear hearers, may this text be fulfilled to you in a gracious sense, and not in this sense of terrible justice! One of the two it must be; for, if you are "rich" as the text uses that term, you must be "sent empty away" in one sense or the other. I pray that, instead, you may be filled with good things because the Spirit of the Lord has caused you to hunger and thirst after righteousness.

II. I shall now briefly use the text WITH REFERENCE TO SAINTS.

Beloved brother and sister in Christ, if your experience at all tallies with mine, I think you will have found that the first clause of this portion of Mary's song is most true to you in your spiritual experiences. I find that, whenever I am hungry,—that is to say, conscious of my utter unworthiness, weakness, insignificance,—then it is that Christ is most precious to me, the promises are peculiarly sweet, the covenant of grace is a dainty morsel, and the assembling of myself with the Lord's people brings me to the King's banqueting-table. Is it so with you? When you are hungry, do you get filled with good things? You remember when you were under the Lord's chastening hand, and much broken in spirit through bodily pain, how precious that promise was, "Thou wilt make all his bed in his sickness." You were laid aside both from the means of grace and the cares of business life, and your soul had time for thought and meditation, and in its hunger the Lord was made very sweet to you. You remember when you were poor, some years ago, when

---

* See *Metropolitan Tabernacle Pulpit*, No. 3,015, "The Two Debtors."

you had to live from hand to mouth, what blessed times you had with your Lord and Master.

You are supposed to be better off now; but you are really worse off if you do not have so much of Christ as you had then. You used, then, to take the promise, "Bread shall be given him; his waters shall be sure;" in a more literal fashion than you do now. A message which came to your soul with quickening power was this, "Man shall not live by bread alone, but by every word that proceedeth out of the mouth of God." You were hungry then, so your Lord filled you with good things. Every now and then, the pangs of this hunger seize us; our spirits sink, our confidence grows dim through the smoke of our sin, and we get such a sense of our sinnership as we have not had, perhaps for months. We feel as if we ought never to have made a profession of religion. We are so ashamed of ourselves that, if we could ship with Jonah to go to Tarshish, we should be glad to flee from the presence of the Lord, and from the presence of his people too. At such a time as that, if we hear a gospel sermon preached to the very chief of sinners, if the preacher opens his mouth wide concerning sovereign grace, and forgiving mercy, and the cleansing power of the precious blood of Jesus, oh, how welcome the message is to us! We go to the sanctuary, not to criticize the preacher, but to seek spiritual food for our souls, and if the preacher does the work which God gave him to do, we are filled with good things.

But, on the other hand, those who reckon themselves to be spiritually rich are "sent empty away." Yes, "sent empty away" from a full gospel! How many people there are, who have such peculiar tastes,—they call them such refined tastes,—that there are only one or two ministers whom they can hear in a radius of twenty miles! It is a sure sign of a bad spiritual appetite when you must always have little dainties all to yourself; or, in other words, when the old-fashioned truths become distasteful to your palate. There are two things that I always like to see on the table; whether at breakfast, dinner, or tea, they are never out of place; and those two things are bread and salt. And the old-fashioned gospel, like bread and salt on the table, ought to be in every sermon; and those whose souls are in a right spiritual condition will always want to hear it. There are some who crave fancy cookery; this dish must be prepared after the Plymouth fashion, and that dish must be spiced according to some other mode; and if it is not made according to the last new fashion in theology, there are some who cannot feed thereon. Oh, to be brought down from such richness as that, and to be made spiritually poor! I am sure that our Bibles would be a hundred times richer to us than they are now if we were a hundred times poorer than we are; by which I mean, that the Bible would be more truly to us what it really is if we had a truer sense of what we really are. As we went down in our own esteem, it would go up; and the doctrines of the Bible, the promises of the Bible,—ay, and even the precepts of the Bible,—would possess a wonderful sweetness to us if we had a greater spiritual hunger. Solomon said, "The full soul loatheth an honeycomb; but to the hungry soul every bitter thing is sweet." There is such a thing as getting full of our own graces, full of our own prayers, full of our own sermons, full of our own good works, full of our own selves; and what state can be worse than this? It is being blown out almost to bursting. Then, soul, empty yourself of yourself; and when you think of yourself as you ought to think, you will abhor yourself, you will see no good in yourself whatever; but you will see the black finger-marks of your fallen nature even upon the bright alabaster works of grace within your soul, and you will mourn over even your best things because you have defiled them. When we become thus empty, God will fill us with good things.

III. Now, lastly, I believe, brethren and sisters in Christ, that our text is true WITH REFERENCE TO CHRISTIANS IN THEIR CAPACITY OF WORKERS FOR CHRIST.

Give me hungry dogs to hunt with, and give me really hungry workers to work with for the Lord Jesus Christ; I mean, men and women who are dissatisfied with the present spiritual condition of the nominal Christian Church, dissatisfied with the progress that is being made, earnestly longing for something better, determinately set on doing something that shall be for God's glory, and the good of the people, crying and sighing for the conversion of souls, not satisfied with ones and twos, but wanting to see the kingdom of Christ come in all its power, and the will of God done on earth as it is done in heaven. Give me men who will not slumber although the professing Church of God slumbers, men who cannot rest because sinners do not find rest in Christ, men who have no peace because Christ has not become the sinner's peace. Give me such men, for they will be filled with good things. A church that longs for the blessing, and will not be content without it, will get it; but, on the other hand, the "rich" church, which says, "We have got the blessing; we are doing very well; we cannot see anything in which we could improve; we preach the gospel, we have all the usual agencies, they are all conducted with propriety, and with a measure of success; everything goes on exceedingly well; on the whole, perhaps we are ahead of the rest of the churches; we ought to let well alone, and not try to get up excitement, or be seeking after what is not attainable, and attempting such great things that we are pretty sure to fail in our attempts;"—such "rich" people will be "sent empty away."

Self-satisfaction is the death of progress. Contentment with worldly goods is a blessing; but contentment in spiritual things is a curse and a sin. What said Paul? "Not as though I had already attained." Some of us think, "If we could get as far as Paul did, we should be satisfied." But Paul said, "Not as though I had already attained;" and then he added, "Forgetting those things which are behind,"—why, some of us wish we had such things to recollect; but he wished to forget all that he had done, and to think only of what remained to be done;—"Forgetting those things which are behind, and reaching forth unto those things which are before, I press toward the mark for the prize of the high calling of God in Christ Jesus." Oh, for this sacred forgetfulness, by way of contentment, of all successes and achievements, so as still to be pressing forward! I would that every believer had, for the glory of God, that spirit which is never satisfied, but always cries for more. I would have the hearts of Christians insatiable as death and the grave, for how can we bear that men should be for ever lost? How can we be quiet while hell is being filled, and souls are perishing day and night? How can we be at ease while God is blasphemed, while Christ is unknown in a great part of the world, and where he is known, he is not beloved? How can we be contented while the black prince of hell seeks to steal the crown rights of King Jesus? Contented and satisfied? Never, till all over this our highly-favoured land Christ shall reign as Sovereign Lord; nay, not then, nor till in every continent and island the nations of the whole world shall have heard the gospel, and vast multitudes have prostrated themselves at Messiah's feet in loyal and loving adoration. Up, saints of God, from your resting-places of inglorious sloth, and begin to cry aloud, and spare not; come to God's throne with a sacred spiritual hunger, for thus shall the Church of God be filled with good things. May God, in his infinite mercy, bless his message, and his shall be the praise and glory for ever. Amen.

Exposition by C. H. Spurgeon.
LUKE I. 26—56.

Verses 26, 27. *And in the sixth month the angel Gabriel was sent from God unto a city of Galilee, named Nazareth, to a virgin espoused to a man whose name was Joseph, of the house of David; and the virgin's name was Mary.*

It was by the temptation of an evil angel that man fell, and Paradise was lost; it was, therefore, most appropriate that good angels should be sent to announce the coming of the Restorer, through whom Paradise is regained: "Gabriel was sent from God unto a city of Galilee, named Nazareth." Christ's coming to earth must be announced in the lowliest of cities, and he must be born in the small Judæan town of Bethlehem; but it was also decreed that he must die at Jerusalem,—in the metropolitan city. Mark the simplicity, and yet the sublimity, of the arrangement by which the meek and lowly Saviour was to be born in our nature. The angel Gabriel was sent from God to a virgin, whose name was Mary.

28, 29. *And the angel came in unto her, and said, Hail, thou that art highly favoured, the Lord is with thee: blessed art thou among women. And when she saw him, she was troubled at his saying, and cast in her mind what manner of salutation this should be.*

The best of news may sometimes cause the greatest perturbation of mind and heart. If you feel troubled when you receive a message from God, do not be astonished, as though some strange thing had happened unto you. See how Mary, who was told that she was to receive the greatest honour and favour possible to a mortal being, was troubled by the angel's speech, perplexed by his extraordinary salutation.

30. *And the angel said unto her, Fear not, Mary: for thou hast found favour with God.*

If we have found favour with God, there is no cause for us to fear. If God is gracious to us, we are raised above all reason for alarm. Some court the fickle favour of men; but, even if they gain it, they may well fear that they may shortly lose it; but the angel said, "Fear not, Mary; for thou hast found favour with God;" and having found that favour, she would never lose it.

31, 32. *And, behold, thou shalt conceive in thy womb, and bring forth a son, and shalt call his name JESUS. He shall be great,—*

How true is that prophecy; "He shall be great." Christ is the greatest of all great ones. How great he is in our esteem! The tongues of men and of angels could not tell all his greatness. "He shall be great,"—

32—37. *And shall be called the Son of the Highest: and the Lord God shall give unto him the throne of his father David: and he shall reign over the house of Jacob for ever; and of his kingdom there shall be no end. Then said Mary unto the angel, How shall this be, seeing I know not a man? And the angel answered and said unto her, The Holy Ghost shall come upon thee, and the power of the Highest shall overshadow thee: therefore also that holy thing which shall be born of thee shall be called the Son of God. And, behold, thy cousin Elisabeth, she hath also conceived a son in her old age: and this is the sixth month with her, who was called barren. For with God nothing shall be impossible.*

It seemed meet that the gospel dispensation should thus begin with two great wonders. The age of wonders has opened upon us now that the day of grace has dawned. Now shall the barren woman keep house, and be the joyful mother of children, according to the ancient prophecy.

38. *And Mary said, Behold the handmaid of the Lord; be it unto me according to thy word.*

Oh, that we all had such a spirit of submission as she had, that we might be willing to place ourselves absolutely at God's disposal, for him to do with us as he pleased!

38. *And the angel of the Lord departed from her.*

His mission was accomplished, so he might go back to the glory from which he had come at God's command.

39—43. *And Mary arose in those days, and went into the hill country with haste, into a city of Juda; and entered into the house of Zacharias, and saluted Elisabeth. And it came to pass, that, when Elisabeth heard the salutation of Mary, the babe leaped in her womb; and Elisabeth was filled with the Holy Ghost: and she spake out with a loud voice, and said, Blessed art thou among women, and blesssed is the fruit of thy womb. And whence is this to me, that the mother of my Lord should come to me?*

The most gracious people are always the most humble people. This question of Elisabeth, "Whence is this to me?" has been one that we have often put concerning ourselves. She was the older woman of the two, but she felt herself highly honoured by this visit from her younger relative, whom the Lord had so wondrously favoured. It is well when Christian people have a high regard for one another, and think less of themselves than they do of others whom God has specially favoured. It is one of the traits in the character of God's true people, that they have this mind in them; while they who think themselves great prove that they are not the Lord's. If you think much of yourself, he thinks little of you.

44, 45. *For, lo, as soon as the voice of thy salutation sounded in mine ears, the babe leaped in my womb for joy. And blessed is she that believed:*

Not only Mary, who believed the angel's message, and was therefore blessed; but every one of us, who believes in God, may share in this benediction.

45, 46. *For there shall be a performance of those things which were told her from the Lord. And Mary said,*

This humble Jewish maiden was a woman of great natural ability. This song of hers is worthy to be sung throughout all ages. It is true that it is mainly taken from the song of Hannah, and other songs of devout persons in former ages; but this shows how Mary had studied the Word of God, and laid it up in her heart. The best preparation that you young people can have for the highest honour and service in your future life is to bathe frequently in the Word of God, and to perfume your whole life by a familiar and accurate acquaintance with Scripture truth. Nothing else can make you so pure, or so prepared for all service which God may yet have for you to perform.

46. *My soul doth magnify the Lord,—*

That is a good beginning. Mary does not magnify herself in her Magnificat; she has nothing to say concerning her own dignity, though she was of a noble lineage; but she sang, "My soul doth magnify the Lord,"—

47. *And my spirit hath rejoiced in God my Saviour.*

She needed a Saviour as much as we do, for she was a sinner like ourselves; and though she was blessed among women, she here indicates that she owed all that blessedness to the grace of God, who had become a Saviour to her, as well as to us.

48. *For he hath regarded the low estate of his handmaiden:*

The family, from which Mary sprang, had become poor, and she dwelt in lowliness at Nazareth.

48, 49. *For, behold, from henceforth all generations shall call me blessed. For he that is mighty hath done to me great things; and holy is his name.*

She was indeed a blessed woman to have such holy thoughts, such reverence for God, such a true idea of his might and majesty, and of the marvellous favour which he had shown to her.

50. *And his mercy is on them that fear him from generation to generation.*

Remember this; it was not mercy to Mary only; it was mercy to us, and mercy to all, who truly trust the Saviour in whom she trusted.

51. *He hath shewed strength with his arm; he hath scattered the proud in the imagination of their hearts.*

Sometimes, we read of God's "finger." That refers to a part of his great power. At other times, we read of his "hand." That is a more brilliant display of his power. But here, as elsewhere, we read of his "arm." This is the majesty of his omnipotence. Pharaoh's magicians told their king that it was the finger of God that wrought the plagues of Egypt, but it was with his outstretched arm that he divided the Red Sea, and overthrew Pharaoh and his hosts: Mary felt that, in the work of salvation we see God's arm; not merely his finger, or his hand.

52. *He hath put down the mighty from their seats, and exalted them of low degree.*

This is what God is constantly doing,—casting down the high and mighty ones, and lifting up the meek and lowly.

53. *He hath filled the hungry with good things; and the rich he hath sent empty away.*

They who are self-satisfied shall, sooner or later, be cast out; but those who look to God alone, and are hungry after him, shall be satisfied with his favour.

54—56. *He hath holpen his servant Israel, in remembrance of his mercy. As he spake to our fathers, to Abraham, and to his seed for ever. And Mary abode with her about three months, and returned to her own house.*

THE COMMISSARIAT OF THE UNIVERSE.

A Sermon

DELIVERED BY

C. H. SPURGEON,

AT THE METROPOLITAN TABERNACLE, NEWINGTON.

"That thou givest them they gather."—Psalm civ. 28.

THIS sentence describes the commissariat of creation. The problem is the feeding of the "creeping things innumerable, both small and great beasts," which swarm the sea, the armies of birds which fill the air, and the vast hordes of animals which people the dry land; and in this sentence we have the problem solved, "That thou givest them they gather." The work is stupendous, but it is done with ease because the Worker is infinite; if he were not at the head of it, the task would never be accomplished. Blessed be God for the great THOU of the text. It is every way our sweetest consolation that the personal God is still at work in the world; leviathan in the ocean, and the sparrow on the bough, may be alike glad of this, and we, the children of the great Father, much more.

The notion of modern philosophers appears to be that the world is like a clock which an omnipotent phantom has set agoing, and left to run on, each wheel acting upon its fellow by rigid law: or, as a brother remarked to me, they think the Lord has wound up the universe like a watch, and put it under his pillow, and gone to sleep. What think you, brethren, do you find pleasure in a world bereaved of its God? To me, such philosophy is dreary, for my soul pines for an infinite love which will give itself to me, and receive my love in return. I am orphaned, indeed, if my Maker will not pity me as his child, and hear my prayers, compassionate my tears, and succour and comfort me. Babes want a mother's heart as much as her hands. Would you wish to be a child brought up by machinery, washed by a mill-wheel, rocked by a pendulum, fed from a pipe, dressed by a steel hand, and, in fine, committed to the care of a wonderful engine which could do everything except love you? You would miss the eyes which weep with you, and smile upon you, the lips which kiss you and speak lovingly to you, and the dear countenance which laughs as you are fondled and pressed to a warm bosom. No, I can neither accept a steam-engine instead of my mother, nor a set of laws in exchange for my God. There is a God who careth for all his creatures, and maketh the grass to grow for the cattle, and herbs for the service of man. There is a Father to whom we speak, and who hears us; one who waters the hills from his chambers, and satisfies the earth with the fruit of his works, to whom we may come boldly in every time of need. Because Jehovah liveth, the creatures are fed; he gives them their daily food, they gather it, and so the work is done.

The general principle of the text is, God gives to his creatures, and his creatures gather. That general principle we shall apply to our own case as men and women, for it is as true of us as it is of the fish of the sea, and the cattle on the hills. "That thou givest them they gather."

I. Our first point is this, WE HAVE ONLY TO GATHER, FOR GOD GIVES.

In temporal things, God gives us day by day our daily bread, and our business is simply to gather it. In the wilderness, the manna fell outside the camp of Israel; they had not to make the manna, but to go out in the morning, and gather it before the sun was hot. Providence has guaranteed to the child of God his necessary food: "Bread shall be given him; his waters shall be sure." Our part in the business is to go forth unto our labour, and gather it. True, in some cases, needful food is not gathered without excessive labour, but this is occasioned by the injustice of man, and not by the arrangements of God; and when true religion shall have fully operated upon all classes of mankind, none shall need to toil like slaves. They shall only need to perform such an amount of labour as shall be healthful and endurable. When no man oppresses his fellow, the work of gathering what God gives will be no hardship, but a wholesome exercise. The sweat of labour will then be a blessed medicine.

In this light let us view our worldly business. We are to go forth unto our work and our labour until the evening, and to expect that bounteous providence will thus enable us to gather what the Lord himself bestows; and if by this means he gives us food and raiment, we are to be therewith content. If our faith can see the hand of God in it all, it will be sweet to pick up the manna from the ground, and eat thereof with gratitude, because it tastes of the place from whence it came.

As to *spirituals*, the principle is true, most emphatically. We have, in the matter of grace, only to gather what God gives. The natural man thinks that he has to earn divine favour, that he has to purchase the blessings of heaven, but he is in grave error; the soul has only to receive that which Jesus freely gives. Mercy is a gift, salvation is a gift, all covenant blessings are gifts; we need not bring a price in our hands, but come empty-handed, and gather what is laid before us, even as the birds gather their food, and the cattle on the hills feed on the herbage which freely grows for them. This is one of the first principles of the gospel. "Every good gift and every perfect gift is from above, and cometh down from the Father of lights;" and it is for us by faith to take our omer, and fill it with the angels' food which has fallen all around us, take it into our tent, and there feast, even to the full. 'Tis God's part to give, 'tis ours to gather. Faith's sphere is that of the fleece which absorbs the dew, or the pool which is filled with the rain. Believer, this is the rule in all spiritual things; you are to be a diligent gatherer, and to strive after high spiritual attainments, but still remember that your heavenly Father knows what you have need of before you ask him. These superior blessings are his gifts, and the surest way of obtaining them is to come to him for them, and receive them by faith. You have not to pluck covenant blessings out of a closed hand, you have only to take from the Lord's open palm what he delights to bestow. For you to be straitened and poor gives no pleasure to him; rather will it delight him to fill you with his favour, and to enrich you with all the blessings of his grace.

If the calm quiet spirit of this thought could enter our minds, how happy we should be! We should then sit down at Jesu's feet with Mary, and leave Martha to fret alone. To-morrow morning, before many of our eyes are open, the sun will be rising, and, as soon as his first beams salute the earth, the birds of every wing will awaken, and, seeing the light, they will begin to sing. But where is your breakfast, little bird? Where is the food for to-day for the nest full of little ones? The birds do not know, neither are they anxious, but they gather the first seed, or crumb, or worm which they find, and continuing to do so all day long, they are satisfied. Yes, and when summer is gone, and the long warm days are over, and cold winter sets in, the birds sit and sing on the bare boughs, though frost is on the ground, for they expect that God will give, and all they have to do is to gather. We may learn much from little birds,—yes, even from little birds in cages; for if those who keep them should forget to give them seed and water, they must die, must they not? And yet they sing. They have no great store, perhaps not enough to last them another day; but it does not fret them, neither do they cease their music, and I believe Luther well translated their song when he said that it meant this,—

"Mortal, cease from care and sorrow!
God provideth for the morrow."

II. Secondly, it is certain that WE CAN ONLY GATHER WHAT GOD GIVES. However eager we may be, there is the end of the matter. The most diligent bird shall not be able to gather more than the Lord has given it; neither shall the most avaricious and covetous man. "It is vain for you to rise up early, to sit up late, to eat the bread of sorrows: for so he giveth his beloved sleep." "Except the Lord build the house, they labour in vain that build it: except the Lord keep the city, the watchman waketh but in vain." What God gives you, you will be able to gather; but if you set about to heap up what your avarice lusts after, no blessing will attend it. What a difference is often seen in two men placed in the same position in life, with the same work to do, and very much the same possessions! You see one of them working cheerfully, happy as a king, sweetening his bread with content and joy in the Lord; while the other murmurs and repines, envying those who are richer, and filled with hard thoughts of God. What makes the one happy and the other wretched? Truly, only that the one has the grace of God to give him contentment, and so is full; and the other has a brutish hunger and greed, and so is left to be his own tormentor. As it is with the poor, so is it with the rich, the heart has more to do with making us happy than our possessions have. He whose soul is full of God, and faith, and contentment, is a truly rich man. The reflection that we can, after all, gather no more than God gives, should make us restful and contented. It teaches us our dependence upon God, and tends to lessen our self-confidence, to moderate our desires, and to abate our cares.

Recollect, dear Christian friends, that *the same remark holds good with regard to spirituals as well as temporals.* You can only gather what the Lord grants you. Before preaching, I was trying to find food for you all, and I began to pray for it, because I remembered that I could only gather for you what the Lord my God gave me. If I bring more than that, it will only be chaff of my own, and not good winnowed corn from his garner. I often need to think of this, for I have to feed a great multitude with spiritual meat almost every day in the week. Where is the poor minister to get the supply from if the Lord does not bring it to him? He waits, therefore, upon his God with humble faith and prayer, expecting that fit matter will be suggested. You also, dear friends, can only obtain, when hearing the Word, what the Holy Spirit gives you. You may hear a thousand sermons, but you will gather nothing that will really quicken or feed your souls unless the Lord gives it to you. Unless the Spirit of the Lord puts fulness into the Word, all the hearing in the world will be nothing worth. The Holy Ghost must take of the things of Christ, and reveal them to the inner man, or you will be surfeited with mere words, or puffed up with human opinions, and nothing more. "That thou givest them they gather," and no more.

So is it when you go out to work for the Lord Jesus Christ among the ungodly. You will win as many souls as God gives you, but no one will be converted by your own power. When we have reason to believe that the Lord has much people in a city, it gives us much comfort in going there. I always do my best for my congregations, because I feel that they are always picked persons, sent to me by my Master: if there are few, they are more than I can edify if he does not help me; and if there be many, so much the more help will my Lord afford me. I can only gather what the Lord gives. We may plant, and we may water too, but God must give the increase. We shall not be a sweet savour unto God, nor a savour of life unto life to any, unless the almighty Spirit of the blessed God shall come forth and work with us.

Should not this lead us to much prayer? No dependence should be placed upon man, or upon the outward form of worship, for the most successful preacher cannot by his own power quicken the dead sinner, or regenerate a depraved soul. The Holy Spirit must be with us, or we prophesy in vain. The most laborious reaper in the Lord's harvest cannot gather more sheaves than his Master gives him. Pray for him, then, that he may not miss his reward; pray for him that he may be strong for labour, that his sickle may be sharp, his arm vigorous, and his harvest plenteous, that he may bring in a glorious load of sheaves to the garner. As for yourselves, when engaged in any service for God, take heed that you rest not in yourselves, for you can receive nothing unless it be given you from above. Your words will be no better than silence, your thoughts no more than day-dreams, and your efforts wasted strength, unless the Lord shall go before you. "Without me ye can do nothing" is a truth you must never forget.

III. Observe, thirdly, that WE MUST GATHER WHAT GOD GIVES, or else we shall get no good by his bountiful giving.

God feeds the creeping things innumerable, but each creature collects the provender for itself. The huge leviathan receives his vast provision, but he must go ploughing through the boundless meadows, and gather up the myriads of minute objects which supply his need. The fish must leap up to catch the fly, the swallow must hawk for its food, the young lions must hunt their prey. "What thou givest them they gather." God has not prepared, in his whole universe, a single corner for an idle being. In no society does the sluggard succeed, and it is not desirable that he should. If a man will not work, he ought to die, for he is of no use alive; he is in everybody's way, and like a fruitless tree he cumbers the ground. God gives, and if a man will not gather, he deserves to starve.

It is so in business; everybody knows that we must be diligent there, for "the hand of the diligent maketh rich." The Book of Proverbs deals very hard blows against sluggards, and Christian ministers do well frequently to denounce the great sin of idleness, which is the mother of a huge family of sins. Idleness is a most contemptible vice; it covers a man with rags, fills him with disease, and makes him a ready servant of the devil. It is a shameful thing that God, "who worketh hitherto," and made us on purpose that we should work, should see us wasting time and strength, and leaving good work unaccomplished. God will not feed you, idle man; his own verdict is, "if he will not work, neither let him eat." If you loaf about, and say, "The Lord will provide," he will probably "provide" you a place in the workhouse, if not in the county jail. If the manna falls near him, and the lazy man will not take the trouble to gather it, his omer will not be filled by miracle, neither will an angel be sent to carry bread and meat to his table. Up, thou sluggard, and gather what the Lord has strewn.

The law of nature and providence holds good in spiritual things. "That thou givest them they gather." There is a spirit abroad in the world—not so powerful now, thank God, as it used to be,—which talks a great deal about grace and predestination, and therein

I rejoice to hear what it has to say; but its inference from those truths is that men are to sit still, to be passive in salvation, and to look upon themselves as so many logs, as if they had no will in the matter, and were never to be called to an account concerning the gospel which they hear. Now, this kind of doctrine virtually teaches that what God gives drops into our mouths, and we need not gather it at all; the very reverse of the Saviour's exhortation to labour for that meat which endureth unto everlasting life. Sovereign grace will not take us to heaven by the hair of our heads, or save us in our sleep, whether we will or no. Such teaching would have been repudiated by the apostles, for it acts like chloroform upon the conscience, and plunges the soul into a deadly lethargy. The fact is, brethren, there is a predestination, and the doctrines of election and effectual grace are true, nor may we deny them; but yet the Lord deals with men as responsible beings, and bids them "strive to enter in at the strait gate," and to "lay hold on eternal life." Such exhortations are evidently intended for free agents, and indicate that our salvation requires energetic action. It would not appear from Scripture that we are to lie dormant, and be merely acted upon, for "the kingdom of heaven suffereth violence, and the violent take it by force." Of men as well as of birds it is true, "what thou givest them *they gather*." God gives you faith, but *you* must believe. God gives you repentance, but *you* must repent. These graces are the work of God, but they are also the acts of man. How often shall we need to remind these brethren that the Holy Ghost does not believe for us? How can he? Is faith to be exercised by proxy? That cannot be. Neither does the Holy Ghost repent for us; it is absurd to entertain such a notion. We must ourselves personally believe and repent. If any man does not repent as his own act and deed, his repentance and faith are not such as are spoken of in Scripture, or required by the gospel. Brethren, we should pray, repent, and believe, as much as if all these were wholly our own, but we are bound to give God all the glory of them, because it is only by his grace that we either can or will perform them. Men must hear the Word, for "faith cometh by hearing;" they must believe the Word, for "without faith it is impossible to please God;" and they must repent of sin, for if sin be not forsaken, pardon is not given. They must fly to the city of refuge, or the avenger of blood will destroy them. They must escape for their lives to the mountain, or the fire from God will overwhelm them in the city of destruction. "That thou givest them they gather." We *must* gather, or we shall not have.

Brethren in Christ, we must not expect spiritual gifts without gathering them. For instance, our souls need food, but we may not expect the Lord to feast us unless we use the means, hear or read his Word, attend to private devotion, and the like. These are channels of grace to us, and woe be to us if we neglect them. If you saw your friend so emaciated that you could count his bones, and so weak that he could scarcely stand, you would enquire what had reduced him so much, for he used to be a strong hearty man. You say to him, "My dear friend, what can be the matter with you?"

You expect him to tell you of some mysterious disease; but no, his tale is far more simple; he confesses that he does not eat, that he has given up having regular meals, and very seldom takes an ounce of nourishment. You quite understand his feebleness and decline, he is injuring his constitution by denying it nutriment. Now, when a Christian man complains that he is full of doubts and fears, and has no joy in the Lord as he used to have, and no enjoyment in prayer or labour for Jesus; if you find out that he neglects all week-night services, never goes to the prayer-meeting, reads anything rather than his Bible, and has no time for meditation, you need not enquire further into his spiritual malady. The man does not gather what God provides. He lets the manna lie outside the camp, and allows the water from the rock to flow untasted, and he must not be astonished that his soul is not in a right condition. Christians will find that, if they neglect the assembling of themselves together, as the manner of some is, and if they forget to wait upon the Lord, and so renew their strength, they will fall into a miserable, weak, low condition, and their souls will be full of doubts, cares, and anxieties, such as they never would have known if they had walked nearer to God, and maintained intimate communion with the Saviour.

As it is with ourselves, *so is it with us in reference to others.* God will give us souls if we pray for them, but we must seek after them. When the Lord calls a man to speak in his name, he intends to give him some success, but he must be on the watch to gather it. Some ministers have preached the gospel long, but have never seen much fruit, because they never tried to gather it; they have had no meetings for enquirers, nor encouraged the young converts to come to them for help. What God has given them they have not gathered. Many professors are always wishing that the church would increase, they would like to see an aggressive work carried on against the world; why do they not set about it? Why stand they gazing up into heaven? Do they expect to see souls converted without means? Dear brethren, it will not do for us to get silly notions into our heads; up to this day, God has been pleased to use instrumentality, and until the second advent he will continue to do so. When the Lord descends from heaven, it will be time enough for us to talk of what he will then do; but till he comes, let us continue to gather the souls he gives us. We are not in such great need of conferences about how to win souls as of men who will do it. I vote for less talk and more work. We cannot have too much prayer, but we certainly need more effort. The Lord said to Moses, "Wherefore criest thou unto me? speak unto the children of Israel, that they *go forward!*" We cry, "Awake, awake, O arm of the Lord!" and the Lord replies, "Awake, awake, put on thy strength, O Zion!" God is awake enough, the arousing is needed by us. We have been praying for his Spirit, and rightly enough; but the Spirit of God is never backward, we are straitened in ourselves. He would use us if we were vessels fit for his use. Oh, that we would yield ourselves fully to the Spirit of God, to be borne which way he wills, even as the clouds are driven by the wind; then he would draw, and we should run; he would give, and we should gather.

IV. The fourth turn of the text gives us the sweet thought that WE MAY GATHER WHAT HE GIVES. We have divine permission to enjoy freely what the Lord bestows.

Poor sinner, whatever the Lord has given in his gospel to sinners, you may freely gather. When the manna fell in the wilderness, no guards were appointed to keep off the people. No enquiry was made as to the character or experience of those who came to gather it; there it was, and no one was denied. Over the heads of the people might have sounded the words, "Whosoever will, let him come, and take of the manna freely." Tests and qualifications there were none, and yet the special design was the feeding of Israel. No discriminating divine cried out, "You must not come unless you feel a law-work within, and are sensible sinners." Not a word of the sort was whispered; and the Lord has appointed no one to keep sinners away from the water of life, but he has chosen many to bid poor souls draw near and drink, and the Holy Ghost himself puts forth his power to draw men to it. Jesus says, "Him that cometh to me I will in no wise cast out;" and I, for one, have no commission to discourage any, nor will I. What he gives you, you may gather. The little birds ask no questions as to whether they may enjoy the seeds or the worms; they see the food, and take it boldly; so, sinners, it is not for you to raise difficulties about the mercy of God. Whosoever believeth on the Lord Jesus Christ shall be saved, and that *whosoever* is a wide word. Thou need'st not say, "I do not know whether I am elected." Neither can I tell you, nor can any other man. "The Lord knoweth them that are his," and none of us know anything about it, except so far as his Spirit teaches us that we ourselves are his. Your thoughts should run in another direction: Christ Jesus came to save sinners, are you a sinner? "Whosoever will, let him come." Are you willing? Then come along with you, and quibble no longer.

God does not guard his great garden of grace as men protect their little patches of ground, wherein they hang up old garments or dead crows to keep the birds away. The Lord giveth freely, and upbraideth not. Certain preachers hang up the dead black crow of their own morbid experience to scare away poor sinners from coming to simple faith in Jesus, but the Lord has no scarecrows in his garden. Do but come, thou blackest of sinners, and he will receive thee. The strangest bird, with speckled wing, may freely gather what mercy gives. Whatever is preached in the gospel as the object of faith, everyone that believes may have; whatever is promised to repentance, everyone that repents may have; and whatever is promised to coming to Christ, everyone that comes to Christ shall have. "That thou givest them they gather," for God gives it to be gathered. He gave the manna on purpose for it to be eaten; he would not have sent bread from heaven if men had not wanted it, and if he had not meant to feed them. Grace must have been meant for sinners; it will suit no other persons. If I have a hard heart, the Spirit of God can soften it; why should he not do so? Here is a foul sinner, and yonder is a fountain filled with blood which cleanses completely; why should he not wash? What was Christ meant for but to be a Saviour? And if he be a Saviour, why should he not save *me?* Surely, when I am thirsty, and I see the water springing up before me, I may as well drink. Sinner, there is a spring open here by the grace of our Lord Jesus, and you have come this way, and therefore I suggest to you, and I pray the Spirit of God also to suggest it to you, that between the fountain and the thirsty soul there ought to be a connection at once begun. God invites you, your need constrains you, may his Spirit draw you; for even now what he has given you may gather!

V. The last thought is, GOD WILL ALWAYS GIVE US SOMETHING TO GATHER.

It is written, "The Lord will provide." The other day, as I walked on a common, I picked up a dead sparrow; going a little further, I found another; and my friend said to me, "I have found another," and he remarked, "It must have been a bad season; these birds must have been starved." "No, no," I said, "you are not going to pick up dead sparrows killed by the weather. That cottager, over the hedge, has some rows of young peas, and he keeps a gun." Men kill the birds, God does not starve them.

Brother, *if you are under the guardian care of God you shall not want.* If you are your own shepherd, you will probably stray into very lean pastures one of these days; but if the Lord is your Shepherd, you shall not want; he will make you to lie down in green pastures. "The young lions do lack, and suffer hunger," for they try to take care of themselves; "but they that seek the Lord," although they are often very simple-minded people, and easily imposed upon, "shall not want any good thing," for God will take care of them. I have often noticed how wonderfully poor widows manage to live and struggle through with large families. When they were dependent upon their husbands, they were often badly off; and when their husbands died, it seemed as if they must starve; but if they are Christian women, they look to God, and God becomes their Husband, and he is a far better husband than the man they have lost. When God takes the children in hand, and becomes their Father, they cannot lack; help is raised up in unexpected quarters, and they are provided for, they can scarcely tell how. If, in providence, we have learned to live by faith in God, we may be sure that he will not fail us. "The Lord will not suffer the soul of the righteous to famish."

Thus is it also in spiritual things. If you are willing to gather, God will always give. Go to the Bible, and say, "Lord, give me a promise," and you will find one suitable to your case. Go and hear his servants whom he has sent; go with hearts ready to receive the Word, and you will not return empty. The Lord will make us speak to your case as much as if we knew all about you. Bring your largest vessel with you, and the Lord will fill it to the brim. Never does a believer open his mouth wide but the Lord fills it. Be you ready to gather, and you may be right well assured that the divine fulness will never cease to supply your need.

Thus, from a very simple text, we have had our lesson; go home, and feed upon what you have gathered, and take care to bless the name of the Lord.

Exposition by C. H. Spurgeon.
PSALM XXXIV.

The title of this Psalm is, "A Psalm of David, when he changed his behaviour before Abimelech (or, Achish); who drove him away, and he departed." It relates to a sad scene in David's life when he had to feign madness in order to escape from his enemies; but I notice that, although the fact is recorded, yet David does not dwell upon it in the Psalm. He had acted as a fool or a madman, but he was not fool enough, or mad enough, to glory in his shame. I have heard some men, whose past lives have been very disgraceful, who, after their professed conversion, have seemed to make a boast of their sin. David does not do that, nor will any other right-minded person. Let us always be ashamed of our sin, even while we magnify the grace of God which has saved us from it. Though we may feel that it is needful to mention it in order to encourage others to hope in the mercy of God, yet we must take care that we never even seem to dwell upon it with any kind of gusto. Thus the Psalm begins:—

Verse 1. *I will bless the LORD at all times:*

"Whether the times are dark or light, whether I feel well or ill, whether the Lord deals with me graciously or severely, I will bless him at all times."

1. *His praise shall continually be in my mouth.*

What a blessed mouthful! If we could but carry out this resolve of David, we should not find so much fault with others as we often do. We shall have little or no opportunity for grumbling and murmuring if praise to Jehovah shall continually be in our mouth.

2. *My soul shall make her boast in the LORD:*

All men are more or less given to boasting, but it seems to be specially characteristic of Englishmen and Americans. Well, there is a right way of boasting; if you can truly say, "My soul shall make her boast in the Lord," you may boast away as much as you like.

2. *The humble shall hear thereof, and be glad.*

Any other kind of boasting makes humble people sad; but when we boast in the Lord, the more we boast the more the humble rejoice.

3. *O magnify the LORD with me, and let us exalt his name together.*

Let each one of us throw his stone upon the cairn to make the heap as high as possible, for every one has some peculiar cause for gratitude and thanksgiving.

4. *I sought the LORD, and he heard me, and delivered me from all my fears.*

It was a very poor way of seeking the Lord when he had got into the hand of the Philistines, and was planning in his own mind a disgraceful way of escaping from them. It was not that calm quiet calling upon God that one would have liked to see in David. Still, God heard him, and that makes the deliverance all the more wonderful.

5. *They looked unto him,*

"All these people that have come at my call to join me in praising the Lord: 'They looked unto him,'"—

5. *And were lightened: and their faces were not ashamed.*

EXPOSITION.

No, not one of them; if they looked to God, light shone from God upon their faces, and their faces glowed with the holy radiance, so they had no reason to be ashamed.

6, 7. *This poor man cried, and the LORD heard him, and saved him out of all his troubles. The angel of the LORD encampeth round about them that fear him, and delivereth them.*

David's deliverance had been so special that he could not help feeling that some special deliverer had been employed on his behalf; "the angel of the Lord" had been sent to his help. Then David, why did you act like a madman? Ah! that was through his want of faith; yet even want of faith must not make us rob God of his glory. What though we were unbelieving, he was faithful; therefore let us give him his due meed of praise. Let us try to blot out the remembrance of our own weakness with our tears, but let us not erase the memory of God's lovingkindness to us.

8. *O taste and see that the LORD is good: blessed is the man that trusteth in him.*

You may not only believe that God is good, but it may become a matter of experience with you: "O taste and see that the Lord is good." You cannot see the goodness of God to perfection without tasting it, so use the sense of taste as well as that of sight. Some people want first to see, and then to taste, but David says, "Taste and see."

9, 10. *O fear the LORD, ye his saints: for there is no want to them that fear him. The young lions do lack,—*

They are strong, cunning, ravenous, yet they "do lack,"—

10. *And suffer hunger:*

They try to take care of themselves, and therefore they get badly taken care of.

10. *But they that seek the LORD shall not want any good thing.*

When God takes care of us, we are well taken care of, though we are not lions, but sheep; for we have a Shepherd, and the lions have not, so we "shall not want any good thing."

11. *Come, ye children, hearken unto me: I will teach you the fear of the LORD.*

I should not wonder but that, when David played the madman, and scrabbled on the doors of the gate, the children in the streets gathered round him, and mocked him. Wherever we have done harm to any, let us try to do them good. So did David; he sought to gather the children about his knees, and to talk to them: "Come, ye children." He does not begin by saying, "Stand off, ye children." There would be no teaching them in that way; you must seek to draw them to yourselves if you would draw them to your Lord. "Come, ye children, hearken unto me: I will teach you the fear of the Lord." Though David had been anointed king, he remained a teacher of children; and the highest honour we can have is, for Christ's sake, to teach the little ones. Children love bright, happy teaching; they naturally desire life and happiness; so David begins :—

12, 13. *What man is he that desireth life, and loveth many days, that he may see good? Keep thy tongue from evil, and thy lips from speaking guile.*

Children's tongues are very active, and they need to be reminded that their tongues must be sanctified, or they will say what is evil. David had both spoken and acted with guile at the court of Achish, so he particularly dwelt upon that matter. "Depart from evil,"—run away from it; not merely do not do it, but get away from it: "Depart from evil, and do good."

15. *The eyes of the LORD are upon the righteous,*

He does not merely give a glance at them now and then, but his eyes rest on them, he is always watching them.

15. *And his ears are open unto their cry.*

The translators put in the words "are open," but they were not needed.

16. *The face of the LORD is against them that do evil,—*

You know what we mean when we say, "I set my face against it." So God sets his face against the wicked. Note how near both the righteous and the wicked are to an observing God. In the first case, his eyes are upon the righteous; in the second, his face "is against them that do evil,"—

16. *To cut off the remembrance of them from the earth.*

He will stamp them out as men do with fire. He will not even let them be remembered; he will take means to ensure that their unholy example shall die with them.

17. *The righteous cry, and the LORD heareth, and delivereth them out of all their troubles.*

That is something to teach the children,—teach them from your own experience, that God does hear and answer prayer; teach them to pray to God always, and to believe that prayer has real and beneficial results: "The Lord heareth, and delivereth them out of all their troubles."

18. *The LORD is nigh unto them that are of a broken heart; and saveth such as be of a contrite spirit.*

We often hear of people who die of a broken heart; but here we read about people who live with a broken heart; and it is the best way of living too, with a heart that is broken for sin, and broken from sin, a heart that in every portion of it feels the power of God.

19. *Many are the afflictions of the righteous:—*

Do not tell the children that the good are always happy, and that the good escape trial, because you will deceive them if you do. "Many are the afflictions of the righteous,"—the happiness, the glory, the heaven of the righteous is not here, but hereafter. "Many are the afflictions of the righteous:—"

19. *But—*

Blessed "but"—

19. *The LORD delivereth him out of them all.*

Not only out of some of them, but "out of them all." The righteous do not get out of them by their own power, but the Lord delivereth them; they have a Divine Helper.

20. *He keepeth all his bones : not one of them is broken.*

The righteous may have skin wounds, and flesh wounds, but they shall not suffer any real hurt. God will not let his people be so injured as to be incapable of holiness. There shall be no bone-breaking in Christ's mystical body, even as not one of the bones of Christ was broken.

21. *Evil shall slay the wicked:*

Sin itself shall slaughter them.

21, 22. *And they that hate the righteous shall be desolate. The LORD redeemeth the soul of his servants : and none of them that trust in him shall be desolate.*

BEGGARS BECOMING PRINCES.

A Sermon

DELIVERED BY

C. H. SPURGEON,

AT THE METROPOLITAN TABERNACLE, NEWINGTON,

On Lord's-day Evening, February 21st, 1864.

"He raiseth up the poor out of the dust, and lifteth up the beggar from the dunghill, to set them among princes, and to make them inherit the throne of glory."—1 Samuel ii. 8.

THIS God sometimes does in providence. History records several very remarkable instances of persons who have sprung from the lowest ranks of society, or from the depths of poverty, yet who have mounted to a throne. When a certain king, in the olden days, was led in chains behind the chariot of his conqueror, he was constantly observed to look at the wheel, and smile; and when he was asked why he did so, he said that it was because he noticed that those spokes of the wheel which were uppermost at one time became the lowest not long after, while those which were lowest in their turn took their place on high, and he would not wonder if it should be the same with him, and that he would again become a king, and that his conqueror would be a captive. So strange are the workings of providence that, however low anyone may be in temporal circumstances, he need not give way to despair, but he may cherish hopes of better times coming to him.

About that matter, however, I have nothing to say to-night; I am going to speak of the far greater changes that have been wrought by grace. We know that many who were "poor" in a spiritual sense, such "beggars" as words can scarcely describe, have been by sovereign grace lifted up from the dunghill of their natural degradation, set among the princes of the blood royal of heaven, and are even now inheriting the throne of glory, or are on their way to it. It is concerning this poverty and its cure that I want to talk to you in the hope that the Holy Spirit may so guide my words that they shall be for the encouragement of those who are seeking salvation by Christ Jesus.

In our text we see, first, *man's sad plight;* and, secondly, *God's infinite grace.*

I. First, then, here is MAN'S SAD PLIGHT. He is described both by his character and by his position; *he is a beggar,* that is his character; *he is on a dunghill,* that is his position.

Fallen man, whether he knows it or not, is spiritually a beggar. What is a beggar? He is one who is penniless. Empty his pockets, and you will not find a single farthing there. Take his old clothes from his back, and see what they will fetch; no one will give a penny for them. He has not a foot of land that he can call his own; and the last six feet which he is pretty sure to have must be given to him by the parish, and it will perhaps be even then given grudgingly. His old hat has almost lost its crown, and his feet can be seen through his very dilapidated shoes. The old proverb says that a beggar can never be bankrupt, but it would be more correct to say that he is never anything else but bankrupt. Do any of you see your own portraits here? I can see just what I was by nature,—utterly penniless. If you turn a natural man inside out, you cannot find a farthing's worth of merit in him. The very rags with which he professes to cover himself are so filthy that he would be far better without them. You may search into a man's thoughts, and words, and actions, you may ransack them, and turn them over again, and again, and again, and you may put the most charitable construction that you can upon them, but if you judge according to truth, and according to the Word of God, which is the only true way of judging, you must say of all that is in man, "Vanity of vanities, all is vanity." Never was a beggar so short of money as a sinner is short of merit.

I want to preach experimentally to-night, so I ask you how many of us have felt this, how many of us are realizing our spiritual poverty now? Never will a man become rich in faith until first he has learned that he is penniless so far as his own merit is concerned. You must be emptied, you must be drained dry, you must be made to feel and to confess that, in your flesh, there dwelleth no good thing, or else the sovereign mercy of God and the riches of his lovingkindness shall never be your heritage.

But a beggar is not only penniless, he is also tradeless. The only thing that he can do is to beg. If he had ever learned a trade, he might turn to some handicraft, and so earn his living. There are many who would be willing to give him a day's work, but there is nothing that he can do. If you should lend him any tools, he would cut his fingers with them, and then come to you to bind them up. He knows nothing, and is good for nothing, he is shiftless, useless, and other men are eager to be rid of him. He is like an ill weed that only cumbers the ground. He is a hopeless, helpless man, unable to earn a penny; and such is every son of Adam spiritually. Not only has he no merit, but it is impossible for him ever to earn any. I have seen the foolish sons of men trying to win merit; hunting shadows, working in their dreams, seeking to build substantial houses upon sandy foundations, or to make garments out of spiders' webs. Yet they have wearied themselves in vain, for not a particle of merit have they ever been able to earn or win. Listen, sinner; there is as great a hope of a beggar getting rich as there is of your attaining to eternal life by any deeds of your own. Nay, some beggars do, by scraping and saving, manage to hoard up what is to them comparative wealth; but you may seek to scrape and to save as much as you can, you may watch your morals, and be careful in your deportment, yet not a step nearer heaven will you be for all your pains. No; you must be born again. God must intervene on your behalf. You must be saved by the grace of God, or not at all, for "by the deeds of the law there shall no flesh be justified in his sight."

> "Not for our duties or deserts,
> But of his own abounding grace,
> He works salvation in our hearts,
> And forms a people for his praise."

Further, though there are exceptions to the rule, it is so generally true that it may form part of the description, a beggar is usually a man without a character. The less that is said about his character, the better. He has a habit of helping himself when others do not help him, only that he helps himself to what does not belong to him. If there is anything lying handy, the beggar is very apt to appropriate it. I suppose that the largest part of beggary results from sin, and that you could hardly read any beggar's true history without at the same time reading the story of wrongdoing. Certainly this is the case concerning spiritual beggary, for the sad state of humanity is not one of misfortune, but of sin. Well do I recollect when this truth stared me in the face, and I saw that my character was such that it would have been an act of justice on God's part if he had shut me up in hell. Ask a convinced sinner about his character, and see what he will say. Before God opens his eyes, and shows him what he really is, he plumes his feathers as proudly as any peacock spreads his fine tail; but when he sees himself as he is in God's sight, he is anxious to hide his head anywhere. He feels that he is such a mass of corruption,—to use Augustine's strong expression, "such a walking dunghill,"—that he loathes himself, and never dares to open his mouth before God except to cry, "Unclean! Unclean!" "I have heard of thee," said Job, "by the hearing of the ear; but now mine eye seeth thee. Wherefore I abhor myself, and repent in dust and ashes." A sight of God will soon show us what our own character is. "The heavens are not clean in his sight," said Eliphaz, "how much more abominable and filthy is man, which drinketh iniquity like water." May the Lord graciously give us this humbling view of ourselves, for we shall never seek true holiness until we are conscious of our own unholiness. That same divine power which reveals to us the light of God also shows us the darkness of self. It is brightness that discovers dimness, holiness that reveals unholiness, and the purity of God that shows the impurity of man.

I trust that these three points have been burned into our minds and hearts by the Holy Spirit; and if they have, thanks be to his holy name for it, for it is true of all of us by nature that we think we are "rich, and increased with goods, and have need of nothing," while, all the time, we are "wretched, and miserable, and poor, and blind, and naked;" but when, by grace, any one of us is brought to say, with David, "I am poor and needy," with him we can add, "yet the Lord thinketh upon me."

Again, the beggar is usually a man without any friends, or without any friends that are any good to him. In driving through various country districts, I have often seen this notice prominently displayed, "All vagrants found begging in this parish will be prosecuted." Yes, that is English law, which reckons begging as a crime; and I suppose it is also an offence to give to beggars, but that is an offence which some people are never likely to commit. Nobody cares to harbour beggars; they apply to a farmer sometimes, and ask to be allowed to sleep in his barn, but he thinks so ill of them that he bids them begone from his premises for he will have nothing to do with them. If the beggar has any friends at all, they are only the companions who share his poverty, who are generally as vile as he himself is, and who can be of little or no service to him. And the natural man, as Adam left him, is one who has no friends to help him. I know that he has those whom he calls his friends, his companions in sin who make their kind of mirth for him; but they are really among his worst enemies, they cannot do him any good. He has no friends who can help him. The angels of God can only look upon him as a spectacle of divine mercy, marvelling that he is still spared, and wondering at his base ingratitude; but there is no hand in the heavens that can help a sinner excepting the hand of the Most High God. The saints on earth may look upon the man with pity, and pray for him;—

"But feeble our compassion proves,
And can but weep where most it loves."

The poverty of sinners is too great for us to cure. We might as well attempt to fill a bag that is full of holes, or to fill to the brim a bottomless vessel, as seek by anything that we can do to bring a sinner nearer to God. No, sinner, apart from God, you have not one friend who can help you. You have no merit with which to help yourself, no power to win any merit, no friend to get any merit for you, and no character to be a recommendation to you. You are a beggar indeed.

Then there is nobody who particularly cares for the beggar's acquaintance. His company is not generally sought after; there are few who make such a supper as that which our Saviour described, to which those who were in the highways and hedges were to be compelled to come in. Men may give the beggar bread, and a place to sleep in, but they put him by himself, for he is not a person whom they would like to have in their houses, they know not what loathsome disease he might impart to any who consorted with him. Now just such is man in his natural state when the Holy Spirit makes him see himself as he is in God's sight. I know that my own moral character was not worse than that of others, and that it was indeed better than the characters of many whom I knew; yet, when the Lord opened my eyes to see myself as I really was in his sight, I felt that I was unfit even to go up to his house, and I wondered how believers could let me join in the hymns they were singing, or take any other part in the service. I have known the time when I would have liked to occupy the worst seat in the chapel, and when I would rather have been where no one could see me, that I might listen to God's Word alone. My going up to the Lord's house, in those days, was like the dog's coming into the dining-room, when he tries to slip under the table unobserved, and to watch for the crumbs that fall to the ground. He feels that he is there only on sufferance; he does not take his seat at the table, for he feels that he has no right to do so. I would not give much for a man's conviction of sin if it does not produce in him a very loathsome idea of himself, and make him marvel how it is that the mercy of God can ever be outstretched to such a wretch, so vile and self-condemned as he is. If there is anyone here in such a condition as this, it is very likely that he is saying, "Why, I feel just like that, but I thought that mine was an utterly hopeless case." No, poor soul, your case is a very hopeful one, for it is the beggar, the loathsome, leprous, foul, filthy beggar, covered with disease and defilement, whom God will lift up from the dunghill, and set among princes, and make him inherit the throne of glory.

To complete the picture, let me add that the beggar is one whose entire dependence is upon charity. He knows that he cannot claim anything from you; as he holds out his hand to you, or follows you with his importunity, he is fully aware that whatever he may get will come to him, not according to law, but rather against law, and simply as an act of grace. Such beggars are we with regard to spiritual gifts. If we are to receive pardon, it must come to us by grace. If we ever become reconciled to God by the death of his Son, it must be by an act of charity which we can do nothing to deserve. The beggar is a man whose only virtues are his boldness and his importunity; and as for you, sinner, there is nothing that becomes you so well as to press boldly to God's throne, and appeal to the graciousness and goodness of his nature, and especially to that display of his love which was given in the person of his bleeding and dying Son. There is nothing more fitting in you than to be importunate, to knock, and knock, and knock again with a holy resolve to take no denial. Your sins are your most urgent reasons for coming to Christ, your rags are your best livery, your emptiness your only fitness, your ruin is that upon which you are to look, and you are to go to Christ in that ruin just as you are. As you go to him, go boldly, for you are asking a great boon from One who has a great heart, you are knocking at the door of the most hospitable King who ever invited beggars to come unto him. Come to him with a holy boldness and perseverance, knowing that you must perish unless he looks upon you with an eye of love; and resolving that, if you must perish, it shall be as a poor mendicant pleading that, for his mercy's sake, he would have pity upon you. No one ever did perish who came to him like that, nor will you.

Thus I have described the character of the spiritual beggar, but it is much blacker than I have painted it. Now we are briefly to consider *the beggar's position*. According to the text, he is on a dunghill; that is the only throne he has by nature.

Why is the spiritual beggar said to be on a dunghill? I think it must be, first, to show that he is as worthless as the rest of the stuff that is there. If the Lord shall only reveal to us our filthy condition as it appears in his sight, we shall feel that it is a positive nuisance, and we shall cry to him, "Take it away, O Lord, take it away!" Sin is an offence to the nostrils of the thrice-holy Jehovah even more than a dunghill can ever be to the most delicately sensitive man or woman; and when we realize our true condition as sinners, we feel that a dunghill is a fitting place for such a mass of defilement and corruption.

Why is the spiritual beggar said to be on a dunghill? I think it is, next, because that is the most suitable place for the best thing that he has. The only thing a man can trust to before he comes to Christ is his own righteousness, and what is the verdict of Scripture upon that? You know well what it is: "We are all as an unclean thing, and all our righteousnesses are as filthy rags." The best things that we have, those that we reckon to be our righteousnesses, are only like filthy rags that find a fitting resting-place on a dunghill. So, if our best things are only fit for such a position, it is no wonder that we ourselves, in our natural state, are relegated to the dunghill with the rest of the unclean things that are thrown away there.

I think the spiritual beggar is also said to be on a dunghill because that place is typical of the best joy that he has. An unconverted man has some joy, some merriment, some pleasure of a certain sort; but what is carnal joy, after all? Think of the character of the places where the ungodly go for their amusement, or of the various ways in which they seek to gratify the lusts of the flesh, and then say if anything is a more appropriate emblem of them than a dunghill with all its filth and abominations. So, when the man who is a beggar with regard to spiritual things mounts his throne, and sits down upon its softest seat, it is only a dunghill!

That dunghill is also an emblem of his end. It is not only a symbol of the corruption that awaits his body after death, but it is also a type of the final doom of both body and soul when they are flung away as worthless refuse fit only for the dunghill. There have been sinners who, even in this life, have had at least a glimpse of the ruin that sin has wrought in them, and who have, as it were, looked into the hell that stood ready to receive them. I have personally witnessed some terrible experiences in which men, helplessly and hopelessly lost, have been upon the very brink of perdition, and I have then understood what it must be to be a spiritual beggar on a dunghill.

I have tried to make the meshes of my net so small that none of you might be able to escape from it, but I see some who seem determined not to be caught by it. They turn on their heel, and say, "All that we have been hearing does not relate to us; we are not beggars, and we are not sitting on a dunghill; we are most respectable members of society." Well then, sirs, why are you here? Why do you read your Bibles? Why do you pray? If you need no mercy, why do you come to the house of mercy, and call upon the God of mercy? We have no gospel to preach to such as you, for even Christ himself said, "I am not come to call the righteous, but sinners to repentance." Go, thou Pharisee, and say as he did in the temple of old, "God, I thank thee, that I am not as other men are;" yet no justification shall drop like blessed dew upon thee; but come, thou publican, thou who darest not lift up so much as thine eyes unto heaven, methinks I hear thee, as thou smitest upon thy breast, dolefully crying, "God be merciful to me a sinner." Thou shalt go down to thy house justified rather than the other: "for every one that exalteth himself shall be abased; and he that humbleth himself shall be exalted." "Pride goeth before destruction, and a haughty spirit before a fall;" but to the humble and the contrite God revealeth the abundance of his mercy, and to the poor in spirit he giveth the riches of his grace.

II. Now, as my time has nearly gone, I must speak very briefly upon the second part of my subject, which is, GOD'S INFINITE GRACE: "He raiseth up the poor out of the dust, and lifteth up the beggar from the dunghill; to set them among princes, and to make them inherit the throne of glory."

As deeply as they fell, so high are they raised; nay, they are raised still higher than they were before, so that Dr. Watts sang truly when he said that God—

"Has made our standing more secure
Than 'twas before we fell."

We lost much through Adam's transgression, but we get all that back, and much more, through Christ's obedience and death, so that where sin abounded, grace doth much more abound, and—

"In Christ the tribes of Adam boast
More blessings than their father lost."

Our text tells us *what is done for the poor beggar upon the dunghill;* he is set among princes, and made to inherit the throne of glory. So, first, he is clothed as princes are clothed. The glorious robe of Christ's righteousness is thrown around this naked beggar, and now he is clad as well as the best of the princes by whom he is surrounded, and he also fares as well as they do. Manna from heaven is his daily portion, and water from the rock constantly supplies his needs; and, like all the saints, in a spiritual fashion he feeds upon the flesh and blood of Christ, who is now his life.

He is also guarded as princes are, and far more securely guarded than any earthly prince unless he also is a child of God, for the strong right arm of the Almighty is his perpetual defence. He is also housed as princes are, for he dwells in the secret place of the Most High, and abides under the shadow of the Almighty. He has a seat at the table of the royalty of heaven, for he is of the blood royal, a son of the Highest, and of the household of God.

Furthermore, he is rich as princes are. Are they heirs of God, and joint-heirs with Jesus Christ? So is he a sharer in that high honour. Are they priests and kings unto God? He also is a priest and a king. Do they say, "Abba, Father"? He too can say the same. Does each of the princes say, with Thomas, "My Lord, and my God"? He too can say, "My Lord, and my God." Have they been pardoned? So has he. Have they acceptance, adoption, calling, regeneration, election, eternal security? He has the same; for, however foul and filthy a sinner may have been, when God calls him by his grace, and adopts him into his family, he gives him, not half the family inheritance, but the whole of it. He does not put off the big sinners with the leavings of the feast. When the father welcomed the prodigal home again, he did not send him to the kitchen among the hired servants, but he killed for him the fatted calf, and gave him a son's place at the table. It would be an eternal mercy if the Lord would allow us just to put our heads within the gates of glory, but that is not his way of rewarding the travail of Christ's soul. Jesus himself prayed, "Father, I will that they also, whom thou hast given me, be with me where I am: that they may behold my glory, which thou hast given me;" and to his disciples he said, "Where I am, there shall also my servant be." That is the position that is reserved even for the chief of sinners, with Christ where he is; what a wonderful change is in store for the beggar from the dunghill!

"To dwell with God, to feel his love,
 Is the full heaven enjoy'd above;
 And the sweet expectation now
 Is the young dawn of heaven below."

See then, sinner, what the Lord does when "he raiseth up the poor out of the dust, and lifteth up the beggar from the dunghill, to set them among princes, and to make them inherit the throne of glory." He gives them the full heritage of the saints on earth, and then crowns it with the glorious inheritance of the saints in heaven. There is nothing good that the Lord keeps back from them. All the promises of this blessed Book, all the blessings guaranteed by the everlasting covenant are theirs most richly to enjoy. Oh, that the Lord would come this very night, and lift up some of you who are like the beggar upon the dunghill, and set you among princes, and make you inherit the throne of glory!

Thus have I hurriedly set before you what is done for the beggar upon the dunghill, and I can only hint at the answer to the next question, *Who does it?* "He raiseth up the poor out of the dust, and lifteth up the beggar from the dunghill." If any of you saw a beggar lying upon a dunghill, and wanted to help him, I expect you would send your servants to lift him up from his unsavoury restingplace; I do not suppose you would go and do it yourselves. It would be very kind for a man to arrange for a beggar in such a position to be taken care of anyhow, and so to do it by proxy; but listen to this. "He raiseth up the poor out of the dust, and (He) lifteth up the beggar from the dunghill." The great Lord of heaven and earth does this work himself, he does not do it by proxy. There are two verses in the 147th Psalm at which I have wondered thousands of times: "He healeth the broken in heart, and bindeth up their wounds. He telleth the number of the stars; he calleth them all by their names." He who looses the bands of Orion, and brings forth Mazzaroth in his season, and guides Arcturus with his sons is the same Lord who bends down in tender pity over the broken in heart, and bindeth up their wounds with a skill and success that no earthly surgeon can ever equal. Oh, the matchless condescension of the great Lord of love that he should thus pity a sinner, love a sinner, embrace a sinner, and lift up a sinner even from a dunghill! No one else can do it. The minister here frankly confesses his inability to do it; not all the holy angels together can do it; only the Spirit of the living God, who first opens our eyes to see our state as beggars, can lead us to look to Jesus Christ, and find in him everlasting riches and eternal salvation.

Now, lastly, *why doth the Lord do this great act of grace?* Why doth he lift up the beggars from the dunghill? I cannot tell you any other reason than this, God does it because he wills to do it. Why does he thus look after some of the chief of sinners, and yet leave many more respectable people to go on in their own way? I know no reason except that he does it because he wills to do it. His name and his nature are both love, and it is characteristic of love to pour itself out on behalf of misery and helplessness. The Lord looketh abroad, and seeth the poor, ruined, helpless soul, and straightway the flood-gates of his heart go up, and out floweth the stream of his lovingkindness and tender mercy.

Perhaps someone asks, "Do I rightly understand you, sir? I do not often go to a place of worship, but I was passing the Tabernacle, and just stepped in; now I am as bad as I well can be, you surely do not mean to say, sir, that God loves me, and such great sinners as I am?" Indeed, my dear friend, I do mean to say it, and to say it upon the authority of God himself. "What! do you mean to tell me that God loves me as I am?" Yes, just as you are. "What! God loves an ungodly man?" Yes; here is a text to prove it: "God, who is rich in mercy, for his great love wherewith he loved us, even when we were dead in sins, hath quickened us together with Christ." Why, if he had not loved us when we were dead in sins, he would never have loved us at all, and we should still have remained dead in trespasses and sins. 'Tis his great grace that lifts a beggar from the dunghill, and sets him among princes. When poor Jeremiah was in the pit, and likely to die of starvation, Ebed-melech the Ethiopian did not go to him, and say, "Come up out of the pit, and I will dress your wounds, and feed you;" but he took men with ropes, and some old rags to put under the prophet's arms, and so drew him out of the dungeon. In like manner, God does not say, "Now, sinner, make yourself a saint, and then I will love you;" but he lets down the great rope of the gospel, which is long enough to reach you wherever you may be, and he lines it with the soft rags of loving invitations, and then he bids you put them beneath your arms, and trust to them as Jeremiah trusted to Ebed-melech's ropes, and so you shall be drawn up out of sin's dungeon. David did not say, "I climbed up out of the horrible pit, and then began to sing." Oh, no; but he said, "He brought me up also out of a horrible pit, out of the miry clay, and set my feet upon a rock, and established my goings. And he hath put a new song in my mouth, even praise unto our God." David's song, like Hannah's, and like Mary's, ascribes all grace and glory to God; and if you put your soul's trust in Jesus, the one and only Saviour, you also will—

> " Give all the glory to his holy name
> For to him all the glory belongs."

Oh, that some spiritual beggar may to-night be lifted up from the dunghill, and set among princes, and the Lord shall have all the praise world without end! Amen.

REDEMPTION
- The Great Liberator—John 8:36
- The Royal Saviour—Acts 5:31
- Exposition of Romans 10
- "The Lamb of God"—John 1:29
- Exposition of John 1:1-34
- The Wordless Book—Ps. 51:7
- Exposition of Psalm 51

THE GREAT LIBERATOR.

A Sermon

DELIVERED ON SUNDAY MORNING, APRIL 17TH, 1864, BY THE

REV. C. H. SPURGEON,

AT THE METROPOLITAN TABERNACLE, NEWINGTON.

"If the Son therefore shall make you free, ye shall be free indeed."—John viii. 36.

BLESSED is that word "free," and blessed is he who spends himself to make men so. Ye did well to crowd your streets and to welcome with your joyous acclamations the man who has broken the yoke from off the neck of the oppressed. Many sons of Italy have done valiantly, but he excels them all, and deserves the love of all the good and brave. *Political slavery is an intolerable evil.* To live, to think, to act, to speak, at the permission of another! Better have no life at all! To depend for my existence upon a despot's will is death itself. Craven spirits may wear the dog-collar which their master puts upon them, and fawn at his feet for the bones of his table, but men who are worthy of the name, had rather feed the vultures on the battle-field. The burden of civil bondage is too heavy for bold spirits to bear with patience, and therefore they fret and murmur beneath it; this murmuring the tyrant loves not, and therefore he throws the sufferers into his dungeons, and bids them wear out their days in captivity. Blessed is he who hurls down the despot bursts the doors of his dungeons, and gives true men their rights. We have never felt, and therefore we know not the bitterness of thraldom. Our emancipators have gone to the world of spirits, bequeathing us an heirloom of liberty, for which we should love their names and reverence their God. If they could have lived on till now, how we should honour them! but as they are gone, we do well to applaud our illustrious guest as if we saw in him the spirit of all our glorious liberators worthily enshrined. Political liberty allows scope for so much of all that is good and ennobling, and its opposite involves so much that is debasing, that the mightiest nation destitute of it is poor indeed, and the poorest of all people, if they be but free, are truly rich.

But, my brethren, men may have political liberty to the very fullest extent, and yet be slaves, for there is such a thing as religious bondage; he who cringes before a priest—he who dreads his anathema, or who creeps at his feet to receive his blessing, is an abject slave. He may call himself a freeman, but his soul is in bondage vile, if superstition makes him wear the chain. To be afraid of the mutterings of a man like myself—to bow before a piece of wood or a yard of painted canvas—to reverence a morsel of bread or a rotten bone, this is mental slavery indeed. They *call* the negro *slave* in the Southern Confederacy, but men who prostrate their reason before the throne of superstition, *are* slaves through and through. To yield obedience to our Lord, to offer prayer to God Most High is perfect freedom; but to tell my heart out to a mortal with a shaven crown—to trust my family secrets and my wife's character to the commands of a man who may be all the while wallowing in debauchery, is worse than the worst form of serfdom. I would sooner serve the most cruel Sultan who ever crushed humanity beneath his iron heel than bow before the Pope or any other priest of man's making. The tyranny of priestcraft is the worst of ills. Ye may cut through the bonds of despots with a sword, but the sword of the Lord himself is needed here. Truth must file these fetters and the Holy Spirit must open these dungeons. Ye may escape from prison, but superstition hangs round a man, and with its deadly influence keeps him ever in its dark and gloomy cell. Scepticism which proposes to snap the chains of superstition only supplants a blind belief with an unhallowed credulity, and leaves the victim as oppressed as ever. Jesus the Son alone can make men truly free. Happy are they whom he has delivered from superstition. Blessed are our eyes that this day we see the light of gospel liberty, and are no longer immured in Popish darkness. Let us remember our privileges and bless God with a loud voice, that the darkness is past and the true light shineth, since the name of Jesus, the preaching of his Word and the power of his truth have, in this respect, in a high degree, made our nation free.

Yet a man may be delivered from the bond of superstition and be still a serf, for he who is not ruled by a priest may still be controlled by the devil or by his own lusts, which is much the same. Our carnal desires and inclinations are domineering lords enough, as those know who follow out their commands. A man may say, " I feel not supernatural terrors; I know no superstitious horrors;" and then, folding his arms, he may boast that he is free; but he may all the while be a slave to his own evil heart; he may be grinding at the mill of avarice, rotting in the reeking dungeon of sensuality, dragged along by the chains of maddened anger, or borne down by the yoke of fashionable custom. He is the free man who is master of himself through the grace of God. He who serves his own passions is the slave of the worst of despots. Talk to me not of dark dungeons beneath the sea level; speak not to me of pits in which men have been immured and forgotten; tell me not of heavy chains nor even of racks and the consuming fire; the slave of sin and Satan, sooner or later, knows greater horrors than these—his doom more terrible because eternal, and his slavery more hopeless because it is one into which he willingly commits himself.

Perhaps there are those present who claim liberty for themselves and say, that they are able to control their passions and have never given away to impure desires. Ay, a man may get as far as that in a modified sense, and yet not be free. Perhaps I address those who, knowing the right, have struggled for it against the wrong. You have reformed yourselves from follies into which you had fallen; you have by diligence brought the flesh somewhat under, in its outward manifestations of sin, and now your life is moral, your conduct is respectable, your reputation high; still for all that it may be that you are conscious that you are not free. Your old sins haunt you, your former corruptions perplex you; you have not found peace, for you have not obtained forgiveness. You have buried your sins beneath the earth of years, but conscience has given them a resurrection, and the ghosts of your past transgressions haunt you; you can scarce sleep at night, because of the recollection of the wrath of God which you deserve; and by day there is a gall put into your sweetest draughts because you know that you have sinned against heaven and that heaven must visit with vengeance your transgression. Ye have not yet come to the full liberty of the children of God, as you will do, if you cast yourselves into the hands of Jesus who looseth the captives. "If the Son therefore shall make you free, ye shall be free indeed;" free as the mere political liberator cannot make you; free as he cannot make you who merely delivers you from superstition; free as reformation cannot make you; free as God alone can make you by his free Spirit. "If the Son therefore shall make you free, ye shall be free indeed."

Now, this morning may the Lord give his servant help from on high, while I try to talk with you. To those who feel to-day their slavery, my message may be profitable. Our *first* point is, that to those who are the bondslaves of Satan, *liberty is possible*. The text would not mock us with a dream: it says, "*If* the Son therefore shall make you free." All who are slaves shall not be set free, but there is the possibility of liberty implied in the text. Blessed "if;" it is like the prison window, through the stony wall, it lets in enough sunshine for us to read the word "hope" with. "*If* the Son therefore shall make you free." *Secondly, there is a false freedom;* you see that in the text—" Ye shall be free *indeed*." it says. There were some who professed to be free, but were not so. The Greek is, " Ye shall be free *really*," for there be some who are free only in the name, and in the shadow of freedom, but who are not free as to the substance. Then *thirdly, real freedom must come to us from the Son*, that glorious Son of God, who, being free, and giving himself to us, gives us freedom. And then we shall close by putting a few personal questions as to whether the Son hath made us free, or whether we still remain slaves.

I. First then, dear friends, our text rings a sweet silver bell of hope in the ear of those who are imprisoned by their sin. FREEDOM IS POSSIBLE: the word "if" implies it. The Son of God can make the prisoner free. No matter who you are, nor what you are, nor how many years you may have remained the slaves of Satan, the Son, the glorious liberator, can make you free. "He is able also to save them to the uttermost, who come unto God by him." Perhaps that which weighs upon you most heavily is a sense of your *past guilt.* "I have offended God: I have offended often, wilfully, atrociously, with many aggravations. On such-and-such a day I offended him in the foulest manner, and with deliberation. On other days I have run greedily in a course of vice. Nothing has restrained me from disobedience, and nothing has impelled me to the service of God. All that his Word says against me, I deserve; and every threatening which his book utters, is justly due to me, and may well be fulfilled. Is there a possibility that I can escape from guilt? Can so foul a sinner as I am be made clean? I know that the leopard cannot lose its spots, nor the Ethiopian change his skin by his own efforts. Is there a power divine which can take away my spots, and change my nature? Sinner, there is. No sin which you have committed need shut you out of heaven. However damnable your iniquities may have been, there is forgiveness with God that he may be feared. You may have gone to the very verge of perdition, but the arm of God's grace is long enough to reach you. You may sit to-day with your tongue padlocked with blasphemy, your hands fast bound by acts of atrocious violence, your heart fettered with corruption, your feet chained fast to the Satanic blocks of unbelief, your whole self locked up in the bondage of corruption, but there is one so mighty to save that he can set *even you* free. "All manner of sin and blasphemy shall be forgiven unto men." "The blood of Jesus Christ his Son cleanseth us from all sin."

In the matter of guilt, then, there is the possibility of freedom. "But can I be freed from *the punishment* of sin?" saith another. "God is just: he must punish sin. It is not possible that the Judge of all the earth should allow such a rebel as I am to escape. Shall I go scot free? Shall I have the same reward with the perfectly righteous? After years of unbelief am I still to be treated as though I had always been a willing and loving child? This is not just: I must be punished." Sinner, there is no need that thou shouldst be cast into hell; nay, thou shalt not be, if thy trust is placed in the bloodshedding upon Calvary. There is an imperative need that sin should be punished, but there is no need that it should be punished in your person. The stern laws of justice demand that sin should meet with satisfaction, but there is no law which demands that it should receive satisfaction from you, for if thou believest, Christ *has* given satisfaction for thee. If thou dost trust Jesus Christ to save thee, be assured that Christ was punished in thy stead, and suffered the whole of wrath divine, so that there is no **fear** of thy being cast into hell. If thou believest, thou canst not be punished, for there is no charge against *thee:* thy sin having been laid on Christ; and there can be no punishment exacted from thee, for Christ has already discharged the whole. God's justice cannot demand two executions for the same offence. O, let not the flames of hell alarm thee, sinner; let not Satan provoke thee to despair by thoughts of the worm that never dies, and of the fire that never can be quenched. Thou needst not go thither: there is a possibility of deliverance for thee; and though thy heart says, "Never, never, shall I escape," trust not thy heart; "God is greater than thy heart, and knoweth all things." Believe thou his testimony, and fly thou to the great Deliverer for liberty. Freedom, then, from punishment is possible through Christ.

I think I hear one say, "Ah! but if I were saved from past sin, and from all the punishment of it, yet still I should submit to *the power of sin* again. I have a wolf within my heart hungering after sin, which will not be satisfied, though it be glutted with evil. The insatiable horseleech of my lust ever crieth, 'Give, give!' Can I be delivered from it? I have been bound with many resolutions, but sin, like Samson, has snapped them as though they were but green withs. I have been shut up in many professions, as though I was now, once for all, a prisoner to morality; but I have taken up posts and bars, and every other restraint which kept me in, and I have gone back to my old uncleannesses. Can I, can I be saved from all these propensities, and all this inbred corruption? My dear friend, there is a hope for thee, that thou mayst be. If thou believest in the Lord Jesus Christ, that same blood by which sin is pardoned enables man to overcome sin. They in heaven washed their robes and made them white in his blood; but they have another note in their song—they *overcame* through the blood of the Lamb. Not only were they delivered from guilt, but from the power of sin. I do not tell you, that in this life Christ himself will make you perfectly free from indwelling sin: there will always be some corruption left in you to struggle with; some Canaanite still in the land to exercise your faith and to teach you the value of a Saviour; but the neck of sin shall be under your foot, God shall lead captive the great Adonibezek of your lust, and you shall cut off his thumbs, so that he cannot handle weapons of war. If the enemy cannot be destroyed, at least his head shall be broken, and he shall never have reigning power over thee—you shall be free from sin, to live no longer therein. Oh! that blessed word "if!" How it sparkles! It may seem but a little star: may it herald the dawning of of the Sun of Righteousness within you—"If the Son therefore shall make you free." "Oh, says one, that is a great 'if' indeed. It cannot be, surely—my guilt pardoned, my punishment remitted, and my nature changed! How can it be?" Dear friend, it may be, and I trust it will be this morning, for this "if" comforts the preacher with a hope of success in delivering the Word; and may it give some hope to the hearers, that perhaps you may be made free yourselves.

But I think I hear another exclaim, "Sir, I am in bondage through *fear of death.* Go where I may, enjoying no assurance of acceptance in Christ, I am afraid to die. I know that I must one of these days close these eyes in the slumbers of the grave, but oh! it is a dread thought to me that I must stand before my God and pass the solemn test. I cannot look into the sepulchre without feeling that it is a cold, damp place, I cannot think of eternity without remembering the terrors which cluster round it to a sinner, 'where their worm dieth not, and where their fire is not quenched.'" Ah, but my dear friend, if the Son make you free, he will deliver you from the fear of death. When sin is pardoned then the law is satisfied, and when the law is satisfied then death becomes a friend. The strength of sin is the law: the law is fulfilled, the strength of sin is broken. The sting of death is sin: sin is pardoned, death has a sting no longer. If thou believest in Christ thou shalt never die, in that sense in which thou dreadest death; thou shalt fall asleep but thou shalt never die. That death of which thou thinkest is not the Christian's portion: it belongs to the ungodly. In it thou shalt have no share, if thou trustest the Saviour. Borne on angels' wings to heaven, up from calamity, imperfection, temptation and trial, shalt thou mount, flitting with the wings of a dove far above the clouds of sorrow, leaving this dusky globe behind thee, thou shalt enter into the splendours of immortality. Thou shalt not die, but wake out of this dying world into a life of glory. Come, soul, if thou trustest in Christ, this "if" shall be no if, but a certainty to-day— the Son shall make you free indeed. I do not think I can bring out the full value of this liberty by merely speaking of the evils which we are delivered *from;* you know, brethren, freedom consists not only in a negative but in a positive—we are not only free *from*, but we are free *to*. We hear of persons receiving the freedom of a city. This implies that certain privileges are bestowed. Now "if the Son therefore shall make you free, you shall be free indeed," in the sense of privilege—you shall be free to call yourself God's child, you shall be free to say, "Abba, Father," without rebuke, you shall be free to claim the protection of that Father's house, and the provision of his bounty; you shall be free to come to his knees with all your trials and tell him all your griefs; you shall be free to plead his promises and to receive the fulfilment of them too; you shall be free to sit at his table, not as a servant is permitted sometimes to sit down when the feast is over to eat the leavings, but you shall sit there as a well-beloved son, to eat the fatted calf while your Father with you, eats, drinks, and is merry; you shall be free to enter into the Church on earth, the mother of us all; free to all her ordinances; free to share in all those boons which Christ hath given to his spouse; and when you die, you shall be free to enter into the rest which remaineth for the people of God; free of the New Jerusalem which is above; free to her harps of gold and to her streets of joy; free to her great banquet which lasteth for ever; free to the heart of God, to the throne of Christ, and to the blessedness of eternity. Oh! how, *how* good it is to think that there is a possibility of a freedom to such privileges as these, and a possibility of it to the vilest of the vile; for some who were grossly guilty, some who had far gone astray have nevertheless enjoyed the fulness of the blessing of the gospel of peace. Look at Paul! No man enters more into the mystery of the gospel than he; he had freedom to do so: he could comprehend with all saints what are the heights and depths, and know the love of Christ which passeth knowledge, and yet it is he, it is he who once foamed out threatenings, who sucked the blood of the saints; it is he who dyed his hands up to the very elbows in murderous gore; it is he who hated Christ, and was a persecutor, and injurious, and yet is he free from evil, and he is free to all the privileges of the chosen of God. And why not you? And why not you? Woman, tottering and trembling, why should not, why should not the Son make thee free? Man, tossed about with many doubts, why should not the great Liberator appear to thee? Can there be a reason why not? Thou hast not read the rolls of predestination and discovered that thy name has been left out. It has not been revealed that for thee there is no atonement, but it is revealed to thee that whosoever believeth on Him is not condemned. And this is the testimony which comes to thee—O that thou wouldst receive it!—"He that believeth on the Lord Jesus Christ, hath everlasting life." O that thou wouldst be bold and trust Christ this morning, and the "if" which is in our text shall become a blessed certainty to thee. So then there is a possibility for freedom. We will pause awhile and then warn you against false freedom.

II. BEWARE OF FALSE LIBERTY. Every good thing is imitated by Satan, who is the master of counterfeits, and hence, liberty—a word fit to be used in heaven, and almost too good for fallen earth—has been used for the very basest of purposes, and men have misnamed the devil's offspring by this angelic title. We have in spiritual matters things called liberty which are no liberty. There is *Antinomian liberty*—God deliver us from that! A man saith, "I am not under the law of God, therefore I will live as I like." A most blessed truth followed by a most atrocious inference. The Christian is not under the law, but under grace—that is a very precious fact: it is much better to serve God because we love him, than because we are afraid of his wrath. To be under the law is to give God the service of a slave who fears the lash; but to be under grace is to serve God out of pure love to him. Oh! to be a child, and to give the obedience of a child and not the homage of a serf! But the Antinomian saith, "I am not under the law, therefore will I live and fulfil my own lust and pleasures." Paul says of those who argue thus, their damnation is just. We have had the pain of knowing some who have said, "I am God's elect: Christ shed his blood for me: I shall never perish;" and then they have gone to the ale-house, they have sung the drunkard's song, and have even used the drunkard's oath. What is this, dear friends, but a strong delusion to believe a lie? They who can do this, must surely have been some time in Satan's oven, to be baked so hard. Why, these must have had their consciences taken out of them. Are they not turned to something worse than brutes? The dog doth not say, "My master feeds me, and he will not destroy me, but is fond of me, therefore will I snarl at him or rend him." Even the ass doth not say, "My master gives me fodder, therefore will I dash my heels into his face." "The ox knoweth its owner, and the ass his master's crib;" but these men only know God to provoke him, and they profess that his love to them gives them a liberty to rebel against his will. God deliver you from any such freedom as this; be not legalists, but love the law of God, and in it make your delight. Abhor all idea of being saved by good works, but O, be as full of good works as if you were to be saved by them. Walk in holiness as if your own walking would make you enter into heaven, and then rest on Christ, knowing that nothing of your own can ever open the gate of the

Celestial City. Eschew and abhor anything like Antinomianism. Do not be afraid of high doctrine. Men sometimes mis-label good sound Calvinism as Antinomianism; do not be afraid of that; do not be alarmed at the ugly word Antinomianism if it does not exist: but the thing itself—flee from it as from a serpent. Shake off the venomous beast into the fire, as Paul did the viper which he found amongst the faggots. When you are gathering up the doctrines of grace to cheer and comfort you, this deadly viper getteth into the midst, and when the fire begins to burn, he cometh out of the heat and fasteneth upon you. Shake him off into the fire of divine love, and there let the monster be consumed. My brethren, if we are loved of God with an everlasting love, and are no more under the law, but free from its curse, let us serve God with all our heart's gratitude to him, let us say, "I am thy servant; I am thy servant, and the son of thine handmaid: thou hast loosed my bonds." Let the loosing of our bonds be an argument for service.

Then again, beloved, there is another kind of freedom of which we must all be aware, it is a *notional professional freedom.* "Free! yes, certainly we are; we are the people of God," say some; not that they have ever passed from death unto life; not that vital godliness is a matter they understand. No; "we always went to Church, or Chapel; we have never stopped away in our lives; we are the most regular of religious people, and we were baptized, and we go to the sacrament, and what is there that we do not do? Who convinceth us of any sin? If we are not free of the Celestial City, who can be? Surely, surely, we enjoy much of the things of God; we sit in God's house, and we feel a pleasure when we listen to the truth. Sacred song bears us on high as well as other men. We sit as God's people sit, and we hear as God's people hear: surely we are free!" Ah! but, dear friends, a man may think himself free, and be a slave still. You know there are many in this world who dream themselves to be what they are not; and you have a faculty of dreaming in the same manner. Christ must have come to you and shown you your slavery, and broken your heart on account of it, or else you are not free; and you must have looked to the wounds of Jesus as the only gates of your escape, and have seen in his hand the only power which could snap your fetters, or else, though you have professed and re-professed, you are as much slaves of Satan as though you were in the pit itself. Beware, I pray you, of hereditary religion. A man cannot hand down his godliness as he doth his goods; and I cannot receive grace as I may receive lands, or gold, or silver. "Ye must be born again." There must be the going up out of Egypt, the leaving the flesh-pots, and the brick-kilns, and advancing through the Red Sea of atonement into the wilderness, and afterwards into the promised rest. Have ye passed from death unto life? If not, beware of having a mere notional, professional liberty.

There are many, too, who have the liberty of *natural self-righteousness* and of *the power of the flesh.* They have fanciful, unfounded hopes of heaven. They have never wronged anybody; they have never done any mischief in the world; they are amiable; they are generous to the poor; they are this, they are that, they are the other; therefore they feel themselves to be free. They never feel their own inability; they can always pray alike and always sing alike; they have no changes; they are not emptied from vessel to vessel; their confidence never wavers; they believe themselves all right, and abide in their confidence. They do not stop to examine: their delusion is too strong and their comfort is much too precious for them to wish to mar it by looking to its foundation, so they go on, on, on, sound asleep, till one of these days, falling over the awful precipice of ruin, they will wake up where waking will be too late. We know there are some such; they are in God's house, but they are not God's sons. You remember the case of Ishmael; it is to that which our Lord seems to allude here. Ishmael was a son of Abraham according to the flesh, but he never was free. His mother being a bondwoman, he was a slave; he might call himself Abraham's son if he would, but being only after the flesh he was still a slave, for it was not in the power of Abraham, in the power of the flesh, to beget anything but bondage, and Ishmael at his best was still the son of the bondwoman. Yet you see he sits at table, he eats and drinks just as merrily as the child of the promise. Nay, in some things he is stronger than Isaac, he has the advantage of age, and I dare say plumes himself on being heir. "Ah!" saith he, "I am the elder one of the family." At last he mocked Isaac: when the boys were at their sports he was violent towards his younger brother, even as many Pharisees are very cruel to true believers. What came of it? Why, "the servant abideth not in the house for ever, but the son abideth ever." and so the day came in which Sarah said, "Cast out the bondwoman and her son," and away went Ishmael. He might cling to his father and say, "I am thy son." "You must go, sir, you are a slave; you were born after the flesh, and therefore you take from your mother your state and condition, and not from your father. Your mother was a bondslave, and so are you, and you must go. The privileges of the children's house are not for you; you must go into the wilderness; you cannot abide here." But Isaac, though feeble and tempted, and tried and vexed, is never sent out of his father's house— never—he abideth ever. This is the position of many. They are very good people in their way; they do their best, but what is their best? It is the offspring of the flesh; and that which is born of the flesh is flesh, consequently their best endeavours only make them slaves in the house, not sons; only he who is born by faith according to the promise, is the free Isaac and abides in the house. The day will come when God will say to every member of the Christian Church, and all who profess religion, "Are ye children by faith in the promise or not?" For if ye are only children according to the flesh he will send you back again into the wilderness, to eternal ruin you must go except the Spirit of God hath given you the spirit of freedom. There was a custom, observed among the Greeks and Romans that when a man died, if he left slaves, they went as a heritage to the elder son, and if the elder son said, "Some of these are my own brethren, though they be slaves, I therefore pronounced them free," they would be free. Emancipation was not always allowed in either Greek or Roman states—a man might not always set a slave free without giving a good reason; but it was always held to be a valid reason if the son; coming into a heritage of slaves, chose to set them free. No question was asked, if the son made them free; the law did not step in. So, dear friends, if the Son shall make *us* free, *we* shall be free *indeed*. If Jesus Christ the great heir according to the promise, the great Mediator whom God hath created heir of all things, by whom also he made the worlds—if he shall say to us who are as Ishmael, " I make you free," then are we free indeed, and neither law, justice, heaven or hell, can bring any argument against us why we should not be free. But do beware of all imaginary freedoms and shun them as you would poison, and God give you to enjoy the glorious liberty of the children of God.

III. TRUE FREEDOM COMES TO US THROUGH HIM WHO IS, IN THE HIGHEST SENSE, "THE SON." No man getteth free except as he cometh to Christ and taketh him to be his all in all. Thou mayst rivet on thy fetters by going to the law, to thine own good works, to thy willings, and thy prayings, and thy doings, but thou wilt never be free until thou comest to Christ. Mark thee, man, if thou wilt come to Christ thou shalt be free this moment from every sort of bondage, but if thou wilt go hither and thither, and try this and that, and the other, thou shalt find all thy tryings end in disappointment, and thou shalt lie down in sorrow and in shame, for none but Jesus, none but Jesus can make us free indeed. Real liberty cometh from him only. Let us think awhile of this real liberty. Remember it is a liberty *righteously bestowed*. Christ has a right to make men free. If I should set a slave free who belonged to his master, he might run for a time; but since I had not the power to give him a legal emancipation, he would be dragged back again. But the Son, who is heir of all things, has a right to make him free whom he wills to make free. The law is on Christ's side. Christ hath such power in heaven and earth committed to him, that if he saith to the sinner, "Thou art free," free he is before high heaven. Before God's great bar thou canst plead the word of Jesus and thou shalt be delivered.

Bethink thee, too, *how dearly this freedom was purchased*. Christ speaks it by his power, but he still bought it by his blood. He makes thee free, sinner, but it is by his own bonds. Thou goest clear, because he bare thy burden for thee. See him bear his agony—" Crushed beneath the millstone of the law, till all his head, his hair, his garments bloody be." See him yonder, dragged to Pilate's hall, bound, whipped like a common felon, scourged like a murderer, and dragged away by hell-hounds through the streets, fastened by those cruel fetters which went through his flesh to the accursed wood. See him yielding up his liberty to the dungeon of death; there the mighty one sleeps in Joseph of Arimathea's tomb. Dearly did he purchase with his own bondage the liberty which he so freely gives. But, though dearly purchased, let us take up that key-note—*he freely gives it*. Jesus asks nothing of us as a preparation for this liberty. He finds us sitting in sackcloth and ashes, and bids us put on the beautiful array of freedom; he discovers us in a darkness which may be felt, sitting in the valley of the shadow of death, and he brings the true light in his hand, and turns our midnight into blazing noon, and all without our help, without our merit, and at first without our will. Christ saveth sinners just as they are; Christ died not for the righteous, but for the ungodly, and his message is grace, pure grace, undiluted by a single condition or requisition which God might make of man. Just as you are, trust your soul with Christ, and though there be in thee no speck of aught that is good, he will save thee and give thee perfect liberty. Dearly hath he bought it, but freely doth he give it, even the faith by which we receive is the gift of God.

It is a liberty which may be *instantaneously received*. The captive goes first through one door and then another, and perhaps a hundred keys must grate in the wards of the lock before he feels the cool fresh air gladdening his brow. But it is not so with the man who believeth. The moment thou believest, thou art free. Thou mayst have been chained at a thousand points, but the instant thou believest in Christ, thou art unfettered and free as the bird of the air. Not more free is the eagle which mounts to his rocky eyrie, and afterwards outsoars the clouds—even he, the bird of God, is not more unfettered than the soul which Christ hath delivered. Cut are the cords, and in an instant you are clear of all, and upward you mount to God. You may have come in here a slave, and you may go out free. God's grace can in a moment give you the condition of freedom and the nature of it. He can make you say, "Abba, Father," with your whole heart, though up to this day you may have been of your father the devil, and his works you have done. In an instant is it wrought. We are told in tropical lands that the sun seems to leap up from under the horizon, and the dead of night is suddenly turned into the lustre of day: so on a sudden doth God's grace often dawn upon the darkness of sinful hearts. You have seen, mayhap, at times after showers of rain have fallen upon the earth, how land which seemed all dry and barren was suddenly covered with green grass, with here and there a lily full in bloom; and so a heart which has been like a desert, when once the shower of Jesus' grace falls on it, blossoms like the garden of the Lord, and yieldeth sweet perfume; and that in a moment. You who have given yourselves up in despair; you who have written your own condemnation; you who have made a league with death and a covenant with hell, and said, "There is no hope, therefore will we go after our iniquities," I charge you hear me, when I declare, that my Lord and Master, who has broken my chains and set me free, can break yours too, and that with one blow.

Mark, that if this be done, it is *done for ever*. When Christ sets free no chains can bind again. Let the Master say to me, "Captive, I have delivered thee," and it is done. Come on, come on, ye fiends of the pit! Mightier is he who is for us than all they who be against us. Come on, come on, temptations of the world, but if the Lord be on our side, whom shall we fear? If he be our defence, who shall be our destruction? Come on, come on, ye foul corruptions, come on, ye machinations and temptations of my own deceitful heart, but he who hath begun the good work in me will carry it on and perfect it to the end. Gather ye, gather ye, gather ye, all your hosts together, ye who are the foes of God and the enemies of man, and come at once with concentrated fury and with hellish might against my spirit, but if God acquitteth who is he that condemneth? Who shall separate us from the love of God which is in Christ Jesus our Lord? Yon black stream of death shall never wash out the mark of Christian liberty. That skeleton monarch bears no yoke which he can put upon a believer's neck. We will shout victory when we are breast-deep amidst the last billows and grapple with the king upon the pale horse: we will throw the rider and win the victory in the last struggle, according as it is written, "Thanks be unto God which giveth us the victory through our Lord Jesus Christ." Sparta and Greece refused to wear the yoke of Persia and broke the proud king's pomp; but we are free in a nobler sense. We refuse the yoke of Satan and will overcome his power as Christ overcame it in the days gone by. Let those who will bend and crouch at the foot of the world's monarch, but as for those whom God has made free, they claim to think, to believe, to act, and to be as their divine instinct commands them, and the Spirit of God enables them—"Where the Spirit of the Lord is there is liberty." "If the Son therefore shall make you free, ye shall be free indeed."

IV. And now we put round the QUESTION, are we free then this morning? Are we free? I will not answer it for you, nor need I just now answer for myself, but I would beseech you to make a searching enquiry into it. If you are free, then remember that *you have changed your lodging-place*, for the slave and the son sleep not in the same room of the house. The things which satisfied you when a slave will not satisfy you now. You wear a garment which a slave may never wear, and you feel an instinct within which the slave can never feel. There is an Abba, Father, cry in you, which was not there once. Is it so? Is it so? If you are free *you live not as you used to do*. You go not to the slave's work, you have not now to toil and sweat to earn the wages of sin which is death, but now as a son serveth his father, you do a son's work and you expect to receive a son's reward, for the gift of God is eternal life through Jesus Christ our Lord. One thing I know, if you are free, then *you are thinking about setting others free;* and if thou hast no zeal for the emancipation of other men thou art a slave thyself. If thou art free *thou hatest all sorts of chains*, all sorts of sin, and thou wilt never willingly put on the fetters any more. Thou livest each day, crying unto him who made thee free at first, to hold thee up that thou fall not into the snare. If thou be free, this is not the world for thee; this is the land of slaves; this is the world of bondage. If thou be free, thy heart has gone to heaven, the land of the free. If thou be free to-day, thy spirit is longing for the time when thou shalt see the great Liberator face to face. If thou be free, thou wilt bide thy time until he call thee; but when he saith, "Friend, come up hither," thou wilt fearlessly mount to the upper spheres, and death and sin shall be no hindrance to thine advent to his glory.

I would we were all free; but if we be not, the next best thing I would is, that those of us who are not free would fret under the fetter; for when the fetters are felt, they shall be broken; when the iron enters into the soul, it shall be snapped; when you long for liberty you shall have it; when you seek for it as for hid treasure, and pant for it as the stag for the waterbrook, God will not deny you. "Seek, and ye shall find; knock, and it shall be opened; ask, and it shall be given you." God 'ead you to seek, and knock, and ask now, for Christ's sake. **Amen.**

THE ROYAL SAVIOUR.

A Sermon

DELIVERED BY

C. H. SPURGEON,

AT THE METROPOLITAN TABERNACLE, NEWINGTON,

On Thursday Evening, February 1st, 1872.

"Him hath God exalted with his right hand to be a Prince and a Saviour, for to give repentance to Israel, and forgiveness of sins."—Acts v. 31.

This was part of the answer of Peter and the other apostles to the question and declaration of the high priest: "Did not we straitly command you that ye should not teach in this name? and, behold, ye have filled Jerusalem with your doctrine, and intend to bring this man's blood upon us." Then Peter and the other apostles replied, "We ought to obey God rather than men. The God of our fathers raised up Jesus, whom ye slew and hanged on a tree;" and, in the verse following our text, they claimed to be witness-bearers for the risen and reigning Prince and Saviour; and, more than that, they declared that they were co-witnesses with "the Holy Ghost, whom God hath given to them that obey him." These apostles were the representatives of Messiah the Prince, acting under his authority, and, so far as they could, filling up the gap caused by his absence. They asserted that their preaching and teaching had been done by divine command, which could not be set aside by any human authority, imperial or ecclesiastical; and that the true Prince of Israel, the Son of David, alone had the power and the right to issue commissions to those who owned allegiance to Jehovah. They declared that Jesus, whom the chief priests had crucified, was still alive, reigning in glory, enthroned at the right hand of God, and that they were only fulfilling his royal commands when they were "standing in the temple, and teaching the people."

Moreover, when the apostles stated that, in addition to being a Prince, Jesus was also a Saviour, and that he had been exalted with his Father's right hand in order that he might "give repentance to Israel, and forgiveness of sins," they gave the very best reason in the world for their preaching, for they were all engaged in preaching that sinners should repent, and in assuring those who did repent that their sins were forgiven for Christ's sake. I cannot conceive of any better argument than this, which the apostles used when answering the high priest:—"You command us not to teach in Christ's name; but the command of the Son of God, our Prince and Saviour, is 'that repentance and remission of sins should be preached in his name among all nations, beginning at Jerusalem;' so, as 'we ought to obey God rather than men,' we have filled Jerusalem with *his* doctrine; and we mean to go on preaching repentance and remission until, as far as we are able, we have filled the whole world with this doctrine." That purpose of Christ was, at least in part, fulfilled by the apostles in their day. God did give repentance and remission of sins to a chosen remnant of Israel; and when the rest of the Jews rejected the testimony of Christ's servants, they said, as Paul and Barnabas did to the Jews at Antioch, "It was necessary that the Word of God should first have been spoken to you: but seeing ye put it from you, and judge yourselves unworthy of everlasting life, lo, we turn to the Gentiles." We must never forget, beloved brethren and sisters in Christ, that we owe the first preaching of the gospel to the Jews. They were, in all lands that were then known, the heralds of Christ, publishing the royal proclamation far and wide. Under the old dispensation, "unto them were committed the oracles of God;" and the gospel of the new covenant was in the first instance entrusted to them, and it was through the Jews that it was made known unto us Gentiles. Let us remember this fact as we contemplate the glorious future both of Jews and Gentiles. Israel as a nation will yet acknowledge her blessed Prince and Saviour. During many centuries, the chosen people, who were of old so highly favoured above all other nations on the face of the earth, have been scattered and peeled, oppressed and persecuted, until sometimes it seemed as if they must be utterly destroyed; yet they shall be restored to their own land, which again shall be a land flowing with milk and honey. Then, when their hearts are turned to Messiah the Prince, and they look upon him whom they have pierced, and mourn over their sin in so long rejecting him, the fulness of the Gentiles shall also come, and Jew and Gentile alike shall rejoice in Christ their Saviour.

In taking such a text as this, I think it is right always to give first the actual meaning of the passage before using it in any other way. This I have already done by showing you what I suppose the apostles meant in replying as they did to the high priest; now let us try to gather other truths from this passage.

I. First, let us learn that ALL WHO RIGHTLY RECEIVE CHRIST RECEIVE HIM BOTH AS PRINCE AND SAVIOUR. He is exalted this day for many purposes,—as a reward for all the pangs he endured upon the cross, as our covenant Head and Representative, and that he may rule over all things for the good of his Church, as Joseph ruled over Egypt for the good of his brethren. Christ is exalted as a pledge of our exaltation, for "we know that, when he shall appear, we shall be like him; for we shall see him as he is."

But our text declares that *God has exalted Jesus that he may be to his own chosen people a Prince and a Saviour;* —not that he may be a Prince only, or a Saviour only, but that he may be both a Prince and a Saviour. He is a Prince, to receive royal honours; a Prince, to be the Leader and Commander of his people; a Prince, whose every word is to be instantly and implicitly obeyed; a Prince, before whom we who love him will gladly bow, even as, in Joseph's dream, his brethren's sheaves made obeisance to his sheaf, and as they themselves afterwards "bowed themselves to him to the earth" when he became a great lord in Egypt. The Lord Jesus Christ is a Prince among men, a Prince in his Church, and a Prince in the highest heavens; indeed, he is more than a Prince as we understand that word, for he is "King of kings and Lord of lords." But he is also a Saviour, to be trusted; a Saviour, to be accepted with our whole heart; a Saviour who exactly meets our need, for we feel that we need to be saved, and we recognize our inability to save ourselves, and we perceive in him the ability, the grace, the power, and everything else that is required in order to save us. So he is a Saviour to be trusted and accepted as well as a Prince to be obeyed and honoured.

Let us never imitate *those who talk of Christ as a Prince, but will not accept him as a Saviour.* There are some who speak respectfully of Christ as a great Leader among men, a most enlightened Teacher, and a holy Man whose life was perfectly consistent with his teaching so that he can be safely followed as an Exemplar; he is their Prince, but that is all. We cannot occupy such a position as that; if we were to say that Christ is our Prince, but not our Saviour, we should have robbed him of that honour which is, perhaps, dearer to him than any other. It was not simply to reign over the sons of men that he came from heaven to earth; he had legions of nobler spirits than those that dwell in bodies of clay, every one of whom would gladly fly at his command to obey his behests. Besides, if he had pleased to do so, he had the power to create unnumbered myriads of holy beings who would have counted it their highest honour to be subservient to his will. Mere dominion is not what Christ craved; from of old his delights were with the sons of men because he had covenanted with his Father that he would save them. Therefore was he called Jesus, because he came to save his people from their sins. In order to accomplish that great purpose, it was necessary for him to take upon himself our nature, and to live a life of perfect obedience to his Father's will, and at last to die a shameful death upon the cross that he might offer the one sacrifice for sins for ever that alone could bring salvation to all who believe in him. We never read that Jesus said to his disciples, "I am longing for the hour when I shall take the reins of government into my hand, and wear upon my head the crown of universal sovereignty;" but we do read that he said to them, "I have a baptism to be baptized with; and how am I straitened till it be accomplished." We never read that he said to the Jews, "I am come to reign over you;" on the contrary, when men would have taken him by force, and made him a king, he hid himself from them. He was a King, but not a man-made king, and his rule was to be a contrast to that of every other monarch. Christ's own description of his mission was, "The Son of man is come to seek and to save that which was lost." Methinks that our royal Saviour puts the saving before the ruling, and if I call him Prince, and deny him the title of Saviour, he will not thank me for such maimed and mutilated honours. No; God exalted him to be a Prince and a Saviour, and we must receive him in both characters, or not at all.

For, mark you, *we cannot really receive Christ as Prince unless we also receive him as Saviour.* If we say that we accept him as our Prince, but reject him as our Saviour, is there, not merely disloyalty, but treason of the deepest dye in that rejection? This gracious Prince tells me that I am lost and undone, and bids me trust to him to save me; if I practically tell him that I do not need him to save me,—and I do that by rejecting him,—I virtually say that he came from heaven to earth on an unnecessary errand, at least so far as I am concerned. If I do not put my trust in his expiatory sacrifice, I say, in effect, that his death upon Calvary was a superfluity, that he foolishly threw away his valuable life in needless self-sacrifice; but that would be rank blasphemy. If I reject Christ as Saviour, I do by that very act reject him as Prince. It is sheer mockery for me to say, "I honour Jesus of Nazareth, the King of the Jews,* but I refuse to be washed from my sin and uncleanness in the fountain filled with his blood; I am willing to accept the Man Christ Jesus as my Exemplar, and I will try, as far as I can, to follow his steps, but I will not accept pardon at his hands." If I talk like that, Christ is neither my Prince nor my Saviour, but I am his enemy; and, unless I repent, and bow before him in real homage, and accept him both as Prince and Saviour, he will at the last condemn me with the rest of his enemies who said, "We will not have this Man to reign over us." You may extol him with your tongue, but the sacrifice of a broken and contrite heart would be far more prized by him than all your empty praises. It is a higher eulogium to Christ to stoop to kiss his piercèd feet, and find in his wounds perfect healing for all the wounds that sin hath made, than to pronounce the most fulsome panegyrics upon his spotless character. He wants not the meaningless flatteries of men, but he thirsts for the trustfulness of souls that are willing to be saved by him. This is the best refreshment he can ever have, as he told his disciples

---

* See *Metropolitan Tabernacle Pulpit*, No. 1,353, "Ecce Rex;" and No. 3,123, "The King of the Jews."

when he had won to himself the soul of that poor fallen woman at Sychar, "My meat is to do the will of him that sent me, and to finish his work."

There are *some who seem willing to accept Christ as Saviour who will not receive him as Lord.* They will not often state the case quite as plainly as that; but, as actions speak more plainly than words, that is what their conduct practically says. How sad it is that some talk about their faith in Christ, yet their faith is not proved by their works! Some even speak as if they understood what we mean by the covenant of grace; yet, alas! there is no good evidence of grace in their lives, but very clear proof of sin (not grace) abounding. I cannot conceive it possible for anyone truly to receive Christ as Saviour and yet not to receive him as Lord. One of the first instincts of a redeemed soul is to fall at the feet of the Saviour, and gratefully and adoringly to cry, "Blessed Master, bought with thy precious blood, I own that I am thine,—thine only, thine wholly, thine for ever. Lord, what wilt thou have me to do?" A man who is really saved by grace does not need to be told that he is under solemn obligations to serve Christ; the new life within him tells him *that.* Instead of regarding it as a burden, he gladly surrenders himself—body, soul, and spirit, to the Lord who has redeemed him, reckoning this to be his reasonable service. Speaking for myself, I can truthfully say that, the moment I knew that Christ was my Saviour, I was ready to say to him,—

> "I am thine, and thine alone,
> This I gladly, fully own;
> And, in all my works and ways,
> Only now would seek thy praise.
>
> "Help me to confess thy name,
> Bear with joy thy cross and shame,
> Only seek to follow thee,
> Though reproach my portion be."

It is not possible for us to accept Christ as our Saviour unless he also becomes our King, for a very large part of salvation consists in our being saved from sin's dominion over us, and the only way in which we can be delivered from the mastery of Satan is by becoming subject to the mastery of Christ. The "strong man armed" cannot keep us under his cruel sway when the stronger One overcomes him, and sets us at liberty. In order that we may be rescued from the power of the prince of darkness, the Prince of light and life and peace must come into our soul; and he must expel the intruder, and take his own rightful place as our Lord and Master, guarding by his own power what he has saved by his own right hand and his holy arm. If it were possible for sin to be forgiven, and yet for the sinner to live just as he lived before, he would not really be saved. He might be saved from some part of the punishment due to sin, but he would still be a most wretched man; for, if there were no other punishment for sin than the slavery and tyranny of sin's own self, that would be punishment enough to make a man's life utterly miserable, like the poor wretch chained to a corpse, and compelled to drag it about with him wherever he went. Let a man once know what sin really is, and he needs nothing else to make him thoroughly unhappy. I was talking, only to-day, with a Christian brother about our crosses, and I said that I thanked God we were not left without a cross to carry. "Ah!" my friend replied, "but there is one cross we would gladly throw away if we could, and that is the heaviest cross of all,—the body of sin and death that is such a burden to us." Yes, that is indeed a grievous burden to true Christians. That is the iron that enters into our very soul. That is the gall of bitterness, the deadly venom of the old dragon's teeth; and therefore brethren and sisters in Christ, we do not really receive Christ as our Saviour unless we also receive him as Prince; but when he comes to reign and rule in our mortal bodies, the tyranny of the usurper is broken, and we know Jesus as the complete Saviour of our body, soul, and spirit. He would not be our Prince if he were not our Saviour, and he would not be our Saviour if he were not our Prince; but what a blessed combination these two offices make!

The man who is taught of God to understand this great truth will be a wise teacher of others. I believe that many errors in doctrine arise through lack of a clear apprehension of Christ's various relationships towards his spiritual Israel. To some, Christ is only a Prince, so they have a sort of lifeless legality. Others live in Antinomian licentiousness because Christ is not the Prince and Lord of their lives. But, beloved, he who receives Christ both as Prince and Saviour has the blessed and happy experience of resigning his own will and subjecting all the passions of his soul to the sacred control of his glorious Prince; and, at the same time, he daily realizes in his soul the cleansing power of the precious blood of Jesus, and so, as Mary sang, his spirit rejoices in God his Saviour. This also is the true Christian practice as well as true Christian doctrine and experience,—to be ever "looking unto Jesus" as my Saviour, feeling that I always want him in that capacity, and that I shall need him to save me even to my last moment on earth; yet also looking up to him as my Prince, seeking to be obedient to him in all things as far as I can learn his will from his Word, and by the teaching of his Holy Spirit, and to conform my whole life to the royal and divine commands that he has issued for my guidance. I have not the time to enlarge upon this truth, but it seems to me that there is a practical lesson to be learned from the fact that all who rightly receive Christ receive him both as Prince and Saviour.

There are preachers who preach mere morality. I trust their number is smaller than it used to be, but there are still too many professedly Christian ministers who are like that notable man who said that he preached morality till there was no morality left in the place. Yet afterwards, when he imitated Paul, and preached Christ crucified, he soon found that vice hid her dishonoured head, and that all the graces and virtues flourished under the shadow of the cross. So have we found it, and therefore, whoever may preach anything else, we shall still stick to the old-fashioned theme that Paul preached, that old, old story which the seeker after novelties condemns as stale, but which, to the man who wants eternal life, and longs for something that will satisfy his conscience and satiate his heart, has a freshness and charm which the lapse of years only intensifies, but does not remove.

II. The second lesson we learn from our text is that REPENTANCE AND REMISSION OF SINS ARE BOTH NEEDED BY THOSE WHO DESIRE TO BE SAVED. Those needs are clearly indicated by Christ's offices as Prince and Saviour; inasmuch as he is a Prince, we must repent of our rebellion against him; and inasmuch as he is a Saviour, he is exalted with his Father's right hand to give us remission as well as repentance, and we must have both these blessings if we are to be saved.

First, *we cannot be saved without repentance.* No remission of sin can be given without repentance; the two things are so joined together by God, as they are in our text, that they cannot be separated. Many mistakes are made as to what true evangelical repentance really is. Just now, some professedly Christian teachers are misleading many by saying that "repentance is only a change of mind." It is true that the original word does convey the idea of a change of mind; but the whole teaching of Scripture concerning the repentance which is not to be repented of is that it is a much more radical and complete change than is implied by our common phrase about changing one's mind. The repentance that does not include sincere sorrow for sin is not the saving grace that is wrought by the Holy Spirit. God-given repentance makes men grieve in their inmost souls over the sin they have committed, and works in them a gracious hatred of evil in every shape and form. We cannot find a better definition of repentance than the one many of us learnt at our mother's knee,—

> "Repentance is to leave
> The sin we loved before,
> And show that we in earnest grieve
> By doing so no more."

I am always afraid of a dry-eyed repentance; and, mark you, if forgiveness could be granted to those who were not sorry for their sin, such forgiveness would tend to aid and abet sin, and would be no better than the Romish heresy that, when you have sinned, all you have to do is to confess it to a priest, pay a certain sum of money according to the regular Roman tariff, and start again on your career of evil. God forbid that we should ever fall into that snare of the devil! If I could keep on living in sin, and loving it as much as ever I did, and yet have remission of it, the accusation of the blasphemer that Christ is the minister of sin would be a just one; but it is not so. On the contrary, we must loathe sin, and leave sin, and have an agonizing desire to be clean delivered from it; otherwise, we can never expect the righteous God to say to us, "Your sins, which are many, are all forgiven."

Besides, if remission could be obtained without repentance, the sinner would be left very much as he was before; indeed, he would be in a worse condition than he was in before. If God *could* say to him, "I forgive you," and yet he remained unrepentant, unregenerated, unconverted, he would still be an enemy of God, for "the carnal mind is enmity against God: for it is not subject to the law of God, neither indeed can be." Forgiveness would only make such a man a more impudent, hardened, self-righteous enemy of God than he was before. If there is not such a thorough Spirit-wrought change in him that he flings away his weapons of rebellion, and casts himself penitently at the feet of his offended Sovereign, I fail to see in what sense we can call him a saved man. No; repentance is the absolutely necessary prelude to remission.

On the other hand, *we cannot be saved without the remission of our sins following upon our redemption.* God exalted Jesus "with his right hand to be a Prince and a Saviour, for to give repentance to Israel, and forgiveness of sins." Note that "repentance" and "forgiveness of sins" are separate and distinct gifts of the exalted Christ. Our repentance does not entitle us to claim from God the pardon of our sin apart from his gracious promise to give it to us. If I get into a man's debt, and then feel sorry that I owe him so much money, that regret will not pay my debt. If I transgress the law of the land, and when I stand in the dock say how grieved I am that I have broken the law, my sorrow will not pay the penalty that I have incurred. The magistrate or judge, in passing sentence upon me, may remit a portion of it because of my contrition, but I have no right to claim even that clemency on his part; and, before God, my sorrow for my sins gives me no claim upon him for the remission of them. No; I must say to him, as Toplady so truly sings,—

> "Let the water and the blood,
> From thy riven side which flowed,
> Be of sin the double cure,
> Cleanse me from its guilt and power.

> "Could my zeal no respite know,
> Could my tears for ever flow,
> All for sin could not atone:
> Thou must save, and thou alone."

Suppose I do now hate some sin that I once loved, or that I hate all sin, no credit is due to me, for that abhorrence of sin is what I ought always to have had. God had the right to claim from me the hatred of sin of every sort, but that hatred does not discharge the debt which I owe to God. I will go further than that, and say that no one ever repents of sin so thoroughly as he does when he knows that it is forgiven. Hence, when Christians begin their new life, they do not repent once, and then leave off repenting; but repentance and faith go hand in hand with them all the way to heaven. Indeed, dear old Rowland Hill used almost to regret that, even in heaven, he might not still have the tear of penitence glistening in his eye; but, of course, that is not possible, for of the redeemed in glory it is expressly declared that "God shall wipe away all tears from their eyes."

III. Thirdly, and very briefly, BOTH REPENTANCE AND REMISSION ARE GIFTS FROM CHRIST. God hath exalted him "to give repentance . . . and forgiveness of sins."

The same Lord who gives the remission also gives the repentance. This is wrought in us by the effectual working of the Holy Spirit, yet it is not HE who repents, he cannot do so, and he has nothing of which he needs to repent; but *we* repent, and though it must always be our own act, yet it is Jesu's gift to us, and the Spirit's work in us. Jesus bestows this gift upon us in his capacity as Saviour, and we never truly repent until we recognize Jesus as our Saviour, and put our whole trust in his atoning sacrifice. Smitten by the cross, our rocky heart is broken, and the streams of penitential tears gush forth even as the water leaped from the rock smitten by the rod of Moses in the wilderness. When Jesus grants the grace of forgiveness, at the same moment he gives the tender heart that mourns that it should have needed forgiveness. I believe that, if this truth were thoroughly understood, it would help many more to receive the Calvinistic system of theology which now puzzles them. I know that, when I first realized that my repentance was the gift of God, the whole doctrine of salvation by grace fell into my soul as by a lightning flash.

The other side of the truth is that *the same Lord who gives the repentance also gives the remission.* No one will dispute the fact that the forgiveness of sins is the free gift of the exalted Saviour. This priceless blessing could never be purchased by us, or deserved by us on account of our feelings, promises, doings, or anything else; it is a gift,—freely, wholly, absolutely a gift of God's grace. It is given *with* repentance, but not given *for* or because of repentance; and wherever remission of sin is given, it works in the soul more and more repentance of sin; but it is, in itself, a gift, independent of repentance, yet given with it, a royal gift from the royal Saviour exalted with his Father's right hand. So that what you have to do, dear friends, is to look to Christ, and to Christ alone, to give you penitence while you are impenitent, and to give you pardon when you are penitent. So, as Hart sings,—

> "Come, ye needy, come and welcome,
> God's free bounty glorify;
> True belief, and true repentance,
> Every grace that brings us nigh,
> Without money,
> Come to Jesus Christ, and buy.

> "Let not conscience make you linger,
> Nor of fitness fondly dream;
> All the *fitness* he requireth,
> Is to feel your need of him:
> *This he gives you;*
> 'Tis the Spirit's rising beam."

Exposition by C. H. Spurgeon.

ROMANS X.

Verse 1. *Brethren, my heart's desire and prayer to God for Israel is, that they might be saved.*

They had hunted Paul from city to city, but the only feeling for them that he had was a wish that they might be saved. Such a wish as that should be in the heart of every Christian; his desire for his bitterest enemy should be that he may be saved.

2. *For I bear them record that they have a zeal of God, but not according to knowledge.*

We should always give people credit for every good thing that there is in them; it will often enable us all the better to point out other matters in which they are deficient. So Paul put it on record, concerning the Jews of his time, that they had a zeal for God, though it was not a zeal "according to knowledge."

3. *For they being ignorant of God's righteousness, and going about to establish their own righteousness, have not submitted themselves unto the righteousness of God.*

They were so busy trying to work out a righteousness of their own that they had never accepted the righteousness which God is prepared freely to give to all those who will receive it at his hands.

4. *For Christ is the end of the law for righteousness to every one that believeth.*

This is the very essence of the gospel, that believing in Christ brings to sinners a righteousness which they can never obtain in any other way.

5, 6. *For Moses describeth the righteousness which is of the law, That the man which doeth those things shall live by them. But the righteousness which is of faith—*

Is of quite another sort, for it—

6—9. *Speaketh on this wise, Say not in thine heart, Who shall ascend into heaven? (that is, to bring Christ down from above:) Or, Who shall descend into the deep? (that is, to bring up Christ again from the dead.) But what saith it? The word is nigh thee, even in thy mouth, and in thy heart: that is, the word of faith, which we preach; that if thou shalt confess with thy mouth the Lord Jesus, and shalt believe in thine heart that God hath raised him from the dead, thou shalt be saved.*

Oh, what a blessedly simple plan of salvation is here revealed! "If thou shalt confess with thy mouth the Lord Jesus, and shalt believe in thine heart that God hath raised him from the dead, thou shalt be saved." The apostle says this plan of salvation is so near to men that it is in their mouth. When anything is in your mouth, how can you make it your own? Why, by swallowing it; and so near is the gospel to every man that he has, as it were, but to drink it down, to make it his very own. It is not up there on the lofty heights, nor down there in the deeps of the abyss, but it is here, and wherever else Christ is preached, and wherever his Word is read. O sinner, "the Word is nigh thee, even in thy mouth, and in thy heart;" then, put it not away from thee, but hold it fast for ever!

10. *For with the heart man be'ieveth unto righteousness; and with the mouth confession is made unto salvation.*

After believing in Christ, the man must confess that he does believe in him. It would be a shame for any believer to try to sneak into heaven without owning that Christ has saved him. If any man is ashamed of his religion, you may depend upon it that it is one of which he has cause to be ashamed; but he who has true saving faith in his heart should never blush to own it. What is there to blush about in being a Christian? Let those blush who are not believers in the Lord Jesus Christ.

11, 12. *For the scripture saith, Whosoever believeth on him shall not be ashamed. For there is no difference between the Jew and the Greek: for the same Lord over all is rich unto all that call upon him.*

Whoever they may be, Jews or Gentiles, rich or poor, learned or illiterate, black or white, if they will but call upon God in prayer, he will not be miserly towards them, but he will be generous towards them in the abundance of the blessings which he will give them in answer to their cry.

13, 14. *For whosoever shall call upon the name of the Lord shall be saved. How then shall they call on him in whom they have not believed?*

They cannot rightly pray without faith, "for he that cometh to God must believe "that he is, and that he is" a rewarder of them that diligently seek him."

14. *And how shall they believe in him of whom they have not heard?*

Those who do not hear the gospel are not likely to believe it, and there are many unbelievers who never seek to hear it, and it is always wrong for a man to refuse to believe any truth before he knows what it really is. There should at least be a sincere searching of the Holy Scriptures, and a candid listening to the preaching of the Word, before it is rejected.

14, 15. *And how shall they hear without a preacher? And how shall they preach, except they be sent? as it is written, How beautiful are the feet of them that preach the gospel of peace, and bring glad tidings of good things!*

The gospel brings gladness wherever it comes. The Word which we preach tells of joys that will last for ever. The gospel shall make the whole world ring with new music when it is received by all; and it shall roll away the mists that now swathe this poor dusky planet, and make it shine out like its sister stars in all the glory of God when once Christ is fully acknowledged here as Lord and Saviour.

16. *But they have not all obeyed the gospel.*

All who have heard the gospel have not obeyed it.

16. *For Esaias saith, Lord, who hath believed our report?*

And what Isaiah said is what we also have to say to-day, "Who hath believed our report? and to whom is the arm of the Lord revealed?"

17. *So then faith cometh by hearing, and hearing by the word of God.*

Salvation comes by faith, and faith comes by hearing, but that hearing must be the hearing of the Word of God. Surely there is no great difficulty in understanding the gospel. This is no maze in which a man may lose himself. Here are no puzzling directions which only the learned can comprehend; oh, no! but here stand the plain, simple, soul-quickening words, "Believe and live."

18, 20. *But I say, Have they not heard? Yes verily, their sound went into all the earth, and their words unto the ends of the world. But I say, Did not Israel know? First Moses saith, I will provoke you to jealousy by them that are no people, and by a foolish nation I will anger you. But Esaias is very bold, and saith, I was found of them that sought me not; I was made manifest unto them that asked not after me.*

Is not that a wonderful text? There are some who have heard the gospel year after year, and who have refused it, and perished; and there are, on the other hand, scattered up and down this world, thousands of people who have never yet heard it, but the very first time they do hear it, they will accept it, and be eternally saved.

21. *But to Israel—*

To God's ancient people, to whom the gospel had been preached when Paul wrote this Epistle: "to Israel"—

21. *He saith, All day long I have stretched forth my hands unto a disobedient and gainsaying people.*

It is strange that many, who first hear the Word, and oftenest hear it, turn away from it, while others, to whom it comes as a complete novelty, are blessed the first time they hear it. I sometimes say that there are some hearers, who regularly occupy these seats, who are just like pieces of india-rubber. They are easily impressed, they yield assent to every truth that is uttered, but they soon get back into their old shape again, and they are exactly the same, after twenty years of hearing the gospel, as they were before, only that they are still more hardened. On the other hand, there will sometimes drop into this house of prayer a thoroughly irreligious man, with a heart as hard as a flint, but the very first tap of the hammer of the gospel breaks the flint so effectually that it is never a flint again, and God's grace renews his heart there and then. It is our earnest desire, on all occasions, whatever hearers are gathered here, that God's saving power may be manifested to all present. So may it be now, for Christ's sake, and to God's glory! Amen.

"THE LAMB OF GOD."

A Sermon

DELIVERED BY

C. H. SPURGEON,

AT THE METROPOLITAN TABERNACLE, NEWINGTON,

On Lord's-day Evening, February 20th, 1870.

"Behold the Lamb of God, which taketh away the sin of the world."—John i. 29.

BEFORE we plunge into our main subject, it is needful to notice what is implied in our text, which is that "the world" was lost through sin, that all mankind had become guilty before God. You, therefore, my dear hearer, are one of those who are thus guilty. Though you may never have broken the laws of your country, nor even the rules of propriety; though you may be both amiable and admirable in your general deportment, yet, for all this, as "there is none righteous, no, not one," you also are included amongst the unrighteous. It matters not what religious professions you may have made, or what outward forms of godliness you may have observed, unless you have a better righteousness than your own, you are a lost sinner. I believe there is now present a brother who, when he was first convinced of sin, strove hard to make himself a better man, under the mistaken idea that this was the way of salvation; and when, one Sabbath night, he heard me say that all the reforms you could ever make upon your old nature would be useless as to the matter of salvation, but that "ye must be born again," he felt very angry, and made a vow that he would never be found listening to me again; yet here he is, rejoicing that the Lord has taught him to see himself as a lost, ruined sinner, and to put his heart's trust in Jesus Christ, the sinner's Saviour.

It is very likely that, if I had time to explain to you, my hearer, the fulness of your sin and the utter ruin of your natural state, you also would grow angry. Yet you would have no cause to be angry, for all that I could say would fall far short of the truth about your real condition in the sight of God; and it is most solemnly important for you to know that, however high you may stand in the ranks of merely moral men, you are a lost soul, and a condemned soul, so long as you remain without living faith in the Lord Jesus Christ. If you are angry with the minister of the gospel who tells you this truth, you are as foolish as a certain Brahmin of whom I have heard. His religion consisted chiefly in not eating any animal food or destroying any kind of life. The missionary told him that it was impossible for him to carry out such a "religion" as that, "for," said he, "in every drop of water that you drink, you swallow thousands of animals, and so destroy vast quantities of animal life." Then he put a drop of water out of the cup from which the Brahmin had been drinking under his microscope, and so convinced him of the truth of what he had said; and when the Brahmin saw the creatures moving in the water, instead of abandoning his false theory, he grew very angry, and dashed the microscope upon the ground. He was not angry, you see, with the fact, but with that which revealed the fact; like the lazy housemaid, who said she was quite sure that she always kept the rooms clean, but that it was the nasty sun that would shine in, and make everything look so dusty! The fault is not in the gospel which we preach, so you should not be angry with it, or with us; the fault is in your own selves, in your own hearts and lives; and if you do not like to be told the truth about sin, it is a sure sign that your heart is not right in the sight of God. It is still true that "every one that doeth evil hateth the light, neither cometh to the light, lest his deeds should be reproved."

Well then, with that truth taken for granted,—that you, whom I am now addressing, have sinned, and are therefore under God's condemnation unless you are trusting in Christ,—we now come directly to our text. We shall take it, not merely as though John the Baptist were speaking it, but as we may now use it from our point of view. It appears to me to be the whole gospel in a very brief form. You may sometimes write much in a very few words, and here you have an epitome of the whole gospel of God in these few syllables: "Behold the Lamb of God, which taketh away the sin of the world." I am going to ask, and to try to answer, three questions: first, *what is to be beheld?* secondly, *what is to be done?* and, thirdly, *why should we do this?*

I. First, then, WHAT IS TO BE BEHELD?

The text mentions *a Lamb*, by which is meant *a sacrifice*. Under the Jewish law, those who had offended brought sacrifices, and offered them to God. These sacrifices were representations of our Lord Jesus Christ, who is "the Lamb of God." Listen, my dear hearer, and I will tell thee the gospel in a few sentences. As God is just, it is inevitable that sin should be punished. If he would pardon thee, how can this be righteously accomplished? Only thus:

Jesus Christ, his Son, came to earth and stood in the room, and place, and stead of all those who believe on him; and God accepted him as the substitutionary sacrifice for all those who put their trust in him. Under the Jewish law, the Lamb was put to death that the man might not be put to death; and, in like manner, Jesus Christ our Lord and Saviour suffered the pangs of death by crucifixion and the greater agony of the wrath of God that we might not suffer the pangs of hell and the wrath eternal which is due to sin. There is no other way of salvation under heaven but this. God cannot relax his justice, and he will by no means clear the guilty; but he laid upon Christ the full punishment that was due to sin, and smote him as though he had been the actual offender, and now, turning round to you, he tells you that, if you trust in Jesus, the merits of his great atoning sacrifice shall be imputed to you, and you shall live for ever in glory because Jesus died upon the cross of Calvary. If any of you would have your sins forgiven, and so enjoy peace with God, you must look by faith to that sacrifice which was offered upon Calvary, and keep your eye of faith fixed there, and sooner or later you will certainly receive the blessings of peace into your souls.

But the text not only mentions a Lamb; it says, "Behold *the* Lamb of God," and I draw your special attention to that expression. It is not merely *a* sacrifice to which you are to look, but *the* sacrifice that God has appointed and ordained to be the one and only sacrifice for sin. This is an all-important point. "The Lord hath laid on him the iniquity of us all. . . . It pleased the Lord to bruise him; he hath put him to grief." If Christ had not been sent of God to be the Saviour of sinners, our faith would have had no firm foundation to rest upon; but as God himself has set forth Christ to be the propitiation for human guilt, then he cannot reject the sinner who accepts that propitiation. I need not raise any question as to whether Christ's atonement is sufficient, for God says that it is; and as he is well satisfied with the sacrifice offered by his only-begotten and well-beloved Son, surely the most troubled conscience may be equally well satisfied with it. Your offence, my friend, was committed against God; if, then, God is content with what Christ has done on your behalf, and so is willing to pardon you, surely you need not enquire any further, but with gratitude you should at once accept the reconciliation which Christ has made. It is "the Lamb of God" whom I have to bid you "behold." It is Jesus Christ, the Son of God, who dies on Calvary, "the Just for the unjust, that he might bring us to God." It was God who appointed him to die as the Substitute for sinners, it was God who accepted his sacrifice when he died; and now Jehovah himself, speaking from his throne of glory, saith to the sinner, "Believe thou on my Son, whom I have set forth as the propitiation for human sin; trust thou in him, and thou shalt be eternally saved."

Still further to bring out the full force of the text, notice the next words, "Behold the Lamb of God, *which taketh away the sin of the world.*" When Jesus Christ was put into our place, our sin was laid upon him; and sin, like anything else, cannot be in two places at one time. If, then, I, being a believer in Jesus, know that all my sin was laid upon Christ, it follows necessarily that I have no sin left upon me. It has become Christ's burden; he has taken it away from me. "Yes," you say, "but then the sin is still on Christ." Ah! but, my hearers, if our Lord Jesus Christ, "his own self bare our sins in his own body up to the tree," he there endured all the punishment that was due to us, or an equivalent for it, and those sins were by that means put away; that is to say, they ceased to be; so they do not exist any longer. All my indebtedness to God was transferred to Christ, and he paid all my debts. Then, where are my debts now? Why, there are none, they are all gone for ever. This is what Christ does for every one who truly trusts in him; he takes that man's sins, suffers what that man ought to have suffered, and puts that man's sins absolutely out of existence, so that they cease to be. Christ has accomplished the great work described to Daniel by the angel Gabriel; he has finished the transgression, made an end of sins,—what a strong expression that is!—made reconciliation for iniquity, and brought in everlasting righteousness. How gloriously he has put sin right away for all who believe in him! "As far as the east is from the west, so far hath he removed our transgressions from us." Of all sinners in the whole world who believe in Jesus Christ, it may be truly said that all their sins are gone past all recall; God has cast them behind his back into the depths of the Red Sea of the Saviour's blood, and they shall not be remembered against them any more for ever. It is thus that the Lamb of God taketh or beareth away sin.

But *whose sin does he take away?* The text saith, "*the sin of the world.*" By this expression, I believe is intended the sin, not of the Jews only, but of Jews and Gentiles alike;—the sin, not of a few sinners only, but of all sinners in the whole world who come to Jesus, and put their trust in him. He has so taken away "the sin of the world" that every sinner in the world who will come to him, and trust in him, shall have all his sins put away for ever. Whether he be Greek or Jew, circumcised or uncircumcised, Barbarian or Scythian, bond or free, if he truly believes in Jesus, it is certain that Christ took all his sins away. Whether he was born eighteen hundred years ago, or whether he shall be born in the ages that are yet to come, does not make any difference to this fact,—Christ hath borne his sins if he trusts in Jesus as his own Saviour. This is the sign and token by which he may assuredly know that he hath a saving and eternal interest in the precious blood of Jesus: "He that believeth on him is not condemned." The gate of grace is set very wide open in our text; if it were not, some poor sinners would be afraid to enter. "Oh!" asks one, "is this mercy for me? Is it for me?" Well, friend, I will ask thee a question,—Wilt thou trust Christ? Wilt thou come to him this very moment, and take the mercy that he freely presents to all who will accept it? If so, I am sure that it is thine, as sure as I am that it is mine.

Possibly, somebody has come in here to-night hoping to hear something new; but I have nothing new to tell, nor do I wish ever to have anything more new than this, "that Christ Jesus came into the world to save sinners;" or this, "God so loved the world, that he gave his only-begotten Son, that whosoever believeth in him should not perish, but have everlasting life." When Dr. Judson went home to America from Burmah, there was a large congregation gathered together, and they requested the returned missionary, the veteran of so many years of service, to address the assembly. He stood up, and simply told the story that I have again told you to-night, the story of Christ suffering in the stead of sinners, and of Christ saving all who trust him. Then he sat down; and one who sat next him said to him, "I am afraid the friends are rather disappointed; they expected to hear something interesting from you." He said, "I have spoken to them, to the best of my ability, upon the most interesting subject in the whole world; what could I have done better than that?" "Yes," said the other; "but, after having been so long abroad, they thought that you would tell them some interesting story; they did not think you would come all the way from Burmah just to tell them only that." The missionary then rose, and said, "I should like to go home feeling that, although I have come all the way from Burmah, I do not know anything that I can tell you that I think is half so good for you to hear, or half so interesting, as the story of the love of Christ in dying to save sinners." The good doctor was right; and I feel, just as he did, that there is nothing so interesting as the story of the cross. You want to hear it, you who are already saved; and you want to hear it, you who are not yet saved. *You* must hear it, for there is no hope of salvation for you except as faith shall come to you by hearing, and specially hearing that portion of the Word of God which deals most closely with the cross of Christ.

One night, a dissolving-view lecture upon the Holy Land was being given; and, as the audience, sitting in darkness, looked at a picture of Jerusalem, they were startled by a voice asking, "Where is Calvary?" Ah! and that is the question that many of you want to ask, "Where is Calvary?" There must you turn your eye, where, betwixt the two thieves, your Saviour died. If you really do look to him as he dies there for guilty sinners, you are saved; and then, whatever else you do not know, you know enough to save you, for you are wise unto life eternal. May the Lord graciously make you thus wise through the effectual working of his ever-blessed Spirit! So then, God in human flesh, the divinely-appointed sacrifice for human guilt, "the Lamb of God," is what you are in our text bidden to "behold."

II. But now, secondly, WHAT ARE WE TO DO?

How are we to have a part and lot in that great sacrifice which Christ offered on Calvary? The answer of the text is, "*Behold*"— that is, look to "*the Lamb of God.*"

"There is life in a look at the Crucified One."

"Behold the Lamb of God" means believe on the Lord Jesus Christ, trust in him as your Saviour, accept God's revelation concerning him, and rely upon him to save you. This is the way of salvation.

Notice *how opposed this is to the idea that we are critically to understand the doctrines of the gospel before we can be saved.* How many persons there are who want to know this and to understand that! They come to us, and say, "Here are two texts that do not seem to us to square with one another, and there are those two doctrines of divine sovereignty and human responsibility which do not appear to be consistent with each other. Must we understand all these mysteries before we can be saved?" O foolish people! they remind me of one who is shipwrecked, and who, as the lifeboat comes up to the sinking ship, or to the spar upon which he is floating, says to the captain, "Before I can get on board that lifeboat, I want to know the exact number of planks there are in it; and I do not think that knowing that would content me, I should like also to know how many rivets and bolts there are in the boat; and I want also to know what is the theory of the operation of the oars upon the waves, and how it is that boats are propelled." If a man ever did talk thus, I am pretty sure that the captain of the lifeboat would exclaim, "What a fool the man is! He is in danger of drowning, yet he talks like this! Come into the boat at once, or we must leave you to perish!" And I also feel that you unconverted sinners have no business to set yourselves up as critics of the Word of God. There is something much simpler than that for you to do, and the text bids you do it. It is this, "Behold the Lamb of God;" do not sit down to manufacture difficulties; "believe on the Lord Jesus Christ, and thou shalt be saved." There are various ways of using a piece of bread. One man may take it, and employ it in rubbing out the pencil marks which he has made upon a sheet of paper. Another man may take it to the analyst, and ask him to see how much alum the baker may have put into it. But the really hungry man, the one who gets the most good out of the piece of bread, eats it; and that is what I recommend you to do with the gospel;—not begin to turn it about this way and that, not ask all manner of questions concerning it, but feed upon it; and the way to feed upon it is to accept and believe it, and especially to put your trust in Jesus Christ, who is the very essence of the gospel.

"Behold the Lamb of God," says the text; then *that command is opposed to the question that troubles so many,—whether they are elect or not.* That is like wanting to read Hebrew before one has learned to speak English. Such people are not content to learn the ABC, the elements, the rudiments of the gospel first, they want to know the gospel's classics, or mathematics, or metaphysics first, but that cannot be. During the recent hard frosts, I have struck an acquaintance with a little friend who, I am afraid, may desert me by-and-by, but our friendship has been exceedingly pleasant to each of us thus far. On the little balcony outside my study windows, I observed a robin frequently coming, so I took an opportunity, one morning, to put some crumbs there, and I have done the same thing every morning since; and my little feathered friend comes close up to the window-frame, and picks up the crumbs, and I do not perceive that he has any difficulty about whether those crumbs were laid there for him, or whether I had an electing love towards him in my heart. There were the crumbs, he wanted them, and he picked them up, and ate them; and I can tell you that, in doing so, he exactly fulfilled my purpose in putting the crumbs there. I thought that he acted very wisely; and I think that, if a poor sinner wants mercy, and he sees that there is mercy to be had, he had better not pause to ask, "Did God decree me to have it?" but go and take it, and he will then find that, in doing so, he is fulfilling God's decrees. My little robin friend is very wise in his way, for he has called a friend of his to join him at the feast on the balcony. How he did it, I do not know; but he managed to tell a blackbird all about the crumbs, and he brought him last Friday morning to see them for himself. The blackbird was rather shy at first, and stood for a while on the iron bar of the balcony; but, after looking in at the study window, he hopped down, and neither he nor the robin asked whether it was my purpose that the blackbird should have any of the crumbs; but there were the crumbs, and they were both hungry, so they came and fed together. So, if any of you find Jesus Christ for yourselves, and you know some poor soul who wants him, do not you begin asking whether it is God's purpose or decree that he also should find the Saviour; you go and invite him to come to Jesus, and then both of you come to the Saviour together; and then, just as the robin and blackbird exactly fulfilled my purpose in throwing out the crumbs, so, when you and your friend too come to Christ, you will rejoice to find that you have both of you fulfilled the eternal purpose of the divine decree of the great heart of God. It is not your business to look into the book of God's secret purposes, but to look to Christ, or, as our text puts it, to "behold the Lamb of God, which taketh away the sin of the world."

Ah! but this beholding of the Lamb of God is a thing to which men cannot readily be brought. I know many whose consciences are truly awakened, and who see themselves as sinners in the sight of God; but, instead of beholding the Lamb of God, they are continually beholding themselves. I do not think that they have any confidence in their own righteousness, but they are afraid that they do not feel their guilt as much as they ought. They think that they are not yet sufficiently awakened, sufficiently humbled, sufficiently penitent, and so on, and thus they fix their eyes upon themselves in the hope of getting peace with God. Suppose that, yesterday, or the day before, you had felt very cold, and therefore you had gone outside your house, and fixed your gaze upon the ice and the snow, do you think that sight would have warmed you? No; you know you would have been getting colder all the time. Suppose you are very poor, and you studiously fix your mind's eye upon your empty pocket, do you think that will enrich you? Or imagine that you have had an accident, and that one of your bones is broken, if you think very seriously of that broken bone, do you think that your consideration will mend it? Yet some sinners seem to imagine that salvation can come to them through their consideration of their lost and ruined condition. My dear unconverted hearers, you are lost whether you know it or not. Take that fact for granted. If you would be saved, look not at yourselves, but "behold the Lamb of God." He has been sent by his Father to be the Saviour of sinners, and it is by trust in him that peace and pardon will come to you. I pray you not to suppose, for a single moment, that your repentance, your tears, or your softened heart can prepare you for Christ. Do not come to Christ because you have a tender heart, but come to Christ to get a tender heart. Do not come to him because you are fit to come, but because you want to be made fit; and remember that—

"All the fitness he requireth
Is to feel your need of him;
This he gives you;
'Tis the Spirit's rising beam."

But do give up looking at yourself, and "behold the Lamb of God."

Let me also, dear friend, *warn you against the notion that your prayers can save you apart from beholding Christ.* I believe that it is both the duty and the privilege of every living soul to pray; but that the first command to a sinner is to pray, I deny. The first command is, "Believe on the Lord Jesus Christ;" and when thou hast done that, thou wilt soon get to praying. I think it is stated, in McCheyne's life, that, after an earnest sermon, he found a man under deep concern of soul; and, after saying a word or two to him, he said, "I cannot stop longer with you myself, but there is one of my elders who will pray with you." The elder did so, and he prayed in so fervent a fashion that it was remarked that he seemed to be like Jacob wrestling with the angel until he prevailed. The man afterwards came to see Mr. McCheyne, and he said to him, "I am very thankful that I was at your church that night; I feel very happy, and I believe I am saved." "Well," said McCheyne, "what makes you feel so happy?" "Oh!" he said, "I have great faith in that good man's prayers." McCheyne at once said, "My friend, I am afraid that good man's prayers will ruin you; if that is where you are putting your confidence, you are utterly mistaken." He was quite right, and your own prayers will be just such an obstacle in your way if you trust to them instead of trusting to Christ. "I know I pray," says one, "and I am very earnest in prayer." Well, I am glad of that as far as it goes; but if you have not something better to trust to than your own prayers, your prayers will ruin you; for the look of faith is not to be given to prayer, but to Christ. Our text says, "Behold the Lamb of God." I have told you what that means,—look by faith to the sacrifice that Christ made for sinners on the cross at Calvary; and if you look to anything else for salvation, you will not find it. Even your prayers, apart from faith in Christ, will not save you from everlasting destruction. O sinner, get away from everything else to Christ!

"None but Jesus, none but Jesus,
Can do helpless sinners good."

This great truth, that believing is the divinely-appointed means of salvation, may be illustrated by the old story of the children of Israel and the serpent of brass. You have heard it scores of times; yet I beg you to listen to it once more. When the people were bitten by the fiery serpents in the wilderness, they were commanded to look to the serpent of brass that was lifted up upon a pole; and whosoever looked, lived. They had nothing to do but to look. Moses lifted up the serpent, and pointed to it, and cried, "Look! Look! Look! and be healed." Possibly, there were some who said they were bitten too badly to look. Well, if they could not or did not look, they would die. They might think it was a proof of their humility to say, "We are too sick to be cured;" but if they did so, they would die whether they were humble or not. O my hearer, do not be lost through a mock humility which is really abominable pride! You are not too great a sinner to be saved. I will venture to say that you will dishonour Christ if you ever think such a thing; so let not that sinful thought destroy you.

There may have been others who said, "We shall not look to the brazen serpent, for we have only got a mere scratch; it will soon be gone." But you know a poison scratch means death; and if your sin were only a scratch, (and it is much more than that,) it would mean eternal damnation for you. So look to Jesus, I implore thee, just as thou art; look now, look and live.

Perhaps there was one who said, "My father had a famous recipe for serpent bites; it was given to him by a celebrated doctor in Egypt; so we will mix up the proper ingredients, and so get cured." Well, if any who were bitten were to act and speak like that, they would all die; the deadly venom would certainly destroy them, whatever ointments they might use. A look at the brazen serpent gave life; but the refusal to look brought death.

There may have been some fine gentlemen there who had imbibed sceptical notions during their life in Egypt. They were so clever that they thought they knew a great deal more than the Lord's servant to whom God had specially revealed the only effectual remedy, so they turned on their heels, and said, "Such a remedy as this is utterly ridiculous; it is not according to the laws of physics that the mere looking at a piece of brass can heal people of the bites of snakes;" so they perished. Notwithstanding all their learning and wit, notwithstanding their jeers at the divinely-appointed remedy, they perished; and nobody in the whole camp was healed except those who were simple enough and wise enough to take God at his word. Then, though they were terribly bitten, and their blood was set on fire by the poison, and though some of them were in a truly desperate state, when they just looked at the serpent of brass, in a moment their blood again flowed healthily through their veins, and their strength returned to them in all its former vigour; and, dear friends, there shall be no soul saved in the whole world except by looking to the crucified Christ of Calvary. All trust in christening, (or even in baptism,) in confirmation, in sacraments, in ceremonies, in priests, and popes, and relics, are all a lie together; but, so long as God's Word remains true, he who looks by faith to Christ alone must and shall be eternally saved. Oh, how can I utter this truth so as to make it plainer, or how shall I plead with you so as to bring you all to trust in Christ? I cannot do this, but I pray the Holy Spirit to do it, for he can; and then you will believe in Jesus, and so receive life everlasting.

III. I must not detain you longer, as our time has fled; otherwise, I was to have answered a third question, WHY SHOULD WE THUS LOOK?

The answer would have been that God has appointed this as the only way of salvation; that those who obey the command of the text will obtain immediate salvation; and that, being saved, they shall have joy and peace in believing; and that those who neglect or refuse to "behold the Lamb of God" must, without doubt, perish everlastingly. Of his infinite mercy, may God graciously grant that none, whom I am now addressing, may refuse to believe in Jesus, but may everyone look unto him, and live, live now, and live for ever.

Exposition by C. H. Spurgeon.

JOHN I. 1—34.

Verse 1. *In the beginning was the Word,—*
Christ the Word has existed from all eternity. He is the eternal Son of the eternal Father; he is really what Melchisedec was metaphorically, "having neither beginning of days, nor end of life." "In the beginning was the Word,"—

1 *And the Word was with God, and the Word was God.*
The Word was as truly God as the Father was God, and as the Spirit was God: "these three are one," and ever have been one. "Very God of very God" is that Jesus whom we trust, and love, and adore.

2—5. *The same was in the beginning with God. All things were made by him; and without him was not any thing made that was made. In him was life; and the life was the light of men. And the light shineth in darkness; and the darkness comprehended it not.*

The light of Christ shone many times amid the darkness that enshrouded the world before his coming to live here in the flesh, yet comparatively few recognized that light, and rejoiced in it. Christ's light shines more brightly now, but the dark, benighted soul of man perceives not the brightness of our spiritual Lord until the Holy Spirit works the mighty miracle of regeneration, and so gives sight to those who have been blind.

6. *There was a man sent from God, whose name was John.*
What a descent it is from "The Word was God" to the "man sent from God, whose name was John"! Jesus himself said concerning John, "Among them that are born of women there hath not risen a greater than John the Baptist;" yet, from the greatest of prophets, what a climb it is to get up to Jesus Christ, the Son of God! "There was a man sent from God, whose name was John."

EXPOSITION. 493

7—9. *The same came for a witness, to bear witness of the Light, that all men through him might believe. He was not that Light, but was sent to bear witness of that Light. That was the true Light, which lighteth every man that cometh into the world.*

That John could not do; he could only bear witness to Christ, the true Light, who alone is able to illuminate, in a larger or lesser degree, "every man that cometh into the world."

10. *He was in the world, and the world was made by him, and the world knew him not.*

Oh, what terrible estrangement sin has caused between God and man! What dreadful ignorance sin has created in the human mind! The world was made by Christ, yet "the world knew him not."

11. *He came unto his own, and his own received him not.*

To those who were chosen as "his own" out of all the nations upon the earth, to those to whom he was specially promised of old, to the descendants of Abraham, Isaac, and Jacob,—to these Jesus came, yet they "received him not."

12. *But—*

This is a blessed "But." Though Christ's own nation, the Jews, as a whole "received him not," there was "a remnant according to the election of grace," there were some who received him. "But"—

12. *As many as received him, to them gave he power to become the sons of God, even to them that believe on his name:*

How came those persons to receive him when others rejected him? There must have been some great change wrought in them to make them different from the rest of their countrymen; and truly there was, for these were twice-born men,—

13. *Which were born, not of blood, nor of the will of the flesh, nor of the will of man, but of God.*

So that those who receive Christ, those who truly believe on Christ, are people who have been born, as others have not been born, by a new birth from heaven, a supernatural birth, so that they are a people set apart by themselves as those who have been twice created, first as human beings just like others, and then as new creatures in Christ Jesus.

14—18. *And the Word was made flesh, and dwelt among us, (and we beheld his glory, the glory as of the only begotten of the Father,) full of grace and truth. John bare witness of him, and cried, saying, This was he of whom I spake, He that cometh after me is preferred before me: for he was before me. And of his fulness have all we received, and grace for grace.† For the law was given by Moses, but grace and truth came by Jesus Christ. No man hath seen God at any time; the only begotten Son, which is in the bosom of the Father, he hath declared him.*

There is no way of knowing God, and being reconciled to God, except as we receive Jesus Christ, his Son, into our hearts, and learn of him, through the Holy Spirit's teaching, all that he delights to reveal to us concerning his Father.

19—23. *And this is the record of John, when the Jews sent priests and Levites from Jerusalem to ask him, Who art thou? And he confessed, and denied not; but confessed, I am not the Christ. And they asked him, What then? Art thou*

Elias? And he saith, I am not. Art thou that prophet? And he answered, No. Then said they unto him, Who art thou? that we may give an answer to them that sent us. What sayest thou of thyself? He said, I am the voice— Not the Word, but "the voice" by which the Word was to be made known: "I am the voice"—

23—27. *Of one crying in the wilderness, Make straight the way of the Lord, as said the prophet Esaias. And they which were sent were of the Pharisees. And they asked him, and said unto him, Why baptizest thou then, if thou be not that Christ, nor Elias, neither that prophet? John answered them, saying, I baptize with water: but there standeth one among you, whom ye know not; he it is, who coming after me is preferred before me, whose shoe's latchet I am not worthy to unloose.*

See the true humility of this faithful servant of Christ. He does not dream of putting his own name side by side with his Master's. The unloosing of shoe latchets was work for a slave to do; but if we are privileged to perform this work for Christ, it will make us as kings before him. To do anything for Christ, to have even a menial's place in his palace, is better than being an emperor among men. May we have the portion of those who are not ashamed to unloose the latchet of Christ's shoes!

28—31. *These things were done in Bethabara beyond Jordon, where John was baptizing. The next day John seeth Jesus coming unto him, and saith, Behold the Lamb of God, which taketh away the sin of the world. This is he of whom I said, After me cometh a man which is preferred before me: for he was before me. And I knew him not:*

"When first I saw him,"—

31—34. *But that he should be made manifest to Israel, therefore am I come baptizing with water. And John bare record, saying, I saw the Spirit descending from heaven like a dove, and it abode upon him. And I knew him not: but he that sent me to baptize with water, the same said unto me, Upon whom thou shalt see the Spirit descending, and remaining on him, the same is he which baptizeth with the Holy Ghost. And I saw, and bare record that this is the Son of God.*

Since John's time, many others have borne similar testimony. We also have received him, and rejoice to say that he has baptized us with the Holy Ghost. All that John said of him is true, and much more than John said is also true. He is the Lamb of God, who has taken upon himself the sin of all who believe in him, and therefore he is able to save unto the uttermost all that come unto God by him. Oh, that all men would receive the testimony concerning him which we find in this blessed Book, and which we delight to repeat in his name!

THE WORDLESS BOOK.

A Sermon

DELIVERED BY

C. H. SPURGEON,

AT THE METROPOLITAN TABERNACLE, NEWINGTON,

On *Thursday Evening, January*, 11*th*, 1866.

"Wash me, and I shall be whiter than snow."—Psalm li. 7.

I DARESAY you have most of you heard of a little book which an old divine used constantly to study, and when his friends wondered what there was in the book, he told them that he hoped they would all know and understand it, but that there was not a single word in it. When they looked at it, they found that it consisted of only three leaves; the first was black, the second was red, and the third was pure white. The old minister used to gaze upon the black leaf to remind himself of his sinful state by nature, upon the red leaf to call to his remembrance the precious blood of Christ, and upon the white leaf to picture to him the perfect righteousness which God has given to believers through the atoning sacrifice of Jesus Christ his Son.

I want you, dear friends, to read this book this evening, and I desire to read it myself. May God the Holy Spirit graciously help us to do so to our profit!

I. First, LET US LOOK AT THE BLACK LEAF.

There is something about this in the text, for the person who used this prayer said, "Wash me," so he was black, and needed to be washed; and the blackness was of such a peculiar kind that a miracle was needed to cleanse it away, so that the one who had been black should become white, and so white that he would be "whiter than snow."

If we consider *David's case when he wrote this Psalm*, we shall see that he was very black. He had committed the horrible sin of adultery, which is so shameful a sin that we can only allude to it with bated breath. It is a sin which involves much unhappiness to others besides the persons who commit it; and it is a sin which,

495

although the guilty ones may repent, cannot be undone. It is altogether a most foul and outrageous crime against God and man, and they who have committed it do indeed need to be washed.

But David's sin was all the greater because of the circumstances in which he was placed. He was like the owner of a great flock, who had no need to take his neighbour's one ewe lamb when he had so many of his own. The sin in his case was wholly inexcusable, for he so well knew what a great evil it was. He was a man who had taken delight in God's law, meditating in it day and night. He was, therefore, familiar with the commandment which expressly forbad that sin; so that, when he sinned in this way, he sinned as one does who takes a draught of poison, not by mistake, but well knowing what will be the consequences of drinking it. It was wilful wickedness on David's part for which there cannot be the slightest palliation.

Nay, more; not only did he know the nature of the sin, but he also knew the sweetness of communion with God, and must have had a clear sense of what it must have meant for him to lose it. His fellowship with the Most High had been so close that he was called "the man after God's own heart." How sweetly has he sung of his delight in the Lord. You know that, in your happiest moments, when you want to praise the Lord with your whole heart, you cannot find any better expression than David has left you in his Psalms. How horrible it is that the man who had been in the third heaven of fellowship with God should have sinned in this foul fashion!

Besides, David had received many providential mercies at the Lord's hands. He was but a shepherd lad, and God took him from feeding his father's flock, and made him king over Israel. The Lord also delivered him out of the paw of the lion and out of the paw of the bear, enabled him to overthrow and slay giant Goliath, and to escape the malice of Saul when he hunted him as a partridge upon the mountains. The Lord preserved him from many perils, and at last firmly established him upon the throne; yet, after all these deliverances and mercies, this man, so highly favoured by God, fell into this gross sin.

Then, also, it was a further aggravation of David's sin that it was committed against Uriah. If you read through the lists of David's mighty men, you will find at the end the name of Uriah the Hittite; he had been with David when he was outlawed by Saul, he had accompanied his leader in his wanderings, he had shared his perils and privations, so it was a shameful return on the part of the king when he stole away the wife of his faithful follower who was at that very time fighting against the king's enemies. Searching through the whole of Scripture, or at least through the Old Testament, I do not know where we have the record of a worse sin committed by one who yet was a true child of God. So David had good reason to pray to the Lord, "Wash me," for he was indeed black with a special and peculiar blackness.

But now, turning from David, let us consider *our own blackness in the sight of God.* Is there not, my dear friend, some peculiar blackness about your case as a sinner before God? I cannot picture it, but I ask you to call it to your remembrance now that your soul may be humbled on account of it. Perhaps you are the child of Christian parents, or you were the subject of early religious impressions, or it may be that you have been in other ways specially favoured by God, yet you have sinned against him, sinned against light and knowledge, sinned against a mother's tears, a father's prayers, and a pastor's admonitions and warnings. You were very ill once, and thought you were going to die, but the Lord spared your life, and restored you to health and strength, yet you went back to your sin as the dog returns to his vomit, or the sow that was washed to her wallowing in the mire. Possibly a sudden sense of guilt alarmed you, so that you could not enjoy your sin, yet you could not break away from it. You spent your money for that which was not bread, and your labour for that which did not satisfy you, yet you went on wasting your substance with riotous living until you came to beggary, but even that did not wean you from your sin. In the house of God you had many solemn warnings, and you went home again and again resolving to repent, yet your resolves soon melted away, like the morning cloud and the early dew, leaving you more hardened than ever. I remember John B. Gough, at Exeter Hall, describing himself in his drinking days as seated upon a wild horse which was hurrying him to his destruction until a stronger hand than his own seized the reins, pulled the horse down upon its haunches, and rescued the reckless rider. It was a terrible picture, yet it was a faithful representation of the conversion of some of us. How we drove the spurs into that wild horse, and urged it to yet greater speed in its mad career until it seemed as if we would even ride over that gracious Being who was determined to save us! That was sin indeed, not merely against the dictates of an enlightened conscience, and against the warnings which were being continually given to us, but it was what the apostle calls treading under foot the Son of God, counting the blood of the covenant an unholy thing, and doing despite unto the Spirit of grace.

Let me, beloved, before I turn away from this black leaf, urge you to study it diligently, and to try to comprehend the blackness of your hearts and the depravity of your lives. That false peace which results from light thoughts of sin is the work of Satan; get rid of it at once if he has wrought it in you. Do not be afraid to look at your sins, do not shut your eyes to them; for you to hide your face from them may be your ruin, but for God to hide his face from them will be your salvation. Look at your sins, and meditate upon them until they even drive you to despair. "What!" says one, "until they drive me to despair?" Yes; I do not mean that despair which arises from unbelief, but that self-despair which is so near akin to confidence in Christ. The more God enables you to see your emptiness, the more eager will you be to avail yourself of Christ's fulness. I have always found that, as my trust in self went up, my trust in Christ went down; and as my trust in self went down, my trust in Christ went up, so I urge you to take an honest view of your own blackness of heart and life, for that will cause you to pray with David, "Wash me, and I shall be whiter than snow." Weigh yourselves in the scales of the sanctuary, for they never err in the slightest degree. You need not exaggerate a single item of your guilt, for just as you are you will find far too much sin within you if the Holy Spirit will enable you to see yourselves as you really are.

II. But now we must turn to the second leaf, THE BLOOD-RED LEAF OF THE WORDLESS BOOK, which brings to our remembrance the precious blood of Christ.

When the sinner cries, "Wash me," there must me some fount of cleansing where he can be washed "whiter than snow." So there is, but there is nothing but the crimson blood of Jesus that can wash out the crimson stain of sin. What is there about Jesus Christ that makes him able to save all who come unto God by him? This is a matter upon which Christians ought to meditate much and often. Try to understand, dear friends, the greatness of the atonement. Live much under the shadow of the cross. Learn to—

> "View the flowing
> Of the Saviour's precious blood,
> By divine assurance knowing
> He has made your peace with God."

Feel that Christ's blood was shed for you, even for you. Never be satisfied till you have learned the mystery of the five wounds; never be content till you are "able to comprehend with all saints what is the breadth, and length, and depth, and height; and to know the love of Christ, which passeth knowledge."

The power of Jesus Christ to cleanse from sin must lie, first, in the greatness of his person. It is not conceivable that the sufferings of a mere man, however holy or great he might have been, could have made atonement for the sins of the whole multitude of the Lord's chosen people. It was because Jesus Christ was one of the persons in the Divine Trinity, it was because the Son of Mary was none other than the Son of God, it was because he who lived, and laboured, and suffered, and died was the great Creator, without whom was not anything made that was made, that his blood has such efficacy that it can wash the blackest sinners so clean that they are "whiter than snow." The death of the best man who ever lived could not make an atonement even for his own sins, much less could it atone for the guilt of others; but when God himself "took upon him the form of a servant, and was made in the likeness of men," and "humbled himself, and became obedient unto death, even the death of the cross," no limit can be set to the value of the atonement that he made. We hold most firmly the doctrine of particular redemption, that Christ loved his Church, and gave himself for it; but we do not hold the doctrine of the limited value of his precious blood. There can be no limit to Deity, there must be infinite value in the atonement which was offered by him who is divine. The only limit of the atonement is in its design, and that design was that Christ should give eternal life to as many as the Father has given him; but in itself the atonement is sufficient for the salvation of the whole world, and if the entire race of mankind could be brought to believe in Jesus, there is enough efficacy in his precious blood to cleanse everyone born of woman from every sin that all of them have ever committed.

But the power of the cleansing blood of Jesus must also lie in the intense sufferings which he endured in making atonement for his people. Never was there another case like that of our precious Saviour. In his merely physical sufferings there may have been some who have endured as much as he did, for the human body is only capable of a certain amount of pain and agony, and others beside our Lord have reached that limit; but there was an element in his sufferings that was never present in any other case. The fact of his dying in the room, and place, and stead of his people, the one great sacrifice for the whole of his redeemed, makes his death altogether unique, so that not even the noblest of the noble army of martyrs can share the glory with him. His mental sufferings also constituted a very vital part of the atonement, the sufferings of his soul were the very soul of his sufferings. If you can comprehend the bitterness of his betrayal by one who had been his follower and friend, and of his desertion by all his disciples, his arraignment for sedition and blasphemy before creatures whom he had himself made; if you can realize what it was for him, who did no sin, to be made sin for us, and to have laid upon him the iniquity of us all; if you can picture to yourself how he loathed sin and shrank from it, you can form some slight idea of what his pure nature must have suffered for our sakes. We do not shrink from sin as Christ did because we are accustomed to it, it was once the element in which we lived, and moved, and had our being; but his holy nature shrank from evil as a sensitive plant recoils from the touch. But the worst of his sufferings must have been when his Father's wrath was poured out upon him as he bore what his people deserved to bear, but which now they will never have to bear.

> "The waves of swelling grief
> Did o'er his bosom roll,
> And mountains of almighty wrath
> Lay heavy on his soul."

For his Father to have to hide his face from him so that he cried in his agony, "My God, my God, why hast thou forsaken me?" must have been a veritable hell to him. This was the tremendous draught of wrath which our Saviour drank for us to its last dregs so that our cup might not have one drop of wrath in it for ever. It must have been a great atonement that was purchased at so great a price.

We may think of the greatness of Christ's atonement in another way. It must have been a great atonement which has safely landed such multitudes of sinners in heaven, and which has saved so many great sinners, and transformed them into such bright saints. It must be a great atonement which is yet to bring innumerable myriads into the unity of the faith, and into the glory of the church of the firstborn, which are written in heaven. It is so great an atonement, sinner, that if thou wilt trust to it, thou shalt be saved by it however many and great thy sins may have been. Art thou afraid that the blood of Christ is not powerful enough to cleanse thee? Dost thou fear that his atonement cannot bear the weight of such a sinner as thou art? I heard, the other day, of a foolish woman at Plymouth who, for a long while, would not go over the Saltash Bridge because she did not think it was safe. When, at length, after seeing the enormous traffic that passed safely over the bridge, she was induced to trust herself to it, she trembled greatly all the time, and was not easy in her mind until she was off it. Of course, everybody laughed at her for thinking that such a ponderous structure could not bear her little weight. There may be some sinner, in this building, who is afraid that the great bridge which eternal mercy has constructed, at infinite cost, across the gulf which separates us from God, is not strong enough to bear his weight. If so, let me assure him that across that bridge of Christ's atoning sacrifice millions of sinners, as vile and foul as he is, have safely passed, and the bridge has not even trembled beneath their weight, nor has any single part of it ever been strained or displaced. My poor fearful friend, your anxiety lest the great bridge of mercy should not be able to bear your weight reminds me of the fable of the gnat that settled on the bull's ear, and then was concerned lest the powerful beast should be incommoded by his enormous weight. It is well that you should have a vivid realization of the weight of your sins, but at the same time you should also realize that Jesus Christ, by virtue of his great atonement, is not only able to bear the weight of your sins, but he can also carry—indeed, he has already carried upon his shoulders the sins of all who shall believe in him right to the end of time; and he has borne them away into the land of forgetfulness, where they shall not be remembered or recovered for ever. So efficacious is the blood of the everlasting covenant that even you, black as you are, may pray, with David, "Wash me, and I shall be whiter than snow."

III. This brings me to THE WHITE LEAF OF THE WORDLESS BOOK, which is just as full of instruction as either the black leaf or the red one: "Wash me, and I shall be *whiter than snow.*"

What a beautiful sight it was, this morning, when we looked out, and saw the ground all covered with snow! The trees were all robed in silver; yet it is almost an insult to the snow to compare it to silver, for silver at its brightest is not worthy to be compared with the marvellous splendour that was to be seen wherever the trees appeared adorned with beautiful festoons above the earth which was robed in its pure white mantle. If we had taken a piece of what we call white paper, and laid it down upon the surface of newly-fallen snow, it would have seemed quite begrimed in comparison with the spotless snow. This morning's scene at once called the text to my mind: "Wash me, and I shall be whiter than snow." You, O black sinner, if you believe in Jesus, shall not only be washed in his precious blood until you become tolerably clean, but you shall be made white, yea, you shall be "whiter than snow." When we have gazed upon the pure whiteness of the snow before it has become defiled, it has seemed as though there could be nothing whiter. I know that, when I have been among the Alps, and have for hours looked upon the dazzling whiteness of the snow, I have been almost blinded by it. If the snow were to lie long upon the ground, and if the whole earth were to be covered with it, we should soon all be blind. The eyes of man have suffered with his soul through sin, and just as our soul would be unable to bear a sight of the unveiled purity of God, our eyes cannot endure to look upon the wondrous purity of the snow. Yet the sinner, black through sin, when brought under the cleansing power of the blood of Jesus, becomes "whiter than snow."

Now, how can a sinner be made "whiter than snow"? Well, first of all, *there is a permanence about the whiteness of a blood-washed sinner which there is not about the snow.* The snow that fell this morning was much of it anything but white this afternoon. Where the thaw had begun to work, it looked yellow even where no foot of man had trodden upon it; and as for the snow in the streets of London, you know how soon its whiteness disappears. But there is no fear that the whiteness which God gives to a sinner will ever depart from him; the robe of Christ's righteousness which is cast around him is permanently white.

> "This spotless robe the same appears
> When ruin'd nature sinks in years;
> No age can change its glorious hue,
> The robe of Christ is ever new."

It is always "whiter than snow." Some of you have to live in smoky, grimy London, but the smoke and the grime cannot discolour the spotless robe of Christ's righteousness. In yourselves, you are stained with sin; but when you stand before God, clothed in the righteousness of Christ, the stains of sin are all gone. David in himself was black and foul when he prayed the prayer of our text, but clothed in the righteousness of Christ he was white and clean. The believer in Christ is as pure in God's sight at one time as he is at another. He does not look upon the varying purity of our sanctification as our ground of acceptance with him; but he looks upon the matchless and immutable purity of the person and work of the Lord Jesus Christ, and he accepts us in Christ, and not because of what we are in ourselves. Hence, when we are once "accepted in the Beloved," we are permanently accepted; and being accepted in him, we are "whiter than snow."

Further, *the whiteness of snow is, after all, only created whiteness.* It is something which God has made, yet it has not the purity which appertains to God himself; but the righteousness which God gives to the believer is a divine righteousness, as Paul says, "He hath made him to be sin for us, who knew no sin; that we might be made the righteousness of God in him." And remember that this is true of the very sinner who before was so black that he had to cry to God, "Wash me, and I shall be whiter than snow." There may be one who came into this building black as night through sin; but if he is enabled now, by grace, to trust in Jesus, his precious blood shall at once cleanse him so completely that he shall be "whiter than snow." Justification is not a work of degrees; it does not progress from one stage to another, but it is the work of a moment, and it is instantaneously complete. God's great gift of eternal life is bestowed in a moment, and you may not be able to discern the exact moment when it is bestowed. Yet you may know even that; for, as soon as you believe in the Lord Jesus Christ, you are born of God, you have passed from death unto life, you are saved, and saved to all eternity. The act of faith is a very simple thing, but it is the most God-glorifying act that a man can perform. Though there is no merit in faith, yet faith is a most ennobling grace, and Christ puts a high honour upon it when he says, "Thy faith hath saved thee; go in peace." Christ puts the crown of salvation upon the head of faith, yet faith will never wear it herself, but lays it at the feet of Jesus, and gives him all the honour and glory.

There may be one in this place who is afraid to think that Christ will save him. My dear friend, do my Master the honour to believe that there are no depths of sin into which you may have gone which are beyond his reach. Believe that there is no sin that is too black to be washed away by the precious blood of Christ, for he has said, "All manner of sin and blasphemy shall be forgiven unto men," and "all manner of sin" must include yours. It is the very greatness of God's mercy that sometimes staggers a sinner. Let me use a homely simile to illustrate my meaning. Suppose you are sitting at your table, carving the joint for dinner, and suppose your dog is under the table, hoping to get a bone or a piece of gristle for his portion. Now, if you were to set the dish with the whole joint on it down on the floor, he would probably be afraid to touch it lest he should get a cut of the whip; he would know that a dog does not deserve such a dinner as that, and that is just your difficulty, poor sinner, you know that you do not deserve such grace as God delights to give. But the fact that it is of grace shuts out the question of merit altogether. "By grace are ye saved through faith; and that not of yourselves: it is the gift of God." God's gifts are like himself, immeasurably great. Perhaps some of you think you would be content with crumbs or bones from God's table. Well, if he were to give me a few crumbs or a little broken meat, I would be grateful for even that, but it would not satisfy me; but when he says to me, "Thou art my son,

I have adopted thee into my family, and thou shalt go no more out for ever;" I do not agree with you that it is too good to be true. It may be too good for you, but it is not too good for God; he gives as only he can give. If I were in great need, and obtained access to the Queen, and after laying my case before her, she said to me, "I feel a very deep interest in your case, here is a penny for you," I should be quite sure that I had not seen the Queen, but that some lady's maid or servant had been making a fool of me. Oh, no! the Queen gives as Queen, and God gives as God; so that the greatness of his gift, instead of staggering us, should only assure us that it is genuine, and that it comes from God. Richard Baxter wisely said, "O Lord, it must be great mercy or no mercy, for little mercy is of no use to me!" So, sinner, go to the great God, with your great sin, and ask for great grace that you may be washed in the great fountain filled with the blood of the great sacrifice, and you shall have the great salvation which Christ has procured, and for it you shall ascribe great praise for ever and ever to Father, Son, and Holy Spirit. God grant that it may be so, for Jesus' sake! Amen.

Exposition by C. H. Spurgeon.

PSALM LI.

It is a Psalm, and therefore it is to be sung. It is dedicated to the chief Musician, and there is music in it, but it needs a trained ear to catch the harmony. The sinner with a broken heart will understand the language and also perceive the sweetness of it; but as for the proud and the self-righteous, they will say, "It is a melancholy dirge," and turn away from it in disgust. There are times, to one under a sense of sin, when there is no music in the world like that of the 51st Psalm, and it is music for the chief Musician, for "there is joy in the presence of the angels of God over one sinner that repenteth;" and this is the Psalm of penitence, and there is joy in it, and it makes joy even to the chief Musican himself.

Verse 1. *Have mercy upon me, O God, according to thy lovingkindness: according unto the multitude of thy tender mercies blot out my transgressions.*

Here is a man of God, a man of God deeply conscious of his sin, crying for mercy, crying with all his heart and soul, and yet with his tear-dimmed eyes looking up to God, and spying out the gracious attributes of Deity, lovingkindness, and tender mercies, multitudes of them. There is no eye that is quicker to see the mercy of God than an eye that is washed with the tears of repentance. When we dare not look upon divine justice, when that burning attribute seems as if it would smite us with blindness, we can turn to that glorious rainbow of grace round about the throne, and rejoice in the lovingkindness and the tender mercies of our God.

2. *Wash me throughly from mine iniquity, and cleanse me from my sin.*

"If washing will not remove it, burn it out, O Lord; but do cleanse me from it; not only from the guilt of it and the consequent punishment, but from the sin itself. Make me clean through and through. 'Wash me throughly from mine iniquity, and cleanse me from my sin.'"

3. *For I acknowledge my transgressions: and my sin is ever before me.*

"As if the record of it were painted on my eyeballs. I cannot look anywhere without seeing it. I seem to taste it in my meat and drink; and when I fall asleep, I dream of it, for thy wrath has come upon me, and now my transgression haunts me wherever I go."

4. *Against thee, thee only, have I sinned, and done this evil in thy sight: that thou mightest be justified when thou speakest, and be clear when thou judgest.*

This is the sting of sin to a truly penitent man, that he has sinned against God. The carnal mind sees nothing in that. If ever it does repent, it repents of doing wrong to man. It only takes the manward side of the transgression; but God's child, though grieved at having wronged man, feels that the deluge of his guilt—that which drowns everything else—is that he has sinned against his God. It is the very token and type and mark of an acceptable repentance that it has an eye to sin as committed against God.

Now observe that the psalmist, having thus sinned, and being thus conscious of his guilt, is now made to see that, if the evil came out of him, it must have been in him at first; he would not have sinned as he had done had there not been an unclean fountain within him.

5, 6. *Behold, I was shapen in iniquity; and in sin did my mother conceive me. Behold, thou desirest truth in the inward parts:—*

Then it is not sufficient for me to be washed outside, and being outwardly moral is not enough. "Thou desirest truth in the inward parts:"—

6. *And in the hidden part thou shalt make me to know wisdom.*

In that part which is even hidden from myself, where sin might lurk without my knowing it, there wouldst thou spy it out. I pray thee, Lord, eject all sin from me, rid me of the most subtle form of iniquity that may be concealed within me.

7. *Purge me with hyssop, and I shall be clean: wash me, and I shall be whiter than snow.*

This is a grand declaration of faith. I know not of such faith as this anywhere else. The faith of Abraham is more amazing; but, to my mind, this faith of poor broken-hearted David, when he saw himself to be black with sin and crimson with crime, and yet could say, "Wash me, and I shall be whiter than snow," is grand faith. It seems to me that a poor, trembling, broken-down sinner, who casts himself upon the infinite mercy of God, brings more glory to God than all the angels that went not astray are ever able to bring to him.

8. *Make me to hear joy and gladness; that the bones which thou hast broken may rejoice.*

Brothers and sisters in Christ, we cannot sin with impunity. Worldlings may do so as far as this life is concerned; but a child of God will find that, to him, sin and smart, if they do not go together, will follow very closely upon one another's heels. Ay, and our Father in heaven chastens his people very sorely, even to the breaking of their bones; and it is only when he applies the promises to our hearts by the gracious operation of his Holy Spirit, and makes the chambers of our soul to echo with the voice of his lovingkindness, that we "hear joy and gladness" again. It is only then that our broken bones are bound up, and begin to rejoice once more.

9. *Hide thy face from my sins,*

David could not bear that God should look upon them.

9. *And blot out all mine iniquities.*

"Put them right out of sight. Turn thy gaze away from them, and then put them out of everybody's sight."

10. *Create in me a clean heart, O God; and renew a right spirit within me.*

"Make me over again; let the image of God in man be renewed in me. Nay, not the image only, but renew the very Spirit of God within me."

11, 12. *Cast me not away from thy presence; and take not thy holy spirit from me, restore unto me the joy of thy salvation;*

"Lift me up, and then keep me up. Let me never sin against thee again."

12, 13. *And uphold me with thy free spirit. Then will I teach transgressors thy ways;*

There are no such teachers of righteousness as those who have smarted under their own personal sin; they can indeed tell to others what the ways of God are. What are those ways? His ways of chastisement,—how he will smite the wandering; his ways of mercy,—how he will restore and forgive the penitent.

13. *And sinners shall be converted unto thee.*

He felt sure that they would be converted; and if anything can be the means of converting sinners, it is the loving faithful testimony of one who has himself tasted that the Lord is gracious. If God has been merciful to you, my brother or my sister, do not hold your tongue about it, but tell to others what he has done for you; let the world know what a gracious God he is.

14. *Deliver me from bloodguiltiness, O God, thou God of my salvation: and my tongue shall sing aloud of thy righteousness.*

I like that confession and that prayer of David. He does not mince matters, for he had guiltily caused the blood of Uriah to be shed, and here he owns it, with great shame, but with equal honesty and truthfulness. As long as you and I call our sins by pretty names, they will not be forgiven. The Lord knows exactly what your sin is, therefore do not try to use polite terms about it. Tell him what it is, that he may know that you know what it is. "Deliver me from bloodguiltiness, O God, thou God of my salvation."

"But surely," says someone, "there is nobody here who needs to pray that prayer." Well, there is one in the pulpit, at least, who often feels that he has need to pray it; for what will happen if I preach not the gospel, or if I preach it not with all my heart? It may be that the blood of souls shall be required at my hands. And my brothers and sisters, if anything in your example should lead others into sin, or if the neglect of any opportunities that are presented to you should lead others to continue in their sin till they perish, will not the sin of bloodguiltiness be possible to you? I think you had better each one pray David's prayer, "Deliver me from bloodguiltiness, O God, thou God of my salvation." "And then, O Lord, if I once get clear of that, 'my tongue shall sing aloud of thy righteousness.'"

15. *O Lord, open thou my lips;*

He is afraid to open them himself lest he should say something amiss. Pardoned sinners are always afraid lest they should err again.

15, 16. *And my mouth shall shew forth thy praise. For thou desirest no sacrifice; else would I give it:*

"Whatever there is in the whole world that thou desirest, I would gladly give it to thee, my God."

16—18. *Thou delightest not in burnt offering. The sacrifices of God are a broken spirit: a broken and a contrite heart, O God, thou wilt not despise. Do good in thy good pleasure unto Zion:—*

You see that the psalmist loves the chosen people of God. With all his faults, his heart is right towards the kingdom under his charge. He feels that he has helped to break down Zion, and to do mischief to Jerusalem, so he prays, "Do good in thy good pleasure unto Zion:"—

18, 19. *Build thou the walls of Jerusalem. Then shalt thou be pleased with the sacrifices of righteousness, with burnt offering and whole burnt offering: then shall they offer bullocks upon thine altar.*

Once get your sin forgiven, and then God will accept your sacrifices. Then bring what you will with all your heart, for an accepted sinner makes an accepted sacrifice, through Jesus Christ.